Economic Report
of the President

Transmitted to the Congress
February 2008

together with
THE ANNUAL REPORT
of the
COUNCIL OF ECONOMIC ADVISERS

UNITED STATES GOVERNMENT PRINTING OFFICE

WASHINGTON : 2008

For sale by the Superintendent of Documents, U.S. Government Printing Office
Internet: bookstore.gpo.gov   Phone: (866) 512-1800;   DC area (202) 512-1800
Fax: (202) 512-2104 Mail Stop: IDCC, Washington, DC 20402-0001

ISBN-13: 978-1-60175-490-5
ISBN-10: 1-60175-490-6

CONTENTS

*For a detailed table of contents of the Council's Report, see page 11

ECONOMIC REPORT
OF THE PRESIDENT

ECONOMIC REPORT OF THE PRESIDENT

To the Congress of the United States:

Over the past 6 years of economic expansion, the American economy has proven its strength and resilience. Job creation grew uninterrupted for a record period of time, inflation remains moderate, unemployment is low, and productivity continues to grow. The economy is built upon a strong foundation, with deep and sophisticated capital markets, flexible labor markets, low taxes, and open trade and investment policies.

Americans should be confident about the long-term strength of our economy, but our economy is undergoing a period of uncertainty, and there are heightened risks to our near-term economic growth. To insure against these risks, I called upon the Congress to enact a growth package that is simple, temporary, and effective in keeping our economy growing and our people working.

There is more we should do to strengthen our economy. First, we must keep taxes low. Unless the Congress acts, most of the tax relief that we have delivered over the past 7 years will be taken away and 116 million American taxpayers will see their taxes rise by an average of $1,800. The tax relief of the past few years has been a key factor in promoting economic growth and job creation and it should be made permanent. We must also work together to tackle unfunded obligations in entitlement programs such as Social Security, Medicare, and Medicaid. I have laid out a detailed plan in my Budget to restrain spending, cut earmarks, and balance the budget by 2012 without raising taxes.

Second, we must trust Americans with the responsibility of homeownership and empower them to weather turbulent times in the market. My Administration has acted aggressively to help credit-worthy homeowners avoid foreclosure. We launched a new initiative called *FHASecure* to help families refinance their homes. I signed legislation to protect families from higher taxes when lenders forgive a portion of their home mortgage debt. We have also brought together the HOPE NOW alliance, which is helping many struggling homeowners avoid foreclosure by facilitating the refinancing and modification of mortgages. The Congress can do more to help American families keep their homes by passing legislation to reform Freddie Mac and Fannie Mae, modernize the Federal Housing Administration, and allow State housing agencies to issue tax-free bonds to help homeowners refinance their mortgages.

Third, we must continue opening new markets for trade and investment. We have an unprecedented opportunity to reduce barriers to global trade and investment through a successful Doha round. The Congress should also approve our pending free trade agreements. I thank the Congress for its approval of a good agreement with Peru, and ask for the approval of agreements with Colombia, Panama, and South Korea. These agreements will benefit our economy by providing greater access for our exports and supporting good jobs for American workers, and they will promote America's strategic interests. I have asked the Congress to reauthorize and reform trade adjustment assistance so that we can help those workers who are displaced by trade to learn new skills and find new jobs.

Fourth, we must make health care more affordable and accessible for all Americans. I have proposed changes in the tax code that would end the bias against those who do not receive health insurance through their employer and would make it easier for many uninsured Americans to obtain insurance. This reform would put private health care coverage within reach for millions. My Budget also improves access to health care by increasing the power of small employers, civic groups, and community organizations to negotiate lower-priced health premiums. These policies would encourage competition among health plans across State lines, help reduce frivolous lawsuits that increase patients' costs, and promote the use of health savings accounts.

Fifth, we must increase our energy security and confront climate change. Last year, I proposed an ambitious plan to reduce U.S. dependence on oil and help cut the growth of greenhouse gas emissions. I am pleased that the Congress responded, and I was able to sign into law a bill that will increase fuel economy and the use of alternative fuels, as well as set new efficiency mandates on appliances, light bulbs, and Federal Government operations. In my State of the Union Message, I proposed that we take the next steps to accelerate techno-logical breakthroughs by funding new technologies to generate coal power that captures carbon emissions, advance emissions-free nuclear power; and invest in advanced battery technology and renewable energy. I am also committing

$2 billion to a new international clean technology fund that will help developing nations make greater use of clean energy sources. Additionally, my Budget proposes to protect the economy against oil supply disruptions by doubling the capacity of the Strategic Petroleum Reserve.

Finally, a strong and vibrant education system is vital to maintaining our Nation's competitive edge and extending economic opportunity to every citizen. Six years ago, we came together to pass the No Child Left Behind Act, and no one can deny its results. Now we must work together to increase accountability, add flexibility for States and districts, reduce the number of high school dropouts, and provide extra help for struggling schools.

Many of these issues are discussed in the 2008 *Annual Report of the Council of Economic Advisers.* The Council has prepared this *Report* to help policymakers understand the economic conditions and issues that underlie my Administration's policy decisions. By relying on the foundation and resilience of our economy, trusting the decisions of individuals and markets and pursuing pro-growth policies, we should have confidence in our prospects for continued prosperity and economic growth.

THE WHITE HOUSE
FEBRUARY 2008

THE ANNUAL REPORT
OF THE
COUNCIL OF ECONOMIC ADVISERS

LETTER OF TRANSMITTAL

COUNCIL OF ECONOMIC ADVISERS
Washington, D.C., February 12, 2008

MR. PRESIDENT:

The Council of Economic Advisers herewith submits its 2008 Annual Report in accordance with the provisions of the Employment Act of 1946 as amended by the Full Employment and Balanced Growth Act of 1978.

Sincerely,

Edward P. Lazear
Chairman

CONTENTS

LIST OF BOXES

Overview

The U.S. economy retains a solid foundation, even as it faces challenges ahead. Toward the end of 2007, there were increasingly mixed economic indicators (see Chapters 1 and 2). Economic growth is expected to continue in 2008. Most market forecasts suggest a slower pace in the first half of 2008, followed by strengthened growth in the second half of the year. The inherent resilience of our economy has enabled it to absorb multiple shocks in recent years, but the President does not take this growth for granted. Recognizing the near-term risks of a broader economic slowdown, the President called on the Congress to enact an economic growth package to protect the health of our economy and encourage job creation. Much of this *Report* examines contributions of pro-growth economic policies and market-based reforms that can further strengthen our economy and allow more Americans to benefit from continued economic expansion.

The United States' commitment to fair and open trade and investment policies is an important factor in our international competitiveness and in the dynamic nature of our economy; export performance has played a notable and growing role in economic growth in recent years (see Chapter 3). Lower tax rates have also contributed to economic performance by easing the burden on labor and capital and enabling consumers to allocate resources more efficiently (see Chapter 5). There remains considerable opportunity to strengthen our economic position by enacting a short-term economic growth package, and by addressing key challenges in the housing and credit markets, rising health care costs, infrastructure financing and the need to diversify our energy portfolios (see Chapters 2, 4, 6, and 7). A mixed economic picture also underscores the need for accurate measures of economic performance. Improvements to economic statistics programs could contribute to a greater understanding of the economy for public policymakers and private decision makers (see Chapter 8).

Chapter 1: The Year in Review
and the Years Ahead

Economic expansion continued for the sixth consecutive year in 2007. This economic growth came despite a weak housing sector, credit tightening, and high energy prices. Sustained growth has resulted from U.S. economic flexibility, openness and other pro-growth policies. Projections of weaker growth in the first half of 2008 and near-term risks of a broader economic slowdown, however, led the President to call on the Congress to enact a short-term economic growth package. Chapter 1 reviews the past year and discusses the Administration's forecast for the years ahead. The key points are:

- Real GDP posted solid 2.5 percent growth during the four quarters of 2007, similar to the pace of a year earlier. Compared with the preceding years of the expansion, the continued reorientation of aggregate demand resulted in more growth from exports and business fixed investment, while residential investment flipped from contributing positively to GDP growth from 2003 to 2005 to subtracting from it in 2006 and 2007.

- Labor markets were tight in the first half of 2007, but conditions slackened somewhat in the second half, with job growth slowing and the unemployment rate edging up to 4.7 percent in the third quarter and to 5.0 percent by December.

- Energy prices dominated the movement of overall inflation in the consumer price index (CPI), with large increases toward the end of the year. Core consumer inflation (which excludes food and energy inflation) moved down from 2.6 percent during the 12 months of 2006 to 2.4 percent in 2007. Food prices rose appreciably faster than core prices.

- Nominal wage gains of 3.7 percent for production workers were offset by the unexpected rise in energy prices. These nominal gains, however, exceeded measures of expected price inflation implying an expectation of real wage gains during the next several years.

- The Administration's forecast calls for the economic expansion to continue in 2008, but at a slower pace. Slower growth is anticipated for the first half of the year, and the average unemployment rate for 2008 is projected to move up from the 2007 level. In 2009 and 2010, real GDP growth is projected to grow at 3 percent, while the unemployment rate is projected to remain stable and below 5 percent.

- The contraction of the secondary market for some mortgage securities and the ensuing write-downs at major financial intermediaries are a new downside risk to this expansion. As of the end of 2007, however, these developments had not greatly affected the nonfinancial economy outside of the housing sector.

Chapter 2: Credit and Housing Markets

In the summer of 2007, the ongoing contraction in the U.S. housing market worsened and credit markets experienced a substantial disruption. Chapter 2 reviews the developments in the housing and credit markets, and describes public and private responses. The key points are:

- Rising delinquencies in subprime mortgages revealed an apparent under-pricing of risk and raised concerns about which market participants were exposed to that risk, but the subprime market was not the only cause for the contraction in credit markets.

- The Federal Reserve provided liquidity and took measures to support financial stability in the financial markets in the wake of the disruptions in the credit markets.

- The Administration focused its response on housing markets and helping homeowners avoid foreclosure—in particular, subprime borrowers facing increases in the interest rate on their adjustable-rate mortgages.

- Participants in the credit and housing markets are actively addressing challenges that were revealed during the summer of 2007. Markets are generally better suited than government to adapting to changes in the economic environment; markets can respond quickly to new information, while government policy often reacts with a lag or has a delayed impact.

- Financial innovations in the mortgage and credit markets have provided a range of economic benefits, but not without some costs. Over time, markets tend to retain valuable innovations and repair or eliminate flawed innovations.

- The macroeconomic effects of the downturn in housing and the credit market disruptions may occur through several channels, including the direct effect on residential investment, the reduction of wealth on personal consumption, and tighter lending standards on business investment.

Chapter 3: The Causes and Consequences of Export Growth

One noteworthy development in recent years has been the rapid growth of U.S. exports. This growth has provided clear benefits to entrepreneurs and workers in export-oriented industries, and to the economy as a whole. Chapter 3 identifies the primary factors that have driven recent export growth and discusses several longer-term trends that have lifted exports over time. More broadly, the chapter addresses the benefits that flow from open trade and investment policies as well as some related challenges. The key points of this chapter are:

- The United States is the world's largest exporter, with $1.5 trillion in goods and services exports in 2006. The United States was the top exporter of services and the second largest exporter of goods, behind only Germany.

- In recent years, factors that have likely contributed to the growth in exports include rising foreign income, the expansion of production in the United States, and changes in exchange rates. One reflection of that growth is that exports accounted for more than a third of U.S. economic growth during 2006 and 2007.

- Over time, falling tariffs and transport and communication costs have likely lowered the cost of many U.S. goods in foreign markets, boosting demand for U.S. exports.

- Open trade and investment policies have increased access to export markets for U.S. producers. Increased investment across borders by U.S. companies facilitates exports.

- Greater export opportunities give U.S. producers incentives to innovate for a worldwide market. Increased innovation and the competition that comes from trade liberalization help raise the living standard of the average U.S. citizen.

- Nearly all economists agree that growth in the volume and value of exports and imports increases the standard of living for the average individual, but they also agree that the gains from trade are not equally distributed and that some individuals bear costs. The Administration has proposed policies to improve training and support to individuals affected by trade disruption.

Chapter 4: The Importance of Health and Health Care

The American health care system is an engine for innovation that develops and broadly disseminates advanced, life-enhancing treatments and offers a wide set of choices for consumers of health care. The health care system provides enormous benefits, but there remain substantial opportunities for improvements that would reduce costs, increase access, and improve quality, thus providing even greater health for Americans. Chapter 4 examines the economics of health and health care. The key points in this chapter are:

- Health can be improved not only through the appropriate consumption of quality health care services, but also through individual behaviors and lifestyle choices such as quitting smoking, eating more nutritious foods, and getting more exercise.
- Health care has enhanced the health of our population; greater efficiency in the health care system, however, could yield even greater health for Americans without increasing health care spending.
- Rapid growth in health care costs and access to health insurance continue to present challenges to the health care system.
- Administration policies focus on reducing cost growth, improving quality, and expanding access to health insurance through an emphasis on private sector and market-based solutions.

Chapter 5: Tax Policy

Economists and policymakers have long debated the appropriate role of the government in a market economy. The government can provide public services and transfer payments to lower-income individuals, but these benefits often come at the cost of higher taxes and lower economic output. The key points in this chapter are:

- The ratio of federal taxation in the United States to gross domestic product (GDP) has fluctuated around an average value of 18.3 percent over the past 40 years; despite the President's 2001 and 2003 tax relief, this ratio was 18.8 percent in 2007, above the 40-year average. Under current law revenues are predicted to grow faster than the economy in coming years, raising the level of taxation well above its historical average.

- Tax reductions in 2001 and 2003 have considerably lowered the tax burden on labor and capital income and reduced distortions to economic decisions. Making these tax cuts permanent can greatly improve long-term economic outcomes.
- In addition to contributing to growth, the tax cuts of 2003 also improved the efficiency of the tax structure primarily by reducing the double taxation of corporate income.
- The business tax structure in the United States still creates substantial distortions. To attract investment from abroad and compete more effectively in foreign markets, the United States must consider how best to address distortions created by the structure of business taxes, as other countries have done.

Chapter 6: The Nation's Infrastructure

Our economy depends on infrastructure that allows goods, people, information, and energy to flow throughout the nation. As our economy grows and our infrastructure faces growing demand, policy should support investments that ensure that existing capacity is used as efficiently as possible. Chapter 6 discusses some of the economic issues associated with major transportation, communication, and power transmission systems. The key points in this chapter are:

- Infrastructure typically requires large capital investments to build and maintain capacity. Once built, however, the cost of allowing an extra person to use the capacity is typically low. This often means that infrastructure cannot be provided efficiently by a competitive market and many types of infrastructure are instead provided by Government-regulated companies or, in some cases, by the Government itself.
- Demands on the U.S. infrastructure grow as the economy expands, and Government policies often determine how effectively infrastructure can accommodate that growth. Properly designed user fees can help ensure efficiency by revealing information about what infrastructure consumers value most.
- The price people pay for using infrastructure should reflect the extra cost associated with its use. This includes the cost of maintaining the infrastructure itself, as well as delays caused by increased congestion.
- The private sector plays an important role in providing infrastructure. However, lack of competition in markets for infrastructure raises concerns about market power, so that Government oversight is sometimes necessary. The Government must continually reassess the need for oversight in the face of changing market conditions.

Chapter 7: Searching for Alternative Energy Solutions

Energy is used for many purposes in our economy: electricity generation, transportation, industrial production, and direct uses by homes and businesses. Energy security and environmental concerns motivate the consideration of policies that diversify our sources of energy. Chapter 7 outlines options for changing the way we produce and consume energy in two sectors of our economy: electricity generation and transportation. The key points in this chapter are:

- The current suite of available alternative energy sources is an important part of achieving our goal, but a number of technical, regulatory, and economic hurdles must be overcome to use them fully.
- There are several promising, but currently unproven, methods of producing and delivering energy that, if successfully developed and deployed, will greatly enhance our Nation's energy portfolio.
- Appropriate and limited government action can play a useful role in helping to realize our energy security goals.

Chapter 8: Improving Economic Statistics

Statistical systems have substantial value for both public policymakers and private decision makers. Chapter 8 examines several key issues in economic statistics, including the role of Federal statistical programs in a dynamic economy, the importance of continuity in statistical series, and ways to improve the value of existing statistical data.

The key points are:

- Robust statistical systems produce products that are important to understanding the changing state of the economy and to formulating sound policy. But statistical systems, like physical infrastructures, become obsolete or depreciate with time if they are not maintained.
- Statistical measures must keep up with the changing nature of the economy to be relevant and useful. For example, it is important that these measures reflect new and growing industries (such as high-technology industries or services) and intangible capital (such as research and development).
- Disruptions in a statistical series render it much less useful to policymakers and other data users. Thus, continuity in statistical series is an important goal.

- More effective statistical use can be made of existing data. In particular, amending relevant legislation to enable full implementation of the Confidential Information Protection and Statistical Efficiency Act (CIPSEA) could greatly improve the quality of Federal statistics.

CHAPTER 1

The Year in Review and the Years Ahead

The expansion of the U.S economy continued for a sixth consecutive year in 2007. Economic growth was solid at 2.5 percent during the four quarters of the year, slightly below the pace during 2006. Payroll job growth set a record for continuous growth, eclipsing the previous record of 48 months. This economic growth came despite a reorientation of the U.S. economy away from housing investment and toward exports and investment in business structures. The persistent tumble in housing investment subtracted roughly a percentage point from real Gross Domestic Product (GDP) growth during the four quarters of the year. Although the quarterly pattern of real GDP was uneven, with strong growth in the second and third quarters and weak growth in the first and fourth quarters, much of the quarter-to-quarter variation can be attributed to net exports, a volatile component of GDP. In the wake of mounting problems with the performance of *subprime* (defined as higher risk) mortgages, financial markets from August onward were unsettled because of concerns about the risk entailed in holding some types of mortgage-backed securities, as well as fears about the financial health of some firms and the possibility of contagion to the nonfinancial economy. To insure against the downside risks from these financial and housing-related developments, the President called for an economic growth package to boost consumption, business investment, and labor demand.

The core CPI (consumer prices excluding food and energy) as well as the *price index* for GDP (covering everything produced in the United States) suggested that inflation had moved lower and into the moderate range by the end of 2007. Food price inflation climbed, however, while energy prices jumped toward the end of the year. In response to these output and inflation developments, the Federal Reserve held the Federal funds rate flat through August. The Federal Reserve then lowered its policy rate by a percentage point from September through December and another 1¼ percentage point in January to ease liquidity concerns in financial markets disturbed by the mortgage market tumble, and to bolster real activity. The Federal Reserve also took other liquidity-enhancing measures, including cutting the discount rate at which it lends to banks, and initiating a new auction approach to provide collateralized loans to banks.

This chapter reviews the economic developments of 2007 and discusses the Administration's forecast for the years ahead. The key points of this chapter are:

- Real GDP posted solid 2.5 percent growth during the four quarters of 2007, similar to the pace of a year earlier. The reorientation of aggregate demand that began in 2006 continued in 2007. Compared with the preceding years of the expansion, this reorientation included more growth from exports and business fixed investment, while residential investment flipped from contributing positively to GDP growth from 2003 to 2005 to subtracting from it in 2006 and 2007.
- Labor markets were tight in the first half of 2007 with job growth averaging 107,000 per month and the jobless rate at 4.5 percent. Labor market conditions slackened somewhat in the second half, with job growth slowing to 82,000 per month and the unemployment rate edging up to 4.7 percent in the third quarter and to 5.0 percent by December.
- Energy prices, which tend to be volatile, dominated the movement of overall inflation in the consumer price index (CPI), with large increases toward the end of the year. Core consumer inflation (which excludes food and energy inflation) moved down from 2.6 percent during the 12 months of 2006 to 2.4 percent in 2007. Food prices rose appreciably faster than core prices.
- Nominal wage gains of 3.7 percent for production workers were offset by the unexpected rise in energy prices. These nominal gains, however, exceeded measures of expected price inflation such as those from the market for the Department of Treasury's inflation-protected securities, about 2.2 percent. As a consequence, the pace of nominal wage increases implies an expectation of real wage gains during the next several years. In the long run, real wages tend to increase with labor productivity.
- The Administration's forecast calls for the economic expansion to continue in 2008, but at a slower pace than in the earlier years of this expansion. Slower growth is anticipated for the first half of the year, and the average unemployment rate for 2008 is projected to move up from the 2007 level. In 2009 and 2010 real GDP growth is projected at 3 percent, thereafter slowing, while the unemployment rate is projected to remain stable and below 5 percent in the 2009–10 period.
- The contraction of the secondary market for some mortgage securities and the ensuing write-downs at major financial intermediaries are a new downside risk to this expansion. As of the end of 2007, however, these developments had not greatly affected the nonfinancial economy outside of the housing sector (which had already been in decline for a year or so before the onset of the mortgage financing problems).
- To insure against the downside risks from these new financial developments, the President proposed tax relief and changes to depreciation schedules that reduce the cost of business investment. The policy changes are expected to boost real GDP growth and job creation.

Developments in 2007 and the Near-Term Outlook

The economy went through a period of rebalancing that began in 2006 and extended into 2007, with faster growth in business structures investment and exports offsetting pronounced declines in homebuilding, while consumer spending growth edged lower.

Consumer Spending and Saving

Real consumer spending slowed to a 2.5 percent growth rate during the four quarters of 2007, somewhat below the growth rates during the preceding 4 years of expansion and below the average rates of the preceding 30 years. Nominal consumer spending (that is consumer spending without adjusting for inflation) pulled back from its 16-year pattern of rising faster than disposable income, and the personal saving rate for the year as a whole ticked up from 0.4 to 0.5 percent. Factors that had pushed down the saving rate during recent years shifted into neutral: the wealth-to-income ratio plateaued and the unemployment rate (which is related to consumer confidence) stopped falling. Energy costs rose rapidly, but consumers continued to purchase similar quantities of energy, which kept the personal saving rate low. The general decline in the personal saving rate during the past 5 years (despite the uptick in 2007) continued a long-term trend that began in the 1980s.

Energy Expenditures

World demand for crude oil increased by 5.5 million barrels per day to 85 million barrels per day between 2003 and the first three quarters of 2007. The United States accounted for only a fraction (0.7 million barrels per day) of this increase, while demand in other OECD countries generally fell. (The OECD, or Organization for Economic Cooperation and Development, comprises 30 key developed economies.) The increase in non-OECD demand totaled 5.3 million barrels per day, with China's per-day consumption alone growing by 2.0 million barrels. In the face of this increase in world oil demand, consumers paid higher prices to maintain their consumption.

Crude oil prices rose again in 2007. The spot price for West Texas Intermediate (a benchmark variety of crude oil) rose to an average of $91 per barrel in the fourth quarter from an average of $66 per barrel in 2006. The price of natural gas, which rose sharply in 2005, then fell during 2006, was little changed on balance in 2007, while electricity prices continued their upward trend.

With the rise in energy prices, the share of energy in total purchases rose sharply. From 2003 to 2007, consumer energy prices increased 41 percent relative to non-energy prices, while real consumption of energy per household fell only 3 percent (according to data from the National Income and Product Accounts). As a result, energy expenditures, which were about 5 percent of consumer purchases in 2003, rose to 6 percent of consumer purchases in 2006 and 2007. Between 2004 and 2006, consumers appear to have maintained both energy and nonenergy consumption by reducing their personal saving, which by 2007 (although up from 2006) averaged only 0.5 percent of disposable personal income. This continued rapid rise in energy prices suggests that consumers' adaptation to these prices remains unfinished. Consumers have chosen to respond to the energy-price shock by using savings to buffer some of its effects, but this response is probably temporary.

Wealth Effects on Consumption and Saving

Household wealth rose rapidly relative to disposable personal income from 2002 through the second quarter of 2007, supporting the growth of consumption and a decline in the saving rate. Over the 2002–07 period, the ratio of household wealth to annual-income increased 0.7 years, to 5.7 years of accumulated income (that is, consumers collectively accumulated an extra 70 percent of a years' income). During the late 1990s and again during 2004–06, a strong rise in household net worth coincided with a sizable increase in consumer spending relative to disposable personal income (Chart 1-1).

Chart 1-1 **Consumption and Net Worth Relative to Disposable Personal Income (DPI)**
Consumption gains from 2004 to 2006 were partly supported by an increase in net worth (wealth). In 2007, wealth grew only as fast as income as housing wealth was held down by flat house prices.

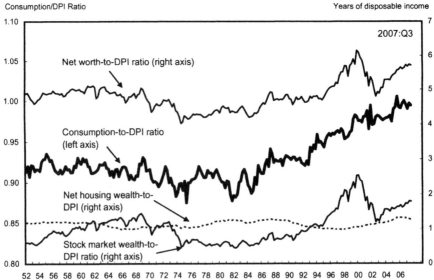

Sources: Department of Commerce (Bureau of Economic Analysis), Federal Reserve Board, and Council of Economic Advisers.

Unlike recent years, however, the 2007 gains did not reflect large increases in housing wealth (net of mortgage debt), which peaked—relative to income—in the first half of 2006, and has edged lower since (see Chart 1-1). The housing price rise of 1.8 percent during the year that ended with the third quarter of 2007 was a substantial deceleration from the 11 percent annual rate during the 3 preceding years and was less than the growth of income. Stock-market wealth rose during the four quarters through the third quarter of 2007 (the most recent wealth data) and accounted for all of the four-quarter gain. By the third quarter of 2007, the overall wealth-to-income ratio was well above its 50-year average.

Projected Consumer Spending

Looking ahead, the path of consumer spending is projected to reflect the recent flattening of the wealth-to-income ratio. Real consumer spending during the four quarters of 2008 is expected to grow 2.1 percent, down from an average of about 3 percent during the past 3 years. This projected rate is less than the projected 2008 growth of *real disposable personal income* (household income less taxes, adjusted for inflation), and so the saving rate is forecasted to continue edging up in 2008. After that, real consumption is projected to increase at about the same pace as real GDP and real income.

Housing Prices

Nationally, nominal house price appreciation slowed to a crawl in 2007, and house prices fell when corrected for inflation. An inflation-adjusted version of the housing price index (the nominal version of which is compiled by the Office of Federal Housing Enterprise Oversight (OFHEO) from home sales and appraisals during refinancing) increased at an average annual rate of 6.3 percent from 2000 to 2005. It then slowed to 4.0 percent during the four quarters of 2006, and declined at a 3.2 percent annual rate during the first three quarters of 2007. (These inflation-adjusted prices are deflated by the consumer price index.) The homes covered by this OFHEO-created housing price index are those which are financed or refinanced by one of the govern-ment-sponsored housing enterprises and must therefore have mortgages below the conforming loan limit (currently $417,000). Another relevant measure of home prices (the S&P/Case-Shiller Index), has fallen 6.7 percent in real terms during the year that ended with the third quarter of 2007; this index covers a smaller portion of the country than the OFHEO measure but is more comprehensive with regard to homes with large mortgages.

The deceleration of housing prices along with falling standards for subprime mortgages in 2005 and 2006 has led to a rising delinquency rate for subprime adjustable-rate mortgages (where the rate on the mortgages resets after an initial period), which severely disrupted the secondary market for nonconforming mortgages in 2007. In contrast, the market for conforming mortgages continued to function well. (Conforming loans must meet certain loan-to-value and documentation requirements in addition to being below the conforming loan limit.) See Chapter 2, "Credit and Housing Markets" for a more extensive analysis.

Residential Investment

Every major measure of housing activity dropped sharply during 2006 and 2007, and the drop in real residential construction was steeper than anticipated in last year's *Report*. Housing starts (the initiation of a homebuilding project), new building permits, and new home sales have fallen more than 40 percent since their annual peaks in 2005. The drop in home-construction activity subtracted an average of almost 1 percentage point at an annual rate from real GDP growth during the last three quarters of 2006 and the four quarters of 2007. Furthermore, even if housing starts level off at their current pace, lags between the beginning and completion of a construction project imply that residential investment will subtract from GDP growth during the first half of 2008.

During 2007, as in 2006, employment in residential construction fell, as did production of construction materials and products associated with new home sales (such as furniture, large appliances, and carpeting). Yet despite these housing sector declines, the overall economy continued to expand (see Box 1-1).

Box 1-1: Indirect Effects of the Housing Sector

Thus far, the sharp drop in homebuilding has not prevented robust activity outside of the housing sector. Employment fell in sectors related to new home construction and housing sales. Despite these repercussions, overall payroll employment continued to increase, and real consumer spending continued to move upward through the end of 2007. The unemployment rate, however, increased, by 0.6 percentage point during the 12 months of the year.

Although residential investment fell sharply, real GDP growth during 2007 was sustained by increases in other forms of investment. As shown in the chart below, private and public nominal nonresidential construction (that is, construction of office buildings, shopping centers, factories, and other business structures) grew rapidly during the year.

continued on the next page

Box 1-1 — continued

Nonresidential construction draws from some of the same resources (such as construction labor and materials) as the residential construction sector. The high level of residential investment during the past couple of years may have limited the growth of investment in nonresidential structures. While the case for housing crowding out other sectors is strongest for nonresidential investment, residential investment competes with all other sectors of production in credit and labor markets. A drop in the share of the economy engaged in housing could provide some room for other sectors to grow.

Construction

Although private residential construction has fallen sharply from its peak, nonresidential investment continues to grow and absorb some of the resources formerly used in the residential sector.

Dollars (billions), seasonally adjusted at an annual rate

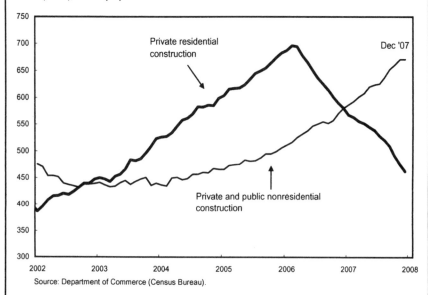

Source: Department of Commerce (Census Bureau).

The housing market could also affect the rest of the economy through the wealth channel. That is, declines in housing prices could reduce household net worth and thereby reduce consumption. The increase in housing prices during 2000–2005 contributed noticeably to the gain in the ratio of household wealth to income (shown earlier in Chart 1-1) and supported growth in consumer spending. In contrast, gains in housing wealth came to a virtual halt during 2007.

In addition to incomes and mortgage rates, the number of homes built is underpinned by demographics. Homebuilding during 2004 and 2005 averaged about 2.0 million units per year, in excess of the 1.8- or 1.9-million unit annual pace of housing starts that would be consistent with some demographic models for a decade-long period, leading to an excess supply of houses on the market. More recently, the 1.2 million unit pace during the fourth quarter of 2007 is well below this long-term demographic target. The pace of homebuilding has now been below this level for long enough that the above-trend production of 2004 and 2005 has been offset by the more recent below-trend production. Yet the construction of new homes continued to fall rapidly through year-end 2007, with the undershooting possibly reflecting uncertain prospects for house prices as well as elevated inventories of unsold new and existing homes. Once prices become firm and inventories return to normal levels, home construction should rebound, but it is difficult to pinpoint when this will occur. The residential sector is not expected to make positive contributions to real GDP growth until 2009.

Business Fixed Investment

During the four quarters of 2007 real business investment in equipment and software (that is, measured at constant prices) grew 3.7 percent, a bit faster than the 2006 pace but notably slower than the 8 percent average pace during the 3 preceding years. Its fastest-growing components during 2007 included computers, software, and communication equipment while investment in industrial equipment grew slowly. Transportation equipment, however, fell substantially due to environmental regulations (on particulate matter emissions issued in 2000 but effective in 2007) that raised truck prices in 2007 and led trucking firms to advance heavy truck purchases into 2006 from 2007.

In contrast to residential investment, real business investment in nonresidential structures grew at a strong 16 percent annual rate over the four quarters of 2007. The gains during 2007 were the second consecutive year of strong growth, which was a marked reversal from the declines during the period from 2001 to 2005. Nearly 70 percent of total growth in nonresidential structures was accounted for by office buildings, lodging facilities, power facilities, and petroleum and natural gas exploration and wells. This sector maintained its ability to borrow funds needed for construction, as net borrowing for nonfinancial corporate commercial mortgages rose 6.5 percent at an annual rate during the first three quarters of 2007.

One risk to the near-term investment forecast is that the recent turmoil in the market for mortgage-backed securities may somehow reduce the funds available for business investment. Most new investment—at least for the corporate sector as a whole—is being financed with internally generated funds for new investment (undistributed profits plus depreciation, also known as *cash flow*) which were at normal levels through the third quarter of 2007. As for the amount that nonfinancial firms must borrow to finance investment (the financing gap), the flows showed no shortfall, at least through the third quarter of 2007 (Chart 1-2). A shortage of investment funds, though possible, appears unlikely. Corporations have been able to finance investment directly through the bond market without penalty as interest rates on 10-year high-grade corporate bonds in the second half of 2007 were little different from the first half of the year. Nevertheless the market for investment funds merits close attention as yields on lower-grade corporate bonds have edged up, the number of newly announced leveraged buyouts have fallen sharply, and the October survey of senior loan officers reported tighter lending standards for loans to large and small companies.

Business investment growth is projected to remain solid in 2008, although probably below the 7½ percent growth rate during the four quarters of 2007. Continued growth in output combined with a tight labor market is expected to maintain strong demand for new capital. In the longer run, real business investment is projected to grow slightly above the growth rate of real GDP.

Chart 1-2 **Net Debt Issuance**
Evidence suggests that the nonfinancial business sector has had no problems borrowing funds through 2007:Q3.

Billion $ (seasonally adjusted annual rate)

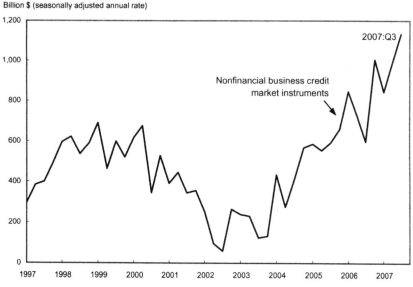

Source: Federal Reserve Board, Flow of Funds.

Business Inventories

Inventory investment was volatile during the past year or so and had a noticeable influence on quarter-to-quarter fluctuations in real GDP, especially the weakness in the first and fourth quarters and the strength in the third quarter. Inventories of motor vehicles on dealer lots and in transit were an important contributor to these fluctuations as they were liquidated during the first half of 2007, and built up in the third quarter before being liquidated again in the fourth quarter. Real nonfarm inventories grew at only an average 0.2 percent annual pace during 2007, a growth rate that is well below the pace of real GDP growth over the same period. Coming off a long-term decline, the inventory-to-sales ratio for manufacturing and trade (in current dollars) rose in late 2006 before being reduced sharply in 2007.

Manufacturing and trade inventories appear to be roughly in line with sales as of November 2007 and do not appear to require dramatic swings in production. Inventory investment is projected to be fairly stable during the next several years, as is generally the case for periods of stable growth. The overall inventory-to-sales ratio is expected to continue trending lower.

Government Purchases

Real Federal consumption and gross investment grew 1.6 percent during 2007, a slowdown from the 2006 pace. Quarterly fluctuations in this spending category were considerable, with nearly all the volatility due to the defense component. Defense spending plunged in the first quarter of 2007 but grew rapidly during the second and third quarters of the year.

The defense appropriations act for fiscal year (FY) 2007 provided $70 billion for operations in Afghanistan and Iraq. The FY 2007 supplemental appropriation for defense provided an additional $107 billion for ongoing operations in Afghanistan and Iraq. Another $70 billion in emergency funding for FY 2008 was provided in the consolidated appropriations act. The first continuing resolution for FY 2008 and the defense appropriations act for FY 2008 provided $17 billion for mine-resistant vehicles and other funding for Afghanistan and Iraq. Another supplemental appropriation for operations in Afghanistan and Iraq is likely for FY 2008.

Nominal Federal revenues grew 12 percent in FY 2006 and 7 percent in FY 2007. These rapid growth rates exceeded growth in outlays and GDP as a whole, and the U.S. fiscal deficit as a share of GDP shrank from 3.6 percent in FY 2004, to 1.9 percent in FY 2006, to 1.2 percent in FY 2007.

Real State and local government purchases rose 3 percent during 2007, the second consecutive year of moderate growth. This followed 3 years of little change. In the wake of the 2001 recession, this sector fell sharply into deficit in 2002. Revenues began to recover in 2003, and the sector was out of deficit by 2005, allowing for an increase in state and local consumption and investment in 2006 and 2007. This pattern of delayed response to downturns resembles the pattern during the business-cycle recovery of the 1990s.

The State and local government sector slipped into a small deficit over the first three quarters of 2007 reflecting strong growth in outlays that were not matched by an increase in revenues. In 2008, only slow growth can be anticipated for this sector's consumption and gross investment because of decelerating housing prices and their effects on property tax receipts—which comprise about 20 percent of this sector's revenues.

Exports and Imports

Real exports of goods and services grew 8 percent during the four quarters 2007, the fourth year of annual growth in excess of 7 percent. The pace of export expansion reflects rapid growth among our trading partners, expanded domestic production capacity, and changes in the terms of trade associated with exchange rate trends between 2002 and 2006 that made American goods cheaper relative to those of some other countries (Chapter 3 analyzes recent export growth in greater detail). Real GDP among our advanced-economy trading partners (that is, the other 29 member countries of the OECD) is estimated to have grown at rates of 3.3 and 2.7 percent during the four quarters of 2006 and 2007, respectively, after growing at an average pace of 2.4 percent during the preceding 3 years. In addition, the economies of some of our major emerging-market trading partners such as China, Singapore, and India are growing at rates of 8 to 11 percent per year, although these countries receive only about 8 percent of our exports. The OECD projects that real GDP among our advanced-economy trading partners will slow to a still-solid 2.4 percent growth rate during the four quarters of 2008. The International Monetary Fund projects that real GDP among the group of emerging market economies will slow to a still-strong 7.4 percent growth rate for 2008 as a whole.

The fastest growth in U.S. goods and services exports was to India, but exports to China, Africa, and the Middle East also grew rapidly. Despite the rapid growth of exports to these emerging economies, the European Union (EU) remains the major overseas export destination, consuming over 25 percent of our exports. By country, Canada accounts for the largest share of U.S. exports, at over 19 percent.

Real imports grew 1.4 percent annual rate during 2007, the slowest pace since 2001. Real imports of nonpetroleum goods grew 1.2 percent during 2007, also the slowest rate of increase since 2001. Real petroleum imports have edged up 2.5 percent during 2007, while nominal imports surged 49 percent due to rising oil prices. The rise in oil prices has been less of a drag on the U.S. economy than similar rises have been because it has been offset by the strong growth in foreign economies, which has boosted U.S. exports.

Indeed, the growth in foreign economies is what has largely induced the multi-year increase in oil prices (Box 1-2).

Box 1-2: Macroeconomic Effects When Oil Price Increases Are Induced by Foreign Demand

The cost of imported crude oil increased nearly $40 per barrel from 2003 to 2007, the largest dollar increase on record. Earlier price increases in 1973, 1979, and 1990 were followed by recessions, a development that has not occurred during the current episode. What has happened recently that has allowed the United States to maintain strong growth in the face of this price surge?

Economic growth outside the United States increased about 2.1 percentage points from the 3.5 percent annual growth rate during the 15 years from 1989 to 2003 to a 5.6 percent annual rate during the 4 years from 2004 to 2007 according to estimates from the International Monetary Fund. The increase in real GDP growth among our trading partners probably caused an increase in both the demand for oil and the price of oil, and also an increase in U.S. exports to our trading partners. Rapidly growing countries (China, Russia, India, and Thailand) accounted for much of the increase in oil demand during the 4 years from 2002 to

Oil Consumption Growth by Country (4 years from 2002 to 2006)
World oil demand (excluding OPEC) rose at a 1.8% annual rate from 2002 to 2006. China, the United States, Russia, India, Thailand, and Canada accounted for more than 70 percent of this growth.

Contribution to world oil consumption growth (percentage points, annual rate)

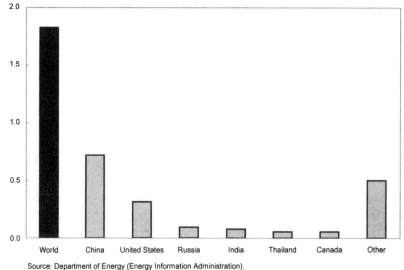

Source: Department of Energy (Energy Information Administration).

continued on the next page

2006 as shown in the chart. Countries showing the largest increases in oil consumption tended to be those showing the largest growth rates during the past 4 years. In addition, U.S. exports grew rapidly to those countries that have recently signed and implemented free trade agreements with the United States (as discussed in Chapter 3).

An increase in real output growth among our trading partners of about 1 percent can be expected to increase our exports by about 1 percent as well. The cumulative 9 percent higher growth among our trading partners (2.1 percent for each of 4 years) could thus have generated as much as $120 billion per year of exports. In comparison, the $40-per-barrel oil price increase added about $150 billion per year to the Nation's bill for oil imports (at 3.7 billion barrels of oil per year).

The *current account deficit* (the excess of imports and income flows to foreigners over exports and foreign income of Americans) averaged 5.5 percent of GDP during the first three quarters of 2007, down from its 2006 average of over 6 percent. The decline in the current account deficit reflects strong export growth and moderate import growth, although domestic investment continues to exceed domestic saving, with foreigners financing the gap between the two.

Employment

Nonfarm payroll employment increased by 1.14 million jobs during 2007, an average pace of about 95,000 jobs per month. The unemployment rate rose slightly over the same period, ticking up 0.6 percentage point to 5.0 percent. The average unemployment rate in 2007 was 4.6 percent, equal to the 2006 average. Both the 2007 average and the December 2007 level of the unemployment rate were below the prevailing rates in each of the three decades of the 1970s, 1980s, and 1990s.

The service-providing sector accounted for all of the year's job gains, as construction employment fell due to continued weakness in the housing market and manufacturing employment continued its downtrend for the tenth consecutive year. (Despite the job losses, manufacturing output continues to increase because of rapid productivity growth.) Employment in mining (which includes oil drilling) rose 5.5 percent during 2007. The goods-producing sector has accounted for a diminishing share of total employment in each of the past five decades. Education and health services (which constituted 13 percent of employment at the end of 2007) added the largest number of jobs, accounting for 47 percent of total job growth.

During the 12 months of 2007, the unemployment rate for the major education groups edged up; it increased 0.3 percentage point for those holding at least a bachelor's degree, 0.4 percentage point for those whose education ended with a high school degree or those with some college, and 1.0 percentage point among those who did not finish high school. By race and ethnicity, the unemployment rate for black Americans rose by 0.7 percentage point, and was about 4 percentage points above the rate for whites, a smaller margin than during most of the past 35 years. Unemployment rates among whites rose 0.4 percentage point, and among Hispanics rose 1.4 percentage points. By sex, the jobless rate for both adult men and adult women increased 0.5 percentage point to 4.4 percent in December 2007.

The median duration of unemployment edged up from 7.5 to 8.4 weeks during the 12 months of 2007, following a substantial decline during the preceding 2 years. The number of long-term unemployed (those who are jobless for 15 weeks or more) rose by 426,000 over the same period. Although this is not a welcome development, increases in unemployment rates (and implicitly increases in duration as well) were built into last year's Administration forecast as the low jobless rates at the end of 2006 were not judged to be sustainable in the long run.

The Administration projects that employment will increase at an average pace of 109,000 jobs per month during the four quarters of 2008, before picking up to 129,000 jobs per month in 2009. In the longer run, the pace of employment growth will slow, reflecting diminishing rates of labor force growth due to the retirement of the baby-boom generation. The Administration also projects that the unemployment rate will edge up from 2007 to 2008 as a whole, before returning to 4.8 percent in 2010, the middle of the range consistent with stable inflation in the long run.

Productivity

Productivity growth has a standard cyclical pattern. It usually falls during a recession, grows rapidly during the early stages of a recovery, but then slows as the recovery matures. The current business cycle began on an unusual note, with strong productivity growth of 4.6 percent at an annual rate (rather than the usual decline) during the three quarters of the 2001 recession. After that, the pattern of productivity followed a more-usual business-cycle pattern with strong (3.1 percent annual rate) growth during the first 3 years of the expansion, followed by a slowing to a 1¾ percent annual rate during the most recent 3-year period. Averaging across the entire 6½-year period since the business-cycle peak in the first quarter of 2001, labor productivity has increased at a 2.7 percent annual rate. This pace is not significantly different from the pace between 1995 and 2001. As can be seen in Chart 1-3, a trend

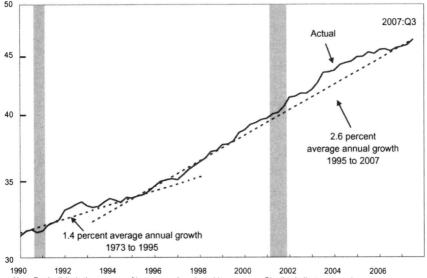

Chart 1-3 **Output per Hour in the Nonfarm Business Sector**
Productivity has trended up at about a 2.6% annual rate since 1995.

Real output per hour (constant $2000, ratio scale)

Note: Productivity is the average of income- and product-side measures. Shading indicates recessions.
Sources: Department of Commerce (Bureau of Economic Analysis) and Department of Labor (Bureau of Labor Statistics).

line with a 2.6 percent annual rate of growth from 1995 to 2007 captures most of the movement of productivity over this period.

The continuation of this roughly 2.6 percent growth in labor productivity is striking, given a flat or diminished contribution from *capital deepening* (the increase in capital services per hour worked). The 1995 to 2001 acceleration may be plausibly accounted for by a pickup in capital deepening and by increases in organizational capital (the investments businesses make to reorganize and restructure themselves, in this instance in response to newly installed information technology). After 2001, a reduced rate of capital deepening—on its own—would have suggested a slowing in the rate of productivity growth. Productivity growth in the recent period therefore appears to be supported by factors that are more difficult to measure than the quantity of capital, such as intangible investments in technology and business practices.

Productivity growth is projected to average 2.5 percent per year during the 6-year span of the budget projection (Table 1-2, later in this chapter), which is about the same as the average annual pace since 1995. The projected growth rate is slightly below the 2.6 percent annual pace discussed in last year's *Report,* and reflects the downward revisions to real GDP and other output measures announced in the annual revisions to the National Income and Product Accounts in July 2006 and July 2007.

Prices and Wages

As measured by the consumer price index (CPI), overall inflation rose from 2.5 percent during the 12 months of 2006 to 4.1 percent during 2007 (Chart 1-4), with the increase due to an acceleration of food and energy prices. Energy prices accelerated from a 2.9 percent increase in 2006 to a 17.4 percent increase in 2007. Food prices increased 4.9 percent during 2007, up sharply from the 2.1 percent pace of the previous year. Core CPI prices (that is, excluding food and energy) increased 2.4 percent during 2007, down from a 2.6 percent increase a year earlier.

Prices of petroleum products climbed 29.4 percent during 2007 while natural gas prices fell slightly. Electricity prices increased 5.2 percent, which was less than the rate of increase a year earlier. As of late-January 2008, futures prices show that market participants expect crude oil prices to edge down during 2008 from their current high level while natural gas prices are expected to rise.

The rapid increase in food prices during 2007 reflects worldwide agricultural supply and demand conditions, such as the drought in Australia (a major wheat exporter), the demand for corn-based ethanol, and short-supply

Chart 1-4 **Consumer Price Inflation**
The increase in overall CPI inflation during 2007 was entirely due to an acceleration in food and energy prices. Core CPI inflation generally edged lower during the year.

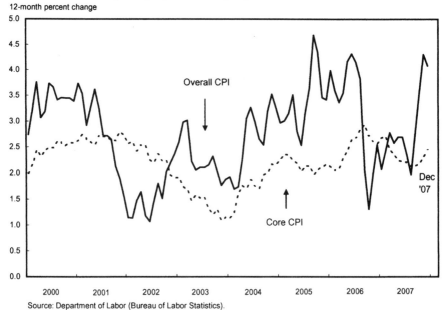

Source: Department of Labor (Bureau of Labor Statistics).

conditions for dairy herds. The supply constraints during 2007 for wheat and dairy products appear temporary and are expected to return toward normal during 2008.

The 0.2 percentage point deceleration of core CPI prices was accounted for primarily by rent of shelter, which slowed to a 3.1 percent rate of increase from a 4.3 percent rate of increase during the 12 months of 2006. The Administration projects that the CPI will increase 2.1 percent in 2008, slightly less that the 2.4 percent rate of increase of the core CPI during 2007; energy and food prices are expected to be little changed in 2008 following their recent large increases.

Hourly compensation (which was about 62 percent of nonfarm business output) has increased at roughly the same 3 percent rate in 2007 as during the preceding 2 years according to the Employment Cost Index (ECI) for the private sector. The wage and salary index grew 3.3 percent, little changed from 3.2 percent a year earlier, while growth of hourly benefits slowed to 2.4 percent. Another measure of hourly compensation from the productivity and cost dataset increased slightly faster than the ECI.

Unit labor costs (labor compensation per unit of output) have put little, if any, upward pressure on inflation thus far, and it appears unlikely that they will over the next year. Unit labor costs grew only 0.7 percent at an annual rate during the first three quarters of 2007 which is less than the 2.6 percent growth in the GDP price index during the same interval.

Average hourly earnings of production or non-supervisory workers (who constitute about 80 percent of total employment on nonfarm payrolls) increased 3.7 percent (in nominal terms) during the 12 months through December 2007—somewhat below the pace a year earlier of 4.3 percent. These nominal hourly earnings were outstripped by the 4.4 percent increase in the overall CPI for wage earners, and so real earnings fell 0.7 percent during 2007 (following a 1.8 percent gain in 2006). Even so, the recent pace of these nominal wage increases is above various measures of expected price inflation (such as those implied by the market for inflation-indexed Treasury securities), and suggests that employers and employees expect a gain in real earnings in 2008. The situation is similar to a year ago, but during 2007, price inflation was higher than expected because of sharp and unanticipated increases in food and energy prices. In the long run, real hourly compensation increases with productivity growth, which is projected to remain solid.

Among the many available measures of inflation, the Administration forecast focuses on two: the consumer price index and the price index for GDP. The CPI measures prices for a fixed basket of consumer goods and services. It is widely reported in the press, and is used to index Social Security benefits, the individual income tax, Federal pensions, and many private-sector contracts. The GDP price index covers prices of all final goods and services produced in the United States, including consumption, investment, and government purchases. In contrast to the CPI, its weights are not fixed, but move to reflect changes in spending patterns. Of the two indexes, the CPI tends to increase more rapidly, in part because it measures a fixed basket of goods and services; the GDP price index increases less rapidly because it reflects the shifting of household and business purchases away from items with increasing relative prices and toward items with decreasing relative prices. Additionally, the GDP price index (which includes investment goods) places a larger weight on computers, which tend to decline in price (on a quality-adjusted basis), while the CPI places a much larger weight on rent and energy.

The "wedge," or difference between the CPI and the GDP measures of inflation, has implications for Federal budget projections. A larger wedge (with the CPI rising faster than the GDP price index) raises the Federal budget deficit because Social Security and Federal pensions rise with the CPI, while Federal revenue tends to increase with the GDP price index. For a given level of nominal income, increases in the CPI also cut Federal revenue because they raise the brackets at which higher income tax rates apply and affect other inflation-indexed features of the tax code.

Is rising inflation a problem for the United States? Although the CPI accelerated to a 4.1 percent rate of increase during 2007, the acceleration was entirely a result of food and energy price increases that are not likely to be repeated. Nor do market participants expect it to be repeated, as is evident from the well-anchored long-run consumer price inflation expectations in the market for inflation-indexed securities. Furthermore, most of the price increases for petroleum do not reflect prices charged by workers or firms in the United States because 65 percent of petroleum is imported. The GDP price index better captures the prices that Americans are charging for their labor and services, and it decelerated to a 2.6 percent increase during 2007 from a year-earlier pace of 2.7 percent. Prices for business investment—which is not captured in the CPI—slowed noticeably in 2007. In sum, long run inflation expectations remain stable, and inflation as measured by the broad-based GDP price index remained moderate in 2007.

Financial Markets

The Wilshire 5000 (a broad stock market index) increased 3.9 percent during 2007, while the Standard and Poor 500 (an index of the 500 largest corporations) increased 3.5 percent. This was the fifth consecutive year of stock market gains, and it followed 3 years of declines.

Yields on 10-year Treasury notes ended 2006 at 4.6 percent—near the low end of the historical range—and fell another 46 basis points during 2007. These yield dropped further in January. The low level of these long-term interest rates was due in part to low and stable long-run inflation expectations.

The Administration's forecast of short-term interest rates is roughly based on financial market data as well as a survey of economic forecasters at the date that the forecast was developed in mid-November. The near-term forecast has been overtaken by events as interest rates have fallen notably since the forecast was finalized. Whatever the starting point, the Administration projects the rate on 91-day Treasury bills to edge up gradually to 4.1 percent by 2011 and then remain at that level. At that level, the real rate (that is, the nominal rate less the rate of inflation) on 91-day Treasury bills would be close to its historical average.

The yield on 10-year Treasury notes on November 15 (when the forecast was finalized) was 4.17 percent. The January decline in this yield means that this near-term forecast has also been overtaken by events. The Administration expects the 10-year rate to increase, eventually reaching a normal spread of about 1.2 percentage points over the 91-day Treasury-bill rate by 2012. An increase in yield also appears to be expected by market participants (as evidenced by higher rates on 20-year Treasury notes than on notes with 10-year maturities). As a result, yields on 10-year notes are expected to increase somewhat further, reaching a plateau at 5.3 percent from 2012 onward.

The Long-Term Outlook Through 2013

During the sixth year of expansion in 2007, the composition of demand was reshuffled, a process that is likely to continue in 2008. The period of somewhat slower-than-normal growth that began in 2007 is likely to continue into 2008. Thereafter, the economy is projected to expand at a roughly steady rate at or just below 3.0 percent. Having reached a level of resource utilization consistent with stable inflation by the end of 2007, inflation will remain in the low-to-moderate range currently suggested by core inflation rates. Payroll job growth is expected to remain solid while the unemployment rate is expected to be little changed over the projection interval (Table 1-1). The forecast is based on conservative economic assumptions that are close to the consensus of professional forecasters. These assumptions provide a sound basis for the Administration's budget projections.

Growth in GDP over the Long Term

The Administration projects that, following a slight pickup of growth from 2008 to 2009, real GDP will increase at a slowly diminishing rate from 2009 through 2013, due to the expected retirement of the baby-boom generation. Indeed, real GDP is projected to decelerate from a 3.0 percent growth rate during the four quarters of 2009 to 2.8 percent by 2013. The average growth rate during this interval is roughly in line with the consensus of private

TABLE 1-1.—*Administration Economic Forecast*[1]

Year	Nominal GDP	Real GDP (chain-type)	GDP price index (chain-type)	Consumer price index (CPI-U)	Unemploy-ment rate (percent)	Interest rate, 91-day Treasury bills[2] (percent)	Interest rate, 10-year Treasury notes (percent)	Nonfarm payroll employ-ment (average monthly change, Q4-to-Q4, thou-sands)[3]
	Percent change, Q4-to-Q4				Level, calendar year			
2006 (actual)........	5.4	2.6	2.7	1.9	4.6	4.7	4.8	192
2007....................	5.1	2.7	2.3	3.9	4.6	4.4	4.7	129
2008....................	4.8	2.7	2.0	2.1	4.9	3.7	4.6	109
2009....................	5.1	3.0	2.0	2.2	4.9	3.8	4.9	129
2010....................	5.0	3.0	2.0	2.3	4.8	4.0	5.1	118
2011....................	5.0	2.9	2.0	2.3	4.8	4.1	5.2	112
2012....................	4.9	2.8	2.0	2.3	4.8	4.1	5.3	102
2013....................	4.9	2.8	2.0	2.3	4.8	4.1	5.3	92

[1] Based on data available as of November 15, 2007.

[2] Secondary market discount basis.

[3] The figures do not reflect the upcoming BLS benchmark which is expected to reduce 2006 and 2007 job growth by a cumulative 300,000 jobs.

Sources: Council of Economic Advisers, Department of Commerce (Bureau of Economic Analysis and Economics and Statistics Administration), Department of Labor (Bureau of Labor Statistics), Department of the Treasury, and Office of Management and Budget.

forecasters for those years. After 2008, the year-by-year pace is close to the estimated growth rate of *potential real* GDP, a measure of the rate of growth of productive capacity. (An economy is said to be growing at its potential rate when all of its resources are utilized and inflation is stable. The supply-side components of potential GDP growth are presented in Table 1-2 and are discussed below.) The unemployment rate is projected to be roughly flat in 2008 and 2009 at around its December 2007 level before edging back down to 4.8 percent thereafter. As discussed below, potential GDP growth is expected to slow in the medium term as productivity growth reverts toward its long-run trend (about 2.5 percent per year), and to slow further during the period from 2008 to 2011 as labor force growth declines due to the retire-ment of the baby-boom generation.

The growth rate of the economy over the long run is determined by its supply-side components, which include population, labor force participation, the ratio of nonfarm business employment to household employment, the length of the workweek, and labor productivity. The Administration's fore-cast for the contribution of the growth rates of different supply-side factors to real GDP growth is shown in Table 1-2.

The labor force participation rate generally fell from 2001 to 2007 and is projected to trend lower through 2013. The recent behavior stands in contrast to the long period of increase from 1960 through 1996. Looking

TABLE 1-2.—*Supply-Side Components of Real GDP Growth, 1953–2013*
[Average annual percent change]

Item	1953 Q2 to 1973 Q4	1973 Q4 to 1995 Q2	1995 Q2 to 2001 Q1	2001 Q1 to 2007 Q3	2007 Q3 to 2013 Q4
1) Civilian noninstitutional population aged 16+[1]	1.6	1.4	1.2	1.2	0.9
2) PLUS: Civilian labor force participation rate	0.2	0.4	0.1	-0.3	-0.2
3) EQUALS: Civilian labor force[2]	1.8	1.8	1.4	0.9	0.7
4) PLUS: Civilian employment rate	-0.1	0.0	0.3	-0.1	0.0
5) EQUALS: Civilian employment[2]	1.7	1.8	1.6	0.8	0.7
6) PLUS: Nonfarm business employment as a share of civilian employment[2,3]	-0.1	0.1	0.4	-0.5	0.0
7) EQUALS: Nonfarm business employment[4]	1.6	1.9	2.0	0.4	0.7
8) PLUS: average weekly hours (nonfarm business)	-0.3	-0.3	-0.1	-0.2	0.0
9) EQUALS: Hours of all persons (nonfarm business)[4]	1.3	1.6	1.9	0.2	0.7
10) PLUS: Output per hour (productivity, nonfarm business)[4]	2.5	1.5	2.4	2.7	2.5
11) EQUALS: Nonfarm business output[4]	3.8	3.1	4.3	2.9	3.2
12) PLUS: Ratio of real GDP to nonfarm business output[5]	-0.2	-0.2	-0.5	-0.3	-0.4
13) EQUALS: Real GDP	3.6	2.8	3.8	2.6	2.8

[1] Adjusted by CEA to smooth discontinuities in the population series since 1990.

[2] BLS research series adjusted to smooth irregularities in the population series since 1990.

[3] Line 6 translates the civilian employment growth rate into the nonfarm business employment growth rate.

[4] Nonfarm employment, workweek, productivity, and output sourced from the BLS productivity and cost database.

[5] Line 12 translates nonfarm business output back into output for all sectors (GDP), which includes the output of farms and general government.

Note: 1953 Q2, 1973 Q4, and 2001 Q1 are NBER business-cycle peaks.
Detail may not add to total because of rounding.

Sources: Council of Economic Advisers, Department of Commerce (Bureau of Economic Analysis) and Department of Labor (Bureau of Labor Statistics).

Box 1-3: Aging and the Pattern of Labor Force Participation

The overall labor force participation rate trended up to 67.1 percent in 1997, and after holding steady between 1997 and 2000, has generally edged lower during the past 7 years. Men's labor force participation rates fell fairly steadily through 2004. Women's labor force participation rose steadily through 1999, and has edged lower since then.

continued on the next page

Box 1-3 — continued

Labor Force Participation Rates for Men and Women (1970–2007)
The female labor force participation rate plateaued from 1999. Men's participation has trended lower, but has fallen only slightly since 2004.

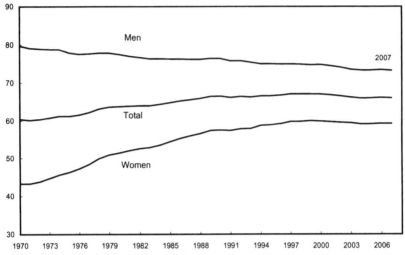

Note: Persons 16 years and over; annual data only.
Source: Department of Labor (Bureau of Labor Statistics).

Participation in the labor force (by working or by looking for a job) declines as people age through their 50s and 60s as is shown for women in the chart below. As a result, the overall rate of labor force participation is projected to decline as the baby-boom cohorts (those born between 1946 and 1964) advance into age brackets with much lower participation rates.

Female participation rises rapidly from age 20 to 24, drops off during the child-rearing years, and then rises again to a maximum in the 40 to 50 age bracket, as shown in the chart above. Looking at how the shape of this age-participation profile has evolved shows some striking changes: The participation rates of women in their 40s moved upward rapidly from the cohorts born in 1928 to those born in 1948, but has not risen any further in the years since. Also, the dip in participation during the child-rearing years has become less pronounced. Neither of these patterns of evolution suggests that the pre-1999 trend of rising female participation will re-emerge. Although participation of women over age 55 rose dramatically from the cohort born in 1938 to the cohort born in 1948, the age-participation profile of the cohort born in 1958 suggests that this trend of rising participation of older women is unlikely to

continued on the next page

Box 1-3 — continued

Female Labor Force Participation Rates by Age
Participation rates edge down after age 50 and fall sharply after age 60. Participation rates of the 1963 cohort (44 years old in 2007) were no higher than those 44-year-olds 5 or 10 years earlier.

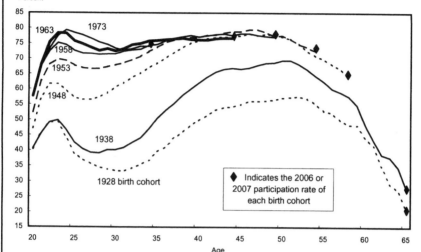

Sources: Department of Commerce (Census Bureau) and Department of Labor (Bureau of Labor Statistics) with interpolations by the Council of Economic Advisers.

continue. This follows because the 1958 cohort shows no advance in participation at age 49 (their age in 2007) compared with somewhat older cohorts (such as the 1948 or 1953 cohorts shown in the chart), hinting that the rising participation rates for older women has plateaued. Also, the drop in participation during the child-rearing years has almost vanished, leaving only a little room for further increase among 25- to 35-year-old women.

ahead, the participation rate is projected to decline, reflecting the aging of the baby-boom cohorts, leading to more retirements and a likely increase in the share of people on disability pensions (Box 1-3).

The Composition of Income over the Long Term

The Administration's economic forecast is used to estimate future government revenues, a purpose that requires a projection of the components of taxable income. The income-side projection is based on the historical stability of labor compensation as a share of gross domestic income (GDI). During the first half of 2007, the labor compensation share of GDI was 56.9 percent (according to the preliminary data available when the projection was finalized), below its 1963–2006 average of 58.0 percent. From this jump-off point, the labor share is projected to slowly return toward its historical average, reaching 57.7 percent by 2013. (Another definition of the labor share—including the imputed wages of the self-employed—is higher, about 62 percent for the nonfarm business sector.)

The labor compensation share of GDI consists of wages and salaries (which are taxable), nonwage compensation (employer contributions to employee pension and insurance funds, which are not taxable), and employer contributions for social insurance (which are not taxable). The Administration forecasts that the wage and salary share of compensation will change little between 2007 and 2013.

As the labor share of GDI increases toward its historical average, the capital share of GDI is expected to edge down from its currently high level before eventually reaching its historical average in 2012. Profits during the first half of 2007 were about 11.6 percent of GDI, well above their post-1959 average of roughly 9 percent. Book profits (also known in the national income accounts as *profits before tax*) are expected to decline as a share of GDI. The GDI share of other taxable income (rent, dividends, proprietors' income, and personal interest income) is projected to edge up slightly over the next 2 years.

Conclusion

The economy entered a period of rebalancing in 2006 and 2007, as higher growth of nonresidential investment and exports offset the lower rates of housing investment. This rebalancing—and the reduced rate of growth that goes with it—is projected to continue in 2008. The bipartisan economic growth package called for by the President would provide insurance against the near-term risks of any broader economic slowdown related to financial and housing-related developments by providing a boost to consumption, business investment, and job creation. The economy is projected to settle into a steady state in which real GDP grows at about 2.9 percent per year, the unemployment rate stays around the level consistent with stable inflation (about 4.8 percent) and inflation remains moderate and stable (about 2.3 on the CPI). Consumer spending is projected to grow in line with disposable income, and business investment and exports are projected to grow a bit faster than GDP as a whole. Economic forecasts are subject to error, and unforeseen positive and negative developments will affect the course of the economy over the next several years. Given the economy's strong basic structure, free mobility of labor, relatively low taxes, well-balanced capital markets, and openness to trade, prospects for continued growth in the years ahead remain good. Later chapters of this *Report* explore how pro-growth policies such as tax reform, fiscal restraint, open commerce, and market-based reforms can enhance our economic performance.

CHAPTER 2

Credit and Housing Markets

In the summer of 2007, the contraction in the U.S. housing market worsened and credit markets experienced a substantial disruption. Default rates on subprime mortgages—particularly more recent vintages of adjustable-rate mortgages—rose rapidly. As a result, investors became worried about how much risk they had exposed themselves to by purchasing financial securities backed by these mortgages. Financial disruptions rippled through the U.S. and world financial markets as yields on many private debt securities rose sharply, while investor demand for those securities dramatically fell. As investors sought the safety of government securities, demand for U.S. Treasury securities spiked upward, driving down their yields.

The Administration and the Federal Reserve independently responded to the subprime mortgage problem and the financial market disruptions. The Administration's policy response addressed problems in the subprime lending market and sought to improve the long-run functioning of the housing and credit markets through programs such as *FHASecure* and HOPE NOW. *FHASecure* expands the Federal Housing Administration's (FHA) ability to offer home mortgage loan refinancing options by giving it the additional flexibility to help not only homeowners who are current on their mortgage payments, but also borrowers in default who had made timely mortgage payments before their loan interest rates reset. HOPE NOW is an example of the government encouraging members of the private sector—including lenders, loan servicers, mortgage counselors, and investors—to identify and reach out to at-risk borrowers and help more families stay in their homes. The Federal Reserve addressed the risks to the economy from financial market disruptions by increasing liquidity and lowering interest rates, and it addressed problems in the subprime mortgage market by joining with its fellow supervisory agencies to work on new consumer protection rules and to issue guidance to lending institutions.

Despite the magnitude of the disruption in financial markets, the impact on the broader real economy was, at least through the fourth quarter of 2007, largely confined to residential investment, which had been weak for about 2 years. Nonetheless, the tightening of credit standards raises the possibility that spending by businesses and consumers could be restrained in the future. Declines in housing wealth may also limit consumer spending.

The credit market disruptions appear to reflect a general repricing of risk that was triggered, though not solely caused, by subprime mortgage delinquencies, which were in turn a partial result of declines in housing appreciation. New financial products, such as certain mortgage-backed securities, also added a layer of complexity to the recent credit market disruptions. These securities markedly expanded liquidity in the mortgage markets and provided many Americans a previously unavailable opportunity to own their own homes.

The key points from this chapter are:

- Rising delinquencies for subprime mortgages revealed an apparent underpricing of risk and raised concerns about which market participants were exposed to that risk, but the subprime market was not the only cause for the contraction in credit markets.
- The Federal Reserve provided liquidity and took measures to support financial stability in the financial markets in the wake of the disruptions in the credit markets.
- The Administration focused its response on housing markets and helping homeowners avoid foreclosure—in particular, subprime borrowers facing increases in the interest rate on their adjustable-rate mortgages.
- Participants in the credit and housing markets are actively addressing challenges that were revealed during the summer of 2007. Markets are generally better suited than government to adapting to changes in the economic environment; markets can respond quickly to new information, while government policy often reacts with a lag or has a delayed impact.
- Financial innovations in the mortgage and credit markets have provided a range of economic benefits, but not without some costs. Over time, markets tend to retain valuable innovations and repair or eliminate flawed innovations.
- The macroeconomic effects of the downturn in housing and the credit market disruptions may occur through several channels, including the direct effect on residential investment, the reduction of wealth on personal consumption, and tighter lending standards on business investment.

What Are Credit Markets?

There are two primary ways to finance any economic activity: through equity or through debt. With *equity financing*, investors take ownership shares in an economic venture, such as investing in a new company, and receive some fraction of the future returns. With *debt* or *credit financing*, a creditor lends a debtor money today, which the debtor must repay with interest in the future. Credit comes in many different forms: credit cards, automobile loans, mortgages, corporate bonds, and government bonds. Securities whose value is derived from underlying assets are called *derivatives* or *derivative securities*. *Credit markets* are the markets in which loans and their derivative securities are traded.

Consider mortgages. Suppose a person wants to purchase a house, but does not have enough cash on hand to buy it. The prospective borrower (the debtor) uses his available cash as a down payment and approaches a lender (the creditor), who lends the borrower the remaining money needed to cover the cost of the house. Over time, the borrower earns income from his job and pays off the mortgage (debt). Because money today is worth more than money tomorrow, the lender charges interest on the amount of the loan (the principal). The interest rate must be set high enough to compensate the lender for bearing the risks associated with the loan but low enough to make the loan attractive to the borrower.

Mortgages, like most forms of credit, are subject to three forms of risk: *credit risk* (the risk that the debtor will default on the loan), *interest rate risk* (the risk that market interest rates will fluctuate), and *prepayment risk* (the risk that the borrower will pay off the loan early). Lenders make money by charging borrowers interest payments on top of the periodic repayments of principal. Therefore, the lender is worse off if these interest payments stop, such as when the borrower defaults on a loan or pays off the loan early in an environment of low interest rates. Mortgage lenders may also face the risk of a loss of principal if a property is foreclosed upon. Loans with greater risk have higher interest rates to compensate the lender for bearing more risk.

Recent Developments in Mortgage Markets

From 2001 to 2007, there was a substantial increase in the use of subprime mortgages. (Box 2-1 defines "subprime mortgages" and other mortgage market terminology.) The share of mortgage originations that were subprime increased from 5 percent in 2001 to more than 20 percent in 2006. Subprime mortgages carry a greater risk than prime mortgages. Many subprime borrowers have poorer credit histories and less reliable sources of income than prime borrowers; they may provide little or no documentation of income or assets from which they can pay the mortgage; and they tend to have high loan-to-value ratios. As a result, compared with prime borrowers, subprime borrowers are more likely to default on their loans.

Box 2-1: Definitions of Select Mortgage Terms

Adjustable-rate mortgage (ARM): Adjustable-rate mortgages have an initial period with a fixed interest rate, after which the interest rate adjusts at set periods. For example, a 3/1 ARM would have a set interest rate for 3 years, but after that the interest rate would adjust every year. The adjusted interest rate is a function of some "index" market interest rate, such as the London Interbank Offer Rate.

Conforming loan limit: The charter-required limit, as determined by Federal regulators, placed on the size of loans that can be purchased by Fannie Mae and Freddie Mac.

Default: A borrower defaults on a mortgage when he or she fails to make timely monthly mortgage payments or otherwise comply with mortgage terms. A mortgage is generally considered in default when payment has not been made for more than 90 days. At this point, foreclosure proceedings against the borrower become a strong possibility.

Delinquency: A borrower is delinquent on a mortgage when he or she fails to make one or more scheduled monthly payments.

Fannie Mae: Fannie Mae is the registered service mark of the Federal National Mortgage Association, a U.S. Government-sponsored enterprise. Fannie Mae buys mortgage loans that meet certain criteria from primary mortgage lenders and sells mortgage-backed securities with guaranteed principal and interest payments. In return for this guaranty, investors pay a fee to Fannie Mae. Fannie Mae also holds some of the mortgages it purchases, and mortgage-backed securities it originates, in its portfolio.

Fixed-rate mortgage (FRM): A mortgage with an interest rate that remains the same throughout the life of the loan.

Foreclosure: A legal process in which a lender seeks recovery of collateral from a borrower (in the case of home mortgages, the home itself is the collateral), with several possible outcomes, including that the borrower sells the property or the lender repossesses the home. Foreclosure laws are based on the statutes of each State.

Freddie Mac: Freddie Mac is the registered service mark of the Federal Home Loan Mortgage Corporation, a U.S. Government-sponsored enterprise. Freddie Mac buys mortgage loans that meet certain criteria from primary mortgage lenders and sells mortgage-backed securities with guaranteed principal and interest payments. In return for this guaranty, investors pay a fee to Freddie Mac. Freddie Mac also holds some of the mortgages it purchases, and mortgage-backed securities it originates, in its portfolio.

Jumbo loan: A loan that exceeds the conforming loan limit.

continued on the next page

Prime loan: Loans made to borrowers that meet stringent lending and underwriting terms and conditions. Prime borrowers have good credit records and meet standard guidelines for documentation of debt-to-income and loan-to-value ratios.

Reset: An interest rate on an adjustable-rate mortgage is said to have reset whenever it is adjusted, or moved, in the direction of the market interest rate that it tracks.

Subprime loan: Loans that meet less stringent lending and underwriting terms and conditions. Subprime borrowers may have weaker credit histories characterized by payment delinquencies; previous charge-offs, judgments, or bankruptcies; low credit scores; high debt-burden ratios; high loan-to-value ratios; or little to no documentation to prove income.

Workout: An adjustment to, or renegotiation of, a loan a lender makes with a borrower, usually with the purpose of avoiding a default or foreclosure on the loan. Types of workouts include modifications to the original loan contract, forbearance agreements (agreements that postpone payments), forgiveness of some debt, and short sales (the lender accepts the proceeds from the home's sale as settlement for the debt even if the proceeds do not cover the entire mortgage amount).

Strong house price appreciation in much of the country beginning in 2003 provided confidence that riskier borrowers could easily refinance mortgages, using their built-up equity, should they be unable to keep up with their monthly mortgage payments. This expectation of house price appreciation, coupled with an increasingly competitive lending environment, led lenders to relax their underwriting standards and offer products with features that lowered monthly payments. Loans with low initial payments, including subprime loans, helped further feed house price appreciation, and increased the risk of eventual default and foreclosure due to their future interest rate resets. Some subprime loans were traditional fixed-rate mortgages (FRMs) that specified a fixed interest rate throughout the life of the loan, while others were adjustable-rate mortgages (ARMs), with interest rates that followed a market interest rate, such as the *London Interbank Offer Rate* (LIBOR), the interest rate at which banks lend to one another using the London market. About 70 percent of subprime ARMs were 2/28 or 3/27 hybrid ARMs. A 2/28 hybrid ARM, for example, has 2 years of payments at a fixed introductory interest rate, after which it *resets* to a higher floating rate, and then floats for the remaining 28 years.

At the same time, the dollar volume of private mortgage-backed securities issued by private sector entities grew rapidly beginning in 2001. Investors were attracted to these securities because of their seemingly high risk-adjusted returns; ARMs apparently shifted interest rate risk from the lender to the borrower, whose mortgage payments would vary according to market interest rates. This provided continued liquidity support for the further expansion of mortgage lending, including poorly underwritten subprime lending. Lenders sold loans on the secondary market, passing risks on to investors who relied primarily on ratings of the securities provided by third-party rating agencies.

There are two important caveats to keep in mind when thinking about credit risk in the mortgage markets. First, defaults and foreclosures are expected even in the best of times. Some individual borrowers will experience difficulties—such as job loss—that may lead them to default on their mortgages. Eliminating defaults and foreclosures caused by such difficulties would be nearly impossible, and efforts to do so by raising credit thresholds would have the unfortunate effect of restricting access to credit—and, therefore, to home ownership—for many prospective borrowers. Second, in well-functioning markets, risks are priced. There is nothing wrong or unnatural about the possibility of higher default and delinquency rates, provided the borrower and lender enter the transaction fully informed. Lenders and investors can compensate for increased risk by setting an appropriately high interest rate. Of course, if information on credit risk is imperfect, the demand for loans in the secondary market will be affected. For example, if credit rating agencies or investors underestimate the default risk of subprime securities, the market may underprice subprime risk, leading to an excess quantity of subprime credit. See Box 2-2 for background on the credit rating agencies.

Box 2-2: Credit Rating Agencies

The securities credit rating industry began in 1909, but it was not until the 1930s that regulators began mandating the use of credit ratings. For example, banks cannot invest in bonds that are rated below investment grade; insurance companies are required to link their capital requirements to the ratings of the bonds they invest in; and the Securities and Exchange Commission's capital requirements require broker-dealers to hold investment-grade bonds in their portfolios.

In order to regulate these ratings the Securities and Exchange Commission created the National Recognized Statistical Rating Organization designation (NRSRO) in 1975. Since then, the NRSRO category has become a de facto license, and like all licenses, it aims to enforce quality but in fact restricts quantity, by granting monopoly power to the incumbent firms. Currently, seven firms are designated

continued on the next page

NRSROs. Critics have described the criteria for entry into the NRSRO designation as opaque, effectively blocking new entry.

The industry came under scrutiny after a large energy company was rated "investment grade" 5 days before its bankruptcy. In September 2006, the Credit Rating Agency Reform Act was passed to increase transparency and competition in the rating industry. Under the new act, a credit rating firm whose ratings have been used by at least 10 investors for 3 years can apply for registration as an NRSRO.

Although the new law is still being implemented, some contend that barriers to entry are still high, and conflicts of interest between the rater and the issuer persist. The President's Working Group on Financial Markets is examining the need for reform of the credit rating agencies.

In 2006, defaults on mortgages began to increase, but, as shown in Chart 2-1, the rise in default rates was concentrated in ARMs, particularly subprime ARMs, while default rates for FRMs were relatively unchanged. The performance of subprime mortgages was particularly poor for more recent vintages. Subprime mortgages originated in 2005 and 2006 have defaulted much more quickly than those originated in 2003 and 2004, for example. By July of 2007, escalating subprime ARM default rates led lenders to sharply curtail new originations of subprime loans.

Chart 2-1 **Percent of Mortgages 90 Days Past Due or In the Process of Foreclosure**
Subprime adjustable-rate mortgages have performed particularly poorly over the past year.
Percent of loans

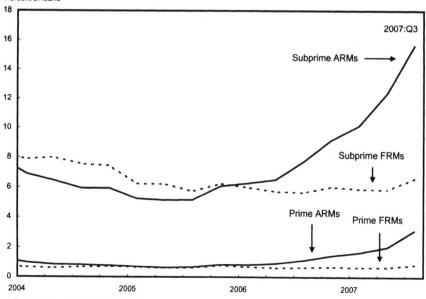

Source: Mortgage Bankers Association.

The current rise in defaults reflects a combination of factors, including flat or falling home prices, weaker underwriting standards (including higher loan-to-value ratios), regional economic weakness, and interest rate resets on subprime ARMs. About 1.8 million owner-occupied loans in subprime mortgage pools are scheduled to reset in 2008 and 2009. For mortgages issued in the past several years, defaults are occurring well before interest rates reset, which suggests soft housing prices and weak underwriting standards may be more important factors. As housing prices began to falter, flat or falling home prices combined with weaker underwriting standards meant that borrowers lost their "equity cushion" and had more difficulty refinancing or selling their homes. Borrowers who had purchased homes (particularly homes for investment purposes) but now owed more than the properties were worth had incentives to stop making mortgage payments in order to minimize their financial losses. Rising interest rates increased the probability of default and foreclosure for borrowers with adjustable-rate mortgages because their monthly payments grew as rates were climbing. The relative importance of these factors may vary geographically, as discussed in Box 2-3.

Worries in late summer about exposure to risk increased in the markets for other mortgages as well. In particular, interest rates on jumbo mortgages (mortgages in excess of the "conforming loan limit" of $417,000) rose, and jumbo mortgage originations slowed. Chart 2-2 shows the increase since the summer of 2007 in interest rates for fixed-rate jumbo mortgages relative to fixed-rate conforming mortgages.

Box 2-3: Geographic Variations in Housing Markets

Home prices vary significantly from neighborhood to neighborhood, State to State, and region to region. In 2006, for example, the median sale price for an existing home sold in the western United States was well over $300,000 compared with just $170,000 in the Midwest. Within California, the median price in San Jose was $775,000, while the median price a few hours away in Sacramento was only $375,000.

Home prices increased from 2001 to 2007 and boomed from 2003 to 2006, rising over 35 percent on average across the Nation, but those gains also showed large regional variations. House prices rose most dramatically in the southeastern and western United States and, to a lesser extent, in New England and the mid-Atlantic. Likewise, the subsequent deceleration (or outright declines) in house prices in 2007 also varied, with the largest changes occurring in those places that had previously shown the most rapid appreciation or were experiencing prolonged economic weakness.

continued on the next page

Box 2-3 — continued

Home Price Appreciation
House price appreciation has varied substantially across cities.

Index (2001:Q1=100)

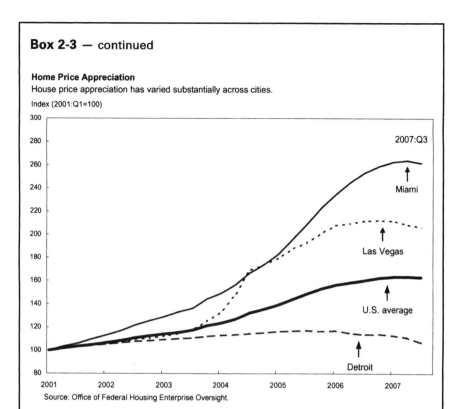

Source: Office of Federal Housing Enterprise Oversight.

Mortgage default rates have also varied substantially across regions. Falling house prices and high loan-to-value ratios have likely lifted delinquency rates in places that had experienced substantial run-ups in prices (such as Las Vegas and Miami), while economic weakness has likely lifted delinquencies in some Midwestern cities.

Concerns about risk also affected the secondary market in which mortgages are bought and *securitized,* that is, bundled together and sold as a single security (see Box 2-4). The government-sponsored enterprises (GSEs), Fannie Mae and Freddie Mac, securitize the majority of prime mortgages below the conforming loan limit. The secondary market for GSE-securitized mortgages remained active through 2007, presumably largely because some investors believe that these securities have an implicit guarantee from the U.S. Federal Government, even though no such guarantee exists. In contrast, the securitization of jumbo mortgages slowed as investors shied away from securities not created by the GSEs.

Chart 2-2 Conforming and Jumbo Mortgage Rates, 30-Year Fixed Rate Mortgages

The spread between jumbo and conforming rates widened following the onset of credit market turmoil in August 2007.

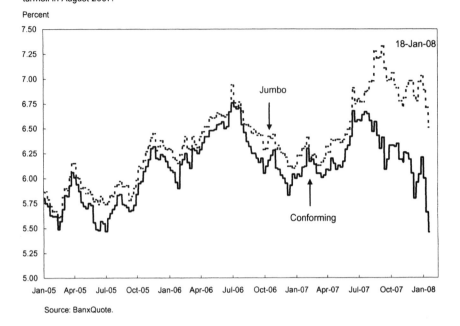

Source: BanxQuote.

Box 2-4: Securitization and Structured Finance

Securitization is the transformation of a collection of individual assets into tradable securities. These "asset-backed securities" are created by financial institutions—including banks and government-sponsored enterprises—from pools of assets, such as mortgages, car loans, credit card loans, corporate receivables, and student loans.

Mortgages make up a large fraction of asset-backed securities. Traditionally, a lender makes a loan to a borrower, in what is called the primary market. In the secondary market, a financial institution buys multiple loans, which, taken together, are essentially a bundle of cash flows. The simplest mortgage-backed security is a pass-through security, for which the interest and principal payments of the individual loans pass through to the holders of the new securities.

Securitization has two major economic benefits: increased risk diversification and increased available capital. With securitization, an investor with $400,000 can own 1 percent portions of 100 $400,000 mortgages rather than having to purchase a single such mortgage. If a single

continued on the next page

Box 2-3 — continued

mortgage defaults, the investor bears a $4,000 loss instead of a full $400,000 loss. If investors are risk-averse, this diversification makes them better off. A security can also include portions of diverse types of mortgages, which further spreads risk if the payment performance on the individual mortgages is not perfectly correlated. Securitization benefits lenders by enabling them to sell loans to those investors who can better handle the risks associated with mortgage borrowers. The sale of mortgages provides lenders with cash that they can then use to supply more mortgages. Investors benefit from the availability of additional securities.

The second economic benefit of securitization is an increase in available capital. More risk-diversified securities draw additional investors into the market, expanding the amount of capital in the market. This increased supply of credit may result in a lower cost of credit for borrowers, which, everything else remaining equal, makes home ownership more accessible.

Credit Market Disruptions in 2007

There were significant disruptions in financial markets in the summer of 2007. Problems became evident in June and July, when several hedge funds reported large losses and a large mortgage lender faced mounting problems. In late July, demand for U.S. Treasury securities jumped due to a "flight-to-quality" as investors shied away from mortgage-related assets, and to a lesser degree, corporate bonds and other relatively riskier assets. The shift away from corporate bonds resulted in a wider spread between interest rates on U.S. Treasuries and those on corporate bonds, following several years of narrow spreads. Conditions in financial markets worsened in early August, when several hedge funds experienced large losses. One European fund even stopped investor redemptions, saying that it was not possible to value certain securities. The disruptions led investors to try to maintain highly liquid positions and to focus on assets that were perceived as less risky and more easily priced.

Credit Market Link to Mortgages

The housing and credit markets are linked through the securitization of mortgages. The resulting mortgage-backed securities are often further packaged into other, more complicated, financial securities. Originations of mortgages that could not be purchased and securitized by Fannie Mae and Freddie Mac slowed sharply in the summer, as investors worried about exposure to risk. This contraction in the secondary market for mortgages had implications for mortgage originations: When banks are unable to sell mortgages they originate, they have fewer funds available for further originations. In addition, banks may be unwilling to hold some of the mortgages they originate because their appetite for risk may differ from that of the investors who previously bought their loans. Securitization problems also emerged for jumbo mortgages, which are not purchased by Fannie Mae and Freddie Mac.

Flight to Quality

When credit markets became disrupted, investors engaged in a "flight to quality," as indicated by the large increase in demand for U.S. Treasury securities. Because investors have high confidence that the U.S. Government will not default on its debt, the demand for U.S. Treasury securities—which include a variety of bills, notes, and bonds—tends to rise during periods of increased financial uncertainty. This increased demand pushes down Treasury yields (which move inversely with prices) relative to private lending rates such as the London Interbank Offered Rate, as shown in Chart 2-3.

Chart 2-3 **Three-month London Interbank Offered Rate and Rates on 3-Month Treasury Bills**
The spread between the London Interbank Offered Rate (LIBOR) and Treasury bill yields widened at the onset of the credit market turmoil in August 2007.

Annualized yield

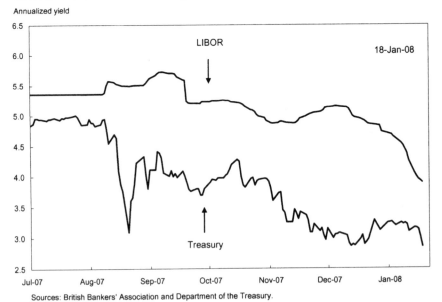

Sources: British Bankers' Association and Department of the Treasury.

Corporate bond yields also rose relative to U.S. Treasury securities. The higher yield on a corporate bond reflects, among other things, the relatively higher likelihood of default (credit risk), the risk of not being able to find a buyer for the bond (liquidity risk), and the potential for default to be correlated with other macroeconomic factors (systemic risk). The spread between the interest rates on corporate bonds and U.S. Treasury notes is therefore a barometer of risk in the market. In late July 2007, these credit spreads spiked upwards, even though they still remained low by historical standards, as Chart 2-4 illustrates.

Financial market participants also showed a preference for making shorter-term, rather than longer-term, loans to one another. This preference reflected a concern among some participants that they might unexpectedly need cash and therefore did not want to have it wrapped up in longer-term loans. Some participants also worried about the potential risk of default among their borrowers. As a result, the costs of borrowing for longer terms rose relative to overnight borrowing.

Chart 2-4 **Spread Between Corporate Bond Yields and Rates on 10-Year Treasury Notes**
In the second half of 2007, rates on corporate bonds rose as investors sought the security of U.S. Treasuries.

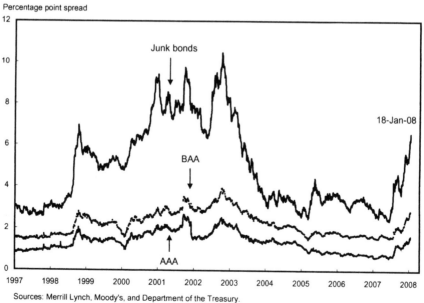

Sources: Merrill Lynch, Moody's, and Department of the Treasury.

Contraction of the Asset-Backed Commercial Paper Market

Another credit market that contracted in 2007 was the asset-backed commercial paper (ABCP) market. As of January 16, 2008, the ABCP market was an $800 billion market, roughly 45 percent of the $1.8 trillion U.S. commercial paper market, which itself is roughly one-fifth the size of the $9 trillion U.S. corporate bond market. Corporations issue short-term loans, called *commercial paper,* to smooth temporary fluctuations in cash flows; the commercial paper market is one market for short-term financing for firms. For example, suppose a firm needs to make certain seasonal payments and has a current cash flow constraint. The firm issues commercial paper into the market in exchange for cash, then repays the loan in 30 or 60 days. This loan is unsecured in that it does not specify collateral in case of default. For blue-chip firms, default is unlikely. However, any firm that defaults on a commercial paper loan is almost surely on the brink of bankruptcy because the default signals to the market that it doesn't have enough cash to pay off the most immediate of its financial obligations.

Commercial paper that is secured by assets (such as a firm's receivables, auto loans, or mortgage-backed securities) is known as *asset-backed commercial paper.* For example, if an automobile manufacturer sells cars but does not receive payment for the cars for 1 month, its receivables account will document the expected cash flow 1 month into the future. Therefore, a bank can issue to the market commercial paper backed by the receivables of the firm. If the firm defaults on its obligations, the holder of the ABCP can receive some payment from the receivables of the firm.

Usually, ABCP is issued by a *special-purpose vehicle* or *conduit* sponsored by a bank that buys assets—such as receivables from multiple corporations—and issues commercial paper backed by these assets to the outside market. Because ABCP conduits issue short-term debt to finance longer-term assets, they must continue to issue new commercial paper to repay maturing commercial paper (a process called *rolling*). Special-purpose vehicles can provide corporations with relatively low-cost access to the short-term financing available in commercial paper markets. These vehicles are not subject to the regulatory capital charge that is mandated for banks that extend credit directly to borrowers. For example, a bank that makes a direct loan to an automobile manufacturer would have to hold capital against that loan. But a bank that sponsored a special-purpose vehicle (which it did not own) could keep the manufacturer as a customer (and earn some fees) without bearing the credit risk of a direct loan and without facing a capital charge. *Structured investment vehicles (SIVs)* are a type of conduit that issues both commercial paper and medium-term notes to finance the purchase of assets. SIVs differ from ABCP conduits in that SIVs have less access to backup credit facilities (called *liquidity support*) in case they are unable to meet their short-term debt obligations.

The credit market disruptions seriously shook the ABCP markets. Investors began to differentiate more between the various types of ABCP and they demanded higher returns on ABCP that had less liquidity support. As a result of this greater investor scrutiny and investor reluctance to purchase commercial paper issued by entities with limited or no backstop liquidity, the volume of outstanding ABCP shrank more than 35 percent, from $1,180 billion in early August 2007 to about $750 billion in late December 2007 (Chart 2-5). Increased concern about risk associated with ABCP and risk in general prompted a flight to quality as investors shifted to low-risk short-term Treasuries. Because ABCP is used to fund SIVs, the reduced demand for ABCP forced banks to either bring the underlying assets (and their associated liabilities) back onto their balance sheets or reduce the size of their SIVs by selling off the assets.

Slower Merger and Acquisition Activity

The relatively low cost of credit contributed to a boom in mergers and acquisitions (M&A) in recent years, but announced M&A deals slowed

Chart 2-5 Commercial Paper Outstanding
The volume of outstanding asset-backed commercial paper contracted sharply in the latter half of 2007.
Billions of dollars

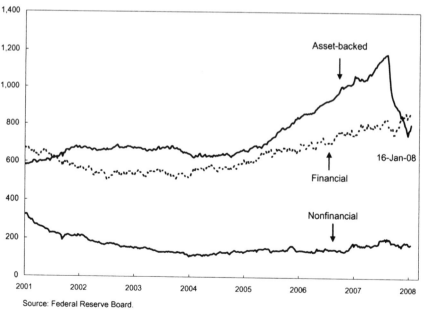

Source: Federal Reserve Board.

sharply following the credit disruptions in mid-2007. The aggregate value of announced M&A deals fell off sharply in late summer after having climbed to the highest levels since 2000–2001, as shown in Chart 2-6. Over the 12 months through August 2007, the value of M&A deals were about $1.65 trillion, but over the following 3 months these deals totaled just $498 billion at an annual rate. Banks that were underwriting *leveraged buyouts* (LBOs)—whereby a company or investor uses debt to finance the purchase of another company's assets—found that buyers were no longer as willing to purchase the debt associated with LBOs, which meant that banks had to keep more of the debt on their own books, possibly limiting the ability of some banks to make further loans.

Equity Markets

Equity markets continued to function amid the disruptions in the credit markets, but implied stock price volatility—an indicator of investor uncertainty—jumped during the summer and remained sensitive to news about credit market developments. Unlike many credit market instruments that trade infrequently and are hard to price, stocks trade in high volumes and are continually repriced, making them much more transparent financial instruments.

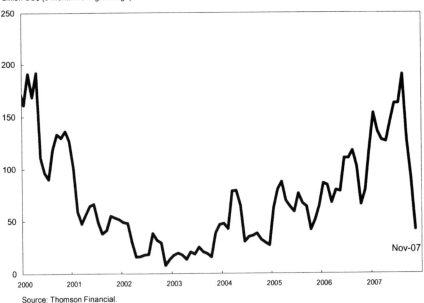

Chart 2-6 **Value of Announced Merger and Acquisition Deals**
North American M&A activity slowed in the latter half of 2007.
Billion US$ (3-month moving average)

Source: Thomson Financial.

International Implications

A notable aspect of the disruptions in the U.S. credit and housing markets was that it was felt globally. Subprime losses appeared not only in the United States but also in the portfolios of banks and investors in Europe, Australia, and Asia, demonstrating how interconnected global capital markets have become. This international diversification provided a clear benefit as the impact of subprime losses were shared, rather than concentrated solely on U.S. investors and financial institutions. In some cases, European banks were more severely affected, at least initially, by the credit market disruptions than were U.S. banks. Lastly, both the European Central Bank and the U.S. Federal Reserve boosted liquidity in similar, and effectively simultaneous, actions (discussed later in this chapter).

Policy Response to Credit Market Disruptions

The mortgage and credit market disruptions of the summer of 2007 shook investor confidence. As in previous financial disruptions, however, these markets again demonstrated their resilience and flexibility. The possibility of gains from trade forces markets to adjust quickly and self-correct. In many cases, the Federal Reserve has better tools at its disposal for addressing certain credit market problems than do fiscal policymakers. For example, the Federal Reserve can act to stave off certain types of liquidity problems, such as short-term cash availability at major banks, but not other liquidity problems, such as a lack of trading in asset-backed commercial paper that results from investors' doubts about the value of the paper.

The Federal Reserve took a variety of actions in the second half of 2007 to maintain financial stability and encourage continued economic growth. In early August 2007, the Federal Reserve used open market operations to inject large amounts of liquidity into financial markets. The Federal Funds rate—the interest rate at which U.S. banks lend to other banks overnight— fell below the target rate. On August 17, 2007, the Federal Reserve made credit more easily available by enacting a 50-basis-point reduction in the *discount rate,* the interest rate that banks are charged when they borrow from the Federal Reserve's discount window. The Federal Reserve also permitted the provision of term financing for terms as long as 30 days, and reiterated the Federal Reserve's policy of accepting a broad range of collateral for loans from the discount window, including home mortgages and related assets. On September 18, 2007, the Federal Reserve reduced the discount rate by an additional 50 basis points and lowered the target Federal Funds rate by 50 basis points. On October 31, 2007, the Federal Funds rate and the discount rate were lowered another 25 basis points.

The Federal Reserve Bank of New York's Open Market Trading Desk announced on November 26 that it would increase the availability of credit in financial markets by conducting certain open market operations for terms that extended past the end of the year. On December 11, 2007, the Federal Funds rate and discount rate were cut another 25 basis points. The following day, the Federal Reserve announced two new actions, in coordination with other central banks actions, that were designed to boost liquidity. The first action was a series of term fund auctions—short-term loans—to depository institutions. The second action was the establishment of temporary currency arrangements with the European Central Bank and the Swiss National Bank that make dollars available to these banks to alleviate dollar funding pressures in their jurisdictions. The Federal Reserve cut rates further in January 2008.

Policy Response to Housing Market Challenges

Housing market policies have been of two types. First are policies that are created to encourage market participants to make use of tools they already possess and provide targeted assistance to borrowers. Second are those that are designed to make changes to the future functioning of the housing market. Policies should be crafted in a manner that avoids unnecessarily restricting access to credit and financial market innovation. Some policies encourage developing private market solutions, such as recommending that lenders develop a mortgage workout plan with borrowers rather than progressing through the foreclosure process. Box 2-5 discusses the challenges of workouts. Policies may also be designed to offer targeted assistance, such as increasing access to FHA-insured loans for subprime borrowers facing interest rate resets. To strengthen the market for the future, other policies address fundamental problems that markets may be slow to address themselves, such as better disclosure of loan terms, total settlement charges, and other mortgage characteristics. In addition, policies that require or provide incentives for lenders and investors to perform quality due diligence would promote true risk-based pricing in the subprime sector, and could make this sector more competitive.

Addressing Current Challenges

The Administration has worked with lenders, loan servicers, mortgage counselors, and investors to develop private sector solutions. The HOPE NOW initiative is an effort to encourage private sector servicers, housing counselors, and investors to work together. The goal is to provide relief to homeowners. The Administration has encouraged market participants who historically have not shared information, resources, or business practices to come together to create a coordinated plan to help homeowners. Importantly, HOPE NOW has no budgetary cost to the Federal Government. HOPE NOW participants have agreed on a new set of industry-wide standards designed to help streamline the mortgage workout process for borrowers with adjustable-rate mortgages who can afford their current mortgage payments, but will have trouble when their interest rates rise. The standards aim to help keep these borrowers' mortgages affordable in three ways: refinancing their existing loans into new private mortgages, moving them into *FHASecure* loans, or freezing their current interest rates for 5 years. HOPE NOW also has an informational component, which has increased outreach to borrowers through mailings, and has supported a toll-free hotline, 1-888-995-HOPE, to provide 24-hour mortgage counseling in multiple languages.

Box 2-5: Mortgage Lending Today

Securitization has helped drive the expansion of home ownership, available credit, and the selection of mortgage products throughout the Nation. Before securitization was a prominent market force, the mortgage industry was characterized by the portfolio lending model. Under this model, a bank made a loan to a borrower and the loan remained on the bank's balance sheet until the loan was paid off. The bank serviced the loan, meaning that it collected interest and principal payments from the borrower, throughout the duration of the loan. If the borrower became delinquent or defaulted on the mortgage, the bank would evaluate the economic feasibility of a mortgage workout plan with the borrower—perhaps by modifying terms or establishing a repayment program for missed payments—versus working through the foreclosure process.

Expanded use of mortgage securitization has partly eclipsed the portfolio lending model and has drawn in new market participants. Now a German businessperson can invest in a hedge fund that purchases mortgage-backed securities, which themselves are pools of mortgages from lenders in Minnesota. The German businessperson is investing in mortgages and supporting the availability of credit for a teacher in Minnesota who wants to buy her first home. Thus securitization provides liquidity and risk diversification in an increasingly integrated world.

The rise of securitization has meant that a third party is needed to service the bundled loans, that is, collect payments from borrowers and distribute payments to investors. Loan servicing has developed into a sophisticated industry. Loan servicers can be commercial banks, community banks, investment banks, and/or third-party corporations. Servicers typically transfer interest and principal payments to master servicers or loan trustees before these payments reach the actual

continued on the next page

The Administration launched a new program at the FHA called *FHASecure* as a targeted response aimed at keeping families in their homes. The FHA was created in 1934 to insure (but not originate) mortgages for qualified low- and moderate-income borrowers, with less-than-perfect credit and little savings for a down payment. This insurance boosts home ownership by enabling borrowers who may have been priced out of the mortgage market to acquire housing on more affordable terms. The FHA works through a network of approved lenders and guarantees that if the borrower defaults on the loan, the FHA will pay the lender the full outstanding balance of the loan. Unlike many subprime lenders, most of the FHA's risk is covered by charging mortgage insurance premiums, not through significantly higher interest rates.

FHASecure can help some creditworthy borrowers who are affected by subprime interest rate resets to refinance their mortgages. The *FHASecure* program applies both to homeowners who are current on their mortgage payments and borrowers who made timely mortgage payments before their loans reset but are now in default. A borrower in default must also have sufficient income to make future mortgage payments under a fixed-rate FHA-insured loan, and a history of on-time mortgage payments before their current loan reset. Making FHA mortgage refinancing options available to more homeowners will help reduce the number of foreclosures and can help bring greater stability to local housing markets.

The President signed a bill to temporarily change the current Federal tax code so that cancelled mortgage debt is not treated as taxable income. Under prior law, if the value of a home declines, and a portion of the debt on the home is forgiven, that portion is treated like taxable income for the borrower. For example, suppose a homeowner owes $120,000 on a mortgage, and the home's value falls to $100,000. If the mortgage lender agrees to take $100,000 from the proceeds of the home's sale and forgive the rest of the debt, the old tax code treated the $20,000 of forgiven debt as income on which the homeowner must pay taxes. Under the new law, the homeowner need not pay taxes on the forgiven debt.

The Administration has also proposed legislation to allow State and local governments to temporarily broaden their tax-exempt bond programs to include mortgage refinancings. Under current law, State and local governments are allowed to issue tax-exempt bonds, called "qualified mortgage bonds," to finance new mortgage loans to first-time home buyers, with some limits on which mortgages can be covered. If passed, this legislation would reduce the cost of State and local housing agency programs that aim to refinance borrowers facing unaffordable rate resets into lower-cost fixed-rate mortgages.

Strengthening the Mortgage Market for the Future

High default rates, which have contributed to recent market disruptions, are more likely if consumers do not understand the terms of their loans. Transparency in mortgage lending helps borrowers find affordable mortgages and avoid predatory lending. Transparent markets lower the chance that borrowers will default on loans. The Administration is working on a new rule under the Real Estate Settlement Procedures Act (RESPA) that would simplify shopping for loans and reduce settlement costs for consumers. RESPA was originally passed in 1974 to protect mortgage borrowers from unnecessarily high settlement charges. This new rule would simplify and improve disclosure requirements for mortgage settlement costs, making it easier for borrowers to shop for loans. The rule would establish a new standard Good Faith Estimate form that loan originators would be required to provide to borrowers in all RESPA-covered transactions. The aim of the rule is to communicate complex information to borrowers so that borrowers will be able to shop effectively for the best loan for them, and understand the obligations they are undertaking when financing a home with a mortgage.

The Federal Reserve is also working to improve transparency through a review of the rules for mortgage lending under the Truth in Lending Act. In December 2007, the Federal Reserve published proposed rules under Regulation Z of the Truth in Lending Act to make mortgage lending more transparent. The new rules would prohibit seven misleading advertising practices, such as using the term "fixed" to refer to a rate that can change, and would require truth-in-lending disclosures to borrowers early enough to use while shopping for a mortgage.

The Federal Reserve is using its rule-making authority under the Home Ownership and Equity Protection Act (HOEPA) to address unfair or deceptive mortgage lending practices. In December 2007, the Federal Reserve proposed—in addition to the rules regarding transparency discussed above—new rules under the Truth in Lending Act that would address unfair mortgage lending. For example, the rules would require subprime lenders to verify income and assets before making a loan and would prohibit subprime lenders from making loans without considering borrowers' ability to repay them. The rules would also prohibit *all* lenders from paying mortgage brokers *yield spread premiums*—fees paid by a lender to a broker for higher-rate loans—without notifying the consumer in advance and from coercing appraisers to misrepresent the value of a home.

The Administration's proposed FHA Modernization legislation aims to reform the FHA to better reflect the way in which the private mortgage market operates, particularly the way it prices risk. From September 2003 to February 2005, FHA loan volume fell precipitously, from 135,000 mortgage endorsements in September 2003 to just 40,000 in February 2005, as Chart 2-7 shows. The drop reflects several factors, including low interest rates that made unassisted mortgages affordable for more families, the private sector's increased use of automated underwriting that allowed the private sector to offer loans on favorable terms to more home buyers, and the increased use of subprime mortgages. In general, it is a positive development when the private sector is offering favorable terms to borrowers who previously would have turned to the FHA. Unfortunately, some borrowers are still underserved, particularly in the subprime market. The FHA's mission is to serve borrowers who are at the margins of home ownership by offering safe, affordable options without compromising underwriting standards. In recent years, the FHA's outdated statutory authority has limited the agency's ability to keep pace with the evolving mortgage market. As a result, borrowers opted for the innovative products and risk-based pricing that were available in the private sector.

FHA Modernization, which was first proposed in the Administration's 2007 budget, is designed to restore a choice to home buyers who cannot qualify for prime financing. The three major elements of FHA reform are to: (1) Allow the FHA to price insurance premiums based on borrower risk; (2) Raise loan limits in high-cost markets so that more families can be served; and (3) Lower the down payment requirements.

Currently, the premiums for FHA mortgage insurance do not vary according to a borrower's credit risk or to the expected cost from defaults. This causes better borrowers to subsidize weaker borrowers (a process called *cross-subsidization*). Charging the same price for all borrowers is a form of average-cost pricing, while charging different prices according to cost (here, risk) is a shift toward marginal-cost pricing, which is more efficient. On top of this, cross-subsidization has driven lower-risk borrowers to seek

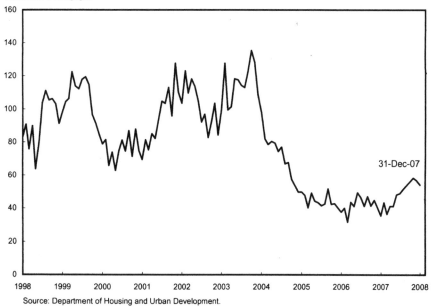

Chart 2-7 **Monthly FHA Mortgage Endorsements**

FHA mortgage endorsements increased in 2007 after having fallen sharply in recent years.

Thousands of mortgages

31-Dec-07

Source: Department of Housing and Urban Development.

alternatives offered in the conventional market. The proposed risk-based pricing addresses this issue by reducing the cost of FHA mortgages for lower-risk borrowers. Risk-based pricing will also enable borrowers to know why they are paying certain costs and what they can do to help lower these costs in the future. The incentives for families to improve their credit histories or save for a down payment are important elements of risk-based pricing. While full risk-based pricing requires a Congressional act to raise the premium caps, a partial, limited version of risk-based pricing can take place through regulation. The new flexibility under the *FHASecure* program includes these regulatory changes in risk-based pricing, and the Administration has called on Congress to pass the broader FHA Modernization legislation to fully implement risk-based pricing.

The second piece of FHA modernization would allow the FHA to insure higher-priced homes. Under current law, the FHA may insure loans that are up to 87 percent of the conforming loan limit. In certain high-cost States, this limit is below the median home price in the State. For example, in California the median home price in 2006 was $500,000, which is more than the current FHA cap of $363,000. Therefore in certain States, the FHA cannot insure many of the homes in the State. The Modernization bill broadens the reach of the FHA program by removing the 87 percent cap and allowing the FHA to insure up to 100 percent of the conforming loan limit.

Finally, the third piece of FHA modernization would eliminate the down payment requirements. Currently, an FHA mortgagor is required to make a 3 percent cash contribution at settlement to be applied to the cost of acquisition of the property. The Administration's proposal removes this 3 percent requirement. Just like risk-based pricing, the change in down payment requirements moves away from the "one size fits all" approach and provides the FHA with the flexibility to insure a variety of mortgage products for different purposes and different borrowers.

Macroeconomic Implications

The potential macroeconomic effects of the housing market weakness and the credit market disruptions may operate through several channels, including residential investment, personal consumption, and business investment. In addition, the production of some manufactured goods used in construction has been weak, and employment in some finance-related sectors has fallen off. Many economists would agree that the downturn in the housing market has likely had some effects on consumption and business investment, but the magnitude of the effects are unknown.

The effect on residential investment is the easiest to quantify. Between the fourth quarter of 2005 and the fourth quarter of 2007, real residential investment dropped about 29 percent and subtracted an average of nearly 0.9 percentage point per quarter at an annual rate from real GDP growth. Single-family housing starts peaked at more than 1.8 million units in January 2006 and then fell more than 55 percent, to below 800,000 units, in December 2007. Inventories of unsold homes are at elevated levels: the inventory-to-sales ratio for existing single-family homes in December 2007—at 9.2 months' supply—was down from the previous few months but still near highs last reached in 1991. As prices for new and existing homes adjust to clear excess inventories, housing starts will stop declining and the drag on GDP growth from residential investment will lessen.

A second effect of the downturn in housing is the potential effect on personal consumption and saving. For many households, their house is their primary asset and a significant source of wealth. A considerable academic literature has shown that increases in wealth tend to boost consumption, though the estimated magnitude of these so-called "wealth effects" is imprecise and may depend upon the type of asset (such as stock market wealth versus housing wealth). In the case of housing wealth, some calculations suggest that a $100 billion decline in the value of the housing stock would reduce the long-run level of annual consumption by between $4 billion and $8 billion. Importantly, consumption responds only gradually to such a change in wealth, which affords fiscal and monetary policy the time to provide an offset.

A third effect of the recent credit market disruptions is that lending standards have been tightened (Chart 2-8) for mortgages and other types of consumer loans as well as for commercial real estate and other types of business lending. Tighter lending standards tend to reduce residential investment by making it more difficult to obtain mortgages. Consumption expenditures are also likely to be lower for two reasons. First, new homeowners may need to save more for their down payments than had previously been the case, which reduces consumption during the period in which they are saving. Second, existing homeowners may find it more difficult to borrow against their home equity or to engage in cash-out refinancings that previously might have boosted their short-term consumption.

On the business side, tighter lending standards would tend make investment more expensive. Historically, business fixed investment has exceeded the internally generated funds of corporations (also known as cash flow) by a substantial margin. The gap between these two measures is financed by issuing equity or taking on corporate debt such as corporate bonds or bank loans. In recent years, this gap has been considerably smaller, which suggests

Chart 2-8 Lending Standards
Banks have been tightening lending standards on a variety of loan products in recent months.

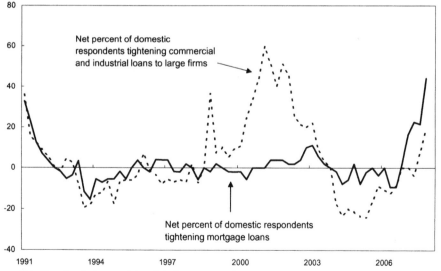

Note: The values for the second through the fourth quarters of 2007 were calculated as a weighted average of prime, subprime, and nontraditional loans using weights estimated by the Council of Economic Advisers.
Source: Federal Reserve Board.

corporations have not needed to borrow funds from other sectors as much as they did in the past. However, this gap is reemerging and firms may need to borrow more in the future, at which point tighter lending standards might become more limiting, though this effect has not been apparent through the third quarter of 2007.

Conclusion

All economic activity requires flows of capital between different parties at different times. This borrowing and lending activity takes place constantly in the world credit markets. These markets are essential to every well-functioning economy because they shift capital from those who supply it (creditors) to those who demand it (debtors). Credit markets include a wide variety of instruments, such as corporate bonds, government bonds, and money market instruments (commercial paper, certificates of deposit, and repurchase agreements, among others). The Federal Reserve's monetary policies influence the general price of borrowing and lending in the economy. Lenders can charge a higher interest payment to compensate themselves for bearing additional risk. Like any market, the credit markets bring together a diverse set of buyers and sellers, and the price of the debt instrument represents an exchange between these two parties.

The summer of 2007 witnessed a contraction in the credit markets that caused the price of borrowing to rise and the quantity of some types of debt offered to the market to shrink. This contraction took place in several markets, including the mortgage lending market and the asset-backed commercial paper market. As markets evolve and adapt to economic conditions, prices and quantities will adjust. The impact on the nonfinancial real economy has been muted to date, notwithstanding the decline in residential investment over the past 2 years. However, the effects of declining home prices in some parts of the country and the tightening of credit standards is likely to have at least some effect on consumer and business spending as time passes.

Monetary policy actions can offset some of the weakening in aggregate demand that results from disruptions in the housing and credit markets, and other government policies can offer targeted assistance. *FHASecure* and FHA Modernization are leading examples of targeted assistance to homeowners and subprime borrowers facing the possibility of foreclosure on their homes. These borrowers purchased their homes during a period in which lenders underpriced risk and offered subprime mortgages at low prices to too many borrowers. *FHASecure* can help those eligible borrowers who were caught off guard by rapidly evolving credit markets and, in some cases, predatory lending. FHA Modernization will encourage a more flexible and better functioning, risk-based mortgage lending market for those with low and moderate incomes.

Beyond such targeted responses, the best course of action is often to simply allow markets to adjust. Financial markets are in a constant process of pricing risk. Economic factors fluctuate daily, and the prices of traded debt instruments reflect investors' attitudes toward the risks associated with these fluctuations. By their very nature, markets have a remarkable resilience and can adapt rapidly to changing economic circumstances, as demonstrated by the response of the markets to the credit market disruptions that began in the summer of 2007. Policies that attempt to protect market participants from the discipline of the market risk delaying necessary adjustments and creating a potential moral hazard problem by giving lenders and borrowers less incentive to make prudent financial decisions in the future.

Markets naturally self-correct, rewarding good strategies and punishing bad ones. Government actions may be less effective at differentiating between the two and may prevent markets from creating products that benefit consumers. In addition, any government actions mitigating the outcomes of risky behavior may create perverse incentives for reckless decisions by borrowers and investors who may come to rely on government interventions. Allowing the market to price mortgage risk will help ensure that subprime mortgages are available to those who can afford to repay them. With enhanced transparency, the market can weed out poor financial products while encouraging positive financial innovations, a process that is crucial to maintaining U.S. competitiveness in the global financial community.

CHAPTER 3

The Causes and Consequences of Export Growth

The rapid growth of U.S. exports has been one of the most important economic developments of the past few years. In the 3 years from the end of 2003 to the end of 2006, real exports grew at an annual average rate of 8.3 percent, more than twice as fast as the overall U.S. economy. This growth has provided clear benefits to the entrepreneurs, owners, and workers of firms in export-oriented industries and, more broadly, to the U.S. economy as a whole. This chapter identifies the factors that have driven recent export growth and discusses several longer-term trends that have lifted exports over time. More broadly, the chapter also addresses the benefits that flow from open trade and investment policies as well as some related challenges.

The key points of this chapter are:

- The United States is the world's largest exporter, with $1.5 trillion in goods and services exports in 2006. The United States was the top exporter of services and second-largest exporter of goods, behind only Germany.

- In recent years, factors that have likely contributed to the growth in exports include rising foreign income, the expansion of production in the United States, and changes in exchange rates. One reflection of that growth is that exports accounted for more than a third of U.S. economic growth during 2006 and 2007.

- Over time, falling tariffs and transport and communication costs have likely lowered the cost of many U.S. goods in foreign markets, boosting demand for U.S. exports.

- Open trade and investment policies have increased access to export markets. Increased investment across borders by U.S. companies facilitates exports.

- Greater export opportunities give U.S. producers incentives to innovate for a worldwide market. Increased innovation and the competition that comes from trade liberalization help raise the living standard of the average U.S. citizen.

- Nearly all economists agree that growth in the volume and value of exports and imports increases the standard of living for the average individual, but they also agree that the gains from trade are not equally distributed and some individuals bear costs. The Administration has proposed policies to improve training and support to individuals affected by trade disruption.

Economists often call attention to the benefits of trade that result from importing goods and services, benefits that have been well-documented in previous issues of the *Economic Report of the President*. Building on that prior work, this chapter focuses on exporting and the benefits that arise from exporting goods and services. Some of the benefits are well known. Others, however, have come to be known more recently as researchers have combined new data with trade theory to provide a better understanding of international trade and international transactions.

The Causes of Recent Export Growth

In 2006, the United States exported nearly $1.5 trillion worth of goods and services. Nominal exports grew by 13 percent from 2005 to 2006, while nominal gross domestic product (GDP) grew 6 percent; 2006 was the third consecutive year in which nominal exports grew faster than the economy as a whole. Chart 3-1, which displays nominal exports as a share of nominal GDP, shows that such rapid export growth is impressive, but also that it is not uncommon for growth in exports to outpace growth in GDP. Exports have grown faster than the economy for much of the past 20 years. That trend was interrupted by the worldwide economic slowdown in 2001 and 2002, but resumed in 2003.

Chart 3-1 **U.S. Exports As a Share of Gross Domestic Product**
Exports as a share of GDP have been increasing for much of the past 20 years.

Percentage of GDP

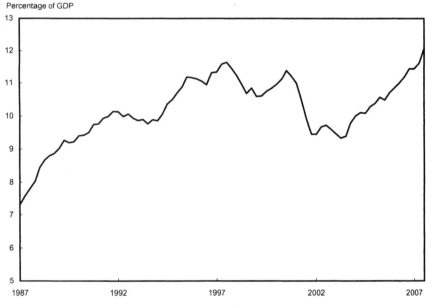

Source: Department of Commerce (Bureau of Economic Analysis).

From 2003 to 2006, the countries and regions contributing to our export growth were also relatively dispersed. Chart 3-2 displays the average annual growth rate of nominal exports to eight different regions. Export growth was positive in each of these regions, and with the exception of Japan, exports increased faster than nominal U.S. output. The fastest-growing markets for U.S. exporters were India and China, where U.S. exports grew at an average annual rate of nearly 27 and 25 percent, respectively. These growth rates imply that exports to India more than doubled and exports to China nearly doubled over this period. Export growth to Eastern Europe and Africa also exceeded 20 percent per year.

America's export growth has occurred not only in traditional export sectors, such as machinery, high-technology products, and agricultural goods. America's services exports have been growing strongly as well, especially private services such as education, finance, business services, professional services, and technical services (Box 3-1). Between 1997 and 2006, the nominal value of private services exports increased by 70 percent, compared with 51 percent for goods exports. Private services comprise 77 percent of U.S. private GDP, so expanding services markets is important to enable continued export growth.

Chart 3-2 **Average Annualized Growth in U.S. Exports to Trading Partners, 2003–2006**
U.S. exports have grown rapidly to all parts of the world.

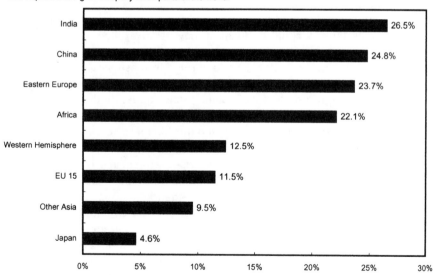

Note: "EU 15" refers to the 15 countries that were members of the European Union as of December 31, 2003. "Other Asia" excludes Mainland China, Japan, and India.
Source: International Monetary Fund, *Direction of Trade Statistics.*

Box 3-1: Trade in Services

Discussions of trade often focus on goods, but trade also involves a wide variety of services such as banking and finance, insurance, information management, medical, legal, tourism, and transportation services. The United States is the world's largest exporter of services, exporting more than $400 billion worth of services in 2006, almost double the amount exported by the United Kingdom, the second largest exporter. The United States runs a trade surplus in services, one indicator that it has a relative advantage over other countries; in 2006, U.S. services exports exceeded imports by nearly $80 billion. Still, services are not traded to the same extent that goods are. Even though private services account for 77 percent of U.S. private GDP, they account for only 28 percent of U.S. exports.

Services have some features that make them more complicated to trade than goods. Most important, goods can be produced, stored, shipped, and consumed at different points in time, but many services must be produced and used simultaneously. Nevertheless, the same basic economic principles that apply to trade in goods also apply to trade in services. The main factors used in the production of many services are skilled labor and high-tech capital, two resources the United States has in abundance. As a result, the United States has an advantage compared to other countries in producing many types of goods and services that rely heavily on these two resources.

Trade in services has benefited from two relatively recent developments. First, advances in telecommunications and information technology have lowered the costs of providing and acquiring services. Thus, while these technical advances may have resulted in the relocation of some business, professional, and technical services, the United States still maintains a sizable trade surplus in these services. In 2006, exports of business, professional, and technical services grew almost 15 percent, to more than $96 billion, and trade in those services generated a surplus of $38 billion. Second, the establishment of facilities abroad by U.S. companies has allowed our business-services providers more direct contact with their customers in other countries.

However, large barriers to trade in services remain. In order to remove these barriers, the Administration is pursuing further liberalization of services trade in the Doha Development Agenda negotiations, multilateral negotiations by members of the World Trade Organization aimed at lowering trade barriers worldwide. Recent free-trade agreements have also included substantial liberalization of the services sectors. One study estimates the long-run effect of a worldwide move to completely free trade in services could translate into enormous economic gains for

continued on the next page

Four factors have contributed to the strong U.S. export performance. First, our trading partners' income growth has boosted their demand for U.S. products. Second, increased productive capacity in the United States has expanded our ability to serve foreign demand. Third, changes in exchange rates since 2002 made American goods cheaper on world markets. Finally, the longer-run decline in transportation costs, lower tariffs, and the removal of other barriers to trade have made it easier for U.S. products to penetrate export markets. Together, these factors not only affect exports, but they also influence the current account, a broader measure of trade and a part of the balance of payments between the United States and the rest of the world (see Box 3-2).

Foreign Income Growth

Perhaps the most important factor driving the recent increase in exports has been the growth of income of our main trading partners. As income increases around the world, demand for U.S. products increases as well. This relationship is depicted in Chart 3-3, which shows the real growth of exports and foreign GDP. There are several aspects of this graph that are noteworthy.

First, foreign GDP growth and U.S. export growth tend to rise or fall together. As other countries become richer, they demand more goods and services, including U.S. goods and services. Strong worldwide expansions, such as those in the late 1980s and the mid-1990s, led to strong U.S. export growth. Weakness in the world economy, such as that during 1998 and 2001, led to weak export growth or even declines. Recent years have experienced a period of strong worldwide growth led by fast-growing emerging markets such as China, relatively strong growth in Europe, and faster GDP growth in Latin America; this growth has been a key driver of rapid U.S. export growth.

Box 3-2: The Current Account Deficit

The *current account* measures the value of international trade in goods and services, investment income flows, and unilateral international transfers. Trade in goods and services is the single largest component of the current account. In 2006, the trade deficit was $759 billion and the current account deficit was $811 billion; that is, the trade deficit accounted for 93 percent of the current account deficit. Exports have grown much faster than imports, and this helped narrow the current account deficit in absolute terms and relative to GDP, as shown in the chart. In the fourth quarter of 2005, the current account deficit totaled $863 billion at an annualized rate, or 6.8 percent of GDP. In the third quarter of 2007, the current account deficit fell to $714 billion at an annualized rate, or 5.1 percent of GDP, as export growth greatly exceeded import growth.

Current Account Deficit As a Share of Gross Domestic Product
After increasing for most of the last 15 years, the current account deficit as a share of GDP has decreased over the last 2 years.

Percentage of GDP

Source: Department of Commerce (Bureau of Economic Analysis).

Chart 3-3 **Real Growth in U.S. Exports and Foreign Gross Domestic Product**
Increases in foreign income are typically associated with export growth.

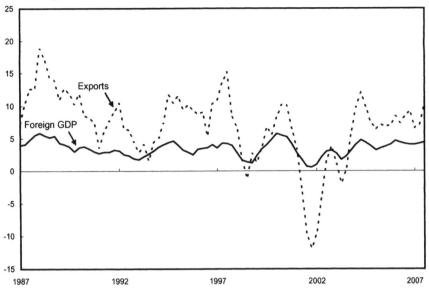

Sources: Department of Commerce (Bureau of Economic Analysis) and Macroeconomic Advisers.

Second, export growth is much more volatile than foreign GDP growth. Exports grew much faster than the world economy during the expansions of the 1980s, the mid-1990s, and the past few years. But export growth fell below worldwide economic growth during the worldwide slowdowns in 1998 and 2001. This type of volatility occurs because changes and expected changes in foreign output typically lead to large changes in investment in those economies; investment is strongly related to demand for capital goods—plants and equipment used in production—and consumer durables—goods used over time, such as refrigerators—which U.S. production helps satisfy. Most U.S. exports of goods are capital goods, consumer durable goods, and inputs that are used to produce them, and are therefore very sensitive to changes in foreign GDP. Capital goods and consumer durables account for 61 percent of nonenergy U.S. merchandise exports. Industrial supplies, which are often used in the production of capital goods and durable goods, account for 14 percent of nonenergy U.S. exports. For example, in 2006, the United States exported almost $85 billion worth of automobiles, auto parts, tractors, and trucks; $46 billion worth of electronic circuits; more than $43 billion worth of airplanes and aircraft; and nearly $21 billion worth of parts and components for office machinery.

Growth in Domestic Production

A second factor that has contributed to the growth in exports is the expansion of the U.S. economy. As the U.S. economy's productive capacity expands, its ability to produce goods and services for export likely expands as well. A key factor in increasing U.S. production, and therefore U.S. capacity to export, has been the growth of labor productivity. Gross output produced per hour of work increased in 88 percent of manufacturing industries from 2004 to 2005, the most recent years for which data are available. Over a longer horizon, output per worker increased in all but 1 of about 85 manufacturing industries. In 2005, 60 percent of manufacturing industries had labor productivity increases of at least 4 percent. The gains were especially high in computer and computer-peripherals manufacturing, apparel and knitting mills, and agricultural chemicals. The growth in output in these sectors has helped to satisfy world demand.

Exchange Rates

From January 2002 through December 2007, the dollar has depreciated 23 percent in nominal terms against a weighted average of currencies. In other words, the cost of buying other currencies has increased by about 23 percent on average. In real terms—controlling for international differences in inflation rates—the average real exchange rate has depreciated by nearly 22 percent; that is, individuals abroad can exchange goods produced in their country and receive about 22 percent more U.S. goods now compared to 2002. Changes in the terms of trade associated with recent exchange rate trends made American goods cheaper relative to those of some other countries.

Trade Costs and Barriers

Falling transportation costs, improved communications, and the removal of tariff and nontariff barriers have also supported the growth in trade. Both exports and imports have benefited.

Over the last half century, there have been dramatic declines in shipping costs as well as striking improvements in the quality of shipping among developed economies. The nature of trade for some emerging economies may now be changing to take advantage of these improvements. Studies indicate that improvements in infrastructure may lower the costs of trade a great deal. The ratio of the value of exports upon arrival to the value when shipped gives a rough measure of the costs associated with freight and insuring the good while in transport. For some export markets there have been noticeable declines in transportation costs, as measured by this ratio. For example, from 2003 to 2006, the average cost of shipping goods to Africa and China decreased by 14 and 12 percentage points, respectively. From 2003 to 2006, for five of the eight regions identified in Chart 3-2, the cost of importing goods from the United States has fallen.

In addition to falling transportation costs, communication costs have declined, facilitating the growth in trade. One example is the growth of e-commerce. One study finds that, on average, the growth in the number of Internet hosts in an economy helped increase that economy's annual export growth from 1997 to 1999. As more of the world's population has gained access to the Internet, the market for U.S. goods and services has expanded and exports have likely increased as well.

Trade liberalization has also been important. Some of the growth of trade can be attributed to successful multilateral reductions in trade barriers through the World Trade Organization (WTO) and its predecessor, the General Agreement on Tariffs and Trade. The United States continues to work with other nations to advance the Doha Development Agenda negotiations, as well as to liberalize trade regionally and bilaterally. When this Administration took office, the United States had free-trade agreements (FTAs) implemented with only 3 countries, Canada, Mexico, and Israel; a fourth, with Jordan, had been signed but was not yet approved by Congress. Through 2007, the Administration has implemented FTAs or completed negotiations with 17 countries. Congress has approved agreements with 14 of these countries, most recently with Peru, while those with Colombia, Panama, and South Korea are awaiting Congressional approval.

Do FTAs contribute to export growth? Over the last 20 years, there has been a virtual explosion in the number of FTAs. Worldwide, there are now more than 200 regional FTAs in force. For many of these FTAs, the removal of tariffs and other trade barriers occurs over 5-year phases and often takes nearly 15 years to have full effect. Recent research shows that in the short run, the average FTA has increased trade between bilateral trading partners by 32 percent after 5 years, 73 percent after 10 years, and 114 percent after 15 years. After 15 years, the average FTA appears to have had no additional effect on trade growth. Therefore, the long-run effect of the average FTA has been roughly a doubling of trade between the two trading partners. In the case of recent U.S. FTAs, nearly all of the tariff cuts and nontariff liberalization occur early in the agreement, and later stages have more modest phase-outs. As a result, we may expect to see much of the increases in trade coming in the first 5 to 10 years of the agreement. As is evident from Chart 3-4, U.S. export growth to recent FTA partners in 2006 from 2005 has, for most countries, been higher than total U.S. export growth. Overall, the FTA partners have been major contributors to the growth in exports. In 2006, the United States exported goods to more than 200 economies. Exports to our 13 trading partners in the FTAs that had been signed and implemented through that year accounted for one-third of the growth of U.S. goods exports between 2005 and 2006.

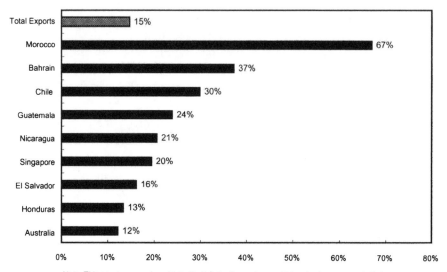

Chart 3-4 **Growth of U.S. Goods Exports to Free Trade Agreement Partners, 2005–2006**
The recent free-trade agreements have provided U.S. businesses access to many new markets. As a result, U.S. nominal exports to these new markets are growing rapidly.

Note: This country group is restricted to U.S. trading partners with free-trade agreements that were both signed and entered into force from 2001 to 2006.
Source: Department of Commerce (Census Bureau).

Exports and Foreign Direct Investment

Many different types of companies engage in international trade. In one form of international trade, U.S. companies invest abroad and operate facilities in foreign countries. Cross-border investment to control a business (with control generally defined as having a 10 percent or greater ownership stake) is known as foreign direct investment (FDI), and FDI facilitates exports.

The United States is strongly committed to open investment (Box 3-3), and the world is more aware of the benefits of open investment today than it was in the past. For much of the early post–World War II era, many countries placed heavy restrictions on investment in both directions. Policies on inbound investment restricted the sectors in which foreign businesses could invest or the level of ownership they could take. Some policies barred acquisitions, and others made it difficult for investors to send profits or capital home.

Spurred in part by the rapid growth of the internationally oriented East Asian economies, by European integration, and by the stagnation of many closed economies, countries have reduced barriers to foreign investment and most now actively seek it. Today, liberalization continues in both developing and advanced economies. In 1992, the United Nations Conference on Trade and Development recorded 77 national regulatory changes around the

Box 3-3: Open Investment and the United States

As a matter of policy, the United States has a longstanding commitment to welcoming foreign direct investment and securing fair, equitable, and nondiscriminatory treatment for U.S. investors abroad. On May 10, 2007, the President issued a Statement on Open Economies reaffirming this commitment, and noted that the Administration is committed to ensuring that the United States continues to be the most attractive place in the world to invest.

This policy stems from recognition of the benefits of open investment. These benefits include the introduction of new technologies, processes, and management techniques into the economy; increased competition that lowers prices for consumers and leads to quality improvements; and the creation of greater international trade and knowledge linkages. Foreign affiliates in the United States tend to have more need for higher-skilled labor than many other firms, paying at least 25 percent greater compensation than private firms that are domestically owned, thus creating an incentive for U.S. workers to keep building skills and to compete for these well-paying jobs. U.S. investment abroad can also strengthen the U.S. economy. It can increase exports, thereby improving U.S. job opportunities. Increased exports provide incentives for firms to hire more people into the more productive, higher-wage industries. Increased trade thereby results in higher average wages for U.S. workers. In addition, there is evidence that firms that invest abroad also increase their domestic investment, and that one activity helps the other.

world that were favorable to FDI. It recorded a peak of 234 such changes in both 2002 and 2004, and a still-robust level of 147 in 2006. But the move toward openness has experienced setbacks as well. In 2006, countries made 37 regulatory changes that were unfavorable to FDI (20 percent of all changes), the highest rate since 1992. Some of these unfavorable changes included restrictions in certain sectors or efforts to nationalize certain sectors, especially natural resource industries.

Another issue facing open investment is that in some limited circumstances, the acquisition of a domestic company by a foreign investor could pose risks to the national security of the host country. For example, such a problem could arise if an adversary of the host country wanted to buy a domestic military contractor. The United States addresses this issue through the interagency Committee on Foreign Investment in the United States (CFIUS), which considers only genuine national security concerns, not economic or other interests. The Foreign Investment and National Security Act of 2007 (FINSA) clarified and improved the CFIUS process and the Act was passed by Congress with strong bipartisan support, reaffirming Congressional trust in CFIUS's role in protecting national security in a manner consistent with the U.S. commitment to open investment. In passing FINSA, Congress stated that the new law is meant "to ensure national security while promoting foreign investment and the creation and maintenance of jobs."

Multinationals and Trade

The United States is both the single leading recipient and leading source of foreign direct investment in the world. In 2006, total cumulative FDI in the United States was almost $1.8 trillion, 15 percent of the world total. That same year, total cumulative FDI from U.S. companies to the rest of the world was almost $2.4 trillion, or 19 percent of the world total.

To understand FDI and how it creates channels for trade, understanding some terms is useful. Firms that carry out direct investment abroad and own companies or branches in more than one country are known as *multinational companies,* or *multinationals.* The company that is the headquarters of the firm does the investing and is known as the *parent.* The parent company is located in the *home country.* The foreign company that the parent owns is known as the *foreign affiliate* and is located in the *host country.* The parent might own as much as 100 percent or as little as 10 percent of the foreign affiliate and still be considered a direct investor. Affiliates that are more than half-owned by direct investors are known as *majority-owned foreign affiliates.* Ownership chains can be complicated: Sometimes a U.S. parent is owned by foreign investors, and is therefore also a foreign affiliate.

The vast majority of U.S. trade is carried out by companies that are part of multinationals. In 2005, the export of goods by U.S. parent companies, by U.S. affiliates of foreign companies, and by unaffiliated companies in the United States to U.S.-owned affiliates abroad amounted to $621 billion, or 69 percent of all U.S. goods exports. Most of these exports—$416 billion—came from U.S. parent companies not otherwise owned by foreign companies, but foreign-owned affiliates in the United States also exported a great deal—$169 billion. A large portion of this multinational-related trade took place *within* multinationals, that is, between parent companies and affiliates. Goods exports from U.S. parent companies to their foreign affiliates and U.S.-based affiliates to their foreign parent companies totaled $267 billion, 30 percent of all U.S. goods exports.

Multinationals are not only goods exporters. They also play an increasing role in the export of services. Between 1997 and 2006, services exports from U.S. parent companies to their foreign affiliates and from U.S. affiliates to their foreign parent companies grew from $51.8 billion to $103.3 billion, or from 22 percent to 26 percent of all U.S. private services exports. Together, they accounted for almost one-third of all the growth in U.S. private services exports. Of the $103.3 billion, U.S. parent companies sold $73.1 billion worth of services to their foreign affiliates, 79 percent more in nominal terms than in 1997. Services exports from U.S.-based affiliates of foreign companies to their foreign parent companies grew even faster. In 2006, these affiliates sold $30.2 billion worth of services to their foreign parent companies, a 175-percent nominal increase from 1997.

The Benefits of Trade and Expanding Export Markets

Promoting free trade is a top priority of this Administration. Trade liberalization, whether it involves multilateral agreements that lower barriers among all the world's countries, or bilateral agreements that permit deeper integration such as by harmonizing laws or institutions, provides a host of economic benefits: lower prices and expanded consumer choice, a larger market for U.S. exports, increased domestic productivity, and closer ties to people and nations around the world. Economists often emphasize the gains from trade from importing goods and services that are relatively more difficult for the domestic economy to produce, but there are also benefits to be gained through exporting.

International trade involves transactions between individuals or firms that reside in different countries. As in any voluntary transaction, the participants in international trade expect to benefit because they value what they receive in the exchange more than what they give. The gains in each individual transaction then aggregate into gains for the economy as a whole. The United States benefits from exporting because it allows us to trade goods that are abundant in national production for goods that are relatively more costly to produce domestically.

Another benefit of policies that encourage free trade and expand markets is that trade encourages specialization and the division of labor. Specialization provides near-term benefits because economies have different endowments of resources and their workforces possess different skills and talents. For example, the United States has a relatively large population of highly skilled workers, but very little tropical land. As a result, the United States exports business and financial services to the world and imports coffee from a variety of tropical countries, such as Colombia.

Specialization raises the living standard for the average citizen because it allows people to consume more goods and services. Exporting allows an economy to use its relatively abundant resources to produce goods and services and export them to economies where the resources required to produce such goods and services are relatively scarce. Because goods are shipped to markets where they are relatively scarce, the United States receives a higher price for these goods than if they were produced and sold only in domestic markets. This increased income allows U.S. citizens to buy more goods and services, including goods and services that are produced in other countries. One study finds that the two major trade agreements of the 1990s—the Uruguay Round of the World Trade Organization and the North American Free Trade Agreement—contribute between $1,300 and $2,000 in annual benefits for the average American family of four.

Some specialization takes the form of interindustry specialization—one country specializes in some goods; another country in others. However, a large proportion of trade involves similar goods within an industry. Such intra-industry trade can occur for several reasons. One of the primary reasons for intra-industry trade is that each producer tailors a product to a specific target audience. In doing so, their output is consumed by a fraction of the total market for that product. Therefore, intra-industry trade typically leads to more varieties; that is, different countries produce goods within the same industry, but they may produce a product with different features or a different style. One recent study that investigates the growth of new varieties from all types of products imported by the United States from 1972 to 2001 finds that new varieties have increased threefold. The welfare gain from this increase in varieties is roughly equal to $900 per person.

The innovation, introduction of new varieties, and expanded competition that come from broadening trade also promote world economic development. As resources are shifted from unproductive sectors to more productive sectors as a result of innovation in an economy such as that of the United States, it becomes more difficult for the country to produce all the goods, new and old. The new goods typically use skilled labor more intensively than the older goods. The production of these new goods in the United States increases the demand for skilled workers and the wages paid to those workers. The increase in the wage paid to skilled workers benefits the United States, not only because it raises the incomes of our workers, but also because it increases the incentives for individuals to acquire more skills. Human capital accumulation is one of the engines that drives economic growth. When the United States begins devoting more resources to producing the new, more profitable goods, it will likely discontinue producing older, less skill-intensive goods, and these goods will need to be produced abroad. Although these older goods were less skill-intensive in the United States, they typically are more skill-intensive in the economy that begins to produce them. This creates greater rewards for skilled workers, which encourages human capital accumulation and promotes growth as well for both trading partners. These benefits are not necessarily equally distributed, as will be discussed in the next section.

Specialization, the division of labor, innovation of products for world markets, and the upgrading of skill that is brought about by trade all create gains in the economy. Are these gains from trade measurable? In fact, research does show that across countries, relative to their income, countries that trade more tend to have higher per capita incomes than those that trade less, and that more trade is a cause of this higher income.

Trade and Labor Markets

The United States has long been committed to free trade and continues to pursue policies and agreements to promote trade liberalization. The consensus among economists is that, in the aggregate, the economic benefits of trade liberalization greatly outweigh its costs. At an individual level, however, those benefits and costs may not be evenly distributed. Some people may particularly benefit—for example, workers who get higher-paying jobs when exporters expand their production—while others bear costs—for example, workers who are displaced because of import competition.

It is important to consider the distributional implications of trade liberalization and, in particular, the impact on workers who may be displaced by import competition. However, it is also important to emphasize that trade liberalization has little, if any, effect on overall employment. In particular, increases in imports are not associated with a higher unemployment rate or lower workforce participation. Chart 3-5 shows the ratio of imports to GDP since 1960, along with the unemployment rate. If trade were a major factor affecting the economy's ability to maintain full employment, these measures would tend to move in tandem. The increase in imports as a percentage of GDP over the past several decades has not led to any noticeable trend in the unemployment rate. Over the past decade, the U.S. economy has experienced historically low unemployment, while imports have grown considerably. Indeed, in recent years, imports as a share of GDP have increased, but this has not resulted in any significant trend in the overall unemployment rate.

Along with trade and trade policies, other factors, such as changes in consumer tastes, domestic competition, and productivity increases, contribute to the churning of the labor market. These other factors can have effects that are similar to those of import competition on the labor market, often on similar individuals and sectors. For example, the United States has seen a vast increase in domestic manufacturing output while the manufacturing workforce has been declining. Import competition in manufacturing industries has played less of a role in the decline of manufacturing employment than has the rapid increase in labor productivity.

The cost for workers in import-competing industries is that increased imports—due to changes in the world economy or policy efforts to liberalize trade—may cause some to lose their jobs or receive lower wages. Among manufacturing industries, the U.S. industries that appear to be most affected

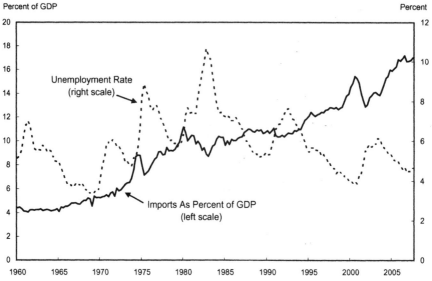

Chart 3-5 Imports and the Unemployment Rate, 1960–2006
Over the long run, there is little connection between increased imports of goods and services and the strength of the labor market.

Percent of GDP

Percent

Unemployment Rate
(right scale)

Imports As Percent of GDP
(left scale)

Sources: Department of Commerce (Bureau of Economic Analysis) and Deparment of Labor (Bureau of Labor Statistics).

by import competition are electrical machinery, apparel, motor vehicles, and non-electrical machinery. Similar to workers displaced from manufacturing more generally, workers displaced from import-competing manufacturing industries tend to have lower earnings upon reemployment. These adverse effects are more a function of such factors as education, skills, and age, rather than something intrinsic to the increase of imports due to trade liberalization. In this way, such trade-induced effects are similar to labor market effects induced by technological change.

While trade liberalization may lead to job loss in some import-competing sectors, it also creates jobs in the industries that produce the goods and services the United States exports and in industries that use imported inputs, and the benefits to the economy resulting from trade liberalization are far greater than the costs. Increased trade does, however, adversely affect some workers. The President recognizes that these workers need help with retraining and reemployment and has called for a reauthorization and reform of the Trade Adjustment Assistance (TAA) program to meet the needs of these displaced workers. The Administration is committed to supporting effective and improved trade-adjustment assistance to workers who are displaced due to import competition.

Despite the overall benefits of trade, there are some who propose suspending our efforts to liberalize trade and even increasing trade barriers as a remedy for the adverse effect of trade on some workers. Increased protectionism, however, has proven itself ineffective as a means to address these concerns. In fact, the cost of protectionism often greatly outweighs the benefits. One study reports that, at the time of the analysis, on average, each job saved in 21 sectors protected by such trade restrictions as high tariffs, import quotas, and other measures cost consumers $170,000 per year in higher prices and reduced purchasing.

Increased protectionism can also have unintended negative effects on domestic industries that use goods produced by protected industries as inputs to their own production. The majority of U.S. imports are intermediate goods; trade restrictions raise the price of these goods and directly harm other domestic industries. By increasing the cost of inputs, protection of one industry can have adverse effects on employment of other industries. Protectionism can also cause companies that use the protected inputs to move jobs and production out of the United States.

Conclusion

Over the last few years there has been a dramatic increase in U.S. exports. This growth is in large part due to increases in foreign demand, increased domestic production, changes in the terms of trade, and reductions in the cost of international transactions. The U.S. economy has benefited substantially from increased trade and, in particular, from the rapid growth of its exports. Exporting firms are typically fast growing and pay higher wages. Thus, increased exports translate into positive benefits for workers in export-oriented industries.

Being more engaged in global trade provides other benefits as well. Trade helps keep prices low and allows for a wider variety of goods and services. Several studies have revealed that there are sizable costs to limiting trade, and benefits to expanding trade. The Administration has worked to lower trade barriers and open markets for U.S. producers through multilateral, regional, and bilateral negotiations. At the global level, the Administration is aggressively pursuing a successful conclusion to the World Trade Organization's Doha Development Agenda, which has the potential to lower trade barriers around the world and help millions of people escape poverty. The Administration is also seeking to advance broad trade agreements in the Americas and the Asia-Pacific region and bilateral free-trade agreements. Bilateral free-trade agreements have been especially progressive in terms of opening markets for services trade, an area in which the United States has a distinct advantage relative to other countries.

The Importance of Health and Health Care

The American health care system is an engine for innovation that develops and broadly disseminates advanced, life-enhancing treatments and offers a wide set of choices for consumers of health care. The current health care system provides enormous benefits, but there are substantial opportunities for reforms that would reduce costs, increase access, enhance quality, and improve the health of Americans.

An individual's health can be maintained or improved in many ways, including through changes in personal behavior and through the appropriate consumption of health care services. While there is substantial health care spending in the United States, the importance of health does provide a strong rationale for this level of spending. But because health care financing and delivery are often inefficient, there are opportunities to advance health and access to health care services without further growth in spending. To improve the efficiency of health care financing and delivery, the Administration has pursued policies that would increase incentives for individuals to purchase consumer-directed health insurance plans. The Administration has also worked to link provider payments to performance, thus rewarding efficient delivery of health care. In the President's State of the Union Address, he proposed changing the tax treatment of health insurance, offering all Americans a standard deduction for buying health insurance. Such a change could play an important role in increasing the efficiency of the American health care system and expanding health insurance coverage.

The key points in this chapter are:

- Health can be improved not only through the consumption of health care services, but also through individual behavior and lifestyle choices such as quitting smoking, eating more nutritious foods, and getting more exercise.
- Health care has enhanced the health of our population; greater efficiency in the health care system, however, could yield even greater health for Americans without increasing health care spending.
- Rapid growth in health care costs and limited access to health insurance continue to present challenges to the health care system.
- Administration policies focus on reducing cost growth, improving quality, and expanding access to health insurance through an emphasis on private sector and market-based solutions.

Health and the Demand for Health Care

The demand for health care is unlike the demand for most consumer products and services because while the desire for consumer products and services comes from direct consumption, the desire for health care is not derived directly from the consumption of the medical procedures themselves; rather, it comes from the direct value of improved health that is produced by health care. For example, demand for an MP3 player is based on the enjoyment that an MP3 player brings to a consumer, but few would choose to get a laparoscopic cholecystectomy for the same reason. Rather, a consumer's desire to have her gallbladder removed is directly related to the positive impact the operation is likely to have on her health. Understanding how health is produced, demanded, and valued is a useful starting point for evaluating the health care system and health care policy.

Demand for Health

People demand health because of its role in facilitating and providing happiness. Health can be defined along two dimensions: the length of life (longevity) and the quality of life. A person derives value from the quality of life directly and indirectly: directly because one's level of health affects the enjoyment of goods and leisure and indirectly because one's level of health enhances productivity (Box 4-1). Enhanced productivity can be rewarded in the labor market through higher wages. The indirect effect of health on productivity suggests that health is an important component of human capital investment. Consistent with the basic principle of our economic system, consumers exercise choice in purchasing health care and other goods and services.

The Production of Health

Health care is only one of the factors that determine health. Other factors include individual behaviors, environmental factors, social factors, education, income, and genetics. If we think of an individual as a producer of health, the key production inputs are the time and money spent on health-improving activities and health care. Health-improving activities can include individual choices regarding exercise, nutrition, and lifestyle. Health care can include hospital care, outpatient visits to medical providers, nursing home care, and medication. Because health can deteriorate from accidents, sudden disease, and the effects of aging, health care inputs are needed not only to maintain current levels of health but also possibly to restore health following an illness or injury.

Box 4-1: Health Effects on Job Productivity

Health can affect job productivity through absenteeism and presenteeism. *Absenteeism,* not being present at the place of work as a result of injury or illness, prevents an individual from contributing to output, and may also affect the ability of coworkers to be productive when tasks require collaboration. *Presenteeism* is the loss of at-work productivity caused by a lack of physical or mental energy needed to complete tasks, increased workplace accidents, and the possible spread of illness to fellow employees. There is evidence that both of these factors are costly. According to the Current Population Survey (CPS), 2.3 percent of workers will have an absence from work during a typical week due to injury or illness. Several studies estimating the extent to which presenteeism affects productivity indicate that, on average, the productivity loss caused by some of the most common conditions (such as allergies, depression, musculoskeletal pain, and respiratory disorders) is between 5 and 18 percent.

Investment in improving and managing health offers opportunities to mitigate some of these costs. An increasing number of employers are instituting at-work wellness programs that provide targeted health management. These programs range from monetary penalties for those with unhealthy lifestyles (such as smoking or uncontrolled diabetes) to subsidizing access to exercise facilities. The benefits are shared by the worker (higher earnings, better quality of life) and the employer (enhanced productivity and decreased health care expenditures). Evidence of the success of these programs, while incomplete and variable, suggests that at-work wellness programs can improve worker health outcomes and provide a positive return to employers. One long-term study of a particularly comprehensive wellness program shows that health care expenditures fell by an average of $225 per employee per year (mostly due to fewer doctor visits and hospital stays), but it took several years to realize these benefits.

Studies of trends in health-improving activities show a mixed picture on whether Americans are investing more in their health. A recent study finds that Americans are smoking less and controlling their cholesterol and blood pressure better (through a combination of health-improving activities and medical inputs). In contrast, there has been a dramatic increase in obesity in the United States in both adults and children during the past few decades. Obesity has more than doubled since the late 1970s, from 15 percent to 34 percent among adults. Among children ages 6 to 19, the incidence of being overweight has tripled. Obesity is an indicator of unhealthy behavior because it often reflects a lack of exercise and overconsumption of unhealthy foods. Also, obesity is associated with a higher risk of many diseases and health conditions, including hypertension, Type 2 diabetes, coronary heart disease, and some cancers.

Trends in Health Spending

Americans are investing more in their health as measured by health care expenditure. In 2006, Americans spent over $7,000 per capita on health care, up from $2,400 in 1980 and $800 in 1960 (all in 2006 dollars). National health care spending has grown more rapidly than the economy as a whole, so health care accounts for an increasing share of the overall economy (Chart 4-1). National health care spending now accounts for about 16 percent of gross domestic product (GDP), up from 9.1 percent in 1980 and only 5.2 percent in 1960.

The primary factor that tends to drive health care expenditure growth is the development and diffusion of new technologies. Knowledge about health and health care conditions continues to expand over time, generating an expanding inventory of new or improved products, techniques, and services. Medical technology may account for about one-half or more of real long-term

Chart 4-1 **National Health Expenditures As a Share of Gross Domestic Product**
Health care expenditures have increased faster than GDP.

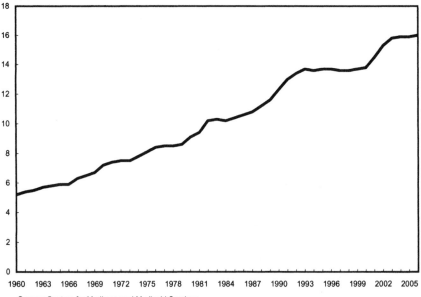

Percent

Source: Centers for Medicare and Medicaid Services.

health care spending growth. Rising incomes are a second important factor because as income increases, a greater proportion of income is typically spent on health care. The aging of the population and increasing disease prevalence is a third important factor contributing to expenditure growth in the United States. Other cited factors include more rapid wage growth in the health sector, greater insurance coverage supported by large government subsidies through both government-sponsored programs and tax subsidies, and the low share of health expenses paid out-of-pocket by health consumers.

Trends in Life Expectancy

Life expectancy is only one of many outcome measures for health, but because it has been reliably and consistently measured over time, it offers a unique historical view of trends in health. United States life expectancy trends since 1900 both from birth and from age 65 are shown in Chart 4-2. In the two panels of this chart, we see life expectancy gains throughout the century. Progress in life expectancy at birth was rapid in the first half of the century, growing from 48 to 68 years. Between 1950 and 1970, life expectancy at birth grew gradually, reaching only 71 by 1970. Progress picked up in the 1970s, with life expectancy reaching age 78 by 2004. There is a contrasting pattern for the life expectancy among those who live to age 65. Life expectancy at age

Chart 4-2 **Life Expectancy at Birth and at Age 65**
Life expectancy at birth increased rapidly in the first half of the century and life expectancy at age 65 increased most rapidly after 1970.

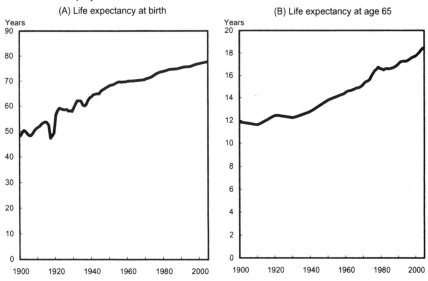

Source: Centers for Disease Control, National Center for Health Statistics, National Vital Statistics Reports, vol.54, No.14, April 19, 2006.

65 showed little progress until the 1930s; in the subsequent 4 decades, life expectancy at 65 rose 3 years to 15 (meaning that in 1930 a person who was 65 could expect to live to age 77, while in 1970 a 65-year-old person could expect to live to age 80). Starting in the 1970s, the pace of improvement accelerated. By 2004, life expectancy at age 65 was 18.5 additional years; a gain of 3.5 years of life over the past 3.5 decades.

Innovations in health and health care can explain the patterns in longevity. Changes in the first half of the 20th century came largely through progress in reducing malnutrition, improving sanitation, and containing infection through improved public health measures and the use of antibiotic agents such as penicillin. After about 20 years of gradual improvement in life expectancy, the rising longevity from 1970 reflects progress in treating life-threatening ailments prevalent among those over 50. As shown in Table 4-1, the largest single contributor to increased longevity has been reduced mortality from heart disease (3.6 years); reduced mortality from strokes added another 1.3 years to life expectancy. Reduced mortality from those two conditions has thus added nearly 5 years to the life expectancy of Americans.

Research suggests that the lower mortality from heart disease and strokes is primarily attributable to advances in intensive medical therapies, non-acute medications to manage high blood pressure and high cholesterol, and changes in individual behavior to reduce risk factors such as smoking and high-fat diets. Improvements in medical treatments alone are believed to account for at least 3 of the 5 years of the life expectancy gain that is attributable to reduced mortality from heart diseases and strokes.

To put these substantial benefits of extending life into a perspective that accounts for the increased spending on health care, it is useful to assess the tradeoff between the cost of the treatments and the benefits of longer life. An influential study has done this and found the benefits of increased spending on cardiovascular treatments to be about four times as large as the costs.

TABLE 4-1.—*Additional Life-Years Due to Reduced Mortality from Selected Causes, for US by Decade, 1950-2000*

(years)

	1950-1960	1960-1970	1970-1980	1980-1990	1990-2000	Total
Infant Mortality	0.47	0.35	0.67	0.22	0.16	1.87
Heart Disease	0.38	0.55	0.96	1.08	0.67	3.63
Cancer	0.01	-0.05	-0.09	-0.05	0.30	0.16
Stroke	0.15	0.24	0.52	0.31	0.07	1.29
Accidents	0.14	-0.09	0.27	0.27	0.09	0.66
Other	0.66	0.00	0.55	-0.28	0.40	1.33
Total	1.80	1.00	2.93	1.54	1.68	8.96

Source: Murphy, K.M., and Topel, R.H. The Value of Life and Longevity (2006). Journal of Political Economy, vol. 11, No. 5, 871-904.

While the study focused on spending on cardiovascular disease, the basic conclusion—aggregate health-spending increases have provided positive returns—is true more broadly. Using the same framework, the total increase in health care spending since 1950 can be justified, in monetary terms, by the life expectancy gains from cardiovascular treatment and neonatal care alone. Gains from other treatment advances (not to mention benefits other than life extension, such as a higher quality of life) thus imply that, over the past half-century, the benefits from greater health care spending in the United States have exceeded their costs. However, the benefits of greater health care spending in relation to costs have not been as favorable since 1980, suggesting potentially diminishing returns from health care spending.

Trends in Health Insurance Coverage

Health insurance helps shield families from the financial risk of the unanticipated health expenses of serious illness or injury, and facilitates access to the health care system, thereby improving health outcomes. Given those benefits, it is a major concern that at any given time, 16 percent of Americans report that they lack health insurance. The primary driver of declining enrollment in private insurance has been the increasing cost of health care and this decline contributes to the rising proportion of uninsured (Chart 4-3).

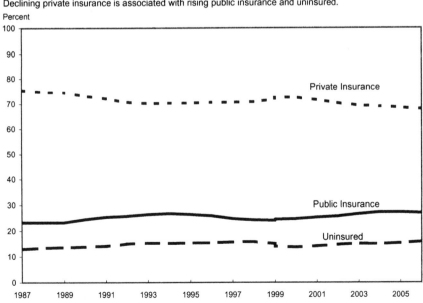

Chart 4-3 **Health Insurance Coverage by Source: 1987 to 2006**
Declining private insurance is associated with rising public insurance and uninsured.

Source: Department of Commerce (Bureau of Census), Current Population Survey, Annual Social and Economic Supplements, 2006.

Addressing Challenges in the
Health Care System

The trends in the U.S. health care system suggest that the rapid growth in health care costs will persist. Health care costs will pose an increasing challenge for consumers of health care and health insurance as expenditures in this sector make up a greater share of household consumption. Taxpayers will also face an increasing challenge as the budgetary burden of Federal and State health care programs continues to expand. (See Box 4-2 for an overview of government health care programs.) Reducing health care cost growth and increasing access while improving health care quality are the goals of Federal health care policy. The Administration's objective has been to develop market-oriented policies to meet these goals by fostering the innovation, flexibility, and choice that are the best aspects of the American health care system. Market-oriented policies must address potential market failures that are at the root of the challenges in the health care system. These problems include insufficient information available to patients, health providers, and insurers; access barriers for lower-income or disadvantaged Americans; and two specific market failures that arise in insurance markets: moral hazard and adverse selection. *Moral hazard* is the tendency for individuals to overuse certain types of health care when insurance covers a sizable fraction of the costs; *adverse selection* is the tendency for insurance to be purchased by those persons who are most likely to need it (and who thus have higher costs). Policies aimed at mitigating these problems can enhance the ability of our market-oriented health care system to achieve the goals of controlled cost growth, improved access to health insurance coverage, and high-quality health care.

Box 4-2: Government Health Care Programs

About 46 percent of health care spending is funded by Federal and State Governments through various health programs. The main government-funded health programs are designed to serve specific populations and include Medicare, Medicaid, the State Children's Health Insurance Program (SCHIP), and the Veterans Health Administration (VHA).

Medicare was enacted in 1965 and covers nearly all individuals aged 65 and older (as well as some younger individuals with disabilities or specific illnesses). Medicare today consists of three basic parts. Part A is hospital insurance, which covers stays in hospitals and nursing facilities. Part A is primarily funded by a 2.9 percent payroll tax (1.45 percent each for workers and employers). Part A is generally provided automatically

continued on next page

Box 4-2 — continued

and without premiums for persons age 65 and older who are eligible for Social Security or Railroad Retirement benefits. Part B is supplementary medical insurance which covers doctor visits and other outpatient services. Part B is voluntary and enrollees pay a monthly premium, yet 94 percent of those eligible elect to enroll. Part D, Medicare's prescription drug benefit which started in 2006, is available on a voluntary basis to individuals who qualify for Medicare Part A, and requires a monthly premium for those beneficiaries who do not qualify for the low-income subsidy. Unlike other parts of Medicare, Part D is administered by a partnership between private insurers and Medicare officials to provide choice of prescription drug plans to beneficiaries and to allow for price competition. Part B and Part D are funded by a combination of premiums from beneficiaries and government revenues (Part D also receives some resources from the States). In 2007, there were 43.4 million beneficiaries enrolled in Part A, 40.6 million in Part B, and 24.4 million in Part D.

Under Fee-for-Service Medicare, health care providers are reimbursed by the Federal Government at predetermined rates for services provided. However, Medicare beneficiaries can opt to enroll in a private Medicare plan under Medicare Advantage through local coordinated care plans offered mostly by local health maintenance organizations (HMOs) and preferred provider organizations (PPOs), regional PPOs, and private fee-for-service providers. Local coordinated care plans make up 72 percent, regional PPO plans 3 percent, and private fee-for-service plans 21 percent of Medicare Advantage plans.

Medicaid was also established in 1965 as a health care program for low-income individuals, in particular those with children. Medicaid is administered by the States, and is funded by both the Federal Government and the States. Like traditional Medicare, Medicaid also reimburses private providers for services at predetermined rates and allows recipients to enroll in Medicaid managed care plans in many States. However, unlike Medicare, these predetermined rates are determined at the State level. In 2006, there were 45.7 million enrollees in Medicaid, of whom 65 percent were in managed care plans. The State Children's Health Insurance Program (SCHIP) was created in 1997 to cover children from low-income families who do not qualify for Medicaid. SCHIP is also administered by the States and funded by both Federal and State Governments, but the Federal contribution towards spending is higher for SCHIP than for Medicaid. In 2006, there were 6.6 million enrollees in SCHIP.

While Medicare, Medicaid, and SCHIP are publicly funded programs, most health care services are delivered by private providers not employed by the government. In contrast, the Veterans Health Administration

continued on next page

(VHA) delivers health care to veterans through a system that is run by the Department of Veterans Affairs. The VHA is a truly public health care system in the sense that the Federal Government owns the VHA hospitals and employs the health care providers.

Rising health care costs are creating budget pressures for government health care programs. Currently, Federal spending on Medicare and Medicaid totals about 4 percent of GDP, or about 20 percent of the Federal budget. Rising health care costs, however, will likely raise those figures in coming decades. If spending grows 1 percent per year faster than GDP (which is somewhat slower than the historical rate of growth over the past 40 years), for example, the Office of Management and Budget projects that in 25 years, spending on these two programs alone could reach 8 percent of GDP. Such spending growth, if it came to pass, would require either unprecedented levels of taxation or dramatic reductions in other government activities.

Moral Hazard and Cost Control

In most markets, consumers decide what to purchase by comparing the benefit of a good or service relative to its cost. In the health care sector, however, consumers often do not learn the prices of goods and services until bills are received weeks or months later. Because health insurance polices cover most health care costs, including the costs of routine, predictable health care services, consumers have little incentive to try to access and act on price information. This moral hazard effect encourages overuse of certain types of heath care, gives little incentive for consumers to consider costs in their search for a provider, and distorts incentives for technological change.

Overuse of health care can occur when the perceived cost of a service is less than the actual cost and, as a result, the service may be used even when its value is less than its cost. This happens, for example, with health insurance coverage that shields consumers from the true cost of a service by having them pay none or only a portion of its cost. To illustrate, consider a consumer's decision to purchase a migraine therapy that costs $100 to produce. If the symptoms are serious enough and would be relieved by the therapy, the consumer might be willing to pay more than $100 for the therapy. The consumer would thus purchase the therapy regardless of how much of the $100 cost was covered by insurance, and the purchase would not be overconsumption. If the customer had milder symptoms, however, insurance may induce overconsumption. Suppose, for example, that the consumer would only be willing to pay $25 to relieve the symptoms. If insurance covered the entire $100 cost, the consumer would purchase the therapy since the $25 benefit exceeds the consumer's effective price of zero. Even if a $10 copayment was required by the insurance benefit, the purchase would still take place. Because the social cost of $100 exceeds the $25 benefit, this purchase would not be socially beneficial and would therefore be considered overconsumption.

Because consumers are less sensitive to the prices of the health care services they consume, the competitive forces that typically keep prices down are weakened. Imagine two hospitals that provide the same service, but hospital A charges $1,000 and is located in an older facility, while hospital B charges $2,000 but is located in an updated facility with a wide array of amenities and equipment on site. Given these choices, a consumer facing the actual price may prefer hospital A, but in a world where few costs are shared with the patient, most people would choose hospital B. This gives hospital B few incentives to control costs given that convenience or amenities have a greater influence on consumer choice than price.

New technological innovations enter a market in which consumers rarely pay more than 10 to 20 percent of the market price out-of-pocket. This influences the value of the innovations that are developed and marketed. If a new product is only slightly more effective than an existing product, for example, it may be highly demanded even if it is priced well above existing alternatives. Because there is a market for new technology with little additional benefit over existing treatments, innovators have sufficient incentive to create new technologies with little marginal value.

Health insurers and their sponsors (employers) recognize that insurance reduces consumer incentives to be responsive to costs. Insurers use a variety of cost-control mechanisms such as utilization review, pre-approval, and drug formularies to attempt to manage costs and, in part, counteract the lack of cost consciousness by consumers. But those mechanisms can only partly offset the problem. In addition, insurance benefits are designed to limit moral hazard by sharing the costs of services received with the beneficiary. Design features to accomplish this goal include deductibles, copayments, and coinsurance. *Deductibles,* the dollar amount that a consumer will have to pay before the insurer pays for any medical expenses, are often less than $500. *Copayments* are a fixed fee paid per visit or per prescription. *Coinsurance* is a percentage of the cost of the service that is the responsibility of the consumer.

These cost sharing mechanisms are underutilized because of a bias created by the tax code. The health insurance premium of employees paid by employers is exempt from income and payroll taxes, but individual spending through deductibles, copayments, and coinsurance is taxable. As a result, there is a tax incentive for employers to compensate employees through generous health insurance plans that limit cost sharing. Thus, the tax code reduces the incentive for optimal health insurance design and ultimately encourages individuals to purchase more health care services than they would otherwise. Health Savings Accounts (HSAs), enacted into law by this Administration in 2004, and the standard deduction for health insurance first proposed by this Administration in 2007, both provide a mechanism for eliminating the tax bias against greater cost sharing. These policies are intended to offer the private sector more opportunities to control costs through greater consumer awareness of the cost of health insurance premiums and health care services.

Health Savings Accounts

Health Savings Accounts are savings accounts of pre-tax dollars, funded by individual or employer contributions, that can be used toward current and future out-of-pocket medical expenses. HSAs are designed to be used in conjunction with high-deductible health plans, reducing reliance on insurance for routine health expenses. The funds in the HSA can be used to pay these routine health expenses directly. Because unspent funds belong to the individual and can accumulate over time, HSAs lead the individual to play a more active role as a health care consumer. In January 2007, HSAs covered 4.5 million people, which is an increase of 1.3 million since January 2006, and 3.5 million since March 2005.

As the consumer plays a greater role and becomes more aware of routine health expenses, provision of inefficient care should be reduced; incentives for providers to adopt cost-effective therapies should increase; and possibly, some health care prices may decline, which may even benefit consumers in traditional insurance plans. Yet the benefit of moving to a high-deductible policy with an HSA will vary in that chronically ill individuals with persistently high spending may find these policies less desirable because their out-of-pocket spending would be consistently high. Consumers in lower tax brackets will derive a smaller tax benefit from HSAs because the value of tax exemption depends on a consumer's marginal tax rate (the tax paid on the next dollar a worker earns).

A Standard Deduction for Health Insurance to Replace the Tax Exemption

The lack of consumer sensitivity to health care prices occurs not just through the consumption of health care services, but through the consumption of health insurance as well. The tax exemption of employer-sponsored health insurance premiums is inefficient because, by providing a larger tax break to families with more-generous employer-sponsored health insurance policies, there is an incentive for health insurance to cover more services than employees would otherwise demand. This occurs because employees can increase after-tax compensation by accepting more of their compensation in the form of health insurance.

The President has proposed to replace the current open-ended tax exclusion for employment-based health insurance with a flat $15,000 standard deduction for health insurance to all families (or $7,500 for individuals), whether that insurance was obtained through their employer or on their own. The amount of this standard deduction would be independent of the actual amount spent on the premium, so families who obtain insurance policies for less than $15,000 (but whose policy satisfies a set of minimum requirements for catastrophic coverage) would still have an exemption for the full $15,000 of compensation from income and payroll taxes. The annual increase in the standard deduction for health insurance would be linked to inflation as measured by the Consumer Price Index.

This policy has two key effects: 1) It would reduce the inefficiency of the current tax treatment of employment-based health insurance and would allow individual consumers to benefit from reducing the cost of their insurance; and 2) it would provide for equitable tax treatment for health insurance purchased inside and outside of employment. The first effect can be shown in the following example. Consider a family of four with an annual income of $50,000 and a health insurance policy worth $10,000 that is sponsored by an employer. Because the marginal tax rate of this family is roughly 30 percent, the current tax exemption for the cost of this insurance policy provides a $3,000 tax break to the family. Another family with the same income and an employer-sponsored health insurance policy worth $20,000 currently receives a tax break of $6,000. One advantage of the proposed standard deduction is that it provides the same tax treatment to all types of health insurance plans. Under the proposed plan, both families would qualify for the flat $15,000 standard deduction and receive the same tax savings of $4,500. The flat tax break provides a strong incentive to obtain health insurance coverage, and it would allow families to reap the tax benefits of health insurance policies with optimal cost-sharing features. Because the tax break is not more generous for those who choose expensive health insurance plans (unlike the tax exemption), consumers will become more conscious of cost when purchasing health insurance and health care.

Health insurance purchases by families and individuals with or without access to employment-based health insurance would receive the same tax benefits under this policy. Currently, tax treatment of health insurance premiums is inequitable because it does not offer the same tax break to families and individuals without access to employment-based insurance, who must instead purchase a private plan in the individual health insurance market. The family considered above with an annual income of $50,000 receives a $3,000 tax break for a health insurance policy worth $10,000 sponsored by an employer, but no tax break for a similar health insurance policy purchased through the individual insurance market. Under the Administration's proposal, those who are currently insured in the individual health insurance market would see a reduction in taxes commensurate with those insured in the group market. As a result, those who are currently uninsured because they have no access to employment-based insurance, would be given a strong incentive to purchase coverage. An uninsured family of four earning $50,000, for example, would receive a tax benefit of $4,500 if they purchased health insurance in the individual market (the value of the $15,000 standard deduction if the family faces a 30 percent marginal tax rate). That tax break would cover nearly half the cost of a family health insurance plan costing $10,000.

The availability of a tax deduction for the purchase of health insurance for individuals and families who are not offered employer-sponsored coverage will make health insurance more affordable for millions of Americans. The Administration estimates that the standard deduction would provide 3 to 5 million individuals with health insurance who did not have it previously. Even with a standard deduction, challenges for affordable coverage remain for individuals with low incomes or with substantial risk of high health expenditures. The Administration's Affordable Choices Initiative addresses these remaining challenges. The initiative facilitates State efforts to make health insurance more affordable for individuals with persistently high medical expenses or limited incomes. Currently, subsidies and payments from the Federal Government are funneled through providers; the objective is to redirect funding toward individuals.

Controlling Costs Through Competitive Insurance Markets

The effective functioning of a competitive marketplace for health insurance requires addressing adverse selection. Adverse selection arises when insurance is most attractive to those persons most likely to need it. If the premium is based on the population average and the policy disproportionately attracts those who spend more than the average, the policy will lose money for the insurer. The policy will then either increase in price or not last in the market. In the extreme, some consumers do not purchase insurance because the only policy available to them is priced for the most expensive consumers.

The problems can be most severe in insurance markets involving small firms and individuals without access to group coverage, because large risk pools mitigate many of the forces that can lead to adverse selection. (However, adverse selection can arise in broad risk pools when competing health plan choices are made available.) To varying degrees, States can minimize adverse selection by permitting providers in the market for individual insurance to rate each individual on the basis of his or her medical risk and past health care expenditure. As a consequence, individuals with chronic illnesses have to pay higher premiums, be denied coverage altogether, or be denied coverage for the condition which is making them ill.

To reduce the extent to which high-risk individuals face higher premiums and to improve the availability of certain health insurance benefits, States have imposed a range of restrictions on insurance underwriting practices as well as coverage mandates on nongroup (and in many cases on group) health insurance plans. These regulations generally include guaranteed issue laws that require insurers to issue insurance to any eligible applicant without regard to current health status or other factors, and community rating laws that prohibit insurers from varying premium rates based on health status and restrict the amount by which insurers are allowed to vary rates based on characteristics such as age or gender. Although these regulations tend to reduce insurance premiums for high-risk individuals, they also increase premiums for lower risk individuals. Those premium increases can have the unintended consequence of encouraging people to wait until they have a health problem before enrolling. If such adverse selection reduces participation of healthier people, premiums will increase and the voluntary insurance market may cease to operate effectively. The result may be less insurance coverage and only limited premium reductions for those who are chronically ill, as those who are healthier choose to forgo coverage entirely rather than pay higher premiums.

The approach of the Administration is one that encourages lower premiums particularly in the individual and small group markets, where adverse selection poses the greatest challenges for competitive insurance markets. The Administration supports a national market for health insurance rather than State-specific markets. This would effectively make insurance available to individuals and small groups under conditions that resemble those now available to employees of many large corporations, which, by self-insuring, are exempt from State insurance regulations and instead operate under the Federal insurance law provisions of the Employee Retirement and Income Security Act (ERISA). Health insurance policies with lower premiums would be more readily available because health insurance policies would not be subject to costly State mandates and regulations. The Administration also supports Association Health Plans—plans that allow small groups to band together to purchase insurance subject to Federal rather than State regulations—because they would reduce adverse selection problems encountered by small employers, achieve economies of scale in negotiating lower rates with participating insurers, and allow for greater participation in a competitive choice system of health insurance plans.

Improving Quality and Costs Through Information and Reimbursement

Because of the complexities of medicine, patients must often rely on experts to determine their diagnosis and select treatments. If the incentives for the expert are different from those that would produce the greatest benefit for the patient, however, the services delivered by the expert may not always be of the greatest benefit to the patient. For example, doctors may have incentives to overstate the value of expensive tests, and most patients lack the expertise to assess these claims.

Physicians determine needed services for patients. Because these decisions are in part subjective, diagnoses and treatments often differ across physicians, sometimes in ways that are not in the patient's or society's best interest. For example, the frequency of spinal surgery is almost eight times higher in some parts of the United States than in others, even though the percentage of people who have back problems does not vary widely between regions. These types of geographic variations in quantity of care exist across a wide range of treatments, yet few differences in outcomes can be detected. Overuse of health care services is one problem, and underuse is another. A classic study evaluated the rate at which clinicians followed processes of care widely recommended through national guidelines and the medical literature. When averaged across all phases of care for the most common or lethal conditions, it was determined that nearly half of patients who met conditions for effective clinical care failed to receive appropriate care.

There is great potential to improve quality and/or reduce costs through reforms that improve information on quality and costs, and align provider payments so that providers are rewarded for the health outcomes of the patients rather than just for the services they perform.

Information on Effectiveness

One of the key impediments to more effective health care delivery is a lack of relevant information—for patients, providers, and payers—on the comparative effectiveness and efficiency of health care options. Such information would be particularly useful for services that are in common practice, generate high costs, employ rapidly changing technologies for which multiple alternative therapies exist, and are in areas with substantial uncertainty. The wide geographic variations in the use of procedures suggest that better information on the effectiveness of different styles of medical practice could result in substantial cost savings.

Health Information Technology

Health information technology (health IT) allows comprehensive management of medical information and the secure exchange of medical information between health care consumers and providers. Broad use of health IT has the potential to help dramatically transform the delivery of health care, making it safer, more effective, and more efficient. While a number of large health care organizations have realized some of these gains through the implementation of multifunctional, interoperable health IT systems, to date, experimental evidence supporting the broad benefits from health IT is more limited. The

Administration supports broad adoption of health IT as a normal cost of doing business, including policies that will encourage physicians and others to adopt electronic health records and through furthering technologies for safe, secure health information exchange.

Value-based Purchasing

Pay for performance or *value-based purchasing* is a payment model that encourages health care providers to meet certain performance measures for quality and efficiency. A recent example is eliminating payments for negative consequences of care. The Centers for Medicare and Medicaid Services (CMS) implemented a provision of the Deficit Reduction Act of 2005, which prevents Medicare from giving hospitals higher payment for the additional costs of treating certain "hospital-acquired conditions"—conditions that result from medical errors or improper care and that can reasonably be expected to be averted. Now big insurers are following Medicare's lead and are moving to ban payments for care resulting from grave mistakes. These changes remove a perverse incentive for hospitals: improving patient safety could reduce revenues and profits. As a result, these reforms should trigger safety improvements and enhance the efficiency of the health care system.

Transparency of Price and Quality Information

Transparency of information on price and quality has been a priority of this Administration. Medicare has provided incentives to providers to submit performance information to CMS and many of these performance measures have been made available on the CMS website so that consumers can compare the quality of providers as they seek care. The administrators and sponsors of Medicare and other Federal health insurance programs have been directed to share with beneficiaries information about prices paid to health care providers and the quality of the services they deliver. The commitment is to transform Medicare by always seeking to improve the connection between expenditures and positive health outcomes without increasing Medicare spending.

Promoting Healthy Behavior

Encouraging healthy behaviors, such as exercising more, eating better, controlling weight gain, and quitting smoking, may be a cost-effective alternative to increased spending on health care. One way to encourage healthy behavior is through health education. For example, much of the beneficial effect of prenatal care is simply related to education about healthy behavior while pregnant. A better understanding of the risks of high cholesterol and blood pressure (and how to reduce those risks through healthy behavior) is credited with being a very highly efficient way to improve health outcomes. Administration policies that aim to increase consumer sensitivity to health care costs have a positive indirect consequence in that they may induce an increase in healthy behaviors.

Conclusion

The health care system in the United States has helped improve the health and well-being of Americans. As health care costs continue to rise, enormous opportunities exist to increase the value of health care and improve health insurance coverage. Addressing these fundamental problems and fulfilling the potential of our health care system will require innovative polices to help Americans get the care that best meets their needs, and to create an environment that rewards high-quality, efficient care. While Federally sponsored health insurance for the most vulnerable Americans through Medicare, Medicaid, and SCHIP remains a priority, private markets offer the best opportunities for controlling costs and providing innovative policies to enhance efficiency, quality, and access. Efficiency of health spending would be improved if tax code reforms were enacted. Reforms could level the playing field between employer-provided and individual health insurance, thus boosting insurance coverage. At the same time, reforms could reward consumers for purchases of higher deductible plans with reasonable copayments that provide insurance for costly medical necessities, but do not encourage unwarranted procedures. By addressing concerns of adverse selection, insurance markets can become more competitive, thereby promoting innovation, choice, access, and efficiency. Finally, health care quality can be addressed by improving the transparency of health care information and by tying reimbursement to the performance of providers.

CHAPTER 5

Tax Policy

Societies face two basic questions with regard to tax policy. The first question concerns the amount of revenue that should be raised. That is, what is the appropriate *level* of taxation? The level of taxation ultimately reflects views about the appropriate size of government. If a society believes that the government should play a large role in the economy, then a high level of tax revenue is necessary. While taxes are necessary to finance the public sector, they have a considerable cost to the economy because they distort incentives and result in lost value of output to society. Without taxes, individuals would decide where to allocate resources depending on where those resources are most productive. Taxes give individuals an incentive to reduce their tax burden by avoiding activities that are taxed; as a result, decisions about working, saving, investing, and spending are influenced by tax considerations, resulting in the loss of output that would have created value for producers, consumers, and workers. The distortions created by taxes have important implications for economic growth and the well-being of Americans.

The second question about tax policy concerns how the tax burden should be distributed across different members of society and different types of activities. That is, what is the appropriate *structure* of taxation? Different tax structures impose different costs on the economy in terms of the distortions they create. A more efficient tax structure raises a given amount of revenue with less distortion. Different tax structures also give rise to different distributions of after-tax income, and some distributions of income may be viewed as more fair than others. A related issue is the timing of taxes. The use of government debt allows the tax burden to be spread across time, raising questions about how to tax different activities and individuals at different points in time.

The key points of this chapter are:

- The ratio of Federal taxation in the United States to gross domestic product (GDP) has fluctuated around an average value of 18.3 percent over the past 40 years; despite the President's 2001 and 2003 tax relief, this ratio was 18.8 percent in 2007, above the 40-year-average. Under current law, revenues are predicted to grow faster than the economy in coming years, raising the level of taxation well above its historical average.
- Tax reductions in 2001 and 2003 have considerably lowered the tax burden on labor and capital income and reduced distortions to economic decisions. Making these tax cuts permanent can greatly improve long-term economic outcomes.

- In addition to contributing to growth, the tax cuts of 2003 also improved the efficiency of the tax structure primarily by reducing the double taxation of corporate income.
- The business tax structure in the United States still creates substantial distortions. To attract investment from abroad and compete more effectively in foreign markets, the United States must consider how best to address distortions created by the structure of business taxes, as other countries have done.

The Size of Government: A Historical View

Economists and policymakers have long debated the appropriate role of the government in a market economy. The government provides some services—such as national defense and law enforcement—that are clearly essential for economic growth, but other functions of government, such as large redistributions of income, are more controversial. A large public sector imposes a cost on the economy primarily because the taxes that are required to finance government programs distort labor supply, saving, and investment decisions, resulting in lost value of output to society. Thus, our Nation faces a tradeoff: a larger government can provide more public services and transfer payments (payments that are not in exchange for goods or services) to lower-income individuals, but these benefits often come at the cost of lower economic output and well being.

The cost from tax distortions can be considerable. One recent study suggests that raising an additional dollar of revenue from the individual income tax costs the economy approximately 30 to 50 cents. That is, if taxes increase by $1, taxpayers bear a cost of $1.30 to $1.50 – the $1 in revenue and 30 to 50 cents from accompanying distortions. This additional cost of 30-50 cents is known as *deadweight loss*. Any government services that are funded with this revenue would have to have a benefit to society of at least $1.30 to justify the increase in taxes.

One measure of the role of government is the size of government spending relative to the economy. Over the past 40 years, Federal *expenditures* have averaged 20.7 percent of GDP. Government activities can be financed by current taxes or borrowing (which will necessitate higher future taxes or lower future spending). Chart 5-1 shows that over the past 40 years, the ratio of Federal *taxes* to GDP has fluctuated around an average value of 18.3 percent. The ratio rose well above that level in the late 1960s, the early 1980s, and the late 1990s. Each of these periods was then followed by several years in which the ratio fell below its long-term average. Recent swings have been particularly pronounced with the ratio reaching a post-World War II high of 20.9 percent in 2000. Tax revenues increased strongly relative to GDP from 1992 to 2000 as a result of rising real incomes, increases in capital gains realizations, and the tax increases of the early 1990s. Tax revenues as a share of GDP tend to rise when real incomes rise and fall when real incomes fall. Beginning in 2001, tax revenues began to decline as the economy slipped into recession and real incomes declined. The ratio of tax revenues to GDP fell to 16.3 percent (a 40-year low) in 2004. Since that time, tax revenues have grown faster than the economy, resulting in a tax-to-GDP ratio of 18.8 percent in 2007, once again above its 40-year average.

While the Federal tax-to-GDP ratio has not exhibited any consistent trend in the past 40 years, it is projected to grow over the next 10 years. Under current law, the President's tax relief of 2001 and 2003 will expire at the end of 2010. At this time, there will be a significant increase in the tax-to-GDP ratio. Moreover, even in the absence of any legislative changes, there is a tendency for the tax-to-GDP ratio to rise. (While the ratio may not rise every year, there is an upward trend over time.) In the past, significant tax cuts (in 1964, 1981, and 2001 to 2003) have maintained the tax-to-GDP ratio at a relatively stable level. The solid line in Chart 5-2 shows the projected tax-to-GDP ratio if the President's 2001 and 2003 tax relief is not extended.

Chart 5-1 **Federal Receipts**
Federal receipts have fluctuated around their historical average with no particular trend.
Percent of GDP

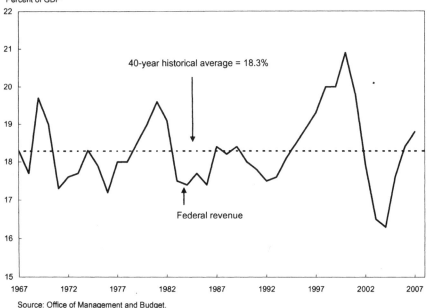

Source: Office of Management and Budget.

Several factors will contribute to rising revenue in the near term, including the expiration of the 2001 and 2003 tax cuts, the Alternative Minimum Tax (AMT), real tax bracket creep, and withdrawals from tax-deferred accounts.

Expiration of the 2001 and 2003 Tax Cuts

The tax cuts of 2001 and 2003 (discussed in detail below) reduced individual tax rates on ordinary income, dividends, and capital gains; increased the child tax credit; reduced the "marriage penalty" (the additional tax that some couples pay as a result of getting married); and began a phase-out of the estate tax. These provisions are set to expire at the end of 2010. If they do, the tax-to-GDP ratio would climb from the 18.8 percent it reached in 2007 to approximately 20 percent. Making the tax cuts permanent would lower this ratio to the 18 to 19 percent range (the dashed line in Chart 5-2), although the ratio would still continue above the 40-year average of 18.3 percent by the end of the 10-year period depicted in the figure.

Chart 5-2 **Federal Receipts Projections**
The tax-to-GDP ratio is projected to rise because tax revenue will grow faster than the economy.

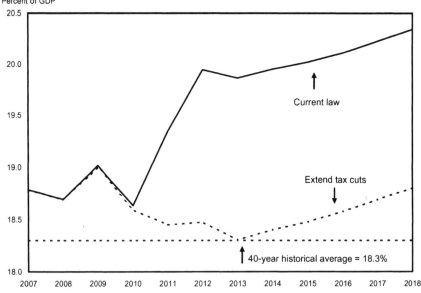

Source: Congressional Budget Office, *Budget and Economic Outlook: Fiscal Years 2008 to 2018.*

Alternative Minimum Tax

Prior to 1969, a handful of high-income taxpayers used deductions and exemptions to substantially reduce or eliminate their income tax liability. This outcome was perceived as unfair, and to address this problem, the Alternative Minimum Tax (AMT) was established. In its current form, the AMT requires taxpayers to compute their tax liability a second way using a broader definition of income that reduces or eliminates many of the deductions and exemptions allowed in the calculation of regular income tax. The taxpayer must pay the greater of the two tax liabilities. In 1970, only 20,000 taxpayers were subject to the AMT. However, in recent years, the AMT increasingly affects middle-income families, primarily because its parameters are not indexed for inflation. Those who are most vulnerable include families with many children (giving rise to a large number of exemptions) and families in high-tax states (giving rise to a large deduction for state taxes). The solution thus far has been to pass a series of temporary "patches" to limit the scope of the AMT. The most recent patch keeps the number of AMT filers stable through 2007 at about 4 million—the same as in 2006—instead of the increase to 25 million that would have occurred had the patch not been enacted. The Administration proposes a similar patch for 2008 in the Budget that will continue to keep the aggregate number of AMT taxpayers roughly constant. If the AMT is not patched in future years, the number of taxpayers affected will continue to climb, resulting in a rising tax-to-GDP ratio. Indexing the AMT parameters for inflation *and* extending the tax cuts would lower the tax-to-GDP ratio below the dotted line in Chart 5-2, unless the revenue loss from AMT indexation were made up via additional taxes.

Real Bracket Creep

Federal taxes as a whole are progressive, meaning that a family's average tax rate (total taxes paid as a percentage of income) rises as its income rises. Recently released estimates suggest that in 2005, taxpayers in the bottom 20 percent of the income distribution faced an average Federal tax rate of 4.3 percent, while taxpayers in the top 20 percent faced an average Federal tax rate of 25.2 percent. (This analysis takes into account individual income taxes, payroll taxes, corporate income taxes, and excise taxes.) Over time, people's nominal incomes (not adjusted for changes in purchasing power) tend to grow. Part of this growth is due only to inflation, but part of it represents an increase in purchasing power (real income growth) as productivity improves and we become more prosperous as a nation. Regular income tax brackets (but not AMT brackets) are indexed for inflation, which prevents people from moving up to higher brackets because of inflation (a phenomenon called *nominal bracket creep*). However, as people's *real* incomes grow, they become subject to higher tax rates. This is called *real bracket creep.* The implication is that, even without explicit tax increases, the median income family (that is, the family whose income places them in the middle of the income distribution) will face a rising average tax rate over the years because median incomes are likely to grow faster than inflation. This will tend to increase the ratio of Federal revenues to GDP.

Withdrawals from Tax-Deferred Accounts

A large amount of individual saving occurs through tax-deferred savings vehicles, including defined benefit pension plans (which provide a specified benefit at retirement) and tax-deferred savings accounts, such as 401(k) plans and traditional Individual Retirement Accounts (IRAs). Individual and employer contributions to these tax-deferred savings vehicles are deductible at the time the contribution is made, and accumulate tax free until retirement. After retirement, payments from these savings vehicles—including benefits paid by defined benefit plans and withdrawals from tax-deferred accounts—are taxable. In comparison, withdrawals from other types of accounts—for example, ordinary savings accounts and Roth IRAs—do not require payment of income tax on the withdrawal, and deposits in these accounts are not tax deductible. At the end of 2002, there was about $9.0 trillion in tax-deferred retirement plans on which tax would be paid at withdrawal. With the aging of the population that is projected to occur, there will be an increase in such payments, resulting in increased government revenue. These withdrawals are different from the previous three factors for two reasons. First, they cause a temporary surge in revenue driven by a demographic shift. Second, their impact will occur over a somewhat longer period than depicted in Chart 5-2. According to a recent study, these withdrawals are likely to increase income tax receipts by about 0.25 percent of GDP over the next 25 years, and twice that amount by the end of 75 years.

The factors discussed above—the expiration of the 2001 and 2003 tax cuts, the expansion of the AMT, real bracket creep, and withdrawals from tax-deferred savings accounts—are built into the tax code. In addition to these internal factors, there are also external pressures for taxes to increase in the future. Total Federal expenditures in 2007 were 20 percent of GDP. However, entitlement programs like Medicare, Medicaid, and Social Security are facing financial pressures from rising medical costs and an aging population. Based on current law, projected benefits under these programs could push entitlement spending alone to 20 percent of GDP in 2080, compared to 10.6 percent in 2007. In the absence of needed reforms to reduce projected spending, this would necessitate unprecedented levels of taxation, deficit spending, or dramatic reductions in the fraction of economic activity devoted to other government activities.

The Impact of Recent Tax Reductions

Taxes transfer resources from individuals to the government. The transfer itself does not represent a net cost to society: any money given up by taxpayers is gained by the government and can be used to fund government programs or transfer payments. However, taxes impose a considerable burden on the economy for several reasons. First, taxes interfere with the efficient allocation of resources by changing the rewards from working, saving, and investing. In the absence of taxes, individuals and firms would allocate resources to activities where they would be most productive. When taxed, individuals alter their behavior. For example, high tax rates on labor income induce individuals to reduce their labor supply, because the incentive for working is lower. High tax rates on capital income (the return earned on capital investments) discourage investment in new capital. A reduction in investment lowers the ratio of capital to labor and in turn reduces worker productivity and wages. As a result of these distortions to work, saving, and investment behavior, output is lost—output that would have created value for producers, consumers, and workers. This loss of output is called the *deadweight loss of taxation.* As discussed above, raising an additional dollar via the individual income tax imposes a direct cost of $1 on taxpayers (which merely represents a transfer to the government) and a deadweight loss of 30 to 50 cents from the lost value of output to society. Second, high tax rates may also encourage some taxpayers to underreport their incomes, giving rise to equity concerns and requiring higher taxes on those who do comply in order to maintain revenue. (While most taxpayers pay the taxes they owe, there is still a gap between the amount of taxes that should be paid and the amount that is actually paid.) Finally, taxes have large compliance costs that reflect the resources taxpayers use to determine and pay their tax liability (including the value of time spent keeping records and doing calculations). In 2004, compliance costs were estimated to be $85 billion for individual income taxes and $40 billion for businesses other than sole proprietorships.

The tax cuts of 2001 and 2003 significantly lowered the tax burden on labor and capital income and reduced distortions. The dividend and capital gains rate cuts enacted in 2003 had an additional benefit to the economy by improving the efficiency of the tax structure. By reducing the existing preference for corporate debt financing over equity financing, these tax cuts reduced the distortion of corporate finance decisions and improved corporate governance.

Labor Supply

Taxes effectively decrease the wage that workers receive for providing labor and therefore distort labor supply decisions by changing the incentive for working. These distortions create efficiency losses. The tax cuts of 2001 significantly decreased the tax rates that workers pay on their earned income, thereby reducing the efficiency losses created by the distortion of their labor supply decisions.

Individuals decide to work based upon whether take-home earnings exceed the value of the leisure they forgo (for this discussion, leisure includes any activities outside the labor market). Take-home pay declines as the *average tax rate,* that is, the fraction of income paid in taxes, rises. Hence, higher average tax rates mean that fewer individuals choose to work. Moreover, higher *marginal tax rates*—the fraction of *additional* income paid in taxes—reduce the incentive for working more hours or in a higher-skilled profession. Increases in both average and marginal tax rates distort labor supply and skill investment decisions and thus generate efficiency losses.

Individuals vary in their responsiveness to average and marginal tax rates, so the efficiency losses from taxes differ by group. Studies show that single mothers and married women are particularly sensitive to high average tax rates. Their cost of working is higher because of child care and other home production demands. The 2001 tax cuts lowered average tax rates at all points of the income distribution, thereby making work decisions more efficient (that is, closer to what they would be in the absence of tax distortions). A recent study suggests that the 2001 tax cuts led single mothers to allocate more of their time to market work. In contrast, several studies suggest that men and single women without children are not affected much by average tax rates when deciding whether to work. The responsiveness of married women to high average tax rates has been falling over time as they become more attached to the labor market (as men have more traditionally been).

High *marginal* income tax rates may discourage workers from working more hours, choosing higher-paid occupations, and investing more in education and other skills that would increase their earnings. To see why higher marginal tax rates have these effects, imagine a worker with only a bachelor's degree deciding between a career as a 40-hour-per-week accountant in a small firm paying around $40,000 per year versus a career as a 70-hour-per-week self-employed consultant with an MBA earning around $80,000 per year. Suppose that the worker would pay $4,000 per year in taxes in the accounting job and $18,000 per year in the consulting job. After taxes, the additional income for the more demanding career would be $26,000 per year. The marginal tax rate would be 35 percent (see Table 5-1).

Now suppose a change in tax policy reduces taxes for the accounting job to $1,000 and increases taxes for the consulting job to $21,000. Instead of a

35 percent marginal tax rate on the additional $40,000 in pre-tax income, there would be a 50 percent marginal tax rate. This change in tax policy reduces the additional return to the more demanding career from $26,000 to just $20,000 per year, a 23 percent drop in the return to the more lucrative career (see Table 5-1).

Factoring in 30 more hours per week working, the greater stress in the consulting job, and the costs of getting the MBA, this tax policy change could induce this worker to choose the less demanding career, thereby creating an efficiency loss. So even if this change in tax policy is revenue neutral (that is, the policy does not change overall average tax rates), the higher marginal taxes would reduce overall economic efficiency because they alter the way wages allocate workers to jobs and decrease incentives to choose higher-paying careers with longer hours, greater intensity demands, and more costly skill investments. The tax cuts in 2001 and 2003 generally reduced marginal tax rates and reduced these distortions, thereby encouraging workers to become more productive.

Saving and Investment

When individuals receive income, they can either spend it on current consumption or save it to fund future consumption. Individual savings gets channeled into capital investments. For example, an individual may save by buying financial assets, such as stocks or bonds. Firms use the funds raised from selling stocks and bonds to finance capital investments, such as buildings or equipment. These investments generate income, which individual savers receive in the form of interest payment on bonds, or dividends and capital gains on stocks. Investment plays an important role in improving the well-being of Americans, as increases in the amount of capital per worker result in productivity increases and economic growth.

TABLE 5-1.—*Comparing the Marginal Tax Rate for a Career Changer Under Two Illustrative Tax Policies*

	Initial Tax Policy		New Tax Policy	
	Accountant	MBA Consultant	Accountant	MBA Consultant
Earnings	$40,000	$80,000	$40,000	$80,000
Taxes	$4,000	$18,000	$1,000	$21,000
After Tax Earnings	$36,000	$62,000	$39,000	$59,000
Change in Earnings (MBA minus Accountant)	$40,000		$40,000	
Change in Taxes	$14,000		$20,000	
Marginal Tax Rate	35%		50%	
Change in After Tax Earnings	$26,000		$20,000	

An important tax policy issue concerns the treatment of income generated by capital investments. Taxes on capital income discourage saving by individuals and investment by businesses. This lowers the capital-to-labor ratio and harms long-run economic growth. Currently, when firms earn income from their capital investments, they may be subject to a firm-level tax on this amount (after subtracting depreciation and interest costs). In addition, individual savers, who provide the funds used to finance these investments, pay income tax on the return on their savings (which includes dividends, capital gains, interest, and rent). As a result, capital income is often taxed at both the firm and the individual level, resulting in double taxation.

Individuals save so they can consume resources in the future, rather than today. Firms invest so that they will be more productive and profitable in the future. Taxes on capital income lower the return to saving and investment, thereby favoring current consumption over future consumption. For example, suppose a corporation is considering the purchase of a machine that will be financed by selling additional shares of stock, and that the rate of return on the investment—net of *depreciation,* or the reduction in the value of the machine—is 10 percent. Suppose further that individual savers are willing to purchase the shares if they receive a return of at least 6 percent. That is, they are willing to sacrifice $1 of current consumption (by buying the shares) in exchange for $1.06 of consumption 1 year from now. The investment is socially beneficial because it generates a 10 percent rate of return, and the savers providing the funds would have settled for 6 percent. At the firm level, the income generated by the machine is subject to the corporate income tax. If the corporate tax rate is 35 percent, and the firm is allowed to deduct actual depreciation, then the after-tax return generated by the machine is 6.5 percent. Suppose the firm then pays its shareholders the entire 6.5 percent return in the form of dividends. If the dividend income tax rate is 15 percent, savers are left with a 5.5 percent after-tax return. The rest of the initial 10 percent return (4.5 percent) goes to the government. Because the 5.5 percent after-tax return is less than the 6 percent that the individual savers require to be willing to forgo current consumption, the investment is not made even though the total return is still 10 percent (4.5 percent to the government plus 5.5 percent to the savers). Consequently, taxes on capital income distort saving and investment decisions. Longer time horizons tend to magnify this distortion because lower after-tax returns get compounded over time.

Firm-level taxes on capital income vary depending on the organizational form of the firm. Some business income, including that of sole proprietorships, Subchapter S corporations, and partnerships, is taxed under the individual income tax system. These firms are known as *flow-through* businesses because they face no firm-level tax; instead, the firms' income flows through to their owners, who pay personal income tax on it. On the other hand, Subchapter

C corporations fall under the corporate tax system. C corporations (hereafter simply referred to as corporations) pay a firm-level tax on the firm's income after deducting costs including wages, interest payments, raw materials, and depreciation.

Current U.S. tax policy is a hybrid of an income tax and a consumption tax. Some capital income is exempt from tax, as it would be under a consumption tax. For example, at the individual level, the return to saving through individual retirement accounts (IRAs) and employer-sponsored retirement plans accumulates free of tax. According to recent estimates, about 35 percent of the return to household financial assets effectively receives consumption tax treatment. The remainder is subject to income tax treatment. At the firm level, firms can often take advantage of accelerated depreciation provisions—which allow them to deduct depreciation from their income before it actually occurs—to lower their tax liability. Accelerated depreciation lowers the tax burden on investment.

The tax reductions of 2001 and 2003 have significantly reduced the tax burden on capital income. By lowering individual income taxes, the 2001 tax cut lowered the top marginal tax rate on flow-through businesses from 39.6 percent to 35 percent. Individuals also pay these reduced tax rates on their interest income. The 2001 tax cuts also included a phased-in elimination of the estate tax (or tax imposed on assets left to one's heirs). Since the estate tax is a tax on wealth, if it were permanently eliminated, it could be expected to increase saving and investment. The tax cuts of 2003 included cuts in dividend and capital gains taxes. As discussed below, if these tax cuts are made permanent, they will have a substantial impact on investment and long-run economic growth.

Corporate Financial Policy and Governance

Tax reforms can result in considerable economic benefits even when they do not lower the overall tax burden. This outcome is accomplished by improving the efficiency of the tax structure, so that the same amount of revenue can be raised with less distortion. The reverse can be true as well: a revenue neutral change, or even a tax cut, can reduce well-being if it is poorly structured.

The tax cuts of 2003 improved the efficiency of the business tax structure by reducing the high tax burden on corporate equity that results from double taxation. For funding investment in new capital, firms generally have a choice between debt (issuing bonds) and equity (retaining earnings or issuing new shares of stock). Corporations pay tax on their revenue minus their costs. Costs include wages, interest, raw materials, and depreciation. Corporate profit is then either paid out to shareholders as dividends, or reinvested in the company (eventually resulting in capital gains for shareholders). Shareholders are taxed at the individual level on any dividends they receive, and on any capital gains they realize when they sell the stock. Double taxation of corporate income imposes a particularly high burden on equity-financed corporate investment. In comparison, because interest payments are deductible to the firm (and taxable to bondholders), corporate debt is only subject to one layer of taxation. Therefore, corporations have a strong incentive to use debt financing, rather than equity financing, for new investment. The overuse of debt financing increases the chances of bankruptcy: when a firm has high debt payments, there is a greater probability that the firm's income will be insufficient to cover these payments. Bankruptcies subject investors to additional costs and risks.

The tax cuts of 2003 also reduced the tax bias against paying dividends compared to retaining earnings. Prior to 2003, long-term capital gains were taxed at a maximum rate of 20 percent, while dividends were potentially subject to the top individual income tax rate (38.6% in 2002). In addition, capital gains income has another tax advantage over dividend income: taxes are deferred until the asset is sold. Thus, capital gains can accumulate tax free, while dividends are taxed when they are paid out. Through compounding, the difference in tax can be substantial, especially over a long period of time.

The tax cuts of 2003 lowered the top tax rate on both qualified dividends and long-term capital gains (capital gains on assets held for more than a year) to 15 percent. While capital gains still have a tax advantage over dividends as a result of deferral, the differential treatment has been reduced considerably. This policy change appears to have had a marked impact on firm behavior. As shown in Chart 5-3, the growth in dividend income received by households increased substantially after 2003. In the 20 years prior to 2003, dividend income grew at an average rate of 5.9 percent per year; following the 2003 tax cut, growth increased to an average of 13.7 percent per year. This result has been confirmed in a number of formal studies. (The 2004 spike in the graph represents a special one-time dividend paid by Microsoft Corporation.)

This increase in dividend payments reflects the reduction in the tax bias against dividends. Paying dividends can have a number of benefits for corporate governance, and there is an efficiency loss when the tax code discourages firms from using dividends when they are appropriate. First, dividends can be used to return funds to shareholders, who can decide how to reinvest them, rather than leaving funds in the hands of corporate managers. Because a portion of managers' pay is independent of the firm's performance, managers' interests generally differ from the interests of shareholders, so managers may have an incentive to use retained earnings in a way that does not maximize the value of the firm. Second, paying dividends can help firms signal their profitability to investors. Thus, corporate governance may suffer if the tax code penalizes dividends relative to capital gains.

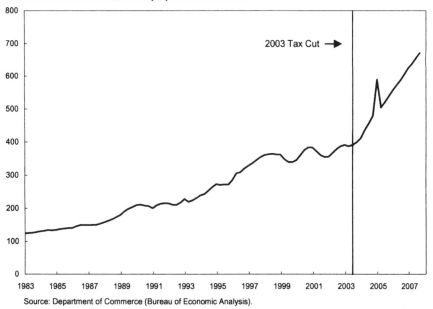

Chart 5-3 **Real Personal Dividend Income**
Dividend payments have increased since the 2003 tax cut.

Billions of chained 2000 dollars, seasonally adjusted at an annual rate

2003 Tax Cut →

Source: Department of Commerce (Bureau of Economic Analysis).

Significance of Tax Cuts to Individuals

The tax cuts since 2001 lowered taxes overall and across all income groups. Average Federal tax rates (which include income, payroll, corporate, and estate taxes) are estimated at 21.7 percent in 2007, but would have been 23.8 percent in the absence of the tax cuts (see Table 5-2). For taxpayers in the bottom 20 percent of the income distribution, Federal tax rates are 3.4 percent, which is lower than the 3.7 percent they would be in the absence of the tax cuts. In addition, over 5 million taxpayers in 2007 are projected to have had their Federal income tax liability completely eliminated by the tax cuts.

TABLE 5-2.—*Estimated Distributional Effects of 2001-2006 Tax Cuts in 2007*

| | Average Federal Tax Rates | | | | | |
	Lowest Quintile	Second Quintile	Third Quintile	Fourth Quintile	Top Quintile	All
With Tax Cuts.............................	3.4	7.3	14.4	18.8	25.9	21.7
Without Tax Cuts.........................	3.7	9.0	16.4	20.7	28.2	23.8
	Share of Federal Taxes					
	Lowest Quintile	Second Quintile	Third Quintile	Fourth Quintile	Top Quintile	All
With Tax Cuts.............................	0.4	2.1	7.4	17.0	73.0	100.0
Without Tax Cuts.........................	0.4	2.3	7.7	17.0	72.4	100.0

Source: Urban Institute/Brookings Institution Tax Policy Center.

The tax cuts increased the share of Federal taxes being paid by high-income taxpayers; the top 20 percent of taxpayers are estimated to have paid 73.0 percent of overall Federal taxes in 2007, but would have paid a somewhat lower share, 72.4 percent, without the tax cuts (see Table 5-2). Conversely, the tax cuts decreased the share of Federal taxes being paid by moderate and middle-income taxpayers; the second and third quintiles (from 20 to 60 percent in the income distribution) are estimated to have paid 9.5 percent (2.1 percent plus 7.4 percent) of overall Federal taxes in 2007, but would have paid 10.0 percent (2.3 percent plus 7.7 percent) without the tax cuts.

In addition to distorting work and skill investment decisions, the tax system can also distort marriage decisions. As discussed in Box 5-1, a progressive tax system cannot simultaneously treat all families with the same income equally and be marriage-neutral. This has resulted in a tax system with marriage bonuses (mostly for couples with dissimilar incomes) and marriage penalties (mostly for couples with similar incomes), although on net it encourages marriage (even before the 2001 tax cuts). It should be noted that both marriage bonuses and penalties distort marriage decisions and potentially generate efficiency losses. However, if marriage generates some greater social good that should be subsidized, marriage bonuses may improve efficiency on net.

The 2001 tax cuts, in general, increased marriage subsidies and reduced marriage penalties in the tax system by: (1) expanding the Earned Income Tax Credit (EITC) for married couples only, (2) expanding the 15 percent bracket only for married couples, (3) expanding the standard deduction only for married couples, and (4) doubling the child tax credit and making it partially refundable. Recent research estimates that the tax cuts, on average, increased the subsidization of marriage by the tax system by about $1,000 per year, although the effect for a particular family depends on family income, number of children, and the share of family income earned by each spouse. It is estimated that these tax changes should eventually increase marriage rates by about 1 to 4 percentage points.

Economic Benefits of Lower Taxes

The previous sections focused on specific ways in which taxes can distort individual behavior. The analysis suggests that recent tax cuts have reduced distortions to labor supply, saving, investment, and corporate governance. A recent study projects that the introduction of the 2003 tax cuts resulted in an immediate increase in GDP in 2003. But because the cuts are temporary, they will have less impact on decisions that generate payoffs far in the future than they would if they were permanent. For example, the decision to undertake education depends on the effect of education on wages over potentially long careers. Thus, they can only have a limited impact on long-term economic

Box 5-1: Marriage Penalty Basics

It is widely acknowledged that a tax system cannot simultaneously accomplish the following three goals:

1. *Progressivity:* average income tax rates rise with family income
2. *Family neutrality:* families with equal incomes pay equal taxes
3. *Marriage neutrality:* taxes paid by a family do not depend on marriage

The inherent conflicts in these three goals can be illustrated by considering a few examples. Consider a couple without children with one spouse who earns $60,000 and another who does not work. Under 2007 tax law, that couple pays $5,592 in Federal income taxes, but would pay a total of $9,236 if they were not married and both were filing individually. The resulting marriage bonus of $3,644 is generated because the nonworking spouse serves as a tax deduction for the higher earning spouse. The current tax system is not marriage-neutral.

Alternatively, suppose that each spouse earns $30,000, resulting in the same family income of $60,000. Current tax law is family-neutral, so this couple pays the same $5,592 as above. If the tax system is changed so that all individuals file separately, each spouse pays $2,796 for a total of $5,592. That is the same as they would pay on a family income of $60,000 but is $3,644 less than the combined tax liability of the family above. A progressive tax system that has all taxpayers file individually cannot be family-neutral.

Finally, if the tax system is changed so that all taxpayers pay 10 percent on all of their income, taxes are $6,000 for each family regardless of whether the couple is married or how the earnings are split between the two spouses. The tax system is marriage- and family-neutral, but it would no longer be progressive, because the average tax rate would be 10 percent for all taxpayers.

performance. Making them permanent can substantially improve economic efficiency. The Treasury Department estimates that if the tax cuts of 2001 and 2003 were made permanent and paid for by reductions in future government spending, economic output would increase by 0.7 percent in the long run.

However, the benefits to the economy might be offset if the extension of the tax cuts results in additional government borrowing or future tax increases, rather than spending cuts. The Treasury Department also estimates that if the tax cuts were made permanent but offset by other revenue raising tax measures in the future, then economic output would decline by 0.9 percent in the long run. The concern about long-term financing for the tax cuts is particularly important because of the likelihood of rising spending pressures in the future. The Office of Management and Budget projects, for example, that under current law total noninterest Federal spending could reach 25 percent of GDP by 2080, compared with 18.2 percent today. The breakdown of projected spending in Chart 5-4 shows that the main driving force behind this increase is the growth in spending on entitlement programs, primarily Medicare, Medicaid, and Social Security, which could reach approximately 20 percent of GDP by 2080. The benefits of making the tax cuts permanent might also be offset if the tax cuts are financed by a reduction in *efficient* government spending (spending whose benefits exceed both the direct cost to the taxpayer and the deadweight loss).

Chart 5-4 **Federal Outlays Projections**
Entitlement spending is projected to approach 20 percent of GDP by 2080.
Percent of GDP

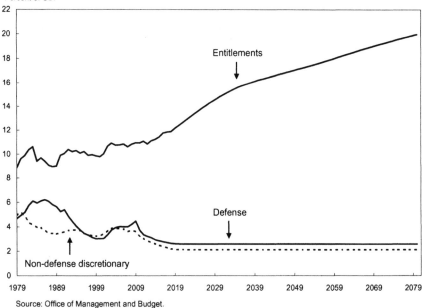

Source: Office of Management and Budget.

The Structure of Business Taxes

Despite recent reforms, the business tax structure still creates a number of distortions in its treatment of capital income. To the extent that the U.S. tax system resembles an income tax, it encourages current consumption rather than saving. Beyond this, however, the tax system imposes differential tax burdens on different types of investments, thereby leading to a misallocation of resources. Ideally, firms should undertake investments that generate the highest rate of return, independent of taxes. If all investment returns are taxed at the same rate, then the projects with the highest returns will still be selected (although investment overall will fall because investment returns overall are taxed). However, if different kinds of investments face different tax rates, then a lower-return project may be selected over a higher-return project because the *after-tax* return could be higher for the lower-return project.

As noted above, the tax burden on investment is affected by both firm-level taxes (such as the corporate income tax) and individual-level taxes on the return to saving (such as dividend and capital gains taxes). The complexity of the tax code makes it difficult to measure the true tax burden on investment returns. For example, corporate earnings are taxed at a maximum Federal rate of 35 percent. However, that tax burden is reduced by accelerated depreciation, special tax preferences for certain activities, and the interest deduction. Also, while some kinds of savings are subject to personal income tax, other kinds (for example, retirement savings accounts) accumulate tax free. A standard approach to quantifying the distortions is to compute the *effective marginal tax rate,* which measures the percentage difference between the before-tax and after-tax returns on a new investment, taking into account the complexities of the tax code, and both firm- and individual-level taxes. The effective marginal tax rate is most relevant when a firm decides whether to undertake a new investment.

Table 5-3 shows the effective marginal tax rates on different kinds of investments. It is clear from the table that tax rates vary considerably across investments, depending on the type of capital involved and the method of financing. Equity-financed corporate investment faces the highest effective tax rate of 40 percent. This is still the case even though the tax cuts of 2003 substantially reduced the double taxation of corporate equity. The tax rate on debt-financed corporate investment is actually negative, a result of the interest deduction combined with accelerated depreciation allowances. Noncorporate investments face a low tax rate because noncorporate firms are treated as flow-through entities and are not subject to double taxation. Owner-occupied housing faces a very low tax rate. The return to an owner-occupied home is the rental value of the home to the occupant, which is not subject to income tax.

These results suggest several distortions. First, housing is favored relative to other capital. While there may be reasons to favor owner-occupied housing, its benefits must be weighed against the value of other kinds of capital. Second, there is a distortion across different types of business investment. For example, equipment is lightly taxed relative to structures and inventories. Third, taxes distort a firm's choice of organizational form. The corporate form of organization is unattractive from a tax standpoint, leading firms to become flow-through entities even in situations in which the corporate form would allow the most effective use of resources. Finally, there is a distortion to corporations' financing decisions, with debt receiving a tax advantage over equity.

There are two broad directions for reform. First, efficiency could be improved by reducing the disparate tax treatment of different kinds of investment. There are a number of reforms that could help to achieve this goal. For example, the Treasury Department estimates that if special preferences were eliminated, the corporate tax rate could be reduced from 35 percent to 31 percent and still raise the same amount of revenue. Further integration of the personal and corporate tax systems would alleviate the double taxation of corporate income. For example, some countries in the Organization for Economic Cooperation and Development (OECD), including the United Kingdom, Canada, and Mexico address the double taxation of capital income by giving investors a tax credit for taxes paid at the corporate level. Second, reducing the tax burden on investment can improve long-run economic performance by increasing the ratio of capital to labor, thereby boosting labor productivity and earnings. There are two ways to reduce the tax burden on investment at the firm level. One is to reduce the corporate tax rate, and the other is to allow full or partial expensing of new investment. *Full expensing* allows the firm to fully deduct the cost of new investments at the time the

TABLE 5-3.—*Effective Marginal Tax Rates on Investment*

Type of Investment	Effective Marginal Tax Rate
Economy (overall)	17%
Business Sector	26
Corporate Sector	29
Method of Financing	
Debt	-2
Equity	40
Type of Asset	
Equipment	25
Structures	34
Land	33
Inventories	33
Noncorporate sector	20
Owner-occupied housing	4

Source: Department of the Treasury (Office of Tax Analysis).

investments are made. A more modest approach would be to allow *partial expensing*, under which a firm could immediately deduct a fraction of the investment's cost. As shown in Box 5-2, full expensing reduces the firm-level tax on new investments to zero.

Box 5-2: Expensing versus Corporate Rate Reductions

Consider a firm that purchases a machine for $100. A year later, the machine produces output worth $50. The firm then sells the machine for $60. Thus, the return from investing $100 in the machine is 10 percent (the firm earns $50 + $60 = $110). The firm can finance the initial $100 investment by borrowing (debt), by reinvesting earnings, or by issuing new shares.

Assume that the firm either reinvests earnings or issues new shares (equity financing). Under an income tax, the firm's net income is $10, the value of the machine's output ($50) plus the proceeds from selling the machine ($60) minus the cost of the machine ($100). If the corporate income tax rate is 35 percent, the firm pays $3.50 in tax on its $10 income, leaving it with $6.50 after taxes (a 6.5 percent after-tax return). Thus, an income tax creates a distortion to the investment decision by lowering the after-tax return on the investment.

In contrast, full expensing allows the firm to deduct the entire $100 cost of the machine up front. Thus, the firm's taxes go down by $35 when it makes the investment, and the effective cost of the machine is $65, rather than $100. The firm earns $50 from the machine's output plus $60 from the sale of the machine, and the total income of $110 is taxed at a rate of 35 percent (because the firm already deducted the cost of the machine upon purchase). Thus, the tax paid is $38.50, and the firm's after-tax income is $71.50. The rate of return is ($71.50 - $65) / $65 = 10 percent, which is the same as it would have been without a tax. Effectively, full expensing makes the government a partner in the investment: the government pays for 35 percent of the investment's cost (via the deduction), and receives 35 percent of its return.

To be most effective in reducing distortions, full expensing would need to be combined with elimination of the interest deduction. Suppose interest payments remain deductible under the full-expensing approach described above and the firm borrows money to fund half of the machine's cost ($50) at a 10 percent interest rate. The effective cost of the machine is $65 due to expensing. Therefore, the firm spends $15 of its own funds ($65 - $50 = $15) for the machine. Next year, the machine generates $110 of income, and the firm pays $55 to the lender (principal

continued on next page

Box 5-2 — continued

plus interest). The firm deducts the interest payment of $5 from its income, resulting in taxable income of $105. At a 35 percent tax rate, the firm's tax liability is $36.75. The firm is left with a profit of $18.25, a return of 22 percent on its initial $15 investment. Thus, the tax on the investment's return is negative (the investment receives a subsidy from the government). If the interest deduction were not allowed, the firm's tax bill would be $38.50 (just as above), and the profit after repaying the lender $55 and paying taxes would be $16.50, a 10 percent rate of return. With full expensing and no interest deductibility, there is no distortion to either the investment decision or the financing decision.

Another alternative is to reduce the corporate rate. Using the same example as above, consider the impact of reducing the corporate tax rate from 35 percent to 10 percent. The firm makes its $100 investment, and next year pays tax on its net income of $10. This leaves the firm with an after-tax return of 9 percent. Since the after-tax return is still below the before-tax return, there is a distortion to the investment decision. However, there is less of a distortion than with the 35 percent tax rate.

In recent years, other countries have taken the approach of cutting the corporate tax rate. A tax rate cut affects all capital, both new and old. In comparison, expensing is targeted to new investment only. Thus, expensing generates a greater increase in investment for any given revenue reduction. Another difference between tax rate cuts and expensing arises because firms sometimes earn returns on their investments that are above the normal, ordinary return. To illustrate this, consider the example in Box 5-2, in which a $100 investment yields a 10 percent rate of return. Suppose that the next best use of the firm's funds would produce a return of 5 percent. The return of 5 percent represents the opportunity cost of the funds, also known as the normal return. As long as the investment return is above the normal return, the firm will undertake the project; thus, taxing any returns that exceed the opportunity cost of funds (called supra-normal returns) does not create any distortions. Expensing exempts only the normal return from taxation; supra-normal returns are subject to taxation. In the example, $5 of the investment's payoff represents compensation for the firm's opportunity cost, and $5 represents a supra-normal return. If the corporate tax rate is 35 percent, full expensing would give the firm a deduction worth $35 this year, and require it to pay a tax of $38.50 next year. Effectively, the firm is able to defer $35 of tax liability for 1 year. The value to the firm of deferring the tax until next year is $1.75 (5 percent of $35). However, next year, the firm must pay $3.50 in additional taxes. Thus, the firm has effectively paid a tax of $1.75 (the $3.50 of additional taxes minus the $1.75 value of deferral), which represents a tax of 35 percent on the $5 supra-normal return. Note that taxing the supra-normal return does not result in any distortions, because the firm's decision to undertake the investment does not depend on the tax. If the normal return were instead 10 percent, then the deferral of tax would be worth $3.50 to the firm, and there would be no effective tax on the investment return. In contrast to expensing, a corporate tax rate cut lowers the tax on both normal and supra-normal returns.

The efficiency of the business tax structure in the United States is particularly important as other countries undertake major corporate tax reforms. Capital is mobile across international borders, and the business tax environment is important in ensuring that the United States continues to attract investment from abroad, and that U.S. firms can compete effectively in foreign countries. In the mid-1980s, the average statutory corporate tax rate (weighted by GDP) across OECD countries was 44 percent. The U.S. tax reform of 1986, which reduced the corporate tax rate from 46 percent to 34 percent, made the United States a relatively low-tax country at the time of the reform. Since that time, however, the OECD-average corporate tax rate has fallen below that of the United States. These comparisons refer to statutory tax rates. The United States has relatively generous accelerated depreciation provisions and a multitude of business-level exemptions and deductions that reduce the tax burden on investment below the statutory rate. However, the effective marginal tax rate on corporate investment is still high: compared to other G7 countries (France, Germany, the United Kingdom, Canada, Italy, and Japan), the United States imposes an above-average marginal effective tax rate on corporate investment for domestic debt and equity holders in the top individual income tax bracket. In contrast, the U.S. *average corporate tax rate* (the total amount of corporate taxes paid as a percentage of corporate operating surplus) is low relative to other countries. This fact highlights the inefficiency and complexity of the corporate tax system. The marginal tax rate represents the additional tax burden a firm faces when it undertakes a new investment; therefore, it is the relevant tax rate for new investment decisions. This distortion is larger in the United States than in other countries. Despite the larger distortion, the corporate tax raises less revenue in the United States than in other countries, as evidenced by the fact that the average tax rate is lower. The implication is that investment incentives could be improved without a reduction in government revenue.

Conclusion

The analysis in this chapter has focused on both the level and structure of taxation. Over the past 40 years, Federal revenues have fluctuated around 18.3% of GDP. Under current law, however, tax revenues are scheduled to rise much faster than GDP in coming years. Furthermore, over longer periods of time, projected growth in entitlement spending will put pressure on taxes to rise. Because taxes distort incentives, these trends have important implications for economic growth. Extending the tax cuts of 2001 and 2003 would improve labor supply and savings incentives and result in less distortion of corporate finance decisions. Combined with control of entitlement spending, and a long-term solution to the Alternative Minimum Tax, this can have a beneficial effect on long-run growth.

The tax cuts of 2001 and 2003 have also improved the efficiency of the tax structure, particularly with respect to the double taxation of corporate income. However, the structure of business taxation still creates a number of distortions and puts the United States at a competitive disadvantage globally. Even revenue-neutral reforms can result in economic gains if they remove unnecessary distortions.

CHAPTER 6

The Nation's Infrastructure

Our economy depends on infrastructure that allows goods, people, information, and energy to flow throughout the Nation. This infrastructure—ports, roads, airports, communication networks, power lines, and many other systems—represents an important input into the economy. Just as firms must use labor and raw materials to produce output, they must also use airports and power lines. Similarly, consumers rely on cell phone towers and highways in their daily lives.

Infrastructure is often provided either directly by government agencies or by firms regulated by the government. Accordingly, the quantity and quality of infrastructure available to a firm or consumer often depends on government policy in addition to market forces. In recent years, the United States has experienced growing demands on its infrastructure, thanks to economic growth and successful deregulation in sectors that are heavy users of infrastructure. The policy challenge is how best to respond to these increased demands.

"Infrastructure" is a broad term, and this brief chapter does not provide a comprehensive review of all of the U.S. infrastructure systems. Instead, it discusses some of the economic issues associated with major transportation, communication, and power transmission systems, and some of the policy challenges in each. The key points of this chapter are:

- Infrastructure typically requires large capital investments to build and maintain capacity. Once built, however, the cost of allowing an extra person to use the capacity is typically low, as long as the number of users is less than the infrastructure's capacity. This cost structure often means that infrastructure cannot be provided efficiently by a competitive market. As a result, many types of infrastructure are instead provided by Government-regulated companies or, in some cases, by the Government itself.

- Demands on the U.S. infrastructure grow as the economy expands, and Government policies often determine how effectively infrastructure can accommodate that growth. Properly designed user fees can help ensure efficiency by revealing information about what infrastructure consumers value most.

- The price people pay for using infrastructure should reflect the extra cost associated with its use. This includes the cost of maintaining the infrastructure itself, as well as delays caused by increased congestion.

- The private sector plays an important role in providing infrastructure. However, lack of competition in markets for infrastructure raises concerns about market power, so that Government oversight is sometimes necessary. Government must continually reassess the need for oversight in the face of changing market conditions.

The Basic Challenge of Infrastructure Policy

As the economy grows, demands on our infrastructure increase. Since 1980, vehicle traffic on U.S. roads has nearly doubled, passenger-miles of air traffic have increased by more than 150 percent, and ton-miles of freight on U.S. railroads have increased by more than 80 percent. The Nation's growing demand for energy resources, together with a greater emphasis on new sources of power, is placing new demands on our energy infrastructure. And the growth of the Internet and information technology means that telecommunications networks are becoming more central to the U.S. economy.

Infrastructure systems—whether pipelines, roads, fiber optic networks, or port facilities—require large investments in long-lived capacity. Once this capacity is in place, however, small increases in usage may cost relatively little to provide. *Marginal cost* refers to the extra cost associated with a small increase in production of a good. Infrastructure investments produce goods, like passenger trips or phone calls, that typically have low marginal cost as long as total demands on the infrastructure do not approach the capacity it was designed to support. Once usage approaches capacity, however, marginal cost can increase substantially as extra use makes the entire system less effective.

These features create certain policy challenges that are common to many types of infrastructure. To illustrate these challenges, imagine a growing city where construction of a new bridge across a river is being considered. The bridge will provide significant benefits relative to the existing options for crossing the river—for example, taking a ferry or traveling several miles to cross at another point.

One possibility is that a private party will construct the bridge, planning to earn a profit by charging tolls. If the private sector builds a bridge, the market for river crossings at any given point will likely be provided by a single monopolist. This is because providing a bridge involves *economies of scale:* it is cheaper to build a single bridge that serves 20,000 people per day than two bridges that each serve 10,000 people per day. Because of economies of scale, the market for bridge crossings is called a *natural monopoly.* Even if there are no artificial barriers to market entry, a monopoly is likely to emerge simply because a single firm can produce the good more cheaply than multiple firms could.

A monopolistic bridge owner may choose to charge prices that are too high from society's perspective. A monopolist will choose a toll that generates the highest possible profit, even though the cost of allowing an extra person to cross the bridge may be very close to zero. This means lost opportunities: some people will choose not to cross because of the high toll, even though the cost of allowing them to cross is very small. The people who choose not to cross may waste time and fuel traveling to a toll-free bridge, or may choose not to cross, perhaps visiting friends less often or not shopping at stores that would require a bridge crossing. Economists refer to this type of foregone benefit as a *deadweight loss,* and it is a key economic reason for preventing monopoly pricing. To avoid this deadweight loss, government often attempts to prevent monopoly pricing of infrastructure, either by regulating the price or by providing the infrastructure itself. While government involvement can address monopoly concerns, it can create other inefficiencies: regulators may lack the information necessary to make efficient choices and may make decisions based on political considerations rather than on a cost-benefit analysis.

If the government builds and operates the bridge, it must make a number of decisions. First, the government must decide how to pay for the bridge. One approach is simply to charge a toll, for each use of the bridge, that is high enough to cover the average cost of providing the bridge. This approach seems sensible: the bridge will be paid for by those people who use it, and their willingness to pay for the bridge reveals that it passes a cost-benefit test. However, this approach is likely to create some inefficiency, because the average cost of providing the bridge will be higher than the extra cost each person imposes when he or she crosses at uncongested times. Thus, some people will choose not to cross even though it would cost the government little or nothing to allow them to cross. This can create a deadweight loss similar to the loss that occurs when a monopolist chooses the toll, though the deadweight loss will generally be smaller than under monopoly pricing.

One response to this problem would be to charge a *two-part tariff:* a fixed charge for a permit to use the bridge, in addition to a per-use toll that would be low to reflect the small marginal cost of using the bridge. This approach creates efficient incentives for those consumers who obtain permits, because the toll they pay for each crossing reflects only the cost of their use. However, some drivers will choose not to obtain a permit, and their failure to use the bridge is a deadweight loss.

Other issues arise if the bridge becomes congested. Suppose that, at peak hours, so many people attempt to use the bridge that traffic jams develop. At such times, each person who uses the bridge contributes to the delay that everyone on the bridge suffers. Congestion means that, from society's perspective, the marginal cost of bridge trips is no longer small: each additional trip makes traffic slower, adding to the delay costs of everyone using the bridge.

When the bridge becomes congested, users of the bridge may urge the government to invest in expanding its capacity. If people can use the bridge for free, frequent users are likely to insist that greater investment is a good idea, while those who do not use the bridge will object to spending tax dollars on the project. If the bridge is financed by tolls that are the same at all times of day, people who use the bridge at peak times will receive the benefit of extra capacity, even though they do not bear the full cost of the expansion. People who use the bridge at uncongested times will pay more in tolls to finance the expansion, but receive no benefit. Thus, peak-time users may support expansion even if the benefits to society do not outweigh the construction costs.

Setting aside the question of whether the bridge should be expanded, the congestion described above reflects a system that encourages inefficient choices. Each person who uses the bridge decides when to cross without considering the costs this creates for others because of increased congestion. Addressing this inefficiency can help ensure that existing capacity is used as efficiently as possible.

The questions of building the bridge—who should provide it, how it should be paid for, and when new capacity should be constructed—are all present to different degrees in debates about the major infrastructure systems in the United States. The next section gives an overview of some of these systems and some of the specific issues they face.

Current State of the Nation's Infrastructure

This section discusses aspects of the U.S. transportation, energy, and communications infrastructure. Economic growth has meant increased demand for transportation, raising questions about how best to address congestion. In energy and communications, changes in technology and market structure are transforming the way that infrastructure serves these sectors.

Roads

Roads play a central role in the U.S. economy. Both firms and consumers depend on cars and trucks in their everyday economic lives. Most U.S. freight shipments take place by road; for example, trucks handle over 70 percent of U.S. freight shipments (by value). On average, drivers travel 29 miles by car each day and spend almost an hour a day behind the wheel. Americans use roads in all parts of their daily lives, from commuting to work to shopping and visiting friends.

The amount of traffic on U.S. roads has been increasing steadily for decades. As traffic has increased, priorities have shifted from building new connections between places to accommodating growing traffic on existing routes (see Box 6-1). Although Federal, State, and local governments have built new roads and added lanes to existing roads, new construction has not kept up with the increases in traffic. Chart 6-1 shows that vehicle miles traveled in the United States have almost doubled since 1980, whereas total lane-miles of road have expanded by less than 6 percent. Put somewhat differently, each mile of road serves more traffic. For example, on urban highways the average number of vehicles using a given mile of road each day has increased from 3,785 in 1980 to 5,527 in 2005. We would not necessarily expect new road investment to match increases in miles driven, because a mile of road that serves 500 vehicles per day may easily accommodate 1,000 vehicles per day without any new construction. But at peak hours, the number of drivers attempting to use many urban roads approaches or exceeds the roads' maximum capacity. In 2004, almost two-thirds of peak-hour travel on urban interstates took place on roads carrying at least 80 percent of their theoretical maximum number of vehicles. More than a third of travel on urban interstates took place on roads carrying at least 95 percent of their theoretical maximum.

Box 6-1: The Interstate Highway System

The Interstate Highway System began when President Eisenhower signed the Federal-Aid Highway Act of 1956, which authorized $25 billion for the construction of 41,000 miles of interstate highway designed to a common standard. One of the original motivations for construction was to move materials and troops in times of emergency. President Eisenhower originally hoped to finance the system with tolls, but the system was instead financed through a fuel tax because of concern that tolls in less densely populated areas would be insufficient to cover the cost of those roads.

The Interstate System has come to play a central role in our Nation's economic life and has lowered the cost of transporting goods around the United States. The construction of the Interstate System may have made important contributions to economic growth, although there is no consensus among economists regarding highways' economic effects, and it is therefore difficult to say what parts of the Interstate System have benefits that outweigh their costs. Today, the local objective of reducing congestion in urban areas has replaced the National objective of connecting distant markets and providing for National defense. Now that interstates connect the country, the priority is to find ways of using these resources as efficiently as possible, and in particular to address congestion on the most heavily traveled interstate corridors.

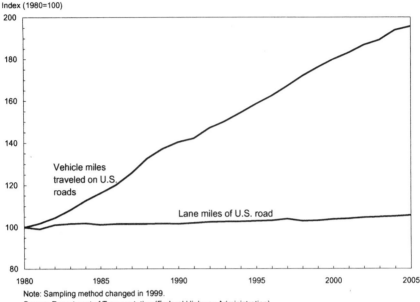

Index (1980=100)

Note: Sampling method changed in 1999.
Source: Department of Transportation (Federal Highway Administration).

When traffic approaches a road's capacity, the road becomes congested, resulting in real costs for drivers and businesses. The extra fuel consumed in all urban areas amounts to 2.87 billion gallons per year—about 2 percent of U.S. gasoline consumption. On average, commuters in urban areas lose almost 38 hours per year due to traffic congestion, and in the largest cities congestion costs the average commuter 54 hours per year. In the largest urban areas, over 40 percent of travel takes place under congested conditions. Congestion is worst in the Nation's largest cities, but is increasing in urbanized areas of every size. Chart 6-2 shows that congestion is increasing even in urbanized areas with fewer than 500,000 residents.

Traffic congestion is the predictable result of a situation in which a scarce resource—road space at rush hour—is made freely available to everyone. Individual drivers choose to travel at the time they find most convenient. When they travel at congested times, however, they contribute to the wasted time, fuel, and increased pollution borne by everyone else on the roadway. Individual drivers do not take this cost into account, so they use the road even though the social costs they create may be greater than the individual benefits they receive. This is the "tragedy of the commons": when a resource is freely available to anyone who wants to use it, it is overused, potentially leaving everyone worse off.

With highway traffic, as with other types of infrastructure, the problem is not simply that so many people use a road, but that they choose to use it at

Chart 6-2 Annual Delay per Peak-Period Traveler, by Urban Area Size, 1982–2005
Traffic flows have deteriorated in urban areas of all sizes.

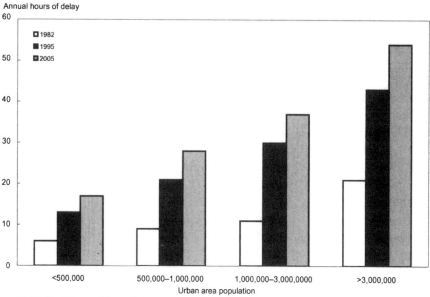

Source: Texas Transportation Institute.

the same time. At hours when many drivers want to travel, a certain amount of delay can be optimal, given the benefits that many drivers receive from traveling at their most preferred time. But as a road becomes very crowded, small increases in the number of cars can cause large decreases in the speed of traffic. When too many people attempt to enter road space at one time, traffic flow "collapses," meaning that a road is able to handle fewer cars in a given amount of time. Spreading out the times at which drivers enter a roadway can permit higher speeds, allowing a road to handle more traffic with the same amount of pavement.

One response to road congestion is to build more roads or widen existing roads. While new construction can be justified in many cases, it is not the solution to all congestion. Road construction is expensive; each additional lane can cost millions of dollars per mile. Furthermore, the tragedy of the commons applies to new capacity as well as to existing capacity. If a new lane makes a road less congested at peak hours, drivers who had previously avoided travel at peak hours will start to use the road at those times. This increase in rush-hour drivers means that the road will again become congested. This phenomenon is often referred to as the "fundamental law of highway congestion": increased capacity induces new traffic at peak times, so that moderate increases in capacity do not eliminate congestion.

A solution that does address the tragedy of the commons is to charge a price for using a road that reflects the extra delay each driver causes. *Congestion pricing* refers to a policy of charging tolls that reflect how crowded a road is at particular times. When drivers are required to pay such a toll, some drivers will choose to travel at less crowded times, take less crowded routes, or take alternative means of transportation. Those for whom it is especially important to travel a particular route at a particular time will pay the toll and be able to travel without inefficient levels of delay.

Congestion pricing has proven effective in many areas in reducing congestion and increasing traffic flows. For example, on a busy 10-mile stretch of State Route 91 in Orange County, California, drivers can choose between free lanes and toll lanes, for which prices adjust during the day on a schedule designed to maintain a free flow of traffic. Speeds in the toll lanes exceed 60 miles per hour even at the busiest time of day, with the result that, at the busiest part of the rush hour, each toll lane can produce almost twice as many vehicle trips each hour as the nontoll lanes. Because prices discourage drivers from entering the toll road when it is already crowded, traffic does not become so dense that flows collapse, and the road is able to serve more drivers during any given period of time.

More and more urban areas are becoming interested in using congestion pricing as a way to alleviate clogged roadways. As part of its Congestion Initiative, the Department of Transportation has developed Urban Partnership Agreements with five cities across the country, working with local authorities to mitigate the increasing congestion. In August 2007, the Secretary of Transportation announced the selection of Miami, Minneapolis/St. Paul, New York, San Francisco, and Seattle as the cities chosen from dozens of applicants to receive a share of $850 million in Federal funds to help alleviate highway congestion and the mounting costs it imposes. Each of these cities has developed plans to use some form of congestion pricing to reduce traffic delays. For example, New York City is proposing "cordon pricing," following an approach that has been successfully implemented in London and Stockholm. Between 6:00 a.m. and 6:00 p.m. on weekdays, cars would pay $8 per day to drive in the busiest parts of Manhattan, while trucks would be charged $21. Vehicles driving in the area could be identified by electronic "E-Z Pass" readers or, for vehicles without the readers, through a license plate recognition system using digital cameras.

New York's plan is targeted at a heavily congested urban area; other cities have followed different approaches targeted at certain roads or stretches of road that are especially congested. On SR-520 in the Seattle area, regional planners are proposing to use demand-based toll rates both to alleviate peak-hour congestion and to raise funds to replace a high-traffic bridge over Lake Washington. Under the plan, toll rates would be updated in real time to reflect current traffic conditions, and in-vehicle transponders and supplemental cameras would collect the toll while drivers travel at highway speed.

Bridges

On August 1, 2007, the I-35W Bridge in Minneapolis collapsed, killing 13 people. This was the first collapse of this magnitude since May 2002, when a barge collided with a bridge in Oklahoma, causing the collapse of a section of I-40 and killing 14 people. The recent tragedy focused national attention on the condition of our highway bridges. Bridge repair and maintenance are important for two reasons: to ensure safety and to maintain or increase the capacity of a bridge to carry traffic.

There are nearly 600,000 bridges in the United States. Bridges are inspected using the National Bridge Inspection Standards, in most cases every 2 years. The Department of Transportation collects this information in the National Bridge Inventory, a database of information on bridge conditions. About 12 percent of the bridges in the United States are classified as "structurally deficient" by the Department of Transportation, meaning that the bridge is subject to certain weight or other restrictions due to its condition. This share has been shrinking as States have focused greater resources on bridge maintenance and repair (see Chart 6-3). These numbers suggest that bridges have become a higher priority for States in recent years.

Chart 6-3 **Condition of U.S. Highway Bridges, 1992–2006**
Bridge conditions have improved in recent years.

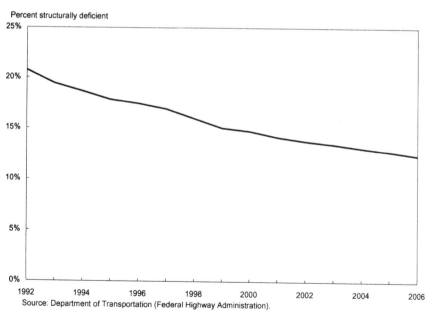

Percent structurally deficient

Source: Department of Transportation (Federal Highway Administration).

Ongoing inspection and maintenance is especially important for bridges. Infrastructure investments should be based on a cost-benefit analysis. In some cases, new projects might seem more appealing to decisionmakers than routine maintenance, but maintenance is essential. One way to encourage investment in projects with the greatest return is to ensure greater transparency in reporting the costs and benefits of different infrastructure projects. For example, by publicly identifying the bridges in greatest need of repair, the National Bridge Inventory may help generate political support for targeting resources where they are most productive.

Railways

Railroads have played a central role in our Nation's history, linking markets over long distances and helping create a national economy. Rail continues to be an important mode of freight transportation, particularly for heavy bulk materials such as coal. Chart 6-4 shows that railroads carry almost one-third of the Nation's freight, measured in terms of ton-miles, but because rail tends to be used for lower-priced goods, this represents a small fraction of the total value of goods shipped. In 1980, the Staggers Rail Act deregulated the freight rail industry. At the time, observers expected prices to increase, but in fact deregulation unleashed significant efficiencies and lower rates. After decades without changes in rates or traffic, shipping rates have fallen substantially in real terms since 1985, while the volume of freight rail traffic has nearly doubled. In the last few years, rising fuel prices have made rail an attractive alternative to trucking, because railways are about three times more fuel efficient than trucks. Increasing highway congestion may also have contributed to increasing demand for rail. As a result of the increased demand for rail shipping, its real price has increased for the first time in many years, and railroads are investing increasing amounts in new capacity.

Railroads serve a variety of customers who face different sets of options for shipping their freight. Some routes are served by only one railroad, while other routes are served by competing railroads. Some products (such as goods in containers) can be economically shipped by road, whereas others (such as coal) may be prohibitively expensive to truck over long distances.

Like roads and other infrastructure, rail systems are very capital intensive, and railroads must pay the cost of maintaining their rail lines and other capital stock regardless of the amount of freight they carry. This creates difficulties for railroads that serve competitive markets. To remain profitable overall, the total revenue from all shipments must cover the railroad's capital costs. But a particular shipment will increase a railroad's profit as long as revenue from that shipment is greater than the marginal cost of that shipment. In markets

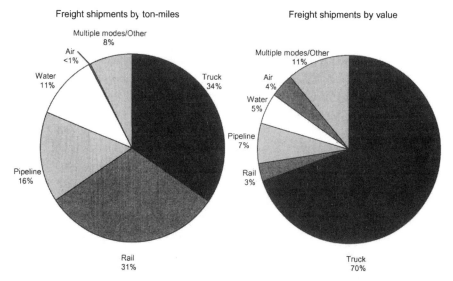

Chart 6-4 **Distribution of U.S. Freight Shipments by Mode**
Rail is used disproportionately for heavier, lower-value shipments.

Freight shipments by ton-miles

Freight shipments by value

Multiple modes/Other
8%

Air
<1%

Water
11%

Truck
34%

Pipeline
16%

Rail
31%

Multiple modes/Other
11%

Air
4%

Water
5%

Pipeline
7%

Rail
3%

Truck
70%

Source: Department of Transportation (Bureau of Transportation Statistics).

where shippers have an alternative to rail, this means that railroads will offer rates to some shippers that do not cover a full share of their capital costs. They make up for this by charging prices that cover more than a shipment's share of capital costs in markets where shippers do not have economical alternatives.

Understandably, many shippers in these markets complain that they pay shipping rates substantially higher than those paid by shippers in more competitive markets. However, the railroads' ability to charge different rates to different shippers plays a vital role in enabling railroads to maintain the large capital investments needed to operate a railroad. If railroads were forced to charge the same price for all freight, many shippers that have alternative shipping options would respond to an increase in rail rates by shifting toward road, water, or other transportation. This reduction in revenue would make railroad capital investments less profitable, and the likely result would be reductions in investment and in rail capacity. In the long run, the result could be even higher shipping rates for those who continued to use rail transportation.

Container Ports

Over 800 billion dollars worth of goods, representing over 40 percent of U.S. trade, passes through U.S. seaports each year. Container trade—that is, goods packed in containers that can be moved from ships to trucks or trains without being unpacked—continues to grow dramatically, more than doubling in the United States since 1995. All of those goods pass through a relatively small number of facilities. A complex system of cranes, berths, skilled labor, warehouses, and ground transportation facilities is necessary to transfer goods from oceangoing ships to the domestic transportation network.

Increases in global containerized trade have meant an increase in the size of container ships. In the late 1980s, shipping companies introduced the first container ships that were too large to use the Panama Canal, and today such "post-Panamax" ships represent at least 30 percent of container shipping capacity. As ships have gotten bigger, port traffic has become more concentrated among those ports with waterways and port facilities capable of handling such large vessels. Today, the 10 busiest U.S. ports handle 85 percent of U.S. container traffic, up from 78 percent in 1995. Chart 6-5 shows that increased concentration has been most noticeable at the 3 busiest U.S. ports (Los Angeles, Long Beach, and New York), where the share of National container traffic increased from 41 percent in 1995 to 49 percent in 2005.

Chart 6-5 **Container Trade at U.S. Marine Ports**
The largest U.S. ports handle a growing share of container shipments.

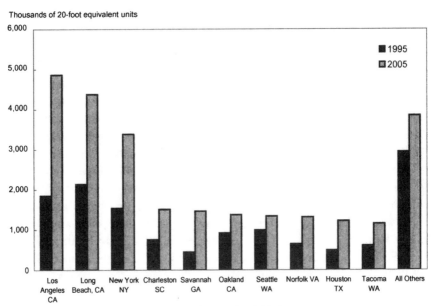

Thousands of 20-foot equivalent units

Source: Department of Transportation (Bureau of Transportation Statistics).

Freight shipments into and out of the United States will continue to grow along with the growth in U.S. trade. This increase in trade flows will place tremendous demands not only on port facilities, but also on the land-based systems that carry traffic to and from the port. For example, the ports of Los Angeles and Long Beach together handle container traffic representing over 10,000 truckloads each day (not to mention goods shipped in tankers, dry bulk, and other ships). All of this traffic must be accommodated on the roads and railways serving the port.

Increased demands on port facilities are creating opportunities for smaller ports to expand their traffic. For example, the Port of Savannah, Georgia, more than tripled its container traffic between 1995 and 2005. Savannah's growth reflects significant investments in expanding warehouses, docks, and rail yards, as well as the desire of shippers to avoid congestion at the larger ports in New York and Los Angeles. Increased U.S. sea trade also creates opportunities for ports in Mexico and Canada, which can connect by road or rail to U.S. markets. For example, a new container port in the town of Prince Rupert, British Columbia, opened in 2007, offering facilities for the largest container ships and rail connections to Chicago and the Midwest.

Faced with growing demands, congested ports have implemented innovative strategies for reducing the attendant strain on local infrastructure. The Ports of Los Angeles and Long Beach developed a program called "PierPass," designed to move traffic to off-peak periods during the nights and weekends. Carriers unloading during peak hours pay a surcharge of $100 for a 40-foot container, and proceeds from the surcharge fund port operations during the weekend and overnight. According to the program, 36 percent of the container volume at the Los Angeles–Long Beach complex is now moved during the off-peak shifts, removing 60,000 trucks from the roads during rush hour each week.

Aviation

Since 1975, the real price of air transportation has fallen, while the number of miles traveled by air has grown by almost 300 percent. An important part of these changes was the deregulation of the airline industry in 1978. By permitting airlines to introduce new flights and schedules, deregulation introduced competitive forces that have led to entry by discount carriers and reductions in the real price of air travel. In 2006, air travel generated approximately $164 billion in revenue, equivalent to approximately 1.2 percent of GDP.

Air travel requires not only planes, but also runways, terminals, and an air traffic control system to maintain a safe distance between planes. The capacity of these systems has not increased as rapidly as the growth of air traffic. Our air traffic control system is largely based on antiquated technology. New investments in infrastructure have been hampered by several factors, including political opposition from communities near airports and the fact that air traffic control is provided by a government bureaucracy that has no financial incentive to respond efficiently to increased demand for its services.

Growing traffic has created congestion in both the Nation's airspace and its airports. The result has been longer flight times and increased delays. Airlines have accounted for congestion, in part, by building more time into their schedules, although delays have grown despite the longer schedules. Chart 6-6 shows that the average scheduled time for a flight from New York's La Guardia airport to Atlanta's Hartsfield-Jackson International Airport has increased from 2 hours and 18 minutes in 1988 to 2 hours and 34 minutes in 2006. The average delay has also increased from 12 minutes in 1988 to over 20 minutes in 2006. This has been the trend for the busiest routes in the continental United States: for the 10 city pairs with the highest number of airline passengers, scheduled times have increased by an average of 14 minutes, and delay has increased by an average of 6 minutes. Delays have also become more severe: for these same routes, the number of flights that are delayed by more than 60 minutes has increased from 2.7 percent to 7.4 percent. The summer of 2007 saw especially severe flight delays, with particularly acute problems in New York (see Box 6-2).

Chart 6-6 **Average Travel Time, New York (LGA) to Atlanta (ATL) 1988–2006**
Scheduled flight times have increased in addition to growing delays.

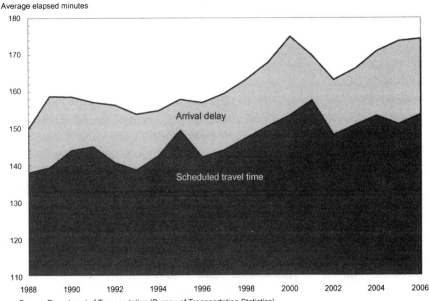

Average elapsed minutes

Source: Department of Transportation (Bureau of Transportation Statistics).

Box 6-2: Delays at New York City Airports

Some of the worst air traffic congestion in the United States occurs in the New York City area. Problems in New York have a large impact on delays nationwide, because a large proportion of U.S. flights travel to, from, or over New York airspace. Delays in New York became especially acute in the summer of 2007, after restrictions were lifted on landings and takeoffs at John F. Kennedy International Airport. With no limitations on how many flights could be scheduled into the airport, the number of scheduled flights increased by 20 percent, and far more flights were scheduled to arrive during peak periods than the airport could handle. The result was long delays: only 56 percent of flights arrived on time during the summer of 2007, with especially severe delays in the peak hours.

In September 2007, the President called on the Secretary of Transportation to seek solutions to mounting air traffic congestion and the frustrations it creates for passengers. The Federal Aviation Administration convened an Aviation Rulemaking Committee to explore ways of relieving congestion, including market-based mechanisms such as congestion pricing or auctions for the right to land or take off at congested times. In December, the Department of Transportation announced that it would limit the number of flights to and from New York airports beginning in spring 2008, while continuing to pursue market-based approaches to reducing congestion in the near term.

History has shown that such market-based solutions can work. In 1968, for example, the Port Authority of New York and New Jersey implemented a congestion-pricing fee on small aircraft by raising the minimum landing fee during peak hours. As expected, travelers responded to the price incentives: general aviation peak hour activity declined by 30 percent, reducing delays at the region's airports.

The Federal Aviation Administration, working with other agencies, has begun an effort to expand capacity by upgrading the air traffic control system. The Next Generation Air Transportation System (NextGen) would use satellites and digital communications to provide both controllers and pilots with a much more accurate picture of where planes are in the airspace. Together with other technologies, these upgrades have the potential to reduce the amount of separation necessary for safe flight, allowing more planes to use a given amount of space and increasing the system's capacity.

Airport congestion reflects capacity constraints and indicates a failure to manage and price that capacity in a way that reflects the costs each plane creates for air traffic control and for other users of congested space. Each plane that lands or takes off at a busy airport takes up roughly the same amount of space and time regardless of size, but the fees paid for using an airport are much higher for larger planes. The airport fees that airlines pay each time they land are based on the weight of a plane, and the national air traffic control system is funded largely by taxes on airline tickets. Both approaches mean that a regional jet carrying 50 passengers pays much less than a large jet carrying 200 passengers, even though each creates roughly the same burden for air traffic control and the same amount of congestion in the airspace. Similarly, fees are the same whether the airport is busy or empty, even though scheduling an arrival at a busy time can generate significant costs for other users. This system creates the wrong incentives, encouraging airlines to use inefficiently small aircraft and to schedule too many flights at the most popular airports and times of day.

The market-based mechanisms discussed earlier in this chapter can help encourage airlines to use airport infrastructure more efficiently. Different options are available for using market-based mechanisms to manage airport congestion. One is to change the structure of landing fees so that planes pay more to land at more congested times and airports. Similar to congestion pricing on roadways, this would encourage airlines and others to schedule flights at times when the airports and airspace are less crowded. Another approach would be to fix the number of landing and takeoff slots available during the busiest times of day, and auction the right to use those slots. Slots would, in effect, be leased for a fixed period of time, with slots turning over and being reauctioned on a regular basis to accommodate new entrants and promote competition. Assigning slots through a market process would have a similar effect to congestion-based fees, because the price of slots at the most popular times would be greater than those at less popular times. Under either approach, airlines would have an incentive to schedule flights at less busy times, and passengers who attach high value to flying at busy times of day would be able to pay a premium to schedule flights at those times with greater confidence that flights will be able to depart on time.

Market-based mechanisms could also improve efficiency when airport capacity is reduced as a result of bad weather or other temporary problems. For example, airlines could pay a premium for the right to land with higher priority when capacity is reduced. Airlines that pay for higher priority could advertise their higher reliability, whereas other airlines might offer price discounts to travelers who were willing to accept a higher probability of delay.

The Electrical Grid

Although they transport electricity rather than goods or people, power lines share important characteristics with roads and other infrastructure. Building transmission lines requires a large capital investment. Once this capacity is built, the marginal cost of transmission is low as long as the amount of power being delivered is less than the capacity of the lines.

The transmission of electric power was once primarily a local affair: a utility generated electricity and distributed it on its own power lines to the surrounding area, with rates set by a local regulator. But over time, the United States has moved from this local model to one in which the Nation is covered by grids of high-voltage transmission lines, and power generated in one place may be used hundreds of miles away. While some power plants continue to serve a particular local population, others take advantage of the grid to sell their electricity on a wholesale market.

By permitting power to be generated in low-cost areas and delivered to high-cost areas, the national electrical grid can allow generating capacity to be used much more efficiently. For example, on the West Coast, long-distance transmission lines allow hydroelectric power from Washington State to be transmitted to California to help meet peak summer demand. Long-distance transmission can make alternative energy sources more viable as the United States attempts to reduce its dependence on fossil fuels (see Chapter 7). For example, production of significant amounts of wind power is economically feasible only in certain areas of the country. Similarly, it is easier to site power plants in certain areas. Long-distance power lines mean that electricity can be produced in areas where production is most efficient and delivered to areas where it is most needed.

The legacy of State-regulated local utilities creates obstacles to developing an efficient national electrical grid. One problem is fragmented ownership of power lines. Different parts of the electrical grid are owned and maintained by a large number of investor-owned utilities and other entities, so that power may need to pass through lines belonging to multiple parties before reaching its destination. This can create coordination problems. Each utility must decide independently how much to invest in the capacity of its power lines, even though these decisions will affect many other parts of the network. It may not make sense for one party to invest in greater capacity unless others make similar investments.

Such problems are exacerbated by the fact that different regulators govern different parts of the electrical grid. Utility investments often must be approved by State or local regulators applying rules designed for the model of a local utility. Regulators in one State may not have incentives to account for the benefits of new transmission capacity for residents of other States. In fact, regulators in an area where production costs are low may object to making it easier for local power generators to sell in areas where production costs are high, because more power will flow to the high-cost market, potentially raising wholesale prices in the local market in the short run. In the long run, however, making trade in electricity easier will lead to greater generating capacity in areas where electricity can be generated at lowest cost. The Federal

Government has taken steps to coordinate interstate transmission projects by giving the Department of Energy the authority to designate certain transmission corridors as high priority and to help develop new capacity in those areas.

Telecommunications

Not long ago, the U.S. telecommunications infrastructure consisted largely of copper wires used to transmit the human voice. Today, information travels any number of ways—satellites, cellular systems, and fiber optic cable, to name some examples—and industry continues to develop new communication technologies. New choices mean consumers and businesses enjoy the benefits of competition among providers. As information technology becomes faster and cheaper, communication infrastructure is allowing workers to telecommute and consumers to shop online.

Broadband Internet Service

Broadband refers to Internet connections that can transmit data at high speeds (the Federal Communications Commission defines a high-speed connection as one that allows transfer rates greater than 200 kilobits per second in at least one direction, but many connections are much faster than this). As recently as 1999, broadband access was very rare, but by 2007 nearly half the country had a broadband connection at home, and the United States had over 80 million high-speed connections. Until 2005, almost all broadband users had either a cable modem or a digital subscriber line (DSL) connection, but recently, mobile wireless subscriptions have increased rapidly (see Chart 6-7).

Like other forms of infrastructure, broadband capacity requires large capital expenditures, and once capacity is installed, the marginal cost of delivering data over a line is close to zero. Telecommunications companies have invested large amounts to expand broadband infrastructure, installing new high-capacity transmission lines and investing in new technology to send data over existing telephone and cable wires.

Despite large fixed costs of deployment, there are multiple broadband providers competing for subscribers in most U.S. markets. The Federal Communications Commission (FCC) reports that by the end of 2006, over 80 percent of U.S. ZIP codes were served by at least four broadband service providers. Nationwide, 79 percent of local telephone subscribers had access to DSL, and 96 percent of cable subscribers had access to cable Internet service.

Broadband service provision remains an extremely dynamic area, and telecommunications providers are exploring new models to determine what type of broadband provision can produce the greatest benefits for consumers. For example, last year, the fastest-growing category of high-speed Internet

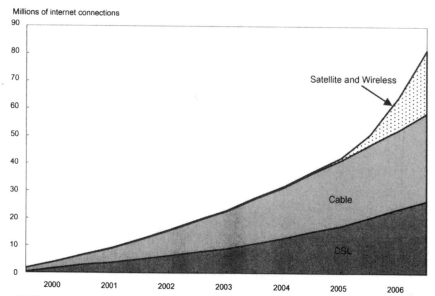

Chart 6-7 **High-Speed Internet Lines in the United States by Type of Connection, 1999–2006**
Broadband connections have grown rapidly.

Millions of internet connections

Satellite and Wireless

Cable

DSL

Note: Fiber and powerline connections are a small fraction of connections and have been omitted.
Source: Federal Communications Commission.

access was in mobile wireless connections—a category that grew from about 3 million connections at the end of 2005 to over 20 million connections at the end of 2006. Broadband providers are also offering dramatically higher transmission speeds, enabling consumers to access new services such as streaming video and voice-over Internet protocol (VOIP). The tremendous value the Internet creates for consumers has provided strong incentives for the private sector both to invest in building out the Internet infrastructure and to innovate in finding new ways of serving the market.

Wireless Communication

Wireless technology, such as that used in cellular phones, has been one of the most dynamic sectors of the economy in recent years, with considerable growth in both the number of users and the quality of services. Today, the United States has 243 million wireless subscribers, up from 16 million at the end of 1993. Several wireless service providers compete to offer communication features that will attract new customers, such as the opportunity to share pictures, download news and other information, or view a map of their current location and directions to their destination.

Wireless communications systems transmit radio signals using specific frequencies of the radio spectrum. If different signals were to use the same frequency, the result would be interference that prevents communication.

To prevent interference, the Government regulates who can use each part of the spectrum. Private sector users obtain licenses from the FCC that grant exclusive permission to transmit signals in a certain area. Certain frequencies are reserved for use by Government agencies, and use of this spectrum is coordinated through the National Telecommunications and Information Administration in the Department of Commerce.

The right to use spectrum is a scarce resource, with many competing demands. Early in the history of radio, the U.S. Government began allocating the right to use spectrum through an administrative process, in which different potential users applied for licenses and the FCC attempted to determine which use would generate the greatest social benefit. This approach requires the Government to evaluate an enormous amount of information about the competing benefits of using resources in different ways. Markets can help solve this problem, because the prices people are willing to pay for a scarce resource reflect all the information they possess about how the resource can be best used.

Recognizing these benefits from market allocation, the U.S. Government has moved to a system in which the right to use spectrum for wireless communication is awarded through auctions. In 1994, the FCC began a series of auctions for the rights to use spectrum for personal communication services. Since then, the FCC has held about 70 spectrum auctions, generating nearly $60 billion in revenue and opening up new opportunities for firms to offer wireless services.

The spectrum auctions have put the right to use spectrum in the hands of those who believe they can use it to generate the greatest value. By creating clear property rights to use particular frequencies, the auctions have given companies the incentives to invest in the resources they have obtained. The result has been a rapid build-out of networks of towers for cellular communication. Chart 6-8 shows that the number of wireless transmitters in the United States has grown from about 20,000 in 1995 to 210,000 in 2007—an increase of 22 percent per year.

Through the President's Spectrum Management Initiative, the Administration has sought ways to ensure that spectrum is used in the way that generates the greatest value. One way to do this is to create incentives for Government users of spectrum to consider the opportunity cost of the spectrum they use. Currently, Government agencies obtain spectrum licenses through an administrative process—in contrast to other valuable resources, such as electricity and labor, for which they must pay. Policies that lead agencies to recognize the cost of using spectrum will encourage them to free up this resource when there are others who could use it more efficiently.

Thousands of wireless sites (transmitters)

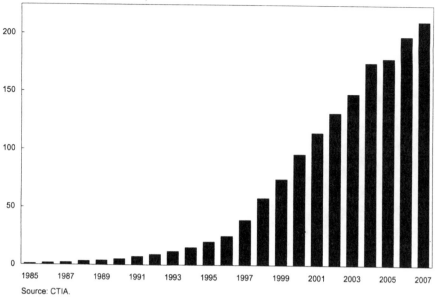

Source: CTIA.

Infrastructure Policy

Though the U.S. infrastructure systems face a diverse set of issues, they have certain features in common, such as high capital costs and limitations to capacity that create the potential for congestion. This section discusses some of the key policy questions that are common to many forms of infrastructure. First, how should infrastructure be paid for? The price of infrastructure should reflect marginal cost, but this may not be sufficient to cover capital costs. Second, how should policymakers set priorities for infrastructure investment? In many cases, the government can look to markets for ideas as to how to best identify which projects have the greatest return. Third, should infrastructure be provided by the private or public sector? Policymakers can often choose between government provision and private sector provision with some degree of government regulation. Fourth, when should infrastructure be provided at the Federal level, and when is it better provided at the State or local level?

How Should Infrastructure Be Paid For?

As discussed at the beginning of this chapter, efficient use of any good or service requires that the price people pay for using the good or service equals the extra cost they impose when they use it. If the price is lower than this cost, people will have an incentive to overuse the good or service. For example, if electricity is available for free, consumers may leave lights on when they are not using them. If the price is higher than the extra cost of providing the good, it will be underused, creating a deadweight loss.

For much infrastructure, the marginal cost of extra use may be very low or close to zero when use is well below capacity. This creates a dilemma in financing infrastructure because encouraging efficient use means setting the price equal to marginal cost. If this price is at or near zero, revenue will not cover the cost of providing infrastructure, requiring either a higher price or some other source of revenue. For some forms of infrastructure, firms address this problem with a *two-part tariff:* a fixed fee for access to the infrastructure, in addition to a per-use fee that reflects the marginal cost of providing the infrastructure. For example, telecommunications providers typically charge users a monthly subscription fee but allow users to transmit as much data as they like at little or no extra charge, reflecting the fact that once a user is connected to the network, extra data transmission involves little or no extra costs. This approach creates efficient incentives for those consumers who subscribe, while still allowing telecommunications providers to finance the cost of their investment.

When roads or other infrastructure become congested, the efficient response is to charge fees that reflect the cost each additional user imposes on others. Congestion prices can lead to efficient decisions about whether and when to use infrastructure and yield information about where additional capacity would be most valuable.

Efficient tolls can also generate revenue that can help pay for infrastructure. Fees collected through congestion pricing can be used to fund expansion of existing infrastructure and reduce current indirect taxes and fees. Under the right circumstances, efficient tolls will be sufficient to completely fund new infrastructure construction—meaning that congestion is reduced, while at the same time roads are financed almost entirely by the drivers who use them during the busiest periods.

How Should Government Set Priorities for Infrastructure Projects?

In competitive markets, firms decide whether to invest in new capacity based on the value that capacity creates for consumers. For example, imagine a coffee shop that has long lines during the morning rush. The shop's owner could shorten the wait by adding an extra cashier. This would cost money, but would please her customers, potentially leading to greater sales. The owner will add a cashier if the extra coffee she can sell will generate enough revenue to justify the extra expense.

In areas in which infrastructure investment is made by private parties, such as broadband or wireless communications, companies undertake exactly this type of analysis. Similarly, when the government decides whether to undertake new infrastructure investment, it should conduct an analysis similar to that of the coffee shop owner, comparing the costs of a new project to the benefits it generates for users. Rigorous cost-benefit analysis should be used to determine whether the benefits of a particular project outweigh its cost and whether the benefits of dollars spent are greater than the social benefits from spending money in other areas.

Private sector firms use the prices consumers are willing to pay to measure the benefits of extra investment. When the government makes investment decisions, however, there is frequently no market price that reflects how much consumers are willing to pay for greater capacity or for a particular new project. When infrastructure is provided for free, one cannot infer from heavy use that users attach a high value to using certain infrastructure. Free access also makes it difficult to evaluate users' stated preferences. For example, residents of a particular area may be strong supporters of expanding a freeway serving their community, given that they are able to use that freeway at no additional charge. But this support is not responsive to the real question that a policymaker would want to answer, which is whether those residents would support the construction project if they had to bear all of its associated costs, in addition to receiving the benefits.

The problem of determining the value users receive from infrastructure projects is another argument on behalf of user fees that reflect marginal cost. When users pay for the infrastructure they use, we can be more confident that the infrastructure produces benefits that reflect the cost.

When Should the Government Regulate or Provide Infrastructure?

As discussed earlier in this chapter, infrastructure is often a *natural monopoly*, meaning that one firm can serve the market more cheaply than multiple firms could. This may create a role for the government to prevent the distortions that result from monopoly pricing. However, large capital costs by themselves do not necessarily imply natural monopoly; when a market is large, it may support multiple firms even though the costs of participating in the market are high. When several firms compete to provide a service, government regulation is not needed to prevent monopoly prices.

Technological innovation has the potential to fundamentally alter the makeup of markets, and government regulation should adapt to changes in market structure. Markets once dominated by monopolies can become competitive over time due to innovation. Regulations should be eliminated as markets become more competitive.

A good example of this phenomenon is telecommunications. Although the industry was once dominated by a single firm or by a few large firms, today numerous providers compete to provide customers with voice, Internet, and video over numerous platforms, including telephone (DSL), cable, fiber-optic, satellite, wireless, and even the electric grid. In the face of such innovation and digital convergence, the government must reassess legacy regulatory regimes and replace regulation with competition wherever possible to most efficiently maximize consumer welfare.

When infrastructure provision is a natural monopoly, economic theory provides no clear answer to the question of whether infrastructure is better provided directly by the government or by a regulated monopolist. In both cases, decisions will be insulated from market discipline. Government regulation of a private firm involves some duplication of effort, because the regulator must examine firm decisions to prevent abuses of monopoly power. But a government agency may not have incentives to produce efficiently, because it does not have the profit motive of the private sector. Private firms may also be able to provide management with stronger incentives to increase efficiency.

Empirical studies of privatization around the world have shown that, in general, private firms in various industries produce and invest more efficiently than state-owned enterprises. Although these privatizations have occurred in a wide variety of different countries and industries, privately run enterprises on average produce more efficiently and invest more in their industry. Recent U.S. experiences have also demonstrated that, in some cases, there can be benefits to greater private sector involvement in provision of transportation infrastructure.

Some urban areas, wanting to improve congested roads in the face of tight budgets, have turned to private investors to build and operate toll roads. In 1990, for example, Virginia authorized a private investment partnership to construct the Dulles Greenway, a 14-mile stretch of highway in a congested part of the Washington, D.C., metropolitan area. The partnership was authorized to collect tolls that would provide no more than a reasonable return on the invested funds. Since construction in the mid-1990s, the road has become an integral part of the region's transportation network, carrying over 50,000 vehicles each day in 2006.

In 2005, the Federal Aviation Administration contracted with Lockheed Martin to take over operation of the FAA's Automated Flight Service Stations. These stations provide general aviation pilots with weather briefings, updates on airport closings, flight plan assistance and emergency communications. The contractor has successfully consolidated operations and reduced costs, and the FAA projects that it will save $2.2 billion over the contract's first 5-year period. The FAA continues to monitor the stations to ensure quality and service levels.

Although private firms have strong incentives to produce efficiently, some argue that they will tend to provide a lower quality of service than the government, because higher quality may yield lower profits. This concern suggests that when government contracts with a private firm to provide public infrastructure, it should pay careful attention to the terms of the contract to ensure that the firm can be held accountable for the quality of the infrastructure.

What Are the Proper Roles for State and Federal Government?

Both the Federal and State Governments provide and regulate infrastructure. For example, most funding for road construction and maintenance is provided by the States, although substantial funds are also raised through Federal taxes on fuel and other transportation goods and then distributed to the States. Similarly, electricity transmission is regulated both by the Federal Energy Regulatory Commission and by State utility regulators.

There are advantages to making decisions about infrastructure policy at the State level. State Governments can tailor infrastructure decisions to local preferences and conditions, rather than providing a single one-size-fits-all policy for the entire country. States that implement policies that their citizens dislike will fail to attract new people and businesses.

Federal provision or regulation can be important when infrastructure in one State provides benefits to residents of other States. For example, power lines transmit electricity across State borders, but State electricity regulators may think only about how regulation affects their own citizens. Federal regulation may be more appropriate when State infrastructure produces national benefits. Similarly, State Governments make decisions about infrastructure investment based on the benefits to their own citizens, and will be reluctant to make investments with their own taxpayers' money if a large share of the benefits goes to out-of-state residents. The Federal Government should take into account the total benefits to the Nation, so when infrastructure projects provide significant cross-state benefits, it may be best to set infrastructure policy at the Federal level.

Conclusion

Infrastructure policy is not simply an engineering problem of how best to build the systems to meet the country's needs. Although Government may play an important role because infrastructure provision is often a natural monopoly, economic incentives matter and must be taken into account. There are two central questions of infrastructure policy. First, what investments in new capacity generate benefits that exceed their costs? Second, how can we ensure that the capacity we invest in is used in the most efficient way possible? By subjecting infrastructure policy decisions to these threshold questions and using market-based solutions where action is taken, Government—at the local, State and Federal levels—will increase certainty that future investments in infrastructure are socially worthwhile and allocated appropriately.

CHAPTER 7

Searching for Alternative Energy Solutions

The United States consumes a great deal of energy in support of the world's largest economy. It produces over 70 quadrillion British Thermal Units (or "Btu," a measure of energy) of primary energy per year—mainly from coal, natural gas, petroleum, and nuclear power—and it consumes 100 quadrillion Btu, more than any other country in the world. The difference—30 quadrillion Btu—is imported, mostly in the form of petroleum. For energy security reasons, the United States seeks to diversify its energy sources and fuels. One way to do this is to pursue the use and development of domestically-produced alternative energy sources. The United States has also been concerned about the environmental effects of current energy use, particularly the emission of air pollutants and carbon dioxide (CO_2). For this reason, the United States has pursued the use of alternative energy sources that have the potential to produce lower emissions than traditional fossil fuels (coal, natural gas, and petroleum), which are the source of about 85 percent of the energy consumed in the United States. Therefore, both energy security and environmental concerns motivate the consideration of policies that diversify our sources of energy. For purposes of this discussion, alternative energy will be defined as alternatives to fossil fuels and will include renewable energy sources (hydroelectric, geothermal, solar, wind, and biomass), as well as nuclear power and emerging technologies.

Alternative energy sources are not the only way to address energy security and environmental concerns. Improved energy efficiency could reduce our energy demand as well as reduce pollution. Environmental concerns could also be addressed by developing ways to use fossil fuels in a less polluting manner, such as through clean coal and carbon capture and storage (CCS) technologies. These are both very important solutions that the Administration is pursuing in tandem with alternative energy solutions; however, this chapter will focus on alternatives to fossil fuel.

This chapter will concentrate on two sectors: electricity generation and transportation. These are not the only two sectors that could benefit from alternative energy. Primary energy consumption (that is, the direct use of energy before it has been subjected to any conversion) can be divided into five major sectors: electricity generation, transportation, and energy end use by industry, commerce and residences. The potential for the direct use of alternative energy by industry, commerce and residences is important; but, because nearly 70 percent of petroleum is used in the transportation sector and the vast majority of coal is used for electricity generation, this chapter will largely focus on these two sectors.

Alternatives for electricity generation include nuclear power, hydropower, biomass, wind, geothermal, and solar power. Alternatives in the transportation sector include developing domestically-produced transportation fuels such as ethanol and biodiesel, and finding new ways to power our cars, such as using electricity for plug-in hybrids or using hydrogen to deliver energy. Our goal over the next several decades is to change the way in which we produce and consume energy for electricity generation and transportation so as to diversify our energy sources. The key points of this chapter are:

- The current suite of available alternative energy sources is an important part of achieving our goal, but a number of technical, regulatory, and economic hurdles must be overcome to use them fully.
- There are several promising, but currently unproven, methods of producing and delivering energy that, if successfully developed and deployed, will greatly enhance our Nation's energy portfolio.
- Appropriate and limited government action can play a useful role in helping to realize our energy security goals.

Energy Sources

The drive for alternative energy is almost a return to our roots, because energy derived from wood biomass is perhaps the oldest source of energy. Two hundred years ago, wood supplied nearly all of our energy needs. It is only over the past two centuries that fossil fuels—fuels formed from the remains of plants and animals—began to dominate as our preferred energy source.

Coal began to be used as a fuel in the 1700s for a number of reasons, including the fact that it burned cleaner and hotter than wood charcoal. Its use spread to the United States during the Industrial Revolution in the early 19th Century, increased with the introduction of steamships and steam-powered railroads, and finally was used for electricity generation in the 1880s.

The market for natural gas developed from 'town gas,' synthesized from coal and used for street and house lighting during the 1800s, and in the 1820s the first well was dug to extract natural gas. In the 1890s, electricity began to replace natural gas for lighting purposes, but beginning in the 1940s, a continental-scale pipeline system evolved to distribute these reserves to urban areas for residential space and water heating, and ultimately for power generation.

The first U.S. oil well was drilled in 1859 in Western Pennsylvania, which spawned the domestic oil industry. After World War II, domestic oil production continued to rise, but failed to keep pace with accelerating consumption. The United States became a net importer of crude oil in 1950. The huge post-war expansion of petroleum consumption in Europe and the Far East was met from foreign sources, notably Iran and Saudi Arabia, while the United States itself became increasingly dependent on petroleum imports. U.S. oil production peaked in 1970, and since then declining domestic oil production and rising domestic consumption have increased petroleum imports. While there have been significant gains in energy efficiency, economic growth in the United States has led to large increases in aviation, trucking, and automobile transportation, and has resulted in increased oil consumption.

While fossil fuels have been the primary source of energy for over a century, alternative energy has been used throughout our history. The first electric car was constructed as early as the 1830s. Hydropower in the form of waterwheels for milling has been used throughout the world for centuries but dramatically increased in the United States in the 1800s with advancements in turbine technology. The first use of hydroelectric power occurred in 1880 at the Wolverine Chair Factory in Grand Rapids, Michigan, and the first U.S. commercial hydroelectric power plant opened in 1882 on the Fox River in Wisconsin. In 1888, the first large windmill was used to generate electricity in Cleveland, Ohio. In 1896, Henry Ford's first car was constructed to run on ethanol. The first commercially available solar water heaters were produced in California in the 1890s. The basis for nuclear power originated in 1942 when Enrico Fermi and other scientists created the first self-sustaining nuclear reactor at the University of Chicago, and the world's first full-scale commercial reactor opened in Cumberland, England in 1956. Today, we continue our search for alternative energy solutions in order to diversify our energy portfolio.

Fossil Fuels

Petroleum accounts for 40 percent of the Nation's total energy consumption (see Chart 7-1), the largest share of any fuel type, and produces almost 40 quadrillion Btu of energy. (A gallon of gasoline contains about 115,000 Btu, while a kilowatt-hour of electricity is equal to 3,413 Btu.) The United States consumes about 20.7 million barrels of petroleum per day, making us the largest oil consuming country in the world. In fact, the United States consumes about 25 percent of the 84.7 million barrels consumed each day worldwide, almost three times the amount of oil consumed by China, the second largest oil-consuming nation. However, China's oil consumption has grown at an average rate of 6.3 percent per year since 1982 compared to an average rate of 1.3 percent per year for the United States.

Chart 7-1 U.S. Energy Consumption and Production (2006)
Fossil fuels accounted for the majority of U.S. energy consumption and production in 2006.

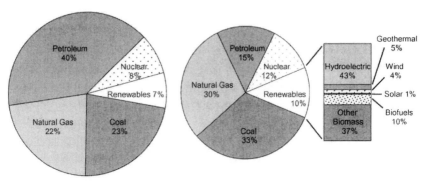

Total Consumption: 100 Quadrillion Btus   Total Production: 71 Quadrillion Btus

Source: Department of Energy (Energy Information Administration).

Chart 7-2 U.S. Energy Consumption by Source and Sector (2006)
The United States consumed 100 quadrillion Btu (quads) of energy in 2006.

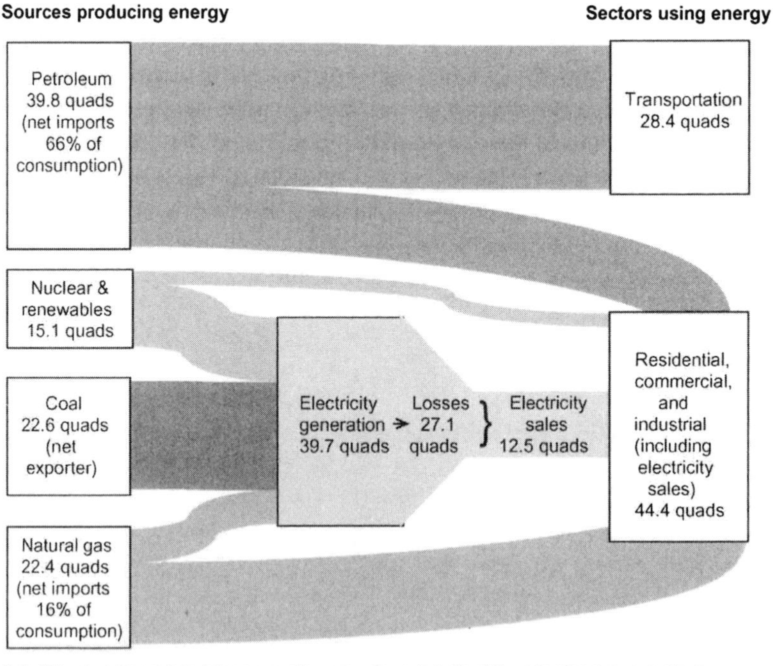

Sources producing energy   **Sectors using energy**

Petroleum
39.8 quads
(net imports
66% of
consumption)

Transportation
28.4 quads

Nuclear &
renewables
15.1 quads

Coal
22.6 quads
(net
exporter)

Electricity   Losses   Electricity
generation ➤ 27.1   sales
39.7 quads   quads   12.5 quads

Residential,
commercial,
and
industrial
(including
electricity
sales)
44.4 quads

Natural gas
22.4 quads
(net imports
16% of
consumption)

Note: This chart does not depict some smaller energy flows, including 2.1 quads of coal consumption by
residential, commercial, and industrial sources; 0.6 quads of petroleum consumption by the electricity-generation
sector; and 0.6 quads of natural gas and 0.5 quads of renewables consumption by the transportation sector.
Source: Department of Energy (Energy Information Administration).

Most of the oil consumed in the United States is used in the transportation sector, absorbing 69 percent of U.S. oil consumption in 2006. The rest is used by the residential, commercial, and industrial sectors, and for electricity generation (see Chart 7-2). The largest domestic sources of oil production are offshore wells in the Gulf of Mexico, and wells in Texas, Alaska, and California. Imported oil primarily comes from Canada, Mexico, Saudi Arabia, Venezuela, and Nigeria; and petroleum is the largest imported energy source for the United States. Because of this reliance on oil, changes in its price can affect the U.S. economy, and in 2008, the price of oil hit record levels (see Box 7-1).

Box 7-1: Oil Prices

In 2008, the nominal price for crude oil reached its highest level ever. This increase was due to several economic, geopolitical, and environmental factors such as growing world demand, limited supply growth, smaller inventories, security concerns in oil producing countries, and a decline in the value of the U.S. dollar.

Some fear that high oil prices reflect a peak in oil production and predict an imminent decline in production in the near future. This type of prediction often assumes static or growing consumption with limited additional discovery or production. As the price of oil rises, however, there is an economic incentive to find new sources or improve extraction techniques. Enhanced oil recovery (EOR) is one example of this type of response. EOR is any technique that can increase the amount of oil that can be recovered from an oil field, but it is most commonly associated with gas injection, particularly using CO_2, which forces the oil to the surface. The Department of Energy estimates that state-of-the-art EOR could potentially add an additional 89 billion barrels to the total recoverable oil resources of the United States, although not all of that is necessarily economically recoverable.

Even if production has peaked, we are unlikely to abruptly run out of oil. As the price rises over time, producers will have an incentive to retain some of the resource to sell at a later date and consumers will have an incentive to transition away from oil consumption. Over time, the price rise will make the adoption of alternative energy sources more and more likely.

The next largest fuel types are coal and natural gas, comprising 23 percent and 22 percent of consumption respectively. In 2006, coal production in the United States reached a record 1,161 million short tons (one short ton equals 2000 pounds), while consumption was 1,114 million short tons. This coal produced 23.8 quadrillion Btu of energy, the vast majority of which was used for electricity generation by the power sector. Coal continues to be a major fuel source for the United States largely due to its domestic abundance. The United States has 18,880 million short tons of recoverable coal reserves at producing mines and an estimated 263,781 million short tons of total recoverable reserves. Domestic coal production comes primarily from three geographical regions—Western, Interior, and Appalachian—and there is a small amount of both imported and exported coal.

In 2006, the United States consumed 21.9 trillion cubic feet (Tcf) of natural gas. By comparison, total world natural gas consumption was 105.5 Tcf, with the United States and Russia combined consuming 36 percent of the world total. U.S. natural gas consumption produced 22.4 quadrillion Btu of energy, with 69 percent used by residential, commercial, and industrial sources and 29 percent used for electricity generation. Domestic gas production comes mainly from the Gulf of Mexico and older-producing areas in Texas, Oklahoma, and Louisiana. Imports, which make up 16 percent of consumption, come mainly by pipeline from Canada.

The Need To Diversify

For more than a century, fossil fuels have satisfied the bulk of America's demand for energy. However, a move to alternative energy sources can hold a number of benefits.

One of the reasons for shifting away from fossil fuels is improved energy security. This term can have multiple meanings, but it is often applied to the desire to reduce the Nation's vulnerability to oil supply disruptions from political or terrorist actions or natural disaster. However, because there is a world market for oil and a world price, the price of oil rises in the case of a disruption no matter the source of supply, be it foreign or domestic. Thus, energy security in this context cannot be obtained by simply shifting from one supplier to another. It requires diversifying the fuels consumed in our energy portfolio, which reduces the amount by which a disruption in any one energy source can affect the economy. In this context, alternative energy technologies for both electricity production and for transportation can dampen the impact of sharply rising prices, and thus provides an energy security benefit.

A second major benefit of alternative energy is that some alternative energy sources have a lower environmental impact than traditional fossil fuels. At the point of generation, wind, nuclear, hydropower, and solar sources produce no local air pollution, such as sulfur dioxide (SO_2) and nitrogen oxides (NO_x).

Also, depending on the fuel and technology used, alternative energy can reduce CO_2 emissions. In 2006, the United States emitted approximately 5.9 billion metric tons of energy-related CO_2, almost 73 percent of which were generated by fossil fuel use for transportation and electricity generation. Approximately one-third of all energy-related CO_2 in the United States came from petroleum use in the transportation sector and 38 percent came from coal and natural gas used to generate electricity (see Chart 7-3). Appropriately chosen alternative energy sources in the transportation and electricity generation sectors may help reduce these emissions.

A third potential benefit of alternative energy is that some believe that it may eventually compete with or cost less than fossil fuels. It is worth noting, however, that reduced energy cost, whether achieved through improved energy efficiency or less expensive energy supply, will result in increased energy demand, a phenomenon known as the *rebound effect*. For example, the Department of Transportation sets mandatory Corporate Average Fuel Economy (CAFE) standards for passenger cars and light trucks. When fuel efficiency standards are raised, vehicles use less gasoline per mile; but, because

Chart 7-3 **U.S. CO_2 emissions from Energy Consumption (2006)**
The United States emitted 5.9 billion metric tons (Gt) of carbon dioxide from energy consumption in 2006.

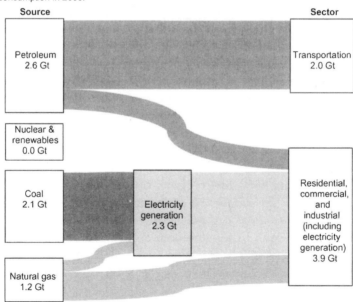

Note: This chart does not depict some smaller emissions flows, including 0.2 Gt of direct emissions from coal by residential, commercial, and industrial sources; 0.3 Gt of emissions from petroleum by the electricity-generation sector; 0.03 Gt of direct emissions from natural gas by the transportation sector; and emissions from non-fuel use.
Source: Department of Energy (Energy Information Administration).

the increased fuel efficiency reduces the cost of driving, people drive more. This leads to less gasoline savings than implied by the change in fuel efficiency. The economic literature puts the rebound effect between 10 percent and 20 percent, which means that a 10 percent improvement in fuel efficiency would actually only produce an 8 to 9 percent improvement in energy consumption.

Alternative Energy Production

While some of the electricity produced in the electric power sector is generated using alternative energy sources, the majority (71 percent) is generated from fossil fuels. In the transportation sector, almost all of the energy consumed comes from fossil fuels. Developing alternative energy sources in these two sectors could move us down the road to enhanced energy security and lower pollution.

Alternatives for Generating Electricity

In the United States, electricity is generated using a wide variety of energy sources, both traditional and alternative. One factor affecting which type of electricity plant will be built at any given time is economics: which energy source will produce the greatest economic return over the lifetime of the plant. However, it is difficult to compare plants that differ in both cost and generation capacity. One way to assess this economic return is to compare the *levelized cost of electricity* (LCOE)—the present value of the total cost of building and operating a generating plant over its financial life, converted into equal payments and amortized over the expected annual generation from the plant. Table 7-1 provides the estimated national average LCOE for various types of electricity generating plants entering service in 2015. The final column of Table 7-1 gives the national average total system LCOE, while the four columns prior to the last give the components that make up this total system cost.

Conventional coal-fired power plants have an average real LCOE of approximately $61 per megawatt hour produced, which is the lowest cost of all electricity generation methods presented. Natural-gas combined cycle plants have an average LCOE of between $65 and $68 per megawatt hour produced, and are closely competitive with coal-fired power plants. On an average LCOE basis, alternative energy based electricity generation is more expensive than both coal and natural gas-based plants, which partially explains their lack of penetration in the market.

The LCOE, however, is not the only consideration in choosing which type of plant to build. Because the demand for electric power varies by time of day and season and because electricity is difficult to store, plants may

TABLE 7-1. —*Estimated Average Levelized Costs*
(2006 $/megawatthour) for Plants Entering Service in 2015

Plant Type	Capacity Factor (%)	Levelized Capital Cost	Fixed Operations & Maintenance (O&M) Cost	Variable Operations & Maintenance Cost (including fuel)	Transmission Investment	Total System Levelized Cost
Fossil Fuel Based Electricity Generation............						
Coal-fired..................						
Conventional Coal.............................	85	$31.4	$3.6	$22.3	$3.6	$60.9
Advanced Coal...................................	85	36.9	5.1	18.4	3.5	63.9
Advanced Coal with CCS	85	52.0	6.0	22.3	3.5	83.8
Natural Gas-fired..................						
Conventional Combined Cycle	87	14.1	1.6	48.7	3.7	68.1
Advanced Combined Cycle.................	87	13.8	1.5	45.8	3.7	64.8
Conventional Combustion Turbine	30	25.7	4.5	72.5	10.8	113.4
Advanced Combustion Turbine	30	24.0	3.9	61.9	10.8	100.6
Alternative Energy Based Electricity Generation..						
Advanced Nuclear................................	90	50.7	8.4	8.2	2.5	69.7
Geothermal....................................	90	47.9	20.1	0.0	4.9	72.9
Biomass.......................................	83	48.3	8.6	18.9	4.0	79.8
Wind..	35	64.6	9.6	0.0	8.2	82.5
Solar Thermal.................................	31.2	122.8	20.7	0.0	10.5	154.0
Solar PV......................................	21.7	268.8	6.1	0.0	13.0	287.9
Conventional Hydropower...................	....	....	....	....	....	....

Source: Department of Energy (Energy Information Administration).

be designed to provide base load power (a constant supply of power), peak load power (when demand is the highest), or to serve as "merchant" plants, selling electricity in the commercial market when it is profitable to do so. The second column in Table 7-1 gives the average capacity factor, which is the ratio of the actual energy produced in a given period to the hypothetical maximum energy output of the plant. While natural gas combustion turbines have a lower capacity factor and a higher LCOE than other fossil fuel based plants, they are attractive as peak load or intermediate load (between base load and peak load) plants. Additionally, fuel prices vary regionally due to transportation costs and resources.

Other factors may also be important in determining what type of plant is built. For example, many states have renewable portfolio standards that require minimum additions to capacity from renewable electricity technologies and there may be tax incentives for alternative energy power generation. The values in Table 7-1 do not reflect these factors. Power producers may also consider environmental factors that could affect technology investment decisions. These considerations may depend on a regulatory environment that differs substantially in different regions of the country. Investors may be concerned that future policies could increase the cost of coal or make it more difficult to dispatch coal-fired power. Finally, LCOE estimates are subject to additional uncertainty not discussed here. For example, actual fuel prices may differ from those assumed for the LCOE estimates. The "best" power generation technology may vary throughout the country, but the LCOE gives some indication of the relative cost of various types of electricity generating plants.

Nuclear Power

There are currently 104 commercial nuclear power reactors in the United States, and they generate approximately 20 percent of the Nation's electricity. While the United States has the largest nuclear capacity of any nation, no new commercial reactor has been ordered and approved for construction since 1978, and all of the plants ordered after 1973 have been cancelled. The last plant to come online was the Watt's Bar reactor in Tennessee in 1996. Despite this, the total nuclear capacity per plant in the Nation has increased over time due to *uprating*, a process by which a plant is upgraded and then a more highly enriched fuel and/or a higher percentage of new fuel is used to generate more power. The Nuclear Regulatory Commission (NRC) has approved 114 power uprate proposals to date and is currently reviewing 13 additional uprate proposals, which would add an additional 1,220 megawatts of electric power. According to NRC, they could receive 24 additional applications for power uprates by 2012. However, there is a limit to our uprate potential, and more reactors will be needed if the United States chooses to get more of its electricity from nuclear power plants. To date, the NRC has received applications for 4 units and a partial application for a fifth unit, and expects to receive applications for as many as 32 units over the next three years. However, there is no requirement that a reactor be built for every license granted.

One advantage to nuclear power is that it has low operating cost, so the cost differential between limited output and full capacity is small. These plants operate at close to full capacity and provide a reliable *base load*, which is a constant supply of the electricity to power lines. Another advantage of nuclear power is that it can produce power using a relatively small amount of fuel without producing air pollutants or CO_2 emissions.

A few of the disadvantages to nuclear power include the length of time required to build a new plant, high capital costs, and the cost of liability insurance. In addition to these economic disadvantages, nuclear power faces a number of obstacles including social opposition to its use, partially due to fears generated from the partial meltdown of the core of the power plant at Three Mile Island in 1979 and the disaster at the Chernobyl nuclear power plant in Ukraine in 1986, as well as additional safety concerns. There is also concern about the current lack of long term storage for the radioactive waste generated that must be properly contained for centuries. In 2002, the President signed a resolution to allow for the storage of nuclear waste at Yucca Mountain in

Nevada. The facility is expected to begin accepting waste in 2017, although limits on funding the facility have in the past delayed the opening and may do so again in the future. Additionally, the Nuclear Waste Policy Act limits the amount of waste that can be stored at the facility to 63,000 metric tons of commercial spent nuclear fuel, and it is estimated that the commercial nuclear facilities currently operating in the United States will produce this much spent fuel before 2017. Unless the capacity at Yucca Mountain is increased by statute or a second site is opened, we will face challenges in storing the commercial spent nuclear fuel generated from nuclear plants.

One possible solution to the storage issue is nuclear recycling. Virtually all of today's nuclear power is generated in an "open fuel cycle" in which enriched uranium fuel is used once and then disposed of. However, only part of this fuel is actually consumed in the process and the residual still has potential energy. Spent nuclear fuel can be recycled to recover some of this remaining energy, and this is done in several nations. A second type of nuclear plant using an "advanced burner reactor" can be designed to consume the residual, producing a "closed fuel cycle" process. It is important, however, that any such recycling program be implemented in such a way so as not to produce weapons-grade nuclear material. This is the central goal of the Global Nuclear Energy Partnership (GNEP) announced by the President in the 2006 State of the Union Address.

Hydropower

Hydropower, which is used almost exclusively to generate commercial electricity, is the largest renewable energy source used by the electric power sector. In 2006, the United States consumed 2.9 quadrillion Btu of conventional hydroelectric power, about 42 percent of all renewable energy consumption. The State of Washington generates the most hydropower among all states, followed by California, Oregon, and New York. Hydropower works by powering turbines with either the force of the current or the fall of water from a reservoir or dam.

The advantage of hydropower is that it is a well-understood renewable power source that can supply both peak load demand, by reserving available water for high value periods, as well as base load demand. Hydroelectric plants do not produce air emissions and there are some positive externalities associated with them because the reservoirs and dams can provide irrigation benefits, recreational opportunities, and flood control. However, hydropower also produces negative ecological effects. Hydropower's largest disadvantages are its negative impact on the surrounding environment, low dissolved oxygen in the water, impacts on the fish and the riverbank habitat, and alteration of fish migration corridors (e.g. salmon runs). Even if the environmental concerns are removed, however, there is limited ability to expand hydropower beyond what is currently available. The total U.S. hydropower capacity, including pumped storage facilities, is about 98 gigawatts, and the Department of Energy estimates that there are only 30 gigawatts of undeveloped capacity remaining in the entire 50 states.

Biomass

Biomass is organic material from plants and animals, such as wood, crops, manure, and some garbage, and is second only to hydroelectric power in providing renewable electricity to the United States. Biomass, excluding biofuels, makes up about 2.5 percent of the Nation's total energy consumption and comprises almost 37 percent of the total renewable energy consumption in the country. Sixty-four percent of this biomass is used directly by the industrial sector to generate power. Only a small portion is used by the power sector to generate electricity.

The main advantage to biomass is that it is a renewable source of energy that can be used either as a dedicated fuel to generate electricity or can be co-fired with other fossil fuels. Compared with coal, biomass produces fewer CO_2, SO_2, and NO_x emissions. If biomass is grown specifically for electricity generation, in a closed loop system, then the only CO_2 emissions come from the harvesting, transportation, and processing operations.

The main disadvantage to electricity generation using biomass is that it currently has an average LCOE above generation using fossil fuels. This is due to a number of factors, including the cost of obtaining the raw material. Also, biomass energy consumption is technically not a zero-emission process.

Geothermal Power

Geothermal energy is contained in underground reservoirs of steam, hot water, and hot dry rocks. Large geothermal power plants use this energy to generate electricity by drilling below the earth's surface in order to release or produce steam, which is used to power turbine generators. After the steam condenses, the water can be injected back into the ground to be used again. Geothermal energy currently makes up about 5 percent of the total renewable production of the country, but it only supplies about 0.4 percent of the Nation's electricity. It is considered an attractive resource because it requires a relatively small plant footprint, requires no storage, has no fuel costs, and can provide continuous base load power. A study by the Government Accountability Office reports that there are at least 400 undeveloped wells and hot springs with potential for future electricity production.

Geothermal power, however, is limited in its ability to provide large amounts of electricity to the country. To be viable, geothermal power requires access to permeable rock systems filled with steam or water at temperatures from 300 to 700 degrees. Sites that meet these conditions are much more prevalent on the West Coast than in other parts of the country. Also, geothermal sites can produce some local pollutants and small amounts of CO_2.

Wind Power

Wind power supplies about 4 percent of our renewable energy and less than 1 percent of the Nation's electricity, a small percentage compared to large wind users such as Denmark, Spain, Portugal, and Germany. However, the use of wind power in the United States is on the rise, and appears to be poised for dramatic increases in the future. In 2006, wind capacity increased by 29 percent, and the United States has led the world in capacity additions in recent years. An estimated 4 gigawatts of wind capacity were added in 2007. This growth is due to the fact that, in some areas, wind is now cost competitive with other sources of energy production, largely because of a government tax credit of 1.9 cents for each kilowatt hour produced (not reflected in Table 7-1).

Wind power is desirable because it is a domestic source of power with no fuel costs or emissions. It has become increasingly popular for two reasons. First, the current generation of windmills produces more power from a given wind resource than past technologies. The amount of electricity generated from a windmill is determined by a number of factors including the turbine size and the capacity factor. The size of the turbine dictates the potential output of the windmill, and the average turbine size has approximately doubled since 2000 to about 1.6 megawatts. The windmill's capacity factor is its actual energy output divided by its potential output. The average capacity factor has shown substantial improvement and is now roughly 35 percent. Second, windmills are increasingly popular because they can be placed on farms, providing a source of lease income, without having a large impact on the surrounding farming activity.

The ability of wind power to grow as an alternative energy source is affected by a number of factors. First, the capacity factor is very sensitive to the average wind speed and it can drop dramatically for sites with less optimal wind profiles, meaning less electricity from each windmill. Second, to maximize the market potential, wind-generated electricity must be integrated with the overall power grid, the system of power lines and transformers that distribute electricity. When wind farms are located in rural areas, some electricity is lost during the transmission to homes and businesses. In addition, since wind energy is generated only when the wind blows and the electricity cannot be economically stored at this time, wind is an intermittent energy source. Finally, there is some public opposition to wind power. Because of the height of the turbine, wind plants produce a large visual footprint, and there is a potential effect on migratory bird and bat populations.

Solar Power

Solar power has captured the imagination of alternative energy advocates and lends itself to creative demonstration projects like the installation of solar panels on the roof of the West Wing of the White House. Solar power is attractive because its output closely aligns with peak electricity demand. The fact is, though, beyond some niche markets, solar power is not yet an economically competitive method of supplying large amounts of electricity. Solar power currently comprises 1 percent of the total renewable energy production and it produces a negligible amount of the Nation's electricity. This is largely because solar power has a levelized cost of electricity above other energy sources.

Solar power generation generally comes in two forms: photovoltaic and thermal. Photovoltaic generation involves the direct conversion of light energy into electricity through the use of semiconducting material like silicon. This technology already has some commercial success for low-power devices like calculators and emergency phones, but is a relatively expensive method of producing large amounts of electricity. At present, photovoltaic generation is generally used when grid connection is difficult or impossible, such as for satellites. However, progress has been made in reducing the cost and improving the efficiency of silicon-based photovoltaic cells as well as newer, thin-film technologies. Photovoltaics can be used for distributed electricity generation at homes and businesses, and may eventually serve as an alternative to bulk power provided by the electricity sector.

Solar thermal devices use direct heat from the sun, concentrating it in some manner to produce heat. Solar power plants focus heat in troughs, dishes, or large power towers to generate electricity, in what is called "concentrating solar power" (CSP) technology. If combined with thermal storage, CSP could reduce the problem of an intermittent power supply. However, currently, CSP plants are expensive. They also require a large amount of space and are considered aesthetically unappealing by some, and thus could be sited away from population centers. This means that there would be transmission losses in moving the electricity to population centers.

Summary of Alternatives for Generating Electricity

There are many alternative sources of energy for generating electricity. Some of them are more promising than others due to costs and other technological barriers. Nuclear power's LCOE is closest to coal and natural gas production and is currently best suited to produce large amounts of electricity without using fossil fuels, but it requires large and expensive plants and is often socially unpopular. Hydropower currently provides the majority of the Nation's renewable electricity production, but it is very limited in its ability to expand. Biomass, geothermal, and wind power are close to economically competitive with nuclear and fossil fuel production and have the potential for expanded use, provided that the constraints described above can be overcome. Finally, while solar power is currently an expensive way to produce large amounts of electricity, it could be an important source of alternative energy if costs can be reduced.

Alternatives for Transportation

Twenty-eight percent of the energy consumed by the United States is used for transportation: cars, trucks, planes, trains, and ships. Unlike the energy used to generate electricity (of which 31 percent is generated using non-fossil fuels), transportation relies almost entirely on petroleum-derived fuels. As with electricity generation, a great emphasis has been placed on finding alternative transportation fuel sources for both energy security and environmental reasons.

One solution is to find an alternative fuel to use in our cars and trucks. At present, corn-based ethanol is the largest alternative fuel source, but other fuels, like biodiesel, are also available. Our current vehicle fleet can burn a gasoline mixture containing up to 10 percent ethanol without any modification; flexible fuel vehicles are already being sold that can operate on 85 percent ethanol; and other alternative fuel vehicles, such as natural gas-powered vehicles, have long been used in niche markets. In addition, investments in second generation biofuels, like cellulosic technologies to convert non-food crop residues, grasses, and forest biomass, are on the rise.

Another alternative energy solution for transportation is to design a different type of car. Hybrid vehicles are part of the current car stock, but other advanced technologies are under development including hydrogen-powered vehicles and plug-in hybrids that would allow consumers to charge on-board batteries and achieve a limited range using electricity.

Corn-Based Ethanol

Ethanol is a fuel made from grains and biomass that can be used as a gasoline supplement for automobiles. By far, the most common raw material or *feedstock* used to produce ethanol in the United States is corn. Since 1978 major manufacturers of fuel tanks have provided the same warranties for use of both unblended gasoline and ethanol blends up to E10 (10 percent ethanol and 90 percent gasoline). Flex-fuel vehicles (FFVs) can use blends containing more than 10 percent ethanol, such as E85, and auto manufacturers can produce FFVs at only a small additional cost. In 2007, of a total 229 million light-duty cars and trucks on the road, an estimated 5.5 million were FFVs, and this portion will likely grow. It is estimated that by 2030, approximately 10 percent of the total U.S. car and truck sales will be FFVs. However, of approximately 170,000 fueling stations in the United States, only 1,183 offer E85, so flex-fuel vehicles have a harder time locating stations offering this fuel.

Ethanol has a number of advantages over oil. First, it is domestically produced, so its use decreases the impact from a disruption in the oil market.

Second, the production of ethanol releases less carbon monoxide emissions (but can increase other pollutants such as nitrogen oxides and non-exhaust volatile organic hydrocarbon) than gasoline use. Finally, depending on how it is produced, ethanol may reduce CO_2 emissions.

Since January 1999, annual ethanol production has increased more than 300 percent, from 1.5 billion gallons to an estimated 6.3 billion gallons in 2007. Including new and expanding plants, one industry group estimates that the United States may soon have the capacity to produce more than 13 billion gallons of ethanol annually. Four major factors have driven the dramatic growth in this market. First, high oil prices have increased the demand for an alternative fuel. While ethanol has one-third less energy content than gasoline, oil prices are high enough for ethanol to compete with gas on an energy-equivalent basis. However, as oil and ethanol prices move, so will the significance of this factor. Second, the elimination of MTBE—a gasoline additive used to produce cleaner fuel in cities with smog problems that was found to contaminate groundwater—has increased the demand for ethanol as a substitute oxygenating agent. Third, there are financial incentives for ethanol production. There is a 51-cent per gallon Federal tax credit for blending ethanol into gasoline (and an associated 54-cent per gallon tariff on imported ethanol) and additional subsidization in some states. Finally, the Energy Policy Act of 2005 mandated the use of 7.5 billion gallons of renewable fuel by 2012, much of which was expected to be met with ethanol. The recently passed Energy Independence and Security Act of 2007 increases this mandate to 36 billion gallons of renewable fuel by 2022, which will likely increase the demand for ethanol.

There are a number of concerns about ethanol. First, some worry that production will outstrip the capacity to blend ethanol into the gasoline supply. (See Box 7-2) Second, the current oil pipeline infrastructure is not capable of transporting ethanol, so it must be shipped by truck, train, and barge. To remain cost competitive, ethanol plants are generally located within 50 miles of where the corn is grown. Ninety percent of the productive capacity is in eight Midwestern States while 80 percent of the U.S. population (and thus, the ethanol demand) lives along the coastline. Rail transport capacity from the Midwest to the coasts is limited, and dedicated ethanol barges (to move ethanol from the Midwest to the Gulf Coast) will take time and money to construct. Third, there are environmental concerns about ethanol production depleting groundwater aquifers and water pollution from fertilizers used to grow crops for biofuels. Finally, there are fiscal concerns, particularly the cost of the 51-cent per gallon blender's credit.

The growing demand for corn-based ethanol as fuel is affecting the overall corn market. Most of the adjustment will take place over the next couple of years, as corn-based ethanol production responds to market signals. Over time, other markets will adjust to higher corn demand, and ethanol substitutes will come online. The Department of Agriculture estimates that acres of planted corn increased to 93.6 million in marketing year 2007/08 and corn production increased to 13.1 billion bushels, an increase of almost 24 percent from marketing year 2006/07. Corn prices are also projected to rise to as much as $3.75 per bushel by 2009/2010 before stabilizing, and the U.S. share of global corn trade is projected to fall to less than 60 percent.

Increased production of ethanol will also affect other crops, particularly soybeans because it competes with corn for cropland. Land devoted to soybeans is expected to decrease from 71 million acres now to 69 million acres by 2009/2010, and the price of soybeans is expected to rise from $5.66 per bushel in 2005 to $7.30 by 2009/2010 before stabilizing. Livestock production will also face higher costs as grain prices rise and the price of its final product (meat, eggs, and milk) will follow. Corn farmers will obtain higher

---

Box 7-2: The Blend Wall

In the United States, nearly all of the ethanol produced is blended into E10 fuel. In 2005, nearly 4 billion gallons of ethanol were blended into 137 billion gallons of gasoline. By 2007, ethanol production is estimated to have grown to 6.3 billion gallons, and the total capacity could eventually reach 13 billion gallons per year. Some worry that production will ultimately outstrip the capacity to blend ethanol into E10. (By definition, ethanol cannot exceed 10 percent of the gasoline pool if it is blended exclusively into E10.) This limit to the use of ethanol (basically, where ethanol supply exceeds demand) is referred to as a "blend wall."

There are a number of reasons why the blend wall is unlikely to pose a significant problem. The United States consumes around 140 billion gallons of gasoline per year, meaning that almost 14 billion gallons of ethanol can be used for E10 alone. In addition, if all existing FFVs used E85, they would consume an additional 3.5 billion gallons of ethanol. Therefore, the total potential demand for ethanol blending is currently around 17.5 billion gallons, and this amount will grow as more FFVs are produced. Even extrapolating the rapid growth in ethanol production, potential demand is well above the production capacity. As the supply of ethanol grows (reducing the price of ethanol) or as the price of oil rises, ethanol looks increasingly attractive compared to oil, and more trucks and rail cars will be devoted to distribution and more E85 pumps will be installed in order to capture the profits of an economically valuable commodity.

prices for their products, but livestock producers will face higher production costs; and government counter-cyclical payments and market loans will likely decrease due to higher commodity prices. On net, however, it is likely farm incomes will rise as consumer prices rise.

Cellulosic Ethanol

Cellulosic ethanol is similar to corn-based ethanol, but it can be produced from a variety of biomass feedstocks such as agricultural plant wastes, industrial plant wastes (such as sawdust and wood pulp), and crops grown specifically for fuel production (such as switchgrass). Because cellulosic ethanol can come from a variety of raw materials, it can be produced in nearly every region of the country and has the potential to supply more fuel per acre than corn. Cellulosic ethanol production also produces less greenhouse gas (CO_2, methane, and nitrous oxide) emissions than either gasoline or corn-based ethanol.

While clearly desirable from both an energy security and an environmental perspective, cellulosic ethanol is not yet commercially available because the conversion technology is only in its introductory stages and is expensive. There are currently no commercial cellulosic ethanol refineries in operation in the United States, but the Department of Energy has announced that it will invest $385 million over the next four years in a cost-sharing program with private companies to fund six biorefinery projects located in California, Georgia, Florida, Kansas, Idaho, and Iowa. By 2012, these refineries are expected to produce 130 million gallons of cellulosic ethanol each year at less than $2 a gallon.

Biodiesel

Biodiesel is a renewable fuel that can be made by chemically combining natural oils and fats with an alcohol. It can be used by vehicles that use diesel fuel, and it is typically blended with petroleum diesel at levels up to 20 percent. Most U.S. biodiesel is made from either soybeans or yellow grease from restaurant cooking oil. Like ethanol, biodiesel is a domestically produced fuel and, depending on how it is produced, its use generates about two-thirds less greenhouse gas emissions than petroleum-based diesel. At present, however, it is economically viable only because of a $1 per gallon tax credit for blending biodiesel from virgin oil (oil in its first-use) and a $0.50 per gallon credit for blending with recycled oil.

Alternative Vehicles

An alternative to developing new fuels is to develop a different type of car that uses less gasoline. Two such vehicles currently exist. Conventional hybrid vehicles combine the internal combustion engine of a standard vehicle with the battery and electric motor of an electric vehicle. This gives them the power, range, and convenient fueling of conventional vehicles, but lower emissions and better gas mileage. Hybrid passenger cars first became available in the United States in 2000 and have gained an increasing share of the U.S. car market, growing to 2.1 percent of the U.S. car sales in 2007. Part of this is due to a tax credit introduced in 2006 for purchasing a hybrid vehicle. This credit of up to $3,400 varies by model and is based on both the lifetime fuel savings and the fuel efficiency of the car measured against a 2002 baseline. However, in order to limit cost to the taxpayer while providing incentive to multiple automakers, this tax credit is phased out for each car manufacturer once it has sold over 60,000 eligible vehicles. A number of manufacturers have already reached this limit.

A second type of alternative vehicle is one powered by natural gas. Though major auto makers sell natural gas-powered cars in Europe, Asia, and South America, they have not sold well in the United States. There are about 150,000 natural gas vehicles in the United States (compared to 5 million worldwide), most of which belong to corporate or government fleets. The low demand for these vehicles is due, in part, to a shorter driving range, smaller trunks due to larger fuel tanks, and a lack of retail stations selling natural gas. However, increased use of natural gas-powered vehicles could both provide both greater fuel diversity and lower CO_2 emissions.

Plug-in Hybrids

Plug-in hybrid cars are a different type of vehicle that has the potential to both improve energy security and decrease pollution. Unlike conventional hybrids, which only recharge the electric battery through braking recovery, a plug-in hybrid is also charged with electricity delivered to the home or business. As a consequence, the vehicle can displace gasoline consumption with electricity that it draws from the grid. Some models under development would run on electricity for about 40 miles. Since 50 percent of personal automobiles travel 20 miles or less daily, plug-in hybrids may consume substantially less gasoline than a conventional hybrid. A recent study suggests that if plug-in hybrids were to be widely adopted and powered with low-carbon generated electricity, they could mitigate a large portion of the Nation's CO_2 emissions from transportation.

The major hurdle to the commercialization of the plug-in hybrid vehicle is the battery. Technology barriers include the battery cost, size and weight, power density, durability, reliability, and safety. With continued improvements, however, plug-in hybrids could eventually become commercially feasible.

Hydrogen-Based Fuel Cell Vehicles

Hydrogen can be used as a fuel with its chemical energy converted to electricity in a fuel cell. Pressurized hydrogen gas is forced through a catalyst and is split into positively charged hydrogen ions and electrons. The hydrogen ions are combined with oxygen to form water and the electrons are used to generate electricity.

There are many possible uses of fuel cells, including primary electricity generation from stationary fuel cells, as well as hydrogen-based fuel cell vehicles. In a fuel cell vehicle, a series of fuel cells generate electricity to power the car's electric motor, and there is no exhaust other than water vapor. Since hydrogen can be produced domestically, fuel cells could provide domestically-fueled vehicles that produce no CO_2 or other harmful emissions from the tailpipe.

While hydrogen has great potential as an alternative fuel, it does face some limitations. Currently, it is more expensive than other energy sources. Production, storage, and delivery are the largest cost categories associated with hydrogen-based energy. Hydrogen can be produced in small quantities where it is needed, such as at a vehicle refueling station, but the production cost can be high. In contrast, larger, centralized facilities can produce hydrogen at a lower cost, but the delivery costs are high. Additionally, the full infrastructure has not been built to accommodate hydrogen fuel, and there are safety concerns with hydrogen pipelines and dispensing systems.

Summary of Alternatives for Transportation

While the United States currently blends corn-based ethanol, the transportation sector still depends on petroleum as its primary energy source. Changes to either the fuel we use or the vehicles themselves will be necessary if we are to substantially reduce this dependency. On the fuel side, we can reduce our reliance on oil by developing alternative fuel like cellulosic ethanol and biodiesel. On the vehicle side, we can develop vehicles that simply do not require gasoline, such as plug-in hybrids or hydrogen-fueled vehicles. Done carefully, these measures will not only enhance energy security but could also reduce CO_2 emissions.

The Road Forward

What we do over the next few years will dictate how quickly we can move away from fossil fuel consumption. The Energy Information Administration projects that, absent any additional action, primary energy consumption in the United States will increase 24 percent to 123.8 quadrillion Btu by 2030, an average annual increase of 0.9 percent per year. Total consumption of coal is projected to grow from 1,114 short tons in 2006 to 1,682 short tons in 2030. Natural gas is expected to increase from 21.8 trillion cubic feet in 2006 to 23.4 trillion cubic feet in 2030. Total consumption of liquid fuels and other petroleum products is projected to grow from 20.7 million barrels per day in 2006 to 24.9 million barrels per day in 2030. Total electricity sales are projected to grow from 3,821 billion kilowatt hours in 2006 to 5,149 billion kilowatt hours in 2030, an average annual increase of 1.3 percent.

Some alternative energy will enter the market as a result of market prices, and as the market fluctuates there will be additional economic incentives to diversify our energy portfolio. If research and development leads to lower renewable energy prices, then sources such as wind power and geothermal energy may eventually become fully cost competitive. Fuel efficiency is expected to increase not only as a result of an increase in the Corporate Average Fuel Economy standards, but also due to price-driven consumer demand and the introduction of more advanced vehicles into the market. Combined total consumption of marketed renewable fuels (including ethanol for gasoline blending) is projected to grow from 6.8 quadrillion Btu in 2006 to 11.5 quadrillion Btu in 2030, with ethanol consumption growing especially rapidly. However, for alternative energy to dramatically penetrate the market, technological and other hurdles must be overcome.

Policy Tools

There are a number of policy tools available to any administration interested in promoting alternative energy and enhancing energy security. The traditional approach is to use research and development grants to subsidize the development of new technologies that are then adopted by the private sector. An alternative is to establish a mandate, through legislation or regulation, and require the private sector to meet it. While both approaches may be useful for advancing the adoption of alternative energy, some worry that these approaches dictate which technology must be adopted. Also, while mandates do not involve direct government expenditure, they are not free. Consumers may have to pay higher prices for some alternative energy in order for the United States to receive the energy security and environmental benefits.

Another approach is to try to overcome the cost gap between conventional and more expensive alternative sources. This can be done through either tax credits or subsidies equal to the cost differential between the two technologies. In either case, there is a public cost either directly through the subsidy or indirectly through the revenue loss on allowed credits. Loan guarantees are another possible tool that can encourage investment by shifting risk to the government, but at the price of some moral hazard: if the government assumes too much of the financial risk, investors may take on highly speculative projects that have little hope of success, shifting the cost onto the Federal taxpayers.

Market-based mechanisms such as cap-and-trade and Pigovian taxes are another possible way to encourage the switch to alternative energy, provided that these programs are workable and can meet the desired objective. Cap-and-trade programs dictate the total permissible emissions or total input desired (the cap) and allow companies to trade the right to make those emissions or produce those quantities (the trade). Trading assures that the desired outcome will be achieved at the lowest cost. For example, the Renewable Fuels Standard (RFS) set in 2005 required that 7.5 billion gallons of gasoline be replaced with renewable fuel by 2012. Obligated parties were to demonstrate compliance with the program by acquiring credits (called renewable identification numbers (*RINs*)) representing the amount of renewable fuel blended into conventional gasoline or used in its neat (unblended) form. Under the trading program, however, obligated parties could purchase these credits from other obligated parties rather than acquire them themselves.

An alternative approach is to set a fixed fee (sometimes called a *Pigovian tax*) for each unit of the traded good. This is theoretically equivalent to a cap-and-trade program when the costs and benefits of the program are known. A hybrid approach is a cap-and-trade program with a *safety valve,* in which the trading of credits occurs normally, but obligated parties can choose to pay a fee (the safety valve) to demonstrate compliance rather than trading. In 2007, the President proposed that the 2005 RFS be increased to 35 billion by 2017, but proposed an automatic safety valve to protect against unforeseen increases in the prices of alternative fuels or their feedstock.

One final policy tool that has shown occasional promise is the use of inducement prizes. When a specific goal is known, the government may choose to award a prize for successfully reaching this goal as a way to spur technological innovation. For example, the government could offer a prize for overcoming the technical barriers associated with the commercialization of hydrogen and fuel cells. Prizes are desirable because they focus on rewarding the actual achievement of the goal using whatever technology gets to the solution first, whereas subsidies, grants, and contracts might only be dispersed to existing technology.

Current Efforts

Diversifying our energy sources and fuels will not come quickly or cheaply and may require incentives for some of the alternative energy options discussed in this chapter. Over the past several years, there have been a number of successful programs promoting alternative energy. In 2006, the President announced his Advanced Energy Initiative, which called for a 22 percent increase in funding for clean-energy research and a significant reduction in our oil imports over time.

To help meet the growing demand for base load electricity generation, there are a number of programs aimed at expanding nuclear energy. The Nuclear Power 2010 program is a joint government and industry effort to develop advanced nuclear plant technology and reduce the technical, regulatory and institutional barriers to the deployment of new nuclear power plants. The United States is also part of two broad international efforts related to the development of nuclear power. The Generation IV International Forum is a cooperative effort to develop competitively priced nuclear energy systems that address nuclear safety, waste, proliferation, and public perception concerns. The goal is to have these systems available for international deployment by 2030. The Global Nuclear Energy Partnership is a group of nineteen countries that seek to expand the use of nuclear energy for peaceful purposes through a proliferation-resistant closed nuclear fuel cycle. Under this program, nations with secure, advanced nuclear capabilities would provide fresh fuel and reprocessing services to other nations who agree to employ nuclear energy for power generation purposes only.

Other efforts are aimed at improving electricity generation from renewable sources. The Department of Energy's Wind Energy Program is focused on the development of technology to make wind power cost-competitive in various areas of the country and to help reduce the barriers to electric grid interconnections. The goal of the Solar America Initiative is to make solar energy cost-competitive with conventional forms of electricity by 2015.

Finally, the recently passed Energy Independence and Security Act of 2007 takes a significant step in the direction of implementing the President's Twenty in Ten plan, which was aimed at reducing domestic gasoline consumption by 20 percent in 10 years. Under this Act, mandatory fuel standards require the production of 36 billion gallons of renewable and alternative fuels by 2022. Also, the Corporate Average Fuel Economy standards will be raised to 35 miles per gallon by 2020, a 40 percent increase from the present level. Because fuel economy standards reduce oil consumption directly (including the rebound effect) and renewable fuels are produced domestically and may generate less CO_2 than oil, both of these measures produce energy security and environmental benefits.

Conclusion

Both energy security and environmental concerns motivate the consideration of policies that move toward alternative energy sources. Currently, 85 percent of our energy consumption comes from fossil fuels, and energy consumption is projected to increase 24 percent by 2030. This means that the incentive to find alternative energy solutions is growing.

Fortunately, some solutions exist. With regard to electricity generation, nuclear power is close to cost competitive and could contribute a larger share to our Nation's energy portfolio. Even though there are some constraints on their use, we should utilize our biomass, geothermal, and wind energy potential where it is economically viable. On the horizon, technological advances and cost reductions might bring in solar power. With regard to transportation, corn-based ethanol and other alternatives already reduce our gasoline consumption. The introduction of cellulosic ethanol in the next few years could reduce it further. In the longer term, introducing new vehicles like plug-in hybrids and hydrogen-based fuel cell cars could dramatically reduce our oil consumption. While none of these solutions can resolve fully our energy security and environmental concerns, together, they provide a potential portfolio of solutions to our search for alternative energy.

CHAPTER 8

Improving Economic Statistics

Statistical systems have substantial value for both public policymakers and private decisionmakers. Administration and Congressional policymakers rely on statistics for budget decisions and related fiscal policy choices, and the Federal Reserve System relies on statistics for formulating sound monetary policy. Private firms combine internal company data with publicly provided statistics to make sales projections and investment decisions. In addition, contracts often use price or wage indexes to adjust payments for inflation.

Statistical systems, like physical infrastructure, become obsolete or depreciate with time. In a dynamic market-based economy, like that of the United States, new industries emerge, old industries contract, and firms find new ways of organizing and conducting their activities. The challenge for those who manage statistical systems is to keep pace with changes in the economy by continually evaluating the relevance and reliability of the statistics that are produced. In addition, it is important to maintain the continuity of statistical time series to facilitate meaningful historical comparisons. Up-to-date, relevant statistics are critical to the public policy process: they help frame policy debates by providing a sense of the size and scope of an issue, as well as the likely benefits and costs associated with a given policy action.

Advisory committees and researchers drawn from other parts of the government and academia help statistical agencies maintain the high quality of the data they collect and publish. They provide advice and engage in academic-style research that ensures that collected data are useful and relevant to issues people care about. Their work also enhances future data products by suggesting ways to improve the statistical system.

The statistical community in government, business, and academia recognizes that statistical agencies can improve the quality, usefulness, and efficiency of their statistical operations through cross-agency sharing of selected business data. Such interagency data sharing facilitates the synchronization of data across agencies, which in turn improves the comparability of different datasets and makes the statistical products of all agencies more valuable. For example, a measure of industry input (such as labor hours) often comes from one agency, while a measure of industry output comes from another agency. If each agency classifies a given firm as belonging to a different industry, then the productivity (output per input) of both industries may be mismeasured. By sharing classification data, agencies can reconcile these differences to ensure that the firm is classified in a consistent manner. In addition to improving the accuracy of government statistics, data synchronization may reduce the reporting burden on survey respondents, thereby improving the efficiency of the Federal statistical system.

The key points in this chapter are:

- Robust statistical systems produce products that are important to understanding the changing state of the economy and to formulating sound policy. But statistical systems, like physical infrastructures, become obsolete or depreciate with time if they are not maintained.
- Statistical measures must keep up with the changing nature of the economy to be relevant and useful. For example, it is important that these measures reflect new and growing industries (such as high-technology industries or services) and intangible capital (such as research and development).
- Disruptions in a statistical series render it much less useful to policy-makers and other data users. Thus, continuity in statistical series is an important goal.
- More effective statistical use can be made of existing data. In particular, amending relevant legislation to enable full implementation of the Confidential Information Protection and Statistical Efficiency Act (CIPSEA) could greatly improve the quality of Federal statistics.

An Overview of the U.S. Statistical System

The U.S. statistical system comprises many organizations inside and outside the U.S. government that produce statistics. Of particular interest in this chapter are Federal statistical agencies (whose principal function is to collect, compile, analyze, and disseminate statistics) and associated organizations, such as the Federal Reserve Board, that produce economic data to inform policy decisions. As of 2007, these organizations produced 38 statistical releases designated as "principal Federal economic indicators." These indicators include everything from agricultural prices to new home sales, the unemployment rate, and gross domestic product (GDP).

Among the Federal statistical agencies, the largest is the Department of Commerce's Census Bureau, which accounted for 39 percent of spending by principal statistical agencies in fiscal year 2007, as shown in Chart 8-1. Spending on statistics by the Federal Reserve and many regulatory and program agencies, as well as by nongovernmental organizations, is excluded from this calculation. The Census Bureau's spending expands even more during years leading up to the Decennial Census. Although the Decennial Census receives a great deal of attention, the Census Bureau conducts numerous other surveys much more frequently.

The Census Bureau accounts for the largest share of Federal statistical spending.

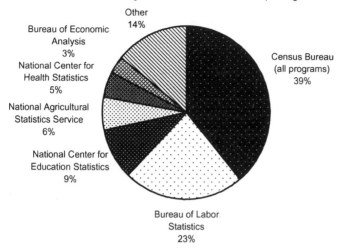

Note: Total does not add up to 100 percent due to rounding error. "Other" includes Department of Agriculture (Economic Research Service), Department of Energy (Energy Information Administration), Department of Justice (Bureau of Justice Statistics), Internal Revenue Service (Statistics of Income Division), National Science Foundation (Science Resources Statistics Division), Department of Transportation (Bureau of Transportation Statistics), and Social Security Administration (Office of Research, Evaluation, and Statistics).
Source: Office of Management and Budget.

The second largest Federal statistical agency, at 23 percent of spending, is the Department of Labor's Bureau of Labor Statistics (BLS), which produces, on a monthly and quarterly basis, the vast majority of U.S. data on employment and prices that are used to provide timely assessments of the current state of the economy. A combined 20 percent of spending is accounted for by the agencies responsible for preparing statistics on education, agriculture, and health.

The Department of Commerce's Bureau of Economic Analysis (BEA) is a relatively small statistical agency, with just 3 percent of spending. Its data products rely substantially on input data collected by other agencies and include the National Income and Product Accounts, which are among the most comprehensive measures of the size and current performance of the U.S. economy. Construction of the national accounts (which includes GDP) makes the BEA a consumer of vast amounts of data from the Census Bureau (such as import and export data) and the BLS (such as wage and salary data), as well as many other public and private sources.

Statistical data may be collected on a regular basis (monthly, quarterly, or annually) or on a relatively infrequent basis (every 5 or 10 years, for example). Chart 8-2 shows the pattern of real spending by several statistical agencies on economic statistics that are produced at least once per year. Examples include the monthly employment report from the BLS; monthly data on durable goods orders and new home sales, quarterly data on services, and official annual estimates of income and poverty from the Census Bureau; and quarterly GDP from the BEA. Chart 8-3 shows the pattern of real spending for several Census Bureau programs that are produced on an infrequent basis (the Decennial Census or the 5-year Economic Census and Census of Governments). In both charts, expenditures on these programs were adjusted for inflation with the Office of Management and Budget's deflator for "all other" Federal outlays (primarily salaries and expenses for nondefense agencies). As shown in Chart 8-2, spending on economic statistics has largely kept up with inflation. Real spending by the BLS has decreased slightly since 2004, after a period of steady growth that began in 1997. The three statistical agencies in Chart 8-2 account for about 50 percent of the total spending on economic statistics (excluding the Decennial Census and periodic spending by the Census Bureau). Total spending on economic statistics by other agencies has remained level.

Chart 8-2 **Real Federal Appropriations for Economic Statistics**
Real spending on economic statistics has been fairly flat in recent years.

Millions of 2007 dollars

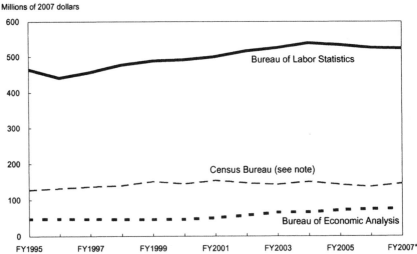

Note: *Figures for fiscal year 2007 are estimated. Census Bureau spending excludes spending on the Decennial Census, Economic Census, and Census of Governments. Bureau of Labor Statistics spending adjusted for the transfer of several large programs from the Employment and Training Administration in 2001.
Sources: Office of Management and Budget and Department of Commerce (Census Bureau, Budget Division).

As shown in Chart 8-3, spending on programs with a 5- or 10-year production cycle exhibits a clear pattern: spending climbs in preparation for the survey during the years immediately preceding the survey, peaks during the year of the survey, and then falls quickly upon completion. For example, real spending (in 2007 dollars) on the Decennial Census, which measures the size of the U.S. population, rose from about $110 million in 1997 to over $5.3 billion in 2000, before quickly falling back. The slight upward trend in decennial funding in the last several years was partly for the development of the American Community Survey, discussed later in this chapter. The 5-year budget cycle of the Economic Census, which measures output and related statistics in the business sector, is also apparent, though the year-to-year changes in spending are considerably smaller. The Census of Governments—which collects data on government organizations, finances, and employment—also picks up every 5 years, but the annual level of spending on this program is relatively small (less than $10 million), so the variations are less noticeable.

Chart 8-3 **Federal Statistical Appropriations for 5- and 10- Year Censuses**
The Decennial Census occurs every 10 years; the Economic Census and the Census of Governments occur every 5 years.

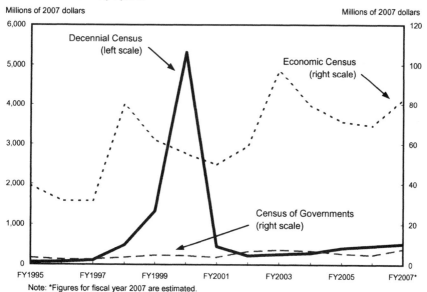

Note: *Figures for fiscal year 2007 are estimated.
Sources: Office of Management and Budget and Department of Commerce (Census Bureau, Budget Division).

Unlike the 5- and 10-year censuses, which are fairly well understood, funding requests for other statistical initiatives, such as new products or needed updates to existing programs, are easily misunderstood. For example, a major redesign of an existing survey's methodology ideally involves running two surveys concurrently (one with the old methodology and one with the new methodology) for a brief period of time so that the effect of the change in methodology can be isolated. Understanding this effect is essential if results from the redesigned survey are to be meaningfully compared to those of the survey being replaced.

The Importance of Statistical Systems

Providing accurate information to households, firms, and policymakers is an important role of government statistical agencies. Most decisionmakers in private industry, in Federal, State, and local governments, and in private households, rely in some way on data collected by Federal agencies. Federal economic statistics are designed to be consistent, unbiased, and reliable over time. These statistics can prove particularly useful if their availability and analysis allow a costly problem to be prevented or remedied more quickly and efficiently.

Private decisionmakers benefit from high-quality statistical systems because they improve the value of the information upon which firms and individuals base their decisions. For example, in formulating investment decisions, industries may use data on final demand or on the output of other industries that buy their output. A firm may examine a variety of labor market data, such as wage rates and educational attainment in the region, when deciding where to open new branches of the company. Airport authorities may study regional economic prospects when considering expansion decisions. Worker organizations and employers may track inflation trends and factor these price changes into their expectations for nominal wage gains. Popular press accounts based on occupational earnings may help students choose colleges, fields of study, or other training that will have long-term implications for their career paths.

State and local governments rely on a wide variety of statistical data to benchmark their performance, to plan for the future, and to readjust their allocation of resources. For example, a State that finds its high school dropout rate rising relative to other States may opt to devote more resources to education. Likewise, a city that finds its crime rate rising relative to other localities may choose to devote more resources to law enforcement. States and cities may study data on local population growth to assess the need for new transportation systems, schools, and other types of physical infrastructure.

Monetary and fiscal policymakers also rely on high-quality, publicly available data for understanding the changing state of the economy, for formulating sound policy on a wide range of macro- and microeconomic issues, and for economic forecasting. For example, monetary policy depends on accurate measures of resource utilization, current employment and unemployment trends, productivity trends, inflation trends (including unit labor costs), and housing market developments. If inflation estimates are overstated, monetary policy might be unnecessarily restrictive. Similarly, if productivity is overstated, policymakers may think that the economy's productive capacity is expanding quickly enough to accommodate rising output without being inflationary, and the resulting monetary policy may not be restrictive enough to limit the risk of inflation. Fiscal policy depends on accurate measures of GDP growth, potential GDP growth, labor markets, and demographic change to forecast future government outlays and revenues. If productivity is growing more slowly than believed, then revenue projections may be too high, and as a result, policymakers may adopt spending plans that are inconsistent with overall budget goals. Thus, a clear understanding of the true trends in these variables is critical to making sound budget projections.

Keeping Up with a Changing Economy

There are many ongoing efforts to update the statistical infrastructure to better reflect the changing economy and to more accurately reflect the economy as it stands now. These efforts include maintaining the relevance of statistical classification systems, better measuring the changing population, improving the measurement of the service-sector output, and measuring the contribution of investment in intangible assets (such as research and development) to economic growth.

Statistical systems rely heavily on the classification of activities, and over time classification structures are changed to better reflect the economy. Sometimes the changes are incremental, such as when an industry is split into two more detailed industries. Other changes are more substantial, such as the transition from the Standard Industrial Classification (SIC) system to the North American Industry Classification System (NAICS). Despite the benefits of NAICS—such as better coverage of advanced technology industries, as well as better international comparability—the transition was nonetheless disruptive to statistical agencies and data users. In particular, the transition to NAICS broke the historical continuity of many data series. Further, the official use of NAICS began in 1997 but not all data series incorporated NAICS classification in the same year. Statistical agencies have extended many of their statistics backward in time on a NAICS basis, but doing so is difficult and time-consuming. There is sometimes inadequate information to cleanly separate SIC-reported industry data into the redefined industries and the greater industry detail under NAICS. Many statistics produced by the BEA and BLS, for example, have been extended back to 1992 or 1990, respectively, and a few series go back further. The Federal Reserve Board extended its industrial production and capacity utilization statistics back to 1972 based on the results of an extensive microdata reclassification research project that was conducted with the Census Bureau's Center for Economic Studies. Despite the improvements that came with NAICS, it can be argued that the classification system has yet to fully capture the character of modern economies. For example, the shift over time from manufacturing to services is still not fully reflected in the level of detail collected, or even in the number of defined industries: The 2007 NAICS recognized nearly 17 percent more private service industries than manufacturing industries (550 versus 472), even though the gross output of private services was about 3 times larger than that of manufacturing in 2005.

The Census Bureau recently introduced the American Community Survey (ACS) to provide more current data on our Nation's population and its characteristics. With a sample size of approximately 3 million addresses, the ACS collects important demographic, housing, social, and economic information for use in the administration of Federal programs and the distribution of Federal spending. The ACS is the Nation's largest household survey and will eliminate the need for the Decennial Census long form in future censuses by providing data for the same detailed geographic locations as the long form. Unlike the long form, however, it will provide single-year estimates for geographic areas with populations of 65,000 or more annually, rather than estimates every 10 years. Smaller geographic areas will be sampled over 3- and 5-year intervals, allowing the Census Bureau to produce estimates down to the census tract or block group. For policymakers who need to make decisions affecting the lives of large numbers of people, having up-to-date estimates of population characteristics is critical to understanding a program's likely beneficiaries and its likely costs.

Another recent improvement to the Federal statistical system has been more accurate and timely measurement of service-sector output. In 2004, the Census Bureau introduced the new Quarterly Services Survey (QSS), the first new principal Federal economic indicator in nearly 30 years. Prior to the introduction of this survey, the 13 private service sectors—which together account for about 55 percent of GDP—were measured, at most, once per year, if covered by the Service Annual Survey. Even at the annual frequency, the available surveys account for just 30 percent of GDP. The only comprehensive measures of service-sector output come every 5 years during the Economic Census. Therefore, the QSS is important because it measures service-sector output much more frequently, which keeps the measures of service-sector activity in the National Income and Product Accounts more current. Even so, the QSS covers a limited portion of the service sector, which means there is room for improvement by broadening the coverage of the survey.

Efforts aimed at understanding the contribution to economic growth of investment in intangible assets, such as spending on research and development (R&D), is another example of the work being done to make statistics better reflect the state of the economy. The BEA, with the support of the National Science Foundation, created a R&D satellite account of the U.S. national accounts, which treats R&D as an investment rather than an expense. Accounting for R&D in this fashion would have boosted the average annual change in real GDP from 1995 to 2004 by nearly one-quarter percentage point, to 3.3 percent. The BLS has created statistical measures of business employment dynamics that help explain the contributions to net changes in employment that come from job losses versus job gains. As the length of the time series increases, these employment measures will be useful for understanding changes in employment over the business cycle. For example, a policy response to a decrease in net employment that results from an increase in gross job losses (i.e., greater layoffs or voluntary separations) may be different from one that results from a decrease in gross job gains (i.e., weaker hiring). The former might reflect transitory industry shifts, while the latter might suggest a generally weaker macroeconomic situation.

Other efforts to better reflect the changing economy include work at the Federal Reserve Board, the BLS, and the BEA to improve price measures to better represent the rapid pace of technological change in high-technology products like computers. When adjusted for improvements in quality, prices are estimated to fall much faster, which raises measures of real output.

Attempts to keep up with the changing economy are complicated by efforts to maintain consistent time series. Long time series are valuable for making historical comparisons and inferring long-run relationships among economic variables. When a time series is short, it is hard to know if there is anything exceptional about a current event. The strength of any conclusions that are drawn is a direct function of variation in data. Short time series have too little cyclical variation. Similarly, panel data—which follows a group of persons, households, or firms over time—are valuable for inferring changes over time from cross-sectional changes due, say, to different population composition.

There are a variety of ways in which economic measures can fail to keep up with the changing nature of the economy. Examples include:

- Firms' increased substitution of purchased services for secondary activities previously done within the firm (such as payroll processing) means that some statistics, such as employment, will document this change as a shift to services. In this example, the data accurately capture the current use of services, but the data do not reflect the *change* in the use of services correctly, as the earlier data classified all activity within the firm (including payroll processing) by the predominant activity of the firm (i.e., construction, manufacturing, etc.).

- Established industries tend to receive a disproportionate share of attention compared to new, growing industries. Industry and product classification codes are more likely to be kept than eliminated, while new industries and products are often poorly measured and tracked, at least initially.
- The growth of *professional employer organizations*—companies that provide employees to firms on a contractual basis—has led to data-reporting problems and, consequently, to inaccurate employment and wage data for industries and localities. Professional employer organizations that report employment centrally, rather than separately for each client, can obscure both the industry and location of the workers and our understanding of employment change and dynamics, negatively affecting data from BLS, the Census Bureau, the BEA, and all derived products.
- The prices for some items may fail to fully reflect changes in the quality of the items. Improvements in quality, if properly accounted for, tend to boost measured real output. The split between consumer and business spending on some products may be updated infrequently, which can lead to misstatements about which components of GDP are growing more rapidly. Both factors tend to result in less reliable estimates of real spending by consumers and businesses.
- Housing and geographic samples for the consumer price index (CPI) become outdated as the population distribution shifts (see Box 8-1).

Improving the Value of Existing Statistical Data

Federal Government statistical agencies are focusing on three ways to improve the value of existing statistical data: Improve the detail in publicly available data products, facilitate well-defined and secure research on the underlying microdata, and synchronize data produced across agencies.

Government agencies strive to improve the usefulness of their data products by providing greater detail while protecting the confidentiality of respondents. The Census Bureau, for example, employs several techniques to avoid disclosing individually identifiable data. *Synthetic data,* modeled on original data, retain the needed statistical properties of the original data but protect the confidentiality of respondents by modifying all or selected variables. The Census Bureau creates synthetic data to obscure the underlying demographic data used in its "On the Map" feature. This feature creates maps showing

Box 8-1: How to Reverse a Decline in Statistical Infrastructure: Improving the Sample for the Consumer Price Index

The housing and geographic area samples for the Consumer Price Index (CPI), currently based on 1990 Decennial Census data, are overdue for an update. Each year these samples become more out of date, in that the samples do not reflect almost 20 years of population growth, demographic changes, and new housing construction. Because of its widespread use to estimate price changes, the accuracy of the CPI influences a range of economic variables in both the public and private sectors. For example, within Federal programs, the CPI is used to adjust Social Security payments, civilian and military retirement payments, and individual income tax brackets for inflation. A study by the Congressional Budget Office found that a 1 percentage point reduction in the growth rate of CPI estimates beginning in January 2006 would have reduced the Federal budget deficit or surplus by $14 billion by the end of 2007 and $153 billion by 2015.

The Administration has proposed to update the 1990 Decennial Census–based housing sample used by the BLS with data from the Census Bureau's new, continuously conducted American Community Survey (ACS) and/or private sector sources. With continuous updating, the sample would never be more than 3 years old. This change would increase the accuracy of the CPI by creating a more representative housing sample, reduce respondent attrition, and reduce potential bias by more accurately reflecting new construction. Moreover, using the ACS to update the geographic sample on which the CPI is based would result in estimates that more accurately reflect the geographic distribution of the population and its characteristics.

commuting patterns and workforce data—where people live and work by age, earnings, and industry—for geographic areas selected by the user. Another method used is *noise addition*—the controlled introduction of variation from reported levels to detailed data that otherwise could not be published, with small compensating adjustments to other data in the same series. The Census Bureau uses this method to ensure that an individual company's data cannot be readily inferred from published Survey of Business Owners data or other estimates.

Government statistical agencies benefit when researchers can subject the data and the methodology behind the statistics to academic scrutiny in a secure research environment that maintains security of the data, restricts access to the level of data essential for an authorized project, and protects the confidentiality of respondents. The analysis of underlying data by academics is an inexpensive way for statistical agencies to improve their data products. For example, academic researchers typically investigate relationships among variables in a single survey, or in several surveys, that are not examined during routine data-processing procedures. Their nonstandardized data reviews can uncover anomalies that should be resolved before the data are released, or provide the basis for future improvements in standardized data-processing routines. In addition, this third-party scrutiny adds to the credibility of the data products. For example, the Census Bureau's Research Data Centers (RDCs) provide secure, restricted access to Census Bureau data for authorized researchers. Likewise, the BLS researcher access program provides secure, restricted access to BLS data. In both cases, researchers must undergo a strict approval process and face significant penalties for violating the laws protecting the confidentiality of responses to government surveys.

Previous research at the RDCs has led to new data products and changed thinking about many important economic issues. For example, an important strand of academic work separated net employment flows—the published employment changes with which people are familiar—into gross job creation and gross job destruction. The quarterly BLS Business Employment Dynamics data release—which reports the number and rates of gross jobs gained at opening and expanding establishments, as well as the number and rates of gross jobs lost at closing and contracting establishments—is an example of a new data product that grew out of this work. Importantly, the Business Employment Dynamics data release is tabulated from already collected company data records, thus creating no additional respondent burden. It is an important example of drawing upon academic research to improve the use of existing data in order to create new data products.

A third way that the Government can improve the value of existing data— and the method that offers the most substantial opportunities—is to allow the BEA, BLS, and Census Bureau to link their business data, while maintaining confidentiality. This linking would result in more accurate and reliable economic indicators, lower budget costs for the agencies, and lower response burdens for survey respondents. For example, at present, both the Census Bureau and the BLS ask firms to break out employment and payroll data by establishment in the Company Organization Survey and Multiple Worksite Report, respectively. If these agencies could share their business data, these two surveys, which are mailed to multiunit companies, could be combined, reducing the response burden of these firms and reducing survey costs for the statistical agencies.

The Administration recognizes that the sharing of key *business* data among Federal statistical agencies has tremendous potential for exploiting synergies among the agencies and for improving the quality of Federal statistics. In 2002, with Administration support, the Congress passed the Confidential

Information Protection and Statistical Efficiency Act (CIPSEA), described in Box 8-2, whose stated purposes were: 1) To protect the confidentiality of information collected by Federal agencies for statistical purposes, and 2) to improve the efficiency of the Federal statistical system by authorizing limited sharing of business data among the Census Bureau, the BEA, and the BLS for exclusively statistical purposes. In 2007, the Office of Management and Budget issued implementation guidance for CIPSEA. The first part—data protection—has been effectively implemented across agencies, but the second part—improving statistical efficiency—cannot be fully enabled without additional legislation. Because business tax data (such as company name and address) are used to construct the Census Bureau's business list, many Census Bureau data products are considered to be comingled with tax information. Therefore, full implementation of CIPSEA would require changes to the portion of the Internal Revenue Service (IRS) code that authorizes the statistical use of business tax data.

Box 8-2: The Confidential Information Protection and Statistical Efficiency Act (CIPSEA)

The two parts of CIPSEA are confidential information protection and statistical efficiency.

Confidential information protection: Subtitle A establishes standardized safeguards to protect the confidentiality of data collected by Federal agencies for exclusively statistical purposes. These safeguards include the assurance that information will not be used against a respondent in any government action and that inappropriate disclosure of confidential data will be considered a felony and carry significant criminal penalties. In other words, data collected for statistical purposes cannot be used for tax, immigration, or other enforcement purposes.

Statistical efficiency: Subtitle B authorizes the sharing of business data among the Census Bureau, the Bureau of Economic Analysis, and the Bureau of Labor Statistics for exclusively statistical purposes in order to:
- Reduce the paperwork burdens imposed on businesses that provide requested information to the Federal Government;
- Improve the comparability and accuracy of Federal economic statistics by allowing these agencies to reconcile differences in business lists; to develop consistent classifications of businesses into industries; and to improve coverage; and
- Increase understanding of the U.S. economy (including key industries and regions), develop more accurate measures of the impact of technology on productivity growth, and enhance the reliability of the Nation's most important economic indicators, such as the National Income and Product Accounts.

A major goal of fully implementing CIPSEA is to better reconcile the BLS Business Establishment List—based on State unemployment insurance records—and the Census Bureau's Business Register—based, in part, on IRS records. One study found that over 30 percent of single-establishment firms had different 6-digit NAICS industry codes in the two lists, and another study revealed large discrepancies in measures of industry-level employment across surveys.

The failure to coordinate data across agencies can lead to noticeable inaccuracies, especially when one needs to calculate a measure that combines data from two agencies. For example, the implications of discrepancies in establishment classifications are particularly acute when measuring labor productivity, which is an important statistic for economic policymakers, including those who project the Federal budget. Labor productivity is the ratio of output, measured by the Census Bureau, and hours worked, as measured by the BLS. Accurate productivity estimates depend upon these labor and hours worked measures being given consistent industry classifications, which is unlikely if the underlying business lists are inconsistent.

Differences in industry classification would also result in discrepancies in the rate of real GDP growth reported by key sectors. For example, in the Computer and Electronic Product Manufacturing Subsector (NAICS 334), the growth in real value added in 2002 would have been 15.6 percent if payroll data from the Census Bureau's Economic Census had been used. Instead, the growth in real value added was published as 7.4 percent, a statistic based on payroll data from the BLS. Without carefully analyzing the confidential business lists used for the Economic Census and the BLS payroll data, it is difficult to know which payroll measure should be used. Some efforts to share data have proven useful in reducing inconsistencies and reducing burden. The BLS has shared industry identifiers with the Census Bureau since 1992 and geographic identifiers since 2002, particularly for new and small businesses. These industry codes covered over 3 million businesses in 2007 alone and now account for about 30 percent of the Census Bureau's business codes. Expanding data sharing would extend this work and further improve consistency and accuracy of key data series.

A 2006 report noted that data sharing might highlight opportunities for understanding data reporting that would better focus resources on activities that would improve the measurement of national economic activity (such as the reporting of stock options). The National Income and Product Accounts provide two measures of national activity, one based on total output (GDP) and one based on total income (gross domestic income or GDI). In theory, these measures should be equal. In practice, they differ by a measurement error called the *statistical discrepancy*. The statistical discrepancy can be persistent: From 1995–2000 real GDI grew 0.6 percentage point faster than real GDP, on average, per year. If the growth rate of the GDI were projected forward instead of the growth rate of GDP, the budget implications could be substantial. An analysis of fiscal year 2006 by the Office of Management and Budget found that if the GDP were persistently understated by 1 percent, the projected cumulative budget deficit would be overstated by $530 billion over a 5-year period.

Better measures of business formation are needed to understand the changing composition of the business sector and the factors that contribute to business and job creation. Data synchronization would help agencies track business formation more accurately and on a more timely basis by reconciling the business lists from the Census Bureau and the BLS. For example, the Census Bureau's Business Register relies heavily on the Economic Censuses (conducted every 5 years) for information on business structure. In the intervening years, however, the Census Bureau makes use of its annual Company Organization Survey, which covers all employers with more than 250 employees, but only a sampling of smaller companies. The Census Bureau's Business Register generally does a good job identifying ownership links among establishments (e.g., when a single firm owns establishments in two different States). However, the information on ownership is weaker for smaller firms because only a subset of these businesses is surveyed during the years between the 5-year censuses. Firm restructuring often contributes to the difficulty of tracking parent–subsidiary relationships. The BLS Business Employment Dynamics accurately measures the universe of business openings and closings on a quarterly frequency but may not always successfully track parent–subsidiary relationships. Combining the strengths of the Census and BLS business lists would improve the ability to discern whether a new establishment is an entirely new firm or a new branch of an existing firm, and therefore improve understanding of business dynamics.

Data synchronization could also help reconcile differences between similar statistics produced by separate agencies. For example, the BLS publishes wages and salary data based on its Quarterly Census of Employment and Wages business list and the Census Bureau publishes payroll data in its County Business Patterns series. A comparison of 2003 private wages and salaries revealed that these two measures differed by significant amounts. For example, the BLS measure of wages and salaries in New Mexico was 4.2 percent higher than the Census Bureau measure, while in Alaska, the BLS measure was 9.5 percent lower. At the national level, BLS data were 0.6 percent (or $25.1 billion) lower than County Business Patterns data, but they were 2 percent (or $6.7 billion) lower for New York. Understanding the sources of these differences (such as differences in reporting and coverage) may yield improved regional measures that would have several implications:

- Distribution of Federal funds to the States: BEA per capita personal income data, based largely on BLS data, are used in the formula that calculates how to distribute the Federal share of Medicaid funding to

States. Wages and salaries and wage-related components account for two-thirds of personal income. In 2003, State private wage levels based on BLS data were $2.5 billion higher in Texas and $7.1 billion lower in Washington than levels based on the Census Bureau's County Business Patterns.

- State tax and budget planning: The dollar difference between BLS and Census measures of wage and salary growth from 2001 to 2002 would result in significantly different projections of State and local government income taxes received: a $165 million discrepancy in New Jersey and a $193 million discrepancy in Massachusetts. The $1.2 billion wage growth difference in New York would yield a $173 million discrepancy in projected State and local tax revenue.

Conclusion

The quality of public policy debates depends, in large part, on the availability of relevant and reliable statistical data. Consistent data series ensure that newly gathered data can be meaningfully compared to previously collected data. At the same time, it is also important that the statistical system maintain the flexibility to create new data products that keep up with the changing nature of the dynamic global economy. The infrastructure required to develop and produce these data, like any infrastructure, requires continuous investment to maintain and improve the system, but not all data improvements are costly. For example, existing economic data on businesses could be improved through the full implementation of the Confidential Information Protection and Statistical Efficiency Act without increasing the reporting burden for respondents, without compromising the confidentiality of the data collected by the Federal statistical agencies, and without significantly raising costs of the data collection and tabulation. Maintaining solid statistical systems ensures that public policymakers and private decisionmakers will have access to the information needed to understand our dynamic economy.

Appendix A

REPORT TO THE PRESIDENT ON THE ACTIVITIES OF THE
COUNCIL OF ECONOMIC ADVISERS DURING 2007

LETTER OF TRANSMITTAL

COUNCIL OF ECONOMIC ADVISERS
Washington, D.C., December 31, 2007

MR. PRESIDENT:

The Council of Economic Advisers submits this report on its activities during calendar year 2007 in accordance with the requirements of the Congress, as set forth in section 10(d) of the Employment Act of 1946 as amended by the Full Employment and Balanced Growth Act of 1978.

Sincerely,

Edward P. Lazear, *Chairman*

Council Members and Their Dates of Service

Name	Position	Oath of office date	Separation date
Edwin G. Nourse	Chairman	August 9, 1946	November 1, 1949
Leon H. Keyserling	Vice Chairman	August 9, 1946	
	Acting Chairman	November 2, 1949	
	Chairman	May 10, 1950	January 20, 1953
John D. Clark	Member	August 9, 1946	
	Vice Chairman	May 10, 1950	February 11, 1953
Roy Blough	Member	June 29, 1950	August 20, 1952
Robert C. Turner	Member	September 8, 1952	January 20, 1953
Arthur F. Burns	Chairman	March 19, 1953	December 1, 1956
Neil H. Jacoby	Member	September 15, 1953	February 9, 1955
Walter W. Stewart	Member	December 2, 1953	April 29, 1955
Raymond J. Saulnier	Member	April 4, 1955	
	Chairman	December 3, 1956	January 20, 1961
Joseph S. Davis	Member	May 2, 1955	October 31, 1958
Paul W. McCracken	Member	December 3, 1956	January 31, 1959
Karl Brandt	Member	November 1, 1958	January 20, 1961
Henry C. Wallich	Member	May 7, 1959	January 20, 1961
Walter W. Heller	Chairman	January 29, 1961	November 15, 1964
James Tobin	Member	January 29, 1961	July 31, 1962
Kermit Gordon	Member	January 29, 1961	December 27, 1962
Gardner Ackley	Member	August 3, 1962	
	Chairman	November 16, 1964	February 15, 1968
John P. Lewis	Member	May 17, 1963	August 31, 1964
Otto Eckstein	Member	September 2, 1964	February 1, 1966
Arthur M. Okun	Member	November 16, 1964	
	Chairman	February 15, 1968	January 20, 1969
James S. Duesenberry	Member	February 2, 1966	June 30, 1968
Merton J. Peck	Member	February 15, 1968	January 20, 1969
Warren L. Smith	Member	July 1, 1968	January 20, 1969
Paul W. McCracken	Chairman	February 4, 1969	December 31, 1971
Hendrik S. Houthakker	Member	February 4, 1969	July 15, 1971
Herbert Stein	Member	February 4, 1969	
	Chairman	January 1, 1972	August 31, 1974
Ezra Solomon	Member	September 9, 1971	March 26, 1973
Marina v.N. Whitman	Member	March 13, 1972	August 15, 1973
Gary L. Seevers	Member	July 23, 1973	April 15, 1975
William J. Fellner	Member	October 31, 1973	February 25, 1975
Alan Greenspan	Chairman	September 4, 1974	January 20, 1977
Paul W. MacAvoy	Member	June 13, 1975	November 15, 1976
Burton G. Malkiel	Member	July 22, 1975	January 20, 1977

Council Members and Their Dates of Service

Name	Position	Oath of office date	Separation date
Charles L. Schultze	Chairman	January 22, 1977	January 20, 1981
William D. Nordhaus	Member	March 18, 1977	February 4, 1979
Lyle E. Gramley	Member	March 18, 1977	May 27, 1980
George C. Eads	Member	June 6, 1979	January 20, 1981
Stephen M. Goldfeld	Member	August 20, 1980	January 20, 1981
Murray L. Weidenbaum	Chairman	February 27, 1981	August 25, 1982
William A. Niskanen	Member	June 12, 1981	March 30, 1985
Jerry L. Jordan	Member	July 14, 1981	July 31, 1982
Martin Feldstein	Chairman	October 14, 1982	July 10, 1984
William Poole	Member	December 10, 1982	January 20, 1985
Beryl W. Sprinkel	Chairman	April 18, 1985	January 20, 1989
Thomas Gale Moore	Member	July 1, 1985	May 1, 1989
Michael L. Mussa	Member	August 18, 1986	September 19, 1988
Michael J. Boskin	Chairman	February 2, 1989	January 12, 1993
John B. Taylor	Member	June 9, 1989	August 2, 1991
Richard L. Schmalensee	Member	October 3, 1989	June 21, 1991
David F. Bradford	Member	November 13, 1991	January 20, 1993
Paul Wonnacott	Member	November 13, 1991	January 20, 1993
Laura D'Andrea Tyson	Chair	February 5, 1993	April 22, 1995
Alan S. Blinder	Member	July 27, 1993	June 26, 1994
Joseph E. Stiglitz	Member	July 27, 1993	
	Chairman	June 28, 1995	February 10, 1997
Martin N. Baily	Member	June 30, 1995	August 30, 1996
Alicia H. Munnell	Member	January 29, 1996	August 1, 1997
Janet L. Yellen	Chair	February 18, 1997	August 3, 1999
Jeffrey A. Frankel	Member	April 23, 1997	March 2, 1999
Rebecca M. Blank	Member	October 22, 1998	July 9, 1999
Martin N. Baily	Chairman	August 12, 1999	January 19, 2001
Robert Z. Lawrence	Member	August 12, 1999	January 12, 2001
Kathryn L. Shaw	Member	May 31, 2000	January 19, 2001
R. Glenn Hubbard	Chairman	May 11, 2001	February 28, 2003
Mark B. McClellan	Member	July 25, 2001	November 13, 2002
Randall S. Kroszner	Member	November 30, 2001	July 1, 2003
N. Gregory Mankiw	Chairman	May 29, 2003	February 18, 2005
Kristin J. Forbes	Member	November 21, 2003	June 3, 2005
Harvey S. Rosen	Member	November 21, 2003	
	Chairman	February 23, 2005	June 10, 2005
Ben S. Bernanke	Chairman	June 21, 2005	January 31, 2006
Katherine Baicker	Member	November 18, 2005	July 11, 2007
Matthew J. Slaughter	Member	November 18, 2005	March 1, 2007
Edward P. Lazear	Chairman	February 27, 2006	

Report to the President on the Activities of the Council of Economic Advisers During 2007

The Council of Economic Advisers was established by the Employment Act of 1946 to provide the President with objective economic analysis and advice on the development and implementation of a wide range of domestic and international economic policy issues.

The Chairman of the Council

Edward P. Lazear continued to chair the Council during 2007. Dr. Lazear is on a leave of absence from the Stanford Graduate School of Business where he is the Jack Steele Parker Professor of Human Resources Management and Economics. He also served as the Morris Arnold Cox Senior Fellow at the Hoover Institution.

Dr. Lazear is responsible for communicating the Council's views on economic matters directly to the President through personal discussions and written reports. He represents the Council at daily White House senior staff meetings, a variety of inter-agency meetings, Cabinet meetings, and other formal and informal meetings with the President. He also travels within the United States and overseas to present the Administration's views on the economy. Dr. Lazear is the Council's chief public spokesperson. He directs the work of the Council and exercises ultimate responsibility for the work of the professional staff.

The Members of the Council

The Council's two other Members were Katherine Baicker who left the Council in July 2007 to become Professor of Health Economics in the Department of Health Policy and Management at Harvard School of Public Health, and Matthew J. Slaughter who left the Council in March 2007 to return to the Tuck School of Business at Dartmouth College as Associate Professor of Business Administration.

The President nominated Dennis W. Carlton and Donald B. Marron to fill these two vacancies.

Macroeconomic Policies

As is its tradition, the Council devoted much time during 2007 to assisting the President in formulating economic policy objectives and designing programs to implement them. In this regard the Chairman kept the President informed, on a continuing basis, of important macroeconomic developments and other major policy issues through regular macroeconomic briefings. The Council prepares for the President, the Vice President, and the White House senior staff regular memoranda that report key economic data and analyze current economic events. Council staff also regularly provides assistance with economic data to other offices within the Executive Office of the President.

The Council, the Department of the Treasury, and the Office of Management and Budget—the Administration's economic "troika"—are responsible for producing the economic forecasts that underlie the Administration's budget proposals. The Council, under the leadership of the Chairman and the Chief Economist, initiates the forecasting process twice each year. In preparing these forecasts, the Council consults with a variety of outside sources, including leading private sector forecasters.

In 2007, the Council took part in discussions on a range of macroeconomic issues. The Council contributed significantly to discussions on the macroeconomic impact of this year's housing and credit market disruptions, and provided analysis and support for the Administration's economic growth package.

The Council works closely with the Department of the Treasury, the Federal Reserve, and other government agencies in providing analyses to the Administration on these topics of concern. It also works closely with the National Economic Council, the Domestic Policy Council, the Office of Management and Budget, and other offices within the Executive Office of the President in assessing the economy and economic policy proposals.

International Economic Policies

The Council was involved in a range of international trade and finance issues, and was an active participant in discussions at the global, regional, and bilateral levels, including the U.S. Trade Policy Review, conducted by the World Trade Organization. On the international trade front, the Council provided empirical analysis of forthcoming free trade agreements and met with policymakers and business leaders in support of the Peru, Colombia, Panama, and South Korea free trade agreements.

Further involvement included extensive analysis related to U.S. economic interaction with China. The Council provided analysis for the Department of the Treasury-led Strategic Economic Dialogue in Beijing, where a host of bilateral economic issues with China were discussed, ranging from financial liberalization, to energy and the environment, to bilateral trade relations.

The Council also prepared in-depth analyses for the President's international itinerary, including travel to the Middle East and Europe, as well as the annual Asia Pacific Economic Cooperation (APEC) summit in Australia.

In the area of investment and security, the Council took part in discussions on the implementation of the Foreign Investment and National Security Act of 2007, which clarified and improved the operations of the Committee on Foreign Investment in the United States (CFIUS). The Council also participated in discussions of individual cases before CFIUS.

The Council participated in discussions concerning the need for greater international financial and trade liberalization with both advanced and emerging market economies. Council Members regularly met with economists and policy officials of foreign countries, finance ministers, other government officials, and members of the private sector to discuss prevailing issues relating to the global economy.

The Council is a leading participant in the Organization for Economic Cooperation and Development (OECD), the principal forum for economic cooperation among the high-income industrial economies. Chairman Lazear, along with other senior Council members, participated in the OECD's Economic Policy Committee (EPC) meeting, as well as the Working Party meetings on macroeconomic policy and coordination.

Microeconomic Policies

A wide variety of microeconomic issues received Council attention during 2007. The Council actively participated in the Cabinet-level National Economic Council and Domestic Policy Council meetings, dealing with issues including health care, labor, energy policy, legal reform, the environment, education, pensions, transportation, and technology.

The Council was active in the examination of health care policy related to the tax treatment of health insurance, health information technology adoption, health insurance for children, veterans health, potential reforms to Medicare, and the promotion of transparency in health price and quality. The Council examined the causes and consequences of rising health care costs and reviewed potential remedies including greater consumer involvement in health care, opening access to insurance across state lines, and improving the connection between health care expenditure and positive health outcomes.

The Council was also active in energy and environmental policy discussions, where it analyzed energy markets, fuel economy issues, and alternatives to oil. This included issues such as the President's Advanced Energy Initiative, bio-energy, the Renewable Fuels Standard, Corporate Average Fuel Economy (CAFE), the Strategic Petroleum Reserve, regulatory reforms, global climate change, and the international trade of energy.

The Council examined transportation policies relating to airports, hybrid vehicles, and congestion pricing. The Council also played a role in the analysis of policy for telecommunications, broadband, and spectrum allocation. Council staff also examined agricultural issues and patent reform.

The Council participated in discussions related to catastrophic risk insurance relating to natural disasters and attacks. The Council also participated in ongoing policy discussions relating to the government's role in terrorism risk insurance.

On labor policy, the Council was involved in the development of the President's comprehensive immigration policy and other proposed immigration reforms. The Council also assisted in Administration evaluation of higher education policies, as well as in the examination of the No Child Left Behind program.

The Council was active in tax policy discussions relating to individual income tax, business tax credits, and corporate taxation, as well as tax issues related to entitlement programs like Social Security. Many additional tax policy discussions were involved in other microeconomic discussions including labor, insurance, pensions, and health care.

The Staff of the Council of Economic Advisers

The professional staff of the Council consists of the Chief of Staff, the Chief Economist, the Director of Macroeconomic Forecasting, the Director of the Statistical Office, nine senior economists, and seven junior staff of staff economists, analysts and research assistants. The professional staff and their areas of concentration at the end of 2007 were:

Chief of Staff
Pierce E. Scranton

Chief Economist
Keith Hall

Consultant
Donald B. Marron

Director of	*Director*
Macroeconomic Forecasting	*Statistical Office*
Steven N. Braun	Adrienne T. Pilot

Senior Economists

Scott Baier..................	International Finance
Erik Durbin	Legal, Transportation, Regulation
Charles Griffiths.........	Agriculture, Environment, Natural Resources
Daniel E. Polsky.........	Health
Korok Ray..................	Public Finance, Technology
Dan Rosenbaum	Labor, Immigration, Education, Welfare
Howard Shatz	International Trade
Sita Slavov.................	Tax, Budget
John Stevens..............	Macroeconomics, Labor, Small Business

Staff Economist

Elizabeth Akers	Labor

Analyst

Kristopher J. Dawsey..	Macroeconomics

Research Assistants

Mark W. Clements .... International Finance and Trade
Joshua K. Goldman.... Microeconomics and Regulation
Elizabeth M. Schultz .. International Finance and US Finance/Banking
Brian T. Waters .... Public Finance and Macroeconomics
Chen Zhao .... Health and Labor

Statistical Office

The Statistical Office administers and updates the Council's statistical information. Duties include preparing material for and overseeing publication of the monthly *Economic Indicators* and the statistical appendix to the *Economic Report of the President*. Staff verifies statistical content in Presidential memoranda and produces background materials for economic analysis. The Office also serves as the Council's liaison to the statistical community.

Brian A. Amorosi .... Program Analyst
Dagmara A. Mocala ... Program Analyst

Administrative Office

The Administrative Office provides general support for the Council's activities. This includes financial management, ethics, human resource management, travel, operations of facilities, security, information technology, and telecommunications management support.

Rosemary M. Rogers .. Administrative Officer
Archana A. Snyder ..... Financial Officer
Doris T. Searles .... Information Management Specialist

Office of the Chairman

Alice H. Williams....... Executive Assistant to the Chairman
Sandra F. Daigle......... Executive Assistant to the Chairman
and Assistant to the Chief of Staff
Lisa D. Branch .... Executive Assistant to the Member
Mary E. Jones .... Executive Assistant to the Member

Staff Support

Sharon K. Thomas ..... Administrative Support Assistant and Assistant to the
Chief Economist

Gary Blank, who served as Chief of Staff, left the Council in August of 2007 to accept a position with Fidelity Investments as Vice President, Policy Analysis.

Jane Tufts, Bruce Kaplan, and Anna Paganelli provided editorial assistance in the preparation of the 2008 *Economic Report of the President.*

Student Interns during the year were: Aaron Epstein, Elisabeth E. Fosslien, Marc Held, Jonathan Jardine, Ashley Jelinek, Kyle Jurado, Jessica Levy, Danyank Lok, Robin Lyu, David Marold, Anthony Ng, Ethan Parker, Jeannine Regalia, William Ross, Kyle Smith, and Zachary Watson.

Our Fellow during the year was Deepa Dhume.

Departures

The Council's senior economists, in most cases, are on leave of absence from academic institutions, government agencies, or private research institutions. Their tenure with the Council is usually limited to 1 or 2 years. The senior economists who resigned during the year were: William Collins (Vanderbilt University), Erik Heitfield (Federal Reserve Board), Bradley Herring (Emory University), Christine McDaniel (Department of the Treasury), Kristin McCue (Census Bureau), Robert Martin (Federal Reserve), David Richardson (TIAA-CREF), and Maryann Wolverton (EPA). The economist who resigned during the year was Benjamin Ho (Cornell University).

The economists are supported by a team of junior staff made up of analysts and research assistants who generally work with the Council for 1 or 2 years before returning to school or other endeavors. The analysts who resigned during 2007 were: Dagmara Tchalakov, Lucas Threinen, Diana Wielocha, and Jonathan Wolfson. Those who served as research assistants at the Council and resigned during 2007 were: Eric Cragun, Nikola Kojucharov, and Gregory Stein.

Public Information

The Council's annual *Economic Report of the President* is an important vehicle for presenting the Administration's domestic and international economic policies. It is available for purchase through the Government Printing Office, and is viewable on the Internet at www.gpoaccess.gov/eop. The Council also publishes the monthly *Economic Indicators,* which is available on-line at www.gpoaccess.gov/indicators. The Council's home page is located at www.whitehouse.gov/cea.

Appendix B
STATISTICAL TABLES RELATING TO INCOME, EMPLOYMENT, AND PRODUCTION

CONTENTS

General Notes

Detail in these tables may not add to totals because of rounding.

Because of the formula used for calculating real gross domestic product (GDP), the chained (2000) dollar estimates for the detailed components do not add to the chained-dollar value of GDP or to any intermediate aggregate. The Department of Commerce (Bureau of Economic Analysis) no longer publishes chained-dollar estimates prior to 1990, except for selected series.

Unless otherwise noted, all dollar figures are in current dollars.

Symbols used:
p Preliminary.
... Not available (also, not applicable).

Data in these tables reflect revisions made by the source agencies through January 29, 2008. In particular, tables containing national income and product accounts (NIPA) estimates reflect revisions released by the Department of Commerce in July 2007.

TABLE B–1.—*Gross domestic product, 1959–2007*

[Billions of dollars, except as noted; quarterly data at seasonally adjusted annual rates]

Year or quarter	Gross domestic product	Personal consumption expenditures				Gross private domestic investment						
							Fixed investment					Change in private inventories
		Total	Durable goods	Non-durable goods	Services	Total	Total	Nonresidential			Residential	
								Total	Struc-tures	Equip-ment and software		
1959	506.6	317.6	42.7	148.5	126.5	78.5	74.6	46.5	18.1	28.4	28.1	3.9
1960	526.4	331.7	43.3	152.8	135.6	78.9	75.7	49.4	19.6	29.8	26.3	3.2
1961	544.7	342.1	41.8	156.6	143.8	78.2	75.2	48.8	19.7	29.1	26.4	3.0
1962	585.6	363.3	46.9	162.8	153.6	88.1	82.0	53.1	20.8	32.3	29.0	6.1
1963	617.7	382.7	51.6	168.2	162.9	93.8	88.1	56.0	21.2	34.8	32.1	5.6
1964	663.6	411.4	56.7	178.6	176.1	102.1	97.2	63.0	23.7	39.2	34.3	4.8
1965	719.1	443.8	63.3	191.5	189.0	118.2	109.0	74.8	28.3	46.5	34.2	9.2
1966	787.8	480.9	68.3	208.7	203.8	131.3	117.7	85.4	31.3	54.0	32.3	13.6
1967	832.6	507.8	70.4	217.1	220.3	128.6	118.7	86.4	31.5	54.9	32.4	9.9
1968	910.0	558.0	80.8	235.7	241.6	141.2	132.1	93.4	33.6	59.9	38.7	9.1
1969	984.6	605.2	85.9	253.1	266.1	156.4	147.3	104.7	37.7	67.0	42.6	9.2
1970	1,038.5	648.5	85.0	272.0	291.5	152.4	150.4	109.0	40.3	68.7	41.4	2.0
1971	1,127.1	701.9	96.9	285.5	319.5	178.2	169.9	114.1	42.7	71.5	55.8	8.3
1972	1,238.3	770.6	110.4	308.0	352.2	207.6	198.5	128.8	47.2	81.7	69.7	9.1
1973	1,382.7	852.4	123.5	343.1	385.8	244.5	228.6	153.3	55.0	98.3	75.3	15.9
1974	1,500.0	933.4	122.3	384.5	426.6	249.4	235.4	169.5	61.2	108.2	66.0	14.0
1975	1,638.3	1,034.4	133.5	420.7	480.2	230.2	236.5	173.7	61.4	112.4	62.7	–6.3
1976	1,825.3	1,151.9	158.9	458.3	534.7	292.0	274.8	192.4	65.9	126.4	82.5	17.1
1977	2,030.9	1,278.6	181.2	497.1	600.2	361.3	339.0	228.7	74.6	154.1	110.3	22.3
1978	2,294.7	1,428.5	201.7	550.2	676.6	438.0	412.2	280.6	93.6	187.0	131.6	25.8
1979	2,563.3	1,592.2	214.4	624.5	753.3	492.9	474.9	333.9	117.7	216.2	141.0	18.0
1980	2,789.5	1,757.1	214.2	696.1	846.9	479.3	485.6	362.4	136.2	226.2	123.2	–6.3
1981	3,128.4	1,941.1	231.3	758.9	950.8	572.4	542.6	420.0	167.3	252.7	122.6	29.8
1982	3,255.0	2,077.3	240.2	787.6	1,049.4	517.2	532.1	426.5	177.6	248.9	105.7	–14.9
1983	3,536.7	2,290.6	280.8	831.2	1,178.6	564.3	570.1	417.2	154.3	262.9	152.9	–5.8
1984	3,933.2	2,503.3	325.5	884.6	1,292.2	735.6	670.2	489.6	177.4	312.2	180.6	65.4
1985	4,220.3	2,720.3	363.5	928.7	1,428.1	736.2	714.4	526.2	194.5	331.7	188.2	21.8
1986	4,462.8	2,899.7	403.0	958.4	1,538.3	746.5	739.9	519.8	176.5	343.3	220.1	6.6
1987	4,739.5	3,100.2	421.7	1,015.3	1,663.3	785.0	757.8	524.1	174.2	349.9	233.7	27.1
1988	5,103.8	3,353.6	453.6	1,083.5	1,816.5	821.6	803.1	563.8	182.8	381.0	239.3	18.5
1989	5,484.4	3,598.5	471.8	1,166.7	1,960.0	874.9	847.3	607.7	193.7	414.0	239.5	27.7
1990	5,803.1	3,839.9	474.2	1,249.9	2,115.9	861.0	846.4	622.4	202.9	419.5	224.0	14.5
1991	5,995.9	3,986.1	453.9	1,284.8	2,247.4	802.9	803.3	598.2	183.6	414.6	205.1	–.4
1992	6,337.7	4,235.3	483.6	1,330.5	2,421.2	864.8	848.5	612.1	172.6	439.6	236.3	16.3
1993	6,657.4	4,477.9	526.7	1,379.4	2,571.8	953.4	932.5	666.6	177.2	489.4	266.0	20.8
1994	7,072.2	4,743.3	582.2	1,437.2	2,723.9	1,097.1	1,033.3	731.4	186.8	544.6	301.9	63.8
1995	7,397.7	4,975.8	611.6	1,485.1	2,879.1	1,144.0	1,112.9	810.0	207.3	602.8	302.8	31.1
1996	7,816.9	5,256.8	652.6	1,555.5	3,048.7	1,240.3	1,209.5	875.4	224.6	650.8	334.1	30.8
1997	8,304.3	5,547.4	692.7	1,619.0	3,235.8	1,389.8	1,317.8	968.7	250.3	718.3	349.1	72.0
1998	8,747.0	5,879.5	750.2	1,683.6	3,445.7	1,509.1	1,438.4	1,052.6	275.2	777.3	385.8	70.8
1999	9,268.4	6,282.5	817.6	1,804.8	3,660.0	1,625.7	1,558.8	1,133.9	282.2	851.7	424.9	66.9
2000	9,817.0	6,739.4	863.3	1,947.2	3,928.8	1,735.5	1,679.0	1,232.1	313.2	918.9	446.9	56.5
2001	10,128.0	7,055.0	883.7	2,017.1	4,154.3	1,614.3	1,646.1	1,176.8	322.6	854.2	469.3	–31.7
2002	10,469.6	7,350.7	923.9	2,079.6	4,347.2	1,582.1	1,570.2	1,066.3	279.2	787.1	503.9	11.9
2003	10,960.8	7,703.6	942.7	2,190.2	4,570.8	1,664.1	1,649.8	1,077.4	277.2	800.2	572.4	14.3
2004	11,685.9	8,195.9	983.9	2,343.7	4,868.3	1,888.6	1,830.0	1,154.5	298.2	856.3	675.5	58.6
2005	12,433.9	8,707.8	1,023.9	2,516.2	5,167.8	2,077.2	2,040.3	1,272.1	334.6	937.5	768.2	36.9
2006	13,194.7	9,224.5	1,048.9	2,688.0	5,487.6	2,209.2	2,162.5	1,397.7	405.1	992.6	764.8	46.7
2004: I	11,405.5	8,010.1	969.6	2,284.2	4,756.3	1,769.6	1,732.6	1,100.4	284.0	816.4	632.2	37.0
II	11,610.3	8,135.0	974.8	2,327.7	4,832.4	1,875.6	1,806.6	1,135.5	293.5	842.0	671.1	69.0
III	11,779.4	8,245.1	986.9	2,353.5	4,904.6	1,929.7	1,864.7	1,172.7	303.4	869.3	692.0	65.0
IV	11,948.5	8,393.3	1,004.1	2,409.3	4,979.9	1,979.5	1,916.1	1,209.5	312.0	897.4	706.6	63.4
2005: I	12,154.0	8,488.8	1,009.7	2,432.1	5,047.0	2,029.6	1,960.4	1,233.1	323.3	909.7	727.3	69.3
II	12,317.4	8,632.6	1,036.0	2,484.3	5,112.3	2,024.7	2,012.5	1,255.7	328.8	926.9	756.8	12.2
III	12,558.8	8,810.5	1,044.1	2,557.0	5,209.4	2,078.5	2,072.7	1,287.0	334.2	952.9	785.7	5.8
IV	12,705.5	8,899.3	1,005.7	2,591.3	5,302.4	2,176.0	2,115.5	1,312.6	352.0	960.5	803.0	60.5
2006: I	12,964.6	9,034.7	1,042.6	2,622.1	5,370.0	2,221.1	2,176.8	1,367.3	375.7	991.7	809.4	44.3
II	13,155.0	9,183.9	1,042.8	2,692.2	5,448.9	2,239.0	2,179.5	1,391.2	400.2	991.1	788.2	59.5
III	13,266.9	9,305.7	1,053.8	2,732.4	5,519.5	2,224.1	2,161.3	1,415.2	416.1	999.1	746.1	62.8
IV	13,392.3	9,373.7	1,056.5	2,705.4	5,611.8	2,152.4	2,132.4	1,417.1	428.4	988.7	715.3	20.0
2007: I	13,551.9	9,540.5	1,074.0	2,759.4	5,707.1	2,117.3	2,118.9	1,431.4	439.6	991.8	687.5	–1.6
II	13,768.8	9,674.0	1,074.7	2,822.7	5,776.5	2,139.1	2,133.9	1,469.1	464.5	1,004.5	664.8	5.1
III	13,970.5	9,785.7	1,081.6	2,846.3	5,857.8	2,162.9	2,127.5	1,500.1	483.1	1,017.1	627.3	35.4

See next page for continuation of table.

[Billions of dollars, except as noted; quarterly data at seasonally adjusted annual rates]

Year or quarter	Net exports of goods and services — Net exports	Exports	Imports	Government consumption expenditures and gross investment — Total	Federal — Total	National defense	Non-defense	State and local	Final sales of domestic product	Gross domestic purchases [1]	Addendum: Gross national product [2]	Percent change from preceding period — Gross domestic product	Gross domestic purchases [1]
1959	0.4	22.7	22.3	110.0	65.4	53.8	11.5	44.7	502.7	506.2	509.3	8.4	8.5
1960	4.2	27.0	22.8	111.6	64.1	53.4	10.7	47.5	523.2	522.2	529.5	3.9	3.2
1961	4.9	27.6	22.7	119.5	67.9	56.5	11.4	51.6	541.7	539.8	548.2	3.5	3.4
1962	4.1	29.1	25.0	130.1	75.3	61.1	14.2	54.9	579.5	581.5	589.7	7.5	7.7
1963	4.9	31.1	26.1	136.4	76.9	61.0	15.9	59.5	612.1	612.8	622.2	5.5	5.4
1964	6.9	35.0	28.1	143.2	78.5	60.3	18.2	64.8	658.8	656.7	668.5	7.4	7.2
1965	5.6	37.1	31.5	151.5	80.4	60.6	19.8	71.0	709.9	713.5	724.4	8.4	8.6
1966	3.9	40.9	37.1	171.8	92.5	71.7	20.8	79.2	774.2	783.9	792.9	9.5	9.9
1967	3.6	43.5	39.9	192.7	104.8	83.5	21.3	87.9	822.7	829.0	838.0	5.7	5.8
1968	1.4	47.9	46.6	209.4	111.4	89.3	22.1	98.0	900.9	908.6	916.1	9.3	9.6
1969	1.4	51.9	50.5	221.5	113.4	89.5	23.8	108.2	975.4	983.2	990.7	8.2	8.2
1970	4.0	59.7	55.8	233.8	113.5	87.6	25.8	120.3	1,036.5	1,034.6	1,044.9	5.5	5.2
1971	.6	63.0	62.3	246.5	113.7	84.6	29.1	132.8	1,118.9	1,126.5	1,134.7	8.5	8.9
1972	-3.4	70.8	74.2	263.5	119.7	87.0	32.7	143.8	1,229.2	1,241.7	1,246.8	9.9	10.2
1973	4.1	95.3	91.2	281.7	122.5	88.2	34.3	159.2	1,366.8	1,378.6	1,395.3	11.7	11.0
1974	-.8	126.7	127.5	317.9	134.6	95.6	39.0	183.4	1,486.0	1,500.8	1,515.5	8.5	8.9
1975	16.0	138.7	122.7	357.7	149.1	103.9	45.1	208.7	1,644.6	1,622.4	1,651.3	9.2	8.1
1976	-1.6	149.5	151.1	383.0	159.7	111.1	48.6	223.3	1,808.2	1,826.9	1,842.1	11.4	12.6
1977	-23.1	159.4	182.4	414.1	175.4	120.9	54.5	238.7	2,008.6	2,054.0	2,051.2	11.3	12.4
1978	-25.4	186.9	212.3	453.6	190.9	130.5	60.4	262.6	2,268.9	2,320.1	2,316.3	13.0	13.0
1979	-22.5	230.1	252.7	500.8	210.6	145.2	65.4	290.2	2,545.3	2,585.9	2,595.3	11.7	11.5
1980	-13.1	280.8	293.8	566.2	243.8	168.0	75.8	322.4	2,795.8	2,802.6	2,823.7	8.8	8.4
1981	-12.5	305.2	317.8	627.5	280.2	196.3	84.0	347.3	3,098.6	3,141.0	3,161.4	12.2	12.1
1982	-20.0	283.2	303.2	680.5	310.8	225.9	84.9	369.7	3,269.9	3,275.0	3,291.5	4.0	4.3
1983	-51.7	277.0	328.6	733.5	342.9	250.7	92.3	390.5	3,542.4	3,588.3	3,573.8	8.7	9.6
1984	-102.7	302.4	405.1	797.0	374.4	281.6	92.8	422.6	3,867.8	4,035.9	3,969.5	11.2	12.5
1985	-115.2	302.0	417.2	879.0	412.8	311.2	101.6	466.2	4,198.4	4,335.5	4,246.8	7.3	7.4
1986	-132.7	320.5	453.3	949.3	438.6	330.9	107.8	510.7	4,456.3	4,595.6	4,480.6	5.7	6.0
1987	-145.2	363.9	509.1	999.5	460.1	350.0	110.0	539.4	4,712.3	4,884.7	4,757.4	6.2	6.3
1988	-110.4	444.1	554.5	1,039.0	462.3	354.9	107.4	576.7	5,085.3	5,214.2	5,127.4	7.7	6.7
1989	-88.2	503.3	591.5	1,099.1	482.2	362.2	120.0	616.9	5,456.7	5,572.5	5,510.6	7.5	6.9
1990	-78.0	552.4	630.3	1,180.2	508.3	374.0	134.3	671.9	5,788.5	5,881.1	5,837.9	5.8	5.5
1991	-27.5	596.8	624.3	1,234.4	527.7	383.2	144.5	706.7	5,996.3	6,023.4	6,026.3	3.3	2.4
1992	-33.2	635.3	668.6	1,271.0	533.9	376.9	157.0	737.0	6,321.4	6,371.0	6,367.4	5.7	5.8
1993	-65.0	655.8	720.9	1,291.2	525.2	362.9	162.4	766.0	6,636.6	6,722.4	6,689.3	5.0	5.5
1994	-93.6	720.9	814.5	1,325.5	519.1	353.7	165.5	806.3	7,008.4	7,165.8	7,098.4	6.2	6.6
1995	-91.4	812.2	903.6	1,369.2	519.2	348.7	170.5	850.0	7,366.5	7,489.0	7,433.4	4.6	4.5
1996	-96.2	868.6	964.8	1,416.0	527.4	354.6	172.8	888.6	7,786.1	7,913.1	7,851.9	5.7	5.7
1997	-101.6	955.3	1,056.9	1,468.7	530.9	349.6	181.3	937.8	8,232.3	8,405.9	8,337.3	6.2	6.2
1998	-159.9	955.9	1,115.9	1,518.3	530.4	345.7	184.7	987.9	8,676.2	8,906.9	8,768.3	5.3	6.0
1999	-260.5	991.2	1,251.7	1,620.8	555.8	360.6	195.2	1,065.0	9,201.5	9,528.9	9,302.2	6.0	7.0
2000	-379.5	1,096.3	1,475.8	1,721.6	578.8	370.3	208.5	1,142.8	9,760.5	10,196.4	9,855.9	5.9	7.0
2001	-367.0	1,032.8	1,399.8	1,825.6	612.9	392.6	220.3	1,212.8	10,159.7	10,495.0	10,171.6	3.2	2.9
2002	-424.4	1,005.9	1,430.3	1,961.1	679.7	437.1	242.5	1,281.5	10,457.7	10,894.0	10,500.2	3.4	3.8
2003	-499.4	1,040.8	1,540.2	2,092.5	756.4	497.2	259.2	1,336.0	10,946.5	11,460.2	11,017.6	4.7	5.2
2004	-615.4	1,182.4	1,797.8	2,216.8	825.6	550.7	274.9	1,391.2	11,627.3	12,301.3	11,762.1	6.6	7.3
2005	-714.6	1,309.4	2,023.9	2,363.4	878.4	588.7	289.8	1,485.0	12,397.0	13,148.5	12,502.4	6.4	6.9
2006	-762.0	1,467.6	2,229.6	2,523.0	932.5	624.3	308.2	1,590.5	13,148.0	13,956.7	13,252.7	6.1	6.1
2004: I	-543.2	1,140.9	1,684.1	2,169.1	806.2	536.5	269.7	1,362.9	11,368.6	11,948.7	11,501.7	6.8	8.0
II	-603.1	1,172.8	1,775.8	2,202.8	821.9	546.5	275.3	1,381.0	11,541.3	12,213.3	11,683.1	7.4	9.2
III	-632.6	1,187.3	1,820.0	2,237.3	839.4	564.9	274.5	1,397.9	11,714.4	12,412.0	11,862.3	6.0	6.7
IV	-682.6	1,228.6	1,911.2	2,258.2	835.0	555.0	280.0	1,423.2	11,885.0	12,631.1	12,001.1	5.9	7.2
2005: I	-671.1	1,260.8	1,931.9	2,306.7	864.0	577.7	286.2	1,442.7	12,084.7	12,825.1	12,224.0	7.1	6.3
II	-679.8	1,301.2	1,981.0	2,339.8	870.4	585.0	285.4	1,469.5	12,305.2	12,997.2	12,385.1	5.5	5.5
III	-725.0	1,316.0	2,041.0	2,394.8	896.0	604.3	291.7	1,498.7	12,553.1	13,283.8	12,645.7	8.1	9.1
IV	-782.4	1,359.6	2,141.9	2,412.5	883.4	587.7	295.7	1,529.0	12,645.0	13,487.8	12,755.0	4.8	6.3
2006: I	-763.3	1,406.6	2,169.9	2,472.1	921.5	610.8	310.7	1,550.6	12,920.3	13,727.9	13,027.5	8.4	7.3
II	-780.4	1,447.4	2,227.8	2,512.5	926.9	620.6	306.3	1,585.7	13,095.5	13,935.4	13,218.9	6.0	6.2
III	-799.1	1,484.5	2,283.6	2,536.1	932.0	620.7	311.3	1,604.1	13,204.1	14,065.9	13,311.9	3.4	3.8
IV	-705.3	1,531.9	2,237.2	2,571.4	949.7	645.2	304.5	1,621.7	13,372.3	14,097.6	13,452.4	3.8	.9
2007: I	-714.2	1,549.9	2,264.0	2,608.3	946.6	634.8	311.7	1,661.7	13,553.5	14,266.1	13,615.1	4.9	4.9
II	-714.2	1,598.7	2,312.9	2,670.0	969.5	654.5	315.0	1,700.5	13,763.6	14,483.0	13,839.4	6.6	6.2
III	-694.7	1,685.7	2,380.4	2,716.5	990.3	673.5	316.8	1,726.2	13,935.0	14,665.1	14,071.6	6.0	5.1

[1] Gross domestic product (GDP) less exports of goods and services plus imports of goods and services.
[2] GDP plus net income receipts from rest of the world.

Source: Department of Commerce (Bureau of Economic Analysis).

Table B–2.—*Real gross domestic product, 1959–2007*

[Billions of chained (2000) dollars, except as noted; quarterly data at seasonally adjusted annual rates]

Year or quarter	Gross domestic product	Personal consumption expenditures				Gross private domestic investment						
		Total	Durable goods	Non-durable goods	Services	Total	Fixed investment					Change in private inven-tories
							Total	Nonresidential			Resi-dential	
								Total	Struc-tures	Equip-ment and software		
1959	2,441.3	1,554.6	....	....	....	266.7	....	....	....	....	....	....
1960	2,501.8	1,597.4	....	....	....	266.6	....	....	....	....	....	....
1961	2,560.0	1,630.3	....	....	....	264.9	....	....	....	....	....	....
1962	2,715.2	1,711.1	....	....	....	298.4	....	....	....	....	....	....
1963	2,834.0	1,781.6	....	....	....	318.5	....	....	....	....	....	....
1964	2,998.6	1,888.4	....	....	....	344.7	....	....	....	....	....	....
1965	3,191.1	2,007.7	....	....	....	393.1	....	....	....	....	....	....
1966	3,399.1	2,121.8	....	....	....	427.7	....	....	....	....	....	....
1967	3,484.6	2,185.0	....	....	....	408.1	....	....	....	....	....	....
1968	3,652.7	2,310.5	....	....	....	431.9	....	....	....	....	....	....
1969	3,765.4	2,396.4	....	....	....	457.1	....	....	....	....	....	....
1970	3,771.9	2,451.9	....	....	....	427.1	....	....	....	....	....	....
1971	3,898.6	2,545.5	....	....	....	475.7	....	....	....	....	....	....
1972	4,105.0	2,701.3	....	....	....	532.1	....	....	....	....	....	....
1973	4,341.5	2,833.8	....	....	....	594.4	....	....	....	....	....	....
1974	4,319.6	2,812.3	....	....	....	550.6	....	....	....	....	....	....
1975	4,311.2	2,876.9	....	....	....	453.1	....	....	....	....	....	....
1976	4,540.9	3,035.5	....	....	....	544.7	....	....	....	....	....	....
1977	4,750.5	3,164.1	....	....	....	627.0	....	....	....	....	....	....
1978	5,015.0	3,303.1	....	....	....	702.6	....	....	....	....	....	....
1979	5,173.4	3,383.4	....	....	....	725.0	....	....	....	....	....	....
1980	5,161.7	3,374.1	....	....	....	645.3	....	....	....	....	....	....
1981	5,291.7	3,422.2	....	....	....	704.9	....	....	....	....	....	....
1982	5,189.3	3,470.3	....	....	....	606.0	....	....	....	....	....	....
1983	5,423.8	3,668.6	....	....	....	662.5	....	....	....	....	....	....
1984	5,813.6	3,863.3	....	....	....	857.7	....	....	....	....	....	....
1985	6,053.7	4,064.0	....	....	....	849.7	....	....	....	....	....	....
1986	6,263.6	4,228.9	....	....	....	843.9	....	....	....	....	....	....
1987	6,475.1	4,369.8	....	....	....	870.0	....	....	....	....	....	....
1988	6,742.7	4,546.9	....	....	....	890.5	....	....	....	....	....	....
1989	6,981.4	4,675.0	....	....	....	926.2	....	....	....	....	....	....
1990	7,112.5	4,770.3	453.5	1,484.0	2,851.7	895.1	886.6	595.1	275.2	355.0	298.9	15.4
1991	7,100.5	4,778.4	427.9	1,480.5	2,900.0	822.2	829.1	563.2	244.6	345.9	270.2	–.5
1992	7,336.6	4,934.8	453.0	1,510.1	3,000.8	889.0	878.3	581.3	229.9	371.1	307.6	16.5
1993	7,532.7	5,099.8	488.4	1,550.4	3,085.7	968.3	953.5	631.9	228.3	417.4	332.7	20.6
1994	7,835.5	5,290.7	529.4	1,603.9	3,176.6	1,099.6	1,042.3	689.9	232.3	467.2	364.8	63.6
1995	8,031.7	5,433.5	552.6	1,638.6	3,259.9	1,134.0	1,109.6	762.5	247.1	523.1	353.1	29.9
1996	8,328.9	5,619.4	595.9	1,680.4	3,356.0	1,234.3	1,209.2	833.6	261.1	578.7	381.3	28.7
1997	8,703.5	5,831.8	646.9	1,725.3	3,468.0	1,387.7	1,320.6	934.2	280.1	658.3	388.6	71.2
1998	9,066.9	6,125.8	720.3	1,794.4	3,615.0	1,524.1	1,455.0	1,037.8	294.5	745.6	418.3	72.6
1999	9,470.3	6,438.6	804.6	1,876.6	3,758.0	1,642.6	1,576.3	1,133.3	293.2	840.2	443.6	68.9
2000	9,817.0	6,739.4	863.3	1,947.2	3,928.8	1,735.5	1,679.0	1,232.1	313.2	918.9	446.9	56.5
2001	9,890.7	6,910.4	900.7	1,986.7	4,023.2	1,598.4	1,629.4	1,180.5	306.1	874.2	448.5	–31.7
2002	10,048.8	7,099.3	964.8	2,037.1	4,100.4	1,557.1	1,544.6	1,071.5	253.8	820.2	469.9	12.5
2003	10,301.0	7,295.3	1,020.6	2,103.0	4,178.8	1,613.1	1,596.9	1,081.8	243.5	843.1	509.4	14.3
2004	10,675.8	7,561.4	1,084.8	2,177.6	4,311.0	1,770.2	1,712.8	1,144.3	246.7	905.1	560.2	54.3
2005	11,003.4	7,803.6	1,137.4	2,255.4	4,427.3	1,869.3	1,831.4	1,225.8	247.8	991.8	597.1	33.2
2006	11,319.4	8,044.1	1,180.5	2,337.7	4,545.5	1,919.5	1,874.7	1,306.8	268.6	1,050.6	569.5	40.3
2004: I	10,543.6	7,475.1	1,066.2	2,156.7	4,262.9	1,685.3	1,647.9	1,099.1	242.9	861.9	540.5	35.0
II	10,634.2	7,520.5	1,071.3	2,164.9	4,294.6	1,766.3	1,698.7	1,127.5	246.5	887.4	561.7	64.9
III	10,728.7	7,585.5	1,091.5	2,181.4	4,325.2	1,800.5	1,736.7	1,160.7	248.7	920.0	567.5	60.1
IV	10,796.4	7,664.3	1,110.1	2,207.5	4,361.1	1,828.8	1,767.7	1,189.7	248.6	951.2	570.9	57.2
2005: I	10,878.4	7,709.4	1,116.0	2,226.8	4,381.3	1,852.6	1,785.3	1,199.5	249.8	960.0	578.3	63.4
II	10,954.1	7,775.2	1,146.3	2,247.2	4,401.3	1,834.3	1,819.8	1,214.1	248.9	977.4	596.4	10.1
III	11,074.3	7,852.8	1,163.5	2,260.9	4,449.1	1,865.3	1,854.9	1,239.5	244.8	1,011.1	606.4	5.9
IV	11,107.2	7,876.9	1,123.8	2,286.8	4,477.5	1,924.9	1,865.6	1,250.0	247.7	1,018.7	607.2	53.6
2006: I	11,238.7	7,961.9	1,167.8	2,312.3	4,501.0	1,945.4	1,901.4	1,289.7	256.5	1,050.2	606.1	38.4
II	11,306.7	8,009.3	1,170.2	2,325.6	4,531.6	1,948.5	1,892.3	1,303.2	266.4	1,050.1	587.5	51.4
III	11,336.7	8,063.8	1,186.3	2,343.9	4,554.0	1,928.2	1,869.6	1,319.4	273.3	1,057.6	555.0	53.9
IV	11,395.5	8,141.2	1,197.6	2,368.8	4,595.5	1,856.2	1,835.5	1,314.8	278.3	1,044.4	529.4	17.4
2007: I	11,412.6	8,215.7	1,223.2	2,386.6	4,630.7	1,816.9	1,815.2	1,321.7	282.6	1,045.3	506.3	.1
II	11,520.1	8,244.3	1,228.4	2,383.8	4,656.7	1,837.4	1,829.3	1,356.6	299.5	1,057.4	490.7	5.8
III	11,658.9	8,302.2	1,241.9	2,396.8	4,689.5	1,859.9	1,826.0	1,387.3	311.1	1,073.5	463.3	30.6

See next page for continuation of table.

[Billions of chained (2000) dollars, except as noted; quarterly data at seasonally adjusted annual rates]

Year or quarter	Net exports of goods and services			Government consumption expenditures and gross investment					Final sales of domestic product	Gross domestic purchases [1]	Addendum: Gross national product [2]	Percent change from preceding period	
	Net exports	Exports	Imports	Total	Federal			State and local				Gross domestic product	Gross domestic purchases [1]
					Total	National defense	Nondefense						
1959	....	77.2	101.9	714.3	....	....	....	....	2,442.7	2,485.9	2,457.4	7.1	7.1
1960	....	90.6	103.3	715.4	....	....	....	....	2,506.8	2,529.6	2,519.4	2.5	1.8
1961	....	91.1	102.6	751.3	....	....	....	....	2,566.8	2,587.6	2,579.3	2.3	2.3
1962	....	95.7	114.3	797.6	....	....	....	....	2,708.5	2,751.4	2,736.9	6.1	6.3
1963	....	102.5	117.3	818.1	....	....	....	....	2,830.3	2,866.0	2,857.2	4.4	4.2
1964	....	114.6	123.6	836.1	....	....	....	....	2,999.9	3,023.2	3,023.6	5.8	5.5
1965	....	117.8	136.7	861.3	....	....	....	....	3,173.8	3,228.6	3,217.3	6.4	6.8
1966	....	126.0	157.1	937.1	....	....	....	....	3,364.8	3,450.3	3,423.7	6.5	6.9
1967	....	128.9	168.5	1,008.9	....	....	....	....	3,467.6	3,545.1	3,510.1	2.5	2.7
1968	....	139.0	193.6	1,040.5	....	....	....	....	3,640.3	3,727.5	3,680.0	4.8	5.1
1969	....	145.7	204.6	1,038.0	....	....	....	....	3,753.7	3,844.1	3,792.0	3.1	3.1
1970	....	161.4	213.4	1,012.9	....	....	....	....	3,787.7	3,837.4	3,798.2	.2	–.2
1971	....	164.1	224.7	990.8	....	....	....	....	3,893.4	3,974.2	3,927.8	3.4	3.6
1972	....	176.5	250.0	983.5	....	....	....	....	4,098.6	4,192.8	4,136.2	5.3	5.5
1973	....	209.7	261.6	980.0	....	....	....	....	4,315.9	4,399.1	4,383.6	5.8	4.9
1974	....	226.3	255.7	1,004.7	....	....	....	....	4,305.5	4,343.8	4,367.5	–.5	–1.3
1975	....	224.9	227.3	1,027.4	....	....	....	....	4,352.5	4,297.0	4,348.4	–.2	–1.1
1976	....	234.7	271.7	1,031.9	....	....	....	....	4,522.3	4,575.0	4,585.3	5.3	6.5
1977	....	240.3	301.4	1,043.3	....	....	....	....	4,721.6	4,818.5	4,800.3	4.6	5.3
1978	....	265.7	327.6	1,074.0	....	....	....	....	4,981.6	5,081.5	5,064.4	5.6	5.5
1979	....	292.0	333.0	1,094.1	....	....	....	....	5,161.2	5,206.8	5,240.1	3.2	2.5
1980	....	323.5	310.9	1,115.4	....	....	....	....	5,196.7	5,108.9	5,227.6	–.2	–1.9
1981	....	327.4	319.1	1,125.6	....	....	....	....	5,265.1	5,244.7	5,349.7	2.5	2.7
1982	....	302.4	315.0	1,145.4	....	....	....	....	5,233.4	5,175.1	5,249.7	–1.9	–1.3
1983	....	294.6	354.8	1,187.3	....	....	....	....	5,454.0	5,477.6	5,482.5	4.5	5.8
1984	....	318.7	441.1	1,227.0	....	....	....	....	5,739.2	5,951.6	5,869.3	7.2	8.7
1985	....	328.3	469.8	1,312.5	....	....	....	....	6,042.1	6,215.8	6,093.4	4.1	4.4
1986	....	353.7	510.0	1,392.5	....	....	....	....	6,271.8	6,443.6	6,290.6	3.5	3.7
1987	....	391.8	540.2	1,426.7	....	....	....	....	6,457.2	6,644.1	6,500.9	3.4	3.1
1988	....	454.6	561.4	1,445.1	....	....	....	....	6,734.5	6,857.9	6,775.2	4.1	3.2
1989	....	506.8	586.0	1,482.5	....	....	....	....	6,962.2	7,060.8	7,015.4	3.5	3.0
1990	–54.7	552.5	607.1	1,530.0	659.1	479.4	178.6	868.4	7,108.5	7,161.6	7,155.2	1.9	1.4
1991	–14.6	589.1	603.7	1,547.2	658.0	474.2	182.8	886.8	7,115.0	7,101.2	7,136.8	–.2	–.8
1992	–15.9	629.7	645.6	1,555.3	646.6	450.7	195.4	906.5	7,331.1	7,338.9	7,371.8	3.3	3.3
1993	–52.1	650.0	702.1	1,541.1	619.6	425.3	194.1	919.5	7,522.3	7,577.2	7,568.6	2.7	3.2
1994	–79.4	706.5	785.9	1,541.3	596.4	404.6	191.7	943.3	7,777.8	7,911.3	7,864.2	4.0	4.4
1995	–71.0	778.2	849.1	1,549.7	580.3	389.2	191.0	968.3	8,010.2	8,098.4	8,069.8	2.5	2.4
1996	–79.6	843.4	923.0	1,564.9	573.5	383.8	189.6	990.5	8,306.5	8,405.7	8,365.3	3.7	3.8
1997	–104.6	943.7	1,048.3	1,594.0	567.6	373.0	194.5	1,025.9	8,636.6	8,807.6	8,737.5	4.5	4.8
1998	–203.7	966.5	1,170.3	1,624.4	561.2	365.3	195.9	1,063.0	8,997.6	9,272.5	9,088.7	4.2	5.3
1999	–296.2	1,008.2	1,304.4	1,686.9	573.7	372.2	201.5	1,113.2	9,404.0	9,767.7	9,504.7	4.5	5.3
2000	–379.5	1,096.3	1,475.8	1,721.6	578.8	370.3	208.5	1,142.8	9,760.5	10,194.4	9,855.9	3.7	4.4
2001	–399.1	1,036.7	1,435.8	1,780.3	601.4	384.9	216.5	1,179.0	9,920.9	10,290.1	9,933.6	.8	.9
2002	–471.3	1,013.3	1,484.6	1,858.8	643.4	413.2	230.2	1,215.4	10,036.5	10,517.7	10,079.0	1.6	2.2
2003	–518.9	1,026.1	1,545.0	1,904.8	687.1	449.0	238.0	1,217.8	10,285.1	10,815.5	10,355.3	2.5	2.8
2004	–593.8	1,126.1	1,719.9	1,931.8	715.9	475.0	240.7	1,215.8	10,619.8	11,261.4	10,746.0	3.6	4.1
2005	–618.0	1,203.4	1,821.5	1,946.3	726.5	482.4	243.9	1,219.6	10,966.9	11,613.1	11,064.7	3.1	3.1
2006	–624.5	1,304.1	1,928.6	1,981.4	742.3	491.5	250.7	1,239.0	11,275.9	11,937.1	11,370.1	2.9	2.8
2004: I	–549.1	1,101.8	1,650.9	1,925.4	709.5	470.2	239.1	1,215.9	10,507.1	11,086.3	10,633.0	3.0	3.6
II	–591.1	1,119.4	1,710.5	1,931.8	713.7	472.5	241.0	1,218.1	10,568.5	11,216.9	10,701.4	3.5	4.8
III	–602.7	1,128.0	1,730.8	1,939.4	724.5	484.8	239.4	1,214.7	10,666.6	11,322.8	10,804.9	3.6	3.8
IV	–632.3	1,155.3	1,787.7	1,930.6	716.0	472.7	243.2	1,214.4	10,737.0	11,419.2	10,844.4	2.5	3.4
2005: I	–624.4	1,172.4	1,796.8	1,936.8	721.0	478.1	242.7	1,215.7	10,813.0	11,493.8	10,941.9	3.1	2.6
II	–601.0	1,199.3	1,800.3	1,942.5	722.2	481.1	240.9	1,220.1	10,940.4	11,546.9	11,014.7	2.8	1.9
III	–604.1	1,205.6	1,809.7	1,957.6	737.3	492.7	244.3	1,220.3	11,064.8	11,670.0	11,151.2	4.5	4.3
IV	–642.6	1,236.4	1,879.0	1,948.2	725.5	477.7	247.8	1,222.5	11,049.5	11,742.0	11,151.1	1.2	2.5
2006: I	–640.1	1,270.6	1,910.7	1,971.8	740.4	485.5	254.8	1,231.3	11,196.1	11,871.3	11,294.0	4.8	4.5
II	–626.6	1,288.4	1,915.0	1,976.5	737.4	488.2	249.0	1,238.9	11,252.1	11,926.1	11,362.5	2.4	1.9
III	–633.8	1,306.6	1,940.4	1,980.2	739.2	486.4	252.7	1,240.9	11,279.7	11,963.6	11,375.9	1.1	1.3
IV	–597.3	1,350.9	1,948.2	1,997.2	752.3	505.8	246.1	1,244.9	11,375.8	11,987.1	11,447.8	2.1	.8
2007: I	–612.1	1,354.7	1,966.8	1,994.7	740.2	491.6	248.4	1,254.2	11,411.6	12,018.7	11,466.7	.6	1.1
II	–573.9	1,379.5	1,953.4	2,014.8	751.0	501.7	248.9	1,263.5	11,512.8	12,088.9	11,580.0	3.8	2.4
III	–533.1	1,441.2	1,974.3	2,033.6	764.0	513.9	249.6	1,269.6	11,626.4	12,188.3	11,744.6	4.9	3.3

[1] Gross domestic product (GDP) less exports of goods and services plus imports of goods and services.
[2] GDP plus net income receipts from rest of the world.

Source: Department of Commerce (Bureau of Economic Analysis).

[Quarterly data are seasonally adjusted]

Year or quarter	Index numbers, 2000=100					Percent change from preceding period [1]				
	Gross domestic product (GDP)			Personal consumption expenditures (PCE)		Gross domestic product (GDP)			Personal consumption expenditures (PCE)	
	Real GDP (chain-type quantity index)	GDP chain-type price index	GDP implicit price deflator	PCE chain-type price index	PCE less food and energy price index	Real GDP (chain-type quantity index)	GDP chain-type price index	GDP implicit price deflator	PCE chain-type price index	PCE less food and energy price index
1959	24.868	20.754	20.751	20.432	21.031	7.1	1.2	1.2	1.6	2.2
1960	25.484	21.044	21.041	20.767	21.382	2.5	1.4	1.4	1.6	1.7
1961	26.077	21.281	21.278	20.985	21.640	2.3	1.1	1.1	1.0	1.2
1962	27.658	21.572	21.569	21.232	21.911	6.1	1.4	1.4	1.2	1.3
1963	28.868	21.801	21.798	21.479	22.175	4.4	1.1	1.1	1.2	1.2
1964	30.545	22.134	22.131	21.786	22.497	5.8	1.5	1.5	1.4	1.5
1965	32.506	22.538	22.535	22.103	22.771	6.4	1.8	1.8	1.5	1.2
1966	34.625	23.180	23.176	22.662	23.246	6.5	2.8	2.8	2.5	2.1
1967	35.496	23.897	23.893	23.237	23.915	2.5	3.1	3.1	2.5	2.9
1968	37.208	24.916	24.913	24.151	24.931	4.8	4.3	4.3	3.9	4.2
1969	38.356	26.153	26.149	25.255	26.089	3.1	5.0	5.0	4.6	4.6
1970	38.422	27.538	27.534	26.448	27.270	.2	5.3	5.3	4.7	4.5
1971	39.713	28.916	28.911	27.574	28.538	3.4	5.0	5.0	4.3	4.6
1972	41.815	30.171	30.166	28.528	29.462	5.3	4.3	4.3	3.5	3.2
1973	44.224	31.854	31.849	30.081	30.533	5.8	5.6	5.6	5.4	3.6
1974	44.001	34.721	34.725	33.191	32.825	−.5	9.0	9.0	10.3	7.5
1975	43.916	38.007	38.002	35.955	35.543	−.2	9.5	9.4	8.3	8.3
1976	46.256	40.202	40.196	37.948	37.716	5.3	5.8	5.8	5.5	6.1
1977	48.391	42.758	42.752	40.410	40.112	4.6	6.4	6.4	6.5	6.4
1978	51.085	45.762	45.757	43.248	42.756	5.6	7.0	7.0	7.0	6.6
1979	52.699	49.553	49.548	47.059	45.735	3.2	8.3	8.3	8.8	7.0
1980	52.579	54.062	54.043	52.078	49.869	−.2	9.1	9.1	10.7	9.0
1981	53.904	59.128	59.119	56.720	54.215	2.5	9.4	9.4	8.9	8.7
1982	52.860	62.738	62.726	59.859	57.776	−1.9	6.1	6.1	5.5	6.6
1983	55.249	65.214	65.207	62.436	60.823	4.5	3.9	4.0	4.3	5.3
1984	59.220	67.664	67.655	64.795	63.352	7.2	3.8	3.8	3.8	4.2
1985	61.666	69.724	69.713	66.936	65.778	4.1	3.0	3.0	3.3	3.8
1986	63.804	71.269	71.250	68.569	68.244	3.5	2.2	2.2	2.4	3.7
1987	65.958	73.204	73.196	70.947	70.772	3.4	2.7	2.7	3.5	3.7
1988	68.684	75.706	75.694	73.755	73.838	4.1	3.4	3.4	4.0	4.3
1989	71.116	78.569	78.556	76.972	76.884	3.5	3.8	3.8	4.4	4.1
1990	72.451	81.614	81.590	80.498	80.156	1.9	3.9	3.9	4.6	4.3
1991	72.329	84.457	84.444	83.419	83.292	−.2	3.5	3.5	3.6	3.9
1992	74.734	86.402	86.385	85.824	86.130	3.3	2.3	2.3	2.9	3.4
1993	76.731	88.390	88.381	87.804	88.332	2.7	2.3	2.3	2.3	2.6
1994	79.816	90.265	90.259	89.654	90.372	4.0	2.1	2.1	2.1	2.3
1995	81.814	92.115	92.106	91.577	92.388	2.5	2.0	2.0	2.1	2.2
1996	84.842	93.859	93.852	93.547	94.124	3.7	1.9	1.9	2.2	1.9
1997	88.658	95.415	95.414	95.124	95.644	4.5	1.7	1.7	1.7	1.6
1998	92.359	96.475	96.472	95.978	96.895	4.2	1.1	1.1	.9	1.3
1999	96.469	97.868	97.868	97.575	98.343	4.5	1.4	1.4	1.7	1.5
2000	100.000	100.000	100.000	100.000	100.000	3.7	2.2	2.2	2.5	1.7
2001	100.751	102.402	102.399	102.094	101.904	.8	2.4	2.4	2.1	1.9
2002	102.362	104.193	104.187	103.542	103.705	1.6	1.7	1.7	1.4	1.8
2003	104.931	106.409	106.404	105.597	105.175	2.5	2.1	2.1	2.0	1.4
2004	108.748	109.462	109.462	108.392	107.338	3.6	2.9	2.9	2.6	2.1
2005	112.086	113.005	113.000	111.588	109.670	3.1	3.2	3.2	2.9	2.2
2006	115.304	116.568	116.567	114.675	112.130	2.9	3.2	3.2	2.8	2.2
2004: I	107.402	108.180	108.175	107.163	106.442	3.0	3.7	3.7	3.5	2.4
II	108.325	109.185	109.178	108.179	107.142	3.5	3.8	3.8	3.8	2.7
III	109.287	109.807	109.793	108.703	107.601	3.6	2.3	2.3	2.0	1.7
IV	109.977	110.677	110.671	109.521	108.169	2.5	3.2	3.2	3.0	2.1
2005: I	110.812	111.745	111.726	110.119	108.858	3.1	3.9	3.9	2.2	2.6
II	111.583	112.455	112.446	111.037	109.422	2.8	2.6	2.6	3.4	2.1
III	112.808	113.422	113.405	112.205	109.878	4.5	3.5	3.5	4.3	1.7
IV	113.143	114.398	114.389	112.989	110.520	1.2	3.5	3.5	2.8	2.4
2006: I	114.482	115.363	115.357	113.480	111.078	4.8	3.4	3.4	1.7	2.0
II	115.175	116.350	116.347	114.670	111.871	2.4	3.5	3.5	4.3	2.9
III	115.481	117.030	117.026	115.406	112.519	1.1	2.4	2.4	2.6	2.3
IV	116.080	117.527	117.522	115.143	113.052	2.1	1.7	1.7	−.9	1.9
2007: I	116.254	118.750	118.745	116.129	113.730	.6	4.2	4.2	3.5	2.4
II	117.349	119.527	119.519	117.345	114.116	3.8	2.6	2.6	4.3	1.4
III	118.763	119.837	119.826	117.873	114.682	4.9	1.0	1.0	1.8	2.0

[1] Quarterly percent changes are at annual rates.

Source: Department of Commerce (Bureau of Economic Analysis).

TABLE B–4.—*Percent changes in real gross domestic product, 1959–2007*

[Percent change from preceding period; quarterly data at seasonally adjusted annual rates]

Year or quarter	Gross domestic product	Personal consumption expenditures				Gross private domestic investment				Exports and imports of goods and services		Government consumption expenditures and gross investment		
		Total	Durable goods	Non-durable goods	Serv-ices	Nonresidential fixed			Resi-dential fixed	Exports	Imports	Total	Federal	State and local
						Total	Struc-tures	Equip-ment and soft-ware						
1959	7.1	5.6	12.1	4.1	5.3	8.0	2.4	11.9	25.4	10.3	10.5	3.4	3.1	3.8
1960	2.5	2.8	2.0	1.5	4.5	5.7	7.9	4.2	−7.1	17.4	1.3	.2	−2.7	4.4
1961	2.3	2.1	−3.8	1.8	4.2	−.6	1.4	−1.9	.3	.5	−.7	5.0	4.2	6.2
1962	6.1	5.0	11.7	3.1	5.0	8.7	4.5	11.6	9.6	5.1	11.3	6.2	8.5	3.1
1963	4.4	4.1	9.7	2.1	4.6	5.6	1.1	8.4	11.8	7.1	2.7	2.6	.1	6.0
1964	5.8	6.0	9.3	4.9	6.1	11.9	10.4	12.8	5.8	11.8	5.3	2.2	−1.3	6.8
1965	6.4	6.3	12.7	5.3	5.3	17.4	15.9	18.3	−2.9	2.8	10.6	3.0	.0	6.7
1966	6.5	5.7	8.4	5.5	5.0	12.5	6.8	16.0	−8.9	6.9	14.9	8.8	11.0	6.3
1967	2.5	3.0	1.6	1.6	4.9	−1.4	−2.5	−.7	−3.1	2.3	7.3	7.7	9.9	5.0
1968	4.8	5.7	11.0	4.6	5.2	4.5	1.5	6.2	13.6	7.9	14.9	3.1	.8	5.9
1969	3.1	3.7	3.5	2.7	4.8	7.6	5.4	8.8	3.0	4.8	5.7	−.2	−3.4	3.4
1970	.2	2.3	−3.2	2.4	4.0	−.5	.3	−1.0	−6.0	10.7	4.3	−2.4	−7.4	2.8
1971	3.4	3.8	10.0	1.8	3.9	.0	−1.6	1.0	27.4	1.7	5.3	−2.2	−7.7	3.1
1972	5.3	6.1	12.7	4.4	5.7	9.2	3.1	12.9	17.8	7.5	11.3	−.7	−4.1	2.2
1973	5.8	4.9	10.3	3.3	4.7	14.6	8.2	18.3	−6	18.9	4.6	−.4	−4.2	2.8
1974	−.5	−.8	−6.9	−2.0	2.3	.8	−2.1	2.6	−20.6	7.9	−2.3	2.5	.9	3.8
1975	−.2	2.3	.0	1.5	3.7	−9.9	−10.5	−9.5	−13.0	−.6	−11.1	2.3	.3	3.7
1976	5.3	5.5	12.8	4.9	4.1	4.9	2.4	6.2	23.6	4.4	19.5	.4	.0	.7
1977	4.6	4.2	9.3	2.4	4.3	11.3	4.1	15.1	21.5	2.4	10.9	1.1	2.1	.4
1978	5.6	4.4	5.3	3.7	4.7	15.0	14.4	15.2	6.3	10.5	8.7	2.9	2.5	3.3
1979	3.2	2.4	−.3	2.7	3.1	10.1	12.7	8.7	−3.7	9.9	1.7	1.9	2.4	1.5
1980	−.2	−.3	−7.8	−.2	1.8	−.3	5.8	−3.6	−21.2	10.8	−6.6	2.0	4.7	−.1
1981	2.5	1.4	1.2	1.2	1.7	5.7	8.0	4.3	−8.0	1.2	2.6	.9	4.8	−2.0
1982	−1.9	1.4	−.1	1.0	2.1	−3.8	−1.7	−5.2	−18.2	−7.6	−1.3	1.8	3.9	.1
1983	4.5	5.7	14.6	3.3	5.5	−1.3	−10.8	5.4	41.4	−2.6	12.6	3.7	6.6	1.2
1984	7.2	5.3	14.6	4.0	4.1	17.7	14.0	19.8	14.8	8.2	24.3	3.3	3.1	3.6
1985	4.1	5.2	10.1	2.7	5.6	6.6	7.1	6.4	1.6	3.0	6.5	7.0	7.8	6.2
1986	3.5	4.1	9.7	3.6	2.9	−2.9	−11.0	1.9	12.3	7.7	8.6	6.1	5.7	6.4
1987	3.4	3.3	1.7	2.4	4.3	−.1	−2.9	1.4	2.0	10.8	5.9	2.5	3.6	1.5
1988	4.1	4.1	6.0	3.3	4.0	5.2	.6	7.5	−1.0	16.0	3.9	1.3	−1.6	3.7
1989	3.5	2.8	2.2	2.8	3.0	5.6	2.0	7.3	−3.0	11.5	4.4	2.6	1.5	3.4
1990	1.9	2.0	−.3	1.6	2.9	.5	1.5	.0	−8.6	9.0	3.6	3.2	2.0	4.1
1991	−.2	.2	−5.6	−.2	1.7	−5.4	−11.1	−2.6	−9.6	6.6	−.6	1.1	−.2	2.1
1992	3.3	3.3	5.9	2.0	3.5	3.2	−6.0	7.3	13.8	6.9	7.0	.5	−1.7	2.2
1993	2.7	3.3	7.8	2.7	2.8	8.7	−.7	12.5	8.2	3.2	8.8	−.9	−4.2	1.4
1994	4.0	3.7	8.4	3.5	2.9	9.2	1.8	11.9	9.6	8.7	11.9	.0	−3.7	2.6
1995	2.5	2.7	4.4	2.2	2.6	10.5	6.4	12.0	−3.2	10.1	8.0	.5	−2.7	2.6
1996	3.7	3.4	7.8	2.6	2.9	9.3	5.6	10.6	8.0	8.4	8.7	1.0	−1.2	2.3
1997	4.5	3.8	8.6	2.7	3.3	12.1	7.3	13.8	1.9	11.9	13.6	1.9	−1.0	3.6
1998	4.2	5.0	11.3	4.0	4.2	11.1	5.1	13.3	7.6	2.4	11.6	1.9	−1.1	3.6
1999	4.5	5.1	11.7	4.6	4.0	9.2	−.4	12.7	6.0	4.3	11.5	3.9	2.2	4.7
2000	3.7	4.7	7.3	3.8	4.5	8.7	6.8	9.4	.8	8.7	13.1	2.1	.9	2.7
2001	.8	2.5	4.3	2.0	2.4	−4.2	−2.3	−4.9	.4	−5.4	−2.7	3.4	3.9	3.2
2002	1.6	2.7	7.1	2.5	1.9	−9.2	−17.1	−6.2	4.8	−2.3	3.4	4.4	7.0	3.1
2003	2.5	2.8	5.8	3.2	1.9	1.0	−4.1	2.8	8.4	1.3	4.1	2.5	6.8	.2
2004	3.6	3.6	6.3	3.5	3.2	5.8	1.3	7.4	10.0	9.7	11.3	1.4	4.2	−2
2005	3.1	3.2	4.9	3.6	2.7	7.1	.5	9.6	6.6	6.9	5.9	.7	1.5	.3
2006	2.9	3.1	3.8	3.6	2.7	6.6	8.4	5.9	−4.6	8.4	5.9	1.8	2.2	1.6
2004: I	3.0	4.4	5.8	4.6	4.1	−2.6	−3	−3.4	4.0	10.0	12.3	1.5	6.1	−1.0
II	3.5	2.4	1.9	1.5	3.0	10.7	6.1	12.4	16.7	6.5	15.2	1.3	2.4	.7
III	3.6	3.5	7.8	3.1	2.9	12.3	3.6	15.5	4.2	3.1	4.8	1.6	6.2	−1.1
IV	2.5	4.2	7.0	4.9	3.4	10.3	−.2	14.3	2.4	10.0	13.8	−1.8	−4.6	−.1
2005: I	3.1	2.4	2.2	3.5	1.9	3.3	2.1	3.8	5.3	6.0	2.1	1.3	2.8	.4
II	2.8	3.5	11.3	3.7	1.8	5.0	−1.6	7.4	13.1	9.5	.8	1.2	.7	1.5
III	4.5	4.1	6.2	2.5	4.4	8.6	−6.3	14.5	6.9	2.1	2.1	3.2	8.6	.0
IV	1.2	1.2	−13.0	4.7	2.6	3.4	4.8	3.1	.5	10.6	16.2	−1.9	−6.2	.7
2006: I	4.8	4.4	16.6	4.5	2.1	13.3	15.0	13.0	−.7	11.5	6.9	4.9	8.4	2.9
II	2.4	2.4	.8	2.3	2.7	4.2	16.4	−.1	−11.7	5.7	.9	1.0	−1.6	2.5
III	1.1	2.8	5.6	3.2	2.0	5.1	10.8	2.9	−20.4	5.7	5.4	.8	.9	.7
IV	2.1	3.9	3.9	4.3	3.7	−1.4	7.4	−4.9	−17.2	14.3	1.6	3.5	7.3	1.3
2007: I	.6	3.7	8.8	3.0	3.1	2.1	6.4	.3	−16.3	1.1	3.9	−.5	−6.3	3.0
II	3.8	1.4	1.7	−.5	2.3	11.0	26.2	4.7	−11.8	7.5	−2.7	4.1	6.0	3.0
III	4.9	2.8	4.5	2.2	2.8	9.3	16.4	6.2	−20.5	19.1	4.4	3.8	7.1	1.9

Note.—Percent changes based on unrounded data.

Source: Department of Commerce (Bureau of Economic Analysis).

TABLE B–5.—*Contributions to percent change in real gross domestic product, 1959–2007*

[Percentage points, except as noted; quarterly data at seasonally adjusted annual rates]

Year or quarter	Gross domestic product (percent change)	Personal consumption expenditures				Gross private domestic investment						
		Total	Durable goods	Non-durable goods	Services	Total	Fixed investment					Change in private inventories
							Total	Nonresidential			Residential	
								Total	Structures	Equipment and software		
1959	7.1	3.55	0.97	1.25	1.33	2.80	1.94	0.73	0.09	0.64	1.21	0.86
1960	2.5	1.73	.17	.44	1.12	.00	.13	.52	.28	.24	-.39	-.13
1961	2.3	1.30	-.31	.53	1.08	-.10	-.04	-.06	.05	-.11	.01	-.05
1962	6.1	3.11	.89	.90	1.31	1.81	1.24	.78	.16	.61	.46	.57
1963	4.4	2.56	.77	.59	1.20	1.00	1.08	.50	.04	.46	.58	-.08
1964	5.8	3.71	.77	1.33	1.61	1.25	1.37	1.07	.36	.71	.30	-.13
1965	6.4	3.91	1.07	1.43	1.42	2.16	1.50	1.65	.57	1.07	-.15	.66
1966	6.5	3.50	.73	1.46	1.31	1.44	.87	1.29	.27	1.02	-.43	.58
1967	2.5	1.81	.13	.42	1.26	-.76	-.28	-.15	-.10	-.05	-.13	-.49
1968	4.8	3.50	.93	1.19	1.38	.90	1.00	.46	.06	.41	.53	-.10
1969	3.1	2.27	.31	.69	1.28	.90	.90	.78	.20	.58	.13	.00
1970	.2	1.42	-.28	.61	1.08	-1.04	-.31	-.06	.01	-.07	-.26	-.73
1971	3.4	2.38	.81	.47	1.09	1.67	1.10	.00	-.06	.07	1.10	.58
1972	5.3	3.80	1.07	1.11	1.61	1.87	1.81	.92	.12	.81	.89	.06
1973	5.8	3.05	.90	.82	1.33	1.96	1.46	1.50	.31	1.19	-.04	.50
1974	-.5	-.47	-.61	-.51	.65	-1.30	-1.04	.09	-.09	.18	-1.13	-.27
1975	-.2	1.42	.00	.37	1.05	-2.98	-1.71	-1.14	-.43	-.70	-.57	-1.27
1976	5.3	3.48	1.04	1.24	1.19	2.84	1.42	.52	.09	.43	.90	1.41
1977	4.6	2.68	.80	.60	1.27	2.43	2.18	1.19	.15	1.04	.99	.25
1978	5.6	2.76	.47	.91	1.38	2.16	2.04	1.69	.54	1.15	.35	.12
1979	3.2	1.52	-.03	.65	.90	.61	1.02	1.23	.52	.71	-.21	-.41
1980	-.2	-.17	-.65	-.04	.52	-2.12	-1.21	-.04	.27	-.30	-1.17	-.91
1981	2.5	.90	.09	.29	.51	1.59	.39	.74	.40	.34	-.35	1.20
1982	-1.9	.87	.00	.23	.65	-2.55	-1.22	-.51	-.09	-.42	-.71	-1.34
1983	4.5	3.65	1.07	.80	1.79	1.45	1.17	-.16	-.57	.41	1.33	.29
1984	7.2	3.44	1.15	.93	1.36	4.63	2.68	2.05	.60	1.44	.64	1.95
1985	4.1	3.31	.83	.61	1.87	-.17	.89	.82	.32	.50	.07	-1.06
1986	3.5	2.62	.83	.78	1.01	-.12	.20	-.36	-.50	.15	.55	-.32
1987	3.4	2.17	.16	.52	1.50	.51	.09	-.01	-.11	.10	.10	.42
1988	4.1	2.66	.53	.70	1.43	.39	.52	.57	.02	.55	-.05	-.14
1989	3.5	1.86	.19	.59	1.07	.64	.47	.61	.07	.54	-.14	.17
1990	1.9	1.34	-.02	.33	1.03	-.53	-.32	.05	.05	.00	-.37	-.21
1991	-.2	.11	-.46	-.05	.62	-1.20	-.94	-.57	-.39	-.18	-.37	-.26
1992	3.3	2.18	.44	.43	1.31	1.07	.79	.32	-.18	.50	.47	.29
1993	2.7	2.23	.59	.56	1.09	1.21	1.14	.83	-.02	.85	.31	.07
1994	4.0	2.52	.66	.71	1.14	1.93	1.30	.91	.05	.87	.39	.63
1995	2.5	1.81	.36	.44	1.01	.48	.94	1.08	.17	.91	-.14	-.46
1996	3.7	2.31	.64	.51	1.15	1.35	1.34	1.01	.16	.85	.33	.02
1997	4.5	2.54	.70	.53	1.31	1.95	1.42	1.33	.21	1.12	.08	.54
1998	4.2	3.36	.93	.78	1.66	1.63	1.60	1.28	.16	1.12	.32	.03
1999	4.5	3.44	.99	.89	1.56	1.33	1.36	1.09	-.01	1.11	.27	-.03
2000	3.7	3.17	.63	.74	1.80	.99	1.09	1.06	.21	.85	.03	-.10
2001	.8	1.74	.37	.40	.97	-1.39	-.50	-.52	-.07	-.44	.02	-.88
2002	1.6	1.90	.61	.50	.79	-.41	-.84	-1.06	-.55	-.51	.22	.43
2003	2.5	1.94	.50	.64	.80	.54	.51	.10	-.11	.21	.41	.04
2004	3.6	2.56	.53	.71	1.32	1.48	1.10	.56	.03	.53	.53	.39
2005	3.1	2.24	.40	.72	1.12	.91	1.09	.70	.01	.69	.39	-.18
2006	2.9	2.15	.31	.74	1.11	.45	.39	.68	.24	.44	-.29	.06
2004: I	3.0	3.12	.49	.92	1.71	.30	-.07	-.28	-.01	-.27	.21	.37
II	3.5	1.73	.16	.31	1.25	3.00	1.88	1.00	.15	.85	.89	1.12
III	3.6	2.46	.64	.62	1.21	1.26	1.41	1.16	.09	1.07	.24	-.14
IV	2.5	2.93	.57	.97	1.39	1.04	1.14	1.00	.00	1.01	.14	-.11
2005: I	3.1	1.68	.18	.71	.79	.89	.68	.36	.06	.30	.32	.21
II	2.8	2.40	.90	.74	.76	-.64	1.26	.51	-.04	.55	.75	-1.90
III	4.5	2.82	.51	.50	1.81	1.15	1.28	.87	-.17	1.04	.42	-.14
IV	1.2	.84	-1.13	.93	1.05	2.13	.38	.35	.12	.23	.03	1.74
2006: I	4.8	3.00	1.23	.91	.86	.78	1.27	1.31	.39	.92	-.05	-.49
II	2.4	1.63	.07	.47	1.10	.13	-.32	.44	.45	-.01	-.76	.46
III	1.1	1.88	.43	.64	.81	-.70	-.80	.53	.31	.21	-1.33	.10
IV	2.1	2.68	.30	.86	1.52	-2.50	-1.19	-.15	.23	-.38	-1.04	-1.31
2007: I	.6	2.56	.67	.61	1.28	-1.36	-.70	.22	.20	.02	-.93	-.65
II	3.8	1.00	.14	-.10	.96	.71	.49	1.12	.78	.34	-.62	.22
III	4.9	2.01	.35	.46	1.20	.77	-.11	.96	.52	.44	-1.08	.89

See next page for continuation of table.

[Percentage points, except as noted; quarterly data at seasonally adjusted annual rates]

Year or quarter	Net exports of goods and services							Government consumption expenditures and gross investment				
	Net exports	Exports			Imports			Total	Federal			State and local
		Total	Goods	Services	Total	Goods	Services		Total	National defense	Non-defense	
1959	0.00	0.45	-0.02	0.48	-0.45	-0.48	0.03	0.76	0.42	-0.23	0.65	0.34
1960	.72	.78	.76	.02	-.06	.05	-.11	.03	-.35	-.17	-.18	.39
1961	.06	.03	.02	.01	.03	.00	.02	1.07	.51	.45	.06	.56
1962	-.21	.25	.17	.08	-.47	-.40	-.07	1.36	1.07	.63	.44	.29
1963	.24	.35	.29	.06	-.12	-.12	.00	.58	.01	-.25	.26	.57
1964	.36	.59	.52	.07	-.23	-.19	-.04	.49	-.17	-.40	.23	.65
1965	-.30	.15	.02	.13	-.45	-.41	-.04	.65	.00	-.19	.19	.66
1966	-.29	.36	.27	.09	-.65	-.49	-.16	1.87	1.24	1.21	.03	.63
1967	-.22	.12	.02	.10	-.34	-.17	-.16	1.68	1.17	1.19	-.02	.51
1968	-.30	.41	.30	.10	-.70	-.68	-.03	.73	.10	.16	-.06	.63
1969	-.04	.25	.20	.05	-.29	-.20	-.09	-.06	-.42	-.49	.06	.37
1970	.34	.56	.44	.12	-.22	-.15	-.07	-.55	-.86	-.83	-.03	.31
1971	-.19	.10	-.02	.11	-.29	-.33	.04	-.50	-.85	-.97	.12	.36
1972	-.21	.42	.43	-.01	-.63	-.57	-.06	-.16	-.42	-.61	.18	.26
1973	.82	1.12	1.01	.11	-.29	-.34	.05	-.08	-.41	-.39	-.02	.33
1974	.75	.58	.46	.12	.18	.17	.00	.52	.08	-.05	.13	.44
1975	.89	-.05	-.16	.10	.94	.87	.07	.48	.03	-.06	.09	.45
1976	-1.08	.37	.31	.05	-1.45	-1.35	-.10	.10	.00	-.02	.03	.09
1977	-.72	.20	.08	.11	-.92	-.84	-.07	.23	.19	.07	.12	.04
1978	.05	.82	.68	.15	-.78	-.67	-.11	.60	.22	.05	.16	.38
1979	.66	.82	.77	.06	-.16	-.14	-.02	.37	.20	.17	.03	.17
1980	1.68	.97	.86	.11	.71	.67	.04	.38	.39	.25	.14	-.01
1981	-.15	.12	-.09	.21	-.27	-.18	-.09	.19	.42	.38	.04	-.23
1982	-.60	-.73	-.67	-.06	.12	.20	-.08	.35	.35	.48	-.13	.01
1983	-1.35	-.22	-.19	-.03	-1.13	-1.00	-.13	.77	.63	.50	.13	.13
1984	-1.58	.63	.46	.17	-2.21	-1.83	-.39	.70	.30	.35	-.05	.40
1985	-.42	.23	.20	.02	-.65	-.52	-.13	1.41	.74	.60	.14	.67
1986	-.30	.54	.26	.28	-.84	-.82	-.02	1.27	.55	.47	.08	.71
1987	.17	.78	.56	.21	-.61	-.39	-.22	.52	.36	.35	.01	.17
1988	.82	1.24	1.04	.20	-.42	-.36	-.07	.27	-.15	-.03	-.12	.42
1989	.52	.99	.75	.24	-.47	-.38	-.10	.52	.14	-.03	.17	.39
1990	.43	.81	.56	.26	-.39	-.26	-.13	.64	.18	.00	.18	.46
1991	.69	.63	.46	.16	.06	.01	.05	.23	-.02	-.07	.06	.24
1992	-.04	.68	.52	.16	-.72	-.77	.05	.11	-.15	-.32	.17	.26
1993	-.59	.32	.23	.09	-.91	-.85	-.06	-.18	-.35	-.33	-.02	.17
1994	-.43	.85	.67	.18	-1.29	-1.18	-.11	.00	-.30	-.27	-.03	.30
1995	.11	1.04	.85	.19	-.93	-.87	-.06	.10	-.20	-.19	-.01	.30
1996	-.14	.91	.68	.22	-1.05	-.94	-.11	.18	-.08	-.07	-.02	.26
1997	-.34	1.30	1.11	.19	-1.64	-1.45	-.19	.34	-.07	-.13	.06	.41
1998	-1.16	.27	.18	.09	-1.43	-1.20	-.23	.34	-.07	-.09	.02	.41
1999	-.99	.47	.29	.18	-1.46	-1.31	-.15	.67	.14	.08	.06	.54
2000	-.86	.93	.84	.09	-1.79	-1.55	-.25	.36	.05	-.02	.07	.31
2001	-.20	-.60	-.48	-.12	.40	.39	.01	.60	.23	.15	.08	.37
2002	-.69	-.23	-.28	.06	-.46	-.41	-.05	.80	.43	.29	.14	.37
2003	-.44	.12	.12	.00	-.56	-.56	.00	.47	.44	.37	.08	.02
2004	-.68	.93	.60	.33	-1.61	-1.33	-.27	.27	.29	.27	.03	-.02
2005	-.23	.70	.53	.17	-.92	-.86	-.06	.14	.11	.07	.03	.04
2006	-.08	.88	.73	.16	-.96	-.83	-.13	.35	.15	.09	.06	.19
2004: I	-.75	.95	.49	.46	-1.70	-1.32	-.37	.29	.41	.36	.06	-.12
II	-1.50	.64	.48	.16	-2.14	-1.92	-.21	.25	.17	.09	.08	.09
III	-.42	.31	.42	-.11	-.73	-.69	-.05	.30	.43	.49	-.06	-.13
IV	-1.07	.97	.49	.49	-2.04	-1.78	-.26	-.35	-.33	-.48	.15	-.01
2005: I	.26	.60	.40	.20	-.34	-.43	.09	.25	.19	.22	-.02	.05
II	.83	.95	.92	.03	-.12	-.13	.01	.22	.05	.12	-.07	.17
III	-.10	.22	.14	.08	-.32	-.32	.00	.60	.59	.46	.13	.01
IV	-1.41	1.07	.87	.20	-2.47	-2.22	-.26	-.37	-.46	-.59	.13	.09
2006: I	.13	1.19	1.10	.10	-1.07	-.83	-.24	.92	.57	.31	.27	.35
II	.49	.61	.49	.13	-.12	-.12	.00	.18	-.11	.11	-.22	.29
III	-.25	.62	.56	.07	-.88	-.84	-.03	.14	.06	-.07	.14	.08
IV	1.25	1.51	.73	.78	-.26	.09	-.35	.66	.50	.74	-.24	.16
2007: I	-.51	.13	.07	.05	-.63	-.57	-.06	-.09	-.46	-.54	.08	.36
II	1.32	.85	.53	.33	.47	.42	.05	.79	.41	.39	.02	.37
III	1.38	2.10	1.96	.14	-.72	-.67	-.05	.74	.50	.47	.03	.24

Source: Department of Commerce (Bureau of Economic Analysis).

TABLE B-6.—Chain-type quantity indexes for gross domestic product, 1959–2007

[Index numbers, 2000=100; quarterly data seasonally adjusted]

Year or quarter	Gross domestic product	Personal consumption expenditures				Gross private domestic investment					
		Total	Durable goods	Non-durable goods	Services	Total	Fixed investment				
							Total	Nonresidential			Residential
								Total	Structures	Equipment and software	
1959	24.868	23.067	10.822	33.491	20.794	15.367	15.736	10.760	36.530	6.065	37.820
1960	25.484	23.702	11.041	33.994	21.720	15.362	15.870	11.371	39.433	6.322	35.129
1961	26.077	24.191	10.622	34.621	22.626	15.261	15.820	11.299	39.966	6.200	35.227
1962	27.658	25.389	11.865	35.710	23.747	17.197	17.248	12.284	41.775	6.917	38.604
1963	28.868	26.436	13.017	36.463	24.830	18.351	18.584	12.966	42.239	7.500	43.154
1964	30.545	28.020	14.222	38.248	26.345	19.863	20.378	14.504	46.626	8.457	45.662
1965	32.506	29.791	16.025	40.277	27.749	22.650	22.459	17.031	54.058	10.007	44.329
1966	34.625	31.484	17.377	42.487	29.129	24.644	23.745	19.160	57.751	11.609	40.362
1967	35.496	32.422	17.648	43.157	30.552	23.517	23.306	18.900	56.284	11.532	39.092
1968	37.208	34.284	19.594	45.126	32.148	24.887	24.935	19.746	57.102	12.250	44.421
1969	38.356	35.558	20.289	46.326	33.691	26.338	26.486	21.246	60.189	13.334	45.733
1970	38.422	36.381	19.631	47.436	35.038	24.608	25.931	21.134	60.364	13.201	42.998
1971	39.713	37.770	21.593	48.294	36.400	27.413	27.894	21.135	59.370	13.332	54.789
1972	41.815	40.082	24.336	50.422	38.469	30.658	31.246	23.072	61.201	15.052	64.526
1973	44.224	42.048	26.849	52.068	40.274	34.249	34.101	26.429	66.200	17.812	64.112
1974	44.001	41.729	25.001	51.020	41.216	31.729	31.971	26.653	64.785	18.268	50.877
1975	43.916	42.688	24.996	51.771	42.743	26.111	28.541	24.022	57.984	16.529	44.271
1976	46.256	45.041	28.187	54.301	44.475	31.387	31.356	25.200	59.390	17.562	54.698
1977	48.391	46.950	30.809	55.609	46.392	36.130	35.863	28.045	61.841	20.208	66.440
1978	51.085	49.012	32.435	57.687	48.558	40.486	40.205	32.243	70.769	23.284	70.623
1979	52.699	50.204	32.325	59.226	50.044	41.776	42.473	35.489	79.731	25.318	68.032
1980	52.579	50.065	29.788	59.137	50.921	37.182	39.708	35.388	84.350	24.407	53.636
1981	53.904	50.779	30.149	59.839	51.773	40.615	40.591	37.398	91.074	25.445	49.336
1982	52.860	51.493	30.128	60.409	52.865	34.918	37.737	35.981	89.528	24.122	40.378
1983	55.249	54.436	34.535	62.417	55.760	38.172	40.491	35.518	79.865	25.420	57.093
1984	59.220	57.325	39.577	64.898	58.026	49.420	47.331	41.788	91.016	30.462	65.566
1985	61.666	60.303	43.577	66.665	61.303	48.963	49.823	44.561	97.502	32.397	66.604
1986	63.804	62.749	47.785	69.060	63.111	48.629	50.403	43.287	86.817	33.011	74.776
1987	65.958	64.840	48.616	70.715	65.843	50.130	50.682	43.259	84.340	33.463	76.269
1988	68.684	67.468	51.549	73.016	68.506	51.309	52.352	45.520	84.885	35.987	75.496
1989	71.116	69.369	52.686	75.044	70.555	53.369	53.928	48.063	86.583	38.624	73.204
1990	72.451	70.782	52.532	76.209	72.583	51.574	52.803	48.302	87.867	38.636	66.887
1991	72.329	70.903	49.564	76.033	73.812	47.378	49.379	45.712	78.091	37.643	60.460
1992	74.734	73.224	52.470	77.553	76.379	51.223	52.312	47.179	73.423	40.387	68.825
1993	76.731	75.672	56.577	79.619	78.540	55.795	56.788	51.287	72.891	45.428	74.446
1994	79.816	78.504	61.321	82.369	80.854	63.358	62.079	55.999	74.180	50.846	81.621
1995	81.814	80.623	64.011	84.152	82.973	65.340	66.090	61.885	78.903	56.930	79.005
1996	84.842	83.382	69.025	86.300	85.424	71.123	72.018	67.661	83.354	62.981	85.331
1997	88.658	86.533	74.935	88.605	88.270	79.961	78.657	75.820	89.432	71.641	86.947
1998	92.359	90.896	83.432	92.154	92.011	87.821	86.657	84.232	94.019	81.137	93.597
1999	96.469	95.537	93.192	96.374	95.652	94.647	93.884	91.980	93.619	91.437	99.254
2000	100.000	100.000	100.000	100.000	100.000	100.000	100.000	100.000	100.000	100.000	100.000
2001	100.751	102.537	104.327	102.027	102.403	92.103	97.047	95.817	97.737	95.136	100.357
2002	102.362	105.340	111.752	104.614	104.366	89.724	91.997	86.969	81.029	89.265	105.149
2003	104.931	108.249	118.214	108.002	106.363	92.949	95.110	87.804	77.735	91.747	113.977
2004	108.748	112.197	125.652	111.833	109.726	102.003	102.012	92.873	78.760	98.505	125.343
2005	112.086	115.791	131.748	115.828	112.687	107.709	109.080	99.490	79.127	107.935	133.608
2006	115.304	119.359	136.735	120.051	115.696	110.607	111.657	106.062	85.770	114.332	127.433
2004: I	107.402	110.917	123.502	110.759	108.502	97.109	98.148	89.210	77.550	93.800	120.936
II	108.325	111.590	124.094	111.178	109.309	101.776	101.175	91.512	78.708	96.575	125.696
III	109.287	112.555	126.432	112.026	110.088	103.748	103.439	94.211	79.410	100.124	126.994
IV	109.977	113.724	128.580	113.369	111.003	105.377	105.287	96.558	79.371	103.519	127.747
2005: I	110.812	114.393	129.271	114.360	111.516	106.749	106.333	97.355	79.776	104.477	129.413
II	111.583	115.370	132.377	115.404	112.626	105.692	108.386	98.545	79.460	106.368	133.463
III	112.808	116.521	134.775	116.110	113.241	107.484	110.481	100.603	78.179	110.030	135.695
IV	113.143	116.878	130.170	117.438	113.964	110.913	111.118	101.457	79.094	110.863	135.860
2006: I	114.482	118.140	135.263	118.749	114.563	112.095	113.245	104.679	81.898	114.291	135.615
II	115.175	118.843	135.542	119.434	115.341	112.274	112.705	105.770	85.063	114.276	131.465
III	115.481	119.652	137.413	120.370	115.911	111.106	111.354	107.090	87.270	115.100	124.190
IV	116.080	120.801	138.720	121.650	116.969	106.955	109.325	106.711	88.849	113.662	118.462
2007: I	116.254	121.906	141.680	122.563	117.865	104.690	108.113	107.277	90.241	113.753	113.301
II	117.349	122.331	142.283	122.419	118.527	105.875	108.956	110.109	95.639	115.075	109.791
III	118.763	123.190	143.852	123.090	119.360	107.172	108.756	112.597	99.330	116.821	103.665

See next page for continuation of table.

TABLE B–6.—*Chain-type quantity indexes for gross domestic product, 1959–2007*—Continued

[Index numbers, 2000=100; quarterly data seasonally adjusted]

Year or quarter	Exports of goods and services			Imports of goods and services			Government consumption expenditures and gross investment				
								Federal			State and local
	Total	Goods	Services	Total	Goods	Services	Total	Total	National defense	Non-defense	
1959	7.043	6.198	9.641	6.908	5.403	15.462	41.489	68.666	89.447	33.305	26.999
1960	8.266	7.651	9.797	7.000	5.314	16.669	41.553	66.779	87.977	30.672	28.182
1961	8.309	7.689	9.857	6.953	5.307	16.385	43.639	69.564	91.851	31.599	29.918
1962	8.729	8.031	10.535	7.742	6.092	17.150	46.329	75.492	97.412	38.144	30.839
1963	9.353	8.662	11.070	7.951	6.339	17.137	47.522	75.540	95.085	42.217	32.696
1964	10.454	9.849	11.733	8.374	6.757	17.579	48.563	74.530	91.304	45.880	34.913
1965	10.747	9.901	12.926	9.265	7.714	18.096	50.028	74.508	89.403	48.995	37.252
1966	11.492	10.589	13.814	10.642	8.930	20.395	54.430	82.737	102.205	49.501	39.590
1967	11.757	10.638	14.905	11.417	9.400	22.887	58.604	90.960	115.571	49.059	41.589
1968	12.681	11.481	16.049	13.118	11.342	23.298	60.436	91.681	117.416	47.912	44.048
1969	13.294	12.082	16.646	13.866	11.963	24.767	60.290	88.525	111.604	49.186	45.534
1970	14.723	13.460	18.128	14.457	12.432	26.059	58.833	81.997	101.477	48.674	46.797
1971	14.973	13.408	19.527	15.229	13.474	25.317	57.553	75.686	89.980	50.961	48.232
1972	16.096	14.849	19.404	16.943	15.307	26.390	57.128	72.574	82.921	54.551	49.291
1973	19.131	18.259	20.775	17.729	16.388	25.500	56.926	69.519	78.322	54.213	50.694
1974	20.643	19.709	22.396	17.327	15.932	25.472	58.360	70.134	77.714	57.023	52.603
1975	20.512	19.252	23.773	15.402	13.924	24.367	59.675	70.360	76.977	58.965	54.536
1976	21.408	20.165	24.476	18.413	17.073	26.049	59.940	70.388	76.706	59.523	54.937
1977	21.923	20.429	26.055	20.426	19.153	27.347	60.598	71.880	77.597	62.089	55.137
1978	24.234	22.712	28.234	22.196	20.871	29.297	62.383	73.681	78.259	65.947	56.938
1979	26.637	25.396	29.103	22.565	21.229	29.700	63.549	75.465	80.648	66.640	57.775
1980	29.506	28.422	30.919	21.066	19.653	29.037	64.790	79.043	84.160	70.373	57.736
1981	29.868	28.114	34.211	21.620	20.058	30.711	65.381	82.818	89.486	71.310	56.577
1982	27.586	25.573	33.263	21.348	19.554	32.346	66.530	86.018	96.244	67.888	56.607
1983	26.875	24.838	32.710	24.041	22.210	34.958	68.964	91.726	103.158	71.398	57.268
1984	29.068	26.801	35.627	29.893	27.584	43.724	71.273	94.550	108.186	70.035	59.322
1985	29.951	27.790	36.051	31.833	29.310	47.050	76.240	101.957	117.355	74.169	63.003
1986	32.259	29.217	41.325	34.561	32.314	47.638	80.885	107.754	124.871	76.764	67.064
1987	35.742	32.456	45.502	36.602	33.812	53.205	82.873	111.674	130.779	76.984	68.041
1988	41.469	38.572	49.616	38.039	35.181	55.010	83.940	109.898	130.161	73.037	70.582
1989	46.233	43.172	54.723	39.706	36.686	57.678	86.110	111.594	129.518	79.075	72.994
1990	50.394	46.810	60.480	41.139	37.770	61.430	88.869	113.873	129.472	85.651	75.991
1991	53.736	50.042	64.082	40.905	37.741	59.849	89.872	113.679	128.050	87.700	77.600
1992	57.439	53.785	67.590	43.748	41.263	58.321	90.342	111.713	121.708	93.749	79.318
1993	59.291	55.534	69.726	47.576	45.423	60.026	89.513	107.056	114.860	93.087	80.459
1994	64.447	60.937	74.097	53.256	51.466	63.421	89.525	103.050	109.259	91.957	82.543
1995	70.982	68.070	78.793	57.539	56.104	65.492	90.015	100.254	105.093	91.613	84.728
1996	76.930	74.086	84.483	62.544	61.337	69.094	90.896	99.091	103.648	90.955	86.668
1997	86.082	84.717	89.509	71.037	70.172	75.600	92.588	98.066	100.733	93.320	89.770
1998	88.164	86.614	92.077	79.299	78.364	84.222	94.354	96.970	98.650	93.985	93.014
1999	91.969	89.907	97.207	88.391	88.078	90.038	97.987	99.122	100.515	96.646	97.409
2000	100.000	100.000	100.000	100.000	100.000	100.000	100.000	100.000	100.000	100.000	100.000
2001	94.565	93.871	96.302	97.291	96.833	99.706	103.412	103.908	103.936	103.859	103.162
2002	92.430	90.143	98.104	100.601	100.377	101.824	107.969	111.169	111.578	110.441	106.354
2003	93.599	91.771	98.148	104.693	105.294	101.857	110.644	118.712	121.239	114.181	106.557
2004	102.723	100.011	109.451	116.546	117.173	113.589	112.210	123.693	128.282	115.441	106.384
2005	109.775	107.542	115.342	123.425	124.937	116.149	113.050	125.524	130.268	116.992	106.721
2006	118.957	118.234	120.897	130.683	132.446	122.180	115.092	128.255	132.722	120.234	108.418
2004: I	100.502	97.543	107.836	111.867	112.096	110.835	111.839	122.580	126.964	114.695	106.393
II	102.108	99.250	109.197	115.903	116.476	113.211	112.212	123.306	127.588	115.604	106.586
III	102.897	100.747	108.243	117.279	118.033	113.712	112.649	125.175	130.930	114.821	106.291
IV	105.385	102.503	112.529	121.135	122.089	116.597	112.138	123.710	127.647	116.644	106.265
2005: I	106.943	103.963	114.325	121.756	123.052	115.549	112.500	124.566	129.104	116.405	106.378
II	109.401	107.322	114.592	121.994	123.368	115.396	112.830	124.787	129.926	115.535	106.763
III	109.976	107.823	115.341	122.630	124.133	115.396	113.710	127.388	133.051	117.182	106.776
IV	112.780	111.059	117.109	127.321	129.196	118.254	113.161	125.353	128.990	118.847	106.968
2006: I	115.898	115.123	117.960	129.472	131.232	120.981	114.533	127.919	131.114	122.227	107.745
II	117.528	116.953	119.103	129.764	131.589	120.953	114.807	127.414	131.848	119.453	108.407
III	119.182	119.047	119.698	131.483	133.574	121.341	115.022	127.708	131.347	121.209	108.584
IV	123.222	121.811	126.828	132.014	133.389	125.445	116.007	129.977	136.577	118.046	108.935
2007: I	123.568	122.091	127.335	133.237	134.755	126.172	115.865	127.886	132.744	119.140	109.748
II	125.833	124.072	130.293	132.363	133.770	125.643	117.028	129.756	135.488	119.414	110.564
III	131.458	131.498	131.576	133.780	135.360	126.189	118.121	132.000	138.775	119.747	111.096

Source: Department of Commerce (Bureau of Economic Analysis).

TABLE B–7.—*Chain-type price indexes for gross domestic product, 1959–2007*

[Index numbers, 2000=100, except as noted; quarterly data seasonally adjusted]

Year or quarter	Gross domestic product	Personal consumption expenditures				Gross private domestic investment						
							Fixed investment					
								Nonresidential				
		Total	Durable goods	Non-durable goods	Services	Total	Total	Total	Structures	Equip-ment and software	Resi-dential
1959	20.754	20.432	45.662	22.765	15.485	29.474	28.262	35.114	15.923	50.882	16.630
1960	21.044	20.767	45.444	23.089	15.887	29.619	28.414	35.275	15.904	51.305	16.743
1961	21.281	20.985	45.551	23.227	16.173	29.538	28.325	35.076	15.810	51.025	16.769
1962	21.572	21.232	45.755	23.412	16.466	29.558	28.346	35.087	15.941	50.774	16.795
1963	21.801	21.479	45.915	23.683	16.701	29.467	28.267	35.088	16.085	50.495	16.663
1964	22.134	21.786	46.142	23.986	17.016	29.634	28.440	35.268	16.316	50.474	16.796
1965	22.538	22.103	45.721	24.423	17.334	30.107	28.926	35.672	16.791	50.520	17.272
1966	23.180	22.662	45.517	25.232	17.810	30.726	29.536	36.206	17.398	50.654	17.899
1967	23.897	23.237	46.228	25.830	18.349	31.538	30.364	37.129	17.943	51.776	18.521
1968	24.916	24.151	47.749	26.820	19.128	32.714	31.582	38.431	18.835	53.167	19.504
1969	26.153	25.255	49.067	28.062	20.106	34.264	33.140	40.018	20.074	54.645	20.853
1970	27.538	26.448	50.148	29.446	21.175	35.713	34.565	41.908	21.390	56.657	21.526
1971	28.916	27.574	51.975	30.359	22.340	37.493	36.306	43.880	23.040	58.340	22.775
1972	30.171	28.528	52.531	31.373	23.304	39.062	37.865	45.367	24.704	59.044	24.158
1973	31.854	30.081	53.301	33.838	24.381	41.172	39.958	47.115	26.619	60.047	26.297
1974	34.721	33.191	56.676	38.702	26.345	45.263	43.890	51.658	30.295	64.474	29.011
1975	38.007	35.955	61.844	41.735	28.595	50.847	49.384	58.763	33.911	74.001	31.706
1976	40.202	37.948	65.278	43.346	30.603	53.654	52.244	62.018	35.571	78.355	33.743
1977	42.758	40.410	68.129	45.911	32.933	57.677	56.342	66.258	38.651	83.011	37.147
1978	45.762	43.248	72.038	48.985	35.464	62.381	61.101	70.695	42.382	87.391	41.696
1979	49.553	47.059	76.830	54.148	38.316	68.027	66.642	76.440	47.313	92.932	46.374
1980	54.062	52.078	83.277	60.449	42.332	74.424	72.887	83.198	51.740	100.868	51.394
1981	59.128	56.720	88.879	65.130	46.746	81.278	79.670	91.245	58.880	108.077	55.587
1982	62.738	59.859	92.358	66.955	50.528	85.455	84.047	96.295	63.566	112.293	58.564
1983	65.214	62.436	94.181	68.386	53.799	85.237	83.912	95.432	61.939	112.530	59.908
1984	67.664	64.795	95.550	70.004	56.680	85.845	84.399	95.195	62.468	111.547	61.630
1985	69.724	66.936	96.620	71.543	59.295	86.720	85.457	95.936	63.940	111.413	63.219
1986	71.269	68.569	97.685	71.273	62.040	88.599	87.501	97.566	65.168	113.178	65.868
1987	73.204	70.947	100.465	73.731	64.299	90.289	89.118	98.435	66.199	113.796	68.561
1988	75.706	73.755	101.921	76.206	67.493	92.354	91.431	100.625	69.016	115.216	70.928
1989	78.569	76.972	103.717	79.842	70.708	94.559	93.641	102.731	71.707	116.657	73.211
1990	81.614	80.498	104.561	84.226	74.197	96.379	95.542	104.695	74.015	118.168	74.930
1991	84.457	83.419	106.080	86.779	77.497	97.749	96.960	106.314	75.355	119.854	75.912
1992	86.402	85.824	106.756	88.105	80.684	97.395	96.670	105.411	75.330	118.444	76.836
1993	88.390	87.804	107.840	88.973	83.345	98.521	97.805	105.487	77.602	117.243	79.941
1994	90.265	89.654	109.978	89.605	85.748	99.813	99.133	106.008	80.388	116.572	82.754
1995	92.115	91.577	110.672	90.629	88.320	100.941	100.292	106.239	83.879	115.224	85.769
1996	93.859	93.547	109.507	92.567	90.844	100.520	100.028	105.011	86.045	112.451	87.610
1997	95.415	95.124	107.068	93.835	93.305	100.157	99.785	103.696	89.381	109.120	89.843
1998	96.475	95.978	104.152	93.821	95.319	99.035	98.861	101.421	93.474	104.259	92.239
1999	97.868	97.575	101.626	96.173	97.393	98.972	98.888	100.057	96.257	101.366	95.780
2000	100.000	100.000	100.000	100.000	100.000	100.000	100.000	100.000	100.000	100.000	100.000
2001	102.402	102.094	98.114	101.531	103.257	101.013	101.023	99.683	105.403	97.708	104.633
2002	104.193	103.542	95.766	102.089	106.018	101.640	101.660	99.513	110.030	95.956	107.240
2003	106.409	105.597	92.366	104.145	109.379	103.191	103.313	99.591	113.872	94.912	112.372
2004	109.462	108.392	90.696	107.626	112.929	106.686	106.845	100.896	120.912	94.600	120.587
2005	113.005	111.588	90.018	111.561	116.726	111.155	111.404	103.778	135.013	94.527	128.653
2006	116.568	114.675	88.857	114.989	120.725	115.090	115.352	106.961	150.806	94.485	134.288
2004: I	108.180	107.163	90.927	105.918	111.582	105.010	105.165	100.123	116.960	94.708	117.027
II	109.185	108.179	90.986	107.530	112.532	106.217	106.382	100.729	119.118	94.872	119.511
III	109.807	108.703	90.415	107.903	113.406	107.246	107.404	101.048	122.026	94.477	121.984
IV	110.677	109.521	90.454	109.153	114.198	108.271	108.429	101.686	125.544	94.344	123.826
2005: I	111.745	110.119	90.470	109.234	115.204	109.653	109.837	102.816	129.388	94.759	125.811
II	112.455	111.037	90.375	110.570	116.165	110.407	110.618	103.439	132.114	94.827	126.933
III	113.422	112.205	89.735	113.113	117.100	111.493	111.759	103.846	136.453	94.240	129.599
IV	114.398	112.989	89.491	113.328	118.434	113.065	113.403	105.009	142.098	94.281	132.270
2006: I	115.363	113.480	89.276	113.405	119.316	114.175	114.485	106.025	146.516	94.423	133.546
II	116.350	114.670	89.110	115.763	120.252	114.891	115.169	106.764	150.294	94.379	134.137
III	117.030	115.406	88.827	116.576	121.209	115.335	115.592	107.267	152.344	94.470	134.390
IV	117.527	115.143	88.213	114.210	122.122	115.958	116.162	107.789	154.071	94.667	135.076
2007: I	118.750	116.129	87.799	115.620	123.252	116.532	116.718	108.301	155.637	94.892	135.736
II	119.527	117.345	87.488	118.413	124.055	116.426	116.636	108.293	155.199	95.002	135.459
III	119.837	117.873	87.091	118.751	124.921	116.325	116.498	108.140	155.392	94.751	135.367

See next page for continuation of table.

TABLE B–7.—*Chain-type price indexes for gross domestic product, 1959–2007*—Continued

[Index numbers, 2000=100, except as noted; quarterly data seasonally adjusted]

Year or quarter	Exports	Imports	Total	Federal Total	Federal National defense	Federal Non-defense	State and local	Final sales of domestic product	Gross domestic purchases Total	Gross domestic purchases Less food and energy	Gross domestic product	Gross domestic purchases Total	Gross domestic purchases Less food and energy
1959	29.433	21.901	15.404	16.450	16.257	16.591	14.475	20.581	20.365	.....	1.2	1.2	.....
1960	29.846	22.110	15.597	16.590	16.383	16.798	14.738	20.872	20.646	.....	1.4	1.4	.....
1961	30.300	22.110	15.909	16.871	16.619	17.296	15.093	21.108	20.865	.....	1.1	1.1	.....
1962	30.375	21.849	16.314	17.228	16.940	17.808	15.564	21.398	21.139	.....	1.4	1.3	.....
1963	30.307	22.273	16.669	17.597	17.320	18.116	15.911	21.629	21.385	.....	1.1	1.2	.....
1964	30.556	22.743	17.132	18.191	17.822	19.036	16.234	21.963	21.725	.....	1.5	1.6	.....
1965	31.529	23.059	17.588	18.658	18.314	19.408	16.685	22.368	22.102	.....	1.8	1.7	.....
1966	32.481	23.596	18.330	19.330	18.950	20.190	17.507	23.010	22.724	.....	2.8	2.8	.....
1967	33.725	23.688	19.099	19.913	19.518	20.815	18.488	23.729	23.389	.....	3.1	2.9	.....
1968	34.461	24.048	20.128	20.995	20.539	22.116	19.475	24.752	24.380	.....	4.3	4.2	.....
1969	35.627	24.675	21.341	22.130	21.664	23.251	20.780	25.988	25.580	.....	5.0	4.9	.....
1970	36.993	26.135	23.079	23.915	23.321	25.478	22.488	27.369	26.964	.....	5.3	5.4	.....
1971	38.358	27.739	24.875	25.957	25.387	27.400	24.087	28.741	28.351	.....	5.0	5.1	.....
1972	40.146	29.682	26.788	28.495	28.319	28.780	25.524	29.994	29.619	.....	4.3	4.5	.....
1973	45.425	34.841	28.743	30.449	30.396	30.394	27.477	31.673	31.343	.....	5.6	5.8	.....
1974	55.965	49.847	31.646	33.162	33.217	32.819	30.500	34.517	34.546	.....	9.0	10.2	.....
1975	61.682	53.997	34.824	36.615	36.460	36.746	33.481	37.789	37.761	.....	9.5	9.3	.....
1976	63.707	55.622	37.118	39.217	39.117	39.209	35.563	39.987	39.938	.....	5.8	5.8	.....
1977	66.302	60.523	39.694	42.180	42.079	42.152	37.872	42.546	42.634	.....	6.4	6.8	.....
1978	70.342	64.798	42.235	44.785	45.035	43.983	40.359	45.551	45.663	.....	7.0	7.1	.....
1979	78.808	75.879	45.775	48.231	48.628	47.099	43.944	49.322	49.669	.....	8.3	8.8	.....
1980	86.801	94.513	50.761	53.299	53.908	51.683	48.858	53.806	54.876	.....	9.1	10.5	.....
1981	93.217	99.594	55.752	58.476	59.229	56.516	53.709	58.859	59.896	.....	9.4	9.1	.....
1982	93.645	96.235	59.414	62.446	63.392	60.020	57.140	62.489	63.296	62.221	6.1	5.7	.....
1983	94.015	92.629	61.778	64.612	65.617	62.038	59.666	64.958	65.515	64.685	3.9	3.5	4.0
1984	94.887	91.829	64.955	68.426	70.290	63.577	62.336	67.399	67.822	67.106	3.8	3.5	3.7
1985	91.983	88.813	66.970	69.974	71.621	65.740	64.739	69.494	69.760	69.232	3.0	2.9	3.2
1986	90.639	88.871	68.175	70.352	71.554	67.395	66.624	71.060	71.338	71.474	2.2	2.3	3.2
1987	92.874	94.251	70.056	71.200	72.281	68.616	69.361	72.985	73.527	73.716	2.7	3.1	3.1
1988	97.687	98.774	71.899	72.704	73.631	70.609	71.485	75.519	76.043	76.429	3.4	3.4	3.7
1989	99.310	100.944	74.139	74.677	75.528	72.826	73.940	78.383	78.934	79.151	3.8	3.8	3.6
1990	99.982	103.826	77.139	77.142	78.010	75.260	77.357	81.440	82.144	82.109	3.9	4.1	3.7
1991	101.313	103.420	79.787	80.232	80.821	79.100	79.681	84.286	84.836	84.942	3.5	3.3	3.5
1992	100.892	103.552	81.719	82.602	83.628	80.411	81.300	86.237	86.828	87.169	2.3	2.3	2.6
1993	100.898	102.671	83.789	84.788	85.313	83.728	83.294	88.226	88.730	89.211	2.3	2.2	2.3
1994	102.033	103.634	86.002	87.061	87.412	86.375	85.472	90.108	90.583	91.213	2.1	2.1	2.2
1995	104.376	106.412	88.358	89.503	89.598	89.351	87.778	91.965	92.483	93.176	2.0	2.1	2.2
1996	102.988	104.529	90.491	91.982	92.379	91.216	89.709	93.736	94.145	94.616	1.9	1.8	1.5
1997	101.232	100.816	92.139	93.533	93.716	93.192	91.414	95.320	95.440	95.865	1.7	1.4	1.3
1998	98.905	95.353	93.469	94.511	94.643	94.268	92.934	96.428	96.060	96.797	1.1	.6	1.0
1999	98.313	95.960	96.079	96.884	96.886	96.880	95.667	97.847	97.556	98.165	1.4	1.6	1.4
2000	100.000	100.000	100.000	100.000	100.000	100.000	100.000	100.000	100.000	100.000	2.2	2.5	1.9
2001	99.624	97.497	102.544	101.907	102.002	101.739	102.868	102.406	101.994	101.882	2.4	2.0	1.9
2002	99.273	96.341	105.507	105.631	105.792	105.345	105.435	104.197	103.583	103.796	1.7	1.6	1.9
2003	101.429	99.685	109.849	110.094	110.751	108.898	109.712	106.430	105.966	105.749	2.1	2.3	1.9
2004	104.997	104.526	114.754	115.322	115.932	114.218	114.431	109.487	109.235	108.587	2.9	3.1	2.7
2005	108.803	111.117	121.435	120.914	122.034	118.807	121.758	113.040	113.225	111.924	3.2	3.7	3.1
2006	112.537	115.610	127.334	125.622	127.027	122.959	128.370	116.603	116.920	115.203	3.2	3.3	2.9
2004: I	103.567	102.047	112.657	113.641	114.112	112.813	112.088	108.206	107.787	107.379	3.7	4.3	3.5
II	104.785	103.872	114.028	115.164	115.679	114.250	113.369	109.212	108.893	108.272	3.8	4.2	3.4
III	105.273	105.212	115.361	115.863	116.521	114.661	115.077	109.830	109.637	108.969	2.3	2.8	2.6
IV	106.362	106.973	116.971	116.621	117.417	115.147	117.191	110.699	110.622	109.728	3.2	3.6	2.8
2005: I	107.552	107.565	119.102	119.840	120.846	117.957	118.677	111.770	111.605	110.804	3.9	3.6	4.0
II	108.506	110.075	120.462	120.512	121.590	118.487	120.443	112.484	112.571	111.507	2.6	3.5	2.6
III	109.171	112.811	122.335	121.534	122.654	119.427	122.825	113.459	113.846	112.247	3.5	4.6	2.7
IV	109.983	114.018	123.839	121.770	123.046	119.355	125.087	114.446	114.878	113.136	3.5	3.7	3.2
2006: I	110.725	113.576	125.379	124.463	125.802	121.927	125.938	115.405	115.645	114.018	3.4	2.7	3.2
II	112.359	116.339	127.125	125.686	127.106	122.990	127.998	116.388	116.850	114.909	3.5	4.2	3.2
III	113.641	117.689	128.076	126.097	127.618	123.204	129.271	117.065	117.575	115.612	2.4	2.5	2.5
IV	113.424	114.834	128.757	126.244	127.582	123.714	130.272	117.553	117.609	116.274	1.7	.1	2.3
2007: I	114.433	115.114	130.765	127.886	129.153	125.503	132.499	118.773	118.702	117.156	4.2	3.8	3.1
II	115.912	118.408	132.527	129.098	130.454	126.539	134.586	119.555	119.809	117.600	2.6	3.8	1.5
III	116.992	120.572	133.588	129.622	131.069	126.876	135.969	119.860	120.330	118.141	1.0	1.8	1.9

[1] Gross domestic product (GDP) less exports of goods and services plus imports of goods and services.
[2] Quarterly percent changes are at annual rates.

Source: Department of Commerce (Bureau of Economic Analysis).

TABLE B–8.—*Gross domestic product by major type of product, 1959–2007*

[Billions of dollars; quarterly data at seasonally adjusted annual rates]

Year or quarter	Gross domestic product	Final sales of domestic product	Change in private inventories	Goods Total Total	Goods Total Final sales	Goods Total Change in private inventories	Durable goods Final sales	Durable goods Change in private inventories[1]	Nondurable goods Final sales	Nondurable goods Change in private inventories[1]	Services[2]	Structures
1959	506.6	502.7	3.9	237.6	233.6	3.9	86.3	2.9	147.3	1.1	206.5	62.5
1960	526.4	523.2	3.2	246.6	243.4	3.2	90.2	1.7	153.2	1.6	217.9	61.9
1961	544.7	541.7	3.0	250.1	247.2	3.0	90.2	–.1	157.0	3.0	231.0	63.6
1962	585.6	579.5	6.1	268.1	262.0	6.1	99.4	3.4	162.6	2.7	249.7	67.8
1963	617.7	612.1	5.6	280.1	274.5	5.6	106.0	2.6	168.5	3.0	265.0	72.7
1964	663.6	658.8	4.8	300.9	296.0	4.8	116.4	3.8	179.7	1.0	284.3	78.4
1965	719.1	709.9	9.2	329.4	320.2	9.2	128.4	6.2	191.8	3.0	305.0	84.7
1966	787.8	774.2	13.6	364.5	350.9	13.6	142.0	10.0	208.9	3.6	335.3	88.0
1967	832.6	822.7	9.9	373.9	364.0	9.9	146.4	4.8	217.6	5.0	369.1	89.6
1968	910.0	900.9	9.1	402.6	393.6	9.1	158.7	4.5	234.8	4.5	407.4	100.0
1969	984.6	975.4	9.2	432.0	422.8	9.2	171.1	6.0	251.7	3.2	444.4	108.3
1970	1,038.5	1,036.5	2.0	446.9	444.9	2.0	173.6	–.2	271.3	2.2	481.9	109.7
1971	1,127.1	1,118.9	8.3	472.9	464.7	8.3	181.1	2.9	283.6	5.3	525.8	128.4
1972	1,238.3	1,229.2	9.1	516.6	507.5	9.1	202.4	6.4	305.1	2.7	574.8	146.9
1973	1,382.7	1,366.8	15.9	597.1	581.2	15.9	236.6	13.0	344.6	2.9	622.7	162.9
1974	1,500.0	1,486.0	14.0	643.3	629.3	14.0	254.5	10.9	374.8	3.1	691.0	165.6
1975	1,638.3	1,644.6	–6.3	691.4	697.7	–6.3	284.5	–7.5	413.2	1.2	780.2	166.7
1976	1,825.3	1,808.2	17.1	777.5	760.4	17.1	321.2	10.8	439.2	6.3	856.6	191.2
1977	2,030.9	2,008.6	22.3	851.5	829.1	22.3	363.8	9.5	465.3	12.8	952.7	226.8
1978	2,294.7	2,268.9	25.8	961.0	935.2	25.8	413.2	18.2	522.0	7.6	1,059.7	273.9
1979	2,563.3	2,545.3	18.0	1,078.1	1,060.1	18.0	472.0	12.8	588.1	5.2	1,171.9	313.3
1980	2,789.5	2,795.8	–6.3	1,145.7	1,152.0	–6.3	500.1	–2.3	651.9	–4.0	1,322.5	321.3
1981	3,128.4	3,098.6	29.8	1,288.2	1,258.3	29.8	542.2	7.3	716.1	22.5	1,487.7	352.6
1982	3,255.0	3,269.9	–14.9	1,277.3	1,292.2	–14.9	539.7	–16.0	752.5	1.1	1,633.2	344.5
1983	3,536.7	3,542.4	–5.8	1,365.0	1,370.8	–5.8	578.1	2.5	792.7	–8.2	1,802.9	368.7
1984	3,933.2	3,867.8	65.4	1,549.6	1,484.2	65.4	650.2	41.4	834.0	24.0	1,957.8	425.8
1985	4,220.3	4,198.4	21.8	1,607.4	1,585.6	21.8	711.0	4.4	874.6	17.4	2,154.1	458.7
1986	4,462.8	4,456.3	6.6	1,657.0	1,650.5	6.6	739.9	–1.9	910.6	8.4	2,325.7	480.1
1987	4,739.5	4,712.3	27.1	1,751.3	1,724.2	27.1	764.9	22.9	959.3	4.2	2,490.5	497.6
1988	5,103.8	5,085.3	18.5	1,903.4	1,884.9	18.5	841.8	22.7	1,043.1	–4.3	2,685.3	515.0
1989	5,484.4	5,456.7	27.7	2,066.6	2,038.9	27.7	917.1	20.0	1,121.9	7.7	2,888.7	529.0
1990	5,803.1	5,788.5	14.5	2,155.8	2,141.3	14.5	950.2	7.7	1,191.1	6.8	3,113.7	533.5
1991	5,995.9	5,996.3	–.4	2,184.7	2,185.1	–.4	944.1	–13.6	1,241.0	13.2	3,311.3	499.9
1992	6,337.7	6,321.4	16.3	2,282.3	2,266.0	16.3	986.1	–3.0	1,279.8	19.3	3,532.7	522.7
1993	6,657.4	6,636.6	20.8	2,387.8	2,367.0	20.8	1,047.9	17.1	1,319.1	3.7	3,711.7	557.8
1994	7,072.2	7,008.4	63.8	2,563.8	2,500.0	63.8	1,125.0	35.7	1,375.0	28.1	3,901.2	607.3
1995	7,397.7	7,366.5	31.1	2,661.1	2,630.0	31.1	1,202.2	33.6	1,427.8	–2.4	4,098.4	638.1
1996	7,816.9	7,786.1	30.8	2,807.0	2,776.3	30.8	1,298.0	19.1	1,478.3	11.7	4,312.7	697.1
1997	8,304.3	8,232.3	72.0	3,007.7	2,935.7	72.0	1,409.1	39.9	1,526.6	32.1	4,548.4	748.2
1998	8,747.0	8,676.2	70.8	3,143.4	3,072.6	70.8	1,487.8	42.8	1,584.8	28.0	4,789.8	813.8
1999	9,268.4	9,201.5	66.9	3,311.3	3,244.4	66.9	1,576.5	40.0	1,667.9	26.9	5,081.8	875.3
2000	9,817.0	9,760.5	56.5	3,449.3	3,392.8	56.5	1,653.3	36.1	1,739.5	20.4	5,425.6	942.1
2001	10,128.0	10,159.7	–31.7	3,412.6	3,444.3	–31.7	1,630.3	–41.8	1,814.0	10.0	5,725.6	989.8
2002	10,469.6	10,457.7	11.9	3,442.4	3,430.5	11.9	1,559.9	15.1	1,870.7	–3.2	6,031.4	995.8
2003	10,960.8	10,946.5	14.3	3,524.2	3,509.9	14.3	1,574.1	11.1	1,935.8	3.2	6,367.4	1,069.2
2004	11,685.9	11,627.3	58.6	3,707.1	3,648.5	58.6	1,615.7	35.2	2,032.8	23.4	6,778.1	1,200.7
2005	12,433.9	12,397.0	36.9	3,874.3	3,837.4	36.9	1,722.9	31.1	2,114.5	5.8	7,213.8	1,345.8
2006	13,194.7	13,148.0	46.7	4,092.4	4,045.8	46.7	1,798.5	20.4	2,247.2	26.3	7,664.8	1,437.5
2004: I	11,405.5	11,368.6	37.0	3,636.5	3,599.5	37.0	1,597.2	29.7	2,002.3	7.2	6,633.2	1,135.9
II	11,610.3	11,541.3	69.0	3,688.2	3,619.2	69.0	1,591.7	41.8	2,027.4	27.2	6,730.3	1,191.8
III	11,779.4	11,714.4	65.0	3,729.8	3,664.9	65.0	1,624.3	41.3	2,040.6	23.7	6,824.7	1,224.8
IV	11,948.5	11,885.0	63.4	3,774.0	3,710.6	63.4	1,649.7	27.8	2,060.9	35.6	6,924.3	1,250.1
2005: I	12,154.0	12,084.7	69.3	3,820.2	3,750.9	69.3	1,672.8	47.8	2,078.1	21.4	7,047.8	1,286.0
II	12,317.4	12,305.2	12.2	3,854.5	3,842.4	12.2	1,725.6	1.5	2,116.8	10.7	7,135.4	1,327.5
III	12,558.8	12,553.1	5.8	3,910.7	3,904.9	5.8	1,761.6	14.8	2,143.4	–9.0	7,283.3	1,364.8
IV	12,705.5	12,645.0	60.5	3,911.9	3,851.4	60.5	1,731.8	60.2	2,119.6	.3	7,388.9	1,404.7
2006: I	12,964.6	12,920.3	44.3	4,020.4	3,976.1	44.3	1,793.9	15.4	2,182.2	29.0	7,502.3	1,441.9
II	13,155.0	13,095.5	59.5	4,089.2	4,029.7	59.5	1,792.0	24.5	2,237.7	35.0	7,608.6	1,457.1
III	13,266.9	13,204.1	62.8	4,128.8	4,066.0	62.8	1,799.5	42.0	2,266.4	20.8	7,706.9	1,431.2
IV	13,392.3	13,372.3	20.0	4,131.3	4,111.3	20.0	1,808.7	–.3	2,302.6	20.3	7,841.3	1,419.7
2007: I	13,551.9	13,553.5	–1.6	4,170.5	4,172.1	–1.6	1,831.3	9	2,340.8	–2.5	7,968.1	1,413.4
II	13,768.8	13,763.6	5.1	4,243.9	4,238.8	5.1	1,861.7	–26.6	2,377.0	31.7	8,100.0	1,424.9
III	13,970.5	13,935.0	35.4	4,335.6	4,300.1	35.4	1,886.9	10.5	2,413.3	25.0	8,221.1	1,413.8

[1] Estimates for durable and nondurable goods for 1996 and earlier periods are based on the Standard Industrial Classification (SIC); later estimates are based on the North American Industry Classification System (NAICS).

[2] Includes government consumption expenditures, which are for services (such as education and national defense) produced by government. In current dollars, these services are valued at their cost of production.

Source: Department of Commerce (Bureau of Economic Analysis).

TABLE B–9.—Real gross domestic product by major type of product, 1959–2007

[Billions of chained (2000) dollars; quarterly data at seasonally adjusted annual rates]

Year or quarter	Gross domestic product	Final sales of domestic product	Change in private inventories	Goods Total — Total	Goods Total — Final sales	Goods Total — Change in private inventories	Durable goods — Final sales	Durable goods — Change in private inventories[1]	Nondurable goods — Final sales	Nondurable goods — Change in private inventories[1]	Services[2]	Structures
1959	2,441.3	2,442.7	12.3	700.7							1,391.1	392.8
1960	2,501.8	2,506.8	10.4	721.1							1,433.0	389.1
1961	2,560.0	2,566.8	9.4	726.7							1,489.4	399.9
1962	2,715.2	2,708.5	19.5	773.8							1,574.3	422.8
1963	2,834.0	2,830.3	18.0	803.4							1,642.4	451.3
1964	2,998.6	2,999.9	15.4	856.4							1,720.1	481.7
1965	3,191.1	3,173.8	29.3	927.3							1,803.6	505.8
1966	3,399.1	3,364.8	42.1	1,005.2							1,916.7	506.4
1967	3,484.6	3,467.6	30.3	1,006.4							2,034.8	499.0
1968	3,652.7	3,640.3	27.4	1,047.9							2,140.4	529.7
1969	3,765.4	3,753.7	27.0	1,082.2							2,212.2	536.5
1970	3,771.9	3,787.4	5.0	1,076.3							2,255.4	513.4
1971	3,898.6	3,893.4	22.3	1,105.7							2,313.6	561.0
1972	4,105.0	4,098.6	23.1	1,180.5							2,393.7	602.7
1973	4,341.5	4,315.9	35.0	1,299.5							2,461.3	615.6
1974	4,319.6	4,305.5	25.9	1,288.1							2,522.8	551.8
1975	4,311.2	4,352.5	–11.3	1,263.7							2,612.1	501.7
1976	4,540.9	4,522.3	30.7	1,359.8							2,676.9	548.7
1977	4,750.5	4,721.6	38.5	1,423.2							2,770.5	600.6
1978	5,015.0	4,981.6	41.1	1,515.6							2,874.9	658.3
1979	5,173.4	5,161.2	25.1	1,517.9							2,943.3	677.0
1980	5,161.7	5,196.7	–8.0	1,567.1							3,004.2	627.8
1981	5,291.7	5,265.1	34.9	1,634.5							3,062.5	619.2
1982	5,189.3	5,233.4	–17.5	1,559.7							3,120.0	566.1
1983	5,423.8	5,454.0	–6.4	1,625.4							3,251.0	607.1
1984	5,813.6	5,739.2	71.3	1,810.9							3,341.1	689.2
1985	6,053.7	6,042.1	23.7	1,851.3							3,520.8	725.1
1986	6,263.6	6,271.8	8.3	1,906.0							3,671.0	735.9
1987	6,475.1	6,457.2	30.3	1,984.9							3,797.3	739.2
1988	6,742.7	6,734.5	20.3	2,108.9							3,930.9	737.9
1989	6,981.4	6,962.2	28.3	2,223.3							4,049.5	732.8
1990	7,112.5	7,108.5	15.4	2,252.7	2,244.3	15.4	872.8	7.2	1,402.1	3.5	4,170.0	718.3
1991	7,100.5	7,115.0	–.5	2,221.5	2,228.9	–.5	852.7	–13.6	1,410.3	6.1	4,251.2	662.8
1992	7,336.6	7,331.1	16.5	2,307.8	2,297.7	16.5	894.7	–3.0	1,434.3	8.7	4,373.7	688.3
1993	7,532.7	7,522.3	20.6	2,394.8	2,380.3	20.6	949.8	16.4	1,457.7	1.5	4,457.5	709.3
1994	7,835.5	7,777.8	63.6	2,550.6	2,493.9	63.6	1,016.4	33.4	1,501.4	12.6	4,558.3	746.0
1995	8,031.7	8,010.2	29.9	2,639.0	2,614.9	29.9	1,096.9	31.0	1,536.9	–1.2	4,654.7	753.5
1996	8,328.9	8,306.5	28.7	2,772.4	2,747.4	28.7	1,193.8	17.8	1,566.5	4.5	4,765.6	803.1
1997	8,703.5	8,636.6	71.2	2,971.3	2,904.6	71.2	1,317.4	38.5	1,593.4	32.4	4,901.1	835.7
1998	9,066.9	8,997.6	72.6	3,132.7	3,063.7	72.6	1,431.8	42.4	1,634.2	29.8	5,057.5	879.1
1999	9,470.3	9,404.0	68.9	3,312.6	3,246.4	68.9	1,554.3	40.4	1,692.6	28.1	5,245.1	913.0
2000	9,817.0	9,760.5	56.5	3,449.3	3,392.8	56.5	1,653.0	36.1	1,739.5	20.4	5,425.6	942.1
2001	9,890.7	9,920.9	–31.7	3,390.9	3,421.9	–31.7	1,655.6	–42.4	1,766.1	10.3	5,553.2	945.6
2002	10,048.8	10,036.5	12.5	3,432.5	3,419.7	12.5	1,610.8	15.5	1,806.2	–2.8	5,693.4	922.1
2003	10,301.0	10,285.1	14.3	3,538.3	3,521.7	14.3	1,669.4	11.2	1,850.5	3.3	5,810.8	952.3
2004	10,675.8	10,619.8	54.3	3,705.4	3,645.6	54.3	1,744.7	34.1	1,900.9	20.8	5,972.7	1,001.4
2005	11,003.4	10,966.9	33.2	3,866.2	3,827.9	33.2	1,867.2	29.5	1,965.6	5.1	6,112.3	1,035.0
2006	11,319.4	11,275.9	40.3	4,057.9	4,011.8	40.3	1,960.3	18.5	2,057.2	21.7	6,255.0	1,033.6
2004: I	10,543.6	10,507.1	35.0	3,644.0	3,605.2	35.0	1,719.4	29.6	1,884.9	6.5	5,922.1	979.7
II	10,634.2	10,568.5	64.9	3,674.9	3,604.4	64.9	1,714.6	40.8	1,888.4	24.9	5,954.0	1,006.7
III	10,728.7	10,666.6	60.1	3,734.2	3,667.7	60.1	1,759.1	39.7	1,909.2	21.2	5,989.4	1,010.0
IV	10,796.4	10,737.0	57.2	3,768.6	3,705.1	57.2	1,785.9	26.3	1,921.0	30.8	6,025.4	1,009.2
2005: I	10,878.4	10,813.0	63.4	3,807.8	3,737.4	63.4	1,808.4	45.5	1,931.7	19.0	6,059.8	1,019.0
II	10,954.1	10,940.4	10.1	3,844.3	3,831.9	10.1	1,865.5	1.6	1,970.8	8.1	6,081.2	1,037.1
III	11,074.3	11,064.8	5.9	3,898.9	3,891.1	5.9	1,912.8	14.3	1,985.3	–7.3	6,146.4	1,040.3
IV	11,107.2	11,049.5	53.6	3,913.7	3,851.2	53.6	1,882.0	56.5	1,974.6	.7	6,161.8	1,043.4
2006: I	11,238.7	11,196.5	38.4	4,004.2	3,959.0	38.4	1,948.0	14.2	2,018.6	23.7	6,199.1	1,054.5
II	11,306.7	11,252.1	51.4	4,049.6	3,990.5	51.4	1,949.9	22.2	2,046.2	29.0	6,230.4	1,050.7
III	11,336.7	11,279.7	53.9	4,083.3	4,021.5	53.9	1,963.8	37.8	2,063.2	17.4	6,261.7	1,023.7
IV	11,395.5	11,375.8	17.4	4,094.5	4,076.2	17.4	1,979.4	–.4	2,100.5	16.9	6,329.0	1,005.4
2007: I	11,412.6	11,411.6	.1	4,096.6	4,100.1	.1	2,007.5	.8	2,099.2	–.6	6,361.8	989.4
II	11,520.1	11,512.8	5.8	4,150.9	4,147.0	5.8	2,048.3	–23.4	2,108.8	25.7	6,411.2	996.7
III	11,658.9	11,626.4	30.6	4,266.8	4,233.5	30.6	2,092.5	9.3	2,151.5	20.6	6,460.9	986.2

[1] Estimates for durable and nondurable goods for 1996 and earlier periods are based on the Standard Industrial Classification (SIC); later estimates are based on the North American Industry Classification System (NAICS).

[2] Includes government consumption expenditures, which are for services (such as education and national defense) produced by government. In current dollars, these services are valued at their cost of production.

Source: Department of Commerce (Bureau of Economic Analysis).

[Billions of dollars; quarterly data at seasonally adjusted annual rates]

Year or quarter	Gross domestic product	Business [1]			Households and institutions			General government [3]			Addendum: Gross housing value added
		Total	Nonfarm [1]	Farm	Total	House-holds	Nonprofit institutions serving households [2]	Total	Federal	State and local	
1959	506.6	408.2	390.9	17.3	40.1	29.8	10.3	58.3	31.9	26.5	36.9
1960	526.4	420.4	402.3	18.2	43.9	32.3	11.7	62.0	33.1	28.9	39.9
1961	544.7	432.0	413.7	18.3	46.7	34.3	12.4	66.0	34.4	31.6	42.8
1962	585.6	464.5	446.1	18.4	50.4	36.7	13.6	70.7	36.5	34.2	46.0
1963	617.7	488.7	470.2	18.5	53.6	38.8	14.8	75.5	38.4	37.1	48.9
1964	663.6	525.6	508.2	17.3	56.9	40.8	16.1	81.1	40.7	40.4	51.6
1965	719.1	571.4	551.5	19.9	61.0	43.3	17.7	86.7	42.4	44.2	54.9
1966	787.8	625.1	604.3	20.8	65.8	45.9	19.9	96.9	47.3	49.6	58.2
1967	832.6	654.5	634.4	20.1	70.9	48.8	22.1	107.2	51.7	55.5	62.1
1968	910.0	714.5	694.0	20.5	76.5	51.6	25.0	119.0	56.4	62.5	65.9
1969	984.6	770.3	747.5	22.8	84.3	55.6	28.7	130.0	60.0	70.0	71.3
1970	1,038.5	803.6	779.9	23.7	91.4	59.4	32.0	143.6	64.1	79.5	76.7
1971	1,127.1	869.9	844.5	25.4	100.9	65.1	35.7	156.4	67.8	88.6	83.9
1972	1,238.3	959.0	929.4	29.7	109.9	70.3	39.5	169.4	71.6	97.9	91.1
1973	1,382.7	1,079.4	1,032.7	46.8	120.0	76.0	44.0	183.3	74.0	109.3	98.3
1974	1,500.0	1,166.9	1,122.6	44.2	131.7	82.5	49.2	201.4	79.6	121.8	106.8
1975	1,638.3	1,268.5	1,222.8	45.6	145.4	90.3	55.1	224.5	87.3	137.1	117.2
1976	1,825.3	1,423.7	1,380.7	43.0	158.1	98.1	60.0	243.5	93.8	149.7	126.6
1977	2,030.9	1,593.5	1,549.9	43.5	172.8	107.3	65.6	264.6	102.1	162.6	140.3
1978	2,294.7	1,813.4	1,762.7	50.7	193.8	120.4	73.4	287.5	109.7	177.8	155.2
1979	2,563.3	2,032.9	1,972.8	60.1	217.4	135.0	82.5	313.0	117.6	195.4	172.5
1980	2,789.5	2,191.1	2,139.7	51.4	249.9	155.5	94.4	348.6	131.3	217.3	199.4
1981	3,128.4	2,459.4	2,394.5	65.0	283.7	176.8	106.9	385.3	147.4	237.9	228.4
1982	3,255.0	2,520.7	2,460.3	60.4	315.3	195.7	119.6	419.0	161.3	257.7	255.4
1983	3,536.7	2,747.2	2,702.3	44.9	344.0	211.7	132.4	445.4	171.3	274.1	277.4
1984	3,933.2	3,071.8	3,007.7	64.2	376.2	230.2	146.0	485.2	192.1	293.1	301.1
1985	4,220.3	3,290.8	3,227.4	63.4	406.0	249.6	156.4	523.5	205.1	318.4	332.9
1986	4,462.8	3,468.8	3,409.4	59.4	438.0	267.4	170.6	556.1	212.6	343.5	359.5
1987	4,739.5	3,669.9	3,608.4	61.6	478.4	287.6	190.8	591.2	223.4	367.8	385.5
1988	5,103.8	3,948.6	3,887.2	61.3	525.1	312.8	212.4	630.1	234.9	395.2	415.5
1989	5,484.4	4,243.2	4,169.7	73.6	569.6	337.0	232.6	671.5	246.6	424.9	443.8
1990	5,803.1	4,462.6	4,386.0	76.6	618.9	362.9	256.0	721.6	258.9	462.6	478.1
1991	5,995.9	4,569.3	4,499.5	69.9	660.7	383.4	277.3	765.9	275.0	490.9	508.5
1992	6,337.7	4,840.4	4,761.7	78.7	697.9	397.2	300.7	799.4	282.1	517.3	531.0
1993	6,657.4	5,096.2	5,025.6	70.6	732.0	413.7	318.3	829.3	286.3	543.0	549.1
1994	7,072.2	5,444.0	5,362.4	81.6	771.3	439.5	331.7	857.0	286.2	570.7	582.0
1995	7,397.7	5,700.6	5,632.0	68.5	815.5	463.3	352.1	881.6	284.7	596.9	613.3
1996	7,816.9	6,056.7	5,966.0	90.7	852.2	484.7	367.5	908.0	288.6	619.3	638.0
1997	8,304.3	6,471.9	6,383.8	88.1	895.8	509.6	386.2	936.7	290.9	645.8	667.7
1998	8,747.0	6,827.1	6,748.2	78.9	949.7	538.0	411.7	970.3	293.1	677.2	700.2
1999	9,268.4	7,243.4	7,174.7	68.8	1,012.3	576.4	435.9	1,012.7	300.9	711.8	747.8
2000	9,817.0	7,666.7	7,595.1	71.5	1,080.7	615.6	465.1	1,069.6	315.4	754.2	794.3
2001	10,128.0	7,841.2	7,768.0	73.1	1,160.4	662.0	498.4	1,126.4	325.7	800.8	849.8
2002	10,469.6	8,040.5	7,969.7	70.8	1,227.3	687.7	539.6	1,201.8	352.9	848.9	876.7
2003	10,960.8	8,411.5	8,323.2	88.3	1,269.2	699.9	569.3	1,280.1	383.9	896.2	878.2
2004	11,685.9	8,987.5	8,872.8	114.7	1,350.0	744.9	605.1	1,348.4	412.6	935.8	929.1
2005	12,433.9	9,603.2	9,502.4	100.9	1,404.7	773.3	631.4	1,425.9	438.9	987.0	964.2
2006	13,194.7	10,192.8	10,097.2	95.7	1,500.3	834.2	666.1	1,501.5	458.6	1,042.9	1,038.2
2004: I	11,405.5	8,757.6	8,640.2	117.4	1,321.7	734.4	587.3	1,326.2	406.2	920.0	915.5
II	11,610.3	8,930.7	8,811.0	119.7	1,338.1	739.2	598.9	1,341.5	411.9	929.6	921.9
III	11,779.4	9,058.1	8,948.6	109.4	1,366.3	751.3	615.0	1,355.0	414.4	940.6	937.5
IV	11,948.5	9,203.6	9,091.4	112.2	1,373.8	754.6	619.2	1,371.0	417.8	953.2	941.4
2005: I	12,154.0	9,367.4	9,265.0	102.4	1,383.5	763.4	620.2	1,403.0	436.8	966.2	952.3
II	12,317.4	9,503.6	9,399.7	103.9	1,396.6	769.0	627.6	1,417.2	436.9	980.2	958.9
III	12,558.8	9,715.2	9,616.9	98.3	1,408.9	773.1	635.8	1,434.7	440.2	994.5	963.7
IV	12,705.5	9,826.7	9,727.9	98.9	1,429.9	787.9	642.0	1,448.8	441.7	1,007.1	981.8
2006: I	12,964.6	10,027.6	9,935.7	92.0	1,464.3	811.2	653.1	1,472.6	454.1	1,018.5	1,009.9
II	13,155.0	10,173.9	10,086.6	87.3	1,490.2	829.1	661.1	1,490.9	457.4	1,033.5	1,031.4
III	13,266.9	10,242.7	10,146.6	96.1	1,512.3	844.6	667.7	1,511.8	460.6	1,051.2	1,050.5
IV	13,392.3	10,327.1	10,219.8	107.3	1,534.5	851.9	682.5	1,530.7	462.3	1,068.5	1,060.9
2007: I	13,551.9	10,435.6	10,319.0	116.6	1,560.0	864.8	695.2	1,556.3	470.8	1,085.5	1,077.4
II	13,768.8	10,604.7	10,479.8	124.9	1,588.9	883.0	705.9	1,575.2	474.6	1,100.5	1,099.3
III	13,970.5	10,761.8	10,627.2	134.6	1,614.5	897.7	716.8	1,594.2	479.3	1,114.9	1,117.6

[1] Gross domestic business value added equals gross domestic product excluding gross value added of households and institutions and of general government. Nonfarm value added equals gross domestic business value added excluding gross farm value added.

[2] Equals compensation of employees of nonprofit institutions, the rental value of nonresidential fixed assets owned and used by nonprofit institutions serving households, and rental income of persons for tenant-occupied housing owned by nonprofit institutions.

[3] Equals compensation of general government employees plus general government consumption of fixed capital.

Source: Department of Commerce (Bureau of Economic Analysis).

TABLE B–11.—*Real gross value added by sector, 1959–2007*

[Billions of chained (2000) dollars; quarterly data at seasonally adjusted annual rates]

Year or quarter	Gross domestic product	Business¹			Households and institutions			General government³			Addendum: Gross housing value added
		Total	Nonfarm¹	Farm	Total	Households	Nonprofit institutions serving households²	Total	Federal	State and local	
1959	2,441.3	1,716.0	1,684.1	21.2	261.7	161.6	97.8	514.5	279.4	236.7	195.0
1960	2,501.8	1,748.8	1,713.5	22.4	279.6	171.4	106.6	532.2	284.6	249.3	207.3
1961	2,560.0	1,782.8	1,747.8	22.6	291.5	179.6	109.6	550.9	290.5	262.1	219.2
1962	2,715.2	1,897.7	1,867.0	22.1	307.7	189.8	115.4	572.5	302.5	271.8	232.8
1963	2,834.0	1,985.4	1,954.3	22.8	320.4	197.7	120.0	589.5	305.2	285.9	244.3
1964	2,998.6	2,111.7	2,086.0	22.1	333.7	205.7	125.4	609.7	308.2	303.1	255.4
1965	3,191.1	2,260.6	2,233.5	23.5	350.2	215.2	132.6	630.3	310.4	321.5	268.9
1966	3,399.1	2,413.6	2,393.2	22.7	366.3	224.0	140.2	669.7	330.7	340.6	281.0
1967	3,484.6	2,459.5	2,434.1	24.5	381.6	233.1	146.5	705.2	352.2	354.9	294.0
1968	3,652.7	2,581.7	2,561.5	23.6	400.4	239.3	161.0	732.7	358.1	376.2	304.6
1969	3,765.4	2,660.3	2,639.1	24.5	417.8	249.1	168.8	751.3	359.0	393.4	318.7
1970	3,771.9	2,659.3	2,636.0	25.1	425.0	254.7	170.0	754.1	343.6	410.8	328.9
1971	3,898.6	2,761.5	2,736.2	26.4	443.0	266.5	176.1	755.3	327.8	427.5	343.8
1972	4,105.0	2,939.8	2,918.4	26.4	460.7	277.7	182.4	753.8	311.8	442.3	360.1
1973	4,341.5	3,145.0	3,131.5	26.2	476.3	287.5	188.2	757.2	300.1	457.8	373.0
1974	4,319.6	3,101.3	3,089.1	25.6	493.9	299.9	193.1	772.6	299.2	474.4	390.7
1975	4,311.2	3,071.2	3,037.5	30.5	513.7	308.0	205.2	785.1	297.5	488.9	402.7
1976	4,540.9	3,272.9	3,249.1	29.1	521.5	313.3	207.5	791.8	297.9	495.3	408.3
1977	4,750.5	3,456.2	3,431.1	30.7	528.3	316.2	211.6	800.1	298.8	502.9	418.3
1978	5,015.0	3,673.3	3,656.8	29.6	552.4	335.1	216.3	815.5	302.5	514.6	436.8
1979	5,173.4	3,796.7	3,774.2	32.2	576.7	350.4	225.3	824.2	302.3	523.7	453.9
1980	5,161.7	3,756.1	3,736.1	31.1	606.9	372.9	232.8	836.0	307.0	530.8	481.9
1981	5,291.7	3,859.5	3,814.7	41.0	626.5	384.7	240.5	840.6	311.7	530.6	501.0
1982	5,189.3	3,743.1	3,691.9	43.1	647.2	391.8	254.4	849.2	316.8	534.0	514.7
1983	5,423.8	3,944.3	3,932.8	26.9	665.9	399.4	265.7	854.6	324.2	531.8	526.2
1984	5,813.6	4,286.3	4,254.3	37.2	687.8	413.3	273.6	865.2	331.5	535.0	543.0
1985	6,053.7	4,484.5	4,434.2	46.7	701.1	423.2	275.9	890.0	341.0	550.3	564.4
1986	6,263.6	4,652.0	4,606.2	44.9	718.5	428.7	289.1	911.9	347.0	566.3	574.9
1987	6,475.1	4,815.5	4,769.8	45.5	745.7	440.3	304.8	931.8	356.1	577.2	588.8
1988	6,742.7	5,023.0	4,987.7	40.9	780.6	457.1	323.1	956.0	360.5	596.9	606.2
1989	6,981.4	5,206.6	5,162.3	46.4	812.3	471.5	340.6	978.8	364.9	615.3	620.3
1990	7,112.5	5,287.0	5,237.9	49.3	841.2	483.2	357.9	1,003.9	371.6	633.6	635.7
1991	7,100.5	5,245.4	5,194.7	50.0	865.3	497.8	367.5	1,014.3	373.8	641.7	657.2
1992	7,336.6	5,456.5	5,395.2	57.5	882.6	502.6	379.9	1,017.7	366.0	652.6	666.2
1993	7,532.7	5,625.9	5,576.0	50.6	904.8	507.9	396.9	1,019.8	358.9	661.6	669.9
1994	7,835.5	5,905.3	5,841.4	60.9	923.1	524.7	398.4	1,019.9	347.2	673.1	690.8
1995	8,031.7	6,076.8	6,030.2	49.6	945.1	534.3	410.8	1,020.6	334.1	686.5	705.7
1996	8,328.9	6,356.0	6,300.4	56.1	957.8	540.8	417.0	1,022.1	325.0	697.2	712.1
1997	8,703.5	6,693.8	6,627.2	64.4	983.5	554.0	429.5	1,030.0	318.8	711.2	726.5
1998	9,066.9	7,017.1	6,955.3	61.6	1,010.4	563.8	446.9	1,041.0	315.2	725.8	735.5
1999	9,470.3	7,376.8	7,314.2	62.9	1,042.3	590.7	451.6	1,051.4	312.7	738.7	767.2
2000	9,817.0	7,666.7	7,595.1	71.5	1,080.7	615.6	465.1	1,069.6	315.4	754.2	794.3
2001	9,890.7	7,691.0	7,625.7	65.6	1,110.0	634.8	475.1	1,089.3	317.0	772.3	815.1
2002	10,048.8	7,806.9	7,736.9	70.1	1,130.9	634.2	496.6	1,110.4	323.3	787.1	809.0
2003	10,301.0	8,050.3	7,974.3	76.0	1,129.1	629.4	499.6	1,123.9	331.9	791.9	789.9
2004	10,675.8	8,387.0	8,304.3	82.1	1,165.6	661.9	504.1	1,129.4	335.2	794.1	825.6
2005	11,003.4	8,692.2	8,604.3	87.0	1,183.1	675.1	508.7	1,139.1	337.4	801.6	841.2
2006	11,319.4	8,965.9	8,877.5	87.5	1,221.5	710.4	513.0	1,146.5	336.9	809.7	883.3
2004: I	10,543.6	8,263.2	8,176.3	84.2	1,158.4	656.3	502.4	1,126.4	334.3	792.0	818.0
II	10,634.2	8,352.3	8,276.4	76.8	1,161.0	657.9	503.4	1,127.0	333.9	793.0	820.7
III	10,728.7	8,434.8	8,354.9	80.2	1,171.1	666.9	504.7	1,129.7	335.2	794.3	832.2
IV	10,796.4	8,498.0	8,409.6	87.4	1,171.8	666.5	505.8	1,134.5	337.4	796.9	831.5
2005: I	10,878.4	8,576.2	8,490.6	84.9	1,174.4	668.0	506.9	1,136.8	337.8	798.8	833.4
II	10,954.1	8,646.0	8,557.4	87.7	1,180.5	672.5	508.6	1,137.7	336.9	800.6	838.3
III	11,074.3	8,762.5	8,674.6	87.0	1,184.5	674.7	510.4	1,139.6	336.7	802.8	840.5
IV	11,107.2	8,784.0	8,694.7	88.3	1,193.1	685.1	509.0	1,142.4	338.1	804.1	852.7
2006: I	11,238.7	8,902.6	8,815.3	86.3	1,209.2	701.2	509.7	1,141.1	335.3	805.8	872.0
II	11,306.7	8,958.5	8,867.9	89.8	1,219.4	710.1	511.3	1,143.6	335.5	808.2	882.8
III	11,336.7	8,972.9	8,885.0	86.9	1,228.5	715.5	515.0	1,149.3	338.3	811.0	889.3
IV	11,395.5	9,029.8	8,941.8	87.1	1,228.8	714.6	516.0	1,152.1	338.4	813.8	888.9
2007: I	11,412.6	9,033.9	8,949.2	84.2	1,238.7	720.3	520.3	1,154.3	337.4	817.0	895.4
II	11,520.1	9,130.9	9,042.6	87.2	1,248.4	725.8	524.5	1,156.8	336.8	820.2	902.2
III	11,658.9	9,258.2	9,167.6	89.2	1,257.7	732.0	527.7	1,161.5	339.9	821.8	909.7

¹ Gross domestic business value added equals gross domestic product excluding gross value added of households and institutions and of general government. Nonfarm value added equals gross domestic business value added excluding gross farm value added.

² Equals compensation of employees of nonprofit institutions, the rental value of nonresidential fixed assets owned and used by nonprofit institutions serving households, and rental income of persons for tenant-occupied housing owned by nonprofit institutions.

³ Equals compensation of general government employees plus general government consumption of fixed capital.

Source: Department of Commerce (Bureau of Economic Analysis).

TABLE B–12.—*Gross domestic product (GDP) by industry, value added, in current dollars and as a percentage of GDP, 1976–2006*

[Billions of dollars; except as noted]

Year	Gross domestic product	Private industries									
		Total private industries	Agriculture, forestry, fishing, and hunting	Mining	Construction	Manufacturing			Utilities	Wholesale trade	Retail trade
						Total manufacturing	Durable goods	Nondurable goods			
						Value added					
1976	1,825.3	1,556.2	50.2	37.5	85.5	386.7	230.2	156.5	41.5	122.7	144.0
1977	2,030.9	1,739.4	51.3	43.4	94.2	438.6	265.0	173.6	45.9	134.9	158.5
1978	2,294.7	1,977.0	59.8	49.5	111.5	489.9	303.4	186.5	50.4	153.4	177.6
1979	2,563.3	2,217.7	70.6	58.4	127.0	543.8	331.1	212.7	51.9	175.8	193.2
1980	2,789.5	2,405.8	62.0	91.3	130.3	556.6	333.9	222.7	60.0	188.7	200.9
1981	3,128.4	2,702.5	75.4	122.9	131.8	616.5	370.4	246.1	70.7	208.3	221.0
1982	3,255.0	2,792.6	71.3	120.0	128.8	603.2	353.4	249.8	81.7	207.9	229.9
1983	3,536.7	3,043.5	57.1	103.1	139.8	653.1	379.3	273.8	91.6	222.9	261.6
1984	3,933.2	3,395.1	77.1	107.2	164.4	724.0	443.5	280.5	102.3	249.4	293.6
1985	4,220.3	3,637.0	77.1	105.4	184.6	740.3	449.2	291.1	109.2	268.3	318.7
1986	4,462.8	3,842.9	74.2	68.9	207.7	766.0	459.3	306.7	114.4	278.5	336.6
1987	4,739.5	4,080.4	79.8	71.5	218.2	811.3	483.8	327.5	123.0	285.3	349.9
1988	5,103.8	4,399.1	80.2	71.4	232.7	876.9	519.0	357.9	122.8	318.1	366.0
1989	5,484.4	4,732.3	92.8	76.0	244.8	927.3	543.2	384.1	135.9	337.4	389.0
1990	5,803.1	4,997.8	96.7	84.9	248.5	947.4	542.7	404.7	142.9	347.7	398.8
1991	5,995.9	5,138.7	89.2	76.0	230.2	957.5	540.9	416.6	152.5	360.5	405.5
1992	6,337.7	5,440.4	99.6	71.3	232.5	996.7	562.8	433.8	157.4	378.9	430.0
1993	6,657.4	5,729.3	93.1	72.1	248.3	1,039.9	593.1	446.8	165.3	401.2	458.0
1994	7,072.2	6,110.5	105.6	73.6	274.4	1,118.8	647.7	471.1	174.6	442.7	493.3
1995	7,397.6	6,407.2	93.1	74.1	287.0	1,177.3	677.2	500.0	181.5	457.0	514.9
1996	7,816.9	6,795.2	113.8	87.5	311.7	1,209.4	706.5	502.9	183.3	489.1	543.8
1997	8,304.3	7,247.5	110.7	92.6	337.6	1,279.8	755.5	524.3	179.6	521.2	574.2
1998	8,747.0	7,652.5	102.4	74.8	374.4	1,343.9	806.9	537.0	180.8	542.9	598.6
1999	9,268.4	8,127.2	93.8	85.4	406.6	1,373.1	820.4	552.7	185.4	577.7	635.5
2000	9,817.0	8,614.3	98.0	121.3	435.9	1,426.2	863.5	560.9	189.3	591.7	662.4
2001	10,128.0	8,869.7	97.9	118.7	469.5	1,341.3	778.9	562.5	202.3	607.1	691.6
2002	10,469.6	9,131.2	95.4	106.5	482.3	1,352.6	774.8	577.9	207.3	615.4	719.6
2003	10,960.8	9,542.3	114.4	143.3	496.2	1,359.3	771.8	587.5	220.0	637.0	751.5
2004	11,685.9	10,194.3	142.2	171.3	539.2	1,427.9	807.5	620.4	240.3	686.7	776.9
2005	12,433.9	10,861.5	128.8	225.7	607.9	1,483.9	840.9	643.0	249.5	723.7	812.7
2006	13,194.7	11,556.0	125.4	262.4	630.0	1,549.7	882.8	666.9	273.4	762.2	848.0
	Percent	Industry value added as a percentage of GDP (percent)									
1976	100.0	85.3	2.7	2.1	4.7	21.2	12.6	8.6	2.3	6.7	7.9
1977	100.0	85.6	2.5	2.1	4.6	21.6	13.1	8.5	2.3	6.6	7.8
1978	100.0	86.2	2.6	2.2	4.9	21.3	13.2	8.1	2.2	6.7	7.7
1979	100.0	86.5	2.8	2.3	5.0	21.2	12.9	8.3	2.0	6.9	7.5
1980	100.0	86.2	2.2	3.3	4.7	20.0	12.0	8.0	2.2	6.8	7.2
1981	100.0	86.4	2.4	3.9	4.2	19.7	11.8	7.9	2.3	6.7	7.1
1982	100.0	85.8	2.2	3.7	4.0	18.5	10.9	7.7	2.5	6.4	7.1
1983	100.0	86.1	1.6	2.9	4.0	18.5	10.7	7.7	2.6	6.3	7.4
1984	100.0	86.3	2.0	2.7	4.2	18.4	11.3	7.1	2.6	6.3	7.5
1985	100.0	86.2	1.8	2.5	4.4	17.5	10.6	6.9	2.6	6.4	7.6
1986	100.0	86.1	1.7	1.5	4.7	17.2	10.3	6.9	2.6	6.2	7.5
1987	100.0	86.1	1.7	1.5	4.6	17.1	10.2	6.9	2.6	6.0	7.4
1988	100.0	86.2	1.6	1.4	4.6	17.2	10.2	7.0	2.4	6.2	7.2
1989	100.0	86.3	1.7	1.4	4.5	16.9	9.9	7.0	2.5	6.2	7.1
1990	100.0	86.1	1.7	1.5	4.3	16.3	9.4	7.0	2.5	6.0	6.9
1991	100.0	85.7	1.5	1.3	3.8	16.0	9.0	6.9	2.5	6.0	6.8
1992	100.0	85.8	1.6	1.1	3.7	15.7	8.9	6.8	2.5	6.0	6.8
1993	100.0	86.1	1.4	1.1	3.7	15.6	8.9	6.7	2.5	6.0	6.9
1994	100.0	86.4	1.5	1.0	3.9	15.8	9.2	6.7	2.5	6.3	7.0
1995	100.0	86.6	1.3	1.0	3.9	15.9	9.2	6.8	2.5	6.2	7.0
1996	100.0	86.9	1.5	1.1	4.0	15.5	9.0	6.4	2.3	6.3	7.0
1997	100.0	87.3	1.3	1.1	4.1	15.4	9.1	6.3	2.2	6.3	6.9
1998	100.0	87.5	1.2	.9	4.3	15.4	9.2	6.1	2.1	6.2	6.8
1999	100.0	87.7	1.0	.9	4.4	14.8	8.9	6.0	2.0	6.2	6.9
2000	100.0	87.7	1.0	1.2	4.4	14.5	8.8	5.7	1.9	6.0	6.7
2001	100.0	87.6	1.0	1.2	4.6	13.2	7.7	5.6	2.0	6.0	6.8
2002	100.0	87.2	.9	1.0	4.6	12.9	7.4	5.5	2.0	5.9	6.9
2003	100.0	87.1	1.0	1.3	4.5	12.4	7.0	5.4	2.0	5.8	6.9
2004	100.0	87.2	1.2	1.5	4.6	12.2	6.9	5.3	2.1	5.9	6.6
2005	100.0	87.4	1.0	1.8	4.9	11.9	6.8	5.2	2.0	5.8	6.5
2006	100.0	87.6	1.0	2.0	4.8	11.7	6.7	5.1	2.1	5.8	6.4

[1] Consists of agriculture, forestry, fishing, and hunting; mining; construction; and manufacturing.
[2] Consists of utilities; wholesale trade; retail trade; transportation and warehousing; information; finance, insurance, real estate, rental, and leasing; professional and business services; educational services, health care, and social assistance; arts, entertainment, recreation, accommodation, and food services; and other services, except government.

Note.—Value added is the contribution of each private industry and of government to gross domestic product. Value added is equal to an industry's gross output minus its intermediate inputs. Current-dollar value added is calculated as the sum of distributions by an industry to its labor and capital which are derived from the components of gross domestic income.

See next page for continuation of table.

TABLE B–12.—*Gross domestic product (GDP) by industry, value added, in current dollars and as a percentage of GDP, 1976–2006*—Continued

[Billions of dollars; except as noted]

Year	Transportation and warehousing	Information	Finance, insurance, real estate, rental, and leasing	Professional and business services	Educational services, health care, and social assistance	Arts, entertainment, recreation, accommodation, and food services	Other services, except government	Government	Private goods-producing industries [1]	Private services-producing industries [2]
					Value added					
1976	68.8	63.5	272.1	105.1	84.0	51.9	42.8	269.1	559.8	996.4
1977	76.2	71.1	304.0	122.7	93.8	58.8	46.1	291.5	627.5	1,111.9
1978	86.7	81.4	347.4	141.9	106.4	67.9	53.2	317.7	710.6	1,266.4
1979	96.6	90.3	390.3	164.0	120.5	77.1	58.2	345.7	799.7	1,417.9
1980	102.3	99.0	442.4	186.3	139.7	83.5	62.6	383.7	840.2	1,565.6
1981	109.9	112.7	498.4	213.2	159.9	93.5	68.5	425.9	946.6	1,755.9
1982	105.9	123.6	539.9	230.9	177.9	100.9	70.7	462.4	923.3	1,869.3
1983	117.8	140.0	604.6	262.5	198.3	112.0	79.2	493.1	953.1	2,090.5
1984	131.4	147.1	670.2	303.8	214.1	121.2	89.3	538.1	1,072.7	2,322.3
1985	136.3	162.9	729.7	340.8	231.3	134.3	98.0	583.3	1,107.4	2,529.5
1986	145.6	173.1	795.1	378.8	252.0	144.9	107.2	620.0	1,116.7	2,726.1
1987	151.1	185.0	840.3	414.1	286.5	152.1	112.3	659.1	1,180.8	2,899.5
1988	161.1	194.0	910.1	466.3	309.1	165.9	124.4	704.7	1,261.3	3,137.8
1989	164.1	210.4	975.4	518.0	347.0	180.2	133.9	752.0	1,341.0	3,391.4
1990	169.4	225.1	1,042.1	569.8	386.7	195.2	142.6	805.3	1,377.4	3,620.4
1991	178.2	235.2	1,103.6	579.3	424.8	202.2	144.2	857.2	1,352.8	3,785.9
1992	186.6	250.9	1,177.4	626.7	463.5	216.2	153.0	897.3	1,400.0	4,040.5
1993	201.0	272.6	1,241.5	659.1	488.0	225.5	163.7	928.1	1,453.4	4,275.9
1994	218.0	294.0	1,297.8	698.4	511.1	235.0	173.2	961.8	1,572.4	4,538.0
1995	226.3	307.6	1,383.0	743.1	533.3	248.3	180.9	990.4	1,631.4	4,775.8
1996	235.2	335.7	1,470.7	810.1	552.5	264.4	188.1	1,021.6	1,722.4	5,072.8
1997	253.7	347.8	1,593.3	896.5	573.1	289.8	197.4	1,056.8	1,820.8	5,426.8
1998	273.7	381.6	1,684.6	976.2	601.5	306.0	211.1	1,094.5	1,895.4	5,757.1
1999	287.4	439.3	1,798.4	1,064.5	634.5	327.8	217.8	1,141.2	1,958.9	6,168.3
2000	301.6	458.3	1,931.0	1,140.8	678.4	350.1	229.1	1,202.7	2,081.5	6,532.8
2001	296.9	476.9	2,059.2	1,165.9	739.3	361.5	241.5	1,258.3	2,027.5	6,842.2
2002	304.6	483.0	2,141.9	1,189.0	799.6	381.5	252.5	1,338.4	2,036.9	7,094.3
2003	316.6	489.1	2,244.6	1,248.9	857.3	398.9	265.3	1,418.4	2,113.3	7,429.1
2004	344.6	530.6	2,378.8	1,338.2	916.3	427.5	273.9	1,491.6	2,280.6	7,913.7
2005	358.5	570.5	2,549.0	1,453.2	961.5	448.4	288.1	1,568.7	2,446.2	8,415.2
2006	385.4	598.8	2,756.6	1,560.9	1,022.3	479.8	301.1	1,649.4	2,567.5	8,988.5
					Industry value added as a percentage of GDP (percent)					
1976	3.8	3.5	14.9	5.8	4.6	2.8	2.3	14.7	30.7	54.6
1977	3.8	3.5	15.0	6.0	4.6	2.9	2.3	14.4	30.9	54.7
1978	3.8	3.5	15.1	6.2	4.6	3.0	2.3	13.8	31.0	55.2
1979	3.8	3.5	15.2	6.4	4.7	3.0	2.3	13.5	31.2	55.3
1980	3.7	3.5	15.9	6.7	5.0	3.0	2.2	13.8	30.1	56.1
1981	3.5	3.6	15.9	6.8	5.1	3.0	2.2	13.6	30.3	56.1
1982	3.3	3.8	16.6	7.1	5.5	3.1	2.2	14.2	28.4	57.4
1983	3.3	4.0	17.1	7.4	5.6	3.2	2.2	14.2	28.4	57.4
1984	3.3	3.7	17.0	7.7	5.4	3.1	2.3	13.9	26.9	59.1
1985	3.3	3.9	17.3	8.1	5.5	3.2	2.3	13.7	27.3	59.0
1986	3.3	3.9	17.8	8.5	5.6	3.2	2.3	13.8	26.2	59.9
1987	3.2	3.9	17.7	8.7	6.0	3.2	2.4	13.9	25.0	61.1
1988	3.2	3.8	17.8	9.1	6.1	3.3	2.4	13.9	24.9	61.2
1989	3.0	3.8	17.8	9.4	6.3	3.3	2.4	13.8	24.7	61.5
1990	2.9	3.9	18.0	9.8	6.7	3.4	2.4	13.7	24.5	61.8
1991	3.0	3.9	18.4	9.7	7.1	3.4	2.5	13.9	23.7	62.4
1992	2.9	4.0	18.6	9.9	7.3	3.4	2.4	14.3	22.6	63.1
1993	3.0	4.1	18.6	9.9	7.3	3.4	2.4	14.2	22.1	63.8
1994	3.1	4.2	18.4	9.9	7.2	3.3	2.4	13.9	21.8	64.2
1995	3.1	4.2	18.7	10.0	7.2	3.4	2.5	13.6	22.2	64.2
1996	3.0	4.3	18.8	10.4	7.1	3.4	2.4	13.4	22.1	64.6
1997	3.1	4.2	19.2	10.8	6.9	3.5	2.4	13.1	22.0	64.9
1998	3.1	4.4	19.3	11.2	6.9	3.5	2.4	12.7	21.9	65.3
1999	3.1	4.7	19.4	11.5	6.8	3.5	2.3	12.5	21.7	65.8
2000	3.1	4.7	19.7	11.6	6.9	3.6	2.3	12.3	21.1	66.6
2001	2.9	4.7	20.3	11.5	7.3	3.6	2.3	12.3	21.2	66.5
2002	2.9	4.6	20.5	11.4	7.6	3.6	2.4	12.4	20.0	67.6
2003	2.9	4.5	20.5	11.4	7.8	3.6	2.4	12.8	19.5	67.8
2004	2.9	4.5	20.4	11.5	7.8	3.7	2.4	12.9	19.3	67.8
2005	2.9	4.6	20.5	11.7	7.7	3.6	2.3	12.8	19.5	67.7
2006	2.9	4.5	20.9	11.8	7.7	3.6	2.3	12.6	19.7	67.7
2006	2.9	4.5	20.9	11.8	7.7	3.6	2.3	12.5	19.5	68.1

Note (cont'd).—Value added industry data shown in Tables B–12 and B–13 are based on the 1997 North American Industry Classification System (NAICS). GDP by industry data based on the Standard Industrial Classification (SIC) are available from the Department of Commerce, Bureau of Economic Analysis.

Source: Department of Commerce (Bureau of Economic Analysis).

| Year | Gross domestic product | Total private industries | Private industries | | | Manufacturing | | | Utilities | Wholesale trade | Retail trade |
			Agriculture, forestry, fishing, and hunting	Mining	Construction	Total manufacturing	Durable goods	Non-durable goods			
					Chain-type quantity indexes for value added (2000=100)						
1976	46.256	43.911	44.589	80.136	73.128	43.369	34.910	59.644	60.220	31.994	36.890
1977	48.391	46.088	46.430	86.262	74.057	46.745	37.736	64.010	59.909	33.611	38.412
1978	51.085	48.802	45.057	88.929	78.442	49.157	40.159	66.062	59.583	37.065	40.654
1979	52.699	50.606	48.573	79.749	81.174	50.843	40.808	70.282	54.661	39.888	40.701
1980	52.579	50.321	47.543	89.978	74.626	48.190	38.476	67.152	51.968	39.782	38.907
1981	53.904	51.720	59.731	90.260	67.939	50.480	39.563	72.303	51.733	42.074	40.035
1982	52.860	50.422	62.961	86.329	59.460	46.795	35.645	69.864	50.698	42.096	39.951
1983	55.249	52.785	43.338	81.175	62.805	50.455	37.953	76.660	52.706	43.770	44.123
1984	59.220	56.789	57.105	88.849	72.200	55.084	44.042	76.466	60.940	49.523	51.232
1985	61.666	59.383	69.555	93.077	79.043	56.582	45.187	78.688	64.406	54.486	54.187
1986	63.804	61.137	68.605	87.529	81.818	56.516	45.550	77.515	64.406	54.486	54.187
1987	65.958	63.367	71.483	91.661	82.448	60.746	48.859	83.572	72.315	53.070	52.138
1988	68.684	66.299	64.678	99.992	85.435	64.212	52.843	85.425	70.613	56.444	56.545
1989	71.116	68.710	71.099	97.072	87.646	65.033	53.696	86.109	79.002	58.603	58.838
1990	72.451	69.905	74.689	96.157	86.543	64.299	52.963	85.419	84.447	57.318	59.794
1991	72.329	69.779	75.398	97.638	79.137	63.412	51.496	85.835	85.285	59.387	59.483
1992	74.734	72.363	83.114	95.694	80.026	65.508	52.742	89.669	85.362	65.037	62.960
1993	76.731	74.291	72.838	97.020	82.010	68.255	55.173	92.943	85.814	67.135	65.351
1994	79.816	77.765	84.616	105.327	86.586	73.496	60.173	98.369	89.518	71.346	69.806
1995	81.814	79.722	73.099	105.681	86.312	76.819	65.218	97.783	93.835	70.800	72.974
1996	84.842	83.179	80.041	98.850	90.694	79.682	69.120	98.443	95.405	77.261	79.407
1997	88.658	87.362	88.315	102.463	93.267	84.518	75.335	100.438	91.161	85.648	86.039
1998	92.359	91.662	86.287	101.682	97.087	90.181	84.355	99.762	90.481	95.431	90.399
1999	96.469	96.183	89.163	104.300	99.411	94.104	89.627	101.298	94.672	100.412	95.686
2000	100.000	100.000	100.000	100.000	100.000	100.000	100.000	100.000	100.000	100.000	100.000
2001	100.751	100.908	93.661	94.715	100.163	94.436	94.031	95.034	95.081	107.003	106.970
2002	102.362	102.354	98.767	88.719	98.201	97.066	95.663	99.056	99.144	108.059	109.294
2003	104.931	105.068	106.173	87.922	96.189	98.168	98.160	98.265	105.990	110.380	113.559
2004	108.748	109.198	113.287	88.770	96.430	103.653	103.873	103.468	112.076	112.614	116.533
2005	112.086	112.910	118.862	86.639	99.028	104.681	108.970	99.416	109.578	114.637	123.659
2006	115.304	116.819	119.941	91.943	93.070	107.738	115.551	98.377	107.085	116.594	129.820
					Percent change from year earlier						
1976	5.3	5.9	−2.8	−0.1	7.3	10.6	10.3	11.1	−0.9	3.5	7.7
1977	4.6	5.0	4.1	7.6	1.3	7.8	8.1	7.3	−.5	5.1	4.1
1978	5.6	5.9	−3.0	3.1	5.9	5.2	6.4	3.2	−.5	10.3	5.8
1979	3.2	3.7	7.8	−10.3	3.5	3.4	1.6	6.4	−8.3	7.6	.1
1980	−.2	−.6	−2.1	12.8	−8.1	−5.2	−5.7	−4.5	−4.9	−.3	−4.4
1981	2.5	2.8	25.6	.3	−9.0	4.8	2.8	7.7	−.5	5.8	2.9
1982	−1.9	−2.5	5.4	−4.4	−12.5	−7.3	−9.9	−3.4	−2.0	.1	−.2
1983	4.5	4.7	−31.2	−6.0	5.6	7.8	6.5	9.7	4.0	4.0	10.4
1984	7.2	7.6	31.8	9.5	15.0	9.2	16.0	−.3	8.8	7.7	9.4
1985	4.1	4.6	21.8	4.8	9.5	2.7	2.6	2.9	6.3	5.0	6.1
1986	3.5	3.0	−1.4	−6.0	3.5	−.1	.8	−1.5	5.7	10.0	5.8
1987	3.4	3.6	4.2	4.7	.8	7.5	7.3	7.8	12.3	−2.6	−3.8
1988	4.1	4.6	−9.5	9.1	3.6	5.7	8.2	2.2	−2.4	6.4	8.5
1989	3.5	3.6	9.9	−2.9	2.6	1.3	1.6	.8	11.9	3.8	4.1
1990	1.9	1.7	5.0	−.9	−1.3	−1.1	−1.4	−.8	6.9	−2.2	1.6
1991	−.2	−.2	.9	1.5	−8.6	−1.4	−2.8	.5	1.0	3.6	−.5
1992	3.3	3.7	10.2	−2.0	1.1	3.3	2.4	4.5	.1	9.5	5.8
1993	2.7	2.7	−12.4	1.4	2.5	4.2	4.6	3.7	.5	3.2	3.8
1994	4.0	4.7	16.2	8.6	5.6	7.7	9.1	5.8	4.3	6.3	6.8
1995	2.5	2.5	−13.6	.3	−.3	4.5	8.4	−.6	4.8	−.8	4.5
1996	3.7	4.3	9.5	−6.5	5.1	3.7	6.0	.7	1.7	9.1	8.8
1997	4.5	5.0	10.3	3.7	2.8	6.1	9.0	2.0	−4.4	10.9	8.4
1998	4.2	4.9	−2.3	−.8	4.1	6.7	12.0	−.7	−.7	11.4	5.1
1999	4.5	4.9	3.3	2.6	2.4	4.4	6.2	1.5	4.6	5.2	5.8
2000	3.7	4.0	12.2	−4.1	.6	6.3	11.6	−1.3	5.6	−.4	4.5
2001	.8	.9	−6.3	−5.3	.2	−5.6	−6.0	−5.0	−4.9	7.0	7.0
2002	1.6	1.4	5.5	−6.3	−2.0	2.8	1.7	4.2	4.3	1.0	2.2
2003	2.5	2.7	7.5	−.9	−2.1	1.1	2.6	−.8	6.9	2.1	3.9
2004	3.6	3.9	6.7	1.0	.3	5.6	5.8	5.3	5.7	2.0	2.6
2005	3.1	3.4	4.9	−2.4	2.7	1.0	4.9	−3.9	−2.2	1.8	6.1
2006	2.9	3.5	.9	6.1	−6.0	2.9	6.0	−1.0	−2.3	1.7	5.0

[1] Consists of agriculture, forestry, fishing, and hunting; mining; construction; and manufacturing.
[2] Consists of utilities; wholesale trade; retail trade; transportation and warehousing; information; finance, insurance, real estate, rental, and leasing; professional and business services; educational services, health care, and social assistance; arts, entertainment, recreation, accommodation, and food services; and other services, except government.

See next page for continuation of table.

Year	Transportation and warehousing	Information	Finance, insurance, real estate, rental, and leasing	Professional and business services	Educational services, health care, and social assistance	Arts, entertainment, recreation, accommodation, and food services	Other services, except government	Government	Private goods-producing industries [1]	Private services-producing industries [2]
	Chain-type quantity indexes for value added (2000=100)									
1976	41.733	26.473	46.720	31.391	54.419	45.554	70.997	74.283	49.103	41.544
1977	43.462	28.460	47.363	34.086	57.878	48.641	71.231	74.973	52.269	43.258
1978	45.697	31.532	50.358	36.884	60.672	52.049	75.107	76.694	54.587	46.163
1979	48.252	34.231	52.965	39.387	63.234	53.512	75.703	77.721	56.085	48.120
1980	47.232	36.394	55.414	40.529	66.887	52.407	74.411	79.023	53.880	48.764
1981	46.178	38.257	56.573	41.554	68.455	54.193	72.329	79.328	55.783	49.923
1982	43.855	38.155	56.986	41.345	68.856	55.695	69.103	79.456	52.029	49.794
1983	49.486	41.017	58.734	44.142	71.153	59.784	72.470	80.178	53.361	52.637
1984	52.121	40.717	61.282	48.913	72.366	62.194	77.498	81.038	59.454	55.727
1985	52.715	42.039	62.812	52.748	73.629	66.167	80.936	83.172	62.569	58.104
1986	53.021	42.672	63.965	56.860	75.166	69.642	82.885	85.105	62.534	60.576
1987	55.690	45.764	65.941	60.050	80.273	68.742	84.221	86.753	66.173	62.256
1988	57.990	47.649	68.652	64.420	80.570	71.515	89.044	88.812	69.104	65.186
1989	59.507	51.150	70.359	68.787	84.002	73.872	92.188	90.984	70.366	68.033
1990	62.281	53.420	71.877	72.073	87.047	76.063	94.369	93.215	69.858	69.877
1991	65.060	54.441	73.051	69.786	89.285	74.232	91.258	93.658	68.214	70.319
1992	68.758	57.568	74.863	72.008	91.728	77.250	92.502	94.134	70.330	73.074
1993	71.988	61.445	76.931	73.224	92.199	78.787	95.195	94.055	72.128	75.047
1994	77.827	65.223	78.506	75.430	92.413	80.604	98.624	94.407	77.818	77.745
1995	80.473	67.996	80.732	77.382	93.503	83.542	99.714	94.250	79.572	79.773
1996	84.585	72.714	82.893	82.053	94.144	86.796	99.072	94.768	82.596	83.377
1997	88.373	74.559	86.786	87.432	94.809	90.310	99.291	95.864	87.229	87.407
1998	91.454	82.252	90.201	91.976	95.603	93.446	101.871	96.923	91.878	91.591
1999	95.301	95.467	94.994	96.898	97.304	96.836	100.236	98.009	95.402	96.434
2000	100.000	100.000	100.000	100.000	100.000	100.000	100.000	100.000	100.000	100.000
2001	97.354	104.034	103.858	99.346	103.186	99.292	98.337	100.794	95.654	102.584
2002	99.531	106.263	104.800	99.192	107.527	101.022	98.667	102.467	96.853	104.107
2003	101.534	109.430	107.288	103.554	112.257	104.138	100.615	103.776	97.402	107.496
2004	110.780	122.221	110.433	107.750	115.949	108.114	100.770	104.252	101.328	111.692
2005	115.372	136.236	115.771	112.083	118.053	109.534	100.185	104.977	102.678	116.164
2006	121.419	146.005	122.523	116.324	122.229	112.916	99.877	105.447	103.543	121.078
	Percent change from year earlier									
1976	8.5	5.2	2.7	5.6	4.7	7.6	4.1	1.6	8.0	4.7
1977	4.1	7.5	1.4	8.6	6.4	6.8	.3	.9	6.4	4.1
1978	5.1	10.8	6.3	8.2	4.8	7.0	5.4	2.3	4.4	6.7
1979	5.6	8.6	5.2	6.8	4.2	2.8	.8	1.3	2.7	4.2
1980	-2.1	6.3	4.6	2.9	5.8	-2.1	-1.7	1.7	-3.9	1.3
1981	-2.2	5.1	2.1	2.5	2.3	3.4	-2.8	.4	3.5	2.4
1982	-5.0	-.3	.7	-.5	.6	2.8	-4.5	.2	-6.7	-.3
1983	12.8	7.5	3.1	6.8	3.3	7.3	4.9	.9	2.6	5.7
1984	5.3	-.7	4.3	10.8	1.7	4.0	6.9	1.1	11.4	5.9
1985	1.1	3.2	2.5	7.8	1.7	6.4	4.4	2.6	5.2	4.3
1986	.6	1.5	1.8	7.8	2.1	5.3	2.4	2.3	-.1	4.3
1987	5.0	7.2	3.1	5.6	6.8	-1.3	1.6	1.9	5.8	2.8
1988	4.1	4.1	4.1	7.3	.4	4.0	5.7	2.4	4.4	4.7
1989	2.6	7.3	2.5	6.8	4.3	3.3	3.5	2.4	1.8	4.4
1990	4.7	4.4	2.2	4.8	3.6	3.0	2.4	2.5	-.7	2.7
1991	4.5	1.9	1.6	-3.2	2.6	-2.4	-3.3	.5	-2.4	.6
1992	5.7	5.7	2.5	3.2	2.7	4.1	1.4	.5	3.1	3.9
1993	4.7	6.7	2.8	1.7	.5	2.0	2.9	-.1	2.6	2.7
1994	8.1	6.1	2.1	3.0	.2	2.3	3.6	.4	7.9	3.6
1995	3.4	4.3	2.8	2.6	1.2	3.6	1.1	-.2	2.3	2.6
1996	5.1	6.9	2.7	6.0	.7	3.9	-.6	.5	3.8	4.5
1997	4.5	2.5	4.7	6.6	.7	4.1	.2	1.2	5.6	4.8
1998	3.5	10.3	3.9	5.2	.8	3.5	2.6	1.1	5.3	4.8
1999	4.2	16.1	5.3	5.4	1.8	3.6	-1.6	1.1	3.8	5.3
2000	4.9	4.7	5.3	3.2	2.8	3.3	-.2	2.0	4.8	3.7
2001	-2.6	4.0	3.9	-.7	3.2	-.7	-1.7	.8	-4.3	2.6
2002	2.2	2.1	.9	-.2	4.2	1.7	.3	1.7	1.3	1.5
2003	2.0	3.0	2.4	4.4	4.4	3.1	2.0	1.3	.6	3.3
2004	9.1	11.7	2.9	4.1	3.3	3.8	.2	.5	4.0	3.9
2005	4.1	11.5	4.8	4.0	1.8	1.3	-.6	.7	1.3	4.0
2006	5.2	7.2	5.8	3.8	3.5	3.1	-.3	.4	.8	4.2

Note.—Data are based on the 1997 North American Industry Classification System (NAICS).
See Note, Table B–12.

Source: Department of Commerce (Bureau of Economic Analysis).

[Billions of dollars; quarterly data at seasonally adjusted annual rates]

Year or quarter	Gross value added of nonfinancial corporate business [1]	Consumption of fixed capital	Net value added Total	Compensation of employees	Taxes on production and imports less subsidies	Net operating surplus Total	Net interest and miscellaneous payments	Business current transfer payments	Corporate profits with inventory valuation and capital consumption adjustments Total	Taxes on corporate rate income	Profits after tax [2]	Addenda: Profits before tax	Inventory valuation adjustment	Capital consumption adjustment
1959	266.0	21.1	244.9	170.8	24.4	49.7	2.9	1.3	45.5	20.7	24.8	43.4	−0.3	2.3
1960	276.4	22.6	253.8	180.4	26.6	46.8	3.2	1.4	42.2	19.1	23.1	40.1	−.2	2.3
1961	283.7	23.2	260.5	184.5	27.6	48.4	3.7	1.5	43.2	19.4	23.8	39.9	.3	3.0
1962	309.8	23.9	285.9	199.3	29.9	56.8	4.3	1.7	50.8	20.6	30.2	44.6	.0	6.1
1963	329.9	25.2	304.7	210.1	31.7	62.9	4.7	1.7	56.5	22.8	33.8	49.7	.1	6.8
1964	356.1	26.4	329.7	225.7	33.9	70.2	5.2	2.0	63.0	23.9	39.2	55.9	−.5	7.7
1965	391.2	28.4	362.8	245.4	36.0	81.4	5.8	2.2	73.3	27.1	46.2	66.1	−1.2	8.4
1966	429.0	31.5	397.4	272.9	37.0	87.6	7.0	2.7	77.9	29.5	48.4	71.4	−2.1	8.5
1967	451.2	34.3	416.8	291.1	39.3	86.4	8.4	2.8	75.2	27.8	47.3	67.6	−1.6	9.1
1968	497.8	37.6	460.2	321.9	45.5	92.8	9.7	3.1	80.0	33.5	46.5	74.0	−3.7	9.7
1969	540.5	42.4	498.1	357.1	50.2	90.8	12.7	3.2	74.9	33.3	41.6	71.2	−5.9	9.6
1970	558.3	46.8	511.5	376.5	54.2	80.7	16.6	3.3	60.9	27.3	33.6	58.5	−6.6	8.9
1971	603.0	50.7	552.4	399.4	59.5	93.4	17.6	3.7	72.1	30.0	42.1	67.4	−4.6	9.3
1972	669.5	56.4	613.2	443.9	63.7	105.6	18.6	4.0	83.0	33.8	49.2	79.2	−6.6	10.5
1973	750.8	62.7	688.1	502.2	70.1	115.8	21.8	4.7	89.4	40.4	49.0	99.4	−19.6	9.5
1974	809.8	74.1	735.7	552.2	74.4	109.1	27.5	4.1	77.5	42.8	34.7	110.1	−38.2	5.6
1975	876.7	87.9	788.7	575.5	80.2	133.1	28.4	5.0	99.6	41.9	57.7	110.7	−10.5	−5
1976	989.7	97.0	892.7	651.4	86.7	154.7	26.0	7.0	121.7	53.5	68.2	138.2	−14.1	−2.4
1977	1,119.4	110.5	1,008.8	735.3	94.6	178.9	28.5	9.0	141.4	60.6	80.9	159.4	−15.7	−2.2
1978	1,272.9	127.8	1,145.1	845.3	102.7	197.0	33.4	9.5	154.1	67.6	86.6	183.7	−23.7	−5.9
1979	1,415.9	147.3	1,268.6	959.9	108.8	200.0	41.8	9.5	148.8	70.6	78.1	197.0	−40.1	−8.1
1980	1,537.1	168.2	1,368.9	1,049.8	121.5	197.6	54.2	10.2	133.2	68.2	65.0	184.0	−42.1	−8.7
1981	1,746.0	191.5	1,554.5	1,161.5	146.7	246.4	67.2	11.4	167.7	66.0	101.7	185.0	−24.6	7.4
1982	1,806.2	211.2	1,594.9	1,203.9	152.9	238.1	77.4	8.8	151.9	48.8	103.1	139.9	−7.5	19.5
1983	1,933.0	217.6	1,715.4	1,266.9	168.0	280.5	77.0	10.5	192.9	61.7	131.2	163.3	−7.4	37.1
1984	2,167.5	230.7	1,936.8	1,406.1	185.0	345.7	86.0	11.7	248.0	75.9	172.0	197.6	−4.0	54.3
1985	2,302.0	247.4	2,054.6	1,504.2	196.6	353.8	91.5	16.1	246.3	71.1	175.2	173.4	.0	72.8
1986	2,387.5	255.3	2,132.2	1,583.1	204.6	344.5	95.1	27.3	222.1	76.2	145.9	149.7	7.1	65.3
1987	2,557.1	266.5	2,290.6	1,687.8	216.8	386.0	96.4	29.9	259.7	94.2	165.5	209.8	−16.2	66.2
1988	2,771.6	281.6	2,490.0	1,812.8	233.8	443.4	109.8	27.4	306.2	104.0	202.3	260.4	−22.2	68.0
1989	2,912.3	301.6	2,610.7	1,914.7	248.2	447.9	142.0	23.0	282.9	101.2	181.7	238.7	−16.3	60.6
1990	3,041.5	319.2	2,722.3	2,012.9	263.5	445.8	146.2	25.4	274.3	98.5	175.8	239.0	−12.9	48.2
1991	3,099.7	341.4	2,758.3	2,048.4	285.7	424.2	135.9	26.7	261.5	88.6	172.9	222.4	4.9	34.2
1992	3,236.0	353.6	2,882.3	2,154.1	302.5	425.7	111.3	25.2	289.2	94.4	194.8	258.2	−2.8	33.8
1993	3,397.8	363.4	3,034.4	2,244.8	318.8	470.8	102.0	29.6	339.2	108.0	231.2	303.3	−4.0	39.9
1994	3,669.5	391.5	3,278.0	2,381.5	349.6	546.9	101.0	30.0	415.9	132.9	283.1	380.1	−12.4	48.3
1995	3,879.5	415.0	3,464.5	2,509.8	356.9	597.8	115.2	30.2	452.5	141.0	311.4	419.3	−18.3	51.5
1996	4,109.5	436.5	3,673.0	2,630.8	369.1	673.1	111.9	38.0	523.2	153.1	370.1	458.5	3.1	61.6
1997	4,401.8	467.1	3,934.7	2,812.9	385.5	736.3	124.0	39.0	573.4	161.9	411.5	494.2	14.1	65.0
1998	4,655.0	493.3	4,161.7	3,045.6	398.7	717.4	143.8	35.2	538.3	158.6	379.7	449.4	20.2	68.7
1999	4,950.8	523.8	4,427.0	3,267.7	416.6	742.7	160.2	45.0	537.6	171.2	366.3	457.9	1.0	78.7
2000	5,272.2	567.8	4,704.3	3,544.4	443.4	716.5	191.7	48.4	476.4	170.2	306.2	423.9	−14.1	66.6
2001	5,293.5	646.8	4,646.7	3,595.9	439.1	611.8	204.0	50.6	357.2	111.7	245.5	310.6	11.3	35.2
2002	5,371.7	643.6	4,728.2	3,611.9	465.5	650.8	167.4	54.0	429.4	97.0	332.3	336.3	−2.2	95.3
2003	5,558.4	657.5	4,900.9	3,703.2	488.5	709.2	152.6	64.4	492.1	135.7	356.4	425.4	−13.6	80.3
2004	5,956.4	687.4	5,269.0	3,865.2	523.9	879.9	138.9	59.3	681.6	191.0	490.7	662.4	−43.1	62.4
2005	6,319.4	742.3	5,577.1	4,078.5	558.7	940.0	132.5	58.3	749.1	263.4	485.7	937.8	−36.2	−152.5
2006	6,689.4	772.8	5,916.6	4,316.7	584.9	1,015.0	133.2	67.6	814.3	288.2	526.0	1,043.2	−36.3	−192.7
2004: I	5,778.1	667.8	5,110.3	3,770.5	512.5	827.4	140.1	64.0	623.3	173.1	450.2	579.0	−33.7	77.9
II	5,907.6	673.7	5,234.0	3,826.4	519.9	887.7	141.7	65.0	681.0	190.0	490.9	661.7	−51.9	71.2
III	6,038.5	717.8	5,320.7	3,899.1	526.3	895.3	138.8	40.2	716.3	201.1	515.2	701.9	−39.6	53.9
IV	6,101.4	690.3	5,411.1	3,965.1	537.0	909.1	135.0	68.1	706.0	199.6	506.4	706.8	−47.2	46.4
2005: I	6,170.9	701.0	5,469.9	3,992.2	545.3	932.4	135.8	73.2	723.4	250.2	473.2	889.5	−45.3	−120.8
II	6,291.1	712.7	5,578.4	4,034.6	556.3	987.5	132.5	74.9	780.2	260.5	519.6	937.8	−19.4	−138.2
III	6,349.9	808.4	5,541.5	4,115.3	563.7	862.5	131.1	19.2	712.2	261.2	450.9	923.1	−32.9	−178.0
IV	6,465.6	747.1	5,718.6	4,171.7	569.4	977.5	130.7	65.9	780.8	281.7	499.1	1,000.8	−47.0	−173.0
2006: I	6,594.1	754.2	5,839.9	4,249.2	576.1	1,014.6	131.8	67.5	815.3	278.3	537.0	1,019.3	−31.4	−172.7
II	6,639.8	767.6	5,872.2	4,269.2	583.9	1,019.1	135.0	66.7	817.5	288.8	528.6	1,061.9	−57.7	−186.7
III	6,739.1	779.5	5,959.6	4,306.4	587.3	1,065.9	132.3	67.2	866.4	300.6	565.8	1,101.4	−35.2	−199.7
IV	6,784.5	789.8	5,994.7	4,442.1	592.1	960.5	133.6	68.9	757.9	285.2	472.7	990.4	−21.0	−211.6
2007: I	6,865.0	795.7	6,069.3	4,494.1	599.7	975.6	136.0	58.5	781.1	298.6	482.5	1,024.9	−40.2	−203.6
II	6,938.0	800.1	6,138.0	4,528.3	607.8	1,001.8	136.2	59.2	806.4	321.6	484.7	1,070.5	−54.7	−209.4
III	6,988.4	802.0	6,186.4	4,583.3	614.2	988.8	136.9	60.0	792.0	310.0	482.0	1,024.5	−20.3	−212.1

[1] Estimates for nonfinancial corporate business for 2000 and earlier periods are based on the Standard Industrial Classification (SIC); later estimates are based on the North American Industry Classification System (NAICS).
[2] With inventory valuation and capital consumption adjustments.

Source: Department of Commerce (Bureau of Economic Analysis).

TABLE B–15.—*Gross value added and price, costs, and profits of nonfinancial corporate business, 1959–2007*

[Quarterly data at seasonally adjusted annual rates]

Year or quarter	Gross value added of nonfinancial corporate business (billions of dollars)[1]		Price per unit of real gross value added of nonfinancial corporate business (dollars)[1,2]									
	Current dollars	Chained (2000) dollars	Total	Compensation of employees (unit labor cost)	Unit nonlabor cost				Corporate profits with inventory valuation and capital consumption adjustments[4]		
					Total	Consumption of fixed capital	Taxes on production and imports[3]	Net interest and miscellaneous payments	Total	Taxes on corporate income	Profits after tax[5]
1959	266.0	980.4	0.271	0.174	0.051	0.022	0.026	0.003	0.046	0.021	0.025
1960	276.4	1,012.0	.273	.178	.053	.022	.028	.003	.042	.019	.023
1961	283.7	1,033.6	.274	.179	.054	.022	.028	.004	.042	.019	.023
1962	309.8	1,120.7	.276	.178	.053	.021	.028	.004	.045	.018	.027
1963	329.9	1,186.7	.278	.177	.053	.021	.028	.004	.048	.019	.028
1964	356.1	1,270.3	.280	.178	.053	.021	.028	.004	.050	.019	.031
1965	391.2	1,375.1	.284	.178	.053	.021	.028	.004	.053	.020	.034
1966	429.0	1,472.6	.291	.185	.053	.021	.027	.005	.053	.020	.033
1967	451.2	1,508.9	.299	.193	.057	.023	.028	.006	.050	.018	.031
1968	497.8	1,604.8	.310	.201	.059	.023	.030	.006	.050	.021	.029
1969	540.5	1,667.6	.324	.214	.065	.025	.032	.008	.045	.020	.025
1970	558.3	1,649.9	.338	.228	.073	.028	.035	.010	.037	.017	.020
1971	603.0	1,716.6	.351	.233	.077	.030	.037	.010	.042	.017	.025
1972	669.5	1,846.4	.363	.240	.078	.031	.037	.010	.045	.018	.027
1973	750.8	1,957.7	.384	.257	.081	.032	.038	.011	.046	.021	.025
1974	809.8	1,925.4	.421	.287	.093	.038	.041	.014	.040	.022	.018
1975	876.7	1,898.8	.462	.303	.106	.046	.045	.015	.052	.022	.030
1976	989.7	2,050.0	.483	.318	.106	.047	.046	.013	.059	.026	.033
1977	1,119.4	2,200.0	.509	.334	.110	.050	.047	.013	.064	.028	.037
1978	1,272.9	2,344.1	.543	.361	.117	.055	.048	.014	.066	.029	.037
1979	1,415.9	2,418.7	.585	.397	.127	.061	.049	.017	.062	.029	.032
1980	1,537.1	2,394.6	.642	.438	.148	.070	.055	.023	.056	.028	.027
1981	1,746.0	2,491.5	.701	.466	.167	.077	.063	.027	.067	.026	.041
1982	1,806.2	2,430.6	.743	.495	.186	.087	.067	.032	.062	.020	.042
1983	1,933.0	2,545.1	.759	.498	.185	.085	.070	.030	.076	.024	.052
1984	2,167.5	2,772.8	.782	.507	.185	.083	.071	.031	.089	.027	.062
1985	2,302.0	2,896.3	.795	.519	.190	.085	.073	.032	.085	.025	.060
1986	2,387.5	2,963.3	.806	.534	.196	.086	.078	.032	.075	.026	.049
1987	2,557.1	3,119.6	.820	.541	.195	.085	.079	.031	.083	.030	.053
1988	2,771.6	3,300.7	.840	.549	.197	.085	.079	.033	.093	.031	.061
1989	2,912.3	3,361.8	.866	.570	.213	.090	.081	.042	.084	.030	.054
1990	3,041.5	3,404.0	.894	.591	.222	.094	.085	.043	.081	.029	.052
1991	3,099.7	3,376.2	.918	.607	.234	.101	.093	.040	.077	.026	.051
1992	3,236.0	3,479.5	.930	.619	.228	.102	.094	.032	.083	.027	.056
1993	3,397.8	3,575.5	.950	.628	.228	.102	.097	.029	.095	.030	.065
1994	3,669.5	3,797.9	.966	.627	.230	.103	.100	.027	.110	.035	.075
1995	3,879.5	3,977.4	.975	.631	.230	.104	.097	.029	.114	.035	.078
1996	4,109.5	4,196.4	.979	.627	.228	.104	.097	.027	.125	.036	.088
1997	4,401.8	4,469.3	.985	.629	.228	.105	.095	.028	.128	.036	.092
1998	4,655.0	4,725.4	.985	.645	.226	.104	.092	.030	.114	.034	.080
1999	4,950.8	5,011.0	.988	.652	.229	.105	.092	.032	.107	.034	.073
2000	5,272.2	5,272.2	1.000	.672	.237	.108	.093	.036	.090	.032	.058
2001	5,293.5	5,224.5	1.013	.688	.257	.124	.094	.039	.068	.021	.047
2002	5,371.7	5,269.7	1.019	.685	.253	.122	.099	.032	.081	.018	.063
2003	5,558.4	5,387.5	1.032	.687	.253	.122	.103	.028	.091	.025	.066
2004	5,956.4	5,652.3	1.054	.684	.250	.122	.103	.025	.121	.034	.087
2005	6,319.4	5,806.6	1.088	.702	.257	.128	.106	.023	.129	.045	.084
2006	6,689.4	6,012.1	1.113	.718	.260	.129	.109	.022	.135	.048	.087
2004: I	5,778.1	5,546.9	1.042	.680	.249	.120	.104	.025	.112	.031	.081
II	5,907.6	5,618.5	1.051	.681	.249	.120	.104	.025	.121	.034	.087
III	6,038.5	5,721.3	1.055	.681	.248	.125	.099	.024	.125	.035	.090
IV	6,101.4	5,722.6	1.066	.693	.251	.121	.106	.024	.123	.035	.088
2005: I	6,170.9	5,727.5	1.077	.697	.254	.122	.108	.024	.126	.044	.083
II	6,291.1	5,802.8	1.084	.695	.255	.123	.109	.023	.134	.045	.090
III	6,349.9	5,808.3	1.093	.709	.262	.139	.100	.023	.123	.045	.078
IV	6,465.6	5,887.8	1.098	.709	.257	.127	.108	.022	.133	.048	.085
2006: I	6,594.1	5,966.9	1.105	.712	.256	.126	.108	.022	.137	.047	.090
II	6,639.8	5,965.7	1.113	.716	.261	.129	.109	.023	.137	.048	.089
III	6,739.1	6,039.7	1.116	.713	.259	.129	.108	.022	.143	.050	.094
IV	6,784.5	6,076.2	1.117	.731	.261	.130	.109	.022	.125	.047	.078
2007: I	6,865.0	6,089.6	1.127	.738	.261	.131	.108	.022	.128	.049	.079
II	6,938.0	6,133.4	1.131	.738	.261	.130	.109	.022	.131	.052	.079
III	6,988.4	6,202.3	1.127	.739	.260	.129	.109	.022	.128	.050	.078

[1] Estimates for nonfinancial corporate business for 2000 and earlier periods are based on the Standard Industrial Classification (SIC); later estimates are based on the North American Industry Classification System (NAICS).
[2] The implicit price deflator for gross value added of nonfinancial corporate business divided by 100.
[3] Less subsidies plus business current transfer payments.
[4] Unit profits from current production.
[5] With inventory valuation and capital consumption adjustments.

Source: Department of Commerce (Bureau of Economic Analysis).

[Billions of dollars; quarterly data at seasonally adjusted annual rates]

Year or quarter	Personal consumption expenditures	Durable goods			Nondurable goods					Services					
		Total [1]	Motor vehicles and parts	Furniture and household equipment	Total [1]	Food	Clothing and shoes	Gasoline and oil	Fuel oil and coal	Total [1]	Housing [2]	Household operation		Transportation	Medical care
												Total [1]	Electricity and gas		
1959	317.6	42.7	18.9	18.1	148.5	80.6	26.4	11.3	4.0	126.5	45.0	18.7	7.6	10.6	16.4
1960	331.7	43.3	19.7	18.0	152.8	82.3	27.0	12.0	3.8	135.6	48.2	20.3	8.3	11.2	17.7
1961	342.1	41.8	17.8	18.3	156.6	84.0	27.6	12.0	3.8	143.8	51.2	21.2	8.8	11.6	19.0
1962	363.3	46.9	21.5	19.3	162.8	86.1	29.0	12.6	3.8	153.6	54.7	22.4	9.4	12.3	21.2
1963	382.7	51.6	24.4	20.7	168.2	88.2	29.8	13.0	4.0	162.9	58.0	23.6	9.9	12.9	23.0
1964	411.4	56.7	26.0	23.2	178.6	93.5	32.4	13.6	4.1	176.1	61.4	25.0	10.4	13.8	26.4
1965	443.8	63.3	29.9	25.1	191.5	100.7	34.1	14.8	4.4	189.0	65.4	26.5	10.9	14.7	28.6
1966	480.9	68.3	30.3	28.2	208.7	109.3	37.4	16.0	4.7	203.8	69.5	28.1	11.5	15.9	31.5
1967	507.8	70.4	30.0	30.0	217.1	112.4	39.2	17.1	4.8	220.3	74.1	30.0	12.2	17.4	34.7
1968	558.0	80.8	36.1	32.9	235.7	122.2	43.2	18.6	4.7	241.6	79.8	32.3	13.0	19.3	40.1
1969	605.2	85.9	38.4	34.7	253.1	131.5	46.5	20.5	4.6	266.1	86.9	35.0	14.1	21.6	45.8
1970	648.5	85.0	35.5	35.7	272.0	143.8	47.8	21.9	4.4	291.5	94.1	37.8	15.3	24.0	51.7
1971	701.9	96.9	44.5	37.8	285.5	149.7	51.7	23.2	4.6	319.5	102.8	41.1	16.9	26.8	58.4
1972	770.6	110.4	51.1	42.4	308.0	161.4	56.4	24.4	5.1	352.2	112.6	45.4	18.8	29.6	65.6
1973	852.4	123.5	56.1	47.9	343.1	179.6	62.5	28.1	6.3	385.8	123.3	49.9	20.4	31.6	73.3
1974	933.4	122.3	49.5	51.5	384.5	201.8	66.0	36.1	7.8	426.6	134.8	55.8	24.0	34.1	82.3
1975	1,034.4	133.5	54.8	54.5	420.7	223.2	70.8	39.7	8.4	480.2	147.7	64.0	29.2	37.9	95.6
1976	1,151.9	158.9	71.3	60.2	458.3	242.5	76.6	43.0	10.1	534.7	162.2	72.5	33.2	42.5	109.1
1977	1,278.6	181.2	83.5	67.2	497.1	262.6	84.1	46.9	11.1	600.2	180.2	81.8	38.5	48.7	125.3
1978	1,428.5	201.7	93.1	74.3	550.2	289.6	94.3	50.1	11.5	676.6	202.4	91.2	43.0	53.4	143.1
1979	1,592.2	214.4	93.5	82.7	624.5	324.7	101.2	66.2	14.4	753.3	227.3	100.3	47.8	59.9	161.0
1980	1,757.1	214.2	87.0	86.7	696.1	356.0	107.3	86.7	15.4	846.9	256.2	113.7	57.5	65.2	184.4
1981	1,941.1	231.3	95.8	92.1	758.9	383.5	117.2	97.9	15.8	950.8	289.7	126.8	64.8	70.3	216.7
1982	2,077.3	240.2	102.9	93.4	787.6	403.4	120.5	94.1	14.5	1,049.4	315.2	142.5	74.2	72.9	243.3
1983	2,290.6	280.8	126.5	106.6	831.2	423.8	130.9	93.1	13.6	1,178.6	341.0	157.0	82.4	81.1	274.3
1984	2,503.3	326.5	152.1	119.0	884.6	447.4	142.5	94.6	13.9	1,292.2	374.5	169.4	86.5	93.2	303.2
1985	2,720.3	363.5	175.9	128.5	928.7	467.6	152.1	97.2	13.6	1,428.1	412.7	181.8	90.8	104.5	331.5
1986	2,899.7	403.0	194.1	143.0	958.4	492.0	163.1	80.1	11.3	1,538.3	448.4	187.7	89.2	111.1	357.5
1987	3,100.2	421.7	195.0	153.4	1,015.3	515.2	174.4	85.4	11.2	1,663.3	483.7	195.4	90.9	120.9	392.2
1988	3,353.6	453.6	209.4	163.7	1,083.5	553.5	185.5	88.3	11.7	1,816.5	521.5	207.3	96.3	133.4	442.8
1989	3,598.5	471.8	215.3	171.6	1,166.7	591.6	198.9	98.6	11.9	1,960.0	557.4	221.1	101.0	142.0	492.5
1990	3,839.9	474.2	212.8	171.6	1,249.9	636.8	204.1	111.2	12.9	2,115.9	597.9	227.3	101.0	147.7	556.0
1991	3,986.1	453.9	193.5	171.7	1,284.8	657.5	208.7	108.5	12.4	2,247.4	631.1	238.6	107.4	145.3	608.9
1992	4,235.3	483.6	213.0	178.7	1,330.5	669.3	221.9	112.4	12.2	2,421.2	658.5	250.7	108.9	157.7	672.2
1993	4,477.9	526.7	234.0	193.4	1,379.4	691.9	229.9	114.1	12.4	2,571.8	683.9	269.9	118.2	172.7	715.1
1994	4,743.3	582.2	260.5	213.4	1,437.2	720.6	238.1	116.2	12.8	2,723.9	726.1	286.2	120.7	190.6	752.9
1995	4,975.8	611.6	266.7	228.6	1,485.1	740.9	241.7	120.2	13.1	2,879.1	764.4	298.7	122.2	207.7	797.9
1996	5,256.8	652.6	284.9	242.9	1,555.5	768.7	250.2	130.4	14.3	3,048.7	800.1	318.5	129.4	226.5	833.5
1997	5,547.4	692.7	305.1	256.2	1,619.0	796.2	258.1	134.4	13.3	3,235.8	842.6	337.0	131.3	245.7	873.0
1998	5,879.5	750.2	336.1	273.1	1,683.6	829.8	270.9	122.4	11.5	3,445.7	894.6	350.5	128.9	259.5	921.4
1999	6,282.5	817.6	370.8	293.9	1,804.8	873.1	286.3	137.9	11.9	3,660.0	948.4	364.8	130.6	276.4	961.1
2000	6,739.4	863.3	386.5	312.9	1,947.2	925.2	297.7	175.7	15.8	3,928.8	1,006.5	390.1	143.3	291.3	1,026.8
2001	7,055.0	883.7	407.9	312.1	2,017.1	967.9	297.7	171.6	15.4	4,154.3	1,073.7	409.0	156.7	292.8	1,113.8
2002	7,350.7	923.9	429.3	323.1	2,079.6	1,001.9	303.5	164.5	14.2	4,347.2	1,123.1	407.7	152.5	288.4	1,206.2
2003	7,703.6	942.7	431.7	331.5	2,190.2	1,046.0	310.9	192.7	16.9	4,570.8	1,161.8	429.4	167.3	297.3	1,300.5
2004	8,195.9	983.9	436.8	355.7	2,343.7	1,113.1	325.0	231.4	18.3	4,868.3	1,226.8	449.0	175.4	308.2	1,395.5
2005	8,707.8	1,023.9	444.9	378.2	2,516.2	1,183.8	341.7	280.7	21.1	5,167.8	1,298.7	481.0	198.7	324.2	1,492.6
2006	9,224.5	1,048.9	434.2	404.1	2,688.0	1,259.3	357.2	318.6	21.6	5,487.6	1,381.3	501.6	209.8	340.6	1,587.7
2004: I	8,010.1	969.6	432.5	347.8	2,284.2	1,090.5	323.6	211.0	17.5	4,756.3	1,201.8	441.6	173.2	303.5	1,357.7
II	8,135.0	974.8	431.6	352.8	2,327.7	1,104.0	321.1	233.0	17.3	4,832.4	1,219.0	445.5	173.3	306.4	1,383.4
III	8,245.1	986.9	436.5	358.6	2,353.5	1,117.0	324.6	232.5	18.4	4,904.6	1,235.2	450.9	174.4	309.4	1,409.3
IV	8,393.3	1,004.1	446.7	363.7	2,409.3	1,140.8	330.6	249.3	19.8	4,979.9	1,251.2	457.8	180.8	313.5	1,431.5
2005: I	8,488.8	1,009.7	442.9	369.3	2,432.1	1,153.0	336.2	245.7	20.3	5,047.0	1,271.2	464.9	185.4	317.2	1,454.8
II	8,632.6	1,036.0	459.0	375.3	2,484.3	1,174.5	342.1	262.8	20.5	5,112.3	1,289.5	470.1	188.7	322.1	1,477.0
III	8,810.5	1,044.1	462.7	380.7	2,557.0	1,193.9	340.2	309.4	21.8	5,209.4	1,307.4	487.4	203.9	326.7	1,503.9
IV	8,899.3	1,005.7	415.1	387.6	2,591.3	1,213.8	348.6	304.8	22.0	5,302.4	1,326.8	501.7	216.9	331.0	1,534.8
2006: I	9,034.7	1,042.6	432.7	400.6	2,622.1	1,236.4	351.3	297.7	20.2	5,370.0	1,347.8	496.8	208.8	334.7	1,558.3
II	9,183.9	1,042.8	431.8	401.8	2,692.2	1,245.9	354.9	341.2	22.1	5,448.9	1,371.1	496.7	206.6	338.4	1,578.6
III	9,305.7	1,053.8	437.6	405.1	2,732.4	1,263.2	359.6	351.0	22.2	5,519.5	1,392.5	503.3	211.3	342.5	1,596.1
IV	9,373.7	1,056.5	434.8	409.0	2,705.4	1,291.7	363.2	284.4	21.9	5,611.8	1,413.9	509.7	212.7	346.8	1,617.9
2007: I	9,540.5	1,074.0	444.5	414.2	2,759.4	1,312.2	371.1	296.2	24.7	5,707.1	1,435.1	520.0	220.6	349.6	1,656.9
II	9,674.0	1,074.7	441.5	414.5	2,822.7	1,322.7	368.4	349.4	24.2	5,776.5	1,455.4	526.2	223.5	355.1	1,674.6
III	9,785.7	1,081.6	437.5	418.6	2,846.3	1,342.4	372.4	341.9	24.0	5,857.8	1,474.9	533.3	227.3	362.5	1,695.0

[1] Includes other items not shown separately.
[2] Includes imputed rental value of owner-occupied housing.

Source: Department of Commerce (Bureau of Economic Analysis).

TABLE B–17.—*Real personal consumption expenditures, 1990–2007*

[Billions of chained (2000) dollars; quarterly data at seasonally adjusted annual rates]

Year or quarter	Personal consumption expenditures	Durable goods			Nondurable goods					Services					
		Total[1]	Motor vehicles and parts	Furniture and household equipment	Total[1]	Food	Clothing and shoes	Gasoline and oil	Fuel oil and coal	Total[1]	Housing[2]	Household operation		Transportation	Medical care
												Total[1]	Electricity and gas	Transportation[1]	
1990	4,770.3	453.5	256.1	119.9	1,484.0	784.4	188.2	141.8	16.7	2,851.7	802.2	266.4	117.4	195.7	797.6
1991	4,778.4	427.9	226.6	121.1	1,480.5	783.3	188.8	140.3	16.6	2,900.0	820.1	269.9	121.1	186.3	824.5
1992	4,934.8	453.0	244.9	127.8	1,510.1	787.9	199.2	146.0	17.0	3,000.8	832.7	277.4	120.4	194.2	863.6
1993	5,099.8	488.4	259.2	141.1	1,550.4	802.2	207.4	149.7	17.4	3,085.7	841.8	291.1	126.8	202.5	877.2
1994	5,290.7	529.4	276.2	156.8	1,603.9	821.8	218.5	151.7	18.2	3,176.6	869.3	303.3	128.8	218.4	887.1
1995	5,433.5	552.6	272.3	173.3	1,638.6	827.1	227.4	154.5	18.7	3,259.9	887.5	312.9	130.2	231.8	906.4
1996	5,619.4	595.9	285.4	193.4	1,680.4	834.7	238.7	157.9	18.4	3,356.0	901.1	327.3	134.7	247.5	922.5
1997	5,831.8	646.9	304.7	216.3	1,725.3	845.2	246.0	162.8	16.9	3,468.0	922.5	340.4	133.7	263.2	942.8
1998	6,125.8	720.3	339.0	244.7	1,794.4	865.6	263.1	170.3	16.0	3,615.0	948.8	357.1	136.7	272.0	970.7
1999	6,438.6	804.6	372.4	280.7	1,876.6	893.6	282.7	176.3	16.4	3,758.0	978.6	371.9	138.1	283.4	989.0
2000	6,739.4	863.3	386.5	312.9	1,947.2	925.2	297.7	175.7	15.8	3,928.8	1,006.5	390.1	143.3	291.3	1,026.8
2001	6,910.4	900.7	405.8	331.8	1,986.7	940.2	303.7	178.3	15.2	4,023.2	1,033.7	391.0	140.9	288.0	1,075.2
2002	7,099.3	964.8	429.0	364.3	2,037.1	954.6	318.3	181.9	15.5	4,100.4	1,042.1	393.2	144.9	280.2	1,136.6
2003	7,295.3	1,020.6	442.1	397.8	2,103.0	977.7	334.2	183.2	15.4	4,178.8	1,051.9	398.8	147.5	280.6	1,180.8
2004	7,561.4	1,084.8	450.8	445.1	2,177.6	1,009.4	350.7	186.7	14.6	4,311.0	1,083.8	408.5	149.1	284.6	1,216.5
2005	7,803.6	1,137.4	451.3	492.2	2,255.4	1,050.0	372.6	186.1	13.2	4,427.3	1,118.3	416.5	153.2	287.8	1,258.2
2006	8,044.1	1,180.5	437.3	550.9	2,337.7	1,091.8	391.1	186.8	12.0	4,545.5	1,148.3	412.9	148.5	291.2	1,300.3
2004: I	7,475.1	1,066.2	448.9	429.1	2,156.7	1,000.8	349.5	186.0	14.9	4,262.9	1,073.3	405.5	149.8	282.3	1,199.0
II	7,520.5	1,071.3	445.7	438.8	2,164.9	1,003.4	345.6	187.2	14.7	4,294.6	1,079.7	407.1	148.6	284.3	1,210.3
III	7,585.5	1,091.5	450.9	451.7	2,181.4	1,008.9	350.2	186.5	14.6	4,325.2	1,087.1	408.8	147.2	285.0	1,223.3
IV	7,664.3	1,110.1	457.8	460.8	2,207.5	1,024.7	357.5	187.0	14.0	4,361.1	1,095.1	412.8	150.9	286.6	1,233.5
2005: I	7,709.4	1,116.0	449.6	472.6	2,226.8	1,032.9	363.4	187.8	14.2	4,381.3	1,104.4	413.8	151.6	287.2	1,240.4
II	7,775.2	1,146.3	464.4	483.4	2,247.2	1,043.1	372.3	186.1	13.5	4,401.3	1,113.9	413.3	150.7	287.6	1,250.3
III	7,852.8	1,163.5	470.7	499.0	2,260.9	1,056.3	372.3	184.3	13.0	4,449.1	1,123.3	422.2	157.8	287.8	1,264.0
IV	7,876.9	1,123.8	420.4	513.8	2,286.8	1,067.6	382.3	186.1	12.3	4,477.5	1,131.6	416.4	152.9	288.7	1,278.1
2006: I	7,961.9	1,167.8	435.7	536.8	2,312.3	1,080.7	386.2	187.2	11.6	4,501.0	1,139.7	406.3	143.7	290.2	1,291.2
II	8,009.3	1,170.2	434.3	544.4	2,325.6	1,084.4	388.0	187.1	12.1	4,531.6	1,146.0	410.9	147.0	289.5	1,298.2
III	8,063.8	1,186.3	439.5	555.4	2,343.9	1,091.4	393.3	188.3	11.8	4,554.0	1,151.0	415.4	150.9	291.0	1,301.4
IV	8,141.2	1,197.6	439.6	566.9	2,368.8	1,110.7	397.0	184.8	12.4	4,595.5	1,156.6	419.1	152.5	294.1	1,310.5
2007: I	8,215.7	1,223.2	451.5	579.9	2,386.6	1,115.3	405.1	184.1	14.1	4,630.7	1,163.7	420.1	153.1	296.0	1,323.2
II	8,244.3	1,228.4	448.2	585.9	2,383.8	1,111.4	407.5	182.8	13.1	4,656.7	1,171.6	421.6	153.6	299.2	1,330.8
III	8,302.2	1,241.9	442.3	601.0	2,396.8	1,115.0	413.7	183.2	12.4	4,689.5	1,178.9	427.9	158.5	301.7	1,338.0

[1] Includes other items not shown separately.
[2] Includes imputed rental value of owner-occupied housing.

Note.—See Table B–2 for data for total personal consumption expenditures for 1959–89.

Source: Department of Commerce (Bureau of Economic Analysis).

Table B–18.—*Private fixed investment by type, 1959–2007*

[Billions of dollars; quarterly data at seasonally adjusted annual rates]

Year or quarter	Private fixed investment	Nonresidential Total nonresidential	Structures	Equipment and software Total	Information processing equipment and software Total	Computers and peripheral equipment	Software	Other	Industrial equipment	Transportation equipment	Other equipment	Residential Total residential [1]	Structures Total [1]	Single family
1959	74.6	46.5	18.1	28.4	4.0	0.0	0.0	4.0	8.5	8.3	7.6	28.1	27.5	16.7
1960	75.7	49.4	19.6	29.8	4.9	.2	.1	4.6	9.4	8.5	7.1	26.3	25.8	14.9
1961	75.2	48.8	19.7	29.1	5.3	.3	.2	4.8	8.8	8.0	7.0	26.4	25.9	14.1
1962	82.0	53.1	20.8	32.3	5.7	.3	.2	5.1	9.3	9.8	7.5	29.0	28.4	15.1
1963	88.1	56.0	21.2	34.8	6.5	.7	.4	5.4	10.0	9.4	8.8	32.1	31.5	16.0
1964	97.2	63.0	23.7	39.2	7.4	.9	.5	5.9	11.4	10.6	9.9	34.3	33.6	17.6
1965	109.0	74.8	28.3	46.5	8.5	1.2	.7	6.7	13.7	13.2	11.0	34.2	33.5	17.8
1966	117.7	85.4	31.3	54.0	10.7	1.7	1.0	8.0	16.2	14.5	12.7	32.3	31.6	16.6
1967	118.7	86.4	31.5	54.9	11.3	1.9	1.2	8.2	16.9	14.3	12.4	32.4	31.6	16.8
1968	132.1	93.4	33.6	59.9	11.9	1.9	1.3	8.7	17.3	17.6	13.0	38.7	37.9	19.5
1969	147.3	104.7	37.7	67.0	14.6	2.4	1.8	10.4	19.1	18.9	14.4	42.6	41.6	19.7
1970	150.4	109.0	40.3	68.7	16.6	2.7	2.3	11.6	20.3	16.2	15.6	41.4	40.2	17.5
1971	169.9	114.1	42.7	71.5	17.3	2.8	2.4	12.2	19.5	18.4	16.3	55.8	54.5	25.8
1972	198.5	128.8	47.2	81.7	19.5	3.5	2.8	13.2	21.4	21.8	19.0	69.7	68.1	32.8
1973	228.6	153.3	55.0	98.3	23.1	3.5	3.2	16.3	26.0	26.6	22.6	75.3	73.6	35.2
1974	235.4	169.5	61.2	108.2	27.0	3.9	3.9	19.2	30.7	26.3	24.3	66.0	64.1	29.7
1975	236.5	173.7	61.4	112.4	28.5	3.6	4.8	20.2	31.3	25.2	27.4	62.7	60.8	29.6
1976	274.8	192.4	65.9	126.4	32.7	4.4	5.2	23.1	34.1	30.0	29.6	82.5	80.4	43.9
1977	339.0	228.7	74.6	154.1	39.2	5.7	5.5	28.0	39.4	39.3	36.3	110.3	107.9	62.2
1978	412.2	280.6	93.6	187.0	48.7	7.6	6.3	34.8	47.7	47.3	43.2	131.6	128.9	72.8
1979	474.9	333.9	117.7	216.2	58.5	10.2	8.1	40.2	56.2	53.6	47.9	141.0	137.8	72.3
1980	485.6	362.4	136.2	226.2	68.8	12.5	9.8	46.4	60.7	48.4	48.3	123.2	119.8	52.9
1981	542.6	420.0	167.3	252.7	81.5	17.1	11.8	52.5	65.5	50.6	55.2	122.6	118.9	52.0
1982	532.1	426.5	177.6	248.9	88.3	18.9	14.0	55.3	62.7	46.8	51.2	105.7	102.0	41.5
1983	570.1	417.2	154.3	262.9	100.1	23.9	16.4	59.8	58.9	53.5	50.4	152.9	148.6	72.5
1984	670.2	489.6	177.4	312.2	121.5	31.6	20.4	69.6	68.1	64.4	58.1	180.6	175.9	86.4
1985	714.4	526.2	194.5	331.7	130.3	33.7	23.8	72.9	72.5	69.0	59.9	188.2	183.1	87.4
1986	739.9	519.8	176.5	343.3	136.8	33.4	25.6	77.7	75.4	70.5	60.7	220.1	214.6	104.1
1987	757.8	524.1	174.2	349.9	141.2	35.8	29.0	76.4	76.7	68.1	63.9	233.7	227.9	117.2
1988	803.1	563.8	182.8	381.0	154.9	38.0	34.2	82.8	84.2	72.9	69.0	239.3	233.2	120.1
1989	847.3	607.7	193.7	414.0	172.6	43.1	41.9	87.6	93.3	67.9	80.2	239.5	233.4	120.9
1990	846.4	622.4	202.9	419.5	177.2	38.6	47.6	90.9	92.1	70.0	80.2	224.0	218.0	112.9
1991	803.3	598.2	183.6	414.6	182.9	37.7	53.7	91.5	89.3	71.5	70.8	205.1	199.4	99.4
1992	848.5	612.1	172.6	439.6	199.9	44.0	57.9	98.1	93.0	74.7	72.0	236.3	230.4	122.0
1993	932.5	666.6	177.2	489.4	217.6	47.9	64.3	105.4	102.2	89.4	80.2	266.0	259.9	140.1
1994	1,033.3	731.4	186.8	544.6	235.2	52.4	68.3	114.6	113.6	107.7	88.1	301.9	295.6	162.3
1995	1,112.9	810.0	207.3	602.8	263.0	66.1	74.6	122.3	129.0	116.1	94.7	302.8	296.5	153.5
1996	1,209.5	875.4	224.6	650.8	290.1	72.8	85.5	131.9	136.5	123.2	101.0	334.1	327.8	170.8
1997	1,317.8	968.7	250.3	718.3	330.3	81.4	107.5	141.4	140.4	135.5	112.1	349.1	342.8	175.2
1998	1,438.4	1,052.6	275.2	777.3	363.4	87.2	124.0	152.2	146.4	144.0	123.5	385.8	379.3	199.4
1999	1,558.8	1,133.9	282.2	851.7	411.0	96.0	152.6	162.4	147.0	167.6	126.0	424.9	417.8	223.8
2000	1,679.0	1,232.1	313.2	918.9	467.6	101.4	176.2	190.0	159.2	160.8	131.2	446.9	439.5	236.8
2001	1,646.1	1,176.8	322.6	854.2	437.0	85.4	174.7	177.0	146.7	141.7	128.8	469.3	461.9	249.1
2002	1,570.2	1,066.3	279.2	787.1	399.4	77.2	167.6	154.5	135.7	126.3	125.7	503.9	496.3	265.9
2003	1,649.8	1,077.4	277.2	800.2	406.7	77.8	171.4	157.5	140.7	118.3	134.5	572.4	564.5	310.6
2004	1,830.0	1,154.5	298.2	856.3	429.6	80.3	183.0	166.4	139.7	142.9	144.0	675.5	667.0	377.6
2005	2,040.3	1,272.1	334.6	937.5	457.4	89.0	193.8	174.6	156.1	159.5	164.6	768.2	759.2	433.5
2006	2,162.5	1,397.7	405.1	992.6	480.9	91.3	203.3	186.2	166.7	171.9	173.2	764.8	755.2	416.0
2004: I	1,732.6	1,100.4	284.0	816.4	424.1	77.7	180.9	165.5	132.8	123.1	136.4	632.2	624.0	353.2
II	1,806.6	1,135.5	293.5	842.0	426.3	77.4	180.3	168.6	136.5	138.3	140.8	671.1	662.7	374.4
III	1,864.7	1,172.7	303.4	869.3	430.3	80.6	183.7	166.0	143.2	148.9	146.9	692.0	683.5	388.1
IV	1,916.1	1,209.5	312.0	897.4	437.9	85.5	187.0	165.4	146.5	161.3	151.8	706.6	698.0	394.5
2005: I	1,960.4	1,233.1	323.3	909.7	448.4	86.0	190.0	172.4	152.6	153.0	155.7	727.3	718.5	410.4
II	2,012.5	1,255.7	328.8	926.9	455.0	88.7	194.3	172.0	150.7	157.0	164.2	756.8	747.8	424.1
III	2,072.7	1,287.0	334.2	952.9	460.6	88.7	194.7	177.1	158.2	161.1	168.0	785.7	776.7	441.3
IV	2,115.5	1,312.6	352.0	960.5	465.7	92.6	196.3	176.7	162.8	161.7	170.4	803.0	793.7	458.3
2006: I	2,176.8	1,367.3	375.7	991.7	479.1	91.7	199.9	187.5	161.5	177.6	173.5	809.4	799.9	463.7
II	2,179.5	1,391.2	400.2	991.1	479.0	91.7	202.6	184.7	168.5	169.5	174.0	788.2	778.6	437.7
III	2,161.3	1,415.2	416.1	999.1	484.9	91.6	204.9	188.4	169.2	172.4	172.6	746.1	736.4	399.5
IV	2,132.4	1,417.1	428.4	988.7	480.5	90.4	205.9	184.3	167.5	168.0	172.7	715.3	705.7	363.1
2007: I	2,118.9	1,431.4	439.6	991.8	497.6	96.6	210.5	190.5	168.1	162.9	163.2	687.5	677.8	334.1
II	2,133.9	1,469.1	464.5	1,004.5	507.7	96.6	216.1	195.0	176.0	153.3	167.5	664.8	655.2	319.1
III	2,127.5	1,500.1	483.1	1,017.1	512.6	95.7	218.5	198.4	180.6	153.3	170.5	627.3	617.7	296.8

[1] Includes other items not shown separately.

Source: Department of Commerce (Bureau of Economic Analysis).

TABLE B–19.—Real private fixed investment by type, 1990–2007

[Billions of chained (2000) dollars; quarterly data at seasonally adjusted annual rates]

Year or quarter	Private fixed investment	Nonresidential										Residential		
		Total nonresidential	Structures	Equipment and software								Total residential[2]	Structures	
				Total	Information processing equipment and software				Industrial equipment	Transportation equipment	Other equipment		Total[2]	Single family
					Total	Computers and peripheral equipment[1]	Software	Other						
1990	886.6	595.1	275.2	355.0	100.7	....	39.9	80.1	109.2	81.0	96.0	298.9	292.6	154.2
1991	829.1	563.2	244.6	345.9	105.9	....	45.1	79.6	102.2	78.8	82.0	270.2	264.0	135.1
1992	878.3	581.3	229.9	371.1	122.2	....	53.0	84.4	104.0	80.2	81.6	307.6	301.4	164.1
1993	953.5	631.9	228.3	417.4	138.2	....	59.3	90.9	112.9	95.1	89.3	332.7	326.4	179.7
1994	1,042.3	689.9	232.3	467.2	155.7	....	65.1	99.4	122.9	111.4	96.5	364.8	358.6	198.9
1995	1,109.6	762.5	247.1	523.1	182.7	....	71.6	107.0	134.9	120.6	101.7	353.1	346.8	180.6
1996	1,209.2	833.6	261.1	578.7	218.9	....	84.1	117.2	139.9	125.4	105.6	381.3	375.1	197.3
1997	1,320.6	934.2	280.1	658.3	269.9	....	108.8	127.3	143.0	135.9	115.8	388.6	382.4	196.6
1998	1,455.0	1,037.8	294.5	745.6	328.9	....	129.4	143.2	148.1	145.4	125.7	418.3	411.9	218.1
1999	1,576.3	1,133.3	293.2	840.2	398.5	....	157.2	158.0	147.9	167.7	126.7	443.6	436.6	234.2
2000	1,679.0	1,232.1	313.2	918.9	467.6	....	176.2	190.0	159.2	160.8	131.2	446.9	439.5	236.8
2001	1,629.4	1,180.5	306.1	874.2	459.0	....	173.8	181.7	145.7	142.8	126.9	448.5	441.1	237.1
2002	1,544.6	1,071.5	253.8	820.2	437.4	....	169.7	161.1	134.5	126.0	122.9	469.9	462.2	246.3
2003	1,596.9	1,081.8	243.5	843.1	462.7	....	177.3	167.1	138.4	113.8	130.4	509.4	501.2	272.6
2004	1,712.8	1,144.3	246.7	905.1	505.7	....	193.6	181.1	134.0	130.6	138.3	560.2	551.2	305.3
2005	1,831.4	1,225.8	247.8	991.8	554.3	....	205.7	191.5	144.3	145.1	151.9	597.1	587.7	328.3
2006	1,874.7	1,306.8	268.6	1,050.6	595.9	....	213.0	204.8	149.6	155.2	156.2	569.5	560.0	302.7
2004: I	1,647.9	1,099.1	242.9	861.9	494.2	....	190.5	179.2	129.1	112.0	132.7	540.5	531.8	295.4
II	1,698.7	1,127.5	246.5	887.4	499.3	....	190.5	183.0	131.5	125.5	135.3	561.7	552.8	305.6
III	1,736.7	1,160.7	248.7	920.0	507.5	....	193.9	181.2	136.9	137.0	140.8	567.5	558.5	310.1
IV	1,767.7	1,189.7	248.6	951.2	521.7	....	199.3	181.0	138.7	147.9	144.5	570.9	561.7	310.1
2005: I	1,785.3	1,199.5	249.8	960.0	537.4	....	201.6	188.9	142.8	138.2	145.7	578.3	569.1	317.5
II	1,819.8	1,214.1	248.9	977.4	548.8	....	206.0	188.3	139.4	142.0	151.6	596.4	587.1	325.7
III	1,854.9	1,239.5	244.8	1,011.1	560.5	....	206.7	194.6	145.9	153.2	154.2	606.4	597.0	332.3
IV	1,865.6	1,250.0	247.7	1,018.7	570.6	....	208.3	194.2	149.2	147.0	156.1	607.2	597.6	337.9
2006: I	1,901.4	1,289.7	256.5	1,050.2	589.8	....	211.0	206.3	147.0	160.3	157.8	606.1	596.3	338.5
II	1,892.3	1,303.2	266.4	1,050.1	592.1	....	212.1	203.3	152.0	153.3	157.9	587.5	577.9	318.8
III	1,869.6	1,319.4	273.3	1,057.6	602.0	....	213.8	207.1	150.9	156.3	155.2	555.0	545.5	291.1
IV	1,835.5	1,314.8	278.3	1,044.4	599.6	....	215.1	202.6	148.4	150.9	153.7	529.4	520.1	262.4
2007: I	1,815.2	1,321.7	282.6	1,045.3	623.3	....	219.9	209.2	147.3	144.8	144.8	506.3	497.1	240.2
II	1,829.3	1,356.6	299.5	1,057.4	638.5	....	225.6	213.4	152.9	135.3	148.0	490.7	481.6	231.2
III	1,826.0	1,387.3	311.1	1,073.5	648.7	....	228.0	216.8	156.0	136.3	150.2	463.3	454.3	215.5

[1] For information on this component, see *Survey of Current Business* Table 5.3.6, Table 5.3.1 (for growth rates), Table 5.3.2 (for contributions), and Table 5.3.3 (for quantity indexes).

[2] Includes other items not shown separately.

Source: Department of Commerce (Bureau of Economic Analysis).

TABLE B–20.—*Government consumption expenditures and gross investment by type, 1959–2007*

[Billions of dollars; quarterly data at seasonally adjusted annual rates]

Year or quarter	Total	Federal		National defense		Gross investment		Nondefense		Gross investment		State and local		Gross investment	
		Total		Total	Con-sumption expenditures	Struc-tures	Equipment and software	Total	Con-sumption expenditures	Struc-tures	Equipment and software	Total	Con-sumption expenditures	Struc-tures	Equipment and software	
1959	110.0	65.4		53.8	40.1	2.5	11.2	11.5	9.8	1.5	0.2	44.7	30.7	12.8	1.1
1960	111.6	64.1		53.4	41.0	2.2	10.1	10.7	8.7	1.7	.3	47.5	33.5	12.7	1.2
1961	119.5	67.9		56.5	42.7	2.4	11.5	11.4	9.0	1.9	.6	51.6	36.6	13.8	1.3
1962	130.1	75.3		61.1	46.6	2.0	12.5	14.2	11.3	2.1	.8	54.9	39.0	14.5	1.3
1963	136.4	76.9		61.0	48.3	1.6	11.0	15.9	12.4	2.3	1.2	59.5	41.9	16.0	1.5
1964	143.2	78.5		60.3	48.8	1.3	10.2	18.2	14.0	2.5	1.6	64.8	45.8	17.2	1.8
1965	151.5	80.4		60.6	50.6	1.1	8.9	19.8	15.1	2.8	1.9	71.0	50.2	19.0	1.9
1966	171.8	92.5		71.7	60.0	1.3	10.5	20.8	15.9	2.8	2.1	79.2	56.1	21.0	2.1
1967	192.7	104.8		83.5	70.0	1.2	12.3	21.3	17.1	2.2	1.9	87.9	62.6	23.0	2.3
1968	209.4	111.4		89.3	77.2	1.2	10.9	22.1	18.3	2.1	1.7	98.0	70.4	25.2	2.4
1969	221.5	113.4		89.5	78.2	1.5	9.9	23.8	20.2	1.9	1.7	108.2	79.9	25.6	2.7
1970	233.8	113.5		87.6	76.6	1.3	9.8	25.8	22.1	2.1	1.7	120.3	91.5	25.8	3.0
1971	246.5	113.7		84.6	77.1	1.8	5.7	29.1	24.9	2.5	1.7	132.8	102.7	27.0	3.1
1972	263.5	119.7		87.0	79.5	1.8	5.7	32.7	28.2	2.7	1.8	143.8	113.2	27.1	3.5
1973	281.7	122.5		88.2	79.4	2.1	6.6	34.3	29.4	3.1	1.8	159.2	126.0	29.1	4.1
1974	317.9	134.6		95.6	84.5	2.2	8.9	39.0	33.4	3.4	2.2	183.4	143.7	34.7	4.9
1975	357.7	149.1		103.9	90.9	2.3	10.7	45.1	38.7	4.1	2.4	208.7	165.1	38.1	5.5
1976	383.0	159.7		111.1	95.8	2.1	13.2	48.6	41.4	4.6	2.7	223.3	179.5	38.1	5.7
1977	414.1	175.4		120.9	104.2	2.4	14.4	54.5	46.5	5.0	3.0	238.7	195.9	36.9	5.9
1978	453.6	190.9		130.5	112.7	2.5	15.3	60.4	50.6	6.1	3.7	262.6	213.2	42.8	6.6
1979	500.8	210.6		145.2	123.8	2.5	18.9	65.4	55.1	6.3	4.0	290.2	233.3	49.0	7.8
1980	566.2	243.8		168.0	143.7	3.2	21.1	75.8	63.8	7.1	4.9	322.4	258.4	55.1	8.9
1981	627.5	280.2		196.3	167.3	3.2	25.7	84.0	71.0	7.7	5.3	347.3	282.3	55.4	9.5
1982	680.5	310.8		225.9	191.2	4.0	30.8	84.9	72.1	6.8	6.0	369.7	304.9	54.2	10.6
1983	733.5	342.9		250.7	208.8	4.8	37.1	92.3	77.7	6.7	7.8	390.5	324.1	54.2	12.2
1984	797.0	374.4		281.6	232.9	4.9	43.8	92.8	77.1	7.0	8.7	422.6	347.7	60.5	14.4
1985	879.0	412.8		311.2	253.7	6.2	51.3	101.6	84.7	7.3	9.6	466.2	381.8	67.6	16.8
1986	949.3	438.6		330.9	268.0	6.8	56.1	107.8	90.3	8.0	9.5	510.7	417.9	74.2	18.6
1987	999.5	460.1		350.0	283.6	7.7	58.8	110.0	90.6	9.0	10.4	539.4	440.9	78.8	19.6
1988	1,039.0	462.3		354.9	293.6	7.4	53.9	107.4	88.9	6.8	11.7	576.7	470.4	84.8	21.5
1989	1,099.1	482.2		362.2	299.5	6.4	56.3	120.0	99.7	6.9	13.4	616.9	502.1	88.7	26.0
1990	1,180.2	508.3		374.0	308.1	6.1	59.8	134.3	111.7	8.0	14.6	671.9	544.6	98.5	28.7
1991	1,234.4	527.7		383.2	319.8	4.6	58.8	144.5	119.7	9.2	15.7	706.7	574.6	103.2	28.9
1992	1,271.0	533.9		376.9	315.3	5.2	56.3	157.0	129.8	10.3	16.9	737.0	602.7	104.2	30.1
1993	1,291.2	525.2		362.9	307.6	5.1	50.1	162.4	134.2	11.2	16.9	766.0	630.3	104.5	31.2
1994	1,325.5	519.1		353.7	300.7	5.7	47.2	165.5	140.1	10.5	14.9	806.3	663.3	108.7	34.3
1995	1,369.2	519.2		348.7	297.3	6.3	45.1	170.5	143.2	10.8	16.5	850.0	696.1	117.3	36.7
1996	1,416.0	527.4		354.6	302.5	6.7	45.4	172.8	143.8	11.2	17.9	888.6	724.8	126.8	36.9
1997	1,468.7	530.9		349.6	304.7	5.7	39.2	181.3	153.0	9.8	18.5	937.8	758.9	139.5	39.4
1998	1,518.3	530.4		345.7	300.7	5.1	39.9	184.7	153.9	10.6	20.2	987.9	801.4	143.6	43.0
1999	1,620.8	555.8		360.6	312.9	5.0	42.8	195.2	162.2	10.6	22.4	1,065.0	858.9	159.7	46.4
2000	1,721.6	578.8		370.3	321.5	6.0	43.8	208.5	177.8	8.3	22.3	1,142.8	917.8	176.0	49.0
2001	1,825.6	612.9		392.6	342.4	4.6	45.6	220.3	189.5	8.3	22.5	1,212.8	969.8	192.4	50.6
2002	1,961.1	679.7		437.1	381.7	4.4	51.0	242.5	209.9	9.9	22.8	1,281.5	1,025.3	205.9	50.2
2003	2,092.5	756.4		497.2	436.8	5.3	55.2	259.2	226.0	10.1	23.1	1,336.0	1,073.8	212.0	50.3
2004	2,216.8	825.6		550.7	482.9	5.6	62.2	274.9	240.8	9.4	24.6	1,391.2	1,120.3	220.3	50.6
2005	2,363.4	878.4		588.7	515.8	5.9	67.0	289.8	252.7	9.4	27.7	1,485.0	1,197.2	236.7	51.1
2006	2,523.0	932.5		624.3	544.8	6.3	73.2	308.2	268.0	10.5	29.7	1,590.5	1,276.5	260.5	53.6
2004: I	2,169.1	806.2		536.5	472.7	5.7	58.0	269.7	236.9	9.3	23.6	1,362.9	1,099.2	213.0	50.7
II	2,202.8	821.9		546.5	480.4	5.3	60.8	275.3	240.8	9.8	24.7	1,381.0	1,110.2	220.4	50.4
III	2,237.3	839.4		564.9	494.1	5.7	65.1	274.5	240.6	9.6	24.2	1,397.9	1,124.8	222.5	50.6
IV	2,258.2	835.0		555.0	484.5	5.7	64.7	280.0	245.0	9.0	25.9	1,423.2	1,147.0	225.3	50.9
2005: I	2,306.7	864.0		577.7	508.1	6.0	63.6	286.2	251.0	9.1	26.1	1,442.7	1,162.9	229.1	50.8
II	2,339.8	870.4		585.0	511.9	5.9	67.2	285.4	249.8	8.7	26.8	1,469.5	1,182.3	236.2	51.0
III	2,394.8	896.0		604.3	529.8	5.9	68.6	291.7	254.3	9.5	28.0	1,498.7	1,208.9	238.7	51.2
IV	2,412.5	883.4		587.7	513.3	6.0	68.4	295.7	255.8	10.2	29.8	1,529.0	1,234.7	242.8	51.6
2006: I	2,472.1	921.5		610.8	535.7	5.5	69.6	310.7	269.2	10.1	31.4	1,550.6	1,247.4	250.7	52.5
II	2,512.5	926.9		620.6	540.0	6.0	74.6	306.3	266.7	10.0	29.6	1,585.7	1,270.0	262.3	53.4
III	2,536.1	932.0		620.7	542.0	6.1	72.6	311.3	271.3	10.1	29.9	1,604.1	1,287.7	262.4	53.9
IV	2,571.4	949.7		645.2	561.5	7.5	76.2	304.5	264.9	11.6	28.0	1,621.7	1,300.8	266.4	54.5
2007: I	2,608.3	946.6		634.8	555.7	6.6	72.4	311.7	274.0	10.2	27.5	1,661.7	1,326.7	279.2	55.9
II	2,670.0	969.5		654.5	573.8	7.0	73.6	315.0	276.0	10.1	28.9	1,700.5	1,355.9	288.0	56.6
III	2,716.5	990.3		673.5	589.6	7.7	76.2	316.8	278.1	10.5	28.1	1,726.2	1,374.3	294.8	57.0

Source: Department of Commerce (Bureau of Economic Analysis).

TABLE B-21.—*Real government consumption expenditures and gross investment by type, 1990–2007*

[Billions of chained (2000) dollars; quarterly data at seasonally adjusted annual rates]

Year or quarter	Total	Government consumption expenditures and gross investment — Federal	National defense	National defense Consumption expenditures	National defense Gross investment Structures	National defense Gross investment Equipment and software	Nondefense Total	Nondefense Consumption expenditures	Nondefense Gross investment Structures	Nondefense Gross investment Equipment and software	State and local Total	State and local Consumption expenditures	State and local Gross investment Structures	State and local Gross investment Equipment and software
1990	1,530.0	659.1	479.4	404.9	8.6	64.2	178.6	156.5	10.6	12.9	868.4	714.2	132.1	25.0
1991	1,547.2	658.0	474.2	404.4	6.4	61.8	182.8	158.4	11.8	13.7	886.8	729.0	136.5	24.8
1992	1,555.3	646.6	450.7	383.5	7.0	58.7	195.4	168.2	13.2	15.0	906.5	746.5	137.0	25.9
1993	1,541.1	619.6	425.3	367.2	6.4	51.1	194.1	166.0	14.1	15.0	919.5	761.4	133.9	26.8
1994	1,541.3	596.4	404.6	350.6	7.1	46.8	191.7	167.3	12.7	13.3	943.3	780.6	134.9	29.5
1995	1,549.7	580.3	389.2	338.1	7.4	43.7	191.0	164.7	12.6	14.7	968.3	798.4	139.5	31.7
1996	1,564.9	573.5	383.8	332.2	7.7	43.8	189.6	161.1	12.7	16.4	990.5	812.8	146.3	32.7
1997	1,594.0	567.6	373.0	328.1	6.4	38.9	194.5	166.6	10.9	17.5	1,025.9	834.9	155.8	36.1
1998	1,624.4	561.2	365.3	319.8	5.5	40.1	195.9	164.8	11.5	19.8	1,063.0	866.4	155.6	41.2
1999	1,686.9	573.7	372.2	324.6	5.2	42.5	201.5	168.1	11.1	22.3	1,113.2	900.3	167.0	45.9
2000	1,721.6	578.8	370.3	321.5	5.0	43.8	208.5	177.8	8.3	22.3	1,142.8	917.8	176.0	49.0
2001	1,780.3	601.4	384.9	334.1	4.4	46.4	216.5	185.8	8.0	22.7	1,179.0	941.2	186.0	51.7
2002	1,858.8	643.4	413.2	356.7	4.2	52.6	230.2	197.3	9.3	23.5	1,215.4	969.4	193.5	52.5
2003	1,904.8	687.1	449.0	387.5	4.8	56.9	238.0	204.5	9.3	24.2	1,217.8	969.8	194.7	53.4
2004	1,931.8	715.9	475.0	407.6	4.8	63.3	240.7	206.7	8.2	25.9	1,215.8	970.8	191.2	54.0
2005	1,946.3	726.5	482.4	411.7	4.7	67.2	243.9	207.9	7.5	29.1	1,219.6	977.7	187.7	54.6
2006	1,981.4	742.3	491.5	416.6	4.6	72.4	250.7	212.6	7.9	31.3	1,239.0	990.9	191.3	57.7
2004: I	1,925.4	709.5	470.2	405.6	5.1	59.7	239.1	205.9	8.4	24.8	1,215.9	969.2	192.6	54.2
II	1,931.8	713.7	472.5	406.4	4.6	62.0	241.0	206.5	8.7	26.0	1,218.1	969.6	194.8	53.7
III	1,939.4	724.5	484.8	414.7	4.8	66.3	239.4	205.6	8.3	25.5	1,214.7	970.7	190.2	54.0
IV	1,930.6	716.0	472.7	403.7	4.7	65.3	243.2	208.6	7.6	27.3	1,214.4	973.5	187.0	54.2
2005: I	1,936.8	721.0	478.1	410.1	4.9	63.8	242.7	208.1	7.5	27.4	1,215.7	973.9	187.9	54.0
II	1,942.5	722.2	481.1	410.3	4.7	67.5	240.9	206.2	7.1	28.2	1,220.1	976.2	189.7	54.4
III	1,957.6	737.3	492.7	420.4	4.6	69.1	244.3	208.0	7.6	29.5	1,220.3	979.2	186.8	54.6
IV	1,948.2	725.5	477.7	406.1	4.6	68.5	247.8	209.5	8.0	31.4	1,222.5	981.4	186.2	55.4
2006: I	1,971.8	740.4	485.5	413.6	4.2	69.4	254.8	215.3	7.8	33.1	1,231.3	985.3	190.2	56.5
II	1,976.5	737.4	488.2	412.5	4.5	73.9	249.0	211.4	7.6	31.1	1,238.9	988.1	194.0	57.4
III	1,980.2	739.2	486.4	412.6	4.5	71.4	252.7	214.8	7.6	31.4	1,240.9	992.7	190.9	58.3
IV	1,997.2	752.3	505.8	427.7	5.4	74.9	246.1	208.8	8.5	29.5	1,244.9	997.5	189.9	58.7
2007: I	1,994.7	740.2	491.6	417.4	4.7	71.3	248.4	212.5	7.4	29.1	1,254.2	1,002.5	193.0	60.1
II	2,014.8	751.0	501.7	426.2	4.9	71.4	248.9	212.0	7.3	30.7	1,263.5	1,007.4	196.5	60.9
III	2,033.6	764.0	513.9	436.0	5.4	74.4	249.6	213.1	7.5	29.9	1,269.6	1,010.7	198.7	61.5

Note.—See Table B–2 for data for total government consumption expenditures and gross investment for 1959-89.

Source: Department of Commerce (Bureau of Economic Analysis).

Table B–22.—*Private inventories and domestic final sales by industry, 1959–2007*

[Billions of dollars, except as noted; seasonally adjusted]

Quarter	Private inventories [1]								Final sales of domestic business [3]	Ratio of private inventories to final sales of domestic business	
	Total [2]	Farm	Mining, utilities, and construction [2]	Manufac- turing	Wholesale trade	Retail trade	Other indus- tries [2]	Non- farm [2]		Total	Non- farm
Fourth quarter:											
1959	132.9	42.1		47.7	16.5	20.5	6.1	90.8	31.6	4.20	2.87
1960	136.2	42.7		48.7	16.9	21.9	6.1	93.5	32.7	4.17	2.86
1961	139.6	44.3		50.1	17.3	21.3	6.6	95.2	34.3	4.07	2.78
1962	147.2	46.7		53.2	18.0	22.7	6.6	100.5	36.0	4.09	2.79
1963	149.7	44.2		55.1	19.5	23.9	7.1	105.5	38.3	3.91	2.75
1964	154.3	42.1		58.6	20.8	25.2	7.7	112.2	41.2	3.75	2.73
1965	169.3	47.1		63.4	22.5	28.0	8.3	122.2	45.3	3.73	2.70
1966	185.7	47.4		73.0	25.8	30.6	8.9	138.3	47.8	3.88	2.89
1967	194.9	45.8		79.9	28.1	30.9	10.1	149.1	50.3	3.87	2.96
1968	208.2	48.9		85.1	29.3	34.2	10.6	159.3	55.4	3.76	2.87
1969	227.7	53.1		92.6	32.5	37.5	12.0	174.6	59.1	3.85	2.95
1970	236.0	52.7		95.5	36.4	38.5	12.9	183.3	62.4	3.78	2.94
1971	253.9	59.5		96.6	39.4	44.7	13.7	194.4	68.0	3.73	2.86
1972	283.9	74.0		102.1	43.1	49.8	14.8	209.9	76.3	3.72	2.75
1973	352.2	102.8		121.5	51.7	58.4	17.7	249.4	84.3	4.18	2.96
1974	406.3	88.2		162.6	66.9	63.9	24.7	318.1	90.4	4.49	3.52
1975	409.3	90.3		162.2	66.5	64.4	25.9	319.0	101.7	4.02	3.14
1976	440.1	85.8		178.7	74.1	73.0	28.5	354.2	111.9	3.93	3.17
1977	482.4	91.0		193.2	84.0	80.9	33.3	391.4	124.8	3.86	3.14
1978	571.4	119.7		219.8	99.0	94.1	38.8	451.7	144.7	3.95	3.12
1979	668.2	135.6		261.8	119.5	104.7	46.6	532.6	160.1	4.17	3.33
1980	739.8	141.1		293.4	139.4	111.7	54.1	598.7	175.0	4.23	3.42
1981	779.2	127.5		313.1	148.8	123.2	66.6	651.7	187.7	4.15	3.47
1982	774.1	131.5		304.6	147.9	123.2	66.8	642.6	195.8	3.95	3.28
1983	797.6	132.5		308.9	153.4	137.6	65.2	665.1	216.8	3.68	3.07
1984	869.3	131.8		344.5	169.1	157.0	66.9	737.6	234.8	3.70	3.14
1985	876.1	125.9		333.3	175.9	171.4	69.5	750.2	250.7	3.49	2.99
1986	858.0	112.9		320.6	182.0	176.2	66.3	745.1	265.7	3.23	2.80
1987	924.2	119.8		339.6	195.8	199.1	69.9	804.4	279.3	3.31	2.88
1988	999.2	130.2		372.4	213.9	213.2	69.5	869.1	305.6	3.27	2.84
1989	1,044.4	129.6		390.5	222.8	231.4	70.1	914.7	324.4	3.22	2.82
1990	1,082.3	133.4		404.5	236.8	236.6	71.0	948.9	337.6	3.21	2.81
1991	1,057.2	123.2		384.1	239.2	240.2	70.5	934.0	347.6	3.04	2.69
1992	1,082.4	132.9		377.6	248.3	249.4	74.3	949.5	372.7	2.90	2.55
1993	1,115.8	132.1		380.1	258.6	268.6	76.5	983.7	393.6	2.83	2.50
1994	1,194.3	134.3		404.3	281.5	293.6	80.6	1,060.0	416.8	2.87	2.54
1995	1,257.0	130.9		424.5	303.7	312.2	85.6	1,126.1	439.2	2.86	2.56
NAICS:											
1996	1,284.4	136.3	31.1	421.0	285.1	328.7	82.1	1,148.1	469.1	2.74	2.45
1997	1,329.5	136.7	33.7	431.7	303.1	337.5	86.9	1,192.9	495.6	2.68	2.41
1998	1,346.8	120.3	37.3	431.5	313.3	353.6	90.9	1,226.5	526.8	2.56	2.33
1999	1,442.2	124.2	39.6	457.7	337.4	383.8	99.5	1,318.0	556.7	2.59	2.37
2000	1,535.9	132.1	44.5	477.0	359.0	409.0	114.4	1,403.8	583.6	2.63	2.41
2001	1,458.3	126.1	47.5	437.9	338.6	395.6	112.6	1,332.2	598.7	2.44	2.23
2002	1,507.8	135.8	49.4	443.6	348.0	419.3	111.7	1,372.0	601.0	2.51	2.28
2003	1,567.3	151.2	58.5	447.0	359.8	436.4	114.3	1,416.1	639.0	2.45	2.22
2004: I	1,605.5	157.0	60.4	457.5	368.9	445.7	116.1	1,448.5	648.1	2.48	2.24
II	1,650.4	165.2	62.9	470.7	376.3	456.9	118.2	1,485.1	658.2	2.51	2.26
III	1,680.7	157.6	65.2	485.7	386.8	464.7	120.7	1,523.1	667.5	2.52	2.28
IV	1,715.0	156.7	69.4	495.1	397.2	472.8	123.7	1,558.2	678.6	2.53	2.30
2005: I	1,756.5	159.2	70.8	512.9	410.0	479.1	124.5	1,597.3	689.5	2.55	2.32
II	1,759.1	155.2	75.3	511.4	414.2	478.1	125.0	1,603.9	704.1	2.50	2.28
III	1,797.5	159.3	81.1	526.7	423.0	481.6	125.8	1,638.2	718.4	2.50	2.28
IV	1,842.3	164.1	90.9	539.0	432.6	489.3	126.4	1,678.1	723.0	2.55	2.32
2006: I	1,853.6	157.0	83.2	548.8	441.4	495.4	127.8	1,696.6	739.5	2.51	2.29
II	1,901.2	156.7	81.7	569.9	459.2	502.3	131.3	1,744.5	749.3	2.54	2.33
III	1,925.8	165.3	83.0	572.4	467.9	503.8	133.4	1,760.5	754.0	2.55	2.33
IV	1,935.8	166.8	84.1	570.0	477.0	504.2	133.6	1,769.0	763.0	2.54	2.32
2007: I	1,991.2	197.0	88.2	577.5	487.9	504.9	135.7	1,794.2	772.7	2.58	2.32
II	2,020.4	196.8	92.1	590.2	494.3	509.4	137.7	1,823.7	783.5	2.58	2.33
III	2,043.8	210.7	88.6	590.3	500.6	515.3	138.3	1,833.0	792.0	2.58	2.31

[1] Inventories at end of quarter. Quarter-to-quarter change calculated from this table is not the current-dollar change in private inventories component of gross domestic product (GDP). The former is the difference between two inventory stocks, each valued at its respective end-of-quarter prices. The latter is the change in the physical volume of inventories valued at average prices of the quarter. In addition, changes calculated from this table are at quarterly rates, whereas change in private inventories is stated at annual rates.

[2] Inventories of construction, mining, and utilities establishments are included in other industries through 1995.

[3] Quarterly totals at monthly rates. Final sales of domestic business equals final sales of domestic product less gross output of general government, gross value added of nonprofit institutions, compensation paid to domestic workers, and space rent for owner-occupied housing. Includes a small amount of final sales by farm and by government enterprises.

Note.—The industry classification of inventories is on an establishment basis. Estimates through 1995 are based on the Standard Industrial Classification (SIC). Beginning with 1996, estimates are based on the North American Industry Classification System (NAICS).

Source: Department of Commerce (Bureau of Economic Analysis).

TABLE B–23.—*Real private inventories and domestic final sales by industry, 1959–2007*

[Billions of chained (2000) dollars, except as noted; seasonally adjusted]

| Quarter | Private inventories [1] | | | | | | | | Final sales of domestic business [3] | Ratio of private inventories to final sales of domestic business | |
	Total [2]	Farm	Mining, utilities, and construction [2]	Manufac-turing	Wholesale trade	Retail trade	Other indus-tries [2]	Non-farm [2]		Total	Non-farm
Fourth quarter:											
1959	428.1	106.9	....	143.5	57.6	63.9	29.8	298.7	131.3	3.26	2.27
1960	438.5	108.3	....	145.4	59.1	68.2	30.8	307.5	134.3	3.27	2.29
1961	448.0	110.4	....	149.8	60.7	66.9	33.9	314.4	140.1	3.20	2.24
1962	467.4	111.8	....	159.8	63.4	71.5	33.8	332.7	145.4	3.21	2.29
1963	485.4	112.9	....	165.9	68.4	75.3	36.2	349.7	153.9	3.15	2.27
1964	500.8	109.8	....	175.1	72.5	79.3	38.4	369.4	163.2	3.07	2.26
1965	530.1	111.8	....	187.4	77.4	87.1	40.1	396.8	177.2	2.99	2.24
1966	572.2	110.7	....	212.5	87.7	94.1	41.1	442.0	180.9	3.16	2.44
1967	602.5	112.8	....	229.3	94.7	94.1	46.0	470.4	185.3	3.25	2.54
1968	629.9	116.1	....	239.8	98.0	101.9	47.3	494.1	195.1	3.23	2.53
1969	656.9	116.1	....	250.9	105.1	108.9	49.7	521.9	198.9	3.30	2.62
1970	661.9	114.2	....	250.9	113.0	109.0	50.3	529.7	201.3	3.29	2.63
1971	684.2	117.5	....	247.9	119.1	123.6	52.1	548.3	211.5	3.24	2.59
1972	707.3	117.9	....	254.6	124.6	133.1	54.7	572.5	228.8	3.09	2.50
1973	742.2	119.3	....	273.5	128.1	143.7	57.5	609.1	236.9	3.13	2.57
1974	768.1	115.7	....	294.1	139.7	141.6	61.3	644.2	228.2	3.37	2.82
1975	756.8	120.4	....	286.7	133.7	134.6	62.9	625.0	238.7	3.17	2.62
1976	787.5	119.1	....	300.4	142.7	144.9	63.6	659.0	250.5	3.14	2.63
1977	826.0	125.0	....	308.8	154.1	153.2	68.4	691.1	263.6	3.13	2.62
1978	867.1	126.7	....	322.9	166.9	163.3	72.5	732.0	283.2	3.06	2.58
1979	892.2	130.2	....	335.3	175.0	163.3	72.4	753.5	289.8	3.08	2.60
1980	884.3	124.3	....	335.7	180.0	158.7	71.2	753.5	289.6	3.05	2.60
1981	919.2	132.5	....	340.2	185.1	167.5	79.2	779.0	287.2	3.20	2.71
1982	901.7	138.6	....	325.0	183.0	163.7	76.8	754.4	286.1	3.15	2.64
1983	895.3	124.4	....	324.5	182.7	177.0	75.9	764.6	307.6	2.91	2.49
1984	966.6	129.6	....	352.8	198.5	198.6	77.0	831.2	324.6	2.98	2.56
1985	990.3	135.3	....	346.6	204.9	214.0	81.4	848.7	339.4	2.92	2.50
1986	998.5	133.5	....	342.9	213.2	217.4	84.4	858.8	352.2	2.84	2.44
1987	1,028.8	126.1	....	351.1	220.6	238.5	86.6	896.5	362.6	2.84	2.47
1988	1,049.1	115.4	....	367.6	229.7	246.1	85.2	929.2	381.6	2.75	2.43
1989	1,077.4	115.4	....	381.4	233.6	260.5	81.4	958.0	392.5	2.75	2.44
1990	1,092.8	120.9	....	390.0	242.0	258.9	78.3	971.2	394.0	2.77	2.46
1991	1,092.3	119.4	....	383.5	246.4	259.5	81.4	972.2	394.6	2.77	2.46
1992	1,108.7	125.1	....	378.9	254.8	264.1	83.9	982.5	415.7	2.67	2.36
1993	1,129.4	119.1	....	382.4	261.0	279.4	86.9	1,010.2	429.8	2.63	2.35
1994	1,193.0	130.3	....	394.1	276.7	299.9	91.1	1,062.2	447.2	2.67	2.38
1995	1,222.8	119.6	....	407.8	289.9	312.0	93.3	1,103.5	464.2	2.63	2.38
NAICS:											
1996	1,251.6	126.4	33.6	409.9	273.3	325.9	82.7	1,125.2	488.3	2.56	2.30
1997	1,322.7	129.3	36.1	430.7	298.3	340.6	88.1	1,193.7	509.2	2.60	2.34
1998	1,395.3	130.7	43.3	449.3	320.9	357.9	94.0	1,264.9	538.0	2.59	2.35
1999	1,464.2	127.8	42.7	466.3	340.6	385.5	101.3	1,336.4	563.4	2.60	2.37
2000	1,520.7	126.4	41.1	474.2	358.2	407.1	113.7	1,394.3	581.0	2.62	2.40
2001	1,488.9	126.5	51.7	452.8	347.5	396.3	113.9	1,362.4	583.6	2.55	2.33
2002	1,501.4	124.0	48.1	447.0	348.8	420.6	112.5	1,377.6	582.5	2.58	2.37
2003	1,515.7	124.4	53.4	437.5	349.6	436.4	113.9	1,391.6	609.7	2.49	2.28
2004: I	1,524.4	125.5	51.9	437.4	351.6	442.6	115.3	1,399.2	613.8	2.48	2.28
II	1,540.7	128.7	51.8	438.9	354.7	449.8	116.5	1,411.8	618.3	2.49	2.28
III	1,555.7	129.9	53.0	438.6	361.8	454.0	118.1	1,425.7	625.1	2.49	2.28
IV	1,570.0	130.3	53.9	440.1	367.6	458.6	119.5	1,439.8	630.9	2.49	2.28
2005: I	1,585.8	129.2	54.3	447.9	374.2	461.2	119.0	1,457.0	635.7	2.49	2.29
II	1,588.3	128.9	56.0	448.0	377.7	458.8	118.5	1,459.9	645.9	2.46	2.26
III	1,589.8	129.3	55.9	448.9	379.3	458.1	117.5	1,460.9	654.2	2.43	2.23
IV	1,603.2	129.8	55.7	451.7	384.1	464.3	117.2	1,473.8	653.4	2.45	2.26
2006: I	1,612.8	130.0	55.4	452.7	388.5	468.3	118.0	1,483.3	663.8	2.43	2.23
II	1,625.7	128.7	57.0	455.8	394.3	470.3	119.4	1,497.7	668.0	2.43	2.24
III	1,639.1	128.0	58.2	458.0	403.3	470.6	120.7	1,512.1	668.8	2.45	2.26
IV	1,643.5	128.9	59.6	457.6	404.9	470.6	121.2	1,515.5	675.4	2.43	2.24
2007: I	1,643.5	130.1	60.6	456.3	406.0	467.3	121.8	1,514.0	677.4	2.43	2.24
II	1,645.0	131.1	61.1	455.3	406.0	468.1	121.9	1,514.4	683.7	2.41	2.21
III	1,652.6	132.1	60.5	456.1	409.5	471.2	122.0	1,520.9	691.0	2.39	2.20

[1] Inventories at end of quarter. Quarter-to-quarter changes calculated from this table are at quarterly rates, whereas the change in private inventories component of gross domestic product (GDP) is stated at annual rates.

[2] Inventories of construction, mining, and utilities establishments are included in other industries through 1995.

[3] Quarterly totals at monthly rates. Final sales of domestic business equals final sales of domestic product less gross output of general government, gross value added of nonprofit institutions, compensation paid to domestic workers, and space rent for owner-occupied housing. Includes a small amount of final sales by farm and by government enterprises.

Note.—The industry classification of inventories is on an establishment basis. Estimates through 1995 are based on the Standard Industrial Classification (SIC). Beginning with 1996, estimates are based on the North American Industry Classification System (NAICS).

See *Survey of Current Business*, Tables 5.7.6A and 5.7.6B, for detailed information on calculation of the chained (2000) dollar inventory series.

Source: Department of Commerce (Bureau of Economic Analysis).

TABLE B–24.—*Foreign transactions in the national income and product accounts, 1959–2007*

[Billions of dollars; quarterly data at seasonally adjusted annual rates]

Year or quarter	Current receipts from rest of the world					Current payments to rest of the world									
	Total	Exports of goods and services			Income receipts	Total	Imports of goods and services			Income payments	Current taxes and transfer payments to rest of the world (net)				Balance on current account, NIPA [2]
		Total	Goods [1]	Services [1]			Total	Goods [1]	Services [1]		Total	From persons (net)	From government (net)	From business (net)	
1959	27.0	22.7	16.5	6.3	4.3	28.2	22.3	15.3	7.0	1.5	4.3	0.5	3.8	0.1	-1.2
1960	31.9	27.0	20.5	6.6	4.9	28.7	22.8	15.2	7.6	1.8	4.1	.5	3.5	.1	3.2
1961	32.9	27.6	20.9	6.7	5.3	28.6	22.7	15.1	7.6	1.8	4.2	.5	3.6	.1	4.3
1962	35.0	29.1	21.7	7.4	5.9	31.1	25.0	16.9	8.1	1.8	4.3	.5	3.6	.1	3.9
1963	37.6	31.1	23.3	7.7	6.5	32.6	26.1	17.7	8.4	2.1	4.4	.7	3.6	.1	5.0
1964	42.3	35.0	26.7	8.3	7.2	34.7	28.1	19.4	8.7	2.3	4.3	.7	3.4	.2	7.5
1965	45.0	37.1	27.8	9.4	7.9	38.8	31.5	22.2	9.3	2.4	4.7	.8	3.7	.2	6.2
1966	49.0	40.9	30.7	10.2	8.1	45.1	37.1	26.3	10.7	3.0	5.0	.8	4.0	.2	3.9
1967	52.1	43.5	32.2	11.3	8.7	48.6	39.9	27.8	12.2	3.3	5.4	1.0	4.1	.2	3.6
1968	58.0	47.9	35.3	12.6	10.1	56.3	46.6	33.9	12.6	4.0	5.7	1.0	4.4	.3	1.7
1969	63.7	51.9	38.3	13.7	11.8	61.9	50.5	36.8	13.7	5.7	5.8	1.1	4.4	.3	1.8
1970	72.5	59.7	44.5	15.2	12.8	68.5	55.8	40.9	14.9	6.4	6.3	1.3	4.7	.4	4.0
1971	77.0	63.0	45.6	17.4	14.0	76.4	62.3	46.6	15.8	6.4	7.6	1.3	5.9	.4	.6
1972	87.1	70.8	51.8	19.0	16.3	90.7	74.2	56.9	17.3	7.7	8.8	1.4	7.0	.5	-3.6
1973	118.8	95.3	73.9	21.3	23.5	109.5	91.2	71.8	19.3	10.9	7.4	1.5	5.2	.7	9.3
1974	156.5	126.7	101.0	25.7	29.8	149.8	127.5	104.5	22.9	14.3	8.1	1.3	5.8	1.0	6.6
1975	166.7	138.7	109.6	29.1	28.0	145.4	122.7	99.0	23.7	15.0	7.6	1.3	5.6	.7	21.4
1976	181.9	149.5	117.8	31.7	32.4	173.0	151.1	124.6	26.5	15.5	6.3	1.3	3.9	1.1	8.9
1977	196.6	159.4	123.7	35.7	37.2	205.6	182.4	152.6	29.8	16.9	6.2	1.3	3.5	1.4	-9.0
1978	233.1	186.9	145.4	41.5	46.3	243.6	212.3	177.4	34.8	24.7	6.7	1.5	3.8	1.4	-10.4
1979	298.5	230.1	184.0	46.1	68.3	297.0	252.7	212.8	39.9	36.4	8.0	1.6	4.3	2.0	1.4
1980	359.9	280.8	225.8	55.0	79.1	348.5	293.8	248.6	45.3	44.9	9.8	1.8	5.5	2.4	11.4
1981	397.3	305.2	239.1	66.1	92.0	390.9	317.8	267.8	49.9	59.1	14.1	5.5	5.4	3.2	6.3
1982	384.2	283.2	215.0	68.2	101.0	384.4	303.2	250.5	52.6	64.5	16.7	6.6	6.7	3.4	-.2
1983	378.9	277.0	207.3	69.7	101.9	410.9	328.6	272.7	56.0	64.8	17.5	6.9	7.2	3.4	-32.1
1984	424.2	302.4	225.6	76.7	121.9	511.2	405.1	336.3	68.8	85.6	20.5	7.8	9.2	3.5	-86.9
1985	414.5	302.0	222.2	79.8	112.4	525.3	417.2	343.3	73.9	85.9	22.2	8.2	11.1	2.9	-110.8
1986	431.9	320.5	226.0	94.5	111.4	571.2	453.3	370.0	83.3	93.6	24.3	9.0	12.2	3.2	-139.2
1987	487.1	363.9	257.5	106.4	123.2	637.9	509.1	414.8	94.3	105.3	23.5	9.9	10.3	3.4	-150.8
1988	596.2	444.1	325.8	118.3	152.1	708.4	554.5	452.1	102.4	128.5	25.5	10.6	10.4	4.5	-112.2
1989	681.0	503.3	369.4	134.0	177.7	769.3	591.5	484.8	106.7	151.5	26.4	11.4	10.4	4.6	-88.3
1990	741.5	552.4	396.6	155.7	189.1	811.5	630.3	508.1	122.3	154.3	26.9	12.0	10.0	4.8	-70.1
1991	765.7	596.8	423.5	173.3	168.9	752.3	624.3	500.7	123.6	138.5	-10.6	13.0	-28.6	5.0	13.5
1992	788.0	635.3	448.0	187.4	152.7	824.9	668.6	544.9	123.6	123.0	33.4	12.3	17.1	3.9	-36.9
1993	812.1	655.8	459.9	195.9	156.2	882.5	720.9	592.8	128.1	124.3	37.3	14.2	17.8	5.4	-70.4
1994	907.3	720.9	510.1	210.8	186.4	1,012.5	814.5	676.8	137.7	160.2	37.8	15.4	15.8	6.6	-105.2
1995	1,046.1	812.2	583.3	228.9	233.9	1,137.1	903.6	757.4	146.1	198.1	35.4	16.2	10.1	9.1	-91.0
1996	1,117.3	868.6	618.3	250.2	248.7	1,217.6	964.8	807.4	157.4	213.7	39.1	18.0	14.1	7.1	-100.3
1997	1,242.0	955.3	687.7	267.6	286.7	1,352.2	1,056.9	885.3	171.5	253.7	41.6	21.0	10.9	9.7	-110.2
1998	1,243.1	955.9	680.9	275.1	287.1	1,430.5	1,115.9	929.0	186.9	265.8	48.8	24.6	11.2	12.9	-187.4
1999	1,312.1	991.2	697.2	294.0	320.8	1,585.9	1,251.7	1,045.5	206.3	287.0	47.2	28.3	11.6	7.3	-273.9
2000	1,478.9	1,096.3	784.3	311.9	382.7	1,875.6	1,475.8	1,243.5	232.3	343.7	56.1	31.5	13.5	11.2	-396.6
2001	1,355.2	1,032.8	731.2	301.6	322.4	1,725.6	1,399.8	1,167.9	231.9	278.8	47.0	33.0	9.5	4.5	-370.4
2002	1,311.6	1,005.9	697.6	308.4	305.7	1,769.9	1,430.3	1,189.3	241.0	275.0	64.5	40.0	14.3	10.3	-458.3
2003	1,377.6	1,040.8	724.4	316.4	336.8	1,889.8	1,540.2	1,283.9	256.2	280.0	69.7	40.2	17.6	11.9	-512.3
2004	1,619.9	1,182.4	818.3	364.1	437.5	2,244.0	1,797.8	1,499.5	298.3	361.3	84.9	43.1	19.2	22.6	-624.1
2005	1,853.5	1,309.4	907.0	402.4	544.1	2,588.5	2,023.9	1,702.0	322.0	475.6	89.0	47.3	27.1	14.6	-735.1
2006	2,159.0	1,467.6	1,030.5	437.1	691.4	2,953.2	2,229.6	1,880.4	349.2	633.4	90.1	48.9	20.3	20.9	-794.1
2004: I	1,548.4	1,140.9	787.6	353.2	407.5	2,087.7	1,684.1	1,399.0	285.1	311.3	92.4	43.0	27.1	22.2	-539.4
II	1,598.1	1,172.8	811.7	361.1	425.4	2,214.4	1,775.8	1,481.3	294.5	352.6	86.0	43.7	16.5	25.8	-616.3
III	1,633.9	1,187.3	826.0	361.3	446.5	2,253.1	1,820.0	1,519.3	300.7	363.5	69.6	43.6	17.1	8.9	-619.2
IV	1,699.2	1,228.6	848.0	380.7	470.6	2,420.9	1,911.2	1,598.4	312.8	417.9	91.7	42.2	16.1	33.4	-721.6
2005: I	1,759.8	1,260.8	869.2	391.5	499.1	2,474.3	1,931.9	1,619.2	312.7	429.0	113.4	49.2	31.7	32.5	-714.5
II	1,824.5	1,301.2	904.0	397.2	523.3	2,534.6	1,981.0	1,662.8	318.1	455.6	98.0	46.6	19.5	31.9	-710.1
III	1,874.1	1,316.0	911.1	404.9	558.1	2,548.8	2,041.0	1,717.0	323.9	471.2	36.6	45.8	23.3	-32.5	-674.7
IV	1,955.4	1,359.6	943.7	415.9	595.9	2,796.4	2,141.9	1,808.9	333.1	546.3	108.2	47.6	34.0	26.5	-841.0
2006: I	2,039.9	1,406.6	985.4	421.2	633.3	2,826.2	2,169.9	1,828.7	341.1	570.4	85.9	45.3	18.3	22.3	-786.3
II	2,136.3	1,447.4	1,016.4	431.0	688.9	2,948.0	2,227.8	1,879.8	348.0	625.0	95.2	49.9	24.1	21.2	-811.7
III	2,194.3	1,484.5	1,047.8	436.7	709.7	3,044.3	2,283.6	1,933.3	350.3	664.7	96.0	49.5	25.4	21.1	-850.1
IV	2,265.7	1,531.9	1,072.3	459.6	733.8	2,994.1	2,237.2	1,879.9	357.3	673.7	83.2	50.6	13.6	18.9	-728.4
2007: I	2,302.0	1,549.9	1,084.0	465.9	752.2	3,058.1	2,264.0	1,902.7	361.4	689.0	105.1	50.4	34.5	20.2	-756.0
II	2,412.9	1,598.7	1,115.2	483.5	814.2	3,143.4	2,312.9	1,947.2	365.7	743.5	86.9	50.5	15.0	21.5	-730.5
III	2,541.3	1,685.7	1,191.3	494.4	855.6	3,232.2	2,380.4	2,007.3	373.2	754.4	97.4	52.2	22.2	23.0	-690.9

[1] Certain goods, primarily military equipment purchased and sold by the Federal Government, are included in services. Beginning with 1986, repairs and alterations of equipment were reclassified from goods to services.
[2] National income and product accounts (NIPA).

Source: Department of Commerce (Bureau of Economic Analysis).

TABLE B–25.—*Real exports and imports of goods and services, 1990–2007*

[Billions of chained (2000) dollars; quarterly data at seasonally adjusted annual rates]

Year or quarter	Exports of goods and services					Imports of goods and services				
	Total	Goods [1]			Services [1]	Total	Goods [1]			Services [1]
		Total	Durable goods	Non-durable goods			Total	Durable goods	Non-durable goods	
1990	552.5	367.2	226.3	145.1	188.7	607.1	469.7	264.7	218.4	142.7
1991	589.1	392.5	243.1	153.7	199.9	603.7	469.3	266.1	215.9	139.0
1992	629.7	421.9	262.5	163.6	210.8	645.6	513.1	294.0	231.9	135.5
1993	650.0	435.6	276.1	162.4	217.5	702.1	564.8	328.8	248.0	139.4
1994	706.5	478.0	309.6	170.1	231.1	785.9	640.0	383.1	266.0	147.3
1995	778.2	533.9	353.6	181.1	245.8	849.1	697.6	427.1	277.0	152.1
1996	843.4	581.1	394.9	186.7	263.5	923.0	762.7	472.8	295.2	160.5
1997	943.7	664.5	466.2	198.7	279.2	1,048.3	872.6	550.3	326.4	175.6
1998	966.5	679.4	481.2	198.5	287.2	1,170.3	974.4	621.8	355.7	195.6
1999	1,008.2	705.2	503.6	201.7	303.2	1,304.4	1,095.2	711.7	384.3	209.1
2000	1,096.3	784.3	569.2	215.1	311.9	1,475.8	1,243.5	820.7	422.8	232.3
2001	1,036.7	736.3	522.2	214.2	300.4	1,435.8	1,204.1	769.4	435.1	231.6
2002	1,013.3	707.0	491.2	216.1	306.0	1,484.6	1,248.2	801.0	447.4	236.5
2003	1,026.1	719.8	499.8	220.3	306.2	1,545.0	1,309.3	835.3	474.2	236.6
2004	1,126.1	784.4	558.6	227.1	341.4	1,719.9	1,457.0	954.4	505.2	263.9
2005	1,203.4	843.5	612.0	234.3	359.8	1,821.5	1,553.6	1,034.2	525.2	269.8
2006	1,304.1	927.4	682.3	249.5	377.1	1,928.6	1,646.6	1,126.7	534.4	283.8
2004: I	1,101.8	765.1	542.5	223.6	336.4	1,650.9	1,393.9	897.8	496.9	257.5
II	1,119.4	778.5	555.8	224.1	340.6	1,710.5	1,448.3	948.9	502.0	263.0
III	1,128.0	790.2	565.3	226.4	337.7	1,730.8	1,467.7	971.1	500.3	264.1
IV	1,155.3	804.0	570.8	234.3	351.0	1,787.7	1,518.1	999.7	521.6	270.8
2005: I	1,172.4	815.4	581.8	235.0	356.6	1,796.8	1,530.1	1,002.1	530.3	268.4
II	1,199.3	841.8	603.5	240.0	357.5	1,800.3	1,534.0	1,020.4	519.0	268.1
III	1,205.6	845.7	616.4	232.4	359.8	1,809.7	1,543.6	1,040.5	511.9	268.1
IV	1,236.4	871.1	646.2	229.8	365.3	1,879.0	1,606.5	1,073.8	539.3	274.7
2006: I	1,270.6	903.0	665.0	242.4	368.0	1,910.7	1,631.8	1,105.5	537.2	281.0
II	1,288.4	917.3	673.2	248.2	371.5	1,915.0	1,636.3	1,118.0	532.0	281.0
III	1,306.6	933.7	685.5	252.5	373.4	1,940.4	1,661.0	1,138.4	537.5	281.9
IV	1,350.9	955.4	705.5	255.0	395.6	1,948.2	1,658.7	1,144.7	531.1	291.4
2007: I	1,354.7	957.6	707.5	255.2	397.2	1,966.8	1,675.6	1,141.8	547.3	293.1
II	1,379.5	973.1	719.5	259.0	406.4	1,953.4	1,663.4	1,136.8	541.0	291.9
III	1,441.2	1,031.4	763.6	273.7	410.4	1,974.3	1,683.2	1,172.1	532.6	293.1

[1] Certain goods, primarily military equipment purchased and sold by the Federal Government, are included in services. Beginning with 1986, repairs and alterations of equipment were reclassified from goods to services.

Note.—See Table B–2 for data for total exports of goods and services and total imports of goods and services for 1959-89.

Source: Department of Commerce (Bureau of Economic Analysis).

TABLE B–26.—*Relation of gross domestic product, gross national product, net national product, and national income, 1959–2007*

[Billions of dollars; quarterly data at seasonally adjusted annual rates]

Year or quarter	Gross domestic product	Plus: Income receipts from rest of the world	Less: Income payments to rest of the world	Equals: Gross national product	Less: Consumption of fixed capital			Equals: Net national product	Less: Statistical discrepancy	Equals: National income
					Total	Private	Government			
1959	506.6	4.3	1.5	509.3	53.0	38.6	14.5	456.3	0.5	455.8
1960	526.4	4.9	1.8	529.5	55.6	40.5	15.0	473.9	−.9	474.9
1961	544.7	5.3	1.8	548.2	57.2	41.6	15.6	491.0	−.6	491.6
1962	585.6	5.9	1.8	589.7	59.3	42.8	16.5	530.5	.4	530.1
1963	617.7	6.5	2.1	622.2	62.4	44.9	17.5	559.8	−.8	560.6
1964	663.6	7.2	2.3	668.5	65.0	46.9	18.1	603.5	.8	602.7
1965	719.1	7.9	2.6	724.4	69.4	50.5	18.9	655.0	1.6	653.4
1966	787.8	8.1	3.0	792.9	75.6	55.5	20.1	717.3	6.3	711.0
1967	832.6	8.7	3.3	838.0	81.5	59.9	21.6	756.5	4.6	751.9
1968	910.0	10.1	4.0	916.1	88.4	65.2	23.1	827.7	4.6	823.2
1969	984.6	11.8	5.7	990.7	97.9	73.1	24.8	892.8	3.2	889.7
1970	1,038.5	12.8	6.4	1,044.9	106.7	80.0	26.7	938.2	7.3	930.9
1971	1,127.1	14.0	6.4	1,134.7	115.0	86.7	28.3	1,019.7	11.6	1,008.1
1972	1,238.3	16.3	7.7	1,246.8	126.5	97.1	29.5	1,120.3	9.1	1,111.2
1973	1,382.7	23.5	10.9	1,395.3	139.3	107.9	31.4	1,256.0	8.6	1,247.4
1974	1,500.0	29.8	14.3	1,515.5	162.5	126.6	35.9	1,353.0	10.9	1,342.1
1975	1,638.3	28.0	15.0	1,651.3	187.7	147.8	40.0	1,463.6	17.7	1,445.9
1976	1,825.3	32.4	15.5	1,842.1	205.2	162.5	42.6	1,637.0	25.1	1,611.8
1977	2,030.9	37.2	16.9	2,051.2	230.0	184.3	45.7	1,821.2	22.3	1,798.9
1978	2,294.7	46.3	24.7	2,316.3	262.3	212.8	49.5	2,054.0	26.6	2,027.4
1979	2,563.3	68.3	36.4	2,595.3	300.1	245.7	54.5	2,295.1	46.0	2,249.1
1980	2,789.5	79.1	44.9	2,823.7	343.0	281.1	61.8	2,480.7	41.4	2,439.3
1981	3,128.4	92.0	59.1	3,161.4	388.1	317.9	70.1	2,773.3	30.9	2,742.4
1982	3,255.0	101.0	64.5	3,291.5	426.9	349.8	77.1	2,864.6	.3	2,864.3
1983	3,536.7	101.9	64.8	3,573.8	443.8	362.1	81.7	3,130.0	45.7	3,084.2
1984	3,933.2	121.9	85.6	3,969.5	472.6	385.6	87.0	3,496.9	14.6	3,482.3
1985	4,220.3	112.4	85.9	4,246.8	506.7	414.0	92.7	3,740.1	16.7	3,723.4
1986	4,462.8	111.4	93.6	4,480.6	531.3	431.8	99.5	3,949.3	47.0	3,902.3
1987	4,739.5	123.2	105.3	4,757.4	561.9	455.3	106.7	4,195.4	21.7	4,173.7
1988	5,103.8	152.1	128.5	5,127.4	597.6	483.5	114.1	4,529.8	−19.5	4,549.4
1989	5,484.4	177.7	151.5	5,510.6	644.3	522.1	122.2	4,866.3	39.7	4,826.6
1990	5,803.1	189.1	154.3	5,837.9	682.5	551.6	130.9	5,155.4	66.2	5,089.1
1991	5,995.9	168.9	138.5	6,026.3	725.9	586.9	139.1	5,300.4	72.5	5,227.9
1992	6,337.7	152.7	123.0	6,367.4	751.9	607.3	144.6	5,615.5	102.7	5,512.8
1993	6,657.4	156.2	124.3	6,689.3	776.4	624.7	151.8	5,912.9	139.5	5,773.4
1994	7,072.2	186.4	160.2	7,098.4	833.7	675.1	158.6	6,264.7	142.5	6,122.3
1995	7,397.7	233.9	198.1	7,433.4	878.4	713.4	165.0	6,555.1	101.2	6,453.9
1996	7,816.9	248.7	213.7	7,851.9	918.1	748.8	169.3	6,933.8	93.7	6,840.1
1997	8,304.3	286.7	253.7	8,337.3	974.4	800.3	174.1	7,362.8	70.7	7,292.2
1998	8,747.0	287.1	265.8	8,768.3	1,030.2	851.2	179.0	7,738.2	−14.6	7,752.8
1999	9,268.4	320.8	287.0	9,302.2	1,101.3	914.3	187.0	8,200.9	−35.7	8,236.7
2000	9,817.0	382.7	343.7	9,855.9	1,187.8	990.8	197.0	8,668.1	−127.2	8,795.2
2001	10,128.0	322.4	278.8	10,171.6	1,281.5	1,075.5	206.0	8,890.2	−89.6	8,979.8
2002	10,469.6	305.7	275.0	10,500.2	1,292.0	1,080.3	211.6	9,208.3	−21.0	9,229.3
2003	10,960.8	336.8	280.0	11,017.6	1,336.5	1,118.3	218.2	9,681.1	48.8	9,632.3
2004	11,685.9	437.5	361.3	11,762.1	1,436.1	1,206.0	230.2	10,326.0	19.1	10,306.8
2005	12,433.9	544.1	475.6	12,502.4	1,609.5	1,357.0	252.4	10,893.0	5.4	10,887.6
2006	13,194.7	691.4	633.4	13,252.7	1,615.2	1,347.5	267.7	11,637.5	−18.1	11,655.6
2004: I	11,405.5	407.5	311.3	11,501.7	1,373.7	1,150.9	222.7	10,128.1	38.0	10,090.0
II	11,610.3	425.4	352.6	11,683.1	1,394.3	1,166.8	227.4	10,288.8	40.8	10,248.0
III	11,779.4	446.5	363.5	11,862.3	1,534.5	1,302.3	232.3	10,327.8	10.0	10,317.8
IV	11,948.5	470.6	417.9	12,001.1	1,442.0	1,203.8	238.2	10,559.1	−12.2	10,571.3
2005: I	12,154.0	499.1	429.0	12,224.0	1,466.6	1,224.9	241.8	10,757.4	−11.1	10,768.5
II	12,317.4	523.3	455.6	12,385.1	1,492.4	1,246.5	245.9	10,892.6	−10.3	10,903.0
III	12,558.8	558.1	471.2	12,645.7	1,903.9	1,637.9	266.0	10,741.8	27.2	10,714.6
IV	12,705.5	595.9	546.3	12,755.0	1,574.9	1,318.9	256.0	11,180.1	15.7	11,164.5
2006: I	12,964.6	633.3	570.4	13,027.5	1,574.8	1,314.8	260.1	11,452.7	−20.9	11,473.6
II	13,155.0	688.9	625.0	13,218.9	1,602.8	1,337.2	265.6	11,616.1	−2.6	11,618.7
III	13,266.9	709.7	664.7	13,311.9	1,628.8	1,358.7	270.1	11,683.1	−2.5	11,685.6
IV	13,392.3	733.8	673.7	13,452.4	1,654.4	1,379.3	275.1	11,798.0	−46.6	11,844.6
2007: I	13,551.9	752.2	689.0	13,615.1	1,670.9	1,389.6	281.3	11,944.2	−66.3	12,010.5
II	13,768.8	814.2	743.5	13,839.4	1,683.4	1,397.4	286.0	12,156.0	−40.8	12,196.8
III	13,970.5	855.6	754.4	14,071.6	1,690.9	1,400.9	290.0	12,380.8	74.8	12,306.0

Source: Department of Commerce (Bureau of Economic Analysis).

TABLE B–27.—*Relation of national income and personal income, 1959–2007*

[Billions of dollars; quarterly data at seasonally adjusted annual rates]

Year or quarter	National income	Less: Corporate profits with inventory valuation and capital consumption adjustments	Less: Taxes on production and imports less subsidies	Less: Contributions for government social insurance	Less: Net interest and miscellaneous payments on assets	Less: Business current transfer payments (net)	Less: Current surplus of government enterprises	Plus: Wage accruals less disbursements	Plus: Personal income receipts on assets	Plus: Personal current transfer receipts	Equals: Personal income
1959	455.8	55.7	40.0	13.8	9.6	1.8	1.0	0.0	34.6	24.2	392.8
1960	474.9	53.8	43.4	16.4	10.6	1.9	.9	.0	37.9	25.7	411.5
1961	491.6	54.9	45.0	17.0	12.5	2.0	.8	.0	40.1	29.5	429.0
1962	530.1	63.3	48.2	19.1	14.2	2.2	.9	.0	44.1	30.4	456.7
1963	560.6	69.0	51.2	21.7	15.2	2.7	1.4	.0	47.9	32.2	479.6
1964	602.7	76.5	54.6	22.4	17.4	3.1	1.3	.0	53.8	33.5	514.6
1965	653.4	87.5	57.8	23.4	19.6	3.6	1.3	.0	59.4	36.2	555.7
1966	711.0	93.2	59.3	31.3	22.4	3.5	1.0	.0	64.1	39.6	603.9
1967	751.9	91.3	64.2	34.9	25.5	3.8	.9	.0	69.0	48.0	648.3
1968	823.2	98.8	72.3	38.7	27.1	4.3	1.2	.0	75.2	56.1	712.0
1969	889.7	95.4	79.4	44.1	32.7	4.9	1.0	.0	84.1	62.3	778.5
1970	930.9	83.6	86.7	46.4	39.1	4.5	.0	.0	93.5	74.7	838.8
1971	1,008.1	98.0	95.9	51.2	43.9	4.3	-.2	.6	101.0	88.1	903.5
1972	1,111.2	112.1	101.4	59.2	47.9	4.9	.5	.0	109.6	97.9	992.7
1973	1,247.4	125.5	112.1	75.5	55.2	6.0	-.4	-.1	124.7	112.6	1,110.7
1974	1,342.1	115.8	121.7	85.2	70.8	7.1	-.9	-.5	146.4	133.3	1,222.6
1975	1,445.9	134.8	131.0	89.3	81.6	9.4	-3.2	.1	162.2	170.0	1,335.0
1976	1,611.8	163.3	141.5	101.3	85.5	9.5	-1.8	.1	178.4	184.0	1,474.8
1977	1,798.9	192.4	152.8	113.1	101.1	8.4	-2.6	.1	205.3	194.2	1,633.2
1978	2,027.4	216.6	162.2	131.3	115.0	10.6	-1.9	.3	234.8	209.6	1,837.7
1979	2,249.1	223.2	171.9	152.7	138.9	13.0	-2.6	-.2	274.7	235.3	2,062.2
1980	2,439.3	201.1	190.9	166.2	181.8	14.4	-4.8	.0	338.7	279.5	2,307.9
1981	2,742.4	226.1	224.5	195.7	232.3	17.6	-4.9	.1	421.9	318.4	2,591.3
1982	2,864.3	209.7	226.4	208.9	271.1	20.1	-4.0	.0	488.4	354.8	2,775.3
1983	3,084.2	264.2	242.5	226.0	285.3	22.5	-3.1	-.4	529.6	383.7	2,960.7
1984	3,482.3	318.6	269.3	257.5	327.1	30.1	-1.9	.2	607.9	400.1	3,289.5
1985	3,723.4	330.3	287.3	281.4	341.3	34.8	.8	-.2	654.0	424.9	3,526.7
1986	3,902.3	319.5	298.9	303.4	366.8	36.6	1.3	.0	695.5	451.0	3,722.4
1987	4,173.7	368.8	317.7	323.1	366.4	33.8	1.2	.0	717.0	467.6	3,947.4
1988	4,549.4	432.6	345.5	361.5	385.3	34.0	2.5	.0	769.3	496.6	4,253.7
1989	4,826.6	426.6	372.1	385.2	432.1	39.2	4.9	.0	878.0	543.4	4,587.8
1990	5,089.1	437.8	398.7	410.1	442.2	39.4	1.6	.1	924.0	595.2	4,878.6
1991	5,227.9	451.2	430.2	430.2	418.2	39.9	5.7	-.1	932.0	666.4	5,051.0
1992	5,512.8	479.3	453.9	455.0	388.5	42.4	7.6	-15.8	910.9	749.4	5,362.0
1993	5,773.4	541.9	467.0	477.7	365.7	40.7	7.2	6.4	901.8	790.1	5,558.5
1994	6,122.3	600.3	513.5	508.2	366.4	43.3	8.6	17.6	950.8	827.3	5,842.5
1995	6,453.9	696.7	524.2	532.8	367.1	46.9	11.4	16.4	1,016.4	877.4	6,152.3
1996	6,840.1	786.2	546.8	555.2	376.2	53.1	12.7	3.6	1,089.2	925.0	6,520.6
1997	7,292.2	868.5	579.1	587.2	415.6	49.9	12.6	-2.9	1,181.7	951.2	6,915.1
1998	7,752.8	801.6	604.4	624.2	487.1	64.7	10.3	-.7	1,283.2	978.6	7,423.0
1999	8,236.7	851.3	629.8	661.4	495.4	67.4	10.1	5.2	1,264.2	1,022.1	7,802.4
2000	8,795.2	817.9	664.6	702.7	559.0	87.1	5.3	.0	1,387.0	1,084.0	8,429.7
2001	8,979.8	767.3	673.3	731.1	566.3	92.8	-1.4	.0	1,380.0	1,193.9	8,724.1
2002	9,229.3	886.3	724.4	750.0	520.9	84.3	.9	.0	1,333.2	1,286.2	8,881.9
2003	9,632.3	993.1	759.3	778.6	524.7	83.8	1.7	15.0	1,336.6	1,351.0	9,163.6
2004	10,306.8	1,231.2	819.2	828.8	491.2	83.0	-4.2	-15.0	1,432.1	1,422.5	9,727.2
2005	10,887.6	1,372.8	863.1	874.8	558.0	66.5	-15.1	5.0	1,617.8	1,520.7	10,301.1
2006	11,655.6	1,553.7	917.6	927.6	598.5	90.2	-13.9	7.5	1,796.5	1,612.5	10,983.4
2004: I	10,090.0	1,184.0	801.1	810.8	497.3	84.8	-2.5	-3.5	1,359.8	1,404.9	9,482.8
II	10,248.0	1,227.4	814.2	822.9	491.8	86.6	-3.3	-21.5	1,384.4	1,415.3	9,629.6
III	10,317.8	1,218.7	823.6	836.1	483.9	67.0	-4.7	-25.0	1,420.1	1,432.7	9,770.9
IV	10,571.3	1,294.8	837.9	845.5	491.8	93.6	-6.5	-10.0	1,564.1	1,437.1	10,025.5
2005: I	10,768.5	1,376.7	845.1	861.0	534.0	94.3	-8.5	.0	1,527.6	1,480.6	10,074.1
II	10,903.0	1,404.0	859.7	867.9	546.7	96.1	-10.4	.0	1,590.0	1,505.2	10,234.1
III	10,714.6	1,297.9	870.4	881.7	568.5	-.3	-27.7	.0	1,643.9	1,560.6	10,328.6
IV	11,164.5	1,412.5	877.0	888.5	583.0	75.8	-13.9	20.0	1,709.5	1,536.2	10,567.4
2006: I	11,473.6	1,515.5	900.1	918.8	592.9	89.1	-11.7	-20.0	1,725.6	1,572.5	10,787.1
II	11,618.7	1,575.5	916.2	920.1	611.0	88.6	-13.4	.0	1,795.7	1,599.1	10,915.5
III	11,685.6	1,592.5	922.9	926.8	594.2	91.4	-14.5	.0	1,828.1	1,630.6	11,030.9
IV	11,844.6	1,531.2	931.1	944.6	596.0	91.8	-16.0	50.0	1,836.6	1,647.7	11,200.2
2007: I	12,010.5	1,547.7	943.8	969.8	599.6	91.8	-17.8	.0	1,882.9	1,710.7	11,469.2
II	12,196.8	1,642.4	956.8	972.2	592.4	92.8	-15.0	25.0	1,930.0	1,717.1	11,577.3
III	12,306.0	1,621.9	967.8	981.5	599.3	94.4	-12.2	25.0	1,976.2	1,742.3	11,746.7

Source: Department of Commerce (Bureau of Economic Analysis).

TABLE B–28.—*National income by type of income, 1959–2007*

[Billions of dollars; quarterly data at seasonally adjusted annual rates]

Year or quarter	National income	Compensation of employees							Proprietors' income with inventory valuation and capital consumption adjustments			Rental income of persons with capital consumption adjustment
		Total	Wage and salary accruals			Supplements to wages and salaries			Total	Farm	Non-farm	
			Total	Govern-ment	Other	Total	Employer contributions for employee pension and insurance funds	Employer contributions for government social insurance				
1959	455.8	281.0	259.8	46.1	213.8	21.1	13.3	7.9	50.7	10.0	40.6	16.2
1960	474.9	296.4	272.9	49.2	223.7	23.6	14.3	9.3	50.8	10.5	40.3	17.1
1961	491.6	305.3	280.5	52.5	228.0	24.8	15.2	9.6	53.2	11.0	42.2	17.9
1962	530.1	327.1	299.4	56.3	243.0	27.8	16.6	11.2	55.4	11.0	44.4	18.8
1963	560.6	345.2	314.9	60.0	254.8	30.4	18.0	12.4	56.5	10.8	45.7	19.5
1964	602.7	370.7	337.8	64.9	272.9	32.9	20.3	12.6	59.4	9.6	49.8	19.6
1965	653.4	399.5	363.8	69.9	293.8	35.7	22.7	13.1	63.9	11.8	52.1	20.2
1966	711.0	442.7	400.3	78.4	321.9	42.3	25.5	16.8	68.2	12.8	55.4	20.8
1967	751.9	475.1	429.0	86.5	342.5	46.1	28.1	18.0	69.8	11.5	58.4	21.2
1968	823.2	524.3	472.0	96.7	375.3	52.3	32.4	20.0	74.3	11.5	62.8	20.9
1969	889.7	577.6	518.3	105.6	412.7	59.3	36.5	22.8	77.4	12.6	64.7	21.2
1970	930.9	617.2	551.6	117.2	434.3	65.7	41.8	23.8	78.4	12.7	65.7	21.4
1971	1,008.1	658.9	584.5	126.8	457.8	74.4	47.9	26.4	84.8	13.2	71.6	22.4
1972	1,111.2	725.1	638.8	137.9	500.9	86.4	55.2	31.2	95.9	16.8	79.1	23.4
1973	1,247.4	811.2	708.8	148.8	560.0	102.5	62.7	39.8	113.5	28.9	84.6	24.3
1974	1,342.1	890.2	772.3	160.5	611.8	118.0	73.3	44.7	113.1	23.2	89.9	24.3
1975	1,445.9	949.1	814.8	176.2	638.6	134.3	87.6	46.7	119.5	21.7	97.8	23.7
1976	1,611.8	1,059.3	899.7	188.9	710.8	159.6	105.2	54.4	132.2	17.0	115.2	22.3
1977	1,798.9	1,180.5	994.2	202.6	791.6	186.4	125.3	61.1	145.7	15.7	130.0	20.7
1978	2,027.4	1,336.1	1,121.2	220.0	901.2	214.9	143.4	71.5	166.6	19.6	147.1	22.1
1979	2,249.1	1,500.8	1,255.8	237.1	1,018.7	245.0	162.4	82.6	180.1	21.8	158.3	23.8
1980	2,439.3	1,651.8	1,377.6	261.5	1,116.2	274.2	185.2	88.9	174.1	11.3	162.8	30.0
1981	2,742.4	1,825.8	1,517.5	285.8	1,231.7	308.3	204.7	103.6	183.0	18.7	164.3	38.0
1982	2,864.3	1,925.8	1,593.7	307.5	1,286.2	332.1	222.4	109.8	176.3	13.1	163.3	38.8
1983	3,084.2	2,042.6	1,684.6	324.8	1,359.8	358.0	238.1	119.9	192.5	6.0	186.5	37.8
1984	3,482.3	2,255.6	1,855.1	348.1	1,507.0	400.5	261.5	139.0	243.3	20.6	222.7	40.2
1985	3,723.4	2,424.7	1,995.5	373.9	1,621.6	429.2	281.5	147.7	262.3	20.8	241.5	41.9
1986	3,902.3	2,570.1	2,114.8	397.0	1,717.9	455.3	297.5	157.9	275.7	22.6	253.1	33.5
1987	4,173.7	2,750.2	2,270.7	422.6	1,848.1	479.5	313.2	166.3	302.2	28.7	273.5	33.5
1988	4,549.4	2,967.2	2,452.9	451.3	2,001.6	514.2	329.6	184.6	341.6	26.8	314.7	40.6
1989	4,826.6	3,145.2	2,596.3	480.2	2,116.2	548.9	355.2	193.7	363.3	33.0	330.3	43.1
1990	5,089.1	3,338.2	2,754.0	517.7	2,236.3	584.2	377.8	206.5	380.6	31.9	348.7	50.7
1991	5,227.9	3,445.2	2,823.0	546.8	2,276.2	622.3	407.1	215.1	377.1	26.7	350.4	60.3
1992	5,512.8	3,635.4	2,964.5	569.2	2,395.3	670.9	442.5	228.4	427.6	34.5	393.0	78.0
1993	5,773.4	3,801.4	3,089.2	586.8	2,502.4	712.2	472.4	239.8	453.8	31.2	422.6	95.6
1994	6,122.3	3,997.2	3,249.8	606.2	2,643.5	747.5	493.3	254.1	473.3	33.9	439.4	119.7
1995	6,453.9	4,193.3	3,435.7	625.5	2,810.2	757.7	493.6	264.0	492.1	22.7	469.5	122.1
1996	6,840.1	4,390.5	3,623.2	644.4	2,978.8	767.3	492.5	274.9	543.2	37.3	505.9	131.5
1997	7,292.2	4,661.7	3,874.7	668.1	3,206.6	787.0	497.5	289.5	576.0	34.2	541.8	128.8
1998	7,752.8	5,019.4	4,182.7	697.3	3,485.5	836.7	529.7	307.0	627.8	29.4	598.4	137.5
1999	8,236.7	5,357.1	4,471.4	729.3	3,742.1	885.7	562.4	323.3	678.3	28.6	649.7	147.3
2000	8,795.2	5,782.7	4,829.2	774.7	4,054.5	953.4	609.9	343.5	728.4	22.7	705.7	150.3
2001	8,979.8	5,942.1	4,942.8	815.9	4,126.9	999.3	642.7	356.6	771.9	19.7	752.2	167.4
2002	9,229.3	6,091.2	4,980.9	865.9	4,115.0	1,110.3	745.1	365.2	768.4	10.6	757.8	152.9
2003	9,632.3	6,325.4	5,127.7	904.4	4,223.3	1,197.7	815.6	382.1	811.3	29.2	782.1	133.0
2004	10,306.8	6,656.4	5,379.5	943.1	4,436.4	1,276.9	868.5	408.3	911.6	37.3	874.3	118.4
2005	10,887.6	7,029.6	5,672.9	980.9	4,691.9	1,356.8	927.7	429.1	969.9	30.8	939.1	42.9
2006	11,655.6	7,448.3	6,025.7	1,020.6	5,005.1	1,422.6	970.7	451.8	1,006.7	19.4	987.4	54.5
2004: I	10,090.0	6,505.6	5,257.4	933.1	4,324.3	1,248.2	848.7	399.5	879.3	40.3	839.1	140.4
II	10,248.0	6,596.7	5,329.7	940.8	4,388.9	1,266.9	861.4	405.5	908.7	39.6	869.1	126.0
III	10,317.8	6,709.7	5,422.8	946.4	4,476.5	1,286.9	874.9	412.0	914.1	33.0	881.1	105.5
IV	10,571.3	6,813.6	5,508.1	952.2	4,555.9	1,305.5	889.1	416.4	944.4	36.5	908.0	101.7
2005: I	10,768.5	6,890.5	5,559.1	971.0	4,588.1	1,331.3	908.9	422.5	948.8	30.1	918.6	87.6
II	10,903.0	6,961.3	5,614.0	977.2	4,636.8	1,347.2	921.6	425.7	971.1	34.0	937.1	74.5
III	10,714.6	7,088.5	5,720.4	984.1	4,736.3	1,368.1	935.6	432.5	967.1	30.9	936.2	–49.8
IV	11,164.5	7,178.3	5,797.9	991.4	4,806.6	1,380.4	944.6	435.8	992.6	28.2	964.4	59.3
2006: I	11,473.6	7,328.7	5,925.6	1,004.4	4,921.1	1,403.1	955.2	447.9	1,000.1	20.8	979.3	59.0
II	11,618.7	7,371.9	5,958.4	1,013.8	4,944.6	1,413.5	965.5	448.0	1,013.5	14.6	998.9	55.4
III	11,685.6	7,442.5	6,015.8	1,027.0	4,988.8	1,426.7	975.4	451.3	1,003.6	18.1	985.5	52.9
IV	11,844.6	7,649.9	6,203.0	1,037.2	5,165.7	1,446.9	986.7	460.2	1,009.8	23.9	985.8	50.9
2007: I	12,010.5	7,764.9	6,294.4	1,051.7	5,242.7	1,470.5	999.2	471.3	1,027.4	29.1	998.3	53.2
II	12,196.8	7,826.9	6,343.9	1,061.9	5,281.9	1,483.0	1,010.9	472.1	1,038.4	33.1	1,005.3	62.1
III	12,306.0	7,917.7	6,418.5	1,072.9	5,345.6	1,499.2	1,022.7	476.4	1,048.7	38.6	1,010.0	68.4

See next page for continuation of table.

[Billions of dollars; quarterly data at seasonally adjusted annual rates]

Year or quarter	Corporate profits with inventory valuation and capital consumption adjustments								Capital consumption adjustment	Net interest and miscellaneous payments	Taxes on production and imports	Less: Subsidies	Business current transfer payments (net)	Current surplus of government enterprises
	Total	Profits with inventory valuation adjustment and without capital consumption adjustment												
		Total	Profits					Inventory valuation adjustment						
			Profits before tax	Taxes on corporate income	Profits after tax									
					Total	Net dividends	Undistributed profits							
1959	55.7	53.5	53.8	23.7	30.0	12.6	17.5	−0.3	2.2	9.6	41.1	1.1	1.8	1.0
1960	53.8	51.5	51.6	22.8	28.8	13.4	15.5	−.2	2.3	10.6	44.6	1.1	1.9	.9
1961	54.9	51.8	51.6	22.9	28.7	13.9	14.8	.3	3.0	12.5	47.0	2.0	2.0	.8
1962	63.3	57.0	57.0	24.1	32.9	15.0	17.9	.0	6.2	14.2	50.4	2.3	2.2	.9
1963	69.0	62.1	62.1	26.4	35.7	16.2	19.5	.1	6.8	15.2	53.4	2.2	2.7	1.4
1964	76.5	68.6	69.1	28.2	40.9	18.2	22.7	−.5	7.9	17.4	57.3	2.7	3.1	1.3
1965	87.5	78.9	80.2	31.1	49.1	20.2	28.9	−1.2	8.6	19.6	60.8	3.0	3.6	1.3
1966	93.2	84.6	86.7	33.9	52.8	20.7	32.1	−2.1	8.6	22.4	63.3	3.9	3.5	1.0
1967	91.3	82.0	83.5	32.9	50.6	21.5	29.1	−1.6	9.3	25.5	68.0	3.8	3.8	.9
1968	98.8	88.8	92.4	39.6	52.8	23.5	29.3	−3.7	10.0	27.1	76.5	4.2	4.3	1.2
1969	95.4	85.5	91.4	40.0	51.4	24.2	27.2	−5.9	9.9	32.7	84.0	4.5	4.9	1.0
1970	83.6	74.4	81.0	34.8	46.2	24.3	21.9	−6.6	9.2	39.1	91.5	4.8	4.5	.0
1971	98.0	88.3	92.9	38.2	54.7	25.0	29.7	−4.6	9.7	43.9	100.6	4.7	4.3	−.2
1972	112.1	101.2	107.8	42.3	65.5	26.8	38.6	−6.6	10.9	47.9	108.1	6.6	4.9	.5
1973	125.5	115.3	134.8	50.0	84.9	29.9	55.0	−19.6	10.2	55.2	117.3	5.2	6.0	−.4
1974	115.8	109.5	147.8	52.8	95.0	33.2	61.8	−38.2	6.2	70.8	125.0	3.3	7.1	−.9
1975	134.8	135.0	145.5	51.6	93.9	33.0	60.9	−10.5	−.2	81.6	135.5	4.5	9.4	−3.2
1976	163.3	165.6	179.7	65.3	114.4	39.0	75.4	−14.1	−2.3	85.5	146.6	5.1	9.5	−1.8
1977	192.4	194.7	210.4	74.4	136.0	44.8	91.2	−15.7	−2.3	101.1	159.9	7.1	8.4	−2.6
1978	216.6	222.4	246.1	84.9	161.3	50.8	110.5	−23.7	−5.8	115.0	171.2	8.9	10.6	−1.9
1979	223.2	231.8	271.9	90.0	181.9	57.5	124.4	−40.1	−8.5	138.9	180.4	8.5	13.0	−2.6
1980	201.1	211.4	253.5	87.2	166.3	64.1	102.2	−42.1	−10.2	181.8	200.7	9.8	14.4	−4.8
1981	226.1	219.1	243.7	84.3	159.4	73.8	85.6	−24.6	7.0	232.3	236.0	11.5	17.6	−4.9
1982	209.7	191.0	198.5	66.5	132.0	77.7	54.3	−7.5	18.6	271.1	241.3	15.0	20.1	−4.0
1983	264.2	226.5	233.9	80.6	153.3	83.5	69.8	−7.4	37.8	285.3	263.7	21.2	22.5	−3.1
1984	318.6	264.6	268.6	97.5	171.1	90.8	80.3	−4.0	54.0	327.1	290.2	21.0	30.1	−1.9
1985	330.3	257.5	257.4	99.4	158.0	97.6	60.5	.0	72.9	341.3	308.5	21.3	34.8	.8
1986	319.5	253.0	246.0	109.7	136.3	106.2	30.1	7.1	66.5	366.8	323.7	24.8	36.6	1.3
1987	368.8	301.4	317.6	130.4	187.2	112.3	74.9	−16.2	67.5	366.4	347.9	30.2	33.8	1.2
1988	432.6	363.9	386.1	141.6	244.4	129.9	114.5	−22.2	68.7	385.3	374.9	29.4	34.0	2.5
1989	426.6	367.4	383.7	146.1	237.7	158.0	79.7	−16.3	59.2	432.1	399.3	27.2	39.2	4.9
1990	437.8	396.6	409.5	145.4	264.1	169.1	95.0	−12.9	41.2	442.2	425.5	26.8	39.4	1.6
1991	451.2	427.9	423.0	138.6	284.4	180.7	103.7	4.9	23.3	418.2	457.5	27.3	39.9	5.7
1992	479.3	458.3	461.1	148.7	312.4	187.9	124.5	−2.8	21.1	388.5	483.8	29.9	42.4	7.6
1993	541.9	513.1	517.1	171.0	346.1	202.8	143.3	−4.0	28.8	365.7	503.4	36.4	40.7	7.2
1994	600.3	564.6	577.1	193.7	383.3	234.7	148.6	−12.4	35.7	366.4	545.6	32.2	43.3	8.6
1995	696.7	656.0	674.3	218.7	455.6	254.2	201.4	−18.3	40.7	367.1	558.2	34.0	46.9	11.4
1996	786.2	736.1	733.0	231.7	501.4	297.6	203.8	3.1	50.1	376.2	581.1	34.3	53.1	12.7
1997	868.5	812.3	798.2	246.1	552.1	334.5	217.6	14.1	56.2	415.6	612.0	32.9	49.9	12.6
1998	801.6	738.5	718.3	248.3	470.0	351.6	118.3	20.2	63.1	487.1	639.8	35.4	64.7	10.3
1999	851.3	776.8	775.9	258.6	517.2	337.4	179.9	1.0	74.5	495.4	674.0	44.2	67.4	10.1
2000	817.9	759.3	773.4	265.2	508.2	377.9	130.3	−14.1	58.6	559.0	708.9	44.3	87.1	5.3
2001	767.3	719.2	707.9	204.1	503.8	370.9	132.9	11.3	48.1	566.3	728.6	55.3	92.8	−1.4
2002	886.3	766.2	768.4	192.6	575.8	399.2	176.6	−2.2	120.1	520.9	762.8	38.4	84.3	.9
2003	993.1	894.5	908.1	243.3	664.8	424.7	240.1	−13.6	98.7	524.7	807.2	47.9	83.8	1.7
2004	1,231.2	1,161.6	1,204.7	307.4	897.3	539.5	357.8	−43.1	69.7	491.2	863.8	44.6	83.0	−4.2
2005	1,372.8	1,543.4	1,579.6	392.9	1,186.7	601.4	585.3	−36.2	−170.6	558.0	921.6	58.5	66.5	−15.1
2006	1,553.7	1,769.5	1,805.8	453.9	1,351.9	698.9	653.0	−36.3	−215.8	598.5	967.3	49.7	90.2	−13.9
2004: I	1,184.0	1,094.6	1,128.3	282.5	845.8	473.9	371.9	−33.7	89.4	497.3	844.8	43.7	82.1	−2.5
II	1,227.4	1,147.7	1,199.6	307.1	892.5	500.7	391.8	−51.9	79.7	491.8	857.1	42.9	86.6	−3.3
III	1,218.7	1,159.7	1,199.3	302.5	896.7	528.5	368.3	−39.6	59.0	483.9	867.8	44.2	67.0	−4.7
IV	1,294.8	1,244.3	1,291.5	337.3	954.2	654.8	299.3	−47.2	50.5	491.8	885.5	47.6	93.6	−6.5
2005: I	1,376.7	1,513.0	1,558.3	389.0	1,169.4	566.0	603.4	−45.3	−136.3	534.0	899.5	54.3	94.3	−8.5
II	1,404.0	1,559.3	1,578.7	393.8	1,184.9	588.1	596.8	−19.4	−155.2	546.7	917.7	58.1	96.1	−10.4
III	1,297.9	1,495.4	1,528.3	373.1	1,155.2	612.6	542.6	−32.9	−197.5	568.5	930.0	59.6	−.3	−27.7
IV	1,412.5	1,605.9	1,653.0	415.6	1,237.3	638.7	598.6	−47.0	−193.5	583.0	939.2	62.2	75.8	−13.9
2006: I	1,515.5	1,708.8	1,740.2	432.8	1,307.3	662.5	644.9	−31.4	−193.3	592.9	953.3	53.2	89.1	−11.7
II	1,575.5	1,784.6	1,842.3	460.0	1,382.4	685.6	696.8	−57.7	−209.1	611.0	965.9	49.7	88.6	−13.4
III	1,592.5	1,816.2	1,851.4	470.4	1,381.0	711.1	670.0	−35.2	−223.7	594.2	971.2	48.3	91.4	−14.5
IV	1,531.2	1,768.2	1,789.2	452.4	1,336.8	736.4	600.3	−21.0	−237.0	596.0	978.9	47.8	91.8	−16.0
2007: I	1,547.7	1,775.6	1,815.8	452.5	1,363.3	759.4	603.9	−40.2	−227.9	599.6	990.8	47.0	91.8	−17.8
II	1,642.4	1,876.8	1,931.5	490.1	1,441.4	784.2	657.2	−54.7	−234.4	592.4	1,004.1	47.3	92.8	−15.0
III	1,621.9	1,859.4	1,879.7	469.4	1,410.2	807.7	602.5	−20.3	−237.4	599.3	1,014.4	46.6	94.4	−12.2

Source: Department of Commerce (Bureau of Economic Analysis).

TABLE B–29.—*Sources of personal income, 1959–2007*

[Billions of dollars; quarterly data at seasonally adjusted annual rates]

| Year or quarter | Personal income | Compensation of employees, received | | | | | | | Proprietors' income with inventory valuation and capital consumption adjustments | | | Rental income of persons with capital consumption adjustment |
| | | Total | Wage and salary disbursements | | | Supplements to wages and salaries | | | Total | Farm | Nonfarm | |
			Total	Private industries	Government	Total	Employer contributions for employee pension and insurance funds	Employer contributions for government social insurance				
1959	392.8	281.0	259.8	213.8	46.1	21.1	13.3	7.9	50.7	10.0	40.6	16.2
1960	411.5	296.4	272.9	223.7	49.2	23.6	14.3	9.3	50.8	10.5	40.3	17.1
1961	429.0	305.3	280.5	228.0	52.5	24.8	15.2	9.6	53.2	11.0	42.2	17.9
1962	456.7	327.1	299.4	243.0	56.3	27.8	16.6	11.2	55.4	11.0	44.4	18.8
1963	479.6	345.2	314.9	254.8	60.0	30.4	18.0	12.4	56.5	10.8	45.7	19.5
1964	514.6	370.7	337.8	272.9	64.9	32.9	20.3	12.6	59.4	9.6	49.8	19.6
1965	555.7	399.5	363.8	293.8	69.9	35.7	22.7	13.1	63.9	11.8	52.1	20.2
1966	603.9	442.7	400.3	321.9	78.4	42.3	25.5	16.8	68.2	12.8	55.4	20.8
1967	648.3	475.1	429.0	342.5	86.5	46.1	28.1	18.0	69.8	11.5	58.4	21.2
1968	712.0	524.3	472.0	375.3	96.7	52.3	32.4	20.0	74.3	11.5	62.8	20.9
1969	778.5	577.6	518.3	412.7	105.6	59.3	36.5	22.8	77.4	12.6	64.7	21.2
1970	838.8	617.2	551.6	434.3	117.2	65.7	41.8	23.8	78.4	12.7	65.7	21.4
1971	903.5	658.3	584.0	457.4	126.6	74.4	47.9	26.4	84.8	13.2	71.6	22.4
1972	992.7	725.1	638.8	501.2	137.6	86.4	55.2	31.2	95.9	16.8	79.1	23.4
1973	1,110.7	811.3	708.8	560.0	148.8	102.5	62.7	39.8	113.5	28.9	84.6	24.3
1974	1,222.6	890.7	772.8	611.8	161.0	118.0	73.3	44.7	113.1	23.2	89.9	24.3
1975	1,335.0	949.0	814.7	638.6	176.1	134.3	87.6	46.7	119.5	21.7	97.8	23.7
1976	1,474.8	1,059.2	899.6	710.8	188.8	159.6	105.2	54.4	132.2	17.0	115.2	22.3
1977	1,633.2	1,180.4	994.1	791.6	202.5	186.4	125.3	61.1	145.7	15.7	130.0	20.7
1978	1,837.7	1,335.8	1,120.9	901.2	219.7	214.9	143.4	71.5	166.6	19.6	147.1	22.1
1979	2,062.2	1,501.0	1,256.0	1,018.7	237.3	245.0	162.4	82.6	180.1	21.8	158.3	23.8
1980	2,307.9	1,651.8	1,377.7	1,116.2	261.5	274.2	185.2	88.9	174.1	11.3	162.8	30.0
1981	2,591.3	1,825.7	1,517.5	1,231.7	285.8	308.3	204.7	103.6	183.0	18.7	164.3	38.0
1982	2,775.3	1,925.9	1,593.7	1,286.2	307.5	332.1	222.4	109.8	176.3	13.1	163.3	38.8
1983	2,960.7	2,043.0	1,685.0	1,359.8	325.2	358.0	238.1	119.9	192.5	6.0	186.5	37.8
1984	3,289.5	2,255.4	1,854.9	1,507.0	347.9	400.5	261.5	139.0	243.3	20.6	222.7	40.2
1985	3,526.7	2,424.9	1,995.7	1,621.6	374.1	429.2	281.5	147.7	262.3	20.8	241.5	41.9
1986	3,722.4	2,570.1	2,114.8	1,717.9	397.0	455.3	297.5	157.9	275.7	22.6	253.1	33.5
1987	3,947.4	2,750.2	2,270.7	1,848.1	422.6	479.5	313.2	166.3	302.2	28.7	273.5	33.5
1988	4,253.7	2,967.2	2,452.9	2,001.6	451.3	514.2	329.6	184.6	341.6	26.8	314.7	40.6
1989	4,587.8	3,145.2	2,596.3	2,116.2	480.2	548.9	355.2	193.7	363.3	33.0	330.3	43.1
1990	4,878.6	3,338.2	2,754.0	2,236.3	517.7	584.2	377.8	206.5	380.6	31.9	348.7	50.7
1991	5,051.0	3,445.3	2,823.0	2,276.2	546.8	622.3	407.1	215.1	377.1	26.7	350.4	60.3
1992	5,362.0	3,651.2	2,980.3	2,411.1	569.2	670.9	442.5	228.4	427.6	34.5	393.0	78.0
1993	5,558.5	3,794.9	3,082.7	2,496.0	586.8	712.2	472.4	239.8	453.8	31.2	422.6	95.6
1994	5,842.5	3,979.6	3,232.1	2,625.9	606.2	747.5	493.3	254.1	473.3	33.9	439.4	119.7
1995	6,152.3	4,177.0	3,419.3	2,793.8	625.5	757.7	493.6	264.0	492.1	22.7	469.5	122.1
1996	6,520.6	4,386.9	3,619.6	2,975.2	644.4	767.3	492.5	274.9	543.2	37.3	505.9	131.5
1997	6,915.1	4,664.6	3,877.6	3,209.5	668.1	787.0	497.5	289.5	576.0	34.2	541.8	128.8
1998	7,423.0	5,020.1	4,183.4	3,486.2	697.3	836.7	529.7	307.0	627.8	29.4	598.4	137.5
1999	7,802.4	5,352.0	4,466.3	3,736.9	729.3	885.7	562.4	323.3	678.3	28.6	649.7	147.3
2000	8,429.7	5,782.7	4,829.2	4,054.5	774.7	953.4	609.9	343.5	728.4	22.7	705.7	150.3
2001	8,724.1	5,942.1	4,942.8	4,126.9	815.9	999.3	642.7	356.6	771.9	19.7	752.2	167.4
2002	8,881.9	6,091.2	4,980.9	4,115.0	865.9	1,110.3	745.1	365.2	768.4	10.6	757.8	152.9
2003	9,163.6	6,310.4	5,112.7	4,208.3	904.4	1,197.7	815.6	382.1	811.3	29.2	782.1	133.0
2004	9,727.2	6,671.4	5,394.5	4,451.4	943.1	1,276.9	868.5	408.3	911.6	37.3	874.3	118.4
2005	10,301.1	7,024.6	5,667.9	4,686.9	980.9	1,356.8	927.7	429.1	969.9	30.8	939.1	42.9
2006	10,983.4	7,440.8	6,018.2	4,997.6	1,020.6	1,422.6	970.7	451.8	1,006.7	19.4	987.4	54.5
2004: I	9,482.8	6,509.1	5,260.9	4,329.3	931.6	1,248.2	848.7	399.5	879.3	40.3	839.1	140.4
II	9,629.6	6,618.2	5,351.2	4,408.9	942.3	1,266.9	861.4	405.5	908.7	39.6	869.1	126.0
III	9,770.9	6,734.7	5,447.8	4,501.5	946.4	1,286.9	874.9	412.0	914.1	33.0	881.1	105.5
IV	10,025.5	6,823.6	5,518.1	4,565.9	952.2	1,305.5	889.1	416.4	944.4	36.5	908.0	101.7
2005: I	10,074.1	6,890.5	5,559.1	4,588.1	971.0	1,331.3	908.9	422.5	948.8	30.1	918.6	87.6
II	10,234.1	6,961.3	5,614.0	4,636.8	977.2	1,347.2	921.6	425.7	971.1	34.0	937.1	74.5
III	10,328.6	7,088.5	5,720.4	4,736.3	984.1	1,368.1	935.6	432.5	967.1	30.9	936.2	–49.8
IV	10,567.4	7,158.3	5,777.9	4,786.6	991.4	1,380.4	944.6	435.8	992.6	28.2	964.4	59.3
2006: I	10,787.1	7,348.7	5,945.6	4,941.1	1,004.4	1,403.1	955.2	447.9	1,000.1	20.8	979.3	59.0
II	10,915.5	7,371.9	5,958.4	4,944.6	1,013.8	1,413.5	965.5	448.0	1,013.5	14.6	998.9	55.4
III	11,030.9	7,442.5	6,015.8	4,988.8	1,027.0	1,426.7	975.4	451.3	1,003.6	18.1	985.5	52.9
IV	11,200.2	7,599.9	6,153.0	5,115.7	1,037.2	1,446.9	986.7	460.2	1,009.8	23.9	985.8	50.9
2007: I	11,469.2	7,764.9	6,294.4	5,242.7	1,051.7	1,470.5	999.2	471.3	1,027.4	29.1	998.3	53.2
II	11,577.3	7,801.9	6,318.9	5,256.9	1,061.9	1,483.0	1,010.9	472.1	1,038.4	33.1	1,005.3	62.1
III	11,746.7	7,892.7	6,393.5	5,320.6	1,072.9	1,499.2	1,022.7	476.4	1,048.7	38.6	1,010.0	68.4

See next page for continuation of table.

[Billions of dollars; quarterly data at seasonally adjusted annual rates]

Year or quarter	Personal income receipts on assets			Personal current transfer receipts								Less: Contributions for government social insurance
					Government social benefits to persons						Other current transfer receipts, from business (net)	
	Total	Personal interest income	Personal dividend income	Total	Total	Old-age, survivors, disability, and health insurance benefits	Government unemployment insurance benefits	Veterans benefits	Family assistance[1]	Other		
1959	34.6	22.0	12.6	24.2	22.9	10.2	2.8	4.6	0.9	4.5	1.3	13.8
1960	37.9	24.5	13.4	25.7	24.4	11.1	3.0	4.6	1.0	4.7	1.3	16.4
1961	40.1	26.2	13.9	29.5	28.1	12.6	4.3	5.0	1.1	5.1	1.4	17.0
1962	44.1	29.1	15.0	30.4	28.8	14.3	3.1	4.7	1.3	5.5	1.5	19.1
1963	47.9	31.7	16.2	32.2	30.3	15.2	3.0	4.8	1.4	5.9	1.9	21.7
1964	53.8	35.6	18.2	33.5	31.3	16.0	2.7	4.7	1.5	6.4	2.2	22.4
1965	59.4	39.2	20.2	36.2	33.9	18.1	2.3	4.9	1.7	7.0	2.3	23.4
1966	64.1	43.4	20.7	39.6	37.5	20.8	1.9	4.9	1.9	8.1	2.1	31.3
1967	69.0	47.5	21.5	48.0	45.8	25.8	2.2	5.6	2.3	9.9	2.3	34.9
1968	75.2	51.6	23.5	56.1	53.3	30.5	2.1	5.9	2.8	11.9	2.8	38.7
1969	84.1	59.9	24.2	62.3	59.0	33.1	2.2	6.7	3.5	13.4	3.3	44.1
1970	93.5	69.2	24.3	74.7	71.7	38.6	4.0	7.7	4.8	16.6	2.9	46.4
1971	101.0	75.9	25.0	88.1	85.4	44.7	5.8	8.8	6.2	20.0	2.7	51.2
1972	109.6	82.8	26.8	97.9	94.8	49.8	5.7	9.7	6.9	22.7	3.1	59.2
1973	124.7	94.8	29.9	112.6	108.6	60.9	4.4	10.4	7.2	25.7	3.9	75.5
1974	146.4	113.2	33.2	133.3	128.6	70.3	6.8	11.8	8.0	31.7	4.7	85.2
1975	162.2	129.3	32.9	170.0	163.1	81.5	17.6	14.5	9.3	40.2	6.8	89.3
1976	178.4	139.5	39.0	184.0	177.3	93.3	15.8	14.4	10.1	43.7	6.7	101.3
1977	205.3	160.6	44.7	194.2	189.1	105.3	12.7	13.8	10.6	46.7	5.1	113.1
1978	234.8	184.0	50.7	209.6	203.2	116.9	9.1	13.9	10.8	52.5	6.5	131.3
1979	274.7	217.3	57.4	235.3	227.1	132.5	9.4	14.4	11.1	59.6	8.2	152.7
1980	338.7	274.7	64.0	279.5	270.8	154.8	15.7	15.0	12.5	72.8	8.6	166.2
1981	421.9	348.3	73.6	318.4	307.2	182.1	15.6	16.1	13.1	80.2	11.2	195.7
1982	488.4	410.8	77.6	354.8	342.4	204.6	25.1	16.4	12.9	83.4	12.4	208.9
1983	529.6	446.3	83.3	383.7	369.9	222.2	26.2	16.6	13.8	91.0	13.8	226.0
1984	607.9	517.2	90.6	400.1	380.4	237.8	15.9	16.4	14.5	95.9	19.7	257.5
1985	654.0	556.6	97.4	424.9	402.6	253.0	15.7	16.7	15.2	102.0	22.3	281.4
1986	695.5	589.5	106.0	451.0	428.0	268.9	16.3	16.7	16.1	109.9	22.9	303.4
1987	717.0	604.9	112.2	467.6	447.4	282.6	14.5	16.6	16.4	117.3	20.2	323.1
1988	769.3	639.5	129.7	496.6	476.0	300.2	13.2	16.9	16.9	128.8	20.6	361.5
1989	878.0	720.2	157.8	543.4	519.9	325.6	14.3	17.3	17.5	145.3	23.5	385.2
1990	924.0	755.2	168.8	595.2	573.1	351.8	18.0	17.8	19.2	166.2	22.2	410.1
1991	932.0	751.7	180.3	666.4	648.5	381.7	26.6	18.3	21.1	200.8	17.9	430.2
1992	910.9	723.4	187.4	749.4	729.8	414.4	38.9	19.3	22.2	234.9	19.6	455.0
1993	901.8	699.6	202.2	790.1	775.7	443.4	34.1	20.1	22.8	255.3	14.4	477.7
1994	950.8	716.8	234.0	827.3	812.2	475.4	23.5	20.1	23.2	270.0	15.1	508.2
1995	1,016.4	763.2	253.2	877.4	858.4	506.8	21.4	20.9	22.6	286.7	19.0	532.8
1996	1,089.2	793.0	296.2	925.0	902.1	537.7	22.0	21.7	20.3	300.4	22.9	555.2
1997	1,181.7	848.7	333.0	951.2	931.8	563.2	19.9	22.5	17.9	308.3	19.4	587.2
1998	1,283.2	933.2	349.9	978.6	952.6	575.1	19.5	23.4	17.4	317.3	26.0	624.2
1999	1,264.2	928.6	335.6	1,022.1	988.0	588.9	20.3	24.3	17.9	336.7	34.1	661.4
2000	1,387.0	1,011.0	376.1	1,084.0	1,041.6	620.8	20.3	25.1	18.4	357.0	42.4	702.7
2001	1,380.0	1,011.0	369.0	1,193.9	1,143.9	668.5	31.7	26.7	18.1	398.9	50.0	731.1
2002	1,333.2	936.1	397.2	1,286.2	1,248.9	707.5	53.2	29.6	17.7	440.9	37.3	750.0
2003	1,336.6	914.1	422.6	1,351.0	1,316.7	741.3	52.8	32.0	18.4	472.2	34.3	778.6
2004	1,432.1	895.1	537.0	1,422.5	1,396.1	788.0	36.0	34.5	18.4	519.2	26.4	828.8
2005	1,617.8	1,018.9	598.9	1,520.7	1,483.1	845.3	31.3	36.9	18.2	551.3	37.6	874.8
2006	1,796.5	1,100.2	696.3	1,612.5	1,585.3	946.4	29.9	39.5	18.2	551.3	27.2	927.6
2004: I	1,359.8	888.1	471.8	1,404.9	1,379.8	775.8	42.6	33.9	18.5	509.0	25.1	810.8
II	1,384.4	885.9	498.5	1,415.3	1,392.6	783.2	35.7	34.2	18.4	521.1	22.7	822.9
III	1,420.1	894.0	526.1	1,432.7	1,396.2	790.4	33.6	34.7	18.3	519.2	36.5	836.1
IV	1,564.1	912.3	651.8	1,437.1	1,415.7	802.8	32.2	35.2	18.3	527.3	21.4	845.5
2005: I	1,527.6	964.0	563.6	1,480.6	1,456.0	828.4	32.3	36.7	18.2	540.3	24.6	861.0
II	1,590.0	1,004.4	585.7	1,505.2	1,479.4	842.7	30.9	36.8	18.2	550.7	25.8	867.9
III	1,643.9	1,033.8	610.1	1,560.6	1,491.1	850.6	30.6	37.1	18.2	554.7	69.5	881.7
IV	1,709.5	1,073.3	636.2	1,536.2	1,505.8	859.5	31.5	37.1	18.2	559.5	30.4	888.5
2006: I	1,725.6	1,065.7	659.9	1,572.5	1,546.9	917.4	30.2	38.8	18.2	542.4	25.7	918.8
II	1,795.7	1,112.7	682.9	1,599.1	1,573.3	940.1	29.2	39.3	18.2	546.4	25.9	920.1
III	1,828.1	1,119.7	708.4	1,630.6	1,603.2	956.1	30.0	39.7	18.3	559.2	27.4	926.8
IV	1,836.6	1,102.8	733.8	1,647.7	1,618.0	972.0	30.3	40.3	18.3	557.0	29.7	944.6
2007: I	1,882.9	1,126.1	756.8	1,710.7	1,683.1	999.4	31.8	41.6	18.4	591.8	27.6	969.8
II	1,930.0	1,148.4	781.6	1,717.1	1,689.4	1,020.1	31.7	43.0	18.5	576.1	27.8	972.2
III	1,976.2	1,171.1	805.0	1,742.3	1,714.4	1,034.6	31.7	43.5	18.7	585.9	28.0	981.5

[1] Consists of aid to families with dependent children and, beginning in 1996, assistance programs operating under the Personal Responsibility and Work Opportunity Reconciliation Act of 1996.

Source: Department of Commerce (Bureau of Economic Analysis).

[Billions of dollars, except as noted; quarterly data at seasonally adjusted annual rates]

Year or quarter	Personal income	Less: Personal current taxes	Equals: Disposable personal income	Less: Personal outlays				Equals: Personal saving	Percent of disposable personal income [2]		
				Total	Personal consumption expenditures	Personal interest payments [1]	Personal current transfer payments		Personal outlays		Personal saving
									Total	Personal consumption expenditures	
1959	392.8	42.3	350.5	323.9	317.6	5.5	0.8	26.7	92.4	90.6	7.6
1960	411.5	46.1	365.4	338.8	331.7	6.2	.8	26.7	92.7	90.8	7.3
1961	429.0	47.3	381.8	349.6	342.1	6.5	1.0	32.2	91.6	89.6	8.4
1962	456.7	51.6	405.1	371.3	363.3	7.0	1.1	33.8	91.7	89.7	8.3
1963	479.6	54.6	425.1	391.8	382.7	7.9	1.2	33.3	92.2	90.0	7.8
1964	514.6	52.1	462.5	421.7	411.4	8.9	1.3	40.8	91.2	89.0	8.8
1965	555.7	57.7	498.1	455.1	443.8	9.9	1.4	43.0	91.4	89.1	8.6
1966	603.9	66.4	537.5	493.1	480.9	10.7	1.6	44.4	91.7	89.5	8.3
1967	648.3	73.0	575.3	520.9	507.8	11.1	2.0	54.4	90.5	88.3	9.5
1968	712.0	87.0	625.0	572.2	558.0	12.2	2.0	52.8	91.6	89.3	8.4
1969	778.5	104.5	674.0	621.4	605.2	14.0	2.2	52.5	92.2	89.8	7.8
1970	838.8	103.1	735.7	666.2	648.5	15.2	2.6	69.5	90.6	88.1	9.4
1971	903.5	101.7	801.8	721.2	701.9	16.6	2.8	80.6	89.9	87.5	10.1
1972	992.7	123.6	869.1	791.9	770.6	18.1	3.1	77.2	91.1	88.7	8.9
1973	1,110.7	132.4	978.3	875.6	852.4	19.8	3.4	102.7	89.5	87.1	10.5
1974	1,222.6	151.0	1,071.6	958.0	933.4	21.2	3.4	113.6	89.4	87.1	10.6
1975	1,335.0	147.6	1,187.4	1,061.9	1,034.4	23.7	3.8	125.6	89.4	87.1	10.6
1976	1,474.8	172.3	1,302.5	1,180.2	1,151.9	23.9	4.4	122.3	90.6	88.4	9.4
1977	1,633.2	197.5	1,435.7	1,310.4	1,278.6	27.0	4.8	125.3	91.3	89.1	8.7
1978	1,837.7	229.4	1,608.3	1,465.8	1,428.5	31.9	5.4	142.5	91.1	88.8	8.9
1979	2,062.2	268.7	1,793.5	1,634.4	1,592.2	36.2	5.9	159.1	91.1	88.8	8.9
1980	2,307.9	298.9	2,009.0	1,807.5	1,757.1	43.6	6.8	201.4	90.0	87.5	10.0
1981	2,591.3	345.2	2,246.1	2,001.8	1,941.1	49.3	11.4	244.3	89.1	86.4	10.9
1982	2,775.3	354.1	2,421.2	2,150.4	2,077.3	59.5	13.6	270.8	88.8	85.8	11.2
1983	2,960.7	352.3	2,608.4	2,374.8	2,290.6	69.2	15.0	233.6	91.0	87.8	9.0
1984	3,289.5	377.4	2,912.0	2,597.3	2,503.3	77.0	16.9	314.8	89.2	86.0	10.8
1985	3,526.7	417.4	3,109.3	2,829.3	2,720.3	90.4	18.6	280.0	91.0	87.5	9.0
1986	3,722.4	437.3	3,285.1	3,016.7	2,899.7	96.1	20.9	268.4	91.8	88.3	8.2
1987	3,947.4	489.1	3,458.3	3,216.9	3,100.2	93.6	23.1	241.4	93.0	89.6	7.0
1988	4,253.7	505.0	3,748.7	3,475.8	3,353.6	96.8	25.4	272.9	92.7	89.5	7.3
1989	4,587.8	566.1	4,021.7	3,734.5	3,598.5	108.2	27.8	287.1	92.9	89.5	7.1
1990	4,878.6	592.8	4,285.8	3,986.4	3,839.9	116.1	30.4	299.4	93.0	89.6	7.0
1991	5,051.0	586.7	4,464.3	4,140.1	3,986.1	118.5	35.6	324.2	92.7	89.3	7.3
1992	5,362.0	610.6	4,751.4	4,385.4	4,235.3	111.8	38.3	366.0	92.3	89.1	7.7
1993	5,558.5	646.6	4,911.9	4,627.9	4,477.9	107.3	42.7	284.0	94.2	91.2	5.8
1994	5,842.5	690.7	5,151.8	4,902.4	4,743.3	112.8	46.3	249.5	95.2	92.1	4.8
1995	6,152.3	744.1	5,408.2	5,157.3	4,975.8	132.7	48.9	250.9	95.4	92.0	4.6
1996	6,520.6	832.1	5,688.5	5,460.0	5,256.8	150.3	52.9	228.4	96.0	92.4	4.0
1997	6,915.1	926.3	5,988.8	5,770.5	5,547.4	163.9	59.2	218.3	96.4	92.6	3.6
1998	7,423.0	1,027.0	6,395.9	6,119.1	5,879.5	174.5	65.2	276.8	95.7	91.9	4.3
1999	7,802.4	1,107.5	6,695.0	6,536.4	6,282.5	181.0	73.0	158.6	97.6	93.8	2.4
2000	8,429.7	1,235.7	7,194.0	7,025.6	6,739.4	204.7	81.5	168.5	97.7	93.7	2.3
2001	8,724.1	1,237.3	7,486.8	7,354.5	7,055.0	212.2	87.2	132.3	98.2	94.2	1.8
2002	8,881.9	1,051.8	7,830.1	7,645.3	7,350.7	196.4	98.2	184.7	97.6	93.9	2.4
2003	9,163.6	1,001.1	8,162.5	7,987.7	7,703.6	182.5	101.5	174.9	97.9	94.4	2.1
2004	9,727.2	1,046.3	8,680.9	8,499.2	8,195.9	191.3	112.1	181.7	97.9	94.4	2.1
2005	10,301.1	1,209.1	9,092.0	9,047.4	8,707.8	217.7	121.8	44.6	99.5	95.8	.5
2006	10,983.4	1,354.3	9,629.1	9,590.3	9,224.5	238.0	127.8	38.8	99.6	95.8	.4
2004: I	9,482.8	1,008.1	8,474.7	8,299.5	8,010.1	180.4	109.1	175.1	97.9	94.5	2.1
II	9,629.6	1,024.5	8,605.1	8,432.9	8,135.0	186.1	111.8	172.2	98.0	94.5	2.0
III	9,770.9	1,062.1	8,708.9	8,553.7	8,245.1	195.0	113.6	155.2	98.2	94.7	1.8
IV	10,025.5	1,090.7	8,934.8	8,710.6	8,393.3	203.5	113.8	224.2	97.5	93.9	2.5
2005: I	10,074.1	1,166.4	8,907.7	8,819.0	8,488.8	208.3	122.0	88.7	99.0	95.3	1.0
II	10,234.1	1,195.5	9,038.6	8,970.8	8,632.6	217.5	120.6	67.8	99.2	95.5	.8
III	10,328.6	1,223.5	9,105.1	9,153.9	8,810.5	222.4	121.0	–48.8	100.5	96.8	–.5
IV	10,567.4	1,251.0	9,316.4	9,245.7	8,899.3	222.6	123.7	70.8	99.2	95.5	.8
2006: I	10,787.1	1,318.6	9,468.5	9,384.0	9,034.7	227.1	122.2	84.5	99.1	95.4	.9
II	10,915.5	1,342.6	9,572.9	9,542.9	9,183.9	231.0	128.0	30.0	99.7	95.9	.3
III	11,030.9	1,355.2	9,675.8	9,677.1	9,305.7	242.3	129.1	–1.4	100.0	96.2	.0
IV	11,200.2	1,401.0	9,799.2	9,757.2	9,373.7	251.6	131.8	42.0	99.6	95.7	.4
2007: I	11,469.2	1,454.7	10,014.5	9,917.5	9,540.5	243.3	133.7	97.0	99.0	95.3	1.0
II	11,577.3	1,477.6	10,099.7	10,069.2	9,674.0	259.5	135.7	30.5	99.7	95.8	.3
III	11,746.7	1,489.2	10,257.5	10,200.9	9,785.7	275.8	139.3	56.7	99.4	95.4	.6

[1] Consists of nonmortgage interest paid by households.
[2] Percents based on data in millions of dollars.

Source: Department of Commerce (Bureau of Economic Analysis).

TABLE B–31.—*Total and per capita disposable personal income and personal consumption expenditures, and per capita gross domestic product, in current and real dollars, 1959–2007*

[Quarterly data at seasonally adjusted annual rates, except as noted]

Year or quarter	Disposable personal income				Personal consumption expenditures				Gross domestic product per capita (dollars)		Population (thousands) [1]
	Total (billions of dollars)		Per capita (dollars)		Total (billions of dollars)		Per capita (dollars)				
	Current dollars	Chained (2000) dollars	Current dollars	Chained (2000) dollars	Current dollars	Chained (2000) dollars	Current dollars	Chained (2000) dollars	Current dollars	Chained (2000) dollars	
1959	350.5	1,715.5	1,979	9,685	317.6	1,554.6	1,793	8,776	2,860	13,782	177,130
1960	365.4	1,759.7	2,022	9,735	331.7	1,597.4	1,835	8,837	2,912	13,840	180,760
1961	381.8	1,819.2	2,078	9,901	342.1	1,630.3	1,862	8,873	2,965	13,932	183,742
1962	405.1	1,908.2	2,171	10,227	363.3	1,711.1	1,947	9,170	3,139	14,552	186,590
1963	425.1	1,979.1	2,246	10,455	382.7	1,781.6	2,022	9,412	3,263	14,971	189,300
1964	462.5	2,122.8	2,410	11,061	411.4	1,888.4	2,144	9,839	3,458	15,624	191,927
1965	498.1	2,253.3	2,563	11,594	443.8	2,007.7	2,283	10,331	3,700	16,420	194,347
1966	537.5	2,371.9	2,734	12,065	480.9	2,121.8	2,446	10,793	4,007	17,290	196,599
1967	575.3	2,475.9	2,895	12,457	507.8	2,185.0	2,555	10,994	4,189	17,533	198,752
1968	625.0	2,588.0	3,114	12,892	558.0	2,310.5	2,780	11,510	4,533	18,196	200,745
1969	674.0	2,668.7	3,324	13,163	605.2	2,396.4	2,985	11,820	4,857	18,573	202,736
1970	735.7	2,781.7	3,587	13,563	648.5	2,451.9	3,162	11,955	5,064	18,391	205,089
1971	801.8	2,907.9	3,860	14,001	701.9	2,545.5	3,379	12,256	5,427	18,771	207,692
1972	869.1	3,046.5	4,140	14,512	770.6	2,701.3	3,671	12,868	5,899	19,555	209,924
1973	978.3	3,252.3	4,616	15,345	852.4	2,833.8	4,022	13,371	6,524	20,484	211,339
1974	1,071.6	3,228.5	5,010	15,094	933.4	2,812.3	4,364	13,148	7,013	20,195	213,898
1975	1,187.4	3,302.6	5,498	15,291	1,034.4	2,876.9	4,789	13,320	7,586	19,961	215,981
1976	1,302.5	3,432.2	5,972	15,738	1,151.9	3,035.5	5,282	13,919	8,369	20,822	218,086
1977	1,435.7	3,552.9	6,517	16,128	1,278.6	3,164.1	5,804	14,364	9,219	21,565	220,289
1978	1,608.3	3,718.8	7,224	16,704	1,428.5	3,303.1	6,417	14,837	10,307	22,526	222,629
1979	1,793.5	3,811.2	7,967	16,931	1,592.2	3,383.4	7,073	15,030	11,387	22,982	225,106
1980	2,009.0	3,857.7	8,822	16,940	1,757.1	3,374.1	7,716	14,816	12,249	22,666	227,726
1981	2,246.1	3,960.0	9,765	17,217	1,941.1	3,422.2	8,439	14,879	13,601	23,007	230,008
1982	2,421.2	4,044.9	10,426	17,418	2,077.3	3,470.3	8,945	14,944	14,017	22,346	232,218
1983	2,608.4	4,177.7	11,131	17,828	2,290.6	3,668.6	9,775	15,656	15,092	23,146	234,333
1984	2,912.0	4,494.1	12,319	19,011	2,503.3	3,863.3	10,589	16,343	16,638	24,593	236,394
1985	3,109.3	4,645.2	13,037	19,476	2,720.3	4,064.0	11,406	17,040	17,695	25,382	238,506
1986	3,285.1	4,791.0	13,649	19,906	2,899.7	4,228.9	12,048	17,570	18,542	26,024	240,683
1987	3,458.3	4,874.5	14,241	20,072	3,100.2	4,369.8	12,766	17,994	19,517	26,664	242,843
1988	3,748.7	5,082.6	15,297	20,740	3,353.6	4,546.9	13,685	18,554	20,827	27,514	245,061
1989	4,021.7	5,224.8	16,257	21,120	3,598.5	4,675.0	14,546	18,898	22,169	28,221	247,387
1990	4,285.8	5,324.2	17,131	21,281	3,839.9	4,770.3	15,349	19,067	23,195	28,429	250,181
1991	4,464.3	5,351.7	17,609	21,109	3,986.1	4,778.4	15,722	18,848	23,650	28,007	253,530
1992	4,751.4	5,536.3	18,494	21,548	4,235.3	4,934.8	16,485	19,208	24,668	28,556	256,922
1993	4,911.9	5,594.2	18,872	21,493	4,477.9	5,099.8	17,204	19,593	25,578	28,940	260,282
1994	5,151.8	5,746.4	19,555	21,812	4,743.3	5,290.7	18,004	20,082	26,844	29,741	263,455
1995	5,408.2	5,905.7	20,287	22,153	4,975.8	5,433.5	18,665	20,382	27,749	30,128	266,588
1996	5,688.5	6,080.9	21,091	22,546	5,256.8	5,619.4	19,490	20,835	28,982	30,881	269,714
1997	5,988.8	6,295.8	21,940	23,065	5,547.4	5,831.8	20,323	21,365	30,424	31,886	272,958
1998	6,395.9	6,663.9	23,161	24,131	5,879.5	6,125.8	21,291	22,183	31,674	32,833	276,154
1999	6,695.0	6,861.3	23,968	24,564	6,282.5	6,438.6	22,491	23,050	33,181	33,904	279,328
2000	7,194.0	7,194.0	25,469	25,469	6,739.4	6,739.4	23,860	23,860	34,755	34,755	282,459
2001	7,486.8	7,333.3	26,224	25,687	7,055.0	6,910.4	24,712	24,205	35,476	34,645	285,490
2002	7,830.1	7,562.2	27,145	26,217	7,350.7	7,099.3	25,483	24,612	36,296	34,837	288,451
2003	8,162.5	7,729.9	28,020	26,535	7,703.6	7,295.3	26,445	25,043	37,626	35,361	291,311
2004	8,680.9	8,008.9	29,517	27,232	8,195.9	7,561.4	27,868	25,711	39,735	36,300	294,096
2005	9,092.0	8,147.9	30,616	27,436	8,707.8	7,803.6	29,322	26,277	41,869	37,052	296,972
2006	9,629.1	8,396.9	32,115	28,005	9,224.5	8,044.1	30,765	26,828	44,007	37,752	299,833
2004: I	8,474.7	7,908.7	28,922	26,990	8,010.1	7,475.1	27,336	25,511	38,924	35,983	293,018
II	8,605.1	7,955.1	29,300	27,087	8,135.0	7,520.5	27,699	25,607	39,532	36,209	293,691
III	8,708.9	8,012.2	29,576	27,210	8,245.1	7,585.5	28,001	25,761	40,004	36,436	294,455
IV	8,934.8	8,158.8	30,265	27,636	8,393.3	7,664.3	28,431	25,961	40,473	36,570	295,222
2005: I	8,907.7	8,089.8	30,106	27,342	8,488.8	7,709.4	28,690	26,056	41,078	36,766	295,878
II	9,038.6	8,140.9	30,477	27,450	8,632.6	7,775.2	29,109	26,217	41,533	36,936	296,567
III	9,105.1	8,115.4	30,622	27,293	8,810.5	7,852.8	29,631	26,410	42,237	37,245	297,339
IV	9,316.4	8,246.0	31,252	27,661	8,899.3	7,876.9	29,853	26,423	42,621	37,259	298,105
2006: I	9,468.5	8,344.2	31,693	27,930	9,034.7	7,961.9	30,241	26,650	43,396	37,618	298,754
II	9,572.9	8,348.6	31,970	27,881	9,183.9	8,009.3	30,671	26,743	43,933	37,760	299,432
III	9,675.8	8,384.5	32,231	27,930	9,305.7	8,063.8	30,999	26,862	44,194	37,764	300,196
IV	9,799.2	8,510.7	32,561	28,280	9,373.7	8,141.2	31,147	27,052	44,500	37,865	300,950
2007: I	10,014.5	8,623.9	33,206	28,595	9,540.5	8,215.7	31,634	27,241	44,935	37,842	301,590
II	10,099.7	8,607.1	33,413	28,475	9,674.0	8,244.3	32,005	27,275	45,552	38,113	302,266
III	10,257.5	8,702.6	33,850	28,719	9,785.7	8,302.2	32,293	27,398	46,103	38,475	303,028

[1] Population of the United States including Armed Forces overseas; includes Alaska and Hawaii beginning in 1960. Annual data are averages of quarterly data. Quarterly data are averages for the period.

Source: Department of Commerce (Bureau of Economic Analysis and Bureau of the Census).

[Billions of dollars, except as noted; quarterly data at seasonally adjusted annual rates]

Year or quarter	Total gross saving	Net saving	Net private saving				Net government saving			Consumption of fixed capital		
		Total net saving	Total	Personal saving	Undistributed corporate profits[1]	Wage accruals less disbursements	Total	Federal	State and local	Total	Private	Government
1959	106.2	53.2	46.0	26.7	19.4	0.0	7.1	3.3	3.8	53.0	38.6	14.5
1960	111.3	55.8	44.3	26.7	17.6	.0	11.5	7.2	4.3	55.6	40.5	15.0
1961	114.3	57.1	50.2	32.2	18.1	.0	6.9	2.6	4.3	57.2	41.6	15.6
1962	124.9	65.7	57.9	33.8	24.1	.0	7.8	2.5	5.2	59.3	42.8	16.5
1963	133.2	70.8	59.7	33.3	26.4	.0	11.1	5.4	5.7	62.4	44.9	17.5
1964	143.4	78.4	71.0	40.8	30.1	.0	7.4	1.0	6.4	65.0	46.9	18.1
1965	158.5	89.1	79.2	43.0	36.2	.0	9.9	3.3	6.5	69.4	50.5	18.9
1966	168.7	93.1	83.1	44.4	38.7	.0	10.0	2.3	7.8	75.6	55.5	20.1
1967	170.5	89.0	91.4	54.4	36.9	.0	-2.4	-9.4	7.0	81.5	59.9	21.6
1968	182.0	93.6	88.4	52.8	35.6	.0	5.2	-2.3	7.5	88.4	65.2	23.1
1969	198.3	100.4	83.7	52.5	31.2	.0	16.7	8.7	8.0	97.9	73.1	24.8
1970	192.7	86.0	94.0	69.5	24.6	.0	-8.1	-15.2	7.1	106.7	80.0	26.7
1971	208.9	93.9	115.8	80.6	34.8	.4	-21.9	-28.4	6.5	115.0	86.7	28.3
1972	237.5	111.0	119.8	77.2	42.9	-.3	-8.8	-24.4	15.6	126.5	97.1	29.5
1973	292.0	152.7	148.3	102.7	45.6	.0	4.4	-11.3	15.7	139.3	107.9	31.4
1974	301.5	139.0	143.4	113.6	29.8	.0	-4.4	-13.8	9.3	162.5	126.6	35.9
1975	297.0	109.2	175.8	125.6	50.2	.0	-66.6	-69.0	2.5	187.7	147.8	40.0
1976	342.1	137.0	181.3	122.3	59.0	.0	-44.4	-51.7	7.4	205.2	162.5	42.6
1977	397.5	167.5	198.5	125.3	73.2	.0	-31.0	-44.1	13.1	230.0	184.3	45.7
1978	478.0	215.7	223.5	142.5	81.0	.0	-7.8	-26.5	18.7	262.3	212.8	49.5
1979	536.7	236.6	234.9	159.1	75.7	.0	1.7	-11.3	13.0	300.1	245.7	54.5
1980	549.4	206.5	251.3	201.4	49.9	.0	-44.8	-53.6	8.8	343.0	281.1	61.8
1981	654.7	266.6	312.3	244.3	68.0	.0	-45.7	-53.3	7.6	388.1	317.9	70.1
1982	629.1	202.2	336.2	270.8	65.4	.0	-134.1	-131.9	-2.2	426.9	349.8	77.1
1983	609.4	165.6	333.7	233.6	100.1	.0	-168.1	-173.0	4.9	443.8	362.1	81.7
1984	773.4	300.9	445.0	314.8	130.3	.0	-144.1	-168.1	23.9	472.6	385.6	87.0
1985	767.5	260.7	413.4	280.0	133.4	.0	-152.6	-175.0	22.3	506.7	414.0	92.7
1986	733.5	202.2	372.0	268.4	103.7	.0	-169.9	-190.8	21.0	531.3	431.8	99.5
1987	796.8	234.9	367.4	241.4	126.1	.0	-132.6	-145.0	12.4	561.9	455.3	106.7
1988	915.0	317.4	434.0	272.9	161.1	.0	-116.6	-134.5	17.9	597.6	483.5	114.1
1989	944.7	300.4	409.7	287.1	122.6	.0	-109.3	-130.1	20.8	644.3	522.1	122.2
1990	940.4	258.0	422.7	299.4	123.3	.0	-164.8	-172.0	7.2	682.5	551.6	130.9
1991	964.1	238.2	456.1	324.2	131.9	.0	-217.9	-213.7	-4.2	725.9	586.9	139.1
1992	948.2	196.3	493.0	366.0	142.7	-15.8	-296.7	-297.4	.7	751.9	607.3	144.6
1993	962.4	186.0	458.6	284.0	168.1	6.4	-272.6	-273.5	.9	776.4	624.7	151.8
1994	1,070.7	237.1	438.9	249.5	171.8	17.6	-201.9	-212.3	10.5	833.7	675.1	158.6
1995	1,184.5	306.2	491.1	250.9	223.8	16.4	-184.9	-197.0	12.0	878.4	713.4	165.0
1996	1,291.1	373.0	489.0	228.4	256.9	3.6	-116.0	-141.8	25.8	918.1	748.8	169.3
1997	1,461.1	486.6	503.3	218.3	287.9	-2.9	-16.7	-55.8	39.1	974.4	800.3	174.1
1998	1,598.7	568.6	477.8	276.8	201.7	-.7	90.8	38.8	52.0	1,030.2	851.2	179.0
1999	1,674.3	573.0	419.0	158.6	255.3	5.2	154.0	103.6	50.4	1,101.3	914.3	187.0
2000	1,770.5	582.7	343.3	168.5	174.8	.0	239.4	189.5	50.0	1,187.8	990.8	197.0
2001	1,657.6	376.1	324.6	132.3	192.3	.0	51.5	46.7	4.8	1,281.5	1,075.5	206.0
2002	1,489.1	197.1	479.2	184.7	294.5	.0	-282.1	-247.9	-34.2	1,292.0	1,080.3	211.6
2003	1,459.0	122.5	515.0	174.9	325.1	15.0	-392.5	-372.1	-20.4	1,336.5	1,118.3	218.2
2004	1,618.1	182.0	551.1	181.7	384.4	-15.0	-369.1	-370.6	1.5	1,436.1	1,206.0	230.2
2005	1,734.6	125.1	428.2	44.6	378.6	5.0	-303.1	-318.3	15.2	1,609.5	1,357.0	252.4
2006	1,866.9	251.7	447.2	38.8	400.9	7.5	-195.4	-220.0	24.6	1,615.2	1,347.5	267.7
2004: I	1,552.4	178.8	597.8	175.1	427.7	-5.0	-419.0	-411.1	-7.9	1,373.7	1,150.9	222.7
II	1,590.0	195.8	571.8	172.2	419.6	-20.0	-376.1	-374.1	-1.9	1,394.3	1,166.8	227.4
III	1,678.3	143.7	517.9	155.2	387.7	-25.0	-374.2	-361.9	-12.3	1,534.5	1,302.3	232.3
IV	1,651.7	209.7	516.9	224.2	302.6	-10.0	-307.1	-335.4	28.3	1,442.0	1,203.8	238.2
2005: I	1,711.0	244.3	510.4	88.7	421.7	.0	-266.0	-298.0	32.0	1,466.6	1,224.9	241.8
II	1,720.8	228.3	490.0	67.8	422.2	.0	-261.6	-287.5	25.9	1,492.4	1,246.5	245.9
III	1,778.4	-125.5	263.4	-48.8	312.2	.0	-388.9	-394.3	5.4	1,903.9	1,637.9	266.0
IV	1,728.2	153.3	448.9	70.8	358.1	20.0	-295.6	-293.2	-2.5	1,574.9	1,318.9	256.0
2006: I	1,875.5	300.7	484.7	84.5	420.2	-20.0	-184.0	-219.6	35.6	1,574.8	1,314.8	260.1
II	1,865.7	262.9	460.0	30.0	430.0	.0	-197.0	-239.9	42.8	1,602.8	1,337.2	265.6
III	1,811.6	182.8	409.7	-1.4	411.1	.0	-226.9	-239.2	12.3	1,628.8	1,358.7	270.1
IV	1,914.9	260.5	434.4	42.0	342.4	50.0	-173.9	-181.5	7.6	1,654.4	1,379.3	275.1
2007: I	1,879.4	208.5	432.8	97.0	335.8	.0	-224.3	-218.5	-5.8	1,670.9	1,389.6	281.3
II	1,913.6	230.2	423.5	30.5	368.0	25.0	-193.4	-206.8	13.4	1,683.4	1,397.4	286.0
III	1,871.7	180.8	426.4	56.7	344.7	25.0	-245.6	-232.6	-13.0	1,690.9	1,400.9	290.0

[1] With inventory valuation and capital consumption adjustments.

See next page for continuation of table.

[Billions of dollars, except as noted; quarterly data at seasonally adjusted annual rates]

Year or quarter	Gross domestic investment, capital account transactions, and net lending, NIPA [2]							Addenda:						
	Gross domestic investment			Capital account transactions (net) [4]	Net lending or net borrowing (−), NIPA [2,5]	Statistical discrepancy	Gross private saving	Gross government saving			Net domestic investment	Gross saving as a percent of gross national income	Net saving as a percent of gross national income
	Total	Total	Gross private domestic investment	Gross government investment [3]					Total	Federal	State and local			
1959	106.7	107.8	78.5	29.3	....	−1.2	0.5	84.6	21.6	13.6	8.0	54.8	20.9	10.4
1960	110.4	107.2	78.9	28.3	....	3.2	−.9	84.8	26.5	17.8	8.7	51.6	21.0	10.5
1961	113.8	109.5	78.2	31.3	....	4.3	−.6	91.8	22.5	13.5	9.0	52.3	20.8	10.4
1962	125.3	121.4	88.1	33.3	....	3.9	.4	100.7	24.3	14.0	10.3	62.2	21.2	11.1
1963	132.4	127.4	93.8	33.6	....	5.0	−.8	104.6	28.6	17.5	11.1	65.0	21.4	11.4
1964	144.2	136.7	102.1	34.6	....	7.5	.8	117.9	25.5	13.4	12.1	71.7	21.5	11.7
1965	160.0	153.8	118.2	35.6	....	6.2	1.6	129.7	28.8	16.0	12.8	84.4	21.9	12.3
1966	175.0	171.1	131.3	39.8	....	3.9	6.3	138.6	30.1	15.5	14.6	95.5	21.4	11.8
1967	175.1	171.6	128.6	43.0	....	3.6	4.6	151.3	19.2	4.7	14.5	90.1	20.5	10.7
1968	186.6	184.8	141.2	43.6	....	1.7	4.6	153.7	28.3	12.5	15.8	96.5	20.0	10.3
1969	201.5	199.7	156.4	43.3	....	1.8	3.2	156.8	41.5	24.2	17.3	101.8	20.1	10.2
1970	200.0	196.0	152.4	43.6	....	4.0	7.3	174.1	18.6	.9	17.7	89.3	18.6	8.3
1971	220.5	219.9	178.2	41.8	....	.6	11.6	202.5	6.4	−11.9	18.3	104.9	18.6	8.4
1972	246.6	250.2	207.6	42.6	....	−3.6	9.1	216.8	20.7	−7.7	28.5	123.7	19.2	9.0
1973	300.7	291.3	244.5	46.8	....	9.3	8.6	256.3	35.8	5.8	30.0	152.1	21.1	11.0
1974	312.3	305.7	249.4	56.3	....	6.6	10.9	270.0	31.5	4.5	27.0	143.2	20.0	9.2
1975	314.7	293.3	230.2	63.1	....	21.4	17.7	323.6	−26.6	−49.3	22.7	105.6	18.2	6.7
1976	367.2	358.4	292.0	66.4	....	8.9	25.1	343.8	−1.7	−30.3	28.6	153.2	18.8	7.5
1977	419.8	428.8	361.3	67.5	....	−9.0	22.3	382.8	14.7	−21.0	35.7	198.8	19.6	8.3
1978	504.6	515.0	438.0	77.1	....	−10.4	26.6	436.3	41.7	−1.5	43.2	252.7	20.9	9.4
1979	582.8	581.4	492.9	88.5	....	1.4	46.0	480.5	56.2	15.7	40.5	281.2	21.1	9.3
1980	590.9	579.5	479.3	100.3	....	11.4	41.4	532.4	17.0	−23.6	40.6	236.6	19.7	7.4
1981	685.6	679.3	572.4	106.9	....	6.3	30.9	630.3	24.4	−19.4	43.9	291.2	20.9	8.5
1982	629.4	629.5	517.2	112.3	−0.2	.0	.3	686.0	−56.9	−94.2	37.3	202.6	19.1	6.1
1983	655.1	687.2	564.3	122.9	−.2	−31.8	45.7	695.8	−86.5	−132.3	45.8	243.4	17.3	4.7
1984	788.0	875.0	735.6	139.4	−.2	−86.7	14.6	830.6	−57.2	−123.5	66.3	402.4	19.6	7.6
1985	784.1	895.0	736.2	158.8	−.3	−110.5	16.7	827.3	−59.9	−126.9	67.0	388.3	18.1	6.2
1986	780.5	919.7	746.5	173.2	−.3	−138.9	47.0	803.9	−70.4	−139.2	68.8	388.4	16.5	4.6
1987	818.5	969.2	785.0	184.3	−.4	−150.4	21.7	822.7	−25.9	−89.8	63.9	407.3	16.8	5.0
1988	895.5	1,007.7	821.6	186.1	−.5	−111.7	−19.5	917.5	−2.5	−75.2	72.7	410.1	17.8	6.2
1989	984.3	1,072.6	874.9	197.7	−.3	−88.0	39.7	931.8	12.9	−66.7	79.6	428.4	17.3	5.5
1990	1,006.7	1,076.7	861.0	215.7	6.6	−76.6	66.2	974.3	−33.8	−104.1	70.3	394.2	16.3	4.5
1991	1,036.6	1,023.2	802.9	220.3	4.5	9.0	72.5	1,042.9	−78.8	−141.5	62.7	297.3	16.2	4.0
1992	1,051.0	1,087.9	864.8	223.1	.6	−37.5	102.7	1,100.4	−152.1	−222.7	70.6	336.0	15.1	3.1
1993	1,102.0	1,172.4	953.4	219.0	1.3	−71.7	139.5	1,083.3	−120.8	−195.5	74.7	395.9	14.7	2.8
1994	1,213.2	1,318.4	1,097.1	221.4	1.7	−106.9	142.5	1,114.0	−43.2	−132.2	88.9	484.7	15.4	3.4
1995	1,285.7	1,376.7	1,144.0	232.7	.9	−91.9	101.2	1,204.5	−19.9	−115.1	95.2	498.4	16.2	4.2
1996	1,384.8	1,485.2	1,240.3	244.9	.7	−101.0	93.7	1,237.8	53.3	−59.7	113.0	567.1	16.6	4.8
1997	1,531.7	1,641.9	1,389.8	252.2	1.0	−111.3	70.7	1,303.6	157.5	26.7	130.7	667.5	17.7	5.9
1998	1,584.1	1,771.5	1,509.1	262.4	.7	−188.1	−14.6	1,328.9	269.8	121.6	148.2	741.3	18.2	6.5
1999	1,638.5	1,912.4	1,625.7	286.8	4.8	−278.7	−35.7	1,333.3	341.0	188.5	152.5	811.2	17.9	6.1
2000	1,643.3	2,040.0	1,735.5	304.5	.8	−397.4	−127.2	1,334.1	436.4	276.6	159.8	852.1	17.7	5.8
2001	1,567.9	1,938.3	1,614.3	324.0	1.1	−371.5	−89.6	1,400.1	257.5	134.9	122.6	656.9	16.2	3.7
2002	1,468.1	1,926.4	1,582.1	344.3	1.4	−459.7	−21.0	1,559.6	−70.5	−159.1	88.6	634.4	14.2	1.9
2003	1,507.8	2,020.0	1,664.1	356.0	3.2	−515.5	48.8	1,633.3	−174.3	−281.7	107.4	683.5	13.3	1.1
2004	1,637.3	2,261.4	1,888.6	372.8	2.4	−626.5	19.1	1,757.0	−138.9	−276.6	137.7	825.3	13.8	1.5
2005	1,739.9	2,475.0	2,077.2	397.8	4.1	−739.1	5.4	1,785.2	−50.6	−219.2	168.6	865.5	13.9	1.0
2006	1,848.8	2,642.9	2,209.2	433.8	3.9	−798.0	−18.1	1,794.6	72.3	−114.6	186.9	1,027.7	14.1	1.9
2004: I	1,590.5	2,129.9	1,769.6	360.3	1.9	−541.3	38.0	1,748.7	−196.3	−319.1	122.9	756.2	13.5	1.6
II	1,630.8	2,247.1	1,875.6	371.5	1.7	−618.0	40.8	1,738.6	−148.6	−280.4	131.8	852.8	13.7	1.7
III	1,688.2	2,307.5	1,929.7	377.8	3.8	−623.0	10.0	1,820.2	−141.9	−267.6	125.7	773.0	14.2	1.2
IV	1,639.5	2,361.2	1,979.5	381.6	2.0	−723.6	−12.2	1,720.7	−68.9	−239.3	170.4	919.2	13.7	1.7
2005: I	1,699.9	2,414.4	2,029.6	384.7	10.4	−724.9	−11.1	1,735.3	−24.3	−200.8	176.5	947.7	14.0	2.0
II	1,710.4	2,420.5	2,024.7	395.8	2.0	−712.2	−10.3	1,736.5	−15.7	−189.5	173.8	928.1	13.9	1.8
III	1,805.6	2,480.3	2,078.5	401.7	1.9	−676.6	27.2	1,901.3	−122.9	−294.6	171.7	576.4	14.1	−1.0
IV	1,743.8	2,584.8	2,176.0	408.8	1.9	−842.9	15.7	1,767.8	−39.7	−192.0	152.4	1,009.9	13.6	1.2
2006: I	1,854.7	2,640.9	2,221.1	419.8	6.9	−793.2	−20.9	1,799.5	76.1	−116.4	192.5	1,066.1	14.4	2.3
II	1,863.2	2,674.9	2,239.0	435.9	4.0	−815.7	−2.6	1,797.1	68.6	−135.2	203.8	1,072.1	14.1	2.0
III	1,809.1	2,659.2	2,224.1	435.1	2.2	−852.2	−2.5	1,768.4	43.2	−132.9	176.2	1,030.4	13.6	1.4
IV	1,868.3	2,596.7	2,152.4	444.2	2.5	−730.9	−46.6	1,813.7	101.2	−74.0	175.2	942.3	14.2	1.9
2007: I	1,813.1	2,569.2	2,117.3	451.8	1.6	−757.7	−66.3	1,822.5	56.9	−110.0	166.9	898.3	13.7	1.5
II	1,872.8	2,603.4	2,139.1	464.3	1.7	−732.3	−40.8	1,820.9	92.7	−96.6	189.3	919.9	13.8	1.7
III	1,946.5	2,637.4	2,162.9	474.4	1.6	−692.4	74.8	1,827.3	44.4	−121.7	166.0	946.5	13.4	1.3

[2] National income and product accounts (NIPA).
[3] For details on government investment, see Table B–20.
[4] Consists of capital transfers and the acquisition and disposal of nonproduced nonfinancial assets.
[5] Prior to 1982, equals the balance on current account, NIPA (see Table B–24).

Source: Department of Commerce (Bureau of Economic Analysis).

TABLE B–33.—*Median money income (in 2006 dollars) and poverty status of families and people, by race, selected years, 1993–2006*

Year	Families[1] Number (millions)	Median money income (in 2006 dollars)[2]	Below poverty level Total Number (millions)	Total Percent	Female householder Number (millions)	Female householder Percent	People below poverty level Number (millions)	Percent	Median money income (in 2006 dollars) of people 15 years old and over with income[2] Males All people	Males Year-round full-time workers	Females All people	Females Year-round full-time workers
ALL RACES												
1993	68.5	$50,782	8.4	12.3	4.4	35.6	39.3	15.1	$28,994	$42,700	$15,177	$30,873
1994	69.3	52,173	8.1	11.6	4.2	34.6	38.1	14.5	29,220	42,528	15,425	31,298
1995	69.6	53,349	7.5	10.8	4.1	32.4	36.4	13.8	29,639	42,299	15,935	31,235
1996	70.2	54,127	7.7	11.0	4.2	32.6	36.5	13.7	30,498	42,915	16,398	31,907
1997	70.9	55,823	7.3	10.3	4.0	31.6	35.6	13.3	31,579	44,149	17,164	32,602
1998	71.6	57,734	7.2	10.0	3.8	29.9	34.5	12.7	32,725	44,782	17,825	33,174
1999[3]	73.2	59,088	6.8	9.3	3.6	27.8	32.8	11.9	33,026	45,316	18,519	33,114
2000[4]	73.8	59,398	6.4	8.7	3.3	25.4	31.6	11.3	33,185	45,534	18,807	34,098
2001	74.3	58,545	6.8	9.2	3.5	26.4	32.9	11.7	33,142	45,709	18,921	34,644
2002	75.6	57,920	7.2	9.6	3.6	26.5	34.6	12.1	32,768	45,398	18,842	34,709
2003	76.2	57,751	7.6	10.0	3.9	28.0	35.9	12.5	32,812	45,498	18,920	34,700
2004[5]	76.9	57,705	7.8	10.2	4.0	28.3	37.0	12.7	32,573	44,476	18,858	34,281
2005	77.4	58,036	7.7	9.9	4.0	28.7	37.0	12.6	32,300	43,571	19,185	34,346
2006	78.5	58,407	7.7	9.8	4.1	28.3	36.5	12.3	32,265	44,958	20,014	34,989
WHITE												
1993	57.9	53,999	5.5	9.4	2.4	29.2	26.2	12.2	30,202	43,738	15,480	31,573
1994	58.4	55,001	5.3	9.1	2.3	29.0	25.4	11.7	30,497	43,641	15,646	32,145
1995	58.9	56,023	5.0	8.5	2.2	26.6	24.4	11.2	31,390	44,027	16,179	31,875
1996	58.9	57,270	5.1	8.6	2.3	27.3	24.7	11.2	31,925	44,455	16,585	32,448
1997	59.5	58,561	5.0	8.4	2.3	27.7	24.4	11.0	32,710	45,239	17,275	33,155
1998	60.1	60,558	4.8	8.0	2.1	24.9	23.5	10.5	34,151	45,948	18,056	33,728
1999[3]	61.1	61,808	4.4	7.3	1.9	22.5	22.2	9.8	34,685	47,449	18,577	33,881
2000[4]	61.3	62,087	4.3	7.1	1.8	21.2	21.6	9.5	34,887	47,129	18,826	35,067
2001	61.6	61,574	4.6	7.4	1.9	22.4	22.7	9.9	34,439	46,454	18,964	35,132
Alone[6]												
2002	62.3	61,229	4.9	7.8	2.0	22.6	23.5	10.2	34,052	46,371	18,871	35,191
2003	62.6	61,136	5.1	8.1	2.2	24.0	24.3	10.5	33,690	46,199	19,099	35,291
2004[5]	63.1	60,547	5.3	8.4	2.3	24.7	25.3	10.8	33,458	45,467	18,892	34,937
2005	63.4	61,262	5.1	8.0	2.3	25.3	24.9	10.6	33,234	45,129	19,281	35,218
2006	64.1	61,280	5.1	8.0	2.4	25.1	24.4	10.3	33,843	45,933	20,082	35,525
Alone or in combination[6]												
2002	63.0	61,023	5.0	7.9	2.1	22.6	24.1	10.3	33,976	46,305	18,834	35,178
2003	63.5	60,956	5.2	8.1	2.2	24.2	25.0	10.6	33,609	46,130	19,065	35,278
2004[5]	64.0	60,399	5.4	8.5	2.3	24.8	26.1	10.9	33,384	45,350	18,860	34,897
2005	64.3	61,062	5.2	8.1	2.4	25.5	25.6	10.7	33,156	44,969	19,229	35,145
2006	65.0	61,198	5.2	8.0	2.4	25.0	25.2	10.4	33,673	45,868	20,039	35,490
BLACK												
1993	8.0	29,599	2.5	31.3	1.9	49.9	10.9	33.1	20,067	32,380	13,064	27,913
1994	8.1	33,226	2.2	27.3	1.7	46.2	10.2	30.6	20,155	32,832	14,185	27,751
1995	8.1	34,116	2.1	26.4	1.7	45.1	9.9	29.3	21,027	32,576	14,399	27,691
1996	8.5	33,938	2.2	26.1	1.7	43.7	9.7	28.4	21,102	34,723	15,063	28,138
1997	8.4	35,825	2.0	23.6	1.6	39.8	9.1	26.5	22,666	33,690	16,343	28,513
1998	8.5	36,323	2.0	23.4	1.6	40.8	9.1	26.1	23,867	33,936	16,228	29,479
1999[3]	8.7	38,540	1.9	21.8	1.5	39.2	8.4	23.6	24,735	36,488	17,880	30,422
2000[4]	8.7	39,428	1.7	19.3	1.3	34.3	8.0	22.5	24,999	35,697	18,594	30,149
2001	8.8	38,263	1.8	20.7	1.4	35.2	8.1	22.7	24,446	36,353	18,543	31,087
Alone[6]												
2002	8.9	37,573	1.9	21.5	1.4	35.8	8.6	24.1	24,164	35,788	18,749	30,960
2003	8.9	37,677	2.0	22.3	1.5	36.9	8.8	24.4	24,102	36,647	18,177	30,281
2004[5]	8.9	37,517	2.0	22.8	1.5	37.6	9.0	24.7	24,220	33,858	18,529	31,110
2005	9.1	36,627	2.0	22.1	1.5	36.1	9.2	24.9	23,396	35,355	18,209	31,359
2006	9.3	38,269	2.0	21.6	1.5	36.6	9.0	24.3	25,064	35,477	19,103	30,936
Alone or in combination[6]												
2002	9.1	37,695	2.0	21.4	1.5	35.7	8.9	23.9	24,106	35,826	18,684	31,048
2003	9.1	37,938	2.0	22.1	1.5	36.8	9.1	24.3	24,046	36,685	18,132	30,339
2004[5]	9.1	37,702	2.1	22.8	1.5	37.6	9.4	24.7	24,244	33,849	18,516	31,161
2005	9.3	36,761	2.1	22.0	1.5	36.2	9.5	24.7	23,350	35,263	18,172	31,362
2006	9.5	38,520	2.0	21.5	1.5	36.4	9.4	24.2	25,075	35,510	19,065	30,984

[1] The term "family" refers to a group of two or more persons related by birth, marriage, or adoption and residing together. Every family must include a reference person.

[2] Current dollar median money income adjusted by consumer price index research series (CPI-U-RS).

[3] Reflects implementation of Census 2000-based population controls comparable with succeeding years.

[4] Reflects household sample expansion.

[5] For 2004, figures are revised to reflect a correction to the weights in the 2005 Annual Social and Economic Supplement.

[6] For white alone, for white alone or in combination, for black alone, and for black alone or in combination. (Black is also black or African American.) Beginning with data for 2002 the Current Population Survey allowed respondents to choose more than one race; for earlier years respondents could report only one race group.

Note.—Poverty thresholds are updated each year to reflect changes in the consumer price index (CPI-U).
For details see publication Series P-60 on the Current Population Survey and Annual Social and Economic Supplements.

Source: Department of Commerce (Bureau of the Census).

TABLE B–34.—*Population by age group, 1929–2007*

[Thousands of persons]

July 1	Total	Age (years)						
		Under 5	5-15	16-19	20-24	25-44	45-64	65 and over
1929	121,767	11,734	26,800	9,127	10,694	35,862	21,076	6,474
1933	125,579	10,612	26,897	9,302	11,152	37,319	22,933	7,363
1939	130,880	10,418	25,179	9,822	11,519	39,354	25,823	8,764
1940	132,122	10,579	24,811	9,895	11,690	39,868	26,249	9,031
1941	133,402	10,850	24,516	9,840	11,807	40,383	26,718	9,288
1942	134,860	11,301	24,231	9,730	11,955	40,861	27,196	9,584
1943	136,739	12,016	24,093	9,607	12,064	41,420	27,671	9,867
1944	138,397	12,524	23,949	9,561	12,062	42,016	28,138	10,147
1945	139,928	12,979	23,907	9,361	12,036	42,521	28,630	10,494
1946	141,389	13,244	24,103	9,119	12,004	43,027	29,064	10,828
1947	144,126	14,406	24,468	9,097	11,814	43,657	29,498	11,185
1948	146,631	14,919	25,209	8,952	11,794	44,288	29,931	11,538
1949	149,188	15,607	25,852	8,788	11,700	44,916	30,405	11,921
1950	152,271	16,410	26,721	8,542	11,680	45,672	30,849	12,397
1951	154,878	17,333	27,279	8,446	11,552	46,103	31,362	12,803
1952	157,553	17,312	28,894	8,414	11,350	46,495	31,884	13,203
1953	160,184	17,638	30,227	8,460	11,062	46,786	32,394	13,617
1954	163,026	18,057	31,480	8,637	10,832	47,001	32,942	14,076
1955	165,931	18,566	32,682	8,744	10,714	47,194	33,506	14,525
1956	168,903	19,003	33,994	8,916	10,616	47,379	34,057	14,938
1957	171,984	19,494	35,272	9,195	10,603	47,440	34,591	15,388
1958	174,882	19,887	36,445	9,543	10,756	47,337	35,109	15,806
1959	177,830	20,175	37,368	10,215	10,969	47,192	35,663	16,248
1960	180,671	20,341	38,494	10,683	11,134	47,140	36,203	16,675
1961	183,691	20,522	39,765	11,025	11,483	47,084	36,722	17,089
1962	186,538	20,469	41,205	11,180	11,959	47,013	37,255	17,457
1963	189,242	20,342	41,626	12,007	12,714	46,994	37,782	17,778
1964	191,889	20,165	42,297	12,736	13,269	46,958	38,338	18,127
1965	194,303	19,824	42,938	13,516	13,746	46,912	38,916	18,451
1966	196,560	19,208	43,702	14,311	14,050	47,001	39,534	18,755
1967	198,712	18,563	44,244	14,200	15,248	47,194	40,193	19,071
1968	200,706	17,913	44,622	14,452	15,786	47,721	40,846	19,365
1969	202,677	17,376	44,840	14,800	16,480	48,064	41,437	19,680
1970	205,052	17,166	44,816	15,289	17,202	48,473	41,999	20,107
1971	207,661	17,244	44,591	15,688	18,159	48,936	42,482	20,561
1972	209,896	17,101	44,203	16,039	18,153	50,482	42,898	21,020
1973	211,909	16,851	43,582	16,446	18,521	51,749	43,235	21,525
1974	213,854	16,487	42,989	16,769	18,975	53,051	43,522	22,061
1975	215,973	16,121	42,508	17,017	19,527	54,302	43,801	22,696
1976	218,035	15,617	42,099	17,194	19,986	55,852	44,008	23,278
1977	220,239	15,564	41,298	17,276	20,499	57,561	44,150	23,892
1978	222,585	15,735	40,428	17,288	20,946	59,400	44,286	24,502
1979	225,055	16,063	39,552	17,242	21,297	61,379	44,390	25,134
1980	227,726	16,451	38,838	17,167	21,590	63,470	44,504	25,707
1981	229,966	16,893	38,144	16,812	21,869	65,528	44,500	26,221
1982	232,188	17,228	37,784	16,332	21,902	67,692	44,462	26,787
1983	234,307	17,547	37,526	15,823	21,844	69,733	44,474	27,361
1984	236,348	17,695	37,461	15,295	21,737	71,735	44,547	27,878
1985	238,466	17,842	37,450	15,005	21,478	73,674	44,602	28,416
1986	240,651	17,963	37,404	15,024	20,942	75,651	44,660	29,008
1987	242,804	18,052	37,333	15,215	20,385	77,338	44,854	29,626
1988	245,021	18,195	37,593	15,198	19,846	78,595	45,471	30,124
1989	247,342	18,508	37,972	14,913	19,442	79,943	45,882	30,682
1990	250,132	18,856	38,632	14,466	19,323	81,291	46,316	31,247
1991	253,493	19,208	39,349	13,992	19,414	82,844	46,874	31,812
1992	256,894	19,528	40,161	13,781	19,314	83,201	48,553	32,356
1993	260,255	19,729	40,904	13,953	19,101	83,766	49,899	32,902
1994	263,436	19,777	41,689	14,228	18,758	84,334	51,318	33,331
1995	266,557	19,627	42,510	14,522	18,391	84,933	52,806	33,769
1996	269,667	19,408	43,172	15,057	17,965	85,527	54,396	34,143
1997	272,912	19,233	43,833	15,433	17,992	85,737	56,283	34,402
1998	276,115	19,145	44,332	15,856	18,250	85,663	58,249	34,619
1999	279,295	19,136	44,755	16,164	18,672	85,408	60,362	34,798
2000 [1]	282,430	19,188	45,159	16,217	19,195	85,171	62,421	35,078
2001 [1]	285,454	19,354	45,202	16,269	19,896	84,973	64,426	35,333
2002 [1]	288,427	19,544	45,177	16,335	20,451	84,744	66,582	35,594
2003 [1]	291,289	19,783	45,117	16,393	20,887	84,486	68,667	35,958
2004 [1]	294,056	20,070	44,978	16,547	21,107	84,331	70,712	36,309
2005 [1]	296,940	20,315	44,827	16,690	21,202	84,256	72,862	36,787
2006 [1]	299,801	20,418	44,665	17,010	21,252	84,312	74,884	37,260
2007	302,045							

[1] Revised total population data are available as follows: 2000, 282,407; 2001, 285,339; 2002, 288,189; 2003, 290,941; 2004, 293,609; 2005, 296,329; and 2006, 299,157.

Note.—Includes Armed Forces overseas beginning with 1940. Includes Alaska and Hawaii beginning with 1950.
All estimates are consistent with decennial census enumerations.

Source: Department of Commerce (Bureau of the Census).

[Monthly data seasonally adjusted, except as noted]

Year or month	Civilian noninsti-tutional population [1]	Civilian labor force						Not in labor force	Civilian labor force participa-tion rate [2]	Civilian employ-ment/population ratio [3]	Unemploy-ment rate, civilian workers [4]
		Total	Employment				Un-employ-ment				
			Total	Agricultural	Non-agricultural						
		Thousands of persons 14 years of age and over								Percent	
1929		49,180	47,630	10,450	37,180		1,550				3.2
1933		51,590	38,760	10,090	28,670		12,830				24.9
1939		55,230	45,750	9,610	36,140		9,480				17.2
1940	99,840	55,640	47,520	9,540	37,980		8,120	44,200	55.7	47.6	14.6
1941	99,900	55,910	50,350	9,100	41,250		5,560	43,990	56.0	50.4	9.9
1942	98,640	56,410	53,750	9,250	44,500		2,660	42,230	57.2	54.5	4.7
1943	94,640	55,540	54,470	9,080	45,390		1,070	39,100	58.7	57.6	1.9
1944	93,220	54,630	53,960	8,950	45,010		670	38,590	58.6	57.9	1.2
1945	94,090	53,860	52,820	8,580	44,240		1,040	40,230	57.2	56.1	1.9
1946	103,070	57,520	55,250	8,320	46,930		2,270	45,550	55.8	53.6	3.9
1947	106,018	60,168	57,812	8,256	49,557		2,356	45,850	56.8	54.5	3.9
		Thousands of persons 16 years of age and over									
1947	101,827	59,350	57,038	7,890	49,148		2,311	42,477	58.3	56.0	3.9
1948	103,068	60,621	58,343	7,629	50,714		2,276	42,447	58.8	56.6	3.8
1949	103,994	61,286	57,651	7,658	49,993		3,637	42,708	58.9	55.4	5.9
1950	104,995	62,208	58,918	7,160	51,758		3,288	42,787	59.2	56.1	5.3
1951	104,621	62,017	59,961	6,726	53,235		2,055	42,604	59.2	57.3	3.3
1952	105,231	62,138	60,250	6,500	53,749		1,883	43,093	59.0	57.3	3.0
1953 [5]	107,056	63,015	61,179	6,260	54,919		1,834	44,041	58.9	57.1	2.9
1954	108,321	63,643	60,109	6,205	53,904		3,532	44,678	58.8	55.5	5.5
1955	109,683	65,023	62,170	6,450	55,722		2,852	44,660	59.3	56.7	4.4
1956	110,954	66,552	63,799	6,283	57,514		2,750	44,402	60.0	57.5	4.1
1957	112,265	66,929	64,071	5,947	58,123		2,859	45,336	59.6	57.1	4.3
1958	113,727	67,639	63,036	5,586	57,450		4,602	46,088	59.5	55.4	6.8
1959	115,329	68,369	64,630	5,565	59,065		3,740	46,960	59.3	56.0	5.5
1960 [5]	117,245	69,628	65,778	5,458	60,318		3,852	47,617	59.4	56.1	5.5
1961	118,771	70,459	65,746	5,200	60,546		4,714	48,312	59.3	55.4	6.7
1962 [5]	120,153	70,614	66,702	4,944	61,759		3,911	49,539	58.8	55.5	5.5
1963	122,416	71,833	67,762	4,687	63,076		4,070	50,583	58.7	55.4	5.7
1964	124,485	73,091	69,305	4,523	64,782		3,786	51,394	58.7	55.7	5.2
1965	126,513	74,455	71,088	4,361	66,726		3,366	52,058	58.9	56.2	4.5
1966	128,058	75,770	72,895	3,979	68,915		2,875	52,288	59.2	56.9	3.8
1967	129,874	77,347	74,372	3,844	70,527		2,975	52,527	59.6	57.3	3.8
1968	132,028	78,737	75,920	3,817	72,103		2,817	53,291	59.6	57.5	3.6
1969	134,335	80,734	77,902	3,606	74,296		2,832	53,602	60.1	58.0	3.5
1970	137,085	82,771	78,678	3,463	75,215		4,093	54,315	60.4	57.4	4.9
1971	140,216	84,382	79,367	3,394	75,972		5,016	55,834	60.2	56.6	5.9
1972 [5]	144,126	87,034	82,153	3,484	78,669		4,882	57,091	60.4	57.0	5.6
1973 [5]	147,096	89,429	85,064	3,470	81,594		4,365	57,667	60.8	57.8	4.9
1974	150,120	91,949	86,794	3,515	83,279		5,156	58,171	61.3	57.8	5.6
1975	153,153	93,775	85,846	3,408	82,438		7,929	59,377	61.2	56.1	8.5
1976	156,150	96,158	88,752	3,331	85,421		7,406	59,991	61.6	56.8	7.7
1977	159,033	99,009	92,017	3,283	88,734		6,991	60,025	62.3	57.9	7.1
1978 [5]	161,910	102,251	96,048	3,387	92,661		6,202	59,659	63.2	59.3	6.1
1979	164,863	104,962	98,824	3,347	95,477		6,137	59,900	63.7	59.9	5.8
1980	167,745	106,940	99,303	3,364	95,938		7,637	60,806	63.8	59.2	7.1
1981	170,130	108,670	100,397	3,368	97,030		8,273	61,460	63.9	59.0	7.6
1982	172,271	110,204	99,526	3,401	96,125		10,678	62,067	64.0	57.8	9.7
1983	174,215	111,550	100,834	3,383	97,450		10,717	62,665	64.0	57.9	9.6
1984	176,383	113,544	105,005	3,321	101,685		8,539	62,839	64.4	59.5	7.5
1985	178,206	115,461	107,150	3,179	103,971		8,312	62,744	64.8	60.1	7.2
1986 [5]	180,587	117,834	109,597	3,163	106,434		8,237	62,752	65.3	60.7	7.0
1987	182,753	119,865	112,440	3,208	109,232		7,425	62,888	65.6	61.5	6.2
1988	184,613	121,669	114,968	3,169	111,800		6,701	62,944	65.9	62.3	5.5
1989	186,393	123,869	117,342	3,199	114,142		6,528	62,523	66.5	63.0	5.3
1990 [5]	189,164	125,840	118,793	3,223	115,570		7,047	63,324	66.5	62.8	5.6
1991	190,925	126,346	117,718	3,269	114,449		8,628	64,578	66.2	61.7	6.8
1992	192,805	128,105	118,492	3,247	115,245		9,613	64,700	66.4	61.5	7.5
1993	194,838	129,200	120,259	3,115	117,144		8,940	65,638	66.3	61.7	6.9
1994 [5]	196,814	131,056	123,060	3,409	119,651		7,996	65,758	66.6	62.5	6.1
1995	198,584	132,304	124,900	3,440	121,460		7,404	66,280	66.6	62.9	5.6
1996	200,591	133,943	126,708	3,443	123,264		7,236	66,647	66.8	63.2	5.4
1997 [5]	203,133	136,297	129,558	3,399	126,159		6,739	66,837	67.1	63.8	4.9
1998 [5]	205,220	137,673	131,463	3,378	128,085		6,210	67,547	67.1	64.1	4.5
1999 [5]	207,753	139,368	133,488	3,281	130,207		5,880	68,385	67.1	64.3	4.2

[1] Not seasonally adjusted.
[2] Civilian labor force as percent of civilian noninstitutional population.
[3] Civilian employment as percent of civilian noninstitutional population.
[4] Unemployed as percent of civilian labor force.

See next page for continuation of table.

[Monthly data seasonally adjusted, except as noted]

Year or month	Civilian noninstitutional population [1]	Civilian labor force					Not in labor force	Civilian labor force participation rate [2]	Civilian employment/ population ratio [3]	Unemployment rate, civilian workers [4]
		Total	Employment			Unemployment				
			Total	Agricultural	Nonagricultural					
	Thousands of persons 16 years of age and over							Percent		
2000 [5,6]	212,577	142,583	136,891	2,464	134,427	5,692	69,994	67.1	64.4	4.0
2001	215,092	143,734	136,933	2,299	134,635	6,801	71,359	66.8	63.7	4.7
2002	217,570	144,863	136,485	2,311	134,174	8,378	72,707	66.6	62.7	5.8
2003 [5]	221,168	146,510	137,736	2,275	135,461	8,774	74,658	66.2	62.3	6.0
2004 [5]	223,357	147,401	139,252	2,232	137,020	8,149	75,956	66.0	62.3	5.5
2005 [5]	226,082	149,320	141,730	2,197	139,532	7,591	76,762	66.0	62.7	5.1
2006 [5]	228,815	151,428	144,427	2,206	142,221	7,001	77,387	66.2	63.1	4.6
2007 [5]	231,867	153,124	146,047	2,095	143,952	7,078	78,743	66.0	63.0	4.6
2004: Jan [5]	222,161	146,830	138,463	2,198	136,219	8,367	75,331	66.1	62.3	5.7
Feb	222,357	146,692	138,529	2,212	136,341	8,162	75,665	66.0	62.3	5.6
Mar	222,550	146,906	138,421	2,180	136,291	8,484	75,644	66.0	62.2	5.8
Apr	222,757	146,839	138,674	2,240	136,481	8,165	75,918	65.9	62.3	5.6
May	222,967	147,058	138,848	2,298	136,553	8,210	75,909	66.0	62.3	5.6
June	223,196	147,454	139,174	2,238	136,746	8,280	75,742	66.1	62.4	5.6
July	223,422	147,706	139,565	2,216	137,365	8,140	75,716	66.1	62.5	5.5
Aug	223,677	147,585	139,585	2,335	137,240	7,999	76,092	66.0	62.4	5.4
Sept	223,941	147,442	139,500	2,248	137,345	7,943	76,499	65.8	62.3	5.4
Oct	224,192	147,816	139,756	2,214	137,613	8,060	76,376	65.9	62.3	5.5
Nov	224,422	148,180	140,245	2,206	137,987	7,935	76,241	66.0	62.5	5.4
Dec	224,640	148,087	140,138	2,179	137,940	7,949	76,553	65.9	62.4	5.4
2005: Jan [5]	224,837	147,981	140,224	2,115	138,099	7,757	76,856	65.8	62.4	5.2
Feb	225,041	148,308	140,354	2,134	138,198	7,954	76,733	65.9	62.4	5.4
Mar	225,236	148,295	140,563	2,183	138,402	7,732	76,942	65.8	62.4	5.2
Apr	225,441	148,912	141,244	2,240	139,037	7,669	76,528	66.1	62.7	5.1
May	225,670	149,276	141,597	2,220	139,364	7,679	76,394	66.1	62.7	5.1
June	225,911	149,244	141,708	2,308	139,236	7,536	76,667	66.1	62.7	5.0
July	226,153	149,479	142,055	2,299	139,804	7,424	76,674	66.1	62.8	5.0
Aug	226,421	149,826	142,457	2,184	140,306	7,369	76,595	66.2	62.9	4.9
Sept	226,693	150,022	142,429	2,176	140,337	7,593	76,671	66.2	62.8	5.1
Oct	226,959	150,061	142,613	2,184	140,483	7,449	76,897	66.1	62.8	5.0
Nov	227,204	150,099	142,564	2,175	140,357	7,535	77,105	66.1	62.7	5.0
Dec	227,425	150,041	142,778	2,111	140,643	7,262	77,384	66.0	62.8	4.8
2006: Jan [5]	227,553	150,111	143,086	2,169	140,901	7,025	77,442	66.0	62.9	4.7
Feb	227,763	150,505	143,362	2,193	141,118	7,143	77,258	66.1	62.9	4.7
Mar	227,975	150,694	143,619	2,165	141,451	7,075	77,280	66.1	63.0	4.7
Apr	228,199	150,904	143,791	2,235	141,557	7,113	77,296	66.1	63.0	4.7
May	228,428	151,126	144,088	2,191	141,859	7,038	77,302	66.2	63.1	4.7
June	228,671	151,386	144,369	2,267	142,006	7,017	77,285	66.2	63.1	4.6
July	228,912	151,471	144,295	2,264	142,116	7,176	77,442	66.2	63.0	4.7
Aug	229,167	151,799	144,671	2,235	142,492	7,128	77,369	66.2	63.1	4.7
Sept	229,420	151,741	144,846	2,166	142,742	6,896	77,678	66.1	63.1	4.5
Oct	229,675	152,130	145,395	2,163	143,256	6,735	77,545	66.2	63.3	4.4
Nov	229,905	152,403	145,583	2,163	143,384	6,820	77,502	66.3	63.3	4.5
Dec	230,108	152,709	145,949	2,257	143,670	6,760	77,399	66.4	63.4	4.4
2007: Jan [5]	230,650	152,958	145,915	2,225	143,691	7,043	77,692	66.3	63.3	4.6
Feb	230,834	152,725	145,888	2,327	143,535	6,837	78,110	66.2	63.2	4.5
Mar	231,034	152,884	146,145	2,202	143,966	6,738	78,150	66.2	63.3	4.4
Apr	231,253	152,542	145,713	2,053	143,678	6,829	78,711	66.0	63.0	4.5
May	231,480	152,776	145,913	2,081	143,799	6,863	78,704	66.0	63.0	4.5
June	231,713	153,085	146,087	1,957	144,066	6,997	78,628	66.1	63.0	4.6
July	231,958	153,182	146,045	1,997	144,096	7,137	78,776	66.0	63.0	4.7
Aug	232,211	152,886	145,753	1,856	143,928	7,133	79,325	65.8	62.8	4.7
Sept	232,461	153,506	146,260	2,065	144,259	7,246	78,955	66.0	62.9	4.7
Oct	232,715	153,306	146,016	2,089	143,933	7,291	79,409	65.9	62.7	4.8
Nov	232,939	153,828	146,647	2,148	144,503	7,181	79,111	66.0	63.0	4.7
Dec	233,156	153,866	146,211	2,248	143,933	7,655	79,290	66.0	62.7	5.0

[5] Not strictly comparable with earlier data due to population adjustments or other changes. See *Employment and Earnings* for details on breaks in series.

[6] Beginning in 2000, data for agricultural employment are for agricultural and related industries; data for this series and for nonagricultural employment are not strictly comparable with data for earlier years. Because of independent seasonal adjustment for these two series, monthly data will not add to total civilian employment.

Note.—Labor force data in Tables B–35 through B–44 are based on household interviews and relate to the calendar week including the 12th of the month. For definitions of terms, area samples used, historical comparability of the data, comparability with other series, etc., see *Employment and Earnings*.

Source: Department of Labor (Bureau of Labor Statistics).

TABLE B–36.—*Civilian employment and unemployment by sex and age, 1960–2007*

[Thousands of persons 16 years of age and over; monthly data seasonally adjusted]

Year or month	Civilian employment							Unemployment						
	Total	Males			Females			Total	Males			Females		
		Total	16-19 years	20 years and over	Total	16-19 years	20 years and over		Total	16-19 years	20 years and over	Total	16-19 years	20 years and over
1960	65,778	43,904	2,361	41,543	21,874	1,768	20,105	3,852	2,486	426	2,060	1,366	286	1,080
1961	65,746	43,656	2,315	41,342	22,090	1,793	20,296	4,714	2,997	479	2,518	1,717	349	1,368
1962	66,702	44,177	2,362	41,815	22,525	1,833	20,693	3,911	2,423	408	2,016	1,488	313	1,175
1963	67,762	44,657	2,406	42,251	23,105	1,849	21,257	4,070	2,472	501	1,971	1,598	383	1,216
1964	69,305	45,474	2,587	42,886	23,831	1,929	21,903	3,786	2,205	487	1,718	1,581	385	1,195
1965	71,088	46,340	2,918	43,422	24,748	2,118	22,630	3,366	1,914	479	1,435	1,452	395	1,056
1966	72,895	46,919	3,253	43,668	25,976	2,468	23,510	2,875	1,551	432	1,120	1,324	405	921
1967	74,372	47,479	3,186	44,294	26,893	2,496	24,397	2,975	1,508	448	1,060	1,468	391	1,078
1968	75,920	48,114	3,255	44,859	27,807	2,526	25,281	2,817	1,419	426	993	1,397	412	985
1969	77,902	48,818	3,430	45,388	29,084	2,687	26,397	2,832	1,403	440	963	1,429	413	1,015
1970	78,678	48,990	3,409	45,581	29,688	2,735	26,952	4,093	2,238	599	1,638	1,855	506	1,349
1971	79,367	49,390	3,478	45,912	29,976	2,730	27,246	5,016	2,789	693	2,097	2,227	568	1,658
1972	82,153	50,896	3,765	47,130	31,257	2,980	28,276	4,882	2,659	711	1,948	2,222	598	1,625
1973	85,064	52,349	4,039	48,310	32,715	3,231	29,484	4,365	2,275	653	1,624	2,089	583	1,507
1974	86,794	53,024	4,103	48,922	33,769	3,345	30,424	5,156	2,714	757	1,957	2,441	665	1,777
1975	85,846	51,857	3,839	48,018	33,989	3,263	30,726	7,929	4,442	966	3,476	3,486	802	2,684
1976	88,752	53,138	3,947	49,190	35,615	3,389	32,226	7,406	4,036	939	3,098	3,369	780	2,588
1977	92,017	54,728	4,174	50,555	37,289	3,514	33,775	6,991	3,667	874	2,794	3,324	789	2,535
1978	96,048	56,479	4,336	52,143	39,569	3,734	35,836	6,202	3,142	813	2,328	3,061	769	2,292
1979	98,824	57,607	4,300	53,308	41,217	3,783	37,434	6,137	3,120	811	2,308	3,018	743	2,276
1980	99,303	57,186	4,085	53,101	42,117	3,625	38,492	7,637	4,267	913	3,353	3,370	755	2,615
1981	100,397	57,397	3,815	53,582	43,000	3,411	39,590	8,273	4,577	962	3,615	3,696	800	2,895
1982	99,526	56,271	3,379	52,891	43,256	3,170	40,086	10,678	6,179	1,090	5,089	4,499	886	3,613
1983	100,834	56,787	3,300	53,487	44,047	3,043	41,004	10,717	6,260	1,003	5,257	4,457	825	3,632
1984	105,005	59,091	3,322	55,769	45,915	3,122	42,793	8,539	4,744	812	3,932	3,794	687	3,107
1985	107,150	59,891	3,328	56,562	47,259	3,105	44,154	8,312	4,521	806	3,715	3,791	661	3,129
1986	109,597	60,892	3,323	57,569	48,706	3,149	45,556	8,237	4,530	779	3,751	3,707	675	3,032
1987	112,440	62,107	3,381	58,726	50,334	3,260	47,074	7,425	4,101	732	3,369	3,324	616	2,709
1988	114,968	63,273	3,492	59,781	51,696	3,313	48,383	6,701	3,655	667	2,987	3,046	558	2,487
1989	117,342	64,315	3,477	60,837	53,027	3,282	49,745	6,528	3,525	658	2,867	3,003	536	2,467
1990	118,793	65,104	3,427	61,678	53,689	3,154	50,535	7,047	3,906	667	3,239	3,140	544	2,596
1991	117,718	64,223	3,044	61,178	53,496	2,862	50,634	8,628	4,946	751	4,195	3,683	608	3,074
1992	118,492	64,440	2,944	61,496	54,052	2,724	51,328	9,613	5,523	806	4,717	4,090	621	3,469
1993	120,259	65,349	2,994	62,355	54,910	2,811	52,099	8,940	5,055	768	4,287	3,885	597	3,288
1994	123,060	66,450	3,156	63,294	56,610	3,005	53,606	7,996	4,367	740	3,627	3,629	580	3,049
1995	124,900	67,377	3,292	64,085	57,523	3,127	54,396	7,404	3,983	744	3,239	3,421	602	2,819
1996	126,708	68,207	3,310	64,897	58,501	3,190	55,311	7,236	3,880	733	3,146	3,356	573	2,783
1997	129,558	69,685	3,401	66,284	59,873	3,260	56,613	6,739	3,577	694	2,882	3,162	577	2,585
1998	131,463	70,693	3,558	67,135	60,771	3,493	57,278	6,210	3,266	686	2,580	2,944	519	2,424
1999	133,488	71,446	3,685	67,761	62,042	3,487	58,555	5,880	3,066	633	2,433	2,814	529	2,285
2000	136,891	73,305	3,671	69,634	63,586	3,519	60,067	5,692	2,975	599	2,376	2,717	483	2,235
2001	136,933	73,196	3,420	69,776	63,737	3,320	60,417	6,801	3,690	650	3,040	3,111	512	2,599
2002	136,485	72,903	3,169	69,734	63,582	3,162	60,420	8,378	4,597	700	3,896	3,781	553	3,228
2003	137,736	73,332	2,917	70,415	64,404	3,002	61,402	8,774	4,906	697	4,209	3,868	554	3,314
2004	139,252	74,524	2,952	71,572	64,728	2,955	61,773	8,149	4,456	664	3,791	3,694	543	3,150
2005	141,730	75,973	2,923	73,050	65,757	3,055	62,702	7,591	4,059	667	3,392	3,531	519	3,013
2006	144,427	77,502	3,071	74,431	66,925	3,091	63,834	7,001	3,753	622	3,131	3,247	496	2,751
2007	146,047	78,254	2,917	75,337	67,792	2,994	64,799	7,078	3,882	623	3,259	3,196	478	2,718
2006: Jan	143,086	76,867	3,017	73,850	66,219	3,058	63,161	7,025	3,679	590	3,089	3,346	505	2,841
Feb	143,362	76,970	3,056	73,913	66,392	3,110	63,282	7,143	3,817	622	3,196	3,326	497	2,829
Mar	143,619	77,237	3,075	74,162	66,382	3,078	63,303	7,075	3,776	631	3,145	3,299	531	2,768
Apr	143,791	77,212	3,058	74,154	66,579	3,120	63,458	7,113	3,837	602	3,235	3,276	442	2,834
May	144,088	77,300	3,117	74,183	66,788	3,132	63,656	7,038	3,866	603	3,262	3,173	412	2,761
June	144,369	77,353	3,116	74,237	67,016	3,129	63,887	7,017	3,747	644	3,103	3,270	507	2,763
July	144,295	77,135	3,070	74,065	67,160	3,122	64,038	7,176	3,857	646	3,210	3,319	519	2,800
Aug	144,671	77,499	3,069	74,429	67,172	3,041	64,131	7,128	3,866	638	3,228	3,262	542	2,720
Sept	144,846	77,945	3,037	74,908	66,901	2,998	63,904	6,896	3,600	652	2,948	3,296	524	2,772
Oct	145,395	78,001	3,061	74,940	67,394	3,089	64,305	6,735	3,640	619	3,021	3,095	496	2,599
Nov	145,583	78,146	3,080	75,066	67,437	3,108	64,330	6,820	3,647	605	3,042	3,173	485	2,688
Dec	145,949	78,324	3,086	75,238	67,625	3,099	64,525	6,760	3,680	596	3,084	3,080	479	2,601
2007: Jan	145,915	78,221	3,067	75,154	67,694	3,047	64,647	7,043	3,846	594	3,252	3,197	485	2,712
Feb	145,888	78,184	3,036	75,148	67,704	3,018	64,686	6,837	3,815	605	3,210	3,021	461	2,561
Mar	146,145	78,297	3,011	75,286	67,849	2,990	64,859	6,738	3,700	576	3,124	3,038	451	2,588
Apr	145,713	78,293	3,013	75,279	67,420	2,941	64,479	6,829	3,743	594	3,149	3,086	488	2,597
May	145,913	78,277	2,934	75,343	67,637	2,926	64,710	6,863	3,776	622	3,154	3,087	479	2,608
June	146,087	78,243	2,951	75,292	67,845	3,017	64,828	6,997	3,859	648	3,212	3,138	485	2,653
July	146,045	78,237	2,914	75,324	67,808	3,016	64,792	7,137	3,887	592	3,295	3,250	476	2,774
Aug	145,753	78,066	2,792	75,274	67,687	2,861	64,826	7,133	3,863	612	3,252	3,270	480	2,790
Sept	146,260	78,229	2,897	75,332	68,030	2,998	65,033	7,246	4,008	650	3,357	3,238	476	2,762
Oct	146,016	78,177	2,903	75,274	67,838	3,011	64,827	7,291	4,032	643	3,389	3,258	462	2,796
Nov	146,647	78,604	2,770	75,834	68,043	3,063	64,980	7,181	3,910	670	3,240	3,271	475	2,796
Dec	146,211	78,260	2,761	75,499	67,951	3,040	64,912	7,655	4,188	683	3,505	3,467	513	2,954

Note.—See footnote 5 and Note, Table B–35.

Source: Department of Labor (Bureau of Labor Statistics).

TABLE B–37.—Civilian employment by demographic characteristic, 1960–2007

[Thousands of persons 16 years of age and over; monthly data seasonally adjusted]

Year or month	All civilian workers	White [1] Total	White Males	White Females	White Both sexes 16-19	Black and other [1] Total	Black and other Males	Black and other Females	Black and other Both sexes 16-19	Black or African American [1] Total	Black or African American Males	Black or African American Females	Black or African American Both sexes 16-19
1960	65,778	58,850	39,755	19,095	3,700	6,928	4,149	2,779	430	....	....	....	....
1961	65,746	58,913	39,588	19,325	3,693	6,833	4,068	2,765	414	....	....	....	....
1962	66,702	59,698	40,016	19,682	3,774	7,003	4,160	2,843	420	....	....	....	....
1963	67,762	60,622	40,428	20,194	3,851	7,140	4,229	2,911	404	....	....	....	....
1964	69,305	61,922	41,115	20,807	4,076	7,383	4,359	3,024	440	....	....	....	....
1965	71,088	63,446	41,844	21,602	4,562	7,643	4,496	3,147	474	....	....	....	....
1966	72,895	65,021	42,331	22,690	5,176	7,877	4,588	3,289	545	....	....	....	....
1967	74,372	66,361	42,833	23,528	5,114	8,011	4,646	3,365	568	....	....	....	....
1968	75,920	67,750	43,411	24,339	5,195	8,169	4,702	3,467	584	....	....	....	....
1969	77,902	69,518	44,048	25,470	5,508	8,384	4,770	3,614	609	....	....	....	....
1970	78,678	70,217	44,178	26,039	5,571	8,464	4,813	3,650	574	....	....	....	....
1971	79,367	70,878	44,595	26,283	5,670	8,488	4,796	3,692	538	....	....	....	....
1972	82,153	73,370	45,944	27,426	6,173	8,783	4,952	3,832	573	7,802	4,368	3,433	509
1973	85,064	75,708	47,085	28,623	6,623	9,356	5,265	4,092	647	8,128	4,527	3,601	570
1974	86,794	77,184	47,674	29,511	6,796	9,610	5,352	4,258	652	8,203	4,527	3,677	554
1975	85,846	76,411	46,697	29,714	6,487	9,435	5,161	4,275	615	7,894	4,275	3,618	507
1976	88,752	78,853	47,775	31,078	6,724	9,899	5,363	4,536	611	8,227	4,404	3,823	508
1977	92,017	81,700	49,150	32,550	7,068	10,317	5,579	4,739	619	8,540	4,565	3,975	508
1978	96,048	84,936	50,544	34,392	7,367	11,112	5,936	5,177	703	9,102	4,796	4,307	571
1979	98,824	87,259	51,452	35,807	7,356	11,565	6,156	5,409	727	9,359	4,923	4,436	579
1980	99,303	87,715	51,127	36,587	7,021	11,588	6,059	5,529	689	9,313	4,798	4,515	547
1981	100,397	88,709	51,315	37,394	6,588	11,688	6,083	5,606	637	9,355	4,794	4,561	505
1982	99,526	87,903	50,287	37,615	5,984	11,624	5,983	5,641	565	9,189	4,637	4,552	428
1983	100,834	88,893	50,621	38,272	5,799	11,941	6,166	5,775	543	9,375	4,753	4,622	416
1984	105,005	92,120	52,462	39,659	5,836	12,885	6,629	6,256	607	10,119	5,124	4,995	474
1985	107,150	93,736	53,046	40,690	5,768	13,414	6,845	6,569	666	10,501	5,270	5,231	532
1986	109,597	95,660	53,785	41,876	5,792	13,937	7,107	6,830	681	10,814	5,428	5,386	536
1987	112,440	97,789	54,647	43,142	5,898	14,652	7,459	7,192	742	11,309	5,661	5,648	587
1988	114,968	99,812	55,550	44,262	6,030	15,156	7,722	7,434	774	11,658	5,824	5,834	601
1989	117,342	101,584	56,352	45,232	5,946	15,757	7,963	7,795	813	11,953	5,928	6,025	625
1990	118,793	102,261	56,703	45,558	5,779	16,533	8,401	8,131	801	12,175	5,995	6,180	598
1991	117,718	101,182	55,797	45,385	5,216	16,536	8,426	8,110	690	12,074	5,961	6,113	494
1992	118,492	101,669	55,959	45,710	4,985	16,823	8,482	8,342	684	12,151	5,930	6,221	492
1993	120,259	103,045	56,656	46,390	5,113	17,214	8,693	8,521	691	12,382	6,047	6,334	494
1994	123,060	105,190	57,452	47,738	5,398	17,870	8,998	8,872	763	12,835	6,241	6,595	552
1995	124,900	106,490	58,146	48,344	5,593	18,409	9,231	9,179	826	13,279	6,422	6,857	586
1996	126,708	107,808	58,888	48,920	5,667	18,900	9,319	9,580	832	13,542	6,456	7,086	613
1997	129,558	109,856	59,998	49,859	5,807	19,701	9,687	10,014	853	13,969	6,607	7,362	631
1998	131,463	110,931	60,604	50,327	6,089	20,532	10,089	10,443	962	14,556	6,871	7,685	736
1999	133,488	112,235	61,139	51,096	6,204	21,253	10,307	10,945	968	15,056	7,027	8,029	691
2000	136,891	114,424	62,289	52,136	6,160	....	....	....	....	15,156	7,082	8,073	711
2001	136,933	114,430	62,212	52,218	5,817	....	....	....	....	15,006	6,938	8,068	637
2002	136,485	114,013	61,849	52,164	5,441	....	....	....	....	14,872	6,959	7,914	611
2003	137,736	114,235	61,866	52,369	5,064	....	....	....	....	14,739	6,820	7,919	516
2004	139,252	115,239	62,712	52,527	5,039	....	....	....	....	14,909	6,912	7,997	520
2005	141,730	116,949	63,763	53,186	5,105	....	....	....	....	15,313	7,155	8,158	536
2006	144,427	118,833	64,883	53,950	5,215	....	....	....	....	15,765	7,354	8,410	618
2007	146,047	119,792	65,289	54,503	4,990	....	....	....	....	16,051	7,500	8,551	566
2006: Jan	143,086	118,078	64,584	53,494	5,210	....	....	....	....	15,490	7,216	8,274	559
Feb	143,362	118,014	64,488	53,526	5,215	....	....	....	....	15,656	7,310	8,346	650
Mar	143,619	118,192	64,709	53,483	5,228	....	....	....	....	15,709	7,340	8,369	602
Apr	143,791	118,412	64,669	53,744	5,250	....	....	....	....	15,691	7,355	8,336	623
May	144,088	118,512	64,671	53,841	5,269	....	....	....	....	15,783	7,372	8,411	644
June	144,369	118,721	64,734	53,987	5,246	....	....	....	....	15,700	7,327	8,373	630
July	144,295	118,878	64,686	54,192	5,252	....	....	....	....	15,682	7,301	8,381	588
Aug	144,671	119,065	64,913	54,152	5,176	....	....	....	....	15,857	7,345	8,512	620
Sept	144,846	119,161	65,166	53,994	5,099	....	....	....	....	15,649	7,298	8,351	583
Oct	145,395	119,523	65,253	54,270	5,167	....	....	....	....	15,901	7,390	8,511	658
Nov	145,583	119,554	65,315	54,239	5,195	....	....	....	....	15,973	7,443	8,530	628
Dec	145,949	119,828	65,407	54,421	5,273	....	....	....	....	16,091	7,548	8,543	627
2007: Jan	145,915	119,742	65,341	54,401	5,185	....	....	....	....	16,242	7,579	8,662	603
Feb	145,888	119,651	65,281	54,370	5,118	....	....	....	....	16,141	7,525	8,615	599
Mar	146,145	120,065	65,531	54,534	5,068	....	....	....	....	15,979	7,385	8,595	592
Apr	145,713	119,505	65,404	54,102	5,029	....	....	....	....	16,048	7,465	8,583	584
May	145,913	119,711	65,393	54,318	4,969	....	....	....	....	15,939	7,407	8,532	562
June	146,087	119,835	65,367	54,468	5,040	....	....	....	....	15,989	7,406	8,583	561
July	146,045	119,713	65,231	54,482	5,009	....	....	....	....	16,172	7,603	8,569	558
Aug	145,753	119,340	64,923	54,417	4,805	....	....	....	....	16,176	7,664	8,512	525
Sept	146,260	119,992	65,153	54,838	4,996	....	....	....	....	16,046	7,536	8,510	541
Oct	146,016	119,883	65,229	54,654	4,985	....	....	....	....	15,946	7,436	8,510	558
Nov	146,647	120,194	65,412	54,782	4,863	....	....	....	....	15,980	7,522	8,458	553
Dec	146,211	119,889	65,237	54,653	4,853	....	....	....	....	15,961	7,470	8,491	556

[1] Beginning in 2003, persons who selected this race group only. Prior to 2003, persons who selected more than one race were included in the group they identified as the main race. Data for "black or African American" were for "black" prior to 2003. Data discontinued for "black and other" series. See Employment and Earnings for details.

Note.—Beginning with data for 2000, since data for all race groups are not shown here, detail will not sum to total. See footnote 5 and Note, Table B–35.

Source: Department of Labor (Bureau of Labor Statistics).

TABLE B–38.—*Unemployment by demographic characteristic, 1960–2007*

[Thousands of persons 16 years of age and over; monthly data seasonally adjusted]

Year or month	All civilian workers	White [1] Total	White Males	White Females	White Both sexes 16-19	Black and other [1] Total	Black and other Males	Black and other Females	Black and other Both sexes 16-19	Black or African American [1] Total	Black or African American Males	Black or African American Females	Black or African American Both sexes 16-19
1960	3,852	3,065	1,988	1,077	575	788	498	290	138	....	....	....	....
1961	4,714	3,743	2,398	1,345	669	971	599	372	159	....	....	....	....
1962	3,911	3,052	1,915	1,137	580	861	509	352	142	....	....	....	....
1963	4,070	3,208	1,976	1,232	708	863	496	367	176	....	....	....	....
1964	3,786	2,999	1,779	1,220	708	787	426	361	165	....	....	....	....
1965	3,366	2,691	1,556	1,135	705	678	360	318	171	....	....	....	....
1966	2,875	2,255	1,241	1,014	651	622	310	312	186	....	....	....	....
1967	2,975	2,338	1,208	1,130	635	638	300	338	203	....	....	....	....
1968	2,817	2,226	1,142	1,084	644	590	277	313	194	....	....	....	....
1969	2,832	2,260	1,137	1,123	660	571	267	304	193	....	....	....	....
1970	4,093	3,339	1,857	1,482	871	754	380	374	235	....	....	....	....
1971	5,016	4,085	2,309	1,777	1,011	930	481	450	249	....	....	....	....
1972	4,882	3,906	2,173	1,733	1,021	977	486	491	288	906	448	458	279
1973	4,365	3,442	1,836	1,606	955	924	440	484	280	846	395	451	262
1974	5,156	4,097	2,169	1,927	1,104	1,058	544	514	318	965	494	470	297
1975	7,929	6,421	3,627	2,794	1,413	1,507	815	692	355	1,369	741	629	330
1976	7,406	5,914	3,258	2,656	1,364	1,492	779	713	355	1,334	698	637	330
1977	6,991	5,441	2,883	2,558	1,284	1,550	784	766	379	1,393	698	695	354
1978	6,202	4,698	2,411	2,287	1,189	1,505	731	774	394	1,330	641	690	360
1979	6,137	4,664	2,405	2,260	1,193	1,473	714	759	362	1,319	636	683	333
1980	7,637	5,884	3,345	2,540	1,291	1,752	922	830	377	1,553	815	738	343
1981	8,273	6,343	3,580	2,762	1,374	1,930	997	933	388	1,731	891	840	357
1982	10,678	8,241	4,846	3,395	1,534	2,437	1,334	1,104	443	2,142	1,167	975	396
1983	10,717	8,128	4,859	3,270	1,387	2,588	1,401	1,187	441	2,272	1,213	1,059	392
1984	8,539	6,372	3,600	2,772	1,116	2,167	1,144	1,022	384	1,914	1,003	911	353
1985	8,312	6,191	3,426	2,765	1,074	2,121	1,095	1,026	394	1,864	951	913	357
1986	8,237	6,140	3,433	2,708	1,070	2,097	1,097	999	383	1,840	946	894	347
1987	7,425	5,501	3,132	2,369	995	1,924	969	955	353	1,684	826	858	312
1988	6,701	4,944	2,766	2,177	910	1,757	888	869	316	1,547	771	776	288
1989	6,528	4,770	2,636	2,135	863	1,757	889	868	331	1,544	773	772	300
1990	7,047	5,186	2,935	2,251	903	1,860	971	889	308	1,565	806	758	268
1991	8,628	6,560	3,859	2,701	1,029	2,068	1,087	981	330	1,723	890	833	280
1992	9,613	7,169	4,209	2,959	1,037	2,444	1,314	1,130	390	2,011	1,067	944	324
1993	8,940	6,655	3,828	2,827	992	2,285	1,227	1,058	373	1,844	971	872	313
1994	7,996	5,892	3,275	2,617	960	2,104	1,092	1,011	360	1,666	848	818	300
1995	7,404	5,459	2,999	2,460	952	1,945	984	961	394	1,538	762	777	325
1996	7,236	5,300	2,896	2,404	939	1,936	984	952	367	1,592	808	784	310
1997	6,739	4,836	2,641	2,195	912	1,903	935	967	359	1,560	747	813	302
1998	6,210	4,484	2,431	2,053	876	1,726	835	891	329	1,426	671	756	281
1999	5,880	4,273	2,274	1,999	844	1,606	792	814	318	1,309	626	684	268
2000	5,692	4,121	2,177	1,944	795	....	....	....	....	1,241	620	621	230
2001	6,801	4,969	2,754	2,215	845	....	....	....	....	1,416	709	706	260
2002	8,378	6,137	3,459	2,678	925	....	....	....	....	1,693	835	858	260
2003	8,774	6,311	3,643	2,668	909	....	....	....	....	1,787	891	895	255
2004	8,149	5,847	3,282	2,565	890	....	....	....	....	1,729	860	868	241
2005	7,591	5,350	2,931	2,419	845	....	....	....	....	1,700	844	856	267
2006	7,001	5,002	2,730	2,271	794	....	....	....	....	1,549	774	775	253
2007	7,078	5,143	2,869	2,274	805	....	....	....	....	1,445	752	693	235
2006: Jan	7,025	5,065	2,761	2,304	789	....	....	....	....	1,513	675	837	239
Feb	7,143	5,067	2,763	2,304	769	....	....	....	....	1,627	794	833	280
Mar	7,075	4,962	2,693	2,269	777	....	....	....	....	1,629	790	839	307
Apr	7,113	5,017	2,764	2,252	743	....	....	....	....	1,608	816	792	253
May	7,038	5,055	2,830	2,225	759	....	....	....	....	1,524	813	710	216
June	7,017	5,036	2,755	2,281	819	....	....	....	....	1,516	756	760	241
July	7,176	5,061	2,748	2,313	791	....	....	....	....	1,659	858	801	286
Aug	7,128	5,106	2,808	2,298	860	....	....	....	....	1,528	782	747	242
Sept	6,896	4,882	2,570	2,311	816	....	....	....	....	1,574	788	787	273
Oct	6,735	4,865	2,626	2,239	798	....	....	....	....	1,471	782	689	246
Nov	6,820	4,899	2,647	2,252	775	....	....	....	....	1,488	751	736	239
Dec	6,760	4,938	2,767	2,170	811	....	....	....	....	1,455	674	781	213
2007: Jan	7,043	5,154	2,871	2,284	791	....	....	....	....	1,415	727	688	246
Feb	6,837	4,986	2,832	2,154	772	....	....	....	....	1,394	733	661	241
Mar	6,738	4,787	2,638	2,149	776	....	....	....	....	1,439	790	648	194
Apr	6,829	4,928	2,731	2,197	773	....	....	....	....	1,435	793	642	258
May	6,863	4,928	2,741	2,187	801	....	....	....	....	1,466	778	688	242
June	6,997	5,083	2,839	2,244	834	....	....	....	....	1,467	775	692	252
July	7,137	5,232	2,921	2,311	800	....	....	....	....	1,421	711	710	206
Aug	7,133	5,256	2,935	2,322	806	....	....	....	....	1,347	660	687	238
Sept	7,246	5,324	3,048	2,275	834	....	....	....	....	1,437	718	719	220
Oct	7,291	5,268	2,959	2,309	810	....	....	....	....	1,483	776	708	215
Nov	7,181	5,235	2,908	2,327	840	....	....	....	....	1,473	756	717	234
Dec	7,655	5,571	3,042	2,529	815	....	....	....	....	1,577	829	748	295

[1] See footnote 1 and Note, Table B–37.

Note.—See footnote 5 and Note, Table B–35.

Source: Department of Labor (Bureau of Labor Statistics).

TABLE B–39.—*Civilian labor force participation rate and employment/population ratio, 1960–2007*

[Percent [1]; monthly data seasonally adjusted]

Year or month	Labor force participation rate							Employment/population ratio						
	All civilian workers	Males	Females	Both sexes 16-19 years	White [2]	Black and other [2]	Black or African American [2]	All civilian workers	Males	Females	Both sexes 16-19 years	White [2]	Black and other [2]	Black or African American [2]
1960	59.4	83.3	37.7	47.5	58.8	64.5		56.1	78.9	35.5	40.5	55.9	57.9	
1961	59.3	82.9	38.1	46.9	58.8	64.1		55.4	77.6	35.4	39.1	55.3	56.2	
1962	58.8	82.0	37.9	46.1	58.3	63.2		55.5	77.7	35.6	39.4	55.4	56.3	
1963	58.7	81.4	38.3	45.2	58.2	63.0		55.4	77.1	35.8	37.4	55.3	56.2	
1964	58.7	81.0	38.7	44.5	58.2	63.1		55.7	77.3	36.3	37.3	55.5	57.0	
1965	58.9	80.7	39.3	45.7	58.4	62.9		56.2	77.5	37.1	38.9	56.0	57.8	
1966	59.2	80.4	40.3	48.2	58.7	63.0		56.9	77.9	38.3	42.1	56.8	58.4	
1967	59.6	80.4	41.1	48.4	59.2	62.8		57.3	78.0	39.0	42.2	57.2	58.2	
1968	59.6	80.1	41.6	48.3	59.3	62.2		57.5	77.8	39.6	42.2	57.4	58.0	
1969	60.1	79.8	42.7	49.4	59.9	62.1		58.0	77.6	40.7	43.4	58.0	58.1	
1970	60.4	79.7	43.3	49.9	60.2	61.8		57.4	76.2	40.8	42.3	57.5	56.8	
1971	60.2	79.1	43.4	49.7	60.1	60.9		56.6	74.9	40.4	41.3	56.8	54.9	
1972	60.4	78.9	43.9	51.9	60.4	60.2	59.9	57.0	75.0	41.0	43.5	57.4	54.1	53.7
1973	60.8	78.8	44.7	53.7	60.8	60.5	60.2	57.8	75.5	42.0	45.9	58.2	55.0	54.5
1974	61.3	78.7	45.7	54.8	61.4	60.3	59.8	57.8	74.9	42.6	46.0	58.3	54.3	53.5
1975	61.2	77.9	46.3	54.0	61.5	59.6	58.8	56.1	71.7	42.0	43.3	56.7	51.4	50.1
1976	61.6	77.5	47.3	54.5	61.8	59.8	59.0	56.8	72.0	43.2	44.2	57.5	52.0	50.8
1977	62.3	77.7	48.4	56.0	62.5	60.4	59.8	57.9	72.8	44.5	46.1	58.6	52.5	51.4
1978	63.2	77.9	50.0	57.8	63.3	62.2	61.5	59.3	73.8	46.4	48.3	60.0	54.7	53.6
1979	63.7	77.8	50.9	57.9	63.9	62.2	61.4	59.9	73.8	47.5	48.5	60.6	55.2	53.8
1980	63.8	77.4	51.5	56.7	64.1	61.7	61.0	59.2	72.0	47.7	46.6	60.0	53.6	52.3
1981	63.9	77.0	52.1	55.4	64.3	61.3	60.8	59.0	71.3	48.0	44.6	60.0	52.6	51.3
1982	64.0	76.6	52.6	54.1	64.3	61.6	61.0	57.8	69.0	47.7	41.5	58.8	50.9	49.4
1983	64.0	76.4	52.9	53.5	64.3	62.1	61.5	57.9	68.8	48.0	41.5	58.9	51.0	49.5
1984	64.4	76.4	53.6	53.9	64.6	62.6	62.2	59.5	70.7	49.5	43.7	60.5	53.6	52.3
1985	64.8	76.3	54.5	54.5	65.0	63.3	62.9	60.1	70.9	50.4	44.4	61.0	54.7	53.4
1986	65.3	76.3	55.3	54.7	65.5	63.7	63.3	60.7	71.0	51.4	44.6	61.5	55.4	54.1
1987	65.6	76.2	56.0	54.7	65.8	64.3	63.8	61.5	71.5	52.5	45.5	62.3	56.8	55.6
1988	65.9	76.2	56.6	55.3	66.2	64.0	63.8	62.3	72.0	53.4	46.8	63.1	57.4	56.3
1989	66.5	76.4	57.4	55.9	66.7	64.7	64.2	63.0	72.5	54.3	47.5	63.8	58.2	56.9
1990	66.5	76.4	57.5	53.7	66.9	64.4	64.0	62.8	72.0	54.3	45.3	63.7	57.9	56.7
1991	66.2	75.8	57.4	51.6	66.6	63.8	63.3	61.7	70.4	53.7	42.0	62.6	56.7	55.4
1992	66.4	75.8	57.8	51.3	66.8	64.6	63.9	61.5	69.8	53.8	41.0	62.4	56.4	54.9
1993	66.3	75.4	57.9	51.5	66.8	63.8	63.2	61.7	70.0	54.1	41.7	62.7	56.3	55.0
1994	66.6	75.1	58.8	52.7	67.1	63.9	63.4	62.5	70.4	55.3	44.3	63.5	57.2	56.1
1995	66.6	75.0	58.9	53.5	67.1	64.3	63.7	62.9	70.8	55.6	44.2	63.8	58.1	57.1
1996	66.8	74.9	59.3	52.3	67.2	64.6	64.1	63.2	70.9	56.0	43.5	64.1	58.6	57.4
1997	67.1	75.0	59.8	51.6	67.5	65.2	64.7	63.8	71.3	56.8	43.4	64.6	59.4	58.2
1998	67.1	74.9	59.8	52.8	67.3	66.0	65.6	64.1	71.6	57.1	45.1	64.7	60.9	59.7
1999	67.1	74.7	60.0	52.0	67.3	65.9	65.8	64.3	71.6	57.4	44.7	64.8	61.3	60.6
2000	67.1	74.8	59.9	52.0	67.3		65.8	64.4	71.9	57.5	45.2	64.9		60.9
2001	66.8	74.4	59.8	49.6	67.0		65.3	63.7	70.9	57.0	42.3	64.2		59.7
2002	66.6	74.1	59.6	47.4	66.8		64.8	62.7	69.7	56.3	39.6	63.4		58.1
2003	66.2	73.5	59.5	44.5	66.5		64.3	62.3	68.9	56.1	36.8	63.0		57.4
2004	66.0	73.3	59.2	43.9	66.3		63.8	62.3	69.2	56.0	36.4	63.1		57.2
2005	66.0	73.3	59.3	43.7	66.3		64.2	62.7	69.6	56.2	36.5	63.4		57.7
2006	66.2	73.5	59.4	43.7	66.5		64.1	63.1	70.1	56.6	36.9	63.8		58.4
2007	66.0	73.2	59.3	41.3	66.4		63.7	63.0	69.8	56.6	34.8	63.6		58.4
2006: Jan	66.0	73.3	59.1	43.4	66.4		63.5	62.9	69.9	56.3	36.8	63.7		57.8
Feb	66.1	73.4	59.2	44.0	66.3		64.4	62.9	69.9	56.4	37.3	63.6		58.4
Mar	66.1	73.5	59.1	44.1	66.3		64.5	63.0	70.1	56.3	37.1	63.6		58.5
Apr	66.1	73.5	59.2	43.5	66.4		64.3	63.0	70.0	56.5	37.2	63.7		58.3
May	66.2	73.5	59.3	43.7	66.4		64.2	63.1	70.0	56.6	37.6	63.7		58.6
June	66.2	73.4	59.5	44.4	66.5		63.8	63.1	70.0	56.7	37.5	63.8		58.2
July	66.2	73.2	59.6	44.1	66.5		64.2	63.0	69.7	56.8	37.1	63.8		58.0
Aug	66.2	73.4	59.5	43.6	66.6		64.2	63.1	70.0	56.7	36.5	63.8		58.6
Sept	66.1	73.5	59.2	43.0	66.5		63.5	63.1	70.3	56.5	36.0	63.8		57.7
Oct	66.2	73.5	59.4	43.3	66.6		64.0	63.3	70.2	56.8	36.7	64.0		58.6
Nov	66.3	73.6	59.5	43.3	66.6		64.2	63.3	70.3	56.8	36.8	63.9		58.7
Dec	66.4	73.7	59.5	43.1	66.7		64.4	63.4	70.4	56.9	36.8	64.0		59.1
2007: Jan	66.3	73.6	59.5	42.6	66.6		64.7	63.3	70.1	56.8	36.2	63.9		59.5
Feb	66.2	73.5	59.3	42.1	66.4		64.2	63.2	70.0	56.8	35.8	63.8		59.1
Mar	66.2	73.4	59.4	41.5	66.5		63.7	63.3	70.1	56.9	35.4	64.0		58.4
Apr	66.0	73.3	59.0	41.5	66.2		63.8	63.0	70.0	56.5	35.1	63.6		58.6
May	66.0	73.3	59.2	41.0	66.3		63.5	63.0	69.9	56.6	34.5	63.7		58.1
June	66.1	73.2	59.3	41.8	66.4		63.6	63.0	69.7	56.7	35.2	63.7		58.2
July	66.0	73.2	59.3	41.2	66.3		64.0	63.0	69.7	56.6	34.9	63.6		58.8
Aug	65.8	72.9	59.2	39.7	66.1		63.6	62.8	69.5	56.5	33.2	63.3		58.7
Sept	66.0	73.1	59.4	41.2	66.4		63.4	62.9	69.5	56.7	34.6	63.6		58.2
Oct	65.9	73.0	59.2	41.2	66.3		63.1	62.7	69.4	56.7	34.6	63.5		57.7
Nov	66.0	73.2	59.3	40.9	66.4		63.1	63.0	69.7	56.6	34.2	63.6		57.8
Dec	66.0	73.1	59.4	41.0	66.3		63.3	62.7	69.3	56.5	34.0	63.4		57.6

[1] Civilian labor force or civilian employment as percent of civilian noninstitutional population in group specified.
[2] See footnote 1, Table B–37.

Note.—Data relate to persons 16 years of age and over.
See footnote 5 and Note, Table B–35.

Source: Department of Labor (Bureau of Labor Statistics).

TABLE B–40.—*Civilian labor force participation rate by demographic characteristic, 1965–2007*

[Percent [1]; monthly data seasonally adjusted]

Year or month	All civilian workers	White [2] Total	White Males Total	White Males 16-19 years	White Males 20 years and over	White Females Total	White Females 16-19 years	White Females 20 years and over	Black and other or black or African American [2] Total	Black Males Total	Black Males 16-19 years	Black Males 20 years and over	Black Females Total	Black Females 16-19 years	Black Females 20 years and over
									Black and other [2]						
1965	58.9	58.4	80.8	54.1	83.9	38.1	39.2	38.0	62.9	79.6	51.3	83.7	48.6	29.5	51.1
1966	59.2	58.7	80.6	55.9	83.6	39.2	42.6	38.8	63.0	79.0	51.4	83.3	49.4	33.5	51.6
1967	59.6	59.2	80.6	56.3	83.5	40.1	42.5	39.8	62.8	78.5	51.1	82.9	49.5	35.2	51.6
1968	59.6	59.3	80.4	55.9	83.2	40.7	43.0	40.4	62.2	77.7	49.7	82.2	49.3	34.8	51.4
1969	60.1	59.9	80.2	56.8	83.0	41.8	44.6	41.5	62.1	76.9	49.6	81.4	49.8	34.6	52.0
1970	60.4	60.2	80.0	57.5	82.8	42.6	45.6	42.2	61.8	76.5	47.4	81.4	49.5	34.1	51.8
1971	60.2	60.1	79.6	57.9	82.3	42.6	45.4	42.3	60.9	74.9	44.7	80.0	49.2	31.2	51.8
1972	60.4	60.4	79.6	60.1	82.0	43.2	48.1	42.7	60.2	73.9	46.0	78.6	48.8	32.3	51.2
									Black or African American [2]						
1972	60.4	60.4	79.6	60.1	82.0	43.2	48.1	42.7	59.9	73.6	46.3	78.5	48.7	32.2	51.2
1973	60.8	60.8	79.4	62.0	81.6	44.1	50.1	43.5	60.2	73.4	45.7	78.4	49.3	34.2	51.6
1974	61.3	61.4	79.4	62.9	81.4	45.2	51.7	44.4	59.8	72.9	46.7	77.6	49.0	33.4	51.4
1975	61.2	61.5	78.7	61.9	80.7	45.9	51.5	45.3	58.8	70.9	42.6	76.0	48.8	34.2	51.1
1976	61.6	61.8	78.4	62.3	80.3	46.9	52.8	46.2	59.0	70.0	41.3	75.4	49.8	32.9	52.5
1977	62.3	62.5	78.5	64.0	80.2	48.0	54.5	47.3	59.8	70.6	43.2	75.6	50.8	32.9	53.6
1978	63.2	63.3	78.6	65.0	80.1	49.4	56.7	48.7	61.5	71.5	44.9	76.2	53.1	37.3	55.5
1979	63.7	63.9	78.6	64.8	80.1	50.5	57.4	49.8	61.4	71.3	43.6	76.3	53.1	36.8	55.4
1980	63.8	64.1	78.2	63.7	79.8	51.2	56.2	50.6	61.0	70.3	43.2	75.1	53.1	34.9	55.6
1981	63.9	64.3	77.9	62.4	79.5	51.9	55.4	51.5	60.8	70.0	41.6	74.5	53.5	34.0	56.0
1982	64.0	64.3	77.4	60.0	79.2	52.4	55.0	52.2	61.0	70.1	39.8	74.7	53.7	33.5	56.2
1983	64.0	64.3	77.1	59.4	78.9	52.7	54.5	52.5	61.5	70.6	39.9	75.2	54.2	33.0	56.8
1984	64.4	64.6	77.1	59.0	78.7	53.3	55.4	53.1	62.2	70.8	41.7	74.8	55.2	35.0	57.6
1985	64.8	65.0	77.0	59.7	78.5	54.1	55.2	54.0	62.9	70.8	44.6	74.4	56.5	37.9	58.6
1986	65.3	65.5	76.9	59.3	78.5	55.0	56.3	54.9	63.3	71.2	43.7	74.8	56.9	39.1	58.9
1987	65.6	65.8	76.8	59.0	78.4	55.7	56.5	55.6	63.8	71.1	43.6	74.7	58.0	39.6	60.0
1988	65.9	66.2	76.9	60.0	78.3	56.4	57.2	56.3	63.8	71.0	43.8	74.6	58.0	37.9	60.1
1989	66.5	66.7	77.1	61.0	78.5	57.2	57.1	57.2	64.2	71.0	44.6	74.4	58.7	40.4	60.6
1990	66.5	66.9	77.1	59.6	78.5	57.4	55.3	57.6	64.0	71.0	40.7	75.0	58.3	36.8	60.6
1991	66.2	66.6	76.5	57.3	78.0	57.4	54.1	57.6	63.3	70.4	37.3	74.6	57.5	33.5	60.0
1992	66.4	66.8	76.5	56.9	78.0	57.7	52.5	58.1	63.9	70.7	40.6	74.3	58.5	35.2	60.8
1993	66.3	66.8	76.2	56.6	77.7	58.0	53.5	58.3	63.2	69.6	39.5	73.2	57.9	34.6	60.2
1994	66.6	67.1	75.9	57.7	77.3	58.9	55.1	59.2	63.4	69.1	40.8	72.5	58.7	36.3	60.9
1995	66.6	67.1	75.7	58.5	77.1	59.0	55.5	59.2	63.7	69.0	40.1	72.5	59.5	39.8	61.4
1996	66.8	67.2	75.8	57.1	77.3	59.1	54.7	59.4	64.1	68.7	39.5	72.3	60.4	38.9	62.6
1997	67.1	67.5	75.9	56.1	77.5	59.5	54.1	59.9	64.7	68.3	37.4	72.2	61.7	39.9	64.0
1998	67.1	67.3	75.6	56.6	77.2	59.4	55.4	59.7	65.6	69.0	40.7	72.5	62.8	42.5	64.8
1999	67.1	67.3	75.6	56.4	77.2	59.6	54.5	59.9	65.8	68.7	38.6	72.4	63.5	38.8	66.1
2000	67.1	67.3	75.5	56.5	77.1	59.5	54.5	59.9	65.8	69.2	39.2	72.8	63.1	39.6	65.4
2001	66.8	67.0	75.1	53.7	76.9	59.4	52.4	59.9	65.3	68.4	37.9	72.1	62.8	37.3	65.2
2002	66.6	66.8	74.8	50.3	76.7	59.3	50.8	60.0	64.8	68.4	37.3	72.1	61.8	34.7	64.4
2003	66.2	66.5	74.2	47.5	76.3	59.2	47.9	59.9	64.3	67.3	31.1	71.5	61.9	33.7	64.6
2004	66.0	66.3	74.1	47.4	76.2	58.9	46.7	59.7	63.8	66.7	30.0	70.9	61.5	32.8	64.2
2005	66.0	66.3	74.1	46.2	76.2	58.9	47.6	59.7	64.2	67.3	32.6	71.3	61.6	32.2	64.4
2006	66.2	66.5	74.3	46.9	76.4	59.0	46.6	59.9	64.1	67.0	32.3	71.1	61.7	35.6	64.2
2007	66.0	66.4	74.0	44.3	76.3	59.0	44.6	60.1	63.7	66.8	29.4	71.2	61.1	31.2	64.0
2006: Jan	66.0	66.4	74.4	47.1	76.5	58.8	47.0	59.6	63.5	65.6	28.7	69.9	61.7	34.4	64.3
Feb	66.1	66.3	74.2	47.2	76.3	58.8	46.5	59.7	64.4	67.3	33.1	71.3	62.1	40.3	64.1
Mar	66.1	66.3	74.3	47.2	76.4	58.7	46.6	59.5	64.5	67.4	33.5	71.4	62.2	38.0	64.5
Apr	66.1	66.4	74.3	46.7	76.4	58.9	46.8	59.8	64.3	67.7	34.0	71.6	61.6	34.7	64.1
May	66.2	66.4	74.3	47.2	76.4	58.9	46.7	59.8	64.2	67.7	33.7	71.6	61.4	33.6	64.1
June	66.2	66.5	74.2	47.3	76.3	59.1	47.1	60.0	63.8	66.7	33.4	70.6	61.4	34.5	64.0
July	66.2	66.5	74.1	46.5	76.2	59.3	47.4	60.2	64.2	67.2	34.1	71.1	61.7	34.0	64.3
Aug	66.2	66.6	74.3	47.1	76.4	59.2	46.6	60.1	64.2	66.8	32.1	70.9	62.1	34.8	64.7
Sept	66.1	66.5	74.2	46.8	76.4	59.0	44.9	60.0	63.5	66.4	28.5	70.8	61.2	37.6	63.5
Oct	66.2	66.6	74.3	46.4	76.5	59.2	45.9	60.1	64.0	67.0	33.2	70.9	61.5	36.5	64.0
Nov	66.3	66.6	74.3	46.0	76.5	59.1	46.3	60.0	64.2	67.0	31.9	71.2	61.9	34.9	64.5
Dec	66.4	66.7	74.5	47.2	76.6	59.2	46.8	60.1	64.4	67.2	29.4	71.6	62.2	35.1	64.8
2007: Jan	66.3	66.6	74.4	46.6	76.6	59.2	45.3	60.1	64.7	67.8	30.7	72.1	62.3	34.3	65.0
Feb	66.2	66.4	74.3	45.6	76.5	59.0	45.0	59.9	64.2	67.3	31.5	71.5	61.7	32.6	64.5
Mar	66.2	66.5	74.3	45.1	76.6	59.1	44.7	60.1	63.7	66.5	28.6	71.0	61.4	31.3	64.3
Apr	66.0	66.2	74.2	45.1	76.4	58.6	43.9	59.7	63.8	67.1	31.5	71.3	61.2	32.6	64.0
May	66.0	66.3	74.1	44.6	76.4	58.8	43.9	59.9	63.5	66.4	30.8	70.6	61.1	30.3	64.1
June	66.1	66.4	74.1	45.5	76.4	59.0	44.6	60.0	63.6	66.2	29.6	70.6	61.4	32.0	64.2
July	66.0	66.3	74.0	44.3	76.3	59.0	44.7	60.1	64.0	67.2	27.1	72.0	61.3	30.7	64.3
Aug	65.8	66.1	73.6	42.8	76.0	58.9	43.2	60.1	63.6	67.2	27.3	71.9	60.7	30.2	63.7
Sept	66.0	66.4	73.9	44.2	76.2	59.3	45.1	60.3	63.4	66.5	28.4	71.0	60.8	29.0	63.9
Oct	65.9	66.3	73.8	44.0	76.1	59.1	44.7	60.1	63.1	66.1	28.8	70.4	60.7	29.4	63.7
Nov	66.0	66.4	73.9	42.0	76.4	59.2	45.3	60.2	63.1	66.5	29.6	70.8	60.3	29.6	63.3
Dec	66.0	66.3	73.8	41.6	76.3	59.2	45.2	60.2	63.3	66.5	31.6	70.7	60.7	32.4	63.4

[1] Civilian labor force as percent of civilian noninstitutional population in group specified.
[2] See footnote 1, Table B–37.

Note.—Data relate to persons 16 years of age and over.
See footnote 5 and Note, Table B–35.

Source: Department of Labor (Bureau of Labor Statistics).

[Percent [1]; monthly data seasonally adjusted]

Year or month	All civilian workers	White [2]							Black and other or black or African American [2]						
		Total	Males			Females			Total	Males			Females		
			Total	16-19 years	20 years and over	Total	16-19 years	20 years and over	Total	Total	16-19 years	20 years and over	Total	16-19 years	20 years and over
									Black and other [2]						
1965	56.2	56.0	77.9	47.1	81.5	36.2	33.7	36.5	57.8	73.7	39.4	78.7	44.1	20.2	47.3
1966	56.9	56.8	78.3	50.1	81.7	37.5	37.5	37.5	58.4	74.0	40.5	79.2	45.1	23.1	48.2
1967	57.3	57.2	78.4	50.2	81.7	38.3	37.7	38.3	58.2	73.8	38.8	79.4	45.0	24.8	47.9
1968	57.5	57.4	78.3	50.3	81.6	38.9	37.8	39.1	58.0	73.3	38.7	78.9	45.2	24.7	48.2
1969	58.0	58.0	78.2	51.1	81.4	40.1	39.5	40.1	58.1	72.8	39.0	78.4	45.9	25.1	48.9
1970	57.4	57.5	76.8	49.6	80.1	40.3	39.5	40.4	56.8	70.9	35.5	76.8	44.9	22.4	48.2
1971	56.6	56.8	75.7	49.2	79.0	39.9	38.6	40.1	54.9	68.1	31.8	74.2	43.9	20.2	47.3
1972	57.0	57.4	76.0	51.5	79.0	40.7	41.3	40.6	54.1	67.3	32.4	73.2	43.3	19.9	46.7
									Black or African American [2]						
1972	57.0	57.4	76.0	51.5	79.0	40.7	41.3	40.6	53.7	66.8	31.6	73.0	43.0	19.2	46.5
1973	57.8	58.2	76.5	54.3	79.2	41.8	43.6	41.6	54.5	67.5	32.8	73.7	43.8	22.0	47.2
1974	57.8	58.3	75.9	54.4	78.6	42.4	44.3	42.2	53.5	65.8	31.4	71.9	43.5	20.9	46.9
1975	56.1	56.7	73.0	50.6	75.7	42.0	42.5	41.9	50.1	60.6	26.3	66.5	41.6	20.2	44.9
1976	56.8	57.5	73.4	51.5	76.0	43.2	44.2	43.1	50.8	60.6	25.8	66.8	42.8	19.2	46.4
1977	57.9	58.6	74.1	54.4	76.5	44.5	45.9	44.4	51.4	61.4	26.4	67.5	43.3	18.5	47.0
1978	59.3	60.0	75.0	56.3	77.2	46.3	48.5	46.1	53.6	63.3	28.5	69.1	45.8	22.1	49.3
1979	59.9	60.6	75.1	55.7	77.3	47.5	49.4	47.3	53.8	63.4	28.7	69.1	46.0	22.4	49.3
1980	59.2	60.0	73.4	53.4	75.6	47.8	47.9	47.8	52.3	60.4	27.0	65.8	45.7	21.0	49.1
1981	59.0	60.0	72.8	51.3	75.1	48.3	46.2	48.5	51.3	59.1	24.6	64.5	45.1	19.7	48.5
1982	57.8	58.8	70.6	47.0	73.0	48.1	44.6	48.4	49.4	56.0	20.3	61.4	44.2	17.7	47.5
1983	57.9	58.9	70.4	47.4	72.6	48.5	44.5	48.9	49.5	56.3	20.4	61.6	44.1	17.0	47.4
1984	59.5	60.5	72.1	49.1	74.3	49.8	47.0	50.0	52.3	59.2	23.9	64.1	46.7	20.1	49.8
1985	60.1	61.0	72.3	49.9	74.3	50.7	47.1	51.0	53.4	60.0	26.3	64.6	48.1	23.1	50.9
1986	60.7	61.5	72.3	49.6	74.3	51.7	47.9	52.0	54.1	60.6	26.5	65.1	48.8	23.8	51.6
1987	61.5	62.3	72.7	49.9	74.7	52.8	49.0	53.1	55.6	62.0	28.5	66.4	50.3	25.8	53.0
1988	62.3	63.1	73.2	51.7	75.1	53.8	50.2	54.0	56.3	62.7	29.4	67.1	51.2	25.8	53.9
1989	63.0	63.8	73.7	52.6	75.4	54.6	50.5	54.9	56.9	62.8	30.4	67.0	52.0	27.1	54.6
1990	62.8	63.7	73.3	51.0	75.1	54.7	48.3	55.2	56.7	62.6	27.7	67.1	51.9	25.8	54.7
1991	61.7	62.6	71.6	47.2	73.5	54.2	45.9	54.8	55.4	61.3	23.8	65.9	50.6	21.5	53.6
1992	61.5	62.4	71.1	46.4	73.1	54.2	44.2	54.9	54.9	59.9	23.6	64.3	50.8	22.1	53.6
1993	61.7	62.7	71.4	46.6	73.3	54.6	45.7	55.2	55.0	60.0	23.6	64.3	50.9	21.6	53.8
1994	62.5	63.5	71.8	48.3	73.6	55.8	47.5	56.4	56.1	60.8	25.4	65.0	52.3	24.5	55.0
1995	62.9	63.8	72.0	49.4	73.8	56.1	48.1	56.7	57.1	61.7	25.2	66.1	53.4	26.1	56.1
1996	63.2	64.1	72.3	48.2	74.2	56.3	47.6	57.0	57.4	61.1	24.9	65.5	54.4	27.1	57.1
1997	63.8	64.6	72.7	48.1	74.7	57.0	47.2	57.8	58.2	61.4	23.7	66.1	55.6	28.5	58.4
1998	64.1	64.7	72.7	48.6	74.7	57.1	49.3	57.7	59.7	62.9	28.4	67.1	57.2	31.8	59.7
1999	64.3	64.8	72.8	49.3	74.8	57.3	48.3	58.0	60.6	63.1	26.7	67.5	58.6	29.0	61.5
2000	64.4	64.9	73.0	49.5	74.9	57.4	48.8	58.0	60.9	63.6	28.9	67.7	58.6	30.6	61.3
2001	63.7	64.2	72.0	46.2	74.0	57.0	46.5	57.7	59.7	62.1	26.4	66.3	57.8	27.0	60.7
2002	62.7	63.4	70.8	42.3	73.1	56.4	44.1	57.3	58.1	61.1	25.6	65.2	55.8	24.9	58.7
2003	62.3	63.0	70.1	39.4	72.5	56.3	41.5	57.3	57.4	59.5	19.9	64.1	55.6	23.4	58.6
2004	62.3	63.1	70.4	39.7	72.8	56.1	40.3	57.2	57.2	59.3	19.3	63.9	55.5	23.6	58.5
2005	62.7	63.4	70.8	38.8	73.3	56.3	41.8	57.4	57.7	60.2	20.8	64.7	55.7	22.4	58.9
2006	63.1	63.8	71.3	40.0	73.7	56.6	41.1	57.7	58.4	60.6	21.7	65.2	56.5	26.4	59.4
2007	63.0	63.8	70.9	37.3	73.5	56.7	39.2	57.9	58.4	60.7	19.5	65.5	56.5	23.3	59.8
2006: Jan	62.9	63.7	71.3	40.2	73.7	56.4	41.5	57.4	57.8	60.0	20.5	64.6	56.0	23.7	59.1
Feb	62.9	63.6	71.1	40.3	73.5	56.4	41.4	57.4	58.4	60.7	22.9	65.1	56.4	28.4	59.1
Mar	63.0	63.6	71.3	40.6	73.7	56.3	41.2	57.4	58.5	60.9	22.2	65.4	56.5	25.1	59.5
Apr	63.0	63.7	71.2	40.0	73.6	56.5	42.0	57.6	58.3	60.9	23.1	65.3	56.2	25.8	59.1
May	63.1	63.7	71.2	40.1	73.6	56.6	42.1	57.6	58.6	60.9	23.7	65.3	56.7	26.7	59.5
June	63.1	63.8	71.2	40.3	73.6	56.7	41.4	57.8	58.2	60.5	22.5	64.9	56.3	26.6	59.2
July	63.0	63.8	71.0	39.9	73.5	56.9	41.8	58.0	58.0	60.2	21.7	64.6	56.3	24.0	59.4
Aug	63.1	63.8	71.2	40.0	73.6	56.8	40.3	58.0	58.6	60.4	21.8	64.9	57.1	26.3	60.1
Sept	63.1	63.8	71.4	39.9	73.9	56.6	39.2	57.8	57.7	59.9	17.3	65.9	55.9	27.7	58.7
Oct	63.3	64.0	71.4	39.7	73.9	56.8	40.3	58.0	58.6	60.6	21.9	65.1	56.9	28.8	59.6
Nov	63.3	63.9	71.4	39.6	73.9	56.8	40.8	57.9	58.7	60.9	21.4	65.5	57.0	26.9	59.9
Dec	63.4	64.0	71.5	40.1	73.9	56.9	41.4	58.0	59.1	61.7	21.4	66.4	57.0	26.6	59.9
2007: Jan	63.3	63.9	71.3	40.0	73.7	56.8	39.8	58.0	59.5	61.8	20.1	66.7	57.7	25.9	60.7
Feb	63.2	63.8	71.2	39.0	73.7	56.7	39.7	57.9	59.1	61.3	20.3	66.1	57.3	25.4	60.4
Mar	63.3	64.0	71.4	38.5	74.0	56.8	39.4	58.1	58.4	60.1	21.3	64.7	57.1	23.8	60.3
Apr	63.0	63.6	71.2	38.6	73.7	56.4	38.6	57.6	58.6	60.6	20.7	65.4	56.9	23.7	60.2
May	63.0	63.7	71.1	37.9	73.7	56.5	38.4	57.8	58.1	60.1	19.9	64.8	56.5	22.8	59.8
June	63.0	63.7	71.0	38.1	73.6	56.7	39.3	57.9	58.2	60.0	19.7	64.7	56.8	22.8	60.1
July	63.0	63.6	70.8	37.5	73.4	56.6	39.3	57.9	58.8	61.5	18.7	66.5	56.6	23.5	59.8
Aug	62.8	63.3	70.4	35.7	73.1	56.5	37.9	57.8	58.7	61.9	18.2	67.0	56.2	21.3	59.6
Sept	62.9	63.4	70.6	37.0	73.2	56.9	39.6	58.1	58.2	60.7	18.8	65.7	56.1	22.0	59.4
Oct	62.7	63.5	70.6	37.0	73.2	56.7	39.3	57.9	57.7	59.8	18.5	64.7	56.0	23.5	59.2
Nov	63.0	63.6	70.8	34.5	73.6	56.8	40.0	58.0	57.8	60.4	19.3	65.3	55.6	22.2	58.8
Dec	62.7	63.4	70.5	34.6	73.3	56.6	39.7	57.8	57.6	59.9	19.1	64.7	55.7	22.6	59.0

[1] Civilian employment as percent of civilian noninstitutional population in group specified.
[2] See footnote 1, Table B–37.

Note.—Data relate to persons 16 years of age and over.
See footnote 5 and Note, Table B–35.

Source: Department of Labor (Bureau of Labor Statistics).

TABLE B–42.—*Civilian unemployment rate, 1960–2007*

[Percent [1]; monthly data seasonally adjusted, except as noted]

Year or month	All civilian workers	Males Total	Males 16-19 years	Males 20 years and over	Females Total	Females 16-19 years	Females 20 years and over	Both sexes 16-19 years	White [2]	Black and other [2]	Black or African American [2]	Asian (NSA) [2,3]	Hispanic or Latino ethnicity [4]	Married men, spouse present	Women who maintain families (NSA) [3]
1960	5.5	5.4	15.3	4.7	5.9	13.9	5.1	14.7	5.0	10.2				3.7	
1961	6.7	6.4	17.1	5.7	7.2	16.3	6.3	16.8	6.0	12.4				4.6	
1962	5.5	5.2	14.7	4.6	6.2	14.6	5.4	14.7	4.9	10.9				3.6	
1963	5.7	5.2	17.2	4.5	6.5	17.2	5.4	17.2	5.0	10.8				3.4	
1964	5.2	4.6	15.8	3.9	6.2	16.6	5.2	16.2	4.6	9.6				2.8	
1965	4.5	4.0	14.1	3.2	5.5	15.7	4.5	14.8	4.1	8.1				2.4	
1966	3.8	3.2	11.7	2.5	4.8	14.1	3.8	12.8	3.4	7.3				1.9	
1967	3.8	3.1	12.3	2.3	5.2	13.5	4.2	12.9	3.4	7.4				1.8	4.9
1968	3.6	2.9	11.6	2.2	4.8	14.0	3.8	12.7	3.2	6.7				1.6	4.4
1969	3.5	2.8	11.4	2.1	4.7	13.3	3.7	12.2	3.1	6.4				1.5	4.4
1970	4.9	4.4	15.0	3.5	5.9	15.6	4.8	15.3	4.5	8.2				2.6	5.4
1971	5.9	5.3	16.6	4.4	6.9	17.2	5.7	16.9	5.4	9.9				3.2	7.3
1972	5.6	5.0	15.9	4.0	6.6	16.7	5.4	16.2	5.1	10.0	10.4			2.8	7.2
1973	4.9	4.2	13.9	3.3	6.0	15.3	4.9	14.5	4.3	9.0	9.4		7.5	2.3	7.1
1974	5.6	4.9	15.6	3.8	6.7	16.6	5.5	16.0	5.0	9.9	10.5		8.1	2.7	7.0
1975	8.5	7.9	20.1	6.8	9.3	19.7	8.0	19.9	7.8	13.8	14.8		12.2	5.1	10.0
1976	7.7	7.1	19.2	5.9	8.6	18.7	7.4	19.0	7.0	13.1	14.0		11.5	4.2	10.1
1977	7.1	6.3	17.3	5.2	8.2	18.3	7.0	17.8	6.2	13.1	14.0		10.1	3.6	9.4
1978	6.1	5.3	15.8	4.3	7.2	17.1	6.0	16.4	5.2	11.9	12.8		9.1	2.8	8.5
1979	5.8	5.1	15.9	4.2	6.8	16.4	5.7	16.1	5.1	11.3	12.3		8.3	2.8	8.3
1980	7.1	6.9	18.3	5.9	7.4	17.2	6.4	17.8	6.3	13.1	14.3		10.1	4.2	9.2
1981	7.6	7.4	20.1	6.3	7.9	19.0	6.8	19.6	6.7	14.2	15.6		10.4	4.3	10.4
1982	9.7	9.9	24.4	8.8	9.4	21.9	8.3	23.2	8.6	17.3	18.9		13.8	6.5	11.7
1983	9.6	9.9	23.3	8.9	9.2	21.3	8.1	22.4	8.4	17.8	19.5		13.7	6.5	12.2
1984	7.5	7.4	19.6	6.6	7.6	18.0	6.8	18.9	6.5	14.4	15.9		10.7	4.6	10.3
1985	7.2	7.0	19.5	6.2	7.4	17.6	6.6	18.6	6.2	13.7	15.1		10.5	4.3	10.4
1986	7.0	6.9	19.0	6.1	7.1	17.6	6.2	18.3	6.0	13.1	14.5		10.6	4.4	9.8
1987	6.2	6.2	17.8	5.4	6.2	15.9	5.4	16.9	5.3	11.6	13.0		8.8	3.9	9.2
1988	5.5	5.5	16.0	4.8	5.6	14.4	4.9	15.3	4.7	10.4	11.7		8.2	3.3	8.1
1989	5.3	5.2	15.9	4.5	5.4	14.0	4.7	15.0	4.5	10.0	11.4		8.0	3.0	8.1
1990	5.6	5.7	16.3	5.0	5.5	14.7	4.9	15.5	4.8	10.1	11.4		8.2	3.4	8.3
1991	6.8	7.2	19.8	6.4	6.4	17.5	5.7	18.7	6.1	11.1	12.5		10.0	4.4	9.3
1992	7.5	7.9	21.5	7.1	7.0	18.6	6.3	20.1	6.6	12.7	14.2		11.6	5.1	10.0
1993	6.9	7.2	20.4	6.4	6.6	17.5	5.9	19.0	6.1	11.7	13.0		10.8	4.4	9.7
1994	6.1	6.2	19.0	5.4	6.0	16.2	5.4	17.6	5.3	10.5	11.5		9.9	3.7	8.9
1995	5.6	5.6	18.4	4.8	5.6	16.1	4.9	17.3	4.9	9.6	10.4		9.3	3.3	8.0
1996	5.4	5.4	18.1	4.6	5.4	15.2	4.8	16.7	4.7	9.3	10.5		8.9	3.0	8.2
1997	4.9	4.9	16.9	4.2	5.0	15.0	4.4	16.0	4.2	8.8	10.0		7.7	2.7	8.1
1998	4.5	4.4	16.2	3.7	4.6	12.9	4.1	14.6	3.9	7.8	8.9		7.2	2.4	7.2
1999	4.2	4.1	14.7	3.5	4.3	13.2	3.8	13.9	3.7	7.0	8.0		6.4	2.2	6.4
2000	4.0	3.9	14.0	3.3	4.1	12.1	3.6	13.1	3.5		7.6	3.6	5.7	2.0	5.9
2001	4.7	4.8	16.0	4.2	4.7	13.4	4.1	14.7	4.2		8.6	4.5	6.6	2.7	6.6
2002	5.8	5.9	18.1	5.3	5.6	14.9	5.1	16.5	5.1		10.2	5.9	7.5	3.6	8.0
2003	6.0	6.3	19.3	5.6	5.7	15.6	5.1	17.5	5.2		10.8	6.0	7.7	3.8	8.5
2004	5.5	5.6	18.4	5.0	5.4	15.5	4.9	17.0	4.8		10.4	4.4	7.0	3.1	8.0
2005	5.1	5.1	18.6	4.4	5.1	14.5	4.6	16.6	4.4		10.0	4.0	6.0	2.8	7.8
2006	4.6	4.6	16.9	4.0	4.6	13.8	4.1	15.4	4.0		8.9	3.0	5.2	2.4	7.1
2007	4.6	4.7	17.6	4.1	4.5	13.8	4.0	15.7	4.1		8.3	3.2	5.6	2.5	6.5
2006: Jan	4.7	4.6	16.4	4.0	4.8	14.2	4.3	15.3	4.1		8.9	3.2	5.7	2.4	8.2
Feb	4.7	4.7	16.9	4.1	4.8	13.8	4.3	15.4	4.1		9.4	3.2	5.5	2.4	7.5
Mar	4.7	4.7	17.0	4.1	4.7	14.7	4.2	15.9	4.0		9.4	3.4	5.3	2.4	7.5
Apr	4.7	4.7	16.5	4.2	4.7	12.4	4.3	14.5	4.1		9.3	3.6	5.3	2.5	7.5
May	4.7	4.8	16.2	4.2	4.5	11.6	4.2	14.0	4.1		8.8	3.0	4.9	2.5	6.3
June	4.6	4.6	17.1	4.0	4.7	13.9	4.1	15.6	4.1		8.8	3.5	5.2	2.5	7.2
July	4.7	4.8	17.4	4.2	4.7	14.3	4.2	15.8	4.1		9.6	2.7	5.2	2.5	7.4
Aug	4.7	4.8	17.2	4.2	4.6	15.1	4.1	16.2	4.1		8.8	2.9	5.4	2.6	6.7
Sept	4.5	4.4	17.7	3.8	4.7	14.9	4.2	16.3	3.9		9.1	2.8	5.4	2.4	6.8
Oct	4.4	4.5	16.8	3.9	4.4	13.8	3.9	15.4	3.9		8.5	2.7	4.7	2.3	6.5
Nov	4.5	4.5	16.4	3.9	4.5	13.5	4.0	15.0	3.9		8.5	3.2	5.0	2.4	6.9
Dec	4.4	4.5	16.2	3.9	4.4	13.4	3.9	14.8	4.0		8.3	2.4	4.9	2.4	6.2
2007: Jan	4.6	4.7	16.2	4.1	4.5	13.7	4.0	15.0	4.1		8.0	3.2	5.7	2.5	6.6
Feb	4.5	4.7	16.6	4.1	4.3	13.2	3.8	15.0	4.0		8.0	2.7	5.2	2.6	6.5
Mar	4.4	4.5	16.1	4.0	4.3	13.1	3.8	14.6	3.8		8.3	3.0	5.2	2.5	6.7
Apr	4.5	4.6	16.5	4.0	4.4	14.2	3.9	15.4	4.0		8.2	3.3	5.5	2.5	6.2
May	4.5	4.6	17.5	4.0	4.4	14.1	3.9	15.8	4.0		8.4	2.9	5.8	2.6	6.3
June	4.6	4.7	18.0	4.1	4.4	13.9	3.9	16.0	4.1		8.4	3.1	5.7	2.4	6.8
July	4.7	4.7	16.9	4.2	4.6	13.6	4.1	15.3	4.2		8.1	3.0	5.9	2.7	6.8
Aug	4.7	4.7	18.0	4.1	4.6	14.4	4.1	16.2	4.2		7.7	3.4	5.5	2.5	6.2
Sept	4.7	4.9	18.3	4.3	4.5	13.7	4.1	16.0	4.2		8.2	3.2	5.7	2.5	6.4
Oct	4.8	4.9	18.1	4.3	4.6	13.3	4.1	15.7	4.2		8.5	3.7	5.6	2.6	6.3
Nov	4.7	4.7	19.5	4.1	4.6	13.4	4.1	16.4	4.2		8.4	3.6	5.7	2.6	6.6
Dec	5.0	5.1	19.8	4.4	4.9	14.4	4.4	17.1	4.4		9.0	3.7	6.3	2.7	6.9

[1] Unemployed as percent of civilian labor force in group specified.
[2] See footnote 1, Table B–37.
[3] Not seasonally adjusted (NSA).
[4] Persons whose ethnicity is identified as Hispanic or Latino may be of any race.

Note.—Data relate to persons 16 years of age and over. See footnote 5 and Note, Table B–35.

Source: Department of Labor (Bureau of Labor Statistics).

TABLE B–43.—*Civilian unemployment rate by demographic characteristics, 1965–2007*

[Percent [1]; monthly data seasonally adjusted]

Year or month	All civilian workers	White [2] Total	Males Total	Males 16-19 years	Males 20 years and over	Females Total	Females 16-19 years	Females 20 years and over	Black and other or black or African American [2] Total	Males Total	Males 16-19 years	Males 20 years and over	Females Total	Females 16-19 years	Females 20 years and over
									Black and other [2]						
1965	4.5	4.1	3.6	12.9	2.9	5.0	14.0	4.0	8.1	7.4	23.3	6.0	9.2	31.7	7.5
1966	3.8	3.4	2.8	10.5	2.2	4.3	12.1	3.3	7.3	6.3	21.3	4.9	8.7	31.3	6.6
1967	3.8	3.4	2.7	10.7	2.1	4.6	11.5	3.8	7.4	6.0	23.9	4.3	9.1	29.6	7.1
1968	3.6	3.2	2.6	10.1	2.0	4.3	12.1	3.4	6.7	5.6	22.1	3.9	8.3	28.7	6.3
1969	3.5	3.1	2.5	10.0	1.9	4.2	11.5	3.4	6.4	5.3	21.4	3.7	7.8	27.6	5.8
1970	4.9	4.5	4.0	13.7	3.2	5.4	13.4	4.4	8.2	7.3	25.0	5.6	9.3	34.5	6.9
1971	5.9	5.4	4.9	15.1	4.0	6.3	15.1	5.3	9.9	9.1	28.8	7.3	10.9	35.4	8.7
1972	5.6	5.1	4.5	14.2	3.6	5.9	14.2	4.9	10.0	8.9	29.7	6.9	11.4	38.4	8.8
									Black or African American [2]						
1972	5.6	5.1	4.5	14.2	3.6	5.9	14.2	4.9	10.4	9.3	31.7	7.0	11.8	40.5	9.0
1973	4.9	4.3	3.8	12.3	3.0	5.3	13.0	4.3	9.4	8.0	27.8	6.0	11.1	36.1	8.6
1974	5.6	5.0	4.4	13.5	3.5	6.1	14.5	5.1	10.5	9.8	33.1	7.4	11.3	37.4	8.8
1975	8.5	7.8	7.2	18.3	6.2	8.6	17.4	7.5	14.8	14.8	38.1	12.5	14.8	41.0	12.2
1976	7.7	7.0	6.4	17.3	5.4	7.9	16.4	6.8	14.0	13.7	37.5	11.4	14.3	41.6	11.7
1977	7.1	6.2	5.5	15.0	4.7	7.3	15.9	6.2	14.0	13.3	39.2	10.7	14.9	43.4	12.3
1978	6.1	5.2	4.6	13.5	3.7	6.2	14.4	5.2	12.8	11.8	36.7	9.3	13.8	40.8	11.2
1979	5.8	5.1	4.5	13.9	3.6	5.9	14.0	5.0	12.3	11.4	34.2	9.3	13.3	39.1	10.9
1980	7.1	6.3	6.1	16.2	5.3	6.5	14.8	5.6	14.3	14.5	37.5	12.4	14.0	39.8	11.9
1981	7.6	6.7	6.5	17.9	5.6	6.9	16.6	5.9	15.6	15.7	40.7	13.5	15.6	42.2	13.4
1982	9.7	8.6	8.8	21.7	7.8	8.3	19.0	7.3	18.9	20.1	48.9	17.8	17.6	47.1	15.4
1983	9.6	8.4	8.8	20.2	7.9	7.9	18.3	6.9	19.5	20.3	48.8	18.1	18.6	48.2	16.5
1984	7.5	6.5	6.4	16.8	5.7	6.5	15.2	5.8	15.9	16.4	42.7	14.3	15.4	42.6	13.5
1985	7.2	6.2	6.1	16.5	5.4	6.4	14.8	5.7	15.1	15.3	41.0	13.2	14.9	39.2	13.1
1986	7.0	6.0	6.0	16.3	5.3	6.1	14.9	5.4	14.5	14.8	39.3	12.9	14.2	39.2	12.4
1987	6.2	5.3	5.4	15.5	4.8	5.2	13.4	4.6	13.0	12.7	34.4	11.1	13.2	34.9	11.6
1988	5.5	4.7	4.7	13.9	4.1	4.7	12.3	4.1	11.7	11.7	32.7	10.1	11.7	32.0	10.4
1989	5.3	4.5	4.5	13.7	3.9	4.5	11.5	4.0	11.4	11.5	31.9	10.0	11.4	33.0	9.8
1990	5.6	4.8	4.9	14.3	4.3	4.7	12.6	4.1	11.4	11.9	31.9	10.4	10.9	29.9	9.7
1991	6.8	6.1	6.5	17.6	5.8	5.6	15.2	5.0	12.5	13.0	36.3	11.5	12.0	36.0	10.6
1992	7.5	6.6	7.0	18.5	6.4	6.1	15.8	5.5	14.2	15.2	42.0	13.5	13.2	37.2	11.8
1993	6.9	6.1	6.3	17.7	5.7	5.7	14.7	5.2	13.0	13.8	40.1	12.1	12.1	37.4	10.7
1994	6.1	5.3	5.4	16.3	4.8	5.2	13.8	4.6	11.5	12.0	37.6	10.3	11.0	32.6	9.8
1995	5.6	4.9	4.9	15.6	4.3	4.8	13.4	4.3	10.4	10.6	37.1	8.8	10.2	34.3	8.6
1996	5.4	4.7	4.7	15.5	4.1	4.7	12.9	4.1	10.5	11.1	36.9	9.4	10.0	30.3	8.7
1997	4.9	4.2	4.2	14.3	3.6	4.2	12.8	3.7	10.0	10.2	36.5	8.5	9.9	28.7	8.8
1998	4.5	3.9	3.9	14.1	3.2	3.9	10.9	3.4	8.9	8.9	30.1	7.4	9.0	25.3	7.9
1999	4.2	3.7	3.6	12.6	3.0	3.8	11.3	3.3	8.0	8.2	30.9	6.7	7.8	25.1	6.8
2000	4.0	3.5	3.4	12.3	2.8	3.6	10.4	3.1	7.6	8.0	26.2	6.9	7.1	22.8	6.2
2001	4.7	4.2	4.2	13.9	3.7	4.1	11.4	3.6	8.6	9.3	30.4	8.0	8.1	27.5	7.0
2002	5.8	5.1	5.3	15.9	4.7	4.9	13.1	4.4	10.2	10.7	31.3	9.5	9.8	28.3	8.8
2003	6.0	5.2	5.6	17.1	5.0	4.8	13.3	4.4	10.8	11.6	36.0	10.3	10.2	30.3	9.2
2004	5.5	4.8	5.0	16.3	4.4	4.7	13.6	4.2	10.4	11.1	35.6	9.9	9.8	28.2	8.9
2005	5.1	4.4	4.4	16.1	3.8	4.4	12.3	3.9	10.0	10.5	36.3	9.2	9.5	30.3	8.5
2006	4.6	4.0	4.0	14.6	3.5	4.0	11.7	3.6	8.9	9.5	32.7	8.3	8.4	25.9	7.5
2007	4.6	4.1	4.1	15.7	3.7	4.0	12.1	3.6	8.3	9.1	33.8	7.9	7.5	25.3	6.7
2006: Jan	4.7	4.1	4.1	14.5	3.6	4.1	11.7	3.7	8.9	8.6	28.6	7.6	9.2	31.1	8.1
Feb	4.7	4.1	4.1	14.7	3.6	4.1	10.9	3.8	9.4	9.8	30.9	8.7	9.1	29.5	7.9
Mar	4.7	4.0	4.0	14.1	3.5	4.1	11.7	3.6	9.4	9.7	33.6	8.4	9.1	33.8	7.7
Apr	4.7	4.1	4.1	14.5	3.6	4.0	10.3	3.7	9.3	10.0	32.3	8.8	8.7	25.7	7.8
May	4.7	4.1	4.2	15.1	3.7	4.0	10.0	3.6	8.8	9.9	29.8	8.8	7.8	20.6	7.1
June	4.6	4.1	4.1	14.8	3.6	4.1	12.1	3.6	8.8	9.4	32.8	8.1	8.3	22.9	7.6
July	4.7	4.1	4.1	14.4	3.6	4.1	11.8	3.7	9.6	10.5	36.3	9.1	8.7	29.3	7.7
Aug	4.7	4.1	4.1	15.0	3.6	4.1	13.4	3.6	8.8	9.6	32.1	8.4	8.1	24.5	7.2
Sept	4.5	3.9	3.8	14.8	3.3	4.1	12.7	3.6	9.1	9.7	39.4	8.3	8.6	26.3	7.6
Oct	4.4	3.9	3.9	14.4	3.4	4.0	12.3	3.5	9.6	9.6	34.0	8.2	7.5	21.2	6.7
Nov	4.5	3.9	3.9	14.0	3.4	4.0	12.0	3.5	8.5	9.2	32.7	7.9	7.9	23.0	7.2
Dec	4.4	4.0	4.0	15.1	3.5	3.8	11.5	3.4	8.3	8.2	27.1	7.3	8.4	24.0	7.6
2007: Jan	4.6	4.1	4.2	14.2	3.7	4.0	12.2	3.6	8.0	8.8	34.3	7.5	7.4	24.3	6.5
Feb	4.5	4.0	4.2	14.4	3.7	3.8	11.8	3.4	8.0	8.9	35.5	7.5	7.1	22.3	6.4
Mar	4.4	3.8	3.9	14.6	3.4	3.8	11.8	3.4	8.3	9.7	25.7	8.9	7.0	23.8	6.2
Apr	4.5	4.0	4.0	14.4	3.5	3.9	12.1	3.5	8.2	9.6	34.3	8.3	7.0	27.1	6.0
May	4.5	4.0	4.0	15.2	3.5	3.9	12.5	3.4	8.4	9.5	35.4	8.2	7.5	24.8	6.7
June	4.6	4.1	4.2	16.3	3.6	4.0	12.0	3.5	8.4	9.5	33.5	8.3	7.5	28.7	6.4
July	4.7	4.2	4.3	15.5	3.8	4.1	12.0	3.6	8.1	8.6	31.1	7.6	7.6	23.5	6.9
Aug	4.7	4.2	4.3	16.5	3.8	4.1	12.2	3.7	7.7	7.9	33.2	6.8	7.5	29.4	6.5
Sept	4.7	4.2	4.5	16.4	3.9	4.0	12.2	3.5	8.2	8.7	33.9	7.5	7.8	24.2	7.1
Oct	4.8	4.2	4.3	15.9	3.8	4.1	12.0	3.6	8.5	9.4	36.0	8.2	7.7	20.1	7.1
Nov	4.7	4.2	4.3	17.8	3.7	4.1	11.8	3.7	8.4	9.1	34.6	7.9	7.8	24.9	7.0
Dec	5.0	4.4	4.5	16.8	3.9	4.4	12.1	4.0	9.0	10.0	39.5	8.4	8.1	30.1	7.0

[1] Unemployed as percent of civilian labor force in group specified.
[2] See footnote 1, Table B–37.

Note.—Data relate to persons 16 years of age and over. See footnote 5 and Note, Table B–35.

Source: Department of Labor (Bureau of Labor Statistics).

[Thousands of persons, except as noted; monthly data seasonally adjusted [1]]

Year or month	Un-employ-ment	Duration of unemployment						Reason for unemployment					
		Less than 5 weeks	5-14 weeks	15-26 weeks	27 weeks and over	Average (mean) duration (weeks)	Median duration (weeks)	Job losers [3]			Job leavers	Re-entrants	New entrants
								Total	On layoff	Other			
1960	3,852	1,719	1,176	503	454	12.8	....	....	....	....	....	....	....
1961	4,714	1,806	1,376	728	804	15.6	....	....	....	....	....	....	....
1962	3,911	1,663	1,134	534	585	14.7	....	....	....	....	....	....	....
1963	4,070	1,751	1,231	535	553	14.0	....	....	....	....	....	....	....
1964	3,786	1,697	1,117	491	482	13.3	....	....	....	....	....	....	....
1965	3,366	1,628	983	404	351	11.8	....	....	....	....	....	....	....
1966	2,875	1,573	779	287	239	10.4	....	....	....	....	....	....	....
1967 [2]	2,975	1,634	893	271	177	8.7	2.3	1,229	394	836	438	945	396
1968	2,817	1,594	810	256	156	8.4	4.5	1,070	334	736	431	909	407
1969	2,832	1,629	827	242	133	7.8	4.4	1,017	339	678	436	965	413
1970	4,093	2,139	1,290	428	235	8.6	4.9	1,811	675	1,137	550	1,228	504
1971	5,016	2,245	1,585	668	519	11.3	6.3	2,323	735	1,588	590	1,472	630
1972	4,882	2,242	1,472	601	566	12.0	6.2	2,108	582	1,526	641	1,456	677
1973	4,365	2,224	1,314	483	343	10.0	5.2	1,694	472	1,221	683	1,340	649
1974	5,156	2,604	1,597	574	381	9.8	5.2	2,242	746	1,495	768	1,463	681
1975	7,929	2,940	2,484	1,303	1,203	14.2	8.4	4,386	1,671	2,714	827	1,892	823
1976	7,406	2,844	2,196	1,018	1,348	15.8	8.2	3,679	1,050	2,628	903	1,928	895
1977	6,991	2,919	2,132	913	1,028	14.3	7.0	3,166	865	2,300	909	1,963	953
1978	6,202	2,865	1,923	766	648	11.9	5.9	2,585	712	1,873	874	1,857	885
1979	6,137	2,950	1,946	706	535	10.8	5.4	2,635	851	1,784	880	1,806	817
1980	7,637	3,295	2,470	1,052	820	11.9	6.5	3,947	1,488	2,459	891	1,927	872
1981	8,273	3,449	2,539	1,122	1,162	13.7	6.9	4,267	1,430	2,837	923	2,102	981
1982	10,678	3,883	3,311	1,708	1,776	15.6	8.7	6,268	2,127	4,141	840	2,384	1,185
1983	10,717	3,570	2,937	1,652	2,559	20.0	10.1	6,258	1,780	4,478	830	2,412	1,216
1984	8,539	3,350	2,451	1,104	1,634	18.2	7.9	4,421	1,171	3,250	823	2,184	1,110
1985	8,312	3,498	2,509	1,025	1,280	15.6	6.8	4,139	1,157	2,982	877	2,256	1,039
1986	8,237	3,448	2,557	1,045	1,187	15.0	6.9	4,033	1,090	2,943	1,015	2,160	1,029
1987	7,425	3,246	2,196	943	1,040	14.5	6.5	3,566	943	2,623	965	1,974	920
1988	6,701	3,084	2,007	801	809	13.5	5.9	3,092	851	2,241	983	1,809	816
1989	6,528	3,174	1,978	730	646	11.9	4.8	2,983	850	2,133	1,024	1,843	677
1990	7,047	3,265	2,257	822	703	12.0	5.3	3,387	1,028	2,359	1,041	1,930	688
1991	8,628	3,480	2,791	1,246	1,111	13.7	6.8	4,694	1,292	3,402	1,004	2,139	792
1992	9,613	3,376	2,830	1,453	1,954	17.7	8.7	5,389	1,260	4,129	1,002	2,285	937
1993	8,940	3,262	2,584	1,297	1,798	18.0	8.3	4,848	1,115	3,733	976	2,198	919
1994	7,996	2,728	2,408	1,237	1,623	18.8	9.2	3,815	977	2,838	791	2,786	604
1995	7,404	2,700	2,342	1,085	1,278	16.6	8.3	3,476	1,030	2,446	824	2,525	579
1996	7,236	2,633	2,287	1,053	1,262	16.7	8.3	3,370	1,021	2,349	774	2,512	580
1997	6,739	2,538	2,138	995	1,067	15.8	8.0	3,037	931	2,106	795	2,338	569
1998	6,210	2,622	1,950	763	875	14.5	6.7	2,822	866	1,957	734	2,132	520
1999	5,880	2,568	1,832	755	725	13.4	6.4	2,622	848	1,774	783	2,005	469
2000	5,692	2,558	1,815	669	649	12.6	5.9	2,517	852	1,664	780	1,961	434
2001	6,801	2,853	2,196	951	801	13.1	6.8	3,476	1,067	2,409	835	2,031	459
2002	8,378	2,893	2,580	1,369	1,535	16.6	9.1	4,607	1,124	3,483	866	2,368	536
2003	8,774	2,785	2,612	1,442	1,936	19.2	10.1	4,838	1,121	3,717	818	2,477	641
2004	8,149	2,696	2,382	1,293	1,779	19.6	9.8	4,197	998	3,199	858	2,408	686
2005	7,591	2,667	2,304	1,130	1,490	18.4	8.9	3,667	933	2,734	872	2,386	666
2006	7,001	2,614	2,121	1,031	1,235	16.8	8.3	3,321	921	2,400	827	2,237	616
2007	7,078	2,542	2,232	1,061	1,243	16.8	8.5	3,515	976	2,539	793	2,142	627
2006: Jan	7,025	2,526	2,219	1,087	1,169	16.9	8.5	3,328	864	2,463	828	2,260	610
Feb	7,143	2,576	2,090	1,176	1,330	17.8	8.9	3,370	879	2,491	846	2,280	694
Mar	7,075	2,704	2,012	1,049	1,278	16.8	8.4	3,444	923	2,521	821	2,166	625
Apr	7,113	2,662	2,133	1,014	1,324	16.7	8.4	3,495	899	2,596	857	2,174	574
May	7,038	2,548	2,199	968	1,336	17.1	8.6	3,473	945	2,527	883	2,131	540
June	7,017	2,678	2,083	979	1,156	16.7	7.7	3,385	988	2,397	810	2,166	640
July	7,176	2,711	2,142	994	1,316	17.1	8.1	3,306	919	2,387	848	2,397	640
Aug	7,128	2,595	2,273	1,017	1,309	17.1	8.4	3,282	898	2,383	851	2,292	655
Sept	6,896	2,584	2,066	1,003	1,254	17.3	8.1	3,231	909	2,322	794	2,279	623
Oct	6,735	2,603	2,066	1,005	1,088	16.4	8.1	3,097	956	2,141	784	2,261	580
Nov	6,820	2,501	2,148	1,038	1,137	16.2	8.2	3,209	973	2,236	796	2,249	588
Dec	6,760	2,650	2,013	994	1,099	16.1	7.5	3,242	968	2,274	803	2,169	592
2007: Jan	7,043	2,596	2,298	995	1,138	16.5	8.2	3,399	1,017	2,382	791	2,195	615
Feb	6,837	2,567	2,181	935	1,216	16.6	8.2	3,449	1,016	2,433	810	2,029	580
Mar	6,738	2,338	2,156	976	1,207	17.2	8.6	3,240	865	2,375	755	2,143	600
Apr	6,829	2,442	2,147	1,066	1,193	17.0	8.6	3,316	1,019	2,297	749	2,169	599
May	6,863	2,467	2,187	1,099	1,137	16.6	8.3	3,375	997	2,379	768	2,149	557
June	6,997	2,505	2,140	1,136	1,159	16.8	8.3	3,418	862	2,555	810	2,125	628
July	7,137	2,496	2,220	1,091	1,311	17.3	8.9	3,629	983	2,646	823	2,082	602
Aug	7,133	2,610	2,201	1,124	1,252	16.9	8.6	3,632	981	2,652	794	2,076	603
Sept	7,246	2,537	2,330	1,112	1,280	16.6	8.9	3,622	963	2,660	839	2,154	685
Oct	7,291	2,508	2,454	1,052	1,315	17.0	8.7	3,731	1,064	2,668	790	2,103	709
Nov	7,181	2,633	2,157	1,014	1,384	17.2	8.7	3,609	979	2,630	783	2,160	669
Dec	7,655	2,793	2,330	1,182	1,243	16.6	8.4	3,857	975	2,882	798	2,343	697

[1] Because of independent seasonal adjustment of the various series, detail will not sum to totals.
[2] For 1967, the sum of the unemployed categorized by reason for unemployment does not equal total unemployment.
[3] Beginning with January 1994, job losers and persons who completed temporary jobs.

Note.—Data relate to persons 16 years of age and over.
See footnote 5 and Note, Table B-35.

Source: Department of Labor (Bureau of Labor Statistics).

[Thousands of persons, except as noted]

Year or month	All programs			State programs					
	Covered employment[1]	Insured unemployment (weekly average)[2,3]	Total benefits paid (millions of dollars)[2,4]	Insured unemployment (weekly average)[3]	Initial claims (weekly average)	Exhaustions (weekly average)[5]	Insured unemployment as percent of covered employment	Benefits paid	
								Total (millions of dollars)[4]	Average weekly check (dollars)[6]
1978	88,804	2,645	9,007	2,359	346	39	3.3	7,717	83.67
1979	92,062	2,592	9,401	2,434	388	39	2.9	8,613	89.67
1980	92,659	3,837	16,175	3,350	488	59	3.9	13,761	98.95
1981	93,300	3,410	15,287	3,047	460	57	3.5	13,262	106.70
1982	91,628	4,592	24,491	4,059	583	80	4.6	20,649	119.34
1983	91,898	3,774	20,968	3,395	438	80	3.9	18,549	123.59
1984	96,474	2,560	13,739	2,475	377	50	2.8	13,237	123.47
1985	99,186	2,699	15,217	2,617	397	49	2.9	14,707	128.11
1986	101,099	2,739	16,563	2,643	378	52	2.8	15,950	135.65
1987	103,936	2,369	14,684	2,300	328	46	2.4	14,211	140.39
1988	107,156	2,135	13,481	2,081	310	38	2.0	13,086	144.74
1989	109,929	2,205	14,569	2,158	330	37	2.1	14,205	151.43
1990	111,500	2,575	18,387	2,522	388	45	2.4	17,932	161.20
1991	109,606	3,406	26,327	3,342	447	67	3.2	25,479	169.56
1992	110,167	3,348	[7] 26,035	3,245	408	74	3.1	25,056	173.38
1993	112,146	2,845	[7] 22,629	2,751	341	62	2.6	21,661	179.41
1994	115,255	2,746	22,508	2,670	340	57	2.4	21,537	181.91
1995	118,068	2,639	21,991	2,572	357	51	2.3	21,226	187.04
1996	120,567	2,656	22,495	2,595	356	53	2.2	21,820	189.27
1997	121,044	2,370	20,324	2,323	323	48	1.9	19,735	192.84
1998	124,184	2,260	19,941	2,222	321	44	1.8	19,431	200.58
1999	127,042	2,223	21,024	2,188	298	44	1.7	20,563	212.10
2000	129,877	2,146	20,983	2,110	301	41	1.6	20,507	221.01
2001	129,636	3,012	32,228	2,974	404	54	2.3	31,680	238.07
2002	128,234	3,624	[8] 42,980	3,585	407	85	2.8	47,251	256.79
2003	127,796	3,573	[8] 42,413	3,531	404	85	2.8	43,159	261.67
2004	129,278	2,999	[8] 36,641	2,950	345	68	2.3	35,776	262.50
2005	131,572	2,709	[8] 32,073	2,661	328	55	2.0	31,238	266.63
2006	133,834	2,521	[8] 30,640	2,476	313	51	1.9	29,800	277.20
2007 [p]		2,612	[8] 31,275	2,571	324	51	....	30,552	287.71
				[**]	[**]		[**]		
2006: Jan		3,385	3,433.5	2,527	291	59	2.0	3,345.7	274.18
Feb		3,043	2,916.2	2,493	303	61	1.9	2,841.5	277.71
Mar		2,653	3,051.9	2,455	307	56	1.9	2,974.6	280.61
Apr		2,662	2,477.4	2,437	312	58	1.9	2,408.6	278.97
May		2,268	2,486.2	2,425	328	52	1.9	2,419.8	277.36
June		2,171	2,273.8	2,435	309	46	1.9	2,215.8	275.16
July		2,639	2,449.5	2,466	313	54	1.9	2,388.2	271.15
Aug		2,267	2,483.6	2,478	317	47	1.9	2,415.8	271.21
Sept		2,092	2,076.9	2,441	315	44	1.9	2,018.4	277.58
Oct		2,283	2,318.4	2,433	314	47	1.9	2,251.0	279.30
Nov		2,221	2,330.2	2,458	325	45	1.9	2,258.3	280.76
Dec		2,633	2,605.9	2,457	320	47	1.9	2,538.1	283.61
2007: Jan		3,163	3,591.5	2,488	311	56	1.9	3,509.8	287.20
Feb		3,104	3,122.7	2,553	337	51	1.9	3,056.3	290.49
Mar		2,741	3,052.2	2,513	317	48	1.9	2,987.0	290.62
Apr		2,833	2,890.7	2,536	327	58	1.9	2,828.3	288.90
May		2,240	2,602.8	2,496	306	52	1.9	2,544.6	288.94
June		2,281	2,297.7	2,527	319	48	1.9	2,248.3	284.23
July		2,705	2,771.3	2,547	307	55	1.9	2,711.8	279.60
Aug		2,272	2,543.1	2,578	324	47	2.0	2,483.9	281.22
Sept		2,346	2,222.2	2,534	313	48	1.9	2,166.4	286.52
Oct		2,259	2,589.2	2,553	326	51	1.9	2,520.5	289.42
Nov		2,274	2,426.4	2,606	339	46	2.0	2,364.2	289.94
Dec [p]		3,070	3,074.5	2,700	342	54	2.0	3,004.0	294.50

[**] Monthly data are seasonally adjusted.

[1] Through 1996, includes persons under the following programs: State, Unemployment Compensation for Federal Employees (UCFE), Railroad Retirement Board (RRB), and Unemployment Compensation for Ex-Servicemembers (UCX). Beginning with 1997, covered employment data are under the State and UCFE programs only. Workers covered by State programs account for about 97 percent of wage and salary earners. Covered employment data beginning 2001 are based on the North American Industry Classification System (NAICS). Prior data are based on the Standard Industrial Classification (SIC).

[2] Includes State, UCFE, RRB, and UCX. Also includes Federal and State extended benefit programs. Does not include Federal Supplemental Benefits (FSB), Special Unemployment Assistance (SUA), Federal Supplemental Compensation, Emergency Unemployment Compensation, and Temporary Extended Unemployment Compensation (TEUC) programs.

[3] Covered workers who have completed at least one week of unemployment.

[4] Annual data are net amounts, and monthly data are gross amounts.

[5] Individuals receiving final payments in benefit year.

[6] For total unemployment only.

[7] Including Emergency Unemployment Compensation, total benefits paid for 1992 and 1993 would be approximately (in millions of dollars): for 1992, 39,990 and for 1993, 34,876.

[8] Including TEUC, total benefits paid (not including RRB program) would be approximately (in millions of dollars): for 2002, 52,709; 2003, 63,097; 2004, 37,932; 2005, 32,051; 2006, 30,588; and 2007, 31,233.

Note.—Insured unemployment and initial claims programs include Puerto Rican sugar cane workers.

Source: Department of Labor (Employment and Training Administration).

[Thousands of persons; monthly data seasonally adjusted]

Year or month	Total	Goods-producing industries						Service-providing industries		
		Total	Natural resources and mining	Con-struc-tion	Manufacturing			Total	Trade, transportation, and utilities [1]	
					Total	Durable goods	Nondurable goods		Total	Retail trade
1960	54,296	19,182	771	2,973	15,438	9,071	6,367	35,114	11,147	5,589
1961	54,105	18,647	728	2,908	15,011	8,711	6,300	35,458	11,040	5,560
1962	55,659	19,203	709	2,997	15,498	9,099	6,399	36,455	11,215	5,672
1963	56,764	19,385	694	3,060	15,631	9,226	6,405	37,379	11,367	5,781
1964	58,391	19,733	697	3,148	15,888	9,414	6,474	38,658	11,677	5,977
1965	60,874	20,595	694	3,284	16,617	9,973	6,644	40,279	12,139	6,262
1966	64,020	21,740	690	3,371	17,680	10,803	6,878	42,280	12,611	6,530
1967	65,931	21,882	679	3,305	17,897	10,952	6,945	44,049	12,950	6,711
1968	68,023	22,292	671	3,410	18,211	11,137	7,074	45,731	13,334	6,977
1969	70,512	22,893	683	3,637	18,573	11,396	7,177	47,619	13,853	7,295
1970	71,006	22,179	677	3,654	17,848	10,762	7,086	48,827	14,144	7,463
1971	71,335	21,602	658	3,770	17,174	10,229	6,944	49,734	14,318	7,657
1972	73,798	22,299	672	3,957	17,669	10,630	7,039	51,499	14,788	8,038
1973	76,912	23,450	693	4,167	18,589	11,414	7,176	53,462	15,349	8,371
1974	78,389	23,364	755	4,095	18,514	11,432	7,082	55,025	15,693	8,536
1975	77,069	21,318	802	3,608	16,909	10,266	6,643	55,751	15,606	8,600
1976	79,502	22,025	832	3,662	17,531	10,640	6,891	57,477	16,128	8,966
1977	82,593	22,972	865	3,940	18,167	11,132	7,035	59,620	16,765	9,359
1978	86,826	24,156	902	4,322	18,932	11,770	7,162	62,670	17,658	9,879
1979	89,932	24,997	1,008	4,562	19,426	12,220	7,206	64,935	18,303	10,180
1980	90,528	24,263	1,077	4,454	18,733	11,679	7,054	66,265	18,413	10,244
1981	91,289	24,118	1,180	4,304	18,634	11,611	7,023	67,172	18,604	10,364
1982	89,677	22,550	1,163	4,024	17,363	10,610	6,753	67,127	18,457	10,372
1983	90,280	22,110	997	4,065	17,048	10,326	6,722	68,171	18,668	10,635
1984	94,530	23,435	1,014	4,501	17,920	11,050	6,870	71,095	19,653	11,223
1985	97,511	23,585	974	4,793	17,819	11,034	6,784	73,926	20,379	11,733
1986	99,474	23,318	829	4,937	17,552	10,795	6,757	76,156	20,795	12,078
1987	102,088	23,470	771	5,090	17,609	10,767	6,842	78,618	21,302	12,419
1988	105,345	23,909	770	5,233	17,906	10,969	6,938	81,436	21,974	12,808
1989	108,014	24,045	750	5,309	17,985	11,004	6,981	83,969	22,510	13,108
1990	109,487	23,723	765	5,263	17,695	10,736	6,959	85,764	22,666	13,182
1991	108,374	22,588	739	4,780	17,068	10,219	6,849	85,787	22,281	12,896
1992	108,726	22,095	689	4,608	16,799	9,945	6,854	86,631	22,125	12,828
1993	110,844	22,219	666	4,779	16,774	9,900	6,873	88,625	22,378	13,021
1994	114,291	22,774	659	5,095	17,021	10,131	6,890	91,517	23,128	13,491
1995	117,298	23,156	641	5,274	17,241	10,372	6,869	94,142	23,834	13,897
1996	119,708	23,410	637	5,536	17,237	10,485	6,752	96,299	24,239	14,143
1997	122,776	23,886	654	5,813	17,419	10,704	6,716	98,890	24,700	14,389
1998	125,930	24,354	645	6,149	17,560	10,910	6,650	101,576	25,186	14,609
1999	128,993	24,465	598	6,545	17,322	10,830	6,492	104,528	25,771	14,970
2000	131,785	24,649	599	6,787	17,263	10,876	6,388	107,136	26,225	15,280
2001	131,826	23,873	606	6,826	16,441	10,335	6,107	107,952	25,983	15,239
2002	130,341	22,557	583	6,716	15,259	9,483	5,775	107,784	25,497	15,025
2003	129,999	21,816	572	6,735	14,510	8,963	5,547	108,182	25,287	14,917
2004	131,435	21,882	591	6,976	14,315	8,924	5,391	109,553	25,533	15,058
2005	133,703	22,190	628	7,336	14,226	8,955	5,272	111,513	25,959	15,280
2006	136,174	22,570	684	7,689	14,197	9,001	5,197	113,605	26,231	15,319
2007 ᴾ	137,969	22,378	722	7,624	14,032	8,890	5,141	115,591	26,472	15,382
2006: Jan	135,110	22,489	655	7,615	14,219	8,984	5,235	112,621	26,157	15,346
Feb	135,410	22,541	661	7,668	14,212	8,986	5,226	112,869	26,187	15,354
Mar	135,659	22,573	669	7,692	14,212	8,999	5,213	113,086	26,225	15,378
Apr	135,803	22,604	678	7,699	14,227	9,020	5,207	113,199	26,207	15,337
May	135,906	22,593	680	7,698	14,215	9,016	5,199	113,313	26,194	15,303
June	136,030	22,613	684	7,691	14,238	9,034	5,204	113,417	26,197	15,296
July	136,252	22,622	690	7,703	14,229	9,023	5,206	113,630	26,226	15,306
Aug	136,438	22,629	692	7,719	14,218	9,021	5,197	113,809	26,227	15,298
Sept	136,636	22,625	694	7,725	14,206	9,017	5,189	114,011	26,241	15,290
Oct	136,745	22,573	700	7,707	14,166	8,996	5,170	114,172	26,258	15,298
Nov	136,941	22,525	699	7,683	14,143	8,972	5,171	114,416	26,320	15,328
Dec	137,167	22,520	705	7,684	14,131	8,972	5,159	114,647	26,345	15,324
2007: Jan	137,329	22,554	706	7,718	14,130	8,952	5,178	114,775	26,378	15,358
Feb	137,419	22,465	711	7,641	14,113	8,943	5,170	114,954	26,393	15,365
Mar	137,594	22,497	715	7,692	14,090	8,928	5,162	115,097	26,436	15,404
Apr	137,716	22,460	717	7,671	14,072	8,921	5,151	115,256	26,427	15,377
May	137,904	22,446	718	7,659	14,069	8,913	5,156	115,458	26,459	15,395
June	137,973	22,436	721	7,665	14,050	8,897	5,153	115,537	26,465	15,383
July	138,066	22,421	726	7,649	14,046	8,900	5,146	115,645	26,489	15,390
Aug	138,159	22,349	728	7,620	14,001	8,873	5,128	115,810	26,494	15,386
Sept	138,203	22,309	728	7,595	13,986	8,862	5,124	115,894	26,518	15,383
Oct	138,362	22,266	728	7,575	13,963	8,845	5,118	116,096	26,510	15,363
Nov ᴾ	138,477	22,221	733	7,538	13,950	8,843	5,107	116,256	26,554	15,395
Dec ᴾ	138,495	22,146	738	7,489	13,919	8,823	5,096	116,349	26,526	15,370

[1] Includes wholesale trade, transportation and warehousing, and utilities, not shown separately.

Note.—Data in Tables B–46 and B–47 are based on reports from employing establishments and relate to full- and part-time wage and salary workers in nonagricultural establishments who received pay for any part of the pay period that includes the 12th of the month. Not comparable with labor force data (Tables B–35 through B–44), which include proprietors, self-employed persons, unpaid family workers, and private household workers; which count persons as employed when they are not at work because of industrial disputes, bad weather, etc., even if they are not paid for the time off; which are based on a

See next page for continuation of table.

[Thousands of persons; monthly data seasonally adjusted]

Year or month	Information	Financial activities	Profes-sional and business services	Education and health services	Leisure and hospitality	Other services	Government Total	Government Federal	Government State	Government Local
							Total	Federal	State	Local
1960	1,728	2,532	3,694	2,937	3,460	1,152	8,464	2,381	1,536	4,547
1961	1,693	2,590	3,744	3,030	3,468	1,188	8,706	2,391	1,607	4,708
1962	1,723	2,656	3,885	3,172	3,557	1,243	9,004	2,455	1,669	4,881
1963	1,735	2,731	3,990	3,288	3,639	1,288	9,341	2,473	1,747	5,121
1964	1,766	2,811	4,137	3,438	3,772	1,346	9,711	2,463	1,856	5,392
1965	1,824	2,878	4,306	3,587	3,951	1,404	10,191	2,495	1,996	5,700
1966	1,908	2,961	4,517	3,770	4,127	1,475	10,910	2,690	2,141	6,080
1967	1,955	3,087	4,720	3,986	4,269	1,558	11,525	2,852	2,302	6,371
1968	1,991	3,234	4,918	4,191	4,453	1,638	11,972	2,871	2,442	6,660
1969	2,048	3,404	5,156	4,428	4,670	1,731	12,330	2,893	2,533	6,904
1970	2,041	3,532	5,267	4,577	4,789	1,789	12,687	2,865	2,664	7,158
1971	2,009	3,651	5,328	4,675	4,914	1,827	13,012	2,828	2,747	7,437
1972	2,056	3,784	5,523	4,863	5,121	1,900	13,465	2,815	2,859	7,790
1973	2,135	3,920	5,774	5,092	5,341	1,990	13,862	2,794	2,923	8,146
1974	2,160	4,023	5,974	5,322	5,471	2,078	14,303	2,858	3,039	8,407
1975	2,061	4,047	6,034	5,497	5,544	2,144	14,820	2,882	3,179	8,758
1976	2,111	4,155	6,287	5,756	5,794	2,244	15,001	2,863	3,273	8,865
1977	2,185	4,348	6,587	6,052	6,065	2,359	15,258	2,859	3,377	9,023
1978	2,287	4,599	6,972	6,427	6,411	2,505	15,812	2,893	3,474	9,446
1979	2,375	4,843	7,312	6,767	6,631	2,637	16,068	2,894	3,541	9,633
1980	2,361	5,025	7,544	7,072	6,721	2,755	16,375	3,000	3,610	9,765
1981	2,382	5,163	7,782	7,357	6,840	2,865	16,180	2,922	3,640	9,619
1982	2,317	5,209	7,848	7,515	6,874	2,924	15,982	2,884	3,640	9,458
1983	2,253	5,334	8,039	7,766	7,078	3,021	16,011	2,915	3,662	9,434
1984	2,398	5,553	8,464	8,193	7,489	3,186	16,159	2,943	3,734	9,482
1985	2,437	5,815	8,871	8,657	7,869	3,366	16,533	3,014	3,832	9,687
1986	2,445	6,128	9,211	9,061	8,156	3,523	16,838	3,044	3,893	9,901
1987	2,507	6,385	9,608	9,515	8,446	3,699	17,156	3,089	3,967	10,100
1988	2,585	6,500	10,090	10,063	8,778	3,907	17,540	3,124	4,076	10,339
1989	2,622	6,562	10,555	10,616	9,062	4,116	17,927	3,136	4,182	10,609
1990	2,688	6,614	10,848	10,984	9,288	4,261	18,415	3,196	4,305	10,914
1991	2,677	6,558	10,714	11,506	9,256	4,249	18,545	3,110	4,355	11,081
1992	2,641	6,540	10,970	11,891	9,437	4,240	18,787	3,111	4,408	11,267
1993	2,668	6,709	11,495	12,303	9,732	4,350	18,989	3,063	4,488	11,438
1994	2,738	6,867	12,174	12,807	10,100	4,428	19,275	3,018	4,576	11,682
1995	2,843	6,827	12,844	13,289	10,501	4,572	19,432	2,949	4,635	11,849
1996	2,940	6,969	13,462	13,683	10,777	4,690	19,539	2,877	4,606	12,056
1997	3,084	7,178	14,335	14,087	11,018	4,825	19,664	2,806	4,582	12,276
1998	3,218	7,462	15,147	14,446	11,232	4,976	19,909	2,772	4,612	12,525
1999	3,419	7,648	15,957	14,798	11,543	5,087	20,307	2,769	4,709	12,829
2000	3,631	7,687	16,666	15,109	11,862	5,168	20,790	2,865	4,786	13,139
2001	3,629	7,807	16,476	15,645	12,036	5,258	21,118	2,764	4,905	13,449
2002	3,395	7,847	15,976	16,199	11,986	5,372	21,513	2,766	5,029	13,718
2003	3,188	7,977	15,987	16,588	12,173	5,401	21,583	2,761	5,002	13,820
2004	3,118	8,031	16,395	16,953	12,493	5,409	21,621	2,730	4,982	13,909
2005	3,061	8,153	16,954	17,372	12,816	5,395	21,804	2,732	5,032	14,041
2006	3,055	8,363	17,552	17,838	13,143	5,432	21,990	2,728	5,080	14,182
2007 ᵖ	3,087	8,446	17,920	18,377	13,565	5,472	22,252	2,714	5,144	14,394
2006: Jan	3,052	8,271	17,316	17,621	12,948	5,417	21,839	2,725	5,034	14,080
Feb	3,058	8,298	17,387	17,666	12,981	5,417	21,875	2,731	5,053	14,091
Mar	3,058	8,314	17,431	17,709	13,022	5,421	21,906	2,731	5,060	14,115
Apr	3,056	8,340	17,458	17,743	13,049	5,424	21,922	2,731	5,064	14,127
May	3,048	8,352	17,499	17,776	13,074	5,432	21,938	2,729	5,073	14,136
June	3,048	8,348	17,539	17,794	13,092	5,431	21,968	2,733	5,075	14,160
July	3,043	8,368	17,592	17,828	13,156	5,427	21,990	2,739	5,078	14,173
Aug	3,051	8,379	17,617	17,894	13,188	5,430	22,023	2,730	5,088	14,205
Sept	3,052	8,408	17,636	17,946	13,209	5,443	22,076	2,729	5,113	14,234
Oct	3,054	8,415	17,662	17,976	13,257	5,450	22,100	2,725	5,109	14,266
Nov	3,057	8,422	17,726	18,018	13,324	5,443	22,106	2,719	5,107	14,280
Dec	3,073	8,438	17,792	18,063	13,373	5,449	22,114	2,713	5,111	14,290
2007: Jan	3,071	8,440	17,804	18,102	13,396	5,444	22,140	2,718	5,117	14,305
Feb	3,084	8,446	17,840	18,138	13,425	5,454	22,174	2,718	5,133	14,323
Mar	3,086	8,445	17,834	18,188	13,449	5,462	22,197	2,716	5,134	14,347
Apr	3,096	8,448	17,859	18,246	13,481	5,470	22,229	2,716	5,140	14,373
May	3,097	8,464	17,893	18,293	13,537	5,479	22,236	2,713	5,133	14,390
June	3,093	8,460	17,886	18,364	13,554	5,481	22,234	2,708	5,139	14,387
July	3,091	8,476	17,911	18,422	13,566	5,480	22,210	2,713	5,143	14,354
Aug	3,087	8,463	17,942	18,484	13,589	5,478	22,273	2,714	5,137	14,422
Sept	3,093	8,439	17,954	18,505	13,630	5,475	22,280	2,710	5,159	14,411
Oct	3,088	8,437	18,024	18,554	13,677	5,477	22,329	2,710	5,162	14,457
Nov ᵖ	3,083	8,421	18,063	18,583	13,712	5,483	22,357	2,711	5,170	14,476
Dec ᵖ	3,070	8,417	18,106	18,627	13,734	5,481	22,388	2,707	5,181	14,500

Note (cont'd).—sample of the working-age population; and which count persons only once—as employed, unemployed, or not in the labor force. In the data shown here, persons who work at more than one job are counted each time they appear on a payroll.

Establishment data for employment, hours, and earnings are classified based on the 2002 North American Industry Classification System (NAICS). For further description and details see *Employment and Earnings.*

Source: Department of Labor (Bureau of Labor Statistics).

TABLE B–47.—*Hours and earnings in private nonagricultural industries, 1960–2007* [1]

[Monthly data seasonally adjusted]

Year or month	Average weekly hours			Average hourly earnings			Average weekly earnings, total private			
	Total private	Manufacturing		Total private		Manufacturing (current dollars)	Level		Percent change from year earlier	
		Total	Overtime	Current dollars	1982 dollars [2]		Current dollars	1982 dollars [2]	Current dollars	1982 dollars [2]
1960	....	39.8	2.5	....	....	$2.15	....	....	....	....
1961	....	39.9	2.4	....	....	2.20	....	....	....	....
1962	....	40.5	2.8	....	....	2.27	....	....	....	....
1963	....	40.6	2.8	....	....	2.34	....	....	....	....
1964	38.5	40.8	3.1	$2.53	$7.86	2.41	$97.41	$302.52	....	....
1965	38.6	41.2	3.6	2.63	8.04	2.49	101.52	310.46	4.2	2.6
1966	38.5	41.4	3.9	2.73	8.13	2.60	105.11	312.83	3.5	.8
1967	37.9	40.6	3.3	2.85	8.21	2.71	108.02	311.30	2.8	−.5
1968	37.7	40.7	3.5	3.02	8.37	2.89	113.85	315.37	5.4	1.3
1969	37.5	40.6	3.6	3.22	8.45	3.07	120.75	316.93	6.1	.5
1970	37.0	39.8	2.9	3.40	8.46	3.23	125.80	312.94	4.2	−1.3
1971	36.8	39.9	2.9	3.63	8.64	3.45	133.58	318.05	6.2	1.6
1972	36.9	40.6	3.4	3.90	8.99	3.70	143.91	331.59	7.7	4.3
1973	36.9	40.7	3.8	4.14	8.98	3.97	152.77	331.39	6.2	−.1
1974	36.4	40.0	3.2	4.43	8.65	4.31	161.25	314.94	5.6	−5.0
1975	36.0	39.5	2.6	4.73	8.48	4.71	170.28	305.16	5.6	−3.1
1976	36.1	40.1	3.1	5.06	8.58	5.09	182.67	309.61	7.3	1.5
1977	35.9	40.3	3.4	5.44	8.66	5.55	195.30	310.99	6.9	.4
1978	35.8	40.4	3.6	5.88	8.69	6.05	210.50	310.93	7.8	.0
1979	35.6	40.2	3.3	6.34	8.41	6.57	225.70	299.34	7.2	−3.7
1980	35.2	39.7	2.8	6.85	8.00	7.15	241.12	281.68	6.8	−5.9
1981	35.2	39.8	2.8	7.44	7.89	7.86	261.89	277.72	8.6	−1.4
1982	34.7	38.9	2.3	7.87	7.87	8.36	273.09	273.09	4.3	−1.7
1983	34.9	40.1	2.9	8.20	7.96	8.70	286.18	277.84	4.8	1.7
1984	35.1	40.7	3.4	8.49	7.96	9.05	298.00	279.55	4.1	.6
1985	34.9	40.5	3.3	8.74	7.92	9.40	305.03	276.55	2.4	−1.1
1986	34.7	40.7	3.4	8.93	7.97	9.59	309.87	276.42	1.6	.0
1987	34.7	40.9	3.7	9.14	7.87	9.77	317.16	273.18	2.4	−1.2
1988	34.6	41.0	3.8	9.44	7.82	10.05	326.62	270.60	3.0	−.9
1989	34.5	40.9	3.8	9.80	7.75	10.35	338.10	267.27	3.5	−1.2
1990	34.3	40.5	3.8	10.20	7.66	10.78	349.75	262.77	3.4	−1.7
1991	34.1	40.4	3.8	10.52	7.59	11.13	358.51	258.67	2.5	−1.6
1992	34.2	40.7	4.0	10.77	7.55	11.40	368.25	258.24	2.7	−.2
1993	34.3	41.1	4.4	11.05	7.54	11.70	378.89	258.45	2.9	.1
1994	34.5	41.7	5.0	11.34	7.54	12.04	391.22	260.29	3.3	.7
1995	34.3	41.3	4.7	11.65	7.54	12.34	400.07	258.78	2.3	−.6
1996	34.3	41.3	4.8	12.04	7.57	12.75	413.28	259.92	3.3	.4
1997	34.5	41.7	5.1	12.51	7.69	13.14	431.86	265.60	4.5	2.2
1998	34.5	41.4	4.8	13.01	7.89	13.45	448.56	272.18	3.9	2.5
1999	34.3	41.4	4.8	13.49	8.01	13.85	463.15	275.03	3.3	1.0
2000	34.3	41.3	4.7	14.02	8.04	14.32	481.01	275.97	3.9	.3
2001	34.0	40.3	4.0	14.54	8.12	14.76	493.79	275.71	2.7	−.1
2002	33.9	40.5	4.2	14.97	8.25	15.29	506.72	279.18	2.6	1.3
2003	33.7	40.4	4.2	15.37	8.28	15.74	518.06	279.13	2.2	.0
2004	33.7	40.8	4.6	15.69	8.24	16.15	529.09	277.88	2.1	−.4
2005	33.8	40.7	4.6	16.13	8.18	16.56	544.33	276.17	2.9	−.6
2006	33.9	41.1	4.4	16.76	8.24	16.80	567.87	279.19	4.3	1.1
2007 [p]	33.8	41.2	4.2	17.41	8.32	17.23	589.36	281.65	3.8	.9
2006: Jan	33.8	40.9	4.5	16.43	8.18	16.69	555.33	276.56	3.6	−.5
Feb	33.8	41.0	4.6	16.49	8.21	16.69	557.36	277.43	3.8	.1
Mar	33.8	41.1	4.5	16.55	8.21	16.71	559.39	277.61	3.9	.3
Apr	33.9	41.2	4.5	16.63	8.20	16.75	563.76	277.99	4.1	.4
May	33.8	41.1	4.5	16.66	8.17	16.77	563.11	276.03	4.0	−.2
June	33.9	41.2	4.5	16.73	8.18	16.78	567.15	277.33	4.7	.2
July	33.9	41.5	4.5	16.79	8.17	16.78	569.18	277.11	4.5	.2
Aug	33.8	41.3	4.4	16.84	8.17	16.83	569.19	276.31	4.4	.4
Sept	33.8	41.1	4.3	16.88	8.25	16.83	570.54	278.99	4.1	2.3
Oct	33.9	41.2	4.3	16.94	8.34	16.88	574.27	282.61	4.2	3.3
Nov	33.8	41.0	4.1	16.99	8.36	16.89	574.26	282.47	4.2	2.4
Dec	33.9	41.0	4.2	17.07	8.36	16.95	578.67	283.25	4.6	2.1
2007: Jan	33.8	40.9	4.1	17.10	8.36	16.98	577.98	282.54	4.1	2.2
Feb	33.7	40.9	4.1	17.16	8.36	17.03	578.29	281.61	3.8	1.5
Mar	33.9	41.2	4.3	17.21	8.32	17.09	583.42	281.92	4.3	1.6
Apr	33.8	41.1	4.2	17.25	8.30	17.18	583.05	280.46	3.4	.9
May	33.8	41.1	4.1	17.32	8.26	17.20	585.42	279.35	4.0	1.2
June	33.9	41.4	4.3	17.40	8.29	17.26	589.86	281.16	4.0	1.4
July	33.8	41.3	4.2	17.45	8.31	17.28	589.81	280.78	3.6	1.3
Aug	33.8	41.4	4.1	17.50	8.35	17.31	591.50	282.13	3.9	2.1
Sept	33.8	41.3	4.1	17.54	8.35	17.32	592.85	282.07	3.9	1.1
Oct	33.8	41.2	4.1	17.57	8.33	17.31	593.87	281.62	3.4	−.4
Nov [p]	33.8	41.3	4.1	17.64	8.29	17.35	596.23	280.27	3.8	−.8
Dec [p]	33.8	41.1	3.9	17.71	8.30	17.35	598.60	280.56	3.4	−.9

[1] For production or nonsupervisory workers; total includes private industry groups shown in Table B–46.

[2] Current dollars divided by the consumer price index for urban wage earners and clerical workers on a 1982=100 base.

Note.—See Note, Table B–46.

Source: Department of Labor (Bureau of Labor Statistics).

TABLE B–48.—*Employment cost index, private industry, 1990–2007*

Year and month	Total private			Goods-producing			Service-providing [1]			Manufacturing		
	Total compensation	Wages and salaries	Benefits [2]	Total compensation	Wages and salaries	Benefits [2]	Total compensation	Wages and salaries	Benefits [2]	Total compensation	Wages and salaries	Benefits [2]
	Indexes on SIC basis, December 2005=100; not seasonally adjusted											
December:												
1990	59.3	62.3	52.9	59.4	63.4	52.3	59.4	61.8	53.4	59.1	63.1	52.1
1991	61.9	64.6	56.2	62.1	65.8	55.5	61.9	64.1	56.7	61.9	65.6	55.2
1992	64.1	66.3	59.1	64.5	67.6	58.7	63.9	65.7	59.4	64.3	67.6	58.3
1993	66.4	68.3	62.0	67.0	69.6	62.0	66.2	67.8	62.0	66.9	69.7	61.8
1994	68.5	70.2	64.3	69.0	71.7	64.1	68.1	69.6	64.4	69.0	71.8	63.9
1995	70.2	72.2	65.7	70.7	73.7	65.2	70.0	71.7	66.0	70.8	73.9	65.0
1996	72.4	74.7	67.0	72.7	76.0	66.4	72.3	74.2	67.3	72.9	76.3	66.5
1997	74.9	77.6	68.5	74.5	78.3	67.3	75.1	77.4	69.2	74.6	78.6	67.4
1998	77.5	80.6	70.2	76.5	81.1	68.1	78.0	80.5	71.4	76.6	81.3	67.9
1999	80.2	83.5	72.6	79.1	83.8	70.5	80.6	83.4	73.8	79.2	84.1	70.3
2000	83.6	86.7	76.7	82.6	87.1	74.3	84.2	86.6	78.1	82.3	87.1	73.6
2001	87.1	90.0	80.6	85.7	90.2	77.3	87.8	89.9	82.5	85.3	90.2	76.3
	Indexes on NAICS basis, December 2005=100; not seasonally adjusted											
2001 [3]	87.3	89.9	81.3	86.0	90.0	78.5	87.8	89.8	82.4	85.5	90.2	77.2
2002	90.0	92.2	84.7	89.0	92.6	82.3	90.4	92.1	85.8	88.7	92.8	81.3
2003	93.6	95.1	90.2	92.6	94.9	88.2	94.0	95.2	91.0	92.4	95.1	87.3
2004	97.2	97.6	96.2	96.9	97.2	96.3	97.3	97.7	96.1	96.9	97.4	96.0
2005	100.0	100.0	100.0	100.0	100.0	100.0	100.0	100.0	100.0	100.0	100.0	100.0
2006	103.2	103.2	103.1	102.5	102.9	101.7	103.4	103.3	103.7	101.8	102.3	100.8
2007: Mar	104.0	104.3	103.2	102.9	103.9	100.9	104.3	104.4	104.1	102.0	103.3	99.6
June	104.9	105.1	104.3	103.9	104.7	102.2	105.2	105.3	105.2	102.9	103.9	101.0
Sept	105.7	106.0	105.0	104.4	105.4	102.4	106.1	106.1	106.0	103.2	104.5	100.7
	Indexes on NAICS basis, December 2005=100; seasonally adjusted											
2006: Mar	100.8	100.8	100.8	100.3	100.8	99.5	100.9	100.8	101.3	100.0	100.7	98.9
June	101.6	101.6	101.5	101.3	101.7	100.3	101.7	101.6	102.0	100.9	101.6	99.7
Sept	102.5	102.4	102.5	101.8	102.2	101.2	102.7	102.5	103.0	101.4	101.8	100.5
Dec	103.3	103.2	103.4	102.6	103.0	101.9	103.5	103.3	104.1	101.9	102.5	101.0
2007: Mar	103.9	104.3	103.1	102.9	104.0	100.9	104.3	104.4	103.9	102.0	103.3	99.5
June	104.8	105.1	104.2	103.8	104.7	102.1	105.2	105.3	105.0	102.8	103.8	100.9
Sept	105.6	105.9	105.0	104.3	105.3	102.3	106.0	106.1	106.0	103.1	104.4	100.7
	Percent change from 12 months earlier, not seasonally adjusted											
December:												
SIC:												
1990	4.6	4.0	6.7	4.8	3.6	7.2	4.6	3.9	6.4	5.0	4.1	7.0
1991	4.4	3.7	6.2	4.5	3.8	6.1	4.2	3.7	6.2	4.7	4.0	6.0
1992	3.6	2.6	5.2	3.9	2.7	5.8	3.2	2.5	4.8	3.9	3.0	5.6
1993	3.6	3.0	4.9	3.9	3.0	5.6	3.6	3.2	4.4	4.0	3.1	6.0
1994	3.2	2.8	3.7	3.0	3.0	3.4	2.9	2.7	3.9	3.1	3.0	3.4
1995	2.5	2.8	2.2	2.5	2.8	1.7	2.8	3.0	2.5	2.6	2.9	1.7
1996	3.1	3.5	2.0	2.8	3.1	1.8	3.3	3.5	2.0	3.0	3.2	2.3
1997	3.5	3.9	2.2	2.5	3.0	1.4	3.9	4.3	2.8	2.3	3.0	1.4
1998	3.5	3.9	2.5	2.7	3.6	1.2	3.9	4.0	3.2	2.7	3.4	.7
1999	3.5	3.6	3.4	3.4	3.3	3.5	3.3	3.6	3.4	3.4	3.4	3.5
2000	4.2	3.8	5.6	4.4	3.9	5.4	4.5	3.8	5.8	3.9	3.6	4.7
2001	4.2	3.8	5.1	3.8	3.6	4.0	4.3	3.8	5.6	3.6	3.6	3.7
NAICS:												
2001 [3]	4.1	3.8	5.2	3.6	3.6	3.7	4.4	3.8	5.6	3.4	3.6	3.5
2002	3.1	2.6	4.2	3.5	2.9	4.8	3.0	2.6	4.1	3.7	2.9	5.3
2003	4.0	3.1	6.5	4.0	2.5	7.2	4.0	3.4	6.1	4.2	2.5	7.4
2004	3.8	2.6	6.7	4.6	2.4	9.2	3.5	2.6	5.6	4.9	2.4	10.0
2005	2.9	2.5	4.0	3.2	2.9	3.8	2.8	2.4	4.1	3.2	2.7	4.2
2006	3.2	3.2	3.1	2.5	2.9	1.7	3.4	3.3	3.7	1.8	2.3	.8
2007: Mar	3.2	3.6	2.2	2.6	3.2	1.3	3.3	3.6	2.6	1.9	2.6	.6
June	3.1	3.3	2.6	2.6	2.8	1.8	3.3	3.5	2.8	1.9	2.2	1.3
Sept	3.1	3.4	2.4	2.4	3.0	1.1	3.3	3.4	2.9	1.8	2.6	.2
	Percent change from 3 months earlier, seasonally adjusted											
2006: Mar	0.7	0.7	0.5	0.1	0.7	-0.7	0.8	0.8	1.0	-0.2	0.5	-1.2
June	.8	.8	.7	1.0	.9	.8	.8	.8	.7	.9	.9	.8
Sept	.9	.8	1.0	.5	.5	.9	1.0	.9	1.0	.5	.2	.8
Dec	.8	.8	.9	.8	.8	.7	.8	.8	1.1	.5	.7	.5
2007: Mar	.6	1.1	-.3	.3	1.0	-1.0	.8	1.1	-.2	.1	.8	-1.5
June	.9	.8	1.1	.9	.7	1.2	.9	.9	1.1	.8	.5	1.4
Sept	.8	.8	.8	.5	.6	.2	.8	.8	1.0	.3	.6	-.2

[1] On Standard Industrial Classification (SIC) basis, data are for service-producing industries.
[2] Employer costs for employee benefits.
[3] Data on North American Industry Classification System (NAICS) basis available beginning with 2001; not strictly comparable with earlier data shown on SIC basis.

Note.—Changes effective with the release of March 2006 data (in April 2006) include changing industry classification to NAICS from SIC and rebasing data to December 2005=100. Complete historical SIC data through December 2005, as well as technical details, are available from the Department of Labor, Bureau of Labor Statistics.
Data exclude farm and household workers.

Source: Department of Labor (Bureau of Labor Statistics).

TABLE B–49.—*Productivity and related data, business and nonfarm business sectors, 1959–2007*

[Index numbers, 1992=100; quarterly data seasonally adjusted]

Year or quarter	Output per hour of all persons — Business sector	Output per hour of all persons — Nonfarm business sector	Output [1] — Business sector	Output [1] — Nonfarm business sector	Hours of all persons [2] — Business sector	Hours of all persons [2] — Nonfarm business sector	Compensation per hour [3] — Business sector	Compensation per hour [3] — Nonfarm business sector	Real compensation per hour [4] — Business sector	Real compensation per hour [4] — Nonfarm business sector	Unit labor costs — Business sector	Unit labor costs — Nonfarm business sector	Implicit price deflator [5] — Business sector	Implicit price deflator [5] — Nonfarm business sector
1959	48.0	51.3	31.4	31.2	65.5	60.9	13.3	13.9	59.9	62.3	27.8	27.1	26.8	26.3
1960	48.9	51.9	32.0	31.8	65.6	61.2	13.9	14.5	61.3	63.9	28.4	27.9	27.1	26.6
1961	50.6	53.5	32.7	32.4	64.6	60.6	14.4	15.0	63.1	65.3	28.5	28.0	27.3	26.8
1962	52.9	55.9	34.8	34.6	65.8	61.9	15.1	15.6	65.2	67.3	28.5	27.8	27.6	27.1
1963	55.0	57.8	36.4	36.2	66.2	62.6	15.6	16.1	66.6	68.7	28.4	27.8	27.7	27.3
1964	56.8	59.6	38.7	38.7	68.1	64.9	16.2	16.6	68.3	69.9	28.5	27.9	28.1	27.6
1965	58.8	61.4	41.4	41.4	70.4	67.4	16.8	17.1	69.7	71.1	28.6	27.9	28.5	28.0
1966	61.2	63.6	44.2	44.4	72.3	69.8	17.9	18.2	72.3	73.2	29.3	28.6	29.2	28.6
1967	62.5	64.7	45.1	45.1	72.1	69.7	19.0	19.2	74.1	75.2	30.3	29.7	30.0	29.5
1968	64.7	66.9	47.3	47.5	73.2	71.0	20.5	20.7	76.9	77.8	31.7	31.0	31.2	30.7
1969	65.0	67.0	48.8	48.9	75.0	73.0	21.9	22.1	78.0	78.8	33.7	33.0	32.6	32.1
1970	66.3	68.0	48.7	48.9	73.5	71.9	23.6	23.7	79.5	79.8	35.6	34.9	34.1	33.5
1971	69.0	70.7	50.6	50.7	73.3	71.7	25.1	25.2	80.9	81.4	36.3	35.7	35.5	35.0
1972	71.2	73.1	53.9	54.1	75.6	74.0	26.7	26.9	83.3	84.0	37.4	36.8	36.8	36.1
1973	73.4	75.3	57.6	58.0	78.5	77.0	28.9	29.1	85.1	85.5	39.4	38.6	38.7	37.4
1974	72.3	74.2	56.8	57.3	78.7	77.2	31.7	31.9	84.0	84.5	43.9	43.0	42.4	41.2
1975	74.8	76.2	56.3	56.3	75.3	73.9	34.9	35.1	84.8	85.2	46.7	46.0	46.6	45.6
1976	77.1	78.7	60.0	60.2	77.8	76.5	38.0	38.1	87.1	87.4	49.2	48.3	49.0	48.1
1977	78.5	80.0	63.3	63.6	80.7	79.5	41.0	41.2	88.3	88.7	52.2	51.5	52.0	51.2
1978	79.3	81.0	67.3	67.8	84.9	83.7	44.5	44.8	89.7	90.3	56.2	55.3	55.6	54.6
1979	79.3	80.7	69.6	70.0	87.7	86.6	48.9	49.1	89.9	90.2	61.6	60.8	60.4	59.2
1980	79.2	80.6	68.8	69.2	87.0	85.9	54.1	54.4	89.6	90.0	68.4	67.5	65.8	64.9
1981	80.8	81.7	70.7	70.7	87.6	86.6	59.3	59.7	89.6	90.2	73.5	73.1	71.8	71.1
1982	80.1	80.8	68.6	68.4	85.6	84.7	63.6	63.9	90.6	91.1	79.4	79.1	75.9	75.5
1983	83.0	84.5	72.3	72.9	87.1	86.3	66.3	66.6	90.6	91.1	79.8	78.9	78.5	77.9
1984	85.2	86.1	78.6	78.9	92.2	91.6	69.1	69.5	90.7	91.1	81.1	80.7	80.8	80.1
1985	87.1	87.5	82.2	82.2	94.3	94.0	72.5	72.6	91.9	92.1	83.2	83.0	82.7	82.5
1986	89.7	90.2	85.3	85.4	95.1	94.7	76.1	76.4	94.9	95.2	84.9	84.7	84.1	83.9
1987	90.1	90.6	88.3	88.4	97.9	97.6	79.0	79.2	95.2	95.5	87.6	87.4	85.9	85.7
1988	91.5	92.1	92.1	92.4	100.6	100.4	83.0	83.1	96.5	96.7	90.7	90.2	88.6	88.3
1989	92.4	92.8	95.4	95.7	103.3	103.1	85.2	85.3	95.0	95.1	92.2	91.9	91.9	91.5
1990	94.4	94.5	96.9	97.1	102.7	102.7	90.6	90.4	96.2	96.0	96.0	95.7	95.1	94.9
1991	95.9	96.1	96.1	96.3	100.2	100.2	95.1	95.0	97.5	97.4	99.1	98.9	98.2	98.1
1992	100.0	100.0	100.0	100.0	100.0	100.0	100.0	100.0	100.0	100.0	100.0	100.0	100.0	100.0
1993	100.4	100.4	103.1	103.4	102.7	102.9	102.2	102.0	99.7	99.5	101.8	101.6	102.1	102.1
1994	101.3	101.5	108.2	108.3	106.8	106.6	103.6	103.7	99.0	99.1	102.3	102.1	103.9	104.0
1995	101.5	102.0	111.4	111.8	109.7	109.6	105.8	105.9	98.7	98.8	104.2	103.8	105.7	105.8
1996	104.5	104.7	116.5	116.8	111.5	111.5	109.5	109.4	99.5	99.5	104.8	104.5	107.4	107.3
1997	106.5	106.4	122.7	122.8	115.2	115.4	113.0	112.8	100.5	100.4	106.1	106.0	109.0	109.1
1998	109.5	109.4	128.6	128.9	117.5	117.9	119.9	119.6	105.2	104.9	109.5	109.3	109.7	109.9
1999	112.8	112.5	135.2	135.6	119.8	120.5	125.8	125.2	108.0	107.5	111.5	111.3	110.7	111.1
2000	116.1	115.7	140.5	140.8	121.0	121.7	134.7	134.2	112.0	111.6	116.0	116.0	112.7	113.3
2001	119.1	118.6	141.0	141.3	118.4	119.2	140.4	139.5	113.5	112.8	117.9	117.7	114.9	115.4
2002	123.9	123.5	143.1	143.4	115.4	116.1	145.3	144.6	115.7	115.1	117.3	117.1	116.1	116.7
2003	128.7	128.0	147.5	147.8	114.6	115.4	151.2	150.4	117.7	117.1	117.5	117.5	117.8	118.3
2004	132.4	131.5	153.7	153.9	116.1	117.0	156.9	155.9	118.9	118.2	118.5	118.5	120.8	121.1
2005	135.0	134.1	159.3	159.5	118.0	118.9	163.2	162.1	119.7	118.9	120.9	120.9	124.5	125.1
2006	136.4	135.4	164.3	164.5	120.5	121.5	169.6	168.5	120.4	119.7	124.3	124.5	128.2	128.9
2003: I	125.8	125.2	144.4	144.6	114.8	115.5	148.1	147.3	115.7	115.2	117.7	117.7	117.3	117.9
II	127.9	126.9	146.0	146.1	114.1	115.1	150.8	149.7	117.8	116.9	117.9	118.0	117.4	118.0
III	130.8	130.1	149.7	150.0	114.5	115.3	152.5	151.7	118.4	117.8	116.6	116.6	118.0	118.4
IV	130.3	129.9	150.1	150.6	115.2	115.9	153.6	152.9	118.9	118.4	117.9	117.7	118.5	118.7
2004: I	131.1	130.2	151.4	151.5	115.5	116.4	153.8	152.9	118.1	117.4	117.3	117.4	119.5	119.7
II	132.3	131.7	153.1	153.4	115.7	116.5	155.8	154.9	118.4	117.7	117.7	117.6	120.5	120.6
III	132.7	132.0	154.6	154.9	116.5	117.3	157.8	156.8	119.2	118.5	118.9	118.8	121.1	121.4
IV	133.4	132.2	155.7	155.9	116.8	117.9	160.2	158.9	120.0	119.0	120.1	120.2	122.1	122.5
2005: I	134.4	133.4	157.2	157.4	117.0	118.0	161.4	160.3	120.3	119.5	120.1	120.2	123.1	123.6
II	134.3	133.5	158.5	158.6	118.0	118.8	161.7	160.9	119.4	118.8	120.4	120.5	123.9	124.5
III	135.9	135.0	160.6	160.8	118.2	119.1	164.2	163.2	119.6	118.8	120.8	120.9	125.0	125.6
IV	135.5	134.5	161.0	161.2	118.8	119.8	165.4	164.2	119.4	118.6	122.0	122.1	126.1	126.8
2006: I	136.4	135.3	163.2	163.4	119.6	120.8	168.2	167.1	120.9	120.1	123.4	123.5	127.0	127.7
II	136.6	135.6	164.2	164.4	120.2	121.2	168.1	167.0	119.3	118.6	123.0	123.2	128.0	128.9
III	136.1	135.0	164.4	164.7	120.8	122.0	168.7	167.5	118.9	118.0	124.0	124.0	128.7	129.4
IV	136.5	135.6	165.5	165.7	121.2	122.2	173.4	172.4	122.8	122.1	127.0	127.1	128.9	129.5
2007: I	136.6	135.9	165.6	165.9	121.2	122.1	175.7	174.9	123.3	122.7	128.6	128.7	130.2	130.6
II	137.8	136.6	167.3	167.6	121.5	122.7	176.8	175.4	122.2	121.2	128.3	128.4	130.9	131.3
III	140.0	138.7	169.7	169.9	121.2	122.5	178.8	177.2	123.0	121.9	127.7	127.7	131.0	131.3

[1] Output refers to real gross domestic product in the sector.
[2] Hours at work of all persons engaged in sector, including hours of proprietors and unpaid family workers. Estimates based primarily on establishment data.
[3] Wages and salaries of employees plus employers' contributions for social insurance and private benefit plans. Also includes an estimate of wages, salaries, and supplemental payments for the self-employed.
[4] Hourly compensation divided by the consumer price index for all urban consumers for recent quarters. The trend from 1978–2006 is based on the consumer price index research series (CPI-U-RS).
[5] Current dollar output divided by the output index.

Source: Department of Labor (Bureau of Labor Statistics).

TABLE B-50.—*Changes in productivity and related data, business and nonfarm business sectors, 1959–2007*

[Percent change from preceding period; quarterly data at seasonally adjusted annual rates]

Year or quarter	Output per hour of all persons		Output [1]		Hours of all persons [2]		Compensation per hour [3]		Real compensation per hour [4]		Unit labor costs		Implicit price deflator [5]	
	Business sector	Nonfarm business sector	Business sector	Nonfarm business sector	Business sector	Nonfarm business sector	Business sector	Nonfarm business sector	Business sector	Nonfarm business sector	Business sector	Nonfarm business sector	Business sector	Nonfarm business sector
1959	3.8	3.8	8.1	8.6	4.2	4.6	4.1	3.9	3.4	3.2	0.3	0.1	0.8	1.3
1960	1.7	1.2	1.9	1.7	.2	.6	4.2	4.3	2.4	2.5	2.4	3.1	1.1	1.2
1961	3.5	3.1	1.9	2.0	-1.5	-1.1	3.9	3.3	2.8	2.3	.4	.2	.8	.8
1962	4.6	4.5	6.4	6.8	1.8	2.2	4.4	4.0	3.4	3.0	-.1	-.5	1.0	1.0
1963	3.9	3.5	4.6	4.7	.7	1.1	3.6	3.4	2.2	2.1	-.3	-.1	.6	.7
1964	3.4	3.0	6.4	6.7	2.9	3.7	3.8	3.1	2.4	1.8	.4	.2	1.1	1.3
1965	3.5	3.1	7.0	7.1	3.4	3.9	3.7	3.3	2.1	1.7	.2	.2	1.6	1.3
1966	4.1	3.6	6.8	7.1	2.6	3.5	6.7	5.9	3.8	3.0	2.6	2.3	2.5	2.3
1967	2.2	1.7	1.9	1.7	-.3	.0	5.7	5.8	2.5	2.7	3.4	4.0	2.7	3.2
1968	3.4	3.4	5.0	5.2	1.5	1.8	8.1	7.8	3.7	3.5	4.5	4.3	4.0	4.0
1969	.5	.1	3.0	3.0	2.5	2.9	7.0	6.8	1.4	1.3	6.5	6.7	4.6	4.5
1970	2.0	1.5	.0	-.1	-2.0	-1.6	7.7	7.2	1.9	1.4	5.6	5.6	4.4	4.5
1971	4.1	4.0	3.8	3.8	-.3	-.2	6.3	6.4	1.8	1.9	2.1	2.3	4.2	4.3
1972	3.2	3.3	6.5	6.7	3.1	3.2	6.3	6.5	3.0	3.2	3.0	3.1	3.6	3.2
1973	3.0	3.1	7.0	7.3	3.8	4.1	8.4	8.2	2.1	1.8	5.2	4.9	5.2	3.6
1974	-1.6	-1.5	-1.4	-1.4	.2	.1	9.6	9.8	-1.3	-1.2	11.4	11.4	9.6	10.2
1975	3.5	2.7	-1.0	-1.7	-4.3	-4.3	10.2	10.1	1.0	.9	6.5	7.2	9.8	10.8
1976	3.1	3.3	6.6	7.0	3.3	3.6	8.6	8.4	2.7	2.5	5.3	5.0	5.3	5.6
1977	1.7	1.6	5.6	5.6	3.8	3.9	8.0	8.1	1.4	1.5	6.2	6.4	6.0	6.3
1978	1.1	1.3	6.3	6.6	5.1	5.2	8.7	8.9	1.6	1.7	7.5	7.5	7.1	6.7
1979	.0	-.3	3.4	3.2	3.4	3.6	9.7	9.6	.1	.0	9.8	10.0	8.5	8.4
1980	-.2	-.2	-1.1	-1.0	-.9	-.8	10.8	10.8	-.3	-.3	11.0	11.0	8.9	9.6
1981	2.1	1.4	2.8	2.1	.7	.7	9.6	9.8	.1	.2	7.4	8.3	9.2	9.6
1982	-.8	-1.1	-3.0	-3.2	-2.3	-2.2	7.2	7.1	1.1	1.0	8.1	8.2	5.7	6.2
1983	3.6	4.5	5.4	6.5	1.8	1.9	4.1	4.2	-.1	.0	.6	-.3	3.4	3.1
1984	2.7	2.0	8.7	8.2	5.8	6.1	4.4	4.2	.1	.0	1.7	2.2	2.9	2.9
1985	2.2	1.6	4.6	4.2	2.3	2.6	4.8	4.6	1.3	1.1	2.5	3.0	2.4	3.0
1986	2.9	3.1	3.7	3.9	.8	.8	5.1	5.2	3.2	3.3	2.1	2.0	1.6	1.7
1987	.5	.5	3.5	3.6	3.0	3.0	3.7	3.7	.4	.4	3.2	3.2	2.2	2.2
1988	1.5	1.7	4.3	4.6	2.7	2.9	5.1	4.9	1.4	1.2	3.5	3.2	3.1	3.0
1989	1.0	.7	3.7	3.5	2.6	2.7	2.7	2.6	-1.6	-1.7	1.7	1.8	3.7	3.6
1990	2.1	1.9	1.5	1.5	-.6	-.4	6.3	6.1	1.3	1.0	4.1	4.1	3.6	3.7
1991	1.6	1.6	-.8	-.8	-2.4	-2.4	4.9	5.1	1.3	1.4	3.3	3.4	3.2	3.4
1992	4.3	4.1	4.0	3.9	-.2	-.2	5.2	5.3	2.6	2.7	.9	1.1	1.8	1.9
1993	.4	.4	3.1	3.3	2.7	2.9	2.2	2.0	-.3	-.5	1.8	1.6	2.1	2.1
1994	1.0	1.1	5.0	4.8	4.0	3.6	1.4	1.7	-.7	-.4	.4	.5	1.8	1.9
1995	.1	.5	2.9	3.2	2.8	2.7	2.1	2.1	-.3	-.3	1.9	1.6	1.8	1.7
1996	3.0	2.7	4.6	4.5	1.6	1.8	3.5	3.4	.8	.7	.5	.7	1.6	· 1.4
1997	1.9	1.6	5.3	5.2	3.4	3.5	3.2	3.1	1.0	.9	1.3	1.4	1.5	1.7
1998	2.8	2.8	4.8	5.0	2.0	2.1	6.1	6.0	4.6	4.5	3.2	3.1	.6	.7
1999	3.1	2.9	5.1	5.2	2.0	2.2	4.9	4.7	2.7	2.5	1.8	1.8	.9	1.1
2000	2.9	2.8	3.9	3.8	1.0	1.0	7.1	7.2	3.7	3.7	4.1	4.2	1.8	1.9
2001	2.6	2.5	.3	.4	-2.2	-2.0	4.2	4.0	1.4	1.2	1.6	1.5	2.0	1.9
2002	4.1	4.1	1.5	1.5	-2.5	-2.6	3.5	3.6	1.9	2.0	-.5	-.5	1.0	1.1
2003	3.8	3.7	3.1	3.1	-.7	-.6	4.1	4.0	1.7	1.7	.2	.3	1.5	1.3
2004	2.9	2.7	4.2	4.1	1.3	1.4	3.7	3.6	1.1	.9	.9	.9	2.6	2.4
2005	2.0	1.9	3.6	3.6	1.6	1.6	4.0	4.0	.6	.7	2.0	2.0	3.1	3.4
2006	1.0	1.0	3.1	3.2	2.1	2.2	3.9	3.9	.6	.6	2.9	2.9	2.9	3.0
2003: I	3.3	3.4	1.1	1.2	-2.2	-2.1	5.5	5.5	1.7	1.7	2.1	2.0	1.9	2.0
II	6.9	5.7	4.6	4.3	-2.2	-1.3	7.5	6.7	7.2	6.4	.6	1.0	.6	.4
III	9.1	10.4	10.4	11.0	1.2	.5	4.6	5.4	2.1	2.9	-4.1	-4.5	1.8	1.3
IV	-1.4	-.5	1.1	1.6	2.5	2.2	2.9	3.3	1.8	2.2	4.3	3.8	1.8	1.1
2004: I	2.4	.9	3.7	2.6	1.2	1.7	.6	-.2	-2.9	-3.6	-1.8	-1.0	3.4	3.4
II	3.9	4.7	4.4	5.0	.5	.3	5.2	5.3	1.0	1.1	1.3	.6	3.6	3.0
III	1.2	.9	4.0	3.8	2.8	3.0	5.3	5.2	3.0	2.9	4.1	4.3	1.8	2.4
IV	2.0	.7	3.0	2.6	1.0	2.0	6.3	5.4	2.6	1.7	4.2	4.7	3.5	3.8
2005: I	3.0	3.7	3.7	3.9	.7	.2	3.0	3.6	1.1	1.6	.0	-.1	3.4	3.8
II	-.3	.3	3.3	3.2	3.6	2.9	.7	1.5	-3.1	-2.4	1.0	1.2	2.6	2.7
III	4.9	4.4	5.5	5.6	.6	1.1	6.2	5.7	.7	.2	1.3	1.3	3.5	3.8
IV	-1.1	-1.4	1.0	.9	2.1	2.4	2.9	2.6	-.5	-.8	4.0	4.1	3.7	3.7
2006: I	2.5	2.5	5.5	5.7	2.9	3.1	7.2	7.2	5.1	5.1	4.6	4.6	2.8	3.0
II	.8	.8	2.5	2.4	1.7	1.6	-.4	-.2	-5.1	-5.0	-1.2	-1.0	3.3	3.7
III	-1.5	-1.6	.6	.8	2.2	2.4	1.6	1.3	-1.6	-1.8	3.1	2.9	2.1	1.6
IV	1.2	1.8	2.6	2.6	1.4	.8	11.4	12.2	13.8	14.6	10.1	10.3	.8	.3
2007: I	.2	.7	.2	.3	.0	-.3	5.5	5.9	1.6	2.0	5.3	5.2	4.1	3.6
II	3.6	2.2	4.4	4.2	.8	2.0	2.4	1.0	-3.3	-4.7	-1.1	-1.1	2.2	2.1
III	6.7	6.3	5.7	5.7	-1.0	-.6	4.7	4.2	2.7	2.3	-2.0	-2.0	.2	-.1

[1] Output refers to real gross domestic product in the sector.
[2] Hours at work of all persons engaged in the sector. See footnote 2, Table B–49.
[3] Wages and salaries of employees plus employers' contributions for social insurance and private benefit plans. Also includes an estimate of wages, salaries, and supplemental payments for the self-employed.
[4] Hourly compensation divided by a consumer price index. See footnote 4, Table B–49.
[5] Current dollar output divided by the output index.

Note.—Percent changes are based on original data and may differ slightly from percent changes based on indexes in Table B–49.

Source: Department of Labor (Bureau of Labor Statistics).

Appendix B – Population, Employment, Wages, and Productivity | 285

TABLE B–51.—*Industrial production indexes, major industry divisions, 1959–2007*

[2002=100; monthly data seasonally adjusted]

Year or month	Total industrial production [1]	Manufacturing				Mining	Utilities
		Total [1]	Durable	Nondurable	Other (non-NAICS) [1]		
1959	24.9	22.6					
1960	25.4	23.0					
1961	25.6	23.1					
1962	27.7	25.1					
1963	29.4	26.7					
1964	31.3	28.5					
1965	34.5	31.6					
1966	37.5	34.4					
1967	38.3	35.1					
1968	40.5	37.1					
1969	42.3	38.7					
1970	40.9	37.0					
1971	41.5	37.5					
1972	45.5	41.5	30.0	61.0	65.6	106.9	50.3
1973	49.2	45.2	33.8	63.8	67.7	107.5	53.2
1974	49.1	45.1	33.6	64.1	68.0	105.9	53.0
1975	44.8	40.4	29.2	59.5	64.9	103.4	54.0
1976	48.3	44.1	31.9	64.9	66.8	104.2	56.4
1977	52.0	47.9	35.1	69.3	73.2	106.6	58.7
1978	54.9	50.8	37.9	71.8	75.7	109.9	60.2
1979	56.6	52.5	39.9	72.2	77.3	113.2	61.6
1980	55.1	50.6	38.1	70.0	80.0	115.3	62.0
1981	55.9	51.2	38.6	70.6	81.9	118.3	62.9
1982	53.1	48.5	35.4	69.5	82.8	112.4	60.9
1983	54.5	50.8	37.2	72.8	85.1	106.5	61.4
1984	59.5	55.9	42.6	76.2	89.0	113.4	65.0
1985	60.3	56.9	43.7	76.6	92.5	111.2	66.4
1986	61.0	58.3	44.5	78.8	94.2	103.1	67.0
1987	64.1	61.6	47.2	83.1	99.7	104.0	70.1
1988	67.4	64.8	50.6	85.8	99.3	106.6	74.1
1989	68.1	65.3	51.2	86.4	97.9	105.4	76.4
1990	68.7	65.9	51.4	87.7	96.7	106.9	77.9
1991	67.7	64.6	49.9	87.4	92.9	104.6	79.8
1992	69.7	67.0	52.5	89.6	91.0	102.2	79.7
1993	72.0	69.5	55.6	90.9	91.8	102.2	82.6
1994	76.0	73.7	60.6	94.1	90.9	104.6	84.2
1995	79.8	77.8	66.0	95.8	90.9	104.4	87.2
1996	83.2	81.4	71.7	96.0	90.2	106.2	89.7
1997	89.2	88.3	80.4	99.6	97.7	108.0	89.7
1998	94.6	94.4	89.2	101.0	104.2	106.5	92.0
1999	99.1	99.5	97.3	101.7	107.6	101.2	94.7
2000	103.6	104.3	105.4	102.3	109.6	103.5	97.4
2001	100.0	100.0	100.4	99.0	103.2	104.5	97.0
2002	100.0	100.0	100.0	100.0	100.0	100.0	100.0
2003	101.1	101.1	102.3	100.1	97.0	99.9	101.9
2004	103.6	104.0	106.3	102.0	97.8	99.2	103.3
2005	106.9	108.0	112.1	104.5	99.6	97.6	105.5
2006	111.1	113.0	120.4	106.7	98.0	100.2	105.2
2007 [p]	113.4	115.2	124.0	107.7	98.7	100.9	109.1
2006: Jan	109.1	111.5	117.5	106.4	98.7	98.7	98.7
Feb	109.4	111.2	117.6	105.9	97.6	98.5	103.7
Mar	110.0	111.7	118.5	105.9	97.8	98.6	105.5
Apr	110.9	112.8	120.3	106.3	99.0	99.7	105.3
May	110.9	112.6	120.1	106.1	98.0	100.7	105.7
June	111.9	113.5	121.3	107.0	98.1	101.1	107.4
July	112.3	113.9	121.7	107.4	98.1	101.0	108.7
Aug	112.5	114.3	122.6	107.5	97.0	99.9	108.8
Sept	112.2	114.3	122.2	107.8	97.2	101.0	104.5
Oct	112.0	113.4	121.2	106.7	99.6	100.9	109.8
Nov	111.5	113.2	121.3	106.2	99.4	100.7	106.8
Dec	112.2	114.4	122.7	107.4	98.7	102.5	102.5
2007: Jan	111.7	113.7	121.2	107.5	98.4	100.2	105.1
Feb	112.5	113.6	121.3	107.2	98.6	100.0	114.1
Mar	112.4	114.4	122.3	107.8	99.1	100.2	106.6
Apr	113.1	114.8	123.2	107.7	99.5	100.2	109.7
May	113.0	114.9	123.4	107.8	99.0	99.9	108.0
June	113.5	115.7	124.7	107.9	99.4	100.4	107.3
July	114.2	116.6	126.2	108.5	99.1	101.3	106.2
Aug	114.1	115.9	125.5	107.7	98.1	100.5	111.5
Sept	114.2	116.1	125.3	108.2	99.4	101.7	109.7
Oct [p]	113.7	115.4	124.8	107.5	98.5	101.6	109.8
Nov [p]	114.0	115.7	125.3	107.6	98.3	102.6	109.8
Dec [p]	114.0	115.7	125.4	107.4	98.4	102.7	109.6

[1] Total industry and total manufacturing series include manufacturing as defined in the North American Industry Classification System (NAICS) plus those industries—logging and newspaper, periodical, book, and directory publishing—that have traditionally been considered to be manufacturing and included in the industrial sector.

Note.—Data based on NAICS; see footnote 1.

Source: Board of Governors of the Federal Reserve System.

[2002=100; monthly data seasonally adjusted]

Year or month	Total industrial production	Final products									Nonindustrial supplies			Materials		
		Total	Consumer goods				Equipment				Total	Construction	Business	Total	Nonenergy	Energy
			Total	Automotive products	Other durable goods	Nondurable goods	Total[1]	Business	Defense and space							
1959	24.9	24.0	30.7	19.1	19.1	37.0	15.9	11.4	46.0	26.0	37.1	21.2	24.7	....	51.0
1960	25.4	24.8	31.9	21.9	19.2	38.2	16.4	11.7	47.2	26.1	36.3	21.9	25.1	....	51.7
1961	25.6	25.0	32.5	20.0	19.8	39.5	16.1	11.4	48.0	26.6	36.6	22.6	25.1	....	52.1
1962	27.7	27.1	34.7	24.2	21.5	41.3	17.9	12.3	53.6	28.3	38.8	24.0	27.3	....	53.9
1963	29.4	28.7	36.6	26.5	23.2	43.2	19.0	12.9	59.9	29.8	40.6	25.5	29.1	....	57.1
1964	31.3	30.3	38.7	27.8	25.4	45.3	20.1	14.5	58.0	31.8	43.1	27.3	31.4	....	59.4
1965	34.5	33.3	41.7	34.2	28.8	47.3	22.7	16.6	64.2	33.9	45.8	29.1	35.1	....	62.1
1966	37.5	36.4	43.9	34.1	31.7	49.5	26.5	19.2	75.5	35.9	47.7	31.4	38.2	....	66.1
1967	38.3	37.9	44.9	30.0	32.1	52.1	28.1	19.6	86.1	37.4	48.9	33.1	37.8	31.0	68.3
1968	40.5	39.7	47.6	35.7	34.4	54.1	29.0	20.5	86.3	39.6	51.5	35.1	40.3	33.2	71.5
1969	42.3	41.0	49.4	35.9	36.7	56.0	29.7	21.8	82.1	41.7	53.7	37.3	42.7	35.3	75.1
1970	40.9	39.5	48.8	30.2	35.5	56.9	27.6	21.0	69.5	41.1	51.8	37.5	41.2	33.2	78.9
1971	41.5	39.9	51.7	38.5	37.6	58.5	25.9	20.0	62.5	42.3	53.5	38.6	41.8	33.8	79.5
1972	45.5	43.3	55.8	41.5	43.1	62.3	28.3	22.7	60.8	47.3	60.7	42.5	46.1	37.9	82.5
1973	49.2	46.7	58.4	45.1	46.0	64.2	32.3	26.4	67.0	50.6	65.8	45.1	50.2	42.0	84.6
1974	49.1	46.6	56.6	38.9	43.3	64.2	34.0	27.9	69.4	50.1	64.3	45.0	50.1	41.9	84.2
1975	44.8	43.9	54.4	37.5	37.9	63.1	30.9	24.7	70.5	45.0	54.6	41.5	44.7	36.1	83.5
1976	48.3	47.0	58.9	42.7	42.6	67.1	32.5	26.3	68.6	48.0	58.9	44.2	48.6	40.2	85.3
1977	52.0	50.9	62.5	48.3	47.6	69.5	36.4	30.6	61.5	52.2	64.1	47.9	52.0	43.6	88.0
1978	54.9	54.1	64.5	48.0	49.8	72.0	40.6	34.6	62.2	55.0	67.8	50.4	54.7	46.4	89.1
1979	56.6	56.0	63.5	43.3	50.1	71.6	45.6	39.2	66.8	56.8	69.6	52.2	56.2	47.7	91.5
1980	55.1	55.7	61.1	33.3	46.5	71.6	47.7	40.1	79.9	54.5	64.4	51.0	54.1	44.9	92.2
1981	55.9	57.1	61.6	34.4	46.9	72.0	50.1	41.4	87.0	55.1	63.4	52.2	54.4	45.1	93.1
1982	53.1	56.0	61.4	33.4	43.5	73.2	47.9	38.0	104.4	53.1	57.6	51.6	50.2	40.6	89.1
1983	54.5	57.0	63.7	38.8	47.1	74.0	47.4	38.1	105.2	56.0	61.7	54.1	51.6	43.5	86.3
1984	59.5	61.9	66.6	43.4	52.7	75.5	54.6	44.2	119.7	61.0	67.2	58.8	56.6	48.5	91.8
1985	60.3	63.6	67.3	43.4	52.8	76.5	57.6	46.2	134.4	62.6	69.0	60.3	56.5	48.7	91.2
1986	61.0	64.7	69.6	46.6	55.9	78.3	56.9	45.7	142.9	64.7	71.4	62.3	56.5	49.7	87.7
1987	64.1	67.6	72.5	49.7	58.9	81.1	60.0	48.7	145.9	68.6	75.9	66.1	59.6	53.0	89.7
1988	67.4	71.2	75.3	52.4	61.9	83.7	64.5	53.4	147.0	70.9	77.6	68.6	62.9	56.4	92.8
1989	68.1	71.9	75.6	54.4	62.6	83.5	66.1	55.3	147.2	71.6	77.3	69.6	63.4	56.8	93.7
1990	68.7	72.7	75.9	50.9	62.5	84.9	67.4	57.3	141.4	72.7	76.6	71.3	63.8	56.9	95.6
1991	67.7	71.8	75.9	47.6	60.8	86.1	65.2	56.4	131.2	71.0	72.4	70.4	62.9	55.7	95.7
1992	69.7	73.5	78.1	55.7	63.5	86.8	66.1	58.7	121.9	73.0	75.5	72.0	65.0	58.5	94.8
1993	72.0	75.9	80.8	61.5	69.2	88.0	68.0	61.2	115.3	75.6	78.9	74.4	67.3	61.2	95.1
1994	76.0	79.3	84.6	68.9	75.8	90.1	70.8	65.0	108.6	79.3	84.7	77.4	71.8	66.3	96.6
1995	79.8	82.7	87.1	71.0	80.3	92.3	75.6	70.8	105.8	82.3	86.7	80.8	76.1	71.3	98.0
1996	83.2	86.0	88.9	73.2	84.3	93.5	81.5	77.8	102.7	85.5	90.6	83.7	79.8	75.3	99.5
1997	89.2	91.6	92.1	78.7	89.6	95.7	91.9	89.7	100.9	91.1	95.1	89.6	86.2	83.3	99.4
1998	94.6	97.0	95.5	83.9	96.1	97.8	101.4	100.3	105.1	96.4	100.2	95.0	91.7	90.0	99.8
1999	99.1	99.7	97.3	92.0	100.4	97.8	106.0	106.5	102.7	100.3	102.8	99.4	98.0	97.8	99.6
2000	103.6	102.9	99.3	93.9	104.8	99.3	111.6	114.6	92.1	104.5	105.1	104.2	104.0	105.0	101.0
2001	100.0	100.8	98.1	90.8	99.2	99.4	107.3	107.6	100.6	100.1	100.5	100.0	99.1	98.8	100.0
2002	100.0	100.0	100.0	100.0	100.0	100.0	100.0	100.0	100.0	100.0	100.0	100.0	100.0	100.0	100.0
2003	101.1	101.2	101.3	105.6	100.9	100.5	100.9	100.2	103.8	101.0	99.8	101.5	100.9	101.3	99.9
2004	103.6	103.3	102.8	105.2	104.3	102.0	104.7	104.5	104.0	103.2	101.8	103.7	104.0	105.6	99.7
2005	106.9	107.6	105.7	102.6	109.1	105.5	112.7	112.8	109.7	107.0	106.7	107.1	106.2	109.4	98.4
2006	111.1	111.5	106.9	99.4	111.6	107.2	124.1	125.9	112.0	110.3	110.4	110.3	111.0	115.7	99.8
2007 P	113.4	114.5	109.1	100.5	111.7	109.9	129.2	132.3	112.1	110.9	108.6	111.8	113.2	118.0	102.0
2006: Jan	109.1	109.2	105.7	102.0	111.2	105.3	118.7	119.7	111.2	109.5	111.3	108.7	108.8	113.9	97.1
Feb	109.4	109.5	106.0	100.9	111.4	105.8	119.1	119.9	111.7	109.3	110.7	108.8	109.3	113.8	98.7
Mar	110.0	110.3	106.7	102.3	111.3	106.5	120.3	121.6	109.9	109.9	111.4	109.4	109.6	114.3	98.5
Apr	110.9	111.2	106.8	101.2	112.7	106.8	123.0	124.6	111.5	110.6	111.6	110.1	110.9	115.7	99.4
May	110.9	110.9	106.4	99.9	112.1	106.4	123.3	124.8	111.8	110.3	111.1	109.9	111.0	115.6	100.2
June	111.9	112.2	107.6	102.8	112.0	107.6	124.7	126.4	112.6	110.9	111.1	110.8	111.9	116.4	101.1
July	112.3	112.5	107.4	97.9	112.3	108.1	126.2	128.1	113.8	111.3	111.6	111.2	112.5	117.0	101.7
Aug	112.5	112.9	107.8	99.6	112.7	108.2	126.6	128.6	113.0	111.4	111.3	111.5	112.6	117.6	100.9
Sept	112.2	112.7	107.6	98.4	112.2	108.2	126.6	128.5	113.6	110.7	110.3	110.8	112.2	117.4	100.0
Oct	112.0	112.4	107.3	94.5	111.0	108.7	126.3	128.4	113.3	110.9	108.4	111.9	112.0	116.4	101.3
Nov	111.5	112.8	107.6	98.2	110.6	108.5	126.9	129.5	112.0	109.6	107.4	110.5	111.3	116.4	100.6
Dec	112.2	113.6	107.8	100.6	111.7	108.2	129.2	132.1	112.5	110.1	109.7	110.3	111.7	116.6	100.2
2007: Jan	111.7	112.7	107.4	95.2	110.8	108.7	126.9	128.8	113.9	110.0	108.4	110.6	111.3	115.9	100.5
Feb	112.5	114.2	109.4	98.7	110.5	110.9	127.1	129.2	113.0	110.2	106.8	111.5	111.8	116.0	101.9
Mar	112.4	113.7	108.6	99.7	110.7	109.6	127.7	130.6	109.8	110.3	107.9	111.2	112.0	116.8	100.5
Apr	113.1	114.3	109.2	102.3	111.8	109.8	128.0	130.9	111.1	110.9	108.3	111.9	112.7	117.5	101.1
May	113.0	114.0	108.8	101.1	112.4	109.4	128.1	131.1	111.0	110.8	109.1	111.5	112.7	117.7	100.9
June	113.5	114.7	109.2	104.1	113.2	109.3	129.4	132.2	112.9	111.2	110.2	111.7	113.2	118.2	101.2
July	114.2	115.4	109.7	105.3	113.2	109.8	130.7	133.9	113.0	111.2	110.9	111.8	114.2	119.6	101.4
Aug	114.1	115.0	109.6	102.8	112.9	110.0	129.9	133.1	112.2	111.3	109.5	113.0	114.3	118.9	103.3
Sept	114.2	115.2	109.5	100.3	112.3	110.4	130.7	134.2	112.3	111.5	109.3	112.3	114.3	119.1	102.8
Oct P	113.7	114.3	108.6	99.2	110.8	109.7	129.6	133.3	112.0	111.0	108.6	112.0	114.1	118.5	103.6
Nov P	114.0	114.6	108.7	100.6	110.9	109.5	130.6	134.1	112.4	110.8	108.3	111.8	114.6	119.3	103.6
Dec P	114.0	114.9	108.8	100.8	110.4	109.7	131.7	135.3	112.5	110.5	107.3	111.8	114.3	118.8	103.6

[1] Includes other items not shown separately.

Note.—See footnote 1 and Note, Table B–51.

Source: Board of Governors of the Federal Reserve System.

TABLE B–53.—*Industrial production indexes, selected manufacturing industries, 1967–2007*

[2002=100; monthly data seasonally adjusted]

Year or month	Durable manufacturing								Nondurable manufacturing					
	Primary metal		Fabri-cated metal prod-ucts	Ma-chinery	Computer and electronic products		Transportation equipment		Apparel	Paper	Printing and sup-port	Chem-ical	Plastics and rubber prod-ucts	Food
	Total	Iron and steel prod-ucts			Total	Se-lected high-tech-nology[1]	Total	Motor vehi-cles and parts						
1967						0.2								
1968						.2								
1969						.2								
1970						.2								
1971						.2								
1972	121.8	129.2	69.3	67.8	1.1	.2	53.2	44.2	170.3	66.1	51.6	47.8	35.2	58.7
1973	141.7	154.9	76.5	78.4	1.3	.3	60.8	50.6	175.4	71.5	54.2	52.4	39.5	58.8
1974	145.3	165.6	75.3	82.2	1.4	.3	56.0	43.4	163.4	74.6	52.6	54.4	38.5	59.4
1975	112.7	122.9	65.0	71.7	1.3	.3	50.7	37.9	159.8	64.5	49.1	47.8	32.9	58.3
1976	119.6	127.5	69.7	74.8	1.5	.4	56.8	48.3	168.8	71.2	52.7	53.5	36.4	63.0
1977	120.7	124.5	75.6	81.8	2.0	.5	61.7	55.0	179.5	74.3	57.1	58.2	42.9	64.1
1978	128.4	133.7	79.4	88.1	2.5	.7	65.7	57.3	184.6	77.7	60.4	61.1	44.4	66.1
1979	131.4	138.5	82.9	93.0	3.1	.9	66.5	52.5	175.0	78.8	62.2	62.5	43.7	65.4
1980	115.3	117.4	78.2	88.5	3.8	1.1	59.0	38.6	177.6	78.6	62.7	59.0	38.9	66.6
1981	115.5	121.7	77.7	87.7	4.4	1.3	56.9	37.7	176.6	79.7	64.3	59.9	41.2	67.5
1982	81.5	74.8	69.6	73.4	5.1	1.6	52.2	33.9	178.9	78.4	69.1	56.1	40.5	70.1
1983	83.5	75.4	70.1	66.3	5.8	1.9	57.6	43.4	184.2	83.5	74.3	59.9	44.0	70.9
1984	91.6	83.0	76.4	77.3	7.4	2.6	65.2	52.0	186.8	87.7	80.9	63.5	50.9	72.3
1985	84.6	77.1	77.4	77.6	8.0	2.8	68.7	54.0	179.5	86.0	84.2	62.9	52.8	74.9
1986	82.6	75.3	76.9	76.4	8.4	2.9	70.3	53.9	181.6	89.5	88.4	65.8	55.0	76.0
1987	88.9	85.7	78.3	77.9	9.5	3.6	72.8	55.9	182.8	92.5	94.9	71.0	60.9	77.7
1988	99.6	99.7	82.3	85.7	10.6	4.2	77.3	59.7	179.4	96.2	98.0	75.1	63.7	79.6
1989	97.4	96.2	81.7	89.0	10.9	4.5	78.8	59.1	170.7	97.2	98.4	76.5	65.8	79.8
1990	96.2	95.1	80.7	86.8	11.9	5.1	76.3	55.5	167.2	97.2	102.1	78.3	67.7	82.3
1991	90.3	86.9	77.0	81.4	12.5	5.5	73.3	53.1	168.1	97.4	98.9	78.0	66.9	83.8
1992	92.4	90.9	79.4	81.2	14.1	6.7	76.0	60.4	171.4	99.7	104.3	79.1	72.0	85.4
1993	96.8	96.4	82.4	87.2	15.8	8.0	78.2	66.8	175.6	100.9	104.6	80.1	77.1	87.6
1994	104.2	104.0	89.5	95.5	18.9	10.6	81.8	76.7	179.1	105.2	105.7	82.1	83.5	88.2
1995	105.4	105.6	95.0	102.3	24.9	15.3	81.9	79.0	179.4	106.8	107.3	83.5	85.6	90.4
1996	107.8	108.2	98.5	105.9	32.0	21.6	83.4	79.6	174.4	103.4	108.0	85.2	88.4	88.6
1997	112.4	111.4	102.9	111.7	43.0	32.0	91.0	85.8	172.2	105.6	110.2	90.2	93.9	91.0
1998	114.3	111.2	106.3	114.5	56.2	45.6	99.0	90.2	162.9	106.4	111.5	91.7	97.3	95.0
1999	114.0	112.0	107.0	112.0	75.5	67.7	104.4	100.1	156.1	107.2	112.4	93.6	102.4	96.0
2000	110.3	110.9	111.2	117.7	101.8	98.8	99.5	99.5	148.5	105.0	113.1	95.0	103.5	97.7
2001	99.8	100.3	103.1	104.1	103.5	101.5	95.7	90.6	127.2	99.0	106.3	93.3	97.4	97.7
2002	100.0	100.0	100.0	100.0	100.0	100.0	100.0	100.0	100.0	100.0	100.0	100.0	100.0	100.0
2003	98.9	100.8	98.9	99.6	111.5	116.7	101.1	103.5	92.3	97.3	96.3	101.4	100.1	101.0
2004	109.3	116.4	99.1	103.7	126.2	132.6	100.8	103.8	79.5	98.0	97.0	105.7	101.3	101.1
2005	107.1	109.9	103.3	110.0	141.0	156.6	104.1	103.7	76.8	98.6	98.9	108.0	102.3	104.5
2006	112.1	117.0	108.9	117.1	169.1	198.1	109.4	101.9	77.8	98.5	103.3	110.3	105.7	107.7
2007 P	110.5	114.4	111.5	118.3	188.8	236.4	111.9	99.5	76.4	96.4	103.7	110.9	108.7	112.7
2006: Jan	112.9	116.0	106.9	112.1	154.7	176.8	108.7	104.2	77.3	100.4	101.3	109.0	104.9	106.9
Feb	112.6	116.8	107.3	112.0	156.0	178.1	108.4	102.9	76.8	98.3	101.8	108.7	105.0	106.2
Mar	111.8	116.8	108.1	114.0	158.9	182.9	109.1	104.3	77.3	97.2	102.3	109.4	105.6	106.7
Apr	114.3	120.2	109.4	116.2	164.0	189.5	110.1	104.3	78.6	97.6	103.9	110.1	106.9	107.8
May	117.1	125.5	108.4	114.1	165.8	192.8	109.3	102.5	78.3	97.8	102.7	110.0	105.9	106.6
June	117.7	126.1	109.1	114.8	169.1	196.0	111.2	104.6	78.9	99.0	103.0	111.1	106.9	106.6
July	115.7	123.3	109.9	119.6	171.6	199.3	109.2	100.3	79.3	98.0	102.7	111.8	108.1	107.0
Aug	114.5	121.8	110.7	121.0	174.0	204.3	110.4	102.2	77.9	98.7	102.7	112.4	107.1	107.0
Sept	112.8	119.8	110.5	120.6	177.2	210.7	109.8	100.9	77.5	99.3	103.1	111.7	106.1	108.5
Oct	109.2	112.3	110.5	118.1	179.3	214.4	107.8	97.3	78.4	98.3	104.1	110.1	104.4	109.4
Nov	103.8	103.9	109.7	117.6	180.0	216.2	110.5	100.7	77.5	97.9	104.3	108.8	103.9	110.0
Dec	102.7	99.5	109.8	122.6	181.7	218.6	111.9	102.4	77.4	99.5	106.3	110.5	105.6	109.8
2007: Jan	107.1	107.6	109.3	116.4	181.3	219.9	108.9	96.4	78.8	96.4	105.6	109.9	106.3	110.0
Feb	107.6	109.2	109.8	115.3	181.5	220.4	110.5	98.7	77.8	97.5	106.0	110.1	105.5	110.8
Mar	108.8	111.1	110.6	118.0	182.3	223.2	110.6	99.4	76.7	97.2	105.6	110.4	107.1	111.7
Apr	111.3	113.8	111.1	117.2	184.2	226.4	111.8	100.8	77.9	97.3	104.7	110.5	108.0	112.5
May	112.1	116.9	110.8	117.6	184.4	228.5	111.5	100.3	77.7	96.7	103.1	110.6	108.5	111.8
June	110.6	115.8	111.7	118.7	187.7	234.4	114.0	102.8	76.9	96.1	102.1	110.8	109.0	112.6
July	114.0	117.8	112.5	119.9	191.6	242.4	114.8	103.6	77.6	96.8	101.7	111.8	109.9	114.0
Aug	112.8	118.0	112.3	117.7	191.8	243.4	114.3	102.2	75.6	96.5	102.5	110.9	109.3	112.9
Sept	109.2	112.8	112.8	120.5	192.8	245.3	112.4	99.1	74.4	96.1	103.2	111.5	110.5	114.3
Oct P	110.5	116.1	112.9	118.7	194.5	248.7	111.4	97.5	74.1	94.7	102.4	111.0	109.6	113.8
Nov P	112.1	118.1	112.6	118.0	197.3	252.6	112.6	98.6	74.0	96.1	102.7	111.5	110.9	113.1
Dec P	110.9	116.0	111.8	118.2	198.8	254.6	112.9	98.2	75.4	95.0	102.3	111.1	109.8	113.9

[1] Computers and peripheral equipment, communications equipment, and semiconductors and related electronic components.

Note.—See footnote 1 and Note, Table B–51.

Source: Board of Governors of the Federal Reserve System.

TABLE B–54.—*Capacity utilization rates, 1959–2007*

[Percent [1]; monthly data seasonally adjusted]

Year or month	Total industry [2]	Manufacturing				Mining	Utilities	Stage-of-process		
		Total [2]	Durable goods	Nondurable goods	Other (non-NAICS) [2]			Crude	Primary and semi-finished	Finished
1959	....	81.6	....	....	....	....	....	....	83.0	81.1
1960	....	80.1	....	....	....	....	....	....	79.8	80.5
1961	....	77.3	....	....	....	....	....	....	77.9	77.2
1962	....	81.4	....	....	....	....	....	....	81.5	81.6
1963	....	83.5	....	....	....	....	....	....	83.8	83.4
1964	....	85.6	....	....	....	....	....	....	87.8	84.6
1965	....	89.5	....	....	....	....	....	....	91.0	88.8
1966	....	91.1	....	....	....	....	....	....	91.4	91.1
1967	87.0	87.2	87.5	86.3	....	81.2	94.5	81.1	85.0	88.2
1968	87.3	87.1	87.3	86.5	....	83.6	95.1	83.4	86.8	87.0
1969	87.4	86.6	87.0	86.2	....	86.8	96.8	85.7	88.1	85.4
1970	81.2	79.4	77.5	82.2	....	89.3	96.3	85.2	81.5	77.9
1971	79.6	77.9	75.1	81.9	....	88.0	94.7	84.4	81.6	75.4
1972	84.6	83.3	81.9	85.3	85.7	90.9	95.2	88.7	88.1	79.4
1973	88.4	87.6	88.5	86.6	84.7	92.0	94.3	90.6	92.2	83.0
1974	85.1	84.4	84.6	84.2	82.7	91.1	87.4	91.3	87.4	80.2
1975	75.6	73.5	71.6	76.0	77.2	89.2	84.5	83.9	75.0	73.5
1976	79.6	78.2	76.3	81.0	77.4	89.7	85.2	87.2	80.0	76.6
1977	83.2	82.4	81.1	84.2	83.4	89.8	85.3	89.1	84.3	79.7
1978	84.9	84.3	83.9	85.0	85.1	89.8	84.2	88.5	85.9	82.1
1979	85.0	84.2	84.4	83.7	85.4	91.1	85.5	89.3	85.9	82.0
1980	80.8	78.7	77.7	79.5	86.9	91.5	85.1	89.1	78.7	79.7
1981	79.7	77.0	75.2	78.9	87.5	91.4	84.3	89.4	77.1	77.9
1982	73.7	71.0	66.5	76.7	87.0	83.7	80.4	81.9	70.4	73.7
1983	74.8	73.5	68.6	79.8	87.6	78.5	79.7	78.8	74.2	73.5
1984	80.4	79.4	76.8	82.4	89.4	84.7	82.9	85.0	81.1	77.6
1985	79.4	78.3	75.8	80.9	90.3	83.4	83.1	83.3	80.0	77.0
1986	78.7	78.4	75.3	81.9	88.8	76.6	82.3	78.6	79.9	77.2
1987	81.1	80.9	77.5	84.8	90.6	79.6	83.9	82.6	82.9	78.6
1988	84.1	83.9	81.8	86.2	88.5	83.7	86.1	86.3	85.9	81.3
1989	83.6	83.1	81.5	85.0	85.4	84.9	86.6	87.0	84.8	81.1
1990	82.4	81.6	79.2	84.5	83.7	86.9	86.0	88.2	82.7	80.3
1991	79.6	78.3	74.8	82.4	81.5	84.9	86.8	85.5	79.7	77.7
1992	80.3	79.4	76.9	82.5	80.9	84.4	85.2	85.5	81.2	77.8
1993	81.4	80.3	78.7	82.3	81.9	85.8	87.7	85.7	83.6	77.8
1994	83.6	82.8	82.0	83.9	81.9	87.6	88.8	87.8	86.6	79.1
1995	84.0	83.1	82.6	83.9	82.2	87.9	89.9	88.6	86.8	79.5
1996	83.1	81.9	81.6	82.5	80.8	90.3	90.4	88.4	85.7	78.7
1997	83.9	83.0	82.7	83.2	84.6	91.2	89.1	90.2	85.9	80.1
1998	82.8	81.7	81.1	82.0	86.5	89.0	91.2	87.3	84.0	80.5
1999	81.9	80.8	80.6	80.4	86.9	86.1	92.5	86.6	84.1	78.5
2000	81.7	80.1	80.1	79.1	88.0	90.8	92.4	88.2	84.3	77.0
2001	76.1	73.9	71.6	75.7	83.5	91.1	88.9	85.3	77.6	72.4
2002	74.8	73.0	69.7	76.2	82.3	86.4	87.7	82.9	77.2	70.6
2003	76.1	74.2	71.3	77.0	82.8	88.2	86.3	84.6	78.3	71.7
2004	78.1	76.6	74.0	78.9	84.8	88.2	84.9	86.5	80.7	73.1
2005	80.2	78.8	76.4	80.8	85.9	87.9	86.0	86.4	82.6	75.5
2006	81.7	80.4	78.9	81.9	84.1	90.7	85.2	88.7	83.4	77.6
2007 [p]	81.6	80.1	78.3	81.9	83.8	90.6	86.2	89.4	82.3	78.4
2006: Jan	81.1	80.3	78.4	82.0	84.8	89.5	80.4	87.4	83.1	76.7
Feb	81.1	79.9	78.1	81.5	83.8	89.3	84.4	87.2	83.4	76.4
Mar	81.4	80.1	78.5	81.5	83.9	89.4	85.7	87.3	83.6	76.9
Apr	81.9	80.7	79.4	81.7	84.9	90.4	85.4	88.2	83.8	77.8
May	81.7	80.3	79.0	81.5	83.9	91.2	85.5	88.9	83.6	77.2
June	82.3	80.8	79.5	82.1	84.0	91.5	86.8	89.2	84.3	77.7
July	82.4	80.9	79.5	82.3	83.9	91.3	87.6	89.5	84.5	77.9
Aug	82.4	81.1	79.8	82.3	82.9	90.2	87.5	89.2	84.4	78.0
Sept	82.0	80.9	79.3	82.5	83.0	91.2	83.9	89.6	83.5	78.0
Oct	81.7	80.1	78.4	81.6	85.0	91.0	88.0	89.1	83.3	77.6
Nov	81.3	79.8	78.2	81.2	84.7	90.7	85.4	88.7	82.0	78.1
Dec	81.6	80.5	78.9	82.0	84.0	92.3	81.8	89.6	81.7	79.0
2007: Jan	81.1	79.8	77.6	82.0	83.8	90.1	83.7	88.2	81.9	77.9
Feb	81.6	79.6	77.5	81.7	83.9	89.9	90.7	88.9	82.7	77.9
Mar	81.4	80.0	77.9	82.1	84.3	90.0	84.7	89.1	82.0	78.2
Apr	81.7	80.2	78.2	82.0	84.5	90.0	87.0	89.2	82.3	78.6
May	81.5	80.1	78.1	82.0	84.0	89.7	85.6	89.2	82.1	78.4
June	81.8	80.5	78.8	82.1	84.4	90.1	85.0	89.3	82.3	78.8
July	82.2	81.0	79.5	82.4	84.1	90.9	84.0	90.0	82.5	79.3
Aug	82.0	80.4	78.9	81.8	83.2	90.2	88.1	89.0	82.9	78.6
Sept	81.9	80.4	78.5	82.1	84.2	91.2	86.6	90.0	82.6	78.6
Oct [p]	81.4	79.8	78.0	81.5	83.4	91.2	86.6	89.4	82.0	78.2
Nov [p]	81.6	79.8	78.1	81.5	83.1	92.1	86.5	90.6	82.1	78.0
Dec [p]	81.4	79.7	78.0	81.3	83.2	92.1	86.2	90.3	81.7	78.3

[1] Output as percent of capacity.
[2] See footnote 1 and Note, Table B–51.

Source: Board of Governors of the Federal Reserve System.

TABLE B-55.—New construction activity, 1964-2007

[Value put in place, billions of dollars; monthly data at seasonally adjusted annual rates]

Year or month	Total new construction	Private construction Total	Residential buildings¹ Total²	New housing units³	Nonresidential buildings and other construction Total	Lodging	Office	Commercial⁴	Manufacturing	Other⁵	Public construction Total	Federal	State and local
1964	75.1	54.9	30.5	24.1	24.4						20.2	3.7	16.5
1965	81.9	60.0	30.2	23.8	29.7						21.9	3.9	18.0
1966	85.8	61.9	28.6	21.8	33.3						23.8	3.8	20.0
1967	87.2	61.8	28.7	21.5	33.1						25.4	3.3	22.1
1968	96.8	69.4	34.2	26.7	35.2						27.4	3.2	24.2
1969	104.9	77.2	37.2	29.2	39.9						27.8	3.2	24.6
1970	105.9	78.0	35.9	27.1	42.1						27.9	3.1	24.8
1971	122.4	92.7	48.5	38.7	44.2						29.7	3.8	25.9
1972	139.1	109.1	60.7	50.1	48.4						30.0	4.2	25.8
1973	153.8	121.4	65.1	54.6	56.3						32.3	4.7	27.6
1974	155.2	117.0	56.0	43.4	61.1						38.1	5.1	33.0
1975	152.6	109.3	51.6	36.3	57.8						43.3	6.1	37.2
1976	172.1	128.2	68.3	50.8	59.9						44.0	6.8	37.2
1977	200.5	157.4	92.0	72.2	65.4						43.1	7.1	36.0
1978	239.9	189.7	109.8	85.6	79.9						50.1	8.1	42.0
1979	272.9	216.2	116.4	89.3	99.8						56.6	8.6	48.1
1980	273.9	210.3	100.4	69.6	109.9						63.6	9.6	54.0
1981	289.1	224.4	99.2	69.4	125.1						64.7	10.4	54.3
1982	279.3	216.3	84.7	57.0	131.6						63.1	10.0	53.1
1983	311.9	248.4	125.8	95.0	122.6						63.5	10.6	52.9
1984	370.2	300.0	155.0	114.6	144.9						70.2	11.2	59.0
1985	403.4	325.6	160.5	115.9	165.1						77.8	12.0	65.8
1986	433.5	348.9	190.7	135.2	158.2						84.6	12.4	72.2
1987	446.6	356.0	199.7	142.7	156.3						90.6	14.1	76.6
1988	462.0	367.3	204.5	142.4	162.8						94.7	12.3	82.5
1989	477.5	379.3	204.3	143.2	175.1						98.2	12.2	86.0
1990	476.8	369.3	191.1	132.1	178.2						107.5	12.1	95.4
1991	432.6	322.5	166.3	114.6	156.2						110.1	12.8	97.3
1992	463.7	347.8	194.4	135.1	148.4						115.8	14.4	101.5
1993	502.4	375.1	225.1	150.9	150.0	4.6	20.0	34.4	23.4	67.7	127.4	14.4	112.9
1994	549.4	419.0	258.6	176.4	160.4	4.7	20.4	39.6	28.8	66.9	130.4	14.4	116.0
1995	567.9	427.9	247.4	171.4	180.5	7.1	23.0	44.1	35.4	70.9	140.0	15.8	124.3
1996	623.3	476.6	281.1	191.1	195.5	10.9	26.5	49.4	38.1	70.6	146.7	15.3	131.4
1997	656.2	502.7	289.0	198.1	213.7	12.9	32.8	53.1	37.6	77.3	153.4	14.1	139.4
1998	706.8	552.0	314.6	224.0	237.4	14.8	40.4	55.7	40.5	86.0	154.8	14.3	140.5
1999	768.8	599.7	350.6	251.3	249.2	16.0	45.1	59.4	35.1	93.7	169.1	14.0	155.1
2000	831.1	649.8	374.5	265.0	275.3	16.3	52.4	64.1	37.6	104.9	181.3	14.2	167.2
2001	864.2	662.2	388.3	279.4	273.9	14.5	49.7	63.6	37.8	108.2	201.9	15.1	186.8
2002	873.1	659.7	421.9	298.8	237.7	10.5	35.3	59.0	22.7	110.2	213.4	16.6	196.9
2003	921.4	705.3	475.9	345.7	229.3	9.9	30.6	57.5	21.4	109.9	216.1	17.9	198.2
2004	1,023.5	803.3	564.8	417.5	238.5	12.0	32.9	63.2	23.7	106.8	220.2	18.3	201.8
2005	1,132.1	898.0	641.3	480.8	256.6	12.7	37.3	66.6	29.9	110.2	234.2	17.3	216.9
2006	1,192.2	937.0	641.3	469.0	295.7	17.7	46.2	72.1	34.3	125.4	255.2	17.6	237.6
2006: Jan	1,203.9	962.9	687.1	514.3	275.7	13.4	39.1	72.5	31.6	119.2	241.1	16.3	224.8
Feb	1,218.6	972.1	696.0	518.0	276.1	14.1	41.0	69.7	30.7	120.5	246.5	16.7	229.8
Mar	1,226.4	973.3	694.5	517.9	278.9	15.2	41.8	69.4	32.0	120.6	253.0	17.5	235.5
Apr	1,216.6	963.8	678.3	504.4	285.6	16.8	43.6	68.7	34.1	122.3	252.8	17.7	235.1
May	1,210.0	954.4	665.9	494.3	288.5	16.8	44.7	70.0	33.2	123.8	255.6	17.2	238.3
June	1,204.0	946.2	650.9	478.9	295.3	18.0	46.2	70.5	35.3	125.2	257.8	16.5	241.3
July	1,192.9	936.5	636.6	465.3	299.9	18.5	48.8	71.6	34.2	126.8	256.4	17.1	239.3
Aug	1,186.3	932.4	625.4	452.8	306.9	18.7	49.4	73.1	38.6	127.2	253.9	16.9	237.0
Sept	1,172.1	919.0	614.4	444.3	304.6	18.8	48.8	74.3	35.9	126.8	253.1	16.5	236.7
Oct	1,164.9	907.3	601.3	430.0	306.0	20.2	48.7	73.0	34.2	129.8	257.6	20.6	237.0
Nov	1,166.3	904.5	590.0	418.7	314.5	21.0	50.4	75.9	35.1	132.1	261.9	19.9	242.0
Dec	1,167.3	896.6	580.7	411.1	315.9	20.5	51.5	76.8	35.2	132.0	270.6	19.8	250.8
2007: Jan	1,160.2	884.4	567.5	398.1	316.9	20.6	54.5	78.6	34.3	128.8	275.9	19.9	255.9
Feb	1,162.2	889.7	562.9	386.1	326.7	22.0	53.5	79.9	35.7	136.6	272.5	18.7	253.8
Mar	1,163.6	886.8	555.6	383.5	331.2	25.0	52.8	80.2	35.0	138.1	276.8	18.5	258.4
Apr	1,166.2	888.0	551.7	378.0	336.3	26.2	52.8	82.3	36.5	138.5	278.1	17.8	260.3
May	1,172.1	888.1	544.8	370.6	343.3	28.1	52.7	82.3	37.4	142.8	284.1	19.0	265.0
June	1,170.5	885.0	538.7	364.7	346.3	28.5	54.3	82.4	36.4	144.7	285.5	19.6	265.9
July	1,161.1	874.4	528.0	357.3	346.4	29.9	53.4	82.1	36.2	144.8	286.7	19.4	267.4
Aug	1,165.3	875.9	520.1	346.6	355.8	30.8	55.9	82.2	36.4	150.6	289.4	20.3	269.2
Sept	1,168.3	874.1	509.0	334.3	365.1	32.0	58.1	83.2	37.3	154.3	294.2	18.9	275.3
Oct ᵖ	1,163.6	866.6	497.1	322.1	369.5	34.4	59.9	83.9	37.4	153.9	297.0	19.8	277.2
Nov ᵖ	1,165.1	860.7	484.9	308.6	375.8	35.1	60.5	84.5	38.5	157.1	304.3	20.2	284.1

¹ Includes farm residential buildings.
² Includes residential improvements, not shown separately.
³ New single- and multi-family units.
⁴ Including farm.
⁵ Health care, educational, religious, public safety, amusement and recreation, transportation, communication, power, highway and street, sewage and waste disposal, water supply, and conservation and development.

Note.—Data beginning with 1993 reflect reclassification.

Source: Department of Commerce (Bureau of the Census).

[Thousands; monthly data at seasonally adjusted annual rates]

Year or month	New housing units started				New housing units authorized[1]				New housing units completed	New houses sold
	Total	1 unit	2 to 4 units[2]	5 units or more	Total	1 unit	2 to 4 units	5 units or more		
1959	1,517.0	1,234.0	283.0		1,208.3	938.3	77.1	192.9		
1960	1,252.2	994.7	257.5		998.0	746.1	64.6	187.4		
1961	1,313.0	974.3	338.7		1,064.2	722.8	67.6	273.8		
1962	1,462.9	991.4	471.5		1,186.6	716.2	87.1	383.3		
1963	1,603.2	1,012.4	590.8		1,334.7	750.2	118.9	465.6		
1964	1,528.8	970.5	108.3	450.0	1,285.8	720.1	100.8	464.9		560
1965	1,472.8	963.7	86.7	422.5	1,240.6	709.9	84.8	445.9		565
1966	1,164.9	778.6	61.2	325.1	971.9	563.2	61.0	347.7		575
1967	1,291.6	843.9	71.7	376.1	1,141.0	650.6	73.0	417.5		461
1968	1,507.6	899.4	80.7	527.3	1,353.4	694.7	84.3	574.4		487
1969	1,466.8	810.6	85.1	571.2	1,322.3	624.8	85.2	612.4	1,319.8	490
1970	1,433.6	812.9	84.9	535.9	1,351.5	646.8	88.1	616.7	1,399.0	448
1971	2,052.2	1,151.0	120.5	780.9	1,924.6	906.1	132.9	885.7	1,418.4	485
1972	2,356.6	1,309.2	141.2	906.2	2,218.9	1,033.1	148.6	1,037.2	1,706.1	656
1973	2,045.3	1,132.0	118.2	795.0	1,819.5	882.1	117.0	820.5	2,003.9	718
1974	1,337.7	888.1	68.0	381.6	1,074.4	643.8	64.3	366.2	2,100.5	634
1975	1,160.4	892.2	64.0	204.3	939.2	675.5	63.9	199.8	1,728.5	519
1976	1,537.5	1,162.4	85.8	289.2	1,296.2	893.6	93.1	309.5	1,317.2	549
1977	1,987.1	1,450.9	121.7	414.4	1,690.0	1,126.1	121.3	442.7	1,377.2	646
1978	2,020.3	1,433.3	125.1	462.0	1,800.5	1,182.6	130.6	487.3	1,657.1	819
1979	1,745.1	1,194.1	122.0	429.0	1,551.8	981.5	125.4	444.8	1,867.5	817
1980	1,292.2	852.2	109.5	330.5	1,190.6	710.4	114.5	365.7	1,870.8	709
1981	1,084.2	705.4	91.2	287.7	985.5	564.3	101.8	319.4	1,501.6	545
1982	1,062.2	662.6	80.1	319.6	1,000.5	546.4	88.3	365.8	1,265.7	436
1983	1,703.0	1,067.6	113.5	522.0	1,605.2	901.5	133.6	570.1	1,005.5	412
1984	1,749.5	1,084.2	121.4	543.9	1,681.8	922.4	142.6	616.8	1,390.3	623
1985	1,741.8	1,072.4	93.5	576.0	1,733.3	956.6	120.1	656.6	1,652.2	639
1986	1,805.4	1,179.4	84.0	542.0	1,769.4	1,077.6	108.4	583.5	1,703.3	688
1987	1,620.5	1,146.4	65.1	408.7	1,534.8	1,024.4	89.3	421.1	1,756.4	750
1988	1,488.1	1,081.3	58.7	348.0	1,455.6	993.8	75.7	386.1	1,668.8	671
1989	1,376.1	1,003.3	55.3	317.6	1,338.4	931.7	67.0	339.8	1,529.8	676
1990	1,192.7	894.8	37.6	260.4	1,110.8	793.9	54.3	262.6	1,422.8	650
1991	1,013.9	840.4	35.6	137.9	948.8	753.5	43.1	152.1	1,308.0	534
1992	1,199.7	1,029.9	30.9	139.0	1,094.9	910.7	45.8	138.4	1,090.8	509
1993	1,287.6	1,125.7	29.4	132.6	1,199.1	986.5	52.3	160.2	1,157.5	610
1994	1,457.0	1,198.4	35.2	223.5	1,371.6	1,068.5	62.2	241.0	1,192.7	666
1995	1,354.1	1,076.2	33.8	244.1	1,332.5	997.3	63.7	271.5	1,346.9	670
1996	1,476.8	1,160.9	45.3	270.8	1,425.6	1,069.5	65.8	290.3	1,312.6	667
1997	1,474.0	1,133.7	44.5	295.8	1,441.1	1,062.4	68.5	310.3	1,412.9	757
1998	1,616.9	1,271.4	42.6	302.9	1,612.3	1,187.6	69.2	355.5	1,400.5	804
1999	1,640.9	1,302.4	31.9	306.6	1,663.5	1,246.7	65.8	351.1	1,474.2	886
2000	1,568.7	1,230.9	38.7	299.1	1,592.3	1,198.0	64.9	329.3	1,604.9	880
2001	1,602.7	1,273.3	36.6	292.8	1,636.7	1,235.6	66.0	335.2	1,573.7	877
2002	1,704.9	1,358.6	38.5	307.9	1,747.7	1,332.6	73.7	341.4	1,570.8	908
2003	1,847.7	1,499.0	33.5	315.2	1,889.2	1,460.9	82.5	345.8	1,648.4	973
2004	1,955.8	1,610.5	42.3	303.0	2,070.1	1,613.4	90.4	366.2	1,678.7	1,086
2005	2,068.3	1,715.8	41.1	311.4	2,155.3	1,682.0	84.0	389.3	1,841.9	1,203
2006	1,800.9	1,465.4	42.7	292.8	1,838.9	1,378.2	76.6	384.1	1,931.4	1,283
2007 p	1,353.7	1,045.9	32.2	275.7	1,380.5	973.3	57.8	349.5	1,500.2	1,051
										774
2006: Jan	2,292	1,837	27	428	2,224	1,686	103	435	2,048	1,185
Feb	2,125	1,808	35	282	2,129	1,633	85	411	2,049	1,084
Mar	1,965	1,610	36	319	2,097	1,551	83	463	2,229	1,126
Apr	1,821	1,510	56	255	1,987	1,492	76	419	2,058	1,097
May	1,944	1,582	50	312	1,918	1,460	83	375	1,901	1,087
June	1,819	1,469	44	306	1,879	1,405	68	406	2,047	1,073
July	1,746	1,434	82	230	1,774	1,319	84	371	1,944	969
Aug	1,646	1,355	40	251	1,731	1,285	78	368	1,881	1,009
Sept	1,721	1,391	29	301	1,654	1,215	71	368	2,019	1,004
Oct	1,470	1,181	38	251	1,560	1,170	65	325	1,919	952
Nov	1,565	1,273	20	272	1,527	1,152	60	315	1,885	987
Dec	1,629	1,241	49	339	1,628	1,181	75	372	1,887	1,019
2007: Jan	1,403	1,123	23	257	1,566	1,127	76	363	1,830	890
Feb	1,487	1,188	30	269	1,541	1,099	72	370	1,628	840
Mar	1,491	1,205	36	250	1,569	1,131	72	366	1,610	830
Apr	1,485	1,195	36	254	1,457	1,075	58	324	1,523	907
May	1,440	1,155	33	252	1,520	1,063	64	393	1,554	861
June	1,468	1,147	38	283	1,413	1,019	52	342	1,496	797
July	1,371	1,058	39	274	1,389	1,008	58	323	1,520	796
Aug	1,347	974	37	336	1,322	934	55	333	1,501	701
Sept	1,182	938	28	216	1,261	877	47	337	1,386	693
Oct	1,274	879	40	355	1,170	809	41	320	1,405	725
Nov p	1,173	818	22	333	1,162	770	51	341	1,411	634
Dec p	1,006	794	16	196	1,080	702	55	323	1,302	604

[1] Authorized by issuance of local building permits in permit-issuing places: 20,000 places beginning with 2004; 19,000 for 1994-2003; 17,000 for 1984-93; 16,000 for 1978-83; 14,000 for 1972-77; 13,000 for 1967-71; 12,000 for 1963-66; and 10,000 prior to 1963.

[2] Monthly data derived.

Note.—Data beginning with 1999 for new housing units started and completed and for new houses sold are based on new estimation methods and are not directly comparable with earlier data.

Source: Department of Commerce (Bureau of the Census).

TABLE B–57.—*Manufacturing and trade sales and inventories, 1967–2007*

[Amounts in millions of dollars; monthly data seasonally adjusted]

Year or month	Total manufacturing and trade			Manufacturing			Merchant wholesalers			Retail trade			Retail and food services sales
	Sales [1]	Inventories [2]	Ratio [3]	Sales [1]	Inventories [2]	Ratio [3]	Sales [1]	Inventories [2]	Ratio [3]	Sales [1,4]	Inventories [2]	Ratio [3]	
SIC: [5]													
1967	90,820	145,681	1.60	46,486	84,646	1.82	19,576	25,786	1.32	24,757	35,249	1.42	
1968	98,685	156,611	1.59	50,229	90,560	1.80	21,012	27,166	1.29	27,445	38,885	1.42	
1969	105,690	170,400	1.61	53,501	98,145	1.83	22,818	29,800	1.31	29,371	42,455	1.45	
1970	108,221	178,594	1.65	52,805	101,599	1.92	24,167	33,354	1.38	31,249	43,641	1.40	
1971	116,895	188,991	1.62	55,906	102,567	1.83	26,492	36,568	1.38	34,497	49,856	1.45	
1972	131,081	203,227	1.55	63,027	108,121	1.72	29,866	40,297	1.35	38,189	54,809	1.44	
1973	153,677	234,406	1.53	72,931	124,499	1.71	38,115	46,918	1.23	42,631	62,989	1.48	
1974	177,912	287,144	1.61	84,790	157,625	1.86	47,982	58,667	1.22	45,141	70,852	1.57	
1975	182,198	288,992	1.59	86,589	159,708	1.84	46,634	57,774	1.24	48,975	71,510	1.46	
1976	204,150	318,345	1.56	98,797	174,636	1.77	50,698	64,622	1.27	54,655	79,087	1.45	
1977	229,513	350,706	1.53	113,201	188,378	1.66	56,136	73,179	1.30	60,176	89,149	1.48	
1978	260,320	400,931	1.54	126,905	211,691	1.67	66,413	86,934	1.31	67,002	102,306	1.53	
1979	297,701	452,640	1.52	143,936	242,157	1.68	79,051	99,679	1.26	74,713	110,804	1.48	
1980	327,233	508,924	1.56	154,391	265,215	1.72	93,099	122,631	1.32	79,743	121,078	1.52	
1981	355,822	545,786	1.53	168,129	283,413	1.69	101,180	129,654	1.28	86,514	132,719	1.53	
1982	347,625	573,908	1.67	163,351	311,852	1.95	95,211	127,428	1.36	89,062	134,628	1.49	
1983	369,286	590,287	1.56	172,547	312,379	1.78	99,225	130,075	1.28	97,514	147,833	1.44	
1984	410,124	649,780	1.53	190,682	339,516	1.73	112,199	142,452	1.23	107,243	167,812	1.49	
1985	422,583	664,039	1.56	194,538	334,749	1.73	113,459	147,409	1.28	114,586	181,881	1.52	
1986	430,419	662,738	1.55	194,657	322,654	1.68	114,960	153,574	1.32	120,803	186,510	1.56	
1987	457,735	709,848	1.50	206,326	338,109	1.59	122,968	163,903	1.29	128,442	207,836	1.55	
1988	497,157	767,222	1.49	224,619	369,374	1.57	134,521	178,801	1.30	138,017	219,047	1.54	
1989	527,039	815,455	1.52	236,698	391,212	1.63	143,760	187,009	1.28	146,581	237,234	1.58	
1990	545,909	840,594	1.52	242,686	405,073	1.65	149,506	195,833	1.29	153,718	239,688	1.56	
1991	542,815	834,609	1.53	239,847	390,950	1.65	148,306	200,448	1.33	154,661	243,211	1.54	
1992	567,176	842,809	1.48	250,394	382,510	1.54	154,150	208,302	1.32	162,632	251,997	1.52	
NAICS: [5]													
1992	540,573	837,045	1.53	242,002	378,762	1.57	147,261	196,914	1.31	151,310	261,369	1.67	168,261
1993	567,580	864,074	1.50	251,708	379,706	1.50	154,018	204,842	1.30	161,854	279,526	1.68	179,858
1994	610,253	927,390	1.46	269,843	399,970	1.44	164,575	221,978	1.29	175,835	305,442	1.66	194,638
1995	655,097	986,160	1.48	289,973	424,843	1.44	179,915	238,392	1.29	185,209	322,925	1.72	204,677
1996	687,350	1,005,600	1.46	299,766	430,518	1.43	190,362	241,083	1.27	197,222	333,999	1.67	217,463
1997	723,879	1,046,786	1.42	319,558	443,622	1.37	198,154	258,570	1.26	206,167	344,594	1.64	227,670
1998	742,837	1,078,644	1.43	324,984	449,083	1.38	202,260	272,315	1.31	215,592	357,246	1.62	238,278
1999	786,634	1,138,209	1.40	335,991	463,563	1.35	216,597	289,564	1.29	234,046	385,082	1.59	257,797
2000	834,325	1,196,628	1.41	350,715	481,633	1.35	234,546	307,962	1.28	249,063	407,033	1.59	274,518
2001	818,615	1,118,784	1.42	330,875	428,108	1.38	232,096	295,658	1.31	255,644	395,018	1.58	282,131
2002	823,714	1,138,707	1.36	326,227	423,082	1.29	236,294	298,808	1.25	261,194	416,817	1.56	288,845
2003	853,596	1,144,702	1.34	334,616	408,226	1.24	246,857	303,343	1.22	272,123	433,133	1.56	301,264
2004	923,319	1,235,243	1.30	359,081	439,821	1.18	274,710	332,815	1.16	289,528	462,607	1.56	320,526
2005	1,001,154	1,312,163	1.27	394,615	479,106	1.18	298,753	357,537	1.16	307,786	475,520	1.51	340,669
2006	1,066,358	1,388,979	1.28	411,663	509,902	1.21	329,336	388,168	1.14	325,359	490,909	1.49	360,871
2007 p										338,618			375,989
2006: Jan	1,058,226	1,319,746	1.25	415,623	483,184	1.16	318,409	358,643	1.13	324,194	477,919	1.47	359,254
Feb	1,048,376	1,320,608	1.26	408,365	482,054	1.18	318,257	362,208	1.14	321,754	476,346	1.48	356,451
Mar	1,054,246	1,331,521	1.26	412,406	486,070	1.18	319,545	363,658	1.14	322,295	481,793	1.49	357,255
Apr	1,060,487	1,338,413	1.26	410,610	490,495	1.19	323,579	368,409	1.14	326,298	479,509	1.47	361,376
May	1,072,137	1,352,522	1.26	419,330	494,016	1.18	328,608	371,812	1.13	324,199	486,694	1.50	359,363
June	1,076,064	1,363,777	1.27	418,185	498,509	1.19	332,492	374,855	1.13	325,387	490,413	1.51	360,488
July	1,080,215	1,371,516	1.27	416,906	502,469	1.21	334,901	378,041	1.13	328,408	491,006	1.50	363,633
Aug	1,086,214	1,379,015	1.27	419,825	504,548	1.20	337,920	382,098	1.13	328,469	492,369	1.50	364,172
Sept	1,063,764	1,384,240	1.30	403,943	508,069	1.26	333,762	384,617	1.15	326,059	491,554	1.51	362,062
Oct	1,061,704	1,386,095	1.31	403,238	508,986	1.26	331,569	385,998	1.16	326,897	491,111	1.50	363,019
Nov	1,063,639	1,388,630	1.31	403,035	509,673	1.26	333,719	389,351	1.17	326,885	489,606	1.50	363,067
Dec	1,081,143	1,388,979	1.28	410,506	509,902	1.24	339,937	388,168	1.14	330,700	490,909	1.48	367,929
2007: Jan	1,070,648	1,391,893	1.30	403,127	509,879	1.26	336,713	390,424	1.16	330,598	491,590	1.49	367,230
Feb	1,073,927	1,394,706	1.30	400,864	510,181	1.27	340,134	392,073	1.15	332,929	492,452	1.48	369,287
Mar	1,092,727	1,394,265	1.28	409,337	511,098	1.25	347,383	393,461	1.13	336,007	489,706	1.46	372,851
Apr	1,100,915	1,399,463	1.27	413,544	513,302	1.24	352,678	394,796	1.12	334,693	491,365	1.47	371,651
May	1,114,765	1,406,612	1.26	417,004	515,362	1.24	357,352	396,604	1.11	340,409	494,646	1.45	377,689
June	1,111,071	1,412,022	1.27	415,010	516,507	1.24	358,788	397,866	1.11	337,273	497,649	1.48	374,740
July	1,123,373	1,418,684	1.26	424,692	517,103	1.22	359,529	398,721	1.11	339,152	502,860	1.48	376,906
Aug	1,119,374	1,423,109	1.27	417,633	516,627	1.24	362,232	401,359	1.11	339,509	505,123	1.49	377,173
Sept	1,127,625	1,429,036	1.27	417,993	519,659	1.24	367,251	403,907	1.10	342,381	505,470	1.48	380,231
Oct	1,137,631	1,431,133	1.26	423,124	520,492	1.23	372,212	403,777	1.08	342,295	506,864	1.48	380,349
Nov p	1,155,674	1,436,735	1.24	428,971	524,452	1.22	380,351	406,153	1.07	346,352	506,130	1.46	384,342
Dec p										344,880			382,928

[1] Annual data are averages of monthly not seasonally adjusted figures.
[2] Seasonally adjusted, end of period. Inventories beginning with January 1982 for manufacturing and December 1980 for wholesale and retail trade are not comparable with earlier periods.
[3] Inventory/sales ratio. Annual data are: beginning with 1982, averages of monthly ratios; for 1967–81, ratio of December inventories to monthly average sales for the year. Monthly ratios are inventories at end of month to sales for month.
[4] Food services included on Standard Industrial Classification (SIC) basis and excluded on North American Industry Classification System (NAICS) basis. See last column for retail and food services sales.
[5] Effective in 2001, data classified based on NAICS. Data on NAICS basis available beginning with 1992. Earlier data based on SIC. Data on both NAICS and SIC basis include semiconductors.

Source: Department of Commerce (Bureau of the Census).

TABLE B–58.—*Manufacturers' shipments and inventories, 1967–2007*

[Millions of dollars; monthly data seasonally adjusted]

Year or month	Shipments[1]			Inventories[2]								
	Total	Durable goods industries	Nondurable goods industries	Total	Durable goods industries				Nondurable goods industries			
					Total	Materials and supplies	Work in process	Finished goods	Total	Materials and supplies	Work in process	Finished goods
SIC:[3]												
1967	46,486	25,233	21,253	84,646	54,896	16,423	24,933	13,540	29,750	11,760	4,431	13,559
1968	50,229	27,624	22,605	90,560	58,732	17,344	27,213	14,175	31,828	12,328	4,852	14,648
1969	53,501	29,403	24,098	98,145	64,598	18,636	30,282	15,680	33,547	12,753	5,120	15,674
1970	52,805	28,156	24,649	101,599	66,651	19,149	29,745	17,757	34,948	13,168	5,271	16,509
1971	55,906	29,924	25,982	102,567	66,136	19,679	28,550	17,907	36,431	13,686	5,678	17,067
1972	63,027	33,987	29,040	108,121	70,067	20,807	30,713	18,547	38,054	14,677	5,998	17,379
1973	72,931	39,635	33,296	124,499	81,192	25,944	35,490	19,758	43,307	18,147	6,729	18,431
1974	84,790	44,173	40,617	157,625	101,493	35,070	42,530	23,893	56,132	23,744	8,189	24,199
1975	86,589	43,598	42,991	159,708	102,590	33,903	43,227	25,460	57,118	23,565	8,834	24,719
1976	98,797	50,623	48,174	174,636	111,988	37,457	46,074	28,457	62,648	25,847	9,929	26,872
1977	113,201	59,168	54,033	188,378	120,877	40,186	50,226	30,465	67,501	27,387	10,961	29,153
1978	126,905	67,731	59,174	211,691	138,181	45,198	58,848	34,135	73,510	29,619	12,085	31,806
1979	143,936	75,927	68,009	242,157	160,734	52,670	69,325	38,739	81,423	32,814	13,910	34,699
1980	154,391	77,419	76,972	265,215	174,788	55,173	76,945	42,670	90,427	36,606	15,884	37,937
1981	168,129	83,727	84,402	283,413	186,443	57,998	80,998	47,447	96,970	38,165	16,194	42,611
1982	163,351	79,212	84,139	311,852	200,444	59,136	86,707	54,601	111,408	44,039	18,612	48,757
1983	172,547	85,481	87,066	312,379	199,854	60,325	86,899	52,630	112,525	44,816	18,691	49,018
1984	190,682	97,940	92,742	339,516	221,330	66,031	98,251	57,048	118,186	45,692	19,328	53,166
1985	194,538	101,279	93,259	334,749	218,193	63,904	98,162	56,127	116,556	44,106	19,442	53,008
1986	194,657	103,238	91,419	322,654	211,997	61,331	97,000	53,666	110,657	42,335	18,124	50,198
1987	206,326	108,128	98,198	338,109	220,799	63,562	102,393	54,844	117,310	45,319	19,270	52,721
1988	224,619	118,458	106,161	369,374	242,468	69,611	112,958	59,899	126,906	49,396	20,559	56,951
1989	236,698	123,158	113,540	391,212	257,513	72,435	122,251	62,827	133,699	50,674	21,653	61,372
1990	242,686	123,776	118,910	405,073	263,209	73,559	124,130	65,520	141,864	52,645	22,817	66,402
1991	239,847	121,000	118,847	390,950	250,019	70,834	114,960	64,225	140,931	53,011	22,815	65,105
1992	250,394	128,489	121,905	382,510	238,105	69,459	104,424	64,222	144,405	54,007	23,532	66,866
NAICS:[3]												
1992	242,002	126,572	115,430	378,762	238,167	69,779	104,184	64,204	140,595	53,144	23,302	64,149
1993	251,708	133,712	117,996	379,706	238,802	72,701	101,961	64,140	140,904	54,249	23,301	63,354
1994	269,843	147,005	122,838	399,970	253,214	78,613	106,515	68,086	146,756	57,138	24,380	65,238
1995	289,973	158,568	131,405	424,843	267,425	85,516	106,595	75,314	157,418	60,725	25,752	70,941
1996	299,766	164,883	134,883	430,518	272,548	86,271	110,493	75,784	157,970	59,121	26,441	72,408
1997	319,558	178,949	140,610	443,622	281,108	92,325	109,882	78,901	162,514	60,189	28,487	73,838
1998	324,984	185,966	139,019	449,083	290,715	93,639	115,177	81,899	158,368	58,265	27,044	73,059
1999	335,991	193,895	142,096	463,563	296,508	97,931	114,061	84,516	167,055	61,141	28,733	77,181
2000	350,715	197,807	152,908	481,633	306,743	106,180	111,225	89,338	174,890	61,542	30,005	83,343
2001	330,875	181,201	149,674	428,108	267,902	91,266	93,996	82,640	160,206	55,751	27,046	77,409
2002	326,227	176,968	149,259	423,082	260,661	88,549	92,449	79,663	162,421	56,550	27,766	78,105
2003	334,616	178,549	156,067	408,226	247,061	82,330	88,753	75,978	161,165	56,843	26,948	77,374
2004	359,081	188,722	170,359	439,821	266,264	92,964	90,735	82,565	173,557	61,035	29,028	83,494
2005	394,615	201,695	192,920	479,106	286,775	99,231	99,286	88,258	192,331	67,744	33,215	91,372
2006	411,663	211,492	200,170	509,902	309,481	107,220	108,898	93,363	200,421	67,327	36,253	96,841
2007 p		212,370			320,716							
2006: Jan	415,623	211,171	204,452	483,184	287,069	98,475	99,354	89,240	196,115	67,954	35,207	92,954
Feb	408,365	211,245	197,120	482,054	286,464	99,037	98,551	88,876	195,590	68,088	33,624	93,878
Mar	412,406	211,645	200,761	486,070	289,312	100,360	100,220	88,732	196,758	68,470	33,609	94,679
Apr	410,610	208,516	202,094	490,495	292,202	101,255	101,856	89,091	198,293	68,592	34,814	94,887
May	419,330	213,746	205,584	494,016	294,341	102,295	102,600	89,446	199,675	70,173	33,923	95,579
June	418,185	214,133	204,052	498,509	296,637	102,868	103,568	90,201	201,872	69,642	36,244	95,986
July	416,906	211,019	205,887	502,469	300,384	104,561	104,755	91,068	202,085	69,386	36,302	96,397
Aug	419,825	215,164	204,661	504,548	301,542	105,697	103,672	92,173	203,006	69,779	36,752	96,475
Sept	403,943	209,152	194,791	508,069	305,166	106,499	105,665	93,002	202,903	69,805	36,111	96,987
Oct	403,238	210,388	192,850	508,986	307,882	107,545	107,125	93,212	201,104	67,696	36,277	97,131
Nov	403,035	209,525	193,510	509,673	308,436	107,433	107,164	93,839	201,237	67,778	36,591	96,868
Dec	410,506	212,817	197,689	509,902	309,481	107,220	108,898	93,363	200,421	67,327	36,253	96,841
2007: Jan	403,127	209,687	193,440	509,879	310,784	107,388	109,616	93,780	199,095	67,573	35,984	95,538
Feb	400,864	206,521	194,343	510,181	311,110	107,073	109,583	94,454	199,071	67,862	36,154	95,055
Mar	409,337	209,287	200,050	511,098	311,315	107,174	109,478	94,663	199,783	67,851	36,591	95,341
Apr	413,544	213,525	200,019	513,302	312,426	107,683	110,369	94,374	200,876	68,351	36,379	96,146
May	417,004	213,967	203,037	515,362	312,653	107,741	111,314	93,598	202,709	68,838	36,756	97,115
June	415,010	211,616	203,394	516,507	312,622	107,180	111,569	93,873	203,885	69,266	36,856	97,763
July	424,692	220,095	204,597	517,103	312,895	106,817	112,389	93,689	204,208	69,549	36,006	98,653
Aug	417,633	215,919	201,714	516,627	312,577	106,426	112,875	93,276	204,050	70,252	35,453	98,345
Sept	417,993	212,135	205,858	519,659	313,607	105,974	113,125	94,508	206,052	71,424	35,724	98,904
Oct	423,124	213,235	209,889	520,492	314,834	106,341	114,419	94,074	205,658	70,857	36,499	98,302
Nov p	428,971	212,706	216,265	524,420	317,222	106,731	115,962	94,497	207,230	70,495	37,256	99,479
Dec p		212,577			320,716							

[1] Annual data are averages of monthly not seasonally adjusted figures.
[2] Seasonally adjusted, end of period. Data beginning with 1982 are not comparable with earlier data.
[3] Effective in 2001, data classified based on North American Industry Classification System (NAICS). Data on NAICS basis available beginning with 1992. Earlier data based on Standard Industrial Classification (SIC). Data on both NAICS and SIC basis include semiconductors.

Source: Department of Commerce (Bureau of the Census).

TABLE B–59.—Manufacturers' new and unfilled orders, 1967–2007

[Amounts in millions of dollars; monthly data seasonally adjusted]

Year or month	New orders[1] Total	Durable goods industries Total	Durable goods industries Capital goods, nondefense	Nondurable goods industries	Unfilled orders[2] Total	Durable goods industries	Nondurable goods industries	Unfilled orders to shipments ratio[2] Total	Durable goods industries	Nondurable goods industries
SIC:[3]										
1967	47,067	25,803	....	21,265	103,711	99,735	3,976	3.66	4.37	0.73
1968	50,657	28,051	6,314	22,606	108,377	104,393	3,984	3.79	4.58	.69
1969	53,990	29,876	7,046	24,114	114,341	110,161	4,180	3.71	4.45	.69
1970	52,022	27,340	6,072	24,682	105,008	100,412	4,596	3.61	4.36	.76
1971	55,921	29,905	6,682	26,016	105,247	100,225	5,022	3.32	4.00	.76
1972	64,182	35,038	7,745	29,144	119,349	113,034	6,315	3.26	3.85	.86
1973	76,003	42,627	9,926	33,376	156,561	149,204	7,357	3.80	4.51	.91
1974	87,327	46,862	11,594	40,465	187,043	181,519	5,524	4.09	4.93	.62
1975	85,139	41,957	9,886	43,181	169,546	161,664	7,882	3.69	4.45	.82
1976	99,513	51,307	11,490	48,206	178,128	169,857	8,271	3.24	3.88	.74
1977	115,109	61,035	13,681	54,073	202,024	193,323	8,701	3.24	3.85	.71
1978	131,629	72,278	17,588	59,351	259,169	248,281	10,888	3.57	4.20	.81
1979	147,604	79,483	21,154	68,121	303,593	291,321	12,272	3.89	4.62	.82
1980	156,359	79,392	21,135	76,967	327,416	315,202	12,214	3.85	4.58	.75
1981	168,025	83,654	21,806	84,371	326,547	314,707	11,840	3.87	4.68	.69
1982	162,140	78,064	19,213	84,077	311,887	300,798	11,089	3.84	4.74	.62
1983	175,451	88,140	19,624	87,311	347,273	333,114	14,159	3.53	4.29	.69
1984	192,879	100,164	23,669	92,715	373,529	359,651	13,878	3.60	4.37	.64
1985	195,706	102,356	24,545	93,351	387,196	372,097	15,099	3.67	4.47	.68
1986	195,204	103,647	23,982	91,557	393,515	376,699	16,816	3.59	4.41	.70
1987	209,389	110,809	26,094	98,579	430,426	408,688	21,738	3.63	4.43	.83
1988	228,270	122,076	31,108	106,194	474,154	452,150	22,004	3.64	4.46	.76
1989	239,572	126,055	32,988	113,516	508,849	487,098	21,751	3.96	4.85	.77
1990	244,507	125,583	33,331	118,924	531,131	509,124	22,007	4.15	5.15	.76
1991	238,805	119,849	30,471	118,957	519,199	495,802	23,397	4.08	5.07	.79
1992	248,212	126,308	31,524	121,905	492,893	469,381	23,512	3.51	4.30	.75
NAICS:[3]										
1992	....	....	....	....	....	450,592	....	....	5.14	....
1993	246,668	128,672	40,681	....	....	425,465	....	....	4.66	....
1994	266,641	143,803	45,175	....	....	434,552	....	....	4.21	....
1995	285,542	154,137	51,011	....	....	447,095	....	....	3.97	....
1996	297,282	162,399	54,066	....	....	488,516	....	....	4.14	....
1997	314,986	174,377	60,697	....	....	512,849	....	....	4.04	....
1998	317,345	178,327	62,133	....	....	496,092	....	....	3.97	....
1999	329,770	187,674	64,392	....	....	505,589	....	....	3.76	....
2000	346,789	193,881	69,278	....	....	549,513	....	....	3.87	....
2001	322,708	173,033	58,204	....	....	513,802	....	....	4.21	....
2002	316,811	167,553	51,817	....	....	461,585	....	....	4.04	....
2003	330,369	174,302	52,891	....	....	477,029	....	....	3.92	....
2004	354,599	184,240	56,079	....	....	495,630	....	....	3.87	....
2005	394,580	201,660	65,625	....	....	570,020	....	....	3.84	....
2006	414,562	214,391	72,429	....	....	684,047	....	....	4.27	....
2007 [p]	....	216,479	74,976	....	....	808,570	....	....	....	....
2006: Jan	406,763	202,311	66,105	....	....	567,567	....	....	3.96	....
Feb	407,631	210,511	68,176	....	....	574,681	....	....	4.03	....
Mar	421,050	220,289	75,340	....	....	590,228	....	....	4.10	....
Apr	413,993	211,899	71,161	....	....	599,629	....	....	4.18	....
May	417,162	211,578	69,848	....	....	604,368	....	....	4.13	....
June	422,357	218,305	71,552	....	....	615,196	....	....	4.17	....
July	419,316	213,429	71,741	....	....	624,281	....	....	4.24	....
Aug	415,676	211,015	67,782	....	....	626,819	....	....	4.18	....
Sept	424,396	229,605	83,984	....	....	653,370	....	....	4.44	....
Oct	403,244	210,394	73,092	....	....	661,059	....	....	4.53	....
Nov	408,606	215,096	72,503	....	....	673,215	....	....	4.62	....
Dec	416,103	218,414	77,700	....	....	684,047	....	....	4.64	....
2007: Jan	398,496	205,056	64,912	....	....	687,768	....	....	4.77	....
Feb	400,493	206,150	68,845	....	....	693,326	....	....	4.81	....
Mar	416,759	216,709	78,375	....	....	706,081	....	....	4.80	....
Apr	418,997	218,978	78,128	....	....	719,366	....	....	4.85	....
May	416,866	213,829	72,788	....	....	725,644	....	....	4.85	....
June	420,992	217,598	77,389	....	....	737,085	....	....	4.97	....
July	435,099	230,502	81,119	....	....	754,340	....	....	4.93	....
Aug	420,076	218,362	71,417	....	....	763,051	....	....	5.06	....
Sept	421,206	215,348	74,935	....	....	771,803	....	....	5.17	....
Oct	424,145	214,256	73,022	....	....	779,374	....	....	5.22	....
Nov [p]	431,698	215,433	76,918	....	....	788,609	....	....	5.28	....
Dec [p]	....	226,601	81,099	....	....	808,570	....	....	....	....

[1] Annual data are averages of monthly not seasonally adjusted figures.
[2] Unfilled orders are seasonally adjusted, end of period. Ratios are unfilled orders at end of period to shipments for period (excludes industries with no unfilled orders). Annual ratios relate to seasonally adjusted data for December.
[3] Effective in 2001, data classified based on North American Industry Classification System (NAICS). Data on NAICS basis available beginning with 1992. Earlier data based on the Standard Industrial Classification (SIC). Data on SIC basis include semiconductors. Data on NAICS basis do not include semiconductors.

Note.—For NAICS basis data beginning with 1992, because there are no unfilled orders for manufacturers' nondurable goods, manufacturers' nondurable new orders and nondurable shipments are the same (see Table B–58).

Source: Department of Commerce (Bureau of the Census).

TABLE B–60.—*Consumer price indexes for major expenditure classes, 1960–2007*

[For all urban consumers; 1982-84=100, except as noted]

Year or month	All items	Food and beverages		Apparel	Housing	Transportation	Medical care	Recreation[2]	Education and communication[2]	Other goods and services	Energy[3]
		Total[1]	Food								
1960	29.6		30.0	45.7		29.8	22.3				22.4
1961	29.9		30.4	46.1		30.1	22.9				22.5
1962	30.2		30.6	46.3		30.8	23.5				22.6
1963	30.6		31.1	46.9		30.9	24.1				22.6
1964	31.0		31.5	47.3		31.4	24.6				22.5
1965	31.5		32.2	47.8		31.9	25.2				22.9
1966	32.4		33.8	49.0		32.3	26.3				23.3
1967	33.4	35.0	34.1	51.0	30.8	33.3	28.2			35.1	23.8
1968	34.8	36.2	35.3	53.7	32.0	34.3	29.9			36.9	24.2
1969	36.7	38.1	37.1	56.8	34.0	35.7	31.9			38.7	24.8
1970	38.8	40.1	39.2	59.2	36.4	37.5	34.0			40.9	25.5
1971	40.5	41.4	40.4	61.1	38.0	39.5	36.1			42.9	26.5
1972	41.8	43.1	42.1	62.3	39.4	39.9	37.3			44.7	27.2
1973	44.4	48.8	48.2	64.6	41.2	41.2	38.8			46.4	29.4
1974	49.3	55.5	55.1	69.4	45.8	45.8	42.4			49.8	38.1
1975	53.8	60.2	59.8	72.5	50.7	50.1	47.5			53.9	42.1
1976	56.9	62.1	61.6	75.2	53.8	55.1	52.0			57.0	45.1
1977	60.6	65.8	65.5	78.6	57.4	59.0	57.0			60.4	49.4
1978	65.2	72.2	72.0	81.4	62.4	61.7	61.8			64.3	52.5
1979	72.6	79.9	79.9	84.9	70.1	70.5	67.5			68.9	65.7
1980	82.4	86.7	86.8	90.9	81.1	83.1	74.9			75.2	86.0
1981	90.9	93.5	93.6	95.3	90.4	93.2	82.9			82.6	97.7
1982	96.5	97.3	97.4	97.8	96.9	97.0	92.5			91.1	99.2
1983	99.6	99.5	99.4	100.2	99.5	99.3	100.6			101.1	99.9
1984	103.9	103.2	103.2	102.1	103.6	103.7	106.8			107.9	100.9
1985	107.6	105.6	105.6	105.0	107.7	106.4	113.5			114.5	101.6
1986	109.6	109.1	109.0	105.9	110.9	102.3	122.0			121.4	88.2
1987	113.6	113.5	113.5	110.6	114.2	105.4	130.1			128.5	88.6
1988	118.3	118.2	118.2	115.4	118.5	108.7	138.6			137.0	89.3
1989	124.0	124.9	125.1	118.6	123.0	114.1	149.3			147.7	94.3
1990	130.7	132.1	132.4	124.1	128.5	120.5	162.8			159.0	102.1
1991	136.2	136.8	136.3	128.7	133.6	123.8	177.0			171.6	102.5
1992	140.3	138.7	137.9	131.9	137.5	126.5	190.1			183.3	103.0
1993	144.5	141.6	140.9	133.7	141.2	130.4	201.4	90.7	85.5	192.9	104.2
1994	148.2	144.9	144.3	133.4	144.8	134.3	211.0	92.7	88.8	198.5	104.6
1995	152.4	148.9	148.4	132.0	148.5	139.1	220.5	94.5	92.2	206.9	105.2
1996	156.9	153.7	153.3	131.7	152.8	143.0	228.2	97.4	95.3	215.4	110.1
1997	160.5	157.7	157.3	132.9	156.8	144.3	234.6	99.6	98.4	224.8	111.5
1998	163.0	161.1	160.7	133.0	160.4	141.6	242.1	101.1	100.3	237.7	102.9
1999	166.6	164.6	164.1	131.3	163.9	144.4	250.6	102.0	101.2	258.3	106.6
2000	172.2	168.4	167.8	129.6	169.6	153.3	260.8	103.3	102.5	271.1	124.6
2001	177.1	173.6	173.1	127.3	176.4	154.3	272.8	104.9	105.2	282.6	129.3
2002	179.9	176.8	176.2	124.0	180.3	152.9	285.6	106.2	107.9	293.2	121.7
2003	184.0	180.5	180.0	120.9	184.8	157.6	297.1	107.5	109.8	298.7	136.5
2004	188.9	186.6	186.2	120.4	189.5	163.1	310.1	108.6	111.6	304.7	151.4
2005	195.3	191.2	190.7	119.5	195.7	173.9	323.2	109.4	113.7	313.4	177.1
2006	201.6	195.7	195.2	119.5	203.2	180.9	336.2	110.9	116.8	321.7	196.9
2007	207.342	203.300	202.916	118.998	209.586	184.682	351.054	111.443	119.577	333.328	207.723
2006: Jan	198.3	194.5	194.1	114.9	200.0	175.9	329.5	109.9	115.7	318.2	189.5
Feb	198.7	194.4	194.0	116.6	200.5	175.8	332.1	110.2	115.7	319.1	186.4
Mar	199.8	194.5	194.0	122.0	201.3	177.4	333.8	110.6	115.6	320.0	188.6
Apr	201.5	194.2	193.7	123.4	201.7	184.1	334.7	111.1	115.8	320.0	201.4
May	202.5	194.7	194.2	122.4	202.2	187.6	335.6	111.2	115.7	320.2	209.3
June	202.9	195.1	194.5	118.9	203.7	187.3	336.0	111.2	115.9	321.5	211.3
July	203.5	195.6	195.0	113.8	204.7	189.0	337.0	111.3	116.3	321.2	215.1
Aug	203.9	196.0	195.5	116.1	205.1	188.5	337.7	111.3	117.5	321.7	214.7
Sept	202.9	196.7	196.2	121.7	205.0	180.6	338.3	111.1	118.4	323.3	199.1
Oct	201.8	197.5	197.1	123.3	204.4	174.8	339.3	111.2	118.5	324.3	181.3
Nov	201.5	197.2	196.8	121.7	204.5	173.9	340.1	111.2	118.1	324.3	180.4
Dec	201.8	197.4	197.0	118.6	204.8	175.4	340.1	110.8	118.0	326.7	185.2
2007: Jan	202.416	199.198	198.812	115.988	206.057	174.463	343.510	111.012	117.815	329.198	183.567
Feb	203.499	200.402	200.000	119.017	207.177	174.799	346.457	111.174	117.971	330.459	184.451
Mar	205.352	200.869	200.403	122.582	208.080	180.346	347.172	111.244	118.231	331.144	196.929
Apr	206.686	201.292	200.820	122.934	208.541	185.231	348.225	111.481	118.301	331.743	207.265
May	207.949	202.225	201.791	121.452	208.902	189.961	349.087	111.659	118.787	332.785	219.071
June	208.352	202.885	202.441	117.225	210.649	189.064	349.510	111.563	118.734	333.378	221.088
July	208.299	203.533	203.121	113.500	211.286	187.690	351.643	111.347	119.025	333.415	217.274
Aug	207.917	204.289	203.885	114.439	211.098	184.480	352.961	111.139	120.311	333.325	209.294
Sept	208.490	205.279	204.941	119.535	210.865	184.532	353.723	111.400	121.273	334.801	209.637
Oct	208.936	206.124	205.796	121.846	210.701	184.952	355.653	111.753	121.557	335.680	207.588
Nov	210.177	206.563	206.277	121.204	210.745	190.677	357.041	111.842	121.409	336.379	219.009
Dec	210.036	206.936	206.704	118.257	210.933	189.984	357.661	111.705	121.506	337.633	217.506

[1] Includes alcoholic beverages, not shown separately.
[2] December 1997=100.
[3] Household energy—gas (piped), electricity, fuel oil, etc.—and motor fuel. Motor oil, coolant, etc. also included through 1982.

Note.—Data beginning with 1983 incorporate a rental equivalence measure for homeowners' costs.
Series reflect changes in composition and renaming beginning in 1998, and formula and methodology changes beginning in 1999.

Source: Department of Labor (Bureau of Labor Statistics).

TABLE B–61.—*Consumer price indexes for selected expenditure classes, 1960–2007*

[For all urban consumers; 1982-84=100, except as noted]

Year or month	Food and beverages				Housing						
		Food					Shelter			Fuels and utilities	
											Household energy
	Total [1]	Total	At home	Away from home	Total [2]	Total [2]	Rent of primary residence	Owners' equivalent rent of primary residence [3]	Total [2]	Total [2]	Gas (piped) and electricity
1960	....	30.0	31.5	25.4	....	25.2	38.7	....	26.0	....	23.3
1961	....	30.4	31.8	26.0	....	25.4	39.2	....	26.3	....	23.5
1962	....	30.6	32.0	26.7	....	25.8	39.7	....	26.3	....	23.5
1963	....	31.1	32.4	27.3	....	26.1	40.1	....	26.6	....	23.5
1964	....	31.5	32.7	27.8	....	26.5	40.5	....	26.6	....	23.5
1965	....	32.2	33.5	28.4	....	27.0	40.9	....	26.6	....	23.5
1966	....	33.8	35.2	29.7	....	27.8	41.5	....	26.7	....	23.6
1967	35.0	34.1	35.1	31.3	30.8	28.8	42.2	....	27.1	21.4	23.7
1968	36.2	35.3	36.3	32.9	32.0	30.1	43.3	....	27.4	21.7	23.9
1969	38.1	37.1	38.0	34.9	34.0	32.6	44.7	....	28.0	22.1	24.3
1970	40.1	39.2	39.9	37.5	36.4	35.5	46.5	....	29.1	23.1	25.4
1971	41.4	40.4	40.9	39.4	38.0	37.0	48.7	....	31.1	24.7	27.1
1972	43.1	42.1	42.7	41.0	39.4	38.7	50.4	....	32.5	25.7	28.5
1973	48.8	48.2	49.7	44.2	41.2	40.5	52.5	....	34.3	27.5	29.9
1974	55.5	55.1	57.1	49.8	45.8	44.4	55.2	....	40.7	34.4	34.5
1975	60.2	59.8	61.8	54.5	50.7	48.8	58.0	....	45.4	39.4	40.1
1976	62.1	61.6	63.1	58.2	53.8	51.5	61.1	....	49.4	43.3	44.7
1977	65.8	65.5	66.8	62.6	57.4	54.9	64.8	....	54.7	49.0	50.5
1978	72.2	72.0	73.8	68.3	62.4	60.5	69.3	....	58.5	53.0	55.0
1979	79.9	79.9	81.8	75.9	70.1	68.9	74.3	....	64.8	61.3	61.0
1980	86.7	86.8	88.4	83.4	81.1	81.0	80.9	....	75.4	74.8	71.4
1981	93.5	93.6	94.8	90.9	90.4	90.5	87.9	....	86.4	87.2	81.9
1982	97.3	97.4	98.1	95.8	96.9	96.9	94.6	....	94.9	95.6	93.2
1983	99.5	99.4	99.1	100.0	99.5	99.1	100.1	102.5	100.2	100.5	101.5
1984	103.2	103.2	102.8	104.2	103.6	104.0	105.3	107.3	104.8	104.0	105.4
1985	105.6	105.6	104.3	108.3	107.7	109.8	111.8	113.2	106.5	104.5	107.1
1986	109.1	109.0	107.3	112.5	110.9	115.8	118.3	119.4	104.1	99.2	105.7
1987	113.5	113.5	111.9	117.0	114.2	121.3	123.1	124.8	103.0	97.3	103.8
1988	118.2	118.2	116.6	121.8	118.5	127.1	127.8	131.1	104.4	98.0	104.6
1989	124.9	125.1	124.2	127.4	123.0	132.8	132.8	137.4	107.8	100.9	107.5
1990	132.1	132.4	132.3	133.4	128.5	140.0	138.4	144.8	111.6	104.5	109.3
1991	136.8	136.3	135.8	137.9	133.6	146.3	143.3	150.4	115.3	106.7	112.6
1992	138.7	137.9	136.8	140.7	137.5	151.2	146.9	155.5	117.8	108.1	114.8
1993	141.6	140.9	140.1	143.2	141.2	155.7	150.3	160.5	121.3	111.2	118.5
1994	144.9	144.3	144.1	145.7	144.8	160.5	154.0	165.8	122.8	111.7	119.2
1995	148.9	148.4	148.8	149.0	148.5	165.7	157.8	171.3	123.7	111.5	119.2
1996	153.7	153.3	154.3	152.7	152.8	171.0	162.0	176.8	127.5	115.2	122.1
1997	157.7	157.3	158.1	157.0	156.8	176.3	166.7	181.9	130.8	117.9	125.1
1998	161.1	160.7	161.1	161.1	160.4	182.1	172.1	187.8	128.5	113.7	121.2
1999	164.6	164.1	164.2	165.1	163.9	187.3	177.5	192.9	128.8	113.5	120.9
2000	168.4	167.8	167.9	169.0	169.6	193.4	183.9	198.7	137.9	122.8	128.0
2001	173.6	173.1	173.4	173.9	176.4	200.6	192.1	206.3	150.2	135.4	142.4
2002	176.8	176.2	175.6	178.3	180.3	208.1	199.7	214.7	143.6	127.2	134.4
2003	180.5	180.0	179.4	182.1	184.8	213.1	205.5	219.9	154.5	138.2	145.0
2004	186.6	186.2	186.2	187.5	189.5	218.8	211.0	224.9	161.9	144.4	150.6
2005	191.2	190.7	189.8	193.4	195.7	224.4	217.3	230.2	179.0	161.6	166.5
2006	195.7	195.2	193.1	199.4	203.2	232.1	225.1	238.2	194.7	177.1	182.1
2007	203.300	202.916	201.245	206.659	209.586	240.611	234.679	246.235	200.632	181.744	186.262
2006: Jan	194.5	194.1	193.4	196.6	200.0	226.8	220.9	233.4	198.7	182.1	188.1
Feb	194.4	194.0	192.6	197.2	200.5	228.3	221.6	234.1	194.6	177.5	182.8
Mar	194.5	194.0	192.3	197.6	201.3	229.9	222.3	234.9	192.3	174.8	179.9
Apr	194.2	193.7	191.5	198.0	201.7	230.7	222.9	235.8	190.8	173.2	177.7
May	194.7	194.2	191.9	198.7	202.2	231.2	223.6	236.9	192.0	174.4	178.8
June	195.1	194.5	192.2	199.2	203.7	232.2	224.4	237.9	197.6	180.4	185.6
July	195.6	195.0	192.6	199.7	204.7	233.6	225.2	238.8	198.5	181.1	186.2
Aug	196.0	195.5	193.1	200.2	205.1	234.2	226.2	239.7	199.0	181.5	186.4
Sept	196.7	196.2	194.1	200.5	205.0	233.9	227.1	240.4	199.6	182.0	187.4
Oct	197.5	197.1	195.1	201.1	204.4	234.8	228.0	241.3	190.1	171.5	176.4
Nov	197.2	196.8	194.3	201.6	204.5	234.9	228.9	242.1	190.6	172.1	177.0
Dec	197.4	197.0	194.3	202.2	204.8	235.1	230.0	242.8	192.6	174.2	179.0
2007: Jan	199.198	198.812	196.671	203.171	206.057	236.504	230.806	243.345	194.378	175.718	181.064
Feb	200.402	200.000	198.193	203.909	207.177	237.972	231.739	244.020	194.890	176.092	181.232
Mar	200.869	200.403	198.766	204.082	208.080	238.980	232.495	244.602	196.414	177.635	182.624
Apr	201.292	200.820	199.020	204.725	208.541	239.735	232.980	244.993	196.393	177.515	182.283
May	202.225	201.791	200.334	205.233	208.902	239.877	233.549	245.236	198.574	179.798	184.737
June	202.885	202.441	200.950	205.934	210.649	240.980	234.071	245.690	206.199	188.040	193.911
July	203.533	203.121	201.401	206.931	211.286	242.067	234.732	246.149	206.140	187.624	193.184
Aug	204.289	203.885	202.126	207.756	211.098	242.238	235.311	246.815	204.334	185.453	190.710
Sept	205.279	204.941	203.193	208.805	210.865	241.990	236.058	247.487	204.264	185.306	190.158
Oct	206.124	205.796	204.333	209.275	210.701	242.405	237.135	248.075	200.836	181.509	185.337
Nov	206.563	206.277	204.745	209.854	210.745	242.207	238.169	248.876	202.161	182.725	184.753
Dec	206.936	206.704	205.208	210.233	210.933	242.372	239.102	249.532	203.006	183.516	185.155

[1] Includes alcoholic beverages, not shown separately.
[2] Includes other items not shown separately.
[3] December 1982=100.

See next page for continuation of table.

[For all urban consumers; 1982-84=100, except as noted]

Year or month	Transportation Total	Private transportation Total²	New vehicles Total²	New vehicles New cars	Used cars and trucks	Motor fuel	Public transportation	Medical care Total	Medical care commodities	Medical care services
1960	29.8	30.6	51.6	51.5	25.0	24.4	22.2	22.3	46.9	19.5
1961	30.1	30.8	51.6	51.5	26.0	24.1	23.2	22.9	46.3	20.2
1962	30.8	31.4	51.4	51.3	28.4	24.3	24.0	23.5	45.6	20.9
1963	30.9	31.6	51.1	51.0	28.7	24.2	24.3	24.1	45.2	21.5
1964	31.4	32.0	50.9	50.9	30.0	24.1	24.7	24.6	45.1	22.0
1965	31.9	32.5	49.8	49.7	29.8	25.1	25.2	25.2	45.0	22.7
1966	32.3	32.9	48.9	48.8	29.0	25.6	26.1	26.3	45.1	23.9
1967	33.3	33.8	49.3	49.3	29.9	26.4	27.4	28.2	44.9	26.0
1968	34.3	34.8	50.7	50.7	....	26.8	28.7	29.9	45.0	27.9
1969	35.7	36.0	51.5	51.5	30.9	27.6	30.9	31.9	45.4	30.2
1970	37.5	37.5	53.1	53.0	31.2	27.9	35.2	34.0	46.5	32.3
1971	39.5	39.4	55.3	55.2	33.0	28.1	37.8	36.1	47.3	34.7
1972	39.9	39.7	54.8	54.7	33.1	28.4	39.3	37.3	47.4	35.9
1973	41.2	41.0	54.8	54.8	35.2	31.2	39.7	38.8	47.5	37.5
1974	45.8	46.2	58.0	57.9	36.7	42.2	40.6	42.4	49.2	41.4
1975	50.1	50.6	63.0	62.9	43.8	45.1	43.5	47.5	53.3	46.6
1976	55.1	55.6	67.0	66.9	50.3	47.0	47.8	52.0	56.5	51.3
1977	59.0	59.7	70.5	70.4	54.7	49.7	50.0	57.0	60.2	56.4
1978	61.7	62.5	75.9	75.8	55.8	51.8	51.5	61.8	64.4	61.2
1979	70.5	71.7	81.9	81.8	60.2	70.1	54.9	67.5	69.0	67.2
1980	83.1	84.2	88.5	88.4	62.3	97.4	69.0	74.9	75.4	74.8
1981	93.2	93.8	93.9	93.7	76.9	108.5	85.6	82.9	83.7	82.8
1982	97.0	97.1	97.5	97.4	88.8	102.8	94.9	92.5	92.3	92.6
1983	99.3	99.3	99.9	99.9	98.7	99.4	99.5	100.6	100.2	100.7
1984	103.7	103.6	102.6	102.8	112.5	97.9	105.7	106.8	107.5	106.7
1985	106.4	106.2	106.1	106.1	113.7	98.7	110.5	113.5	115.2	113.2
1986	102.3	101.2	110.6	110.6	108.8	77.1	117.0	122.0	122.8	121.9
1987	105.4	104.2	114.4	114.6	113.1	80.2	121.1	130.1	131.0	130.0
1988	108.7	107.6	116.5	116.9	118.0	80.9	123.3	138.6	139.9	138.3
1989	114.1	112.9	119.2	119.2	120.4	88.5	129.5	149.3	150.8	148.9
1990	120.5	118.8	121.4	121.0	117.6	101.2	142.6	162.8	163.4	162.7
1991	123.8	121.9	126.0	125.3	118.1	99.4	148.9	177.0	176.8	177.1
1992	126.5	124.6	129.2	128.4	123.2	99.0	151.4	190.1	188.1	190.5
1993	130.4	127.5	132.7	131.5	133.9	98.0	167.0	201.4	195.0	202.9
1994	134.3	131.4	137.6	136.0	141.7	98.5	172.0	211.0	200.7	213.4
1995	139.1	136.3	141.0	139.0	156.5	100.0	175.9	220.5	204.5	224.2
1996	143.0	140.0	143.7	141.4	157.0	106.3	181.9	228.2	210.4	232.4
1997	144.3	141.0	144.3	141.7	151.1	106.2	186.7	234.6	215.3	239.1
1998	141.6	137.9	143.4	140.7	150.6	92.2	190.3	242.1	221.8	246.8
1999	144.4	140.5	142.9	139.6	152.0	100.7	197.7	250.6	230.7	255.1
2000	153.3	149.1	142.8	139.6	155.8	129.3	209.6	260.8	238.1	266.0
2001	154.3	150.0	142.1	138.9	158.7	124.7	210.6	272.8	247.6	278.8
2002	152.9	148.8	140.0	137.3	152.0	116.6	207.4	285.6	256.4	292.9
2003	157.6	153.6	137.9	134.7	142.9	135.8	209.3	297.1	262.8	306.0
2004	163.1	159.4	137.1	133.9	133.3	160.4	209.1	310.1	269.3	321.3
2005	173.9	170.2	137.9	135.2	139.4	195.7	217.3	323.2	276.0	336.7
2006	180.9	177.0	137.6	136.4	140.0	221.0	226.6	336.2	285.9	350.6
2007	184.682	180.778	136.254	135.865	135.747	239.070	230.002	351.054	289.999	369.302
2006: Jan	175.9	172.1	139.3	137.7	139.3	199.2	219.9	329.5	282.0	342.9
Feb	175.8	171.9	139.3	137.5	139.5	198.1	221.3	332.1	283.1	346.1
Mar	177.4	173.5	138.8	136.9	140.0	205.8	222.6	333.8	284.3	348.0
Apr	184.1	180.4	138.4	136.5	140.4	235.4	225.3	334.7	285.3	348.8
May	187.6	183.9	137.7	136.2	140.9	250.9	229.2	335.6	286.3	349.7
June	187.3	183.2	137.2	135.8	141.5	248.4	234.3	336.0	286.3	350.3
July	189.0	184.9	136.9	135.6	142.1	255.6	237.4	337.0	287.1	351.2
Aug	188.5	184.5	136.4	135.4	142.4	254.4	234.3	337.7	287.6	352.1
Sept	180.6	176.5	136.3	135.7	141.0	220.1	229.5	338.3	288.1	352.7
Oct	174.8	170.7	136.8	136.3	139.3	193.8	226.9	339.3	288.1	354.0
Nov	173.9	170.0	136.8	136.6	137.3	191.4	220.4	340.1	286.6	355.6
Dec	175.4	171.8	137.1	136.9	136.2	199.3	217.8	340.1	285.9	356.0
2007: Jan	174.463	170.562	137.603	137.204	135.257	193.900	221.403	343.510	288.088	359.757
Feb	174.799	170.775	137.340	136.844	134.597	195.377	224.061	346.457	287.703	363.908
Mar	180.346	176.468	137.228	136.589	134.382	220.515	225.893	347.172	286.940	365.164
Apr	185.231	181.478	136.963	136.400	134.363	242.944	227.567	348.225	288.349	366.070
May	189.961	186.376	136.295	135.787	134.481	265.781	228.251	349.087	288.661	367.127
June	189.064	185.175	135.820	135.479	135.067	260.655	233.389	349.510	288.508	367.758
July	187.690	183.619	135.415	135.009	136.024	252.909	235.767	351.643	290.257	370.008
Aug	184.480	180.408	135.204	134.888	137.138	238.194	233.112	352.961	291.164	371.461
Sept	184.532	180.586	134.927	134.637	137.142	239.104	230.694	353.723	291.340	372.432
Oct	184.952	180.919	135.344	135.169	136.950	239.048	232.725	355.653	292.161	374.750
Nov	190.677	186.839	136.250	136.003	136.616	262.282	233.758	357.041	293.201	376.250
Dec	189.984	186.134	136.664	136.371	136.943	258.132	233.408	357.661	293.610	376.940

Source: Department of Labor (Bureau of Labor Statistics).

[For all urban consumers; 1982-84=100, except as noted]

Year or month	All items (CPI-U)[1]	Commodities — All commodities	Commodities less food	Services	All items less food	All items less energy	All items less food and energy	All items less medical care	CPI-U-X1 (Dec. 1982 = 97.6)[2]	CPI-U-RS (Dec. 1977 = 100)[3]	C-CPI-U (Dec. 1999 = 100)[4]
1960	29.6	33.6	36.0	24.1	29.7	30.4	30.6	30.2	32.2		
1961	29.9	33.8	36.1	24.5	30.0	30.7	31.0	30.5	32.5		
1962	30.2	34.1	36.3	25.0	30.3	31.1	31.4	30.8	32.8		
1963	30.6	34.4	36.6	25.5	30.7	31.5	31.8	31.1	33.3		
1964	31.0	34.8	36.9	26.0	31.1	32.0	32.3	31.5	33.7		
1965	31.5	35.2	37.2	26.6	31.6	32.5	32.7	32.0	34.2		
1966	32.4	36.1	37.7	27.6	32.3	33.5	33.5	33.0	35.2		
1967	33.4	36.8	38.6	28.8	33.4	34.4	34.7	33.7	36.3		
1968	34.8	38.1	40.0	30.3	34.9	35.9	36.3	35.1	37.7		
1969	36.7	39.9	41.7	32.4	36.8	38.0	38.4	37.0	39.4		
1970	38.8	41.7	43.4	35.0	39.0	40.3	40.8	39.2	41.3		
1971	40.5	43.2	45.1	37.0	40.8	42.0	42.7	40.8	43.1		
1972	41.8	44.5	46.1	38.4	42.0	43.4	44.0	42.1	44.4		
1973	44.4	47.8	47.7	40.1	43.7	46.1	45.6	44.8	47.2		
1974	49.3	53.5	52.8	43.8	48.0	50.6	49.4	49.8	51.9		
1975	53.8	58.2	57.6	48.0	52.5	55.1	53.9	54.3	56.2		
1976	56.9	60.7	60.5	52.0	56.0	58.2	57.4	57.2	59.4		
1977	60.6	64.2	63.8	56.0	59.6	61.9	61.0	60.8	63.2		
1978	65.2	68.8	67.5	60.8	63.9	66.7	65.5	65.4	67.5	104.4	
1979	72.6	76.6	75.3	67.5	71.2	73.4	71.9	72.9	74.0	114.4	
1980	82.4	86.0	85.7	77.9	81.5	81.9	80.8	82.8	82.3	127.1	
1981	90.9	93.2	93.1	88.1	90.4	90.1	89.2	91.4	90.1	139.2	
1982	96.5	97.0	96.9	96.0	96.3	96.1	95.8	96.8	95.6	147.6	
1983	99.6	99.8	100.0	99.4	99.7	99.6	99.6	99.6	99.6	153.9	
1984	103.9	103.2	103.1	104.6	104.0	104.3	104.6	103.7	103.9	160.2	
1985	107.6	105.4	105.2	109.9	108.0	108.4	109.1	107.2	107.6	165.7	
1986	109.6	104.4	101.7	115.4	109.8	112.6	113.5	108.8	109.6	168.7	
1987	113.6	107.7	104.3	120.2	113.6	117.2	118.2	112.6	113.6	174.4	
1988	118.3	111.5	107.7	125.7	118.3	122.3	123.4	117.0	118.3	180.8	
1989	124.0	116.7	112.0	131.9	123.7	128.1	129.0	122.4	124.0	188.6	
1990	130.7	122.8	117.4	139.2	130.3	134.7	135.5	128.8	130.7	198.0	
1991	136.2	126.6	121.3	146.3	136.1	140.9	142.1	133.8	136.2	205.1	
1992	140.3	129.1	124.2	152.0	140.8	145.4	147.3	137.5	140.3	210.3	
1993	144.5	131.5	126.3	157.9	145.1	150.0	152.2	141.2	144.5	215.5	
1994	148.2	133.8	127.9	163.1	149.0	154.1	156.5	144.7	148.2	220.1	
1995	152.4	136.4	129.8	168.7	153.1	158.7	161.2	148.6	152.4	225.4	
1996	156.9	139.9	132.6	174.1	157.5	163.1	165.6	152.8	156.9	231.4	
1997	160.5	141.8	133.4	179.4	161.1	167.1	169.5	156.3	160.5	236.4	
1998	163.0	141.9	132.0	184.2	163.4	170.9	173.4	158.6	163.0	239.7	
1999	166.6	144.4	134.0	188.8	167.0	174.4	177.0	162.0	166.6	244.7	
2000	172.2	149.2	139.2	195.3	173.0	178.6	181.3	167.3	172.2	252.9	102.0
2001	177.1	150.7	138.9	203.4	177.8	183.5	186.1	171.9	177.1	260.0	104.3
2002	179.9	149.7	136.0	209.8	180.5	187.7	190.5	174.3	179.9	264.2	105.6
2003	184.0	151.2	136.5	216.5	184.7	190.6	193.2	178.1	184.0	270.1	107.8
2004	188.9	154.7	138.8	222.8	189.4	194.4	196.6	182.7	188.9	277.4	110.5
2005	195.3	160.2	144.5	230.1	196.0	198.7	200.9	188.7	195.3	286.7	113.7
2006	201.6	164.0	148.0	238.9	202.7	203.7	205.9	194.7	201.6	296.1	116.9
2007	207.342	167.509	149.720	246.848	208.098	208.925	210.729	200.080	207.342	304.5	119.822
2006: Jan	198.3	161.3	144.7	234.9	199.0	200.8	202.6	191.6	198.3	291.2	115.2
Feb	198.7	161.4	144.9	235.7	199.5	201.6	203.6	191.9	198.7	291.8	115.5
Mar	199.8	162.8	146.8	236.6	200.8	202.6	204.9	193.0	199.8	293.5	116.1
Apr	201.5	165.5	150.6	237.1	202.8	203.0	205.5	194.7	201.5	295.9	116.8
May	202.5	166.9	152.3	237.7	203.9	203.3	205.7	195.6	202.5	297.3	117.3
June	202.9	166.3	151.3	239.2	204.3	203.6	205.9	196.1	202.9	297.9	117.5
July	203.5	166.4	151.3	240.2	204.9	203.9	206.2	196.6	203.5	298.8	117.7
Aug	203.9	166.6	151.4	240.9	205.4	204.4	206.7	197.1	203.9	299.5	117.9
Sept	202.9	164.4	148.0	241.1	204.1	204.9	207.2	196.0	202.9	298.0	117.7
Oct	201.8	162.5	145.1	240.9	202.6	205.6	207.8	194.9	201.8	296.4	117.2
Nov	201.5	161.8	144.3	240.9	202.3	205.3	207.6	194.5	201.5	295.9	117.0
Dec	201.8	162.1	144.7	241.2	202.6	205.1	207.3	194.8	201.8	296.4	117.1
2007: Jan	202.416	161.978	143.775	242.540	203.035	205.993	208.009	195.295	202.416	297.3	117.427
Feb	203.499	162.890	144.558	243.793	204.101	207.106	209.112	196.298	203.499	298.9	118.030
Mar	205.352	165.710	148.240	244.671	206.195	207.850	209.923	198.179	205.352	301.6	118.962
Apr	206.686	167.777	150.894	245.265	207.680	208.243	210.311	199.512	206.686	303.6	119.552
May	207.949	169.767	153.228	245.793	208.991	208.400	210.316	200.779	207.949	305.4	120.041
June	208.352	168.921	151.825	247.450	209.353	208.636	210.474	201.178	208.352	306.0	120.230
July	208.299	167.938	150.225	248.331	209.179	208.980	210.756	201.042	208.299	305.9	120.157
Aug	207.917	166.955	148.591	248.555	208.607	209.399	211.111	200.598	207.917	305.4	120.077
Sept	208.490	167.952	149.541	248.700	209.100	210.000	211.628	201.159	208.490	306.2	120.423
Oct	208.936	168.664	150.180	248.878	209.478	210.714	212.318	201.544	208.936	306.9	120.699
Nov	210.177	171.043	153.234	248.974	210.846	210.888	212.435	202.770	210.177	308.7	121.178
Dec	210.036	170.511	152.344	249.225	210.610	210.890	212.356	202.600	210.036	308.5	121.088

[1] Consumer price index, all urban consumers.

[2] CPI-U-X1 reflects a rental equivalence approach to homeowners' costs for the CPI-U for years prior to 1983, the first year for which the official index incorporates such a measure. CPI-U-X1 is rebased to the December 1982 value of the CPI-U (1982-84=100) and is identical with CPI-U data from December 1982 forward. Data prior to 1967 estimated by moving the series at the same rate as the CPI-U for each year.

[3] Consumer price index research series (CPI-U-RS) using current methods introduced in June 1999. Data for 2007 are preliminary. All data are subject to revision annually.

[4] Chained consumer price index (C-CPI-U) introduced in August 2002. Data for 2006 and 2007 are subject to revision.

Source: Department of Labor (Bureau of Labor Statistics).

TABLE B–63.—*Changes in special consumer price indexes, 1960–2007*

[For all urban consumers; percent change]

Year or month	All items		All items less food		All items less energy		All items less food and energy		All items less medical care	
	Dec. to Dec.[1]	Year to year	Dec. to Dec.[1]	Year to year	Dec. to Dec.[1]	Year to year	Dec. to Dec.[1]	Year to year	Dec. to Dec.[1]	Year to year
1960	1.4	1.7	1.0	1.7	1.3	1.7	1.0	1.3	1.3	1.3
1961	.7	1.0	1.3	1.0	.7	1.0	1.3	1.3	.3	1.0
1962	1.3	1.0	1.0	1.0	1.3	1.3	1.3	1.3	1.3	1.0
1963	1.6	1.3	1.6	1.3	1.9	1.3	1.6	1.3	1.6	1.0
1964	1.0	1.3	1.0	1.3	1.3	1.6	1.2	1.6	1.0	1.3
1965	1.9	1.6	1.6	1.6	1.9	1.6	1.5	1.2	1.9	1.6
1966	3.5	2.9	3.5	2.2	3.4	3.1	3.3	2.4	3.4	3.1
1967	3.0	3.1	3.3	3.4	3.2	2.7	3.8	3.6	2.7	2.1
1968	4.7	4.2	5.0	4.5	4.9	4.4	5.1	4.6	4.7	4.2
1969	6.2	5.5	5.6	5.4	6.5	5.8	6.2	5.8	6.1	5.4
1970	5.6	5.7	6.6	6.0	5.4	6.1	6.6	6.3	5.2	5.9
1971	3.3	4.4	3.0	4.6	3.4	4.2	3.1	4.7	3.2	4.1
1972	3.4	3.2	2.9	2.9	3.5	3.3	3.0	3.0	3.4	3.2
1973	8.7	6.2	5.6	4.0	8.2	6.2	4.7	3.6	9.1	6.4
1974	12.3	11.0	12.2	9.8	11.7	9.8	11.1	8.3	12.2	11.2
1975	6.9	9.1	7.3	9.4	6.6	8.9	6.7	9.1	6.7	9.0
1976	4.9	5.8	6.1	6.7	4.8	5.6	6.1	6.5	4.5	5.3
1977	6.7	6.5	6.4	6.4	6.7	6.4	6.5	6.3	6.7	6.3
1978	9.0	7.6	8.3	7.2	9.1	7.8	8.5	7.4	9.1	7.6
1979	13.3	11.3	14.0	11.4	11.1	10.0	11.3	9.8	13.4	11.5
1980	12.5	13.5	13.0	14.5	11.7	11.6	12.2	12.4	12.5	13.6
1981	8.9	10.3	9.8	10.9	8.5	10.0	9.5	10.4	8.8	10.4
1982	3.8	6.2	4.1	6.5	4.2	6.7	4.5	7.4	3.6	5.9
1983	3.8	3.2	4.1	3.5	4.5	3.6	4.8	4.0	3.6	2.9
1984	3.9	4.3	3.9	4.3	4.4	4.7	4.7	5.0	3.9	4.1
1985	3.8	3.6	4.1	3.8	4.0	3.9	4.3	4.3	3.5	3.4
1986	1.1	1.9	.5	1.7	3.8	3.9	3.8	4.0	.7	1.5
1987	4.4	3.6	4.6	3.5	4.1	4.1	4.2	4.1	4.3	3.5
1988	4.4	4.1	4.2	4.1	4.7	4.4	4.7	4.4	4.2	3.9
1989	4.6	4.8	4.5	4.6	4.6	4.7	4.4	4.5	4.5	4.6
1990	6.1	5.4	6.3	5.3	5.2	5.2	5.2	5.0	5.9	5.2
1991	3.1	4.2	3.3	4.5	3.9	4.6	4.4	4.9	2.7	3.9
1992	2.9	3.0	3.2	3.5	3.0	3.2	3.3	3.7	2.7	2.8
1993	2.7	3.0	2.7	3.1	3.1	3.2	3.2	3.3	2.6	2.7
1994	2.7	2.6	2.6	2.7	2.6	2.7	2.6	2.8	2.5	2.5
1995	2.5	2.8	2.7	2.8	2.9	3.0	3.0	3.0	2.5	2.7
1996	3.3	3.0	3.1	2.9	2.9	2.8	2.6	2.7	3.3	2.8
1997	1.7	2.3	1.8	2.3	2.1	2.5	2.2	2.4	1.6	2.3
1998	1.6	1.6	1.5	1.4	2.4	2.3	2.4	2.3	1.5	1.5
1999	2.7	2.2	2.8	2.2	2.0	2.0	1.9	2.1	2.6	2.1
2000	3.4	3.4	3.5	3.6	2.6	2.4	2.6	2.4	3.3	3.3
2001	1.6	2.8	1.3	2.8	2.8	2.7	2.7	2.6	1.4	2.7
2002	2.4	1.6	2.6	1.5	1.8	2.3	1.9	2.4	2.2	1.4
2003	1.9	2.3	1.5	2.3	1.5	1.5	1.1	1.4	1.8	2.2
2004	3.3	2.7	3.4	2.5	2.2	2.0	2.2	1.8	3.2	2.6
2005	3.4	3.4	3.6	3.5	2.2	2.2	2.2	2.2	3.3	3.3
2006	2.5	3.2	2.6	3.4	2.5	2.5	2.6	2.5	2.5	3.2
2007	4.1	2.8	4.0	2.7	2.8	2.6	2.4	2.3	4.0	2.8

	Percent change from preceding month									
	Unad-justed	Seasonally adjusted	Unad-justed	Seasonally adjusted	Unad-justed	Seasonally adjusted	Unad-justed	Seasonally adjusted	Unad-justed	Seasonally adjusted
2006: Jan	0.8	0.6	0.8	0.6	0.3	0.2	0.2	0.1	0.8	0.6
Feb	.2	.1	.3	.1	.4	.2	.5	.2	.2	.1
Mar	.6	.3	.7	.3	.5	.2	.6	.2	.6	.3
Apr	.9	.6	1.0	.6	.2	.2	.3	.3	.9	.6
May	.5	.5	.5	.6	.1	.2	.1	.2	.5	.6
June	.2	.2	.2	.2	.1	.3	.1	.3	.3	.2
July	.3	.4	.3	.3	.1	.2	.1	.2	.3	.5
Aug	.2	.3	.2	.2	.2	.2	.2	.2	.3	.3
Sept	−.5	−.5	−.6	−.6	.2	.2	.2	.2	−.6	−.6
Oct	−.5	−.4	−.7	−.6	.3	.1	.3	.1	−.6	−.5
Nov	−.1	.0	−.1	.0	−.1	.1	−.1	.1	−.2	.0
Dec	.1	.4	.1	.6	−.1	.1	−.1	.1	.2	.5
2007: Jan	.3	.2	.2	.0	.4	.3	.3	.3	.3	.1
Feb	.5	.4	.5	.3	.5	.3	.5	.2	.5	.4
Mar	.9	.6	1.0	.7	.4	.1	.4	.1	1.0	.6
Apr	.6	.4	.7	.4	.2	.2	.2	.2	.7	.4
May	.6	.7	.6	.7	.1	.2	.0	.1	.6	.7
June	.2	.2	.2	.1	.1	.3	.1	.2	.2	.2
July	.0	.1	−.1	.1	.2	.2	.1	.2	−.1	.1
Aug	−.2	−.1	−.3	−.2	.2	.2	.2	.2	−.2	−.2
Sept	.3	.3	.2	.2	.3	.2	.2	.2	.3	.3
Oct	.2	.3	.2	.2	.3	.2	.3	.2	.2	.3
Nov	.6	.8	.7	.9	.1	.3	.1	.3	.6	.8
Dec	−.1	.3	−.1	.3	.0	.2	.0	.2	−.1	.3

[1] Changes from December to December are based on unadjusted indexes.

Source: Department of Labor (Bureau of Labor Statistics).

Year	All items		Commodities				Services				Medical care [2]		Energy [3]	
			Total		Food		Total		Medical care					
	Dec. to Dec. [1]	Year to year	Dec. to Dec. [1]	Year to year	Dec. to Dec. [1]	Year to year	Dec. to Dec. [1]	Year to year	Dec. to Dec. [1]	Year to year	Dec. to Dec. [1]	Year to year	Dec. to Dec. [1]	Year to year
1929	0.6	0.0			2.5	1.2								
1933	.8	-5.1			6.9	-2.8								
1939	.0	-1.4	-0.7	-2.0	-2.5	-2.5	0.0	0.0	1.2	1.2	1.0	0.0		
1940	.7	.7	1.4	.7	2.5	1.7	.8	.8	.0	.0	.0	1.0		
1941	9.9	5.0	13.3	6.7	15.7	9.2	2.4	.8	1.2	.0	1.0	.0		
1942	9.0	10.9	12.9	14.5	17.9	17.6	2.3	3.1	3.5	3.5	3.8	2.9		
1943	3.0	6.1	4.2	9.3	3.0	11.0	2.3	2.3	5.6	4.5	4.6	4.7		
1944	2.3	1.7	2.0	1.0	.0	-1.2	2.2	2.2	3.2	4.3	2.6	3.6		
1945	2.2	2.3	2.9	3.0	3.5	2.4	.7	1.5	3.1	3.1	2.6	2.6		
1946	18.1	8.3	24.8	10.6	31.3	14.5	3.6	1.4	9.0	5.1	8.3	5.0		
1947	8.8	14.4	10.3	20.5	11.3	21.7	5.6	4.3	6.4	8.7	6.9	8.0		
1948	3.0	8.1	1.7	7.2	-.8	8.3	5.9	6.1	6.9	7.1	5.8	6.7		
1949	-2.1	-1.2	-4.1	-2.7	-3.9	-4.2	3.7	5.1	1.6	3.3	1.4	2.8		
1950	5.9	1.3	7.8	.7	9.8	1.6	3.6	3.0	4.0	2.4	3.4	2.0		
1951	6.0	7.9	5.9	9.0	7.1	11.0	5.2	5.3	5.3	4.7	5.8	5.3		
1952	.8	1.9	-.9	1.3	-1.0	1.8	4.4	4.5	5.8	6.7	4.3	5.0		
1953	.7	.8	-.3	-.3	-1.1	-1.4	4.2	4.3	3.4	3.5	3.5	3.6		
1954	-.7	.7	-1.6	-.9	-1.8	-.4	2.0	3.1	2.6	3.4	2.3	2.9		
1955	.4	-.4	-.3	-.9	-.7	-1.4	2.0	2.0	3.2	2.6	3.3	2.2		
1956	3.0	1.5	2.6	1.0	2.9	.7	3.4	2.5	3.8	3.8	3.2	3.8		
1957	2.9	3.3	2.8	3.2	2.8	3.2	4.2	4.3	4.8	4.3	4.7	4.2		
1958	1.8	2.8	1.2	2.1	2.4	4.5	2.7	3.7	4.6	5.3	4.5	4.6	-0.9	0.0
1959	1.7	.7	.6	.0	-1.0	-1.7	3.9	3.1	4.9	4.5	3.8	4.4	4.7	1.9
1960	1.4	1.7	1.2	.9	3.1	1.0	2.5	3.4	3.7	4.3	3.2	3.7	1.3	2.3
1961	.7	1.0	.0	.6	-.7	1.3	2.1	1.7	3.5	3.6	3.1	2.7	-1.3	.4
1962	1.3	1.0	.9	.9	1.3	.7	1.6	2.0	2.9	3.5	2.2	2.6	2.2	.4
1963	1.6	1.3	1.5	.9	2.0	1.6	2.4	2.0	2.8	2.9	2.5	2.6	-.9	.0
1964	1.0	1.3	.9	1.2	1.3	1.3	1.6	2.0	2.3	2.3	2.1	2.1	.0	-.4
1965	1.9	1.6	1.4	1.1	3.5	2.2	2.7	2.3	3.6	3.2	2.8	2.4	1.8	1.8
1966	3.5	2.9	2.5	2.6	4.0	5.0	4.8	3.8	8.3	5.3	6.7	4.4	1.7	1.7
1967	3.0	3.1	2.5	1.9	1.2	.9	4.3	4.3	8.0	8.8	6.3	7.2	1.7	2.1
1968	4.7	4.2	4.0	3.5	4.4	3.5	5.8	5.2	7.1	7.3	6.2	6.0	1.7	1.7
1969	6.2	5.5	5.4	4.7	7.0	5.1	7.7	6.9	7.3	8.2	6.2	6.7	2.9	2.5
1970	5.6	5.7	3.9	4.5	2.3	5.7	8.1	8.0	8.1	7.0	7.4	6.6	4.8	2.8
1971	3.3	4.4	2.8	3.6	4.3	3.1	4.1	5.7	5.4	7.4	4.6	6.2	3.1	3.9
1972	3.4	3.2	3.4	3.0	4.6	4.2	3.4	3.8	3.7	3.5	3.3	3.3	2.6	2.6
1973	8.7	6.2	10.4	7.4	20.3	14.5	6.2	4.4	6.0	4.5	5.3	4.0	17.0	8.1
1974	12.3	11.0	12.8	11.9	12.0	14.3	11.4	9.2	13.2	10.4	12.6	9.3	21.6	29.6
1975	6.9	9.1	6.2	8.8	6.6	8.5	8.2	9.6	10.3	12.6	9.8	12.0	11.4	10.5
1976	4.9	5.8	3.3	4.3	.5	3.0	7.2	8.3	10.8	10.1	10.0	9.5	7.1	7.1
1977	6.7	6.5	6.1	5.8	8.1	6.3	8.0	7.7	9.0	9.9	8.9	9.6	7.2	9.5
1978	9.0	7.6	8.8	7.2	11.8	9.9	9.3	8.6	9.3	8.5	8.8	8.4	7.9	6.3
1979	13.3	11.3	13.0	11.3	10.2	11.0	13.6	11.0	10.5	9.8	10.1	9.2	37.5	25.1
1980	12.5	13.5	11.0	12.3	10.2	8.6	14.2	15.4	10.1	11.3	9.9	11.0	18.0	30.9
1981	8.9	10.3	6.0	8.4	4.3	7.8	13.0	13.1	12.6	10.7	12.5	10.7	11.9	13.6
1982	3.8	6.2	3.6	4.1	3.1	4.1	4.3	9.0	11.2	11.8	11.0	11.6	1.3	1.5
1983	3.8	3.2	2.9	2.9	2.7	2.1	4.8	3.5	6.2	8.7	6.4	8.8	-.5	.7
1984	3.9	4.3	2.7	3.4	3.8	3.8	5.4	5.2	5.8	6.0	6.1	6.2	.2	1.0
1985	3.8	3.6	2.5	2.1	2.6	2.3	5.1	5.1	6.8	6.1	6.8	6.3	1.8	.7
1986	1.1	1.9	-2.0	-.9	3.8	3.2	4.5	5.0	7.9	7.7	7.7	7.5	-19.7	-13.2
1987	4.4	3.6	4.6	3.2	3.5	4.1	4.3	4.2	5.6	6.6	5.8	6.6	8.2	.5
1988	4.4	4.1	3.8	3.5	5.2	4.1	4.8	4.6	6.9	6.4	6.9	6.5	.5	.8
1989	4.6	4.8	4.1	4.7	5.6	5.8	5.1	4.9	8.6	7.7	8.5	7.7	5.1	5.6
1990	6.1	5.4	6.6	5.2	5.3	5.8	5.7	5.5	9.9	9.3	9.6	9.0	18.1	8.3
1991	3.1	4.2	1.2	3.1	1.9	2.9	4.6	5.1	8.0	8.9	7.9	8.7	-7.4	.4
1992	2.9	3.0	2.0	2.0	1.5	1.2	3.6	3.9	7.0	7.6	6.6	7.4	2.0	.5
1993	2.7	3.0	1.5	1.9	2.9	2.2	3.8	3.9	5.9	6.5	5.4	5.9	-1.4	1.2
1994	2.7	2.6	2.3	1.7	2.9	2.4	2.9	3.3	5.4	5.2	4.9	4.8	2.2	.4
1995	2.5	2.8	1.4	1.9	2.1	2.8	3.5	3.4	4.4	5.1	3.9	4.5	-1.3	.6
1996	3.3	3.0	3.2	2.6	4.3	3.3	3.3	3.2	3.2	3.7	3.0	3.5	8.6	4.7
1997	1.7	2.3	.2	1.4	1.5	2.6	2.8	3.0	2.9	2.9	2.8	2.8	-3.4	1.3
1998	1.6	1.6	.4	.1	2.3	2.2	2.6	2.7	3.2	3.2	3.4	3.2	-8.8	-7.7
1999	2.7	2.2	2.7	1.8	1.9	2.1	2.6	2.5	3.6	3.4	3.7	3.5	13.4	3.6
2000	3.4	3.4	2.7	3.3	2.8	2.3	3.9	3.4	4.6	4.3	4.2	4.1	14.2	16.9
2001	1.6	2.8	-1.4	1.0	2.8	3.2	3.7	4.1	4.8	4.8	4.7	4.6	-13.0	3.8
2002	2.4	1.6	1.2	-.7	1.5	1.8	3.2	3.1	5.6	5.1	5.0	4.7	10.7	-5.9
2003	1.9	2.3	.5	1.0	3.6	2.2	2.8	3.2	4.2	4.5	3.7	4.0	6.9	12.2
2004	3.3	2.7	3.6	2.3	2.7	3.4	3.1	2.9	4.9	5.0	4.2	4.4	16.6	10.9
2005	3.4	3.4	2.7	3.6	2.3	2.4	3.8	3.3	4.5	4.8	4.3	4.2	17.1	17.0
2006	2.5	3.2	1.3	2.4	2.1	2.4	3.4	3.8	4.1	4.1	3.6	4.0	2.9	11.2
2007	4.1	2.8	5.2	2.1	4.9	4.0	3.3	3.3	5.9	5.3	5.2	4.4	17.4	5.5

[1] Changes from December to December are based on unadjusted indexes.
[2] Commodities and services.
[3] Household energy—gas (piped), electricity, fuel oil, etc.—and motor fuel. Motor oil, coolant, etc. also included through 1982.

Source: Department of Labor (Bureau of Labor Statistics).

TABLE B-65.—*Producer price indexes by stage of processing, 1959–2007*

[1982=100]

Year or month	Total finished goods	Finished goods								Total finished consumer goods
		Consumer foods			Finished goods excluding consumer foods					
		Total	Crude	Processed	Total	Consumer goods			Capital equipment	
						Total	Durable	Nondurable		
1959	33.1	34.8	37.3	34.7	....	33.3	43.9	28.2	32.7	33.3
1960	33.4	35.5	39.8	35.2	....	33.5	43.8	28.4	32.8	33.6
1961	33.4	35.4	38.0	35.3	....	33.4	43.6	28.4	32.9	33.6
1962	33.5	35.7	38.4	35.6	....	33.4	43.4	28.4	33.0	33.7
1963	33.4	35.3	37.8	35.2	....	33.4	43.1	28.5	33.1	33.5
1964	33.5	35.4	38.9	35.2	....	33.3	43.3	28.4	33.4	33.6
1965	34.1	36.8	39.0	36.8	....	33.6	43.2	28.8	33.8	34.2
1966	35.2	39.2	41.5	39.2	....	34.1	43.4	29.3	34.6	35.4
1967	35.6	38.5	39.6	38.8	35.0	34.7	44.1	30.0	35.8	35.6
1968	36.6	40.0	42.5	40.0	35.9	35.5	45.1	30.6	37.0	36.5
1969	38.0	42.4	45.9	42.3	36.9	36.3	45.9	31.5	38.3	37.9
1970	39.3	43.8	46.0	43.9	38.2	37.4	47.2	32.5	40.1	39.1
1971	40.5	44.5	45.8	44.7	39.6	38.7	48.9	33.5	41.7	40.2
1972	41.8	46.9	48.0	47.2	40.4	39.4	50.0	34.1	42.8	41.5
1973	45.6	56.5	63.6	55.8	42.0	41.2	50.9	36.1	44.2	46.0
1974	52.6	64.4	71.6	63.9	48.8	48.2	55.5	44.0	50.5	53.1
1975	58.2	69.8	71.7	70.3	54.7	53.2	61.0	48.9	58.2	58.2
1976	60.8	69.6	76.7	69.0	58.1	56.5	63.7	52.4	62.1	60.4
1977	64.7	73.3	79.5	72.7	62.2	60.6	67.4	56.8	66.1	64.3
1978	69.8	79.9	85.8	79.4	66.7	64.9	73.6	60.0	71.3	69.4
1979	77.6	87.3	92.3	86.8	74.6	73.5	80.8	69.3	77.5	77.5
1980	88.0	92.4	93.9	92.3	86.7	87.1	91.0	85.1	85.8	88.6
1981	96.1	97.8	104.4	97.2	95.6	96.1	96.4	95.8	94.6	96.6
1982	100.0	100.0	100.0	100.0	100.0	100.0	100.0	100.0	100.0	100.0
1983	101.6	101.0	102.4	100.9	101.8	101.2	102.8	100.5	102.8	101.3
1984	103.7	105.4	111.4	104.9	103.2	102.2	104.5	101.1	105.2	103.3
1985	104.7	104.6	102.9	104.8	104.6	103.3	106.5	101.7	107.5	103.8
1986	103.2	107.3	105.6	107.4	101.9	98.5	108.9	93.3	109.7	101.4
1987	105.4	109.5	107.1	109.6	104.0	100.7	111.5	94.9	111.7	103.6
1988	108.0	112.6	109.8	112.7	106.5	103.1	113.8	97.3	114.3	106.2
1989	113.6	118.7	119.6	118.6	111.8	108.9	117.6	103.8	118.8	112.1
1990	119.2	124.4	123.0	124.4	117.4	115.3	120.4	111.5	122.9	118.2
1991	121.7	124.1	119.3	124.4	120.9	118.7	123.9	115.0	126.7	120.5
1992	123.2	123.3	107.6	124.4	123.1	120.8	125.7	117.3	129.1	121.7
1993	124.7	125.7	114.4	126.5	124.4	121.7	128.0	117.6	131.4	123.0
1994	125.5	126.8	111.3	127.9	125.1	121.6	130.9	116.2	134.1	123.3
1995	127.9	129.0	118.8	129.8	127.5	124.0	132.7	118.8	136.7	125.6
1996	131.3	133.6	129.2	133.8	130.5	127.6	134.2	123.3	138.3	129.5
1997	131.8	134.5	126.6	135.1	130.9	128.2	133.7	124.3	138.2	130.2
1998	130.7	134.3	127.2	134.8	129.5	126.4	132.9	122.2	137.6	128.9
1999	133.0	135.1	125.5	135.9	132.3	130.5	133.0	127.9	137.6	132.0
2000	138.0	137.2	123.5	138.3	138.1	138.4	133.9	138.7	138.8	138.2
2001	140.7	141.3	127.7	142.4	140.4	141.4	134.0	142.8	139.7	141.5
2002	138.9	140.1	128.5	141.0	138.3	138.8	133.0	139.8	139.1	139.4
2003	143.3	145.9	130.0	147.2	142.4	144.7	133.1	148.4	139.5	145.3
2004	148.5	152.7	138.2	153.9	147.2	150.9	135.0	156.6	141.4	151.7
2005	155.7	155.7	140.2	156.9	155.5	161.9	136.6	172.0	144.6	160.4
2006	160.4	156.7	151.3	157.1	161.0	169.2	136.9	182.6	146.9	166.0
2007 p	166.6	166.9	169.6	166.7	166.2	175.6	138.2	191.8	149.5	173.5
2006: Jan	159.9	157.1	157.7	157.0	160.3	168.7	137.3	181.7	145.8	165.7
Feb	158.0	153.8	133.2	155.6	158.8	166.2	137.5	177.9	146.2	163.0
Mar	159.1	154.4	139.7	155.6	160.1	168.0	137.4	180.6	146.4	164.5
Apr	160.7	154.8	156.7	154.5	161.9	170.7	137.1	184.7	146.6	166.5
May	161.2	154.2	139.1	155.5	162.7	171.9	137.1	186.5	146.7	167.2
June	161.8	156.1	144.8	157.0	163.0	172.3	136.7	187.2	146.7	168.0
July	161.7	156.4	139.1	157.9	162.8	172.5	134.1	188.8	145.8	168.3
Aug	162.3	158.3	161.5	157.9	163.1	172.5	135.1	188.4	146.4	168.8
Sept	160.3	159.2	166.0	158.6	160.3	168.2	135.6	181.7	146.7	165.9
Oct	158.9	158.4	161.2	158.1	158.8	165.5	136.9	177.1	147.5	163.8
Nov	159.8	157.9	145.6	158.9	160.0	166.7	139.1	177.8	148.8	164.5
Dec	160.5	160.1	171.2	159.0	160.3	167.2	138.5	178.9	148.6	165.5
2007: Jan	160.1	161.1	164.2	160.8	159.6	166.0	138.3	177.1	148.9	164.9
Feb	161.8	163.9	178.4	162.4	161.0	167.9	138.4	180.0	149.2	167.1
Mar	164.1	166.3	187.4	164.2	163.2	171.2	138.2	185.2	149.1	170.2
Apr	165.9	166.8	182.1	165.3	165.3	174.5	137.7	190.4	149.1	172.7
May	167.5	166.8	161.7	167.4	167.4	177.6	137.7	195.0	149.1	174.8
June	167.2	166.3	147.5	168.3	167.1	177.2	137.7	194.5	149.0	174.4
July	168.5	166.4	152.9	167.9	168.8	179.7	137.6	198.1	149.1	176.2
Aug	166.1	166.3	146.5	168.4	165.8	175.3	137.2	191.8	149.0	173.0
Sept [1]	167.4	168.3	160.5	169.2	166.9	176.9	136.9	194.4	149.0	174.8
Oct [1]	168.6	169.6	180.0	168.7	168.0	177.9	139.5	194.6	150.5	175.9
Nov [1]	171.3	169.4	177.2	168.7	171.5	182.9	140.1	201.6	150.8	179.4
Dec [1]	170.6	172.0	197.3	169.6	169.9	180.6	139.5	198.5	150.6	178.5

[1] Data have been revised through August 2007; data are subject to revision four months after date of original publication.

See next page for continuation of table.

TABLE B–65.—Producer price indexes by stage of processing, 1959–2007—Continued

[1982=100]

Year or month	Intermediate materials, supplies, and components								Crude materials for further processing				
	Total	Foods and feeds[2]	Other	Materials and components		Processed fuels and lubricants	Containers	Supplies	Total	Foodstuffs and feedstuffs	Other		
				For manufacturing	For construction						Total	Fuel	Other
1959	30.8	....	30.5	33.3	32.9	16.2	33.0	33.5	31.1	38.8	....	10.4	28.1
1960	30.8	....	30.7	33.3	32.7	16.6	33.4	33.3	30.4	38.4	....	10.5	26.9
1961	30.6	....	30.3	32.9	32.2	16.8	33.2	33.7	30.2	37.9	....	10.5	27.2
1962	30.6	....	30.2	32.7	32.1	16.7	33.6	34.5	30.5	38.6	....	10.4	27.1
1963	30.7	....	30.1	32.7	32.2	16.6	33.2	35.0	29.9	37.5	....	10.5	26.7
1964	30.8	....	30.3	33.1	32.5	16.2	32.9	34.7	29.6	36.6	....	10.5	27.2
1965	31.2	....	30.7	33.6	32.8	16.5	33.5	35.0	31.1	39.2	....	10.6	27.7
1966	32.0	....	31.3	34.3	33.6	16.8	34.5	36.5	33.1	42.7	....	10.9	28.3
1967	32.2	41.8	31.7	34.5	34.0	16.9	35.0	36.8	31.3	40.3	21.1	11.3	26.5
1968	33.0	41.5	32.5	35.3	35.7	16.5	35.9	37.1	31.8	40.9	21.6	11.5	27.1
1969	34.1	42.9	33.6	36.5	37.7	16.6	37.2	37.8	33.9	44.1	22.5	12.0	28.4
1970	35.4	45.6	34.8	38.0	38.3	17.7	39.0	39.7	35.2	45.2	23.8	13.8	29.1
1971	36.8	46.7	36.2	38.9	40.8	19.5	40.8	40.8	36.0	46.1	24.7	15.7	29.4
1972	38.2	49.5	37.7	40.4	43.0	20.1	42.7	42.5	39.9	51.5	27.0	16.8	32.3
1973	42.4	70.3	40.6	44.1	46.5	22.2	45.2	51.7	54.5	72.6	34.3	18.6	42.9
1974	52.5	83.6	50.5	56.0	55.0	33.6	53.3	56.8	61.4	76.4	44.1	24.8	54.5
1975	58.0	81.6	56.6	61.7	60.1	39.4	60.0	61.8	61.6	77.4	43.7	30.6	50.0
1976	60.9	77.4	60.0	64.0	64.1	42.3	63.1	65.8	63.4	76.8	48.2	34.5	54.9
1977	64.9	79.6	64.1	67.4	69.3	47.7	65.9	69.3	65.5	77.5	51.7	42.0	56.3
1978	69.5	84.8	68.6	72.0	76.5	49.9	71.0	72.9	73.4	87.3	57.5	48.2	61.9
1979	78.4	94.5	77.4	80.9	84.2	61.6	79.4	80.2	85.9	100.0	69.6	57.3	75.5
1980	90.3	105.5	89.4	91.7	91.3	85.0	89.1	89.9	95.3	104.6	84.6	69.4	91.8
1981	98.6	104.6	98.2	98.7	97.9	100.6	96.7	96.9	103.0	103.9	101.8	84.8	109.8
1982	100.0	100.0	100.0	100.0	100.0	100.0	100.0	100.0	100.0	100.0	100.0	100.0	100.0
1983	100.6	103.6	100.5	101.2	102.8	95.4	100.4	101.8	101.3	101.8	100.7	105.1	98.8
1984	103.1	105.7	103.0	104.1	105.6	95.7	105.9	104.1	103.5	104.7	102.2	105.1	101.0
1985	102.7	97.3	103.0	103.3	107.3	92.8	109.0	104.4	95.8	94.8	96.9	102.7	94.3
1986	99.1	96.2	99.3	102.2	108.1	72.7	110.3	105.6	87.7	93.2	81.6	92.2	76.0
1987	101.5	99.2	101.7	105.3	109.8	73.3	114.5	107.7	93.7	96.2	87.9	84.1	88.5
1988	107.1	109.5	106.9	113.2	116.1	71.2	120.1	113.7	96.0	106.1	85.5	82.1	85.9
1989	112.0	113.8	111.9	118.1	121.3	76.4	125.4	118.1	103.1	111.2	93.4	85.3	95.8
1990	114.5	113.3	114.5	118.7	122.9	85.9	127.7	119.4	108.9	113.1	101.5	84.8	107.3
1991	114.4	111.1	114.6	118.1	124.5	85.3	128.1	121.4	101.2	105.5	94.6	82.9	97.5
1992	114.7	110.7	114.9	117.9	126.5	84.5	127.7	122.7	100.4	105.1	93.5	84.0	94.2
1993	116.2	112.7	116.4	118.9	132.0	84.7	126.4	125.0	102.4	108.4	94.7	87.1	94.1
1994	118.5	114.8	118.7	122.1	136.6	83.1	129.7	127.0	101.8	106.5	94.8	82.4	97.0
1995	124.9	114.8	125.5	130.4	142.1	84.2	148.8	132.1	102.7	105.8	96.8	72.1	105.8
1996	125.7	128.1	125.6	128.6	143.6	90.0	141.1	135.9	113.8	121.5	104.5	92.6	105.7
1997	125.6	125.4	125.7	128.3	146.5	89.3	136.0	135.9	111.1	112.2	106.4	101.3	103.5
1998	123.0	116.2	123.4	126.1	146.8	81.1	140.8	134.8	96.8	103.9	88.4	86.7	84.5
1999	123.2	111.1	123.9	124.6	148.9	84.6	142.5	134.2	98.2	98.7	94.3	91.2	91.1
2000	129.2	111.7	130.1	128.1	150.7	102.0	151.6	136.9	120.6	100.2	130.4	136.9	118.0
2001	129.7	115.9	130.5	127.4	150.6	104.5	153.1	138.7	121.0	106.1	126.8	151.4	101.5
2002	127.8	115.5	128.5	126.1	151.3	96.3	152.1	138.9	108.1	99.5	111.4	117.3	101.0
2003	133.7	125.9	134.2	129.7	153.6	112.6	153.7	141.5	135.3	113.5	148.2	185.7	116.9
2004	142.6	137.1	143.0	137.9	166.4	124.3	159.3	146.7	159.0	127.0	179.2	211.4	149.2
2005	154.0	133.8	155.1	146.0	176.6	150.0	167.1	151.9	182.2	122.7	223.4	279.7	176.7
2006	164.0	135.2	165.4	155.9	188.4	162.8	175.0	157.0	184.8	119.3	230.6	241.5	210.0
2007 P	170.6	154.4	171.5	162.4	192.4	173.9	180.3	161.7	207.3	146.7	246.7	237.5	238.8
2006: Jan	161.6	135.0	163.0	151.2	184.2	167.2	170.5	155.3	199.0	119.3	255.7	332.9	195.0
Feb	160.7	133.6	162.1	151.9	185.0	160.1	171.2	155.6	182.9	116.6	229.3	269.0	192.1
Mar	161.2	133.8	162.6	152.7	185.5	160.0	173.1	155.9	178.4	114.2	223.4	243.9	197.7
Apr	163.1	133.0	164.6	153.9	186.7	165.6	172.8	156.2	183.0	113.1	232.4	239.6	213.8
May	164.9	133.1	166.5	156.3	188.2	167.4	173.3	156.5	186.9	112.7	239.6	238.4	225.4
June	166.1	133.9	167.6	157.3	189.2	169.4	176.3	156.8	181.6	116.9	226.7	212.4	221.0
July	166.6	135.2	168.2	158.2	190.2	169.2	176.6	157.2	186.2	118.8	233.4	212.7	230.9
Aug	167.4	134.6	169.0	158.6	190.7	171.5	177.1	157.5	191.1	119.3	241.8	244.2	225.4
Sept	165.4	135.2	166.9	158.4	191.0	161.6	178.0	157.5	183.8	121.3	227.1	228.9	212.0
Oct	162.9	135.7	164.2	158.1	190.4	149.9	177.5	158.2	167.0	124.8	194.7	164.1	200.4
Nov	163.3	138.6	164.6	157.4	189.6	153.9	176.8	158.6	186.6	127.5	227.2	250.5	199.6
Dec	164.1	140.4	165.3	157.1	189.6	157.5	176.8	159.3	191.2	126.9	235.7	261.5	206.1
2007: Jan	163.3	142.6	164.3	157.3	190.3	152.0	178.1	159.6	180.0	128.7	212.9	212.6	199.4
Feb	164.3	147.2	165.2	157.6	190.6	156.1	178.1	160.1	197.0	138.8	235.1	253.4	209.7
Mar	166.6	149.8	167.5	158.7	191.2	164.6	178.1	160.4	202.1	142.0	241.5	255.8	218.0
Apr	169.1	151.0	170.0	160.6	192.1	171.6	179.2	160.7	204.2	143.7	243.9	248.3	225.7
May	171.1	151.6	172.1	162.8	192.8	176.2	179.6	160.8	208.0	148.1	246.6	258.1	224.2
June	172.0	154.5	172.8	162.8	193.1	178.1	179.7	161.4	209.7	148.4	249.6	260.4	227.6
July	173.6	155.9	174.5	164.5	193.5	183.0	180.2	161.9	210.3	150.0	249.2	236.9	243.6
Aug	171.5	156.3	172.3	163.4	193.5	175.3	180.5	162.0	202.8	147.8	237.6	211.7	242.2
Sept[1]	172.3	158.5	173.0	163.4	193.3	178.8	180.7	162.1	204.7	151.9	237.5	195.4	253.6
Oct[1]	172.1	159.7	172.8	163.9	193.2	176.2	182.2	162.8	209.9	149.8	248.7	211.8	260.5
Nov[1]	176.5	161.3	177.3	166.3	192.9	191.0	183.1	163.9	228.4	152.7	279.4	251.8	282.8
Dec[1]	175.3	164.9	175.9	166.3	193.0	184.4	183.5	164.6	230.5	158.9	277.9	253.8	279.0

[2] Intermediate materials for food manufacturing and feeds.

Source: Department of Labor (Bureau of Labor Statistics).

TABLE B–66.—Producer price indexes by stage of processing, special groups, 1974–2007

[1982=100]

Year or month	Finished goods						Intermediate materials, supplies, and components				Crude materials for further processing			
	Total	Foods	Energy	Excluding foods and energy			Total	Foods and feeds [1]	Energy	Other	Total	Food-stuffs and feed-stuffs	Energy	Other
				Total	Capital equipment	Consumer goods excluding foods and energy								
1974	52.6	64.4	26.2	53.6	50.5	55.5	52.5	83.6	33.1	54.0	61.4	76.4	27.8	83.3
1975	58.2	69.8	30.7	59.7	58.2	60.6	58.0	81.6	38.7	60.2	61.6	77.4	33.3	69.3
1976	60.8	69.6	34.3	63.1	62.1	63.7	60.9	77.4	41.5	63.8	63.4	76.8	35.3	80.2
1977	64.7	73.3	39.7	66.9	66.1	67.3	64.9	79.6	46.8	67.6	65.5	77.5	40.4	79.8
1978	69.8	79.9	42.3	71.9	71.3	72.2	69.5	84.8	49.1	72.5	73.4	87.3	45.2	87.8
1979	77.6	87.3	57.1	78.3	77.5	78.8	78.4	94.5	61.1	80.7	85.9	100.0	54.9	106.2
1980	88.0	92.4	85.2	87.1	85.8	87.8	90.3	105.5	84.9	90.3	95.3	104.6	73.1	113.1
1981	96.1	97.8	101.5	94.6	94.6	94.6	98.6	104.6	100.5	97.7	103.0	103.9	97.7	111.7
1982	100.0	100.0	100.0	100.0	100.0	100.0	100.0	100.0	100.0	100.0	100.0	100.0	100.0	100.0
1983	101.6	101.0	95.2	103.0	102.8	103.1	100.6	103.6	95.3	101.6	101.3	101.8	98.7	105.3
1984	103.7	105.4	91.2	105.5	105.2	105.7	103.1	105.7	95.5	104.7	103.5	104.7	98.0	111.7
1985	104.7	104.6	87.6	108.1	107.5	108.4	102.7	97.3	92.6	105.2	95.8	94.8	93.3	104.9
1986	103.2	107.3	63.0	110.6	109.7	111.1	99.1	96.2	72.6	104.9	87.7	93.2	71.8	103.1
1987	105.4	109.5	61.8	113.3	111.7	114.2	101.5	99.2	73.0	107.8	93.7	96.2	75.0	115.7
1988	108.0	112.6	59.8	117.0	114.3	118.5	107.1	109.5	70.9	115.2	96.0	106.1	67.7	133.0
1989	113.6	118.7	65.7	122.1	118.8	124.0	112.0	113.8	76.1	120.2	103.1	111.2	75.9	137.9
1990	119.2	124.4	75.0	126.6	122.9	128.8	114.5	113.3	85.5	120.9	108.9	113.1	85.9	136.3
1991	121.7	124.1	78.1	131.1	126.7	133.7	114.4	111.1	85.1	121.4	101.2	105.5	80.4	128.2
1992	123.2	123.3	77.8	134.2	129.1	137.3	114.7	110.7	84.3	122.0	100.4	105.1	78.8	128.4
1993	124.7	125.7	78.0	135.8	131.4	138.5	116.2	112.7	84.6	123.8	102.4	108.4	76.7	140.2
1994	125.5	126.8	77.0	137.1	134.1	139.0	118.5	114.8	83.0	127.1	101.8	106.5	72.1	156.2
1995	127.9	129.0	78.1	140.0	136.7	141.9	124.9	114.8	84.1	135.2	102.7	105.8	69.4	173.6
1996	131.3	133.6	83.2	142.0	138.3	144.3	125.7	128.1	89.8	134.0	113.8	121.5	85.0	155.8
1997	131.8	134.5	83.4	142.4	138.2	145.1	125.6	125.4	89.0	134.2	111.1	112.2	87.3	156.5
1998	130.7	134.3	75.1	143.7	137.6	147.7	123.0	116.2	80.8	133.5	96.8	103.9	68.6	142.1
1999	133.0	135.1	78.8	146.1	137.6	151.7	123.2	111.1	84.3	133.1	98.2	98.7	78.5	135.2
2000	138.0	137.2	94.1	148.0	138.8	154.0	129.2	111.7	101.7	136.6	120.6	100.2	122.1	145.2
2001	140.7	141.3	96.7	150.0	139.7	156.9	129.7	115.9	104.1	136.4	121.0	106.1	122.3	130.7
2002	138.9	140.1	88.8	150.2	139.1	157.6	127.8	115.5	95.9	135.8	108.1	99.5	102.0	135.7
2003	143.3	145.9	102.0	150.5	139.5	157.9	133.7	125.9	111.9	138.5	135.3	113.5	147.2	152.5
2004	148.5	152.7	113.0	152.7	141.4	160.3	142.6	131.7	123.2	146.5	159.0	127.0	174.6	193.0
2005	155.7	155.7	132.6	156.4	144.6	164.3	154.0	133.8	149.2	154.6	182.2	122.7	234.0	202.4
2006	160.4	156.7	145.9	158.7	146.9	166.7	164.0	135.2	162.8	163.8	184.8	119.3	226.9	244.5
2007 p	166.6	166.9	156.4	161.7	149.5	170.0	170.6	154.4	174.6	168.4	207.3	146.7	233.0	283.3
2006: Jan	159.9	157.1	145.7	157.9	145.8	166.0	161.6	135.0	166.5	159.7	199.0	119.3	274.5	216.1
Feb	158.0	153.8	139.1	158.3	146.2	166.5	160.7	133.6	160.5	160.3	182.9	116.6	233.6	224.0
Mar	159.1	154.4	143.1	158.5	146.4	166.7	161.2	133.8	160.4	161.0	178.4	114.2	223.6	227.7
Apr	160.7	154.8	149.6	158.5	146.6	166.5	163.1	133.0	165.9	162.0	183.0	113.1	231.6	239.4
May	161.2	154.2	151.9	158.7	146.7	166.9	164.3	133.1	168.1	163.7	186.9	112.7	233.5	259.5
June	161.8	156.1	153.1	158.6	146.7	166.6	166.1	133.9	169.9	164.7	181.6	116.9	216.9	255.4
July	161.7	156.4	155.4	157.5	145.8	165.4	166.3	133.9	169.3	165.6	186.2	118.8	224.7	259.3
Aug	162.3	158.3	155.0	158.0	146.4	165.8	167.4	134.6	170.9	166.2	191.1	119.3	240.2	250.9
Sept	160.3	159.2	144.3	158.3	146.7	166.1	165.4	135.2	161.3	166.1	183.8	121.3	218.1	253.8
Oct	158.9	158.4	136.8	159.1	147.5	166.9	162.9	135.7	149.7	166.0	167.0	124.8	174.3	247.9
Nov	159.8	157.9	137.9	160.3	148.8	168.1	163.3	138.6	153.9	165.3	186.6	127.5	220.5	248.1
Dec	160.5	160.1	139.1	160.3	148.6	168.1	164.1	140.4	156.8	165.4	191.2	126.9	230.9	252.3
2007: Jan	160.1	161.1	135.6	160.6	148.9	168.5	163.3	142.6	151.8	165.5	180.0	128.7	195.9	255.5
Feb	161.8	163.9	139.0	161.2	149.2	169.2	164.3	147.2	155.7	165.5	197.0	138.8	223.9	265.6
Mar	164.1	166.3	147.4	161.0	149.1	169.0	166.6	149.8	164.0	166.2	202.1	142.0	224.7	284.5
Apr	165.9	166.8	155.4	161.0	149.1	169.0	169.1	151.0	170.5	167.7	204.2	143.7	226.5	288.4
May	167.5	166.8	161.9	161.3	149.1	169.5	171.1	151.6	176.7	168.6	208.0	148.1	233.0	282.8
June	167.2	166.3	160.9	161.3	149.0	169.6	172.0	154.5	179.2	169.0	209.7	148.4	238.0	281.5
July	168.5	166.4	166.4	161.4	149.1	169.7	173.6	155.9	184.2	169.6	210.3	150.0	236.8	284.0
Aug	166.1	166.3	155.6	161.5	149.0	170.0	171.5	156.3	177.0	168.8	202.8	147.8	221.7	284.7
Sept [2]	167.4	168.3	159.6	161.5	149.0	169.9	172.3	158.5	179.9	168.9	204.7	151.9	219.9	289.2
Oct [2]	168.6	168.3	163.0	160.5	150.5	171.6	172.1	159.7	178.0	169.2	209.9	149.8	232.9	294.0
Nov [2]	171.3	169.4	170.5	163.5	150.8	172.1	176.5	161.3	192.3	170.8	228.4	152.7	272.5	294.6
Dec [2]	170.6	172.0	164.7	163.5	150.6	172.3	175.3	164.9	186.0	170.8	230.5	158.9	270.6	294.8

[1] Intermediate materials for food manufacturing and feeds.
[2] Data have been revised through August 2007; data are subject to revision four months after date of original publication.

Source: Department of Labor (Bureau of Labor Statistics).

[1982=100]

Year or month	Farm products and processed foods and feeds			Industrial commodities				
	Total	Farm products	Processed foods and feeds	Total	Textile products and apparel	Hides, skins, leather, and related products	Fuels and related products and power	Chemicals and allied products [1]
1959	37.6	40.2	35.6	30.5	48.1	35.9	13.7	34.8
1960	37.7	40.1	35.6	30.5	48.6	34.6	13.9	34.8
1961	37.7	39.7	36.2	30.4	47.8	34.9	14.0	34.5
1962	38.1	40.4	36.5	30.4	48.2	35.3	14.0	33.9
1963	37.7	39.6	36.8	30.3	48.2	34.3	13.9	33.5
1964	37.5	39.0	36.7	30.5	48.5	34.4	13.5	33.6
1965	39.0	40.7	38.0	30.9	48.8	35.9	13.8	33.9
1966	41.6	43.7	40.2	31.5	48.9	39.4	14.1	34.0
1967	40.2	41.3	39.8	32.0	48.9	38.1	14.4	34.2
1968	41.1	42.3	40.6	32.8	50.7	39.3	14.3	34.1
1969	43.4	45.0	42.7	33.9	51.8	41.5	14.6	34.2
1970	44.9	45.8	44.6	35.2	52.4	42.0	15.3	35.0
1971	45.8	46.6	45.5	36.5	53.3	43.4	16.6	35.6
1972	49.2	51.6	48.0	37.8	55.5	50.0	17.1	35.6
1973	63.9	72.7	58.9	40.3	60.5	54.5	19.4	37.6
1974	71.3	77.4	68.0	49.2	68.0	55.2	30.1	50.2
1975	74.0	77.0	72.6	54.9	67.4	56.5	35.4	62.0
1976	73.6	78.8	70.8	58.4	72.4	63.9	38.3	64.0
1977	75.9	79.4	74.0	62.5	75.3	68.3	43.6	65.9
1978	83.0	87.7	80.6	67.0	78.1	76.1	46.5	68.0
1979	92.3	99.6	88.5	75.7	82.5	96.1	58.9	76.0
1980	98.3	102.9	95.9	88.0	89.7	94.7	82.8	89.0
1981	101.1	105.2	98.9	97.4	97.6	99.3	100.2	98.4
1982	100.0	100.0	100.0	100.0	100.0	100.0	100.0	100.0
1983	102.0	102.4	101.8	101.1	100.3	103.2	95.9	100.3
1984	105.5	105.5	105.4	103.3	102.7	109.0	94.8	102.9
1985	100.7	95.1	103.5	103.7	102.9	108.9	91.4	103.7
1986	101.2	92.9	105.4	100.0	103.2	113.0	69.8	102.6
1987	103.7	95.5	107.9	102.6	105.1	120.4	70.2	106.4
1988	110.0	104.9	112.7	106.3	109.2	131.4	66.7	116.3
1989	115.4	110.9	117.8	111.6	112.3	136.3	72.9	123.0
1990	118.6	112.2	121.9	115.8	115.0	141.7	82.3	123.6
1991	116.4	105.7	121.9	116.5	116.3	138.9	81.2	125.6
1992	115.9	103.6	122.1	117.4	117.8	140.4	80.4	125.9
1993	118.4	107.1	124.0	119.0	118.0	143.7	80.0	128.2
1994	119.1	106.3	125.5	120.7	118.3	148.5	77.8	132.1
1995	120.5	107.4	127.0	125.5	120.8	153.7	78.0	142.5
1996	129.7	122.4	133.3	127.3	122.4	150.5	85.8	142.1
1997	127.0	112.9	134.0	127.7	122.6	154.2	86.1	143.6
1998	122.7	104.6	131.6	124.8	122.9	148.0	75.3	143.9
1999	120.3	98.4	131.1	126.5	121.1	146.0	80.5	144.2
2000	122.0	99.5	133.1	134.8	121.4	151.5	103.5	151.0
2001	126.2	103.8	137.3	135.7	121.3	158.4	105.3	151.8
2002	123.9	99.0	136.2	132.4	119.9	157.6	93.2	151.9
2003	132.8	111.5	143.4	139.1	119.8	162.3	112.9	161.8
2004	142.0	123.3	151.2	147.6	121.0	164.5	126.9	174.4
2005	141.3	118.5	153.1	160.2	122.8	165.4	156.4	192.0
2006	141.2	117.0	153.8	168.8	124.5	168.4	166.7	205.8
2007 ᴾ	157.7	143.3	165.1	175.2	125.9	173.5	177.7	214.8
2006: Jan	141.2	117.4	153.6	168.3	123.8	164.9	175.6	203.7
Feb	138.6	111.9	152.6	165.7	124.1	165.6	163.5	203.4
Mar	138.3	111.0	152.6	166.3	124.2	166.6	163.8	203.4
Apr	138.1	111.3	152.2	168.8	124.2	167.8	170.5	203.1
May	137.8	109.8	152.5	170.6	124.5	168.3	172.9	205.7
June	140.1	113.8	153.8	170.6	124.5	168.8	171.5	207.9
July	141.1	115.5	154.4	171.3	124.6	169.0	173.4	208.3
Aug	141.7	118.5	153.7	172.4	124.7	169.1	176.6	209.8
Sept	142.8	120.3	154.6	169.2	124.8	169.0	163.8	207.6
Oct	143.7	123.2	154.3	165.4	125.0	169.8	148.5	206.9
Nov	144.9	124.5	155.5	168.0	125.2	170.2	158.4	204.5
Dec	146.2	127.0	156.2	168.9	125.0	171.2	161.8	205.3
2007: Jan	147.5	127.1	158.2	166.8	125.1	173.6	152.4	206.0
Feb	152.9	137.5	160.6	169.1	125.4	174.1	160.2	206.7
Mar	155.1	140.6	162.4	171.6	125.4	174.9	167.9	208.8
Apr	156.1	141.3	163.4	173.9	125.3	176.0	174.7	210.7
May	157.5	142.7	164.8	176.0	125.4	175.6	181.3	213.7
June	158.0	141.8	166.2	176.4	125.7	174.7	182.4	215.0
July	158.6	143.4	166.2	177.9	126.0	171.6	186.7	217.1
Aug	157.8	140.4	166.6	174.9	126.2	172.6	176.3	215.0
Sept ²	160.5	146.4	167.6	175.7	126.3	172.3	179.1	217.0
Oct ²	160.8	147.8	167.5	176.7	126.3	172.1	180.5	217.9
Nov ²	162.1	150.6	167.9	182.3	126.7	172.0	198.4	224.6
Dec ²	166.1	159.6	169.4	180.7	126.7	171.8	192.6	225.2

[1] Prices for some items in this grouping are lagged and refer to one month earlier than the index month.
[2] Data have been revised through August 2007; data are subject to revision four months after date of original publication.

See next page for continuation of table.

TABLE B–67.—*Producer price indexes for major commodity groups, 1959–2007*—Continued

[1982=100]

Year or month	Industrial commodities—Continued									
	Rubber and plastic products	Lumber and wood products	Pulp, paper, and allied products	Metals and metal products	Machinery and equipment	Furniture and household durables	Non-metallic mineral products	Transportation equipment		Miscellaneous products
								Total	Motor vehicles and equipment	
1959	42.6	34.7	33.7	30.6	32.8	48.0	30.3		39.9	33.4
1960	42.7	33.5	34.0	30.6	33.0	47.8	30.4		39.3	33.6
1961	41.1	32.0	33.0	30.5	33.0	47.5	30.5		39.2	33.7
1962	39.9	32.2	33.4	30.2	33.0	47.2	30.5		39.2	33.9
1963	40.1	32.8	33.1	30.3	33.1	46.9	30.3		38.9	34.2
1964	39.6	33.5	33.0	31.1	33.3	47.1	30.4		39.1	34.4
1965	39.7	33.7	33.3	32.0	33.7	46.8	30.4		39.2	34.7
1966	40.5	35.2	34.2	32.8	34.7	47.4	30.7		39.2	35.3
1967	41.4	35.1	34.6	33.2	35.9	48.3	31.2		39.8	36.2
1968	42.8	39.8	35.0	34.0	37.0	49.7	32.4		40.9	37.0
1969	43.6	44.0	36.0	36.0	38.2	50.7	33.6	40.4	41.7	38.1
1970	44.9	39.9	37.5	38.7	40.0	51.9	35.3	41.9	43.3	39.8
1971	45.2	44.7	38.1	39.4	41.4	53.1	38.2	44.2	45.7	40.8
1972	45.3	50.7	39.3	40.9	42.3	53.8	39.4	45.5	47.0	41.5
1973	46.6	62.2	42.3	44.0	43.7	55.7	40.7	46.1	47.4	43.3
1974	56.4	64.5	52.5	57.0	50.0	61.8	47.8	50.3	51.4	48.1
1975	62.2	62.1	59.0	61.5	57.9	67.5	54.4	56.7	57.6	53.4
1976	66.0	72.2	62.1	65.0	61.3	70.3	58.2	60.5	61.2	55.6
1977	69.4	83.0	64.6	69.3	65.2	73.2	62.6	64.6	65.2	59.4
1978	72.4	96.9	67.7	75.3	70.3	77.5	69.6	69.5	70.0	66.7
1979	80.5	105.5	75.9	86.0	76.7	82.8	77.6	75.3	75.8	75.5
1980	90.1	101.5	86.3	95.0	86.0	90.7	88.4	82.9	83.1	93.6
1981	96.4	102.8	94.8	99.6	94.4	95.9	96.7	94.3	94.6	96.1
1982	100.0	100.0	100.0	100.0	100.0	100.0	100.0	100.0	100.0	100.0
1983	100.8	107.9	103.3	101.8	102.7	103.4	101.6	102.8	102.2	104.8
1984	102.3	108.0	110.3	104.8	105.1	105.7	105.4	105.2	104.1	107.0
1985	101.9	106.6	113.3	104.4	107.2	107.1	108.6	107.9	106.4	109.4
1986	101.9	107.2	116.1	103.2	108.8	108.2	110.0	110.5	109.1	111.6
1987	103.0	112.8	121.8	107.1	110.4	109.9	110.0	112.5	111.7	114.9
1988	109.3	118.9	130.4	118.7	113.2	113.1	111.2	114.3	113.1	120.2
1989	112.6	126.7	137.8	124.1	117.4	116.9	112.6	117.7	116.2	126.5
1990	113.6	129.7	141.2	122.9	120.7	119.2	114.7	121.5	118.2	134.2
1991	115.1	132.1	142.9	120.2	123.0	121.2	117.2	126.4	122.1	140.8
1992	115.1	146.6	145.2	119.2	123.4	122.2	117.3	130.4	124.9	145.3
1993	116.0	174.0	147.3	119.2	124.0	123.7	120.0	133.7	128.0	145.4
1994	117.6	180.0	152.5	124.8	125.1	126.1	124.2	137.2	131.4	141.9
1995	124.3	178.1	172.2	134.5	126.6	128.2	129.0	139.7	133.0	145.4
1996	123.8	176.1	168.7	131.0	126.5	130.4	131.0	141.7	134.1	147.7
1997	123.2	183.8	167.9	131.8	125.9	130.8	133.2	141.6	132.7	150.9
1998	122.6	179.1	171.7	127.8	124.9	131.3	135.4	142.2	131.4	156.0
1999	122.5	183.6	174.1	124.6	124.3	131.7	138.9	141.8	131.7	166.6
2000	125.5	178.2	183.7	128.1	124.0	132.6	142.5	143.8	132.3	170.8
2001	127.2	174.4	184.8	125.4	123.7	133.2	144.3	145.2	131.5	181.3
2002	126.8	173.3	185.9	125.9	122.9	133.5	146.2	144.6	129.9	182.4
2003	130.1	177.4	190.0	129.2	121.9	133.9	148.2	145.7	129.6	179.6
2004	133.8	195.6	195.7	149.6	122.1	135.1	153.2	148.6	131.0	183.2
2005	143.8	196.5	202.6	160.8	123.7	139.4	164.2	151.0	131.5	195.1
2006	153.8	194.4	209.8	181.6	126.2	142.6	179.9	152.6	131.0	205.6
2007 ᴾ	155.0	192.4	216.8	193.5	127.3	144.7	186.1	155.0	132.1	210.5
2006: Jan	153.0	197.5	205.4	168.6	124.0	142.0	174.1	152.1	131.4	202.1
Feb	153.2	198.4	206.8	170.9	124.2	142.2	175.3	152.4	131.6	203.0
Mar	153.0	198.6	207.5	172.0	125.3	142.2	176.6	152.7	131.7	204.1
Apr	153.1	198.3	207.8	176.9	125.7	142.2	178.1	152.8	131.5	205.3
May	153.2	198.6	209.2	184.2	125.8	142.0	179.2	152.8	131.4	206.2
June	153.1	195.4	210.1	184.9	126.1	142.3	179.9	152.5	130.9	206.7
July	153.8	193.9	210.8	187.5	126.5	142.5	181.8	149.9	127.4	206.3
Aug	154.1	191.4	211.3	187.0	127.0	142.9	182.4	150.9	128.6	206.9
Sept	154.3	191.8	211.8	187.7	127.4	143.2	183.0	151.4	129.1	206.1
Oct	155.0	188.7	212.0	187.3	127.3	143.5	182.8	153.0	130.8	206.3
Nov	154.9	189.4	212.2	186.0	127.3	143.4	182.7	155.5	133.9	207.3
Dec	154.7	190.3	212.2	186.5	127.4	143.2	182.7	155.1	133.2	207.0
2007: Jan	154.2	192.1	213.5	185.7	127.8	143.9	185.3	155.0	132.7	207.7
Feb	154.0	192.7	214.0	187.2	127.3	144.5	185.4	155.0	132.5	211.0
Mar	153.8	193.3	215.1	191.1	127.2	144.4	185.9	154.6	132.1	210.6
Apr	153.9	193.3	215.1	195.4	127.4	144.6	186.5	154.3	131.8	209.9
May	154.2	193.1	215.8	196.3	127.2	144.9	186.3	154.2	131.6	210.3
June	154.4	193.7	216.1	195.9	127.2	144.9	186.3	154.4	131.6	210.0
July	154.8	194.4	217.2	196.6	127.1	144.8	186.0	154.4	131.3	209.7
Aug	155.7	193.2	217.6	195.5	127.0	144.5	186.3	154.2	130.9	209.7
Sept ²	155.5	192.5	217.5	193.9	127.3	144.8	186.5	153.9	130.3	211.1
Oct ²	156.1	190.9	218.9	194.5	127.2	144.9	185.9	156.7	133.5	212.0
Nov ²	156.6	189.7	220.4	195.2	127.1	144.9	186.0	157.1	134.1	211.6
Dec ²	157.1	189.4	220.5	194.3	127.5	145.3	186.2	156.5	133.2	212.2

Source: Department of Labor (Bureau of Labor Statistics).

[Percent change]

Year or month	Total finished goods		Finished consumer foods		Finished goods excluding consumer foods						Finished energy goods		Finished goods excluding foods and energy	
					Total		Consumer goods		Capital equipment					
	Dec. to Dec.[1]	Year to year	Dec. to Dec.[1]	Year to year	Dec. to Dec.[1]	Year to year	Dec. to Dec.[1]	Year to year	Dec. to Dec.[1]	Year to year	Dec. to Dec.[1]	Year to year	Dec. to Dec.[1]	Year to year
1965	3.3	1.8	9.1	4.0			0.9	0.9	1.5	1.2				
1966	2.0	3.2	1.3	6.5			1.8	1.9	3.8	2.4				
1967	1.7	1.1	–.3	–1.8			2.0	1.8	3.1	3.5				
1968	3.1	2.8	4.6	3.9	2.5	2.6	2.0	2.3	3.0	3.4				
1969	4.9	3.8	8.1	6.0	3.3	2.8	2.8	2.3	4.8	3.5				
1970	2.1	3.4	–2.3	3.3	4.3	3.5	3.8	3.0	4.8	4.7				
1971	3.3	3.1	5.8	1.6	2.0	3.7	2.1	3.5	2.4	4.0				
1972	3.9	3.2	7.9	5.4	2.3	2.0	2.1	1.8	2.1	2.6				
1973	11.7	9.1	22.7	20.5	6.6	4.0	7.5	4.6	5.1	3.3				
1974	18.3	15.4	12.8	14.0	21.1	16.2	20.3	17.0	22.7	14.3			17.7	11.4
1975	6.6	10.6	5.6	8.4	7.2	12.1	6.8	10.4	8.1	15.2	16.3	17.2	6.0	11.4
1976	3.8	4.5	–2.5	–.3	6.2	6.2	6.0	6.2	6.5	6.7	11.6	11.7	5.7	5.7
1977	6.7	6.4	6.9	5.3	6.8	7.1	6.7	7.3	7.2	6.4	12.0	15.7	6.2	6.0
1978	9.3	7.9	11.7	9.0	8.3	7.2	8.5	7.1	8.0	7.9	8.5	6.5	8.4	7.5
1979	12.8	11.2	7.4	9.3	14.8	11.8	17.6	13.3	8.8	8.7	58.1	35.0	9.4	8.9
1980	11.8	13.4	7.5	5.8	13.4	16.2	14.1	18.5	11.4	10.7	27.9	49.2	10.8	11.2
1981	7.1	9.2	1.5	5.8	8.7	10.3	8.6	10.3	9.2	10.3	14.1	19.1	7.7	8.6
1982	3.6	4.1	2.0	2.2	4.2	4.6	4.2	4.1	3.9	5.7	–.1	–1.5	4.9	5.7
1983	.6	1.6	2.3	1.0	.0	1.8	–.9	1.2	2.0	2.8	–9.2	–4.8	1.9	3.0
1984	1.7	2.1	3.5	4.4	1.1	1.4	.8	1.0	1.8	2.3	–4.2	–4.2	2.0	2.4
1985	1.8	1.0	.6	–.8	2.2	1.4	2.1	1.1	2.7	2.2	–.2	–3.9	2.7	2.5
1986	–2.3	–1.4	2.8	2.6	–4.0	–2.6	–6.6	–4.6	2.1	2.0	–38.1	–28.1	2.7	2.3
1987	2.2	2.1	–.2	2.1	3.2	2.1	4.1	2.2	1.3	1.8	11.2	–1.9	2.1	2.4
1988	4.0	2.5	5.7	2.8	3.2	2.4	3.1	2.4	3.6	2.3	–3.6	–3.2	4.3	3.3
1989	4.9	5.2	5.2	5.4	4.8	5.0	5.3	5.6	3.8	3.9	9.5	9.9	4.2	4.4
1990	5.7	4.9	2.6	4.8	6.9	5.0	8.7	5.9	3.4	3.5	30.7	14.2	3.5	3.7
1991	–.1	2.1	–1.5	–.2	.3	3.0	–.7	2.9	2.5	3.1	–9.6	4.1	3.1	3.6
1992	1.6	1.2	1.6	–.6	1.6	1.8	1.6	1.8	1.7	1.9	–.3	–.4	2.0	2.4
1993	.2	1.2	2.4	1.9	–.4	1.1	–1.4	.7	1.8	1.8	–4.1	.3	.4	1.2
1994	1.7	.6	1.1	.9	1.9	.6	2.0	–.1	2.0	2.1	3.5	–1.3	1.6	1.0
1995	2.3	1.9	1.9	1.7	2.3	1.9	2.3	2.0	2.2	1.9	1.1	1.4	2.6	2.1
1996	2.8	2.7	3.4	3.6	2.6	2.4	3.7	2.9	.4	1.2	11.7	6.5	.6	1.4
1997	–1.2	.4	–.8	.7	–1.2	.3	–1.5	.5	–.6	.0	–6.4	.2	.0	.3
1998	.0	–.8	.1	–.1	–.1	–1.1	–.1	–1.4	.0	–.4	–11.7	–10.0	2.5	.9
1999	2.9	1.8	.8	.6	3.5	2.2	5.1	3.2	.3	.0	18.1	4.9	.9	1.7
2000	3.6	3.8	1.7	1.6	4.1	4.4	5.5	6.1	1.2	.0	16.6	19.4	1.3	1.3
2001	–1.6	2.0	1.8	3.0	–2.6	1.7	–3.9	2.2	.0	.6	–17.1	2.8	.9	1.4
2002	1.2	–1.3	–.6	–.8	1.7	–1.5	2.9	–1.8	–.6	–.4	12.3	–8.2	–.5	.1
2003	4.0	3.2	7.7	4.1	3.0	3.0	4.1	4.3	.8	.3	11.4	14.9	1.0	.2
2004	4.2	3.6	3.1	4.7	4.5	3.4	5.5	4.3	2.4	1.4	13.4	10.8	2.3	1.5
2005	5.4	4.8	1.7	2.0	6.4	5.6	8.8	7.3	1.2	2.3	23.9	17.3	1.4	2.4
2006	1.1	3.0	1.7	.6	1.0	3.5	.4	4.5	2.3	1.6	–2.0	10.0	2.0	1.5
2007 [p]	6.3	3.9	7.4	6.5	6.0	3.2	8.0	3.8	1.3	1.8	18.4	7.2	2.0	1.9

	Percent change from preceding month													
	Unadjusted	Seasonally adjusted	Unadjusted	Seasonally adjusted	Unadjusted	Seasonally adjusted	Unadjusted	Seasonally adjusted	Unadjusted	Seasonally adjusted	Unadjusted	Seasonally adjusted	Unadjusted	Seasonally adjusted
2006: Jan	0.8	0.3	–0.3	0.0	1.0	0.4	1.3	0.4	0.3	0.3	2.7	0.2	0.5	0.4
Feb	–1.2	–1.1	–2.1	–2.0	–.9	–.7	–1.5	–1.2	.3	.3	–4.5	–3.9	.3	.3
Mar	.7	.4	.4	.4	.8	.4	1.1	.6	.1	.1	2.9	1.3	.1	.2
Apr	1.0	.7	.3	.5	1.1	.7	1.6	1.0	.1	.2	4.5	2.6	.0	.1
May	.3	.2	–.4	–.8	.5	.4	.7	.5	.1	.2	1.5	1.1	.1	.2
June	.4	.5	1.2	1.2	.2	.4	.2	.5	.0	.1	.8	1.1	–.1	.1
July	–.1	–.1	.2	.1	–.1	–.2	.1	.0	–.6	–.4	1.5	.7	–.7	–.5
Aug	.4	.4	1.2	1.2	.2	.1	.0	–.1	.4	.4	–.3	–.5	.3	.4
Sept	–1.2	–1.1	.6	.4	–1.7	–1.4	–2.5	–2.1	.2	.3	–6.9	–5.9	.2	.3
Oct	–.9	–1.5	–.5	–.4	–.9	–1.8	–1.6	–2.4	.5	–.3	–5.2	–5.8	.5	–.4
Nov	.6	1.6	–.3	.1	.8	2.0	.7	2.4	.9	1.0	.8	5.4	.8	.9
Dec	.4	.7	1.4	1.1	.2	.6	.3	1.0	–.1	.0	.9	2.4	.0	.1
2007: Jan	–.2	–.6	.6	1.0	–.4	–1.0	–.7	–1.5	.2	.1	–2.5	–4.3	.2	.2
Feb	1.1	1.2	1.7	1.7	.9	1.1	1.1	1.4	.2	.3	2.5	3.0	.4	.4
Mar	1.4	1.0	1.5	1.6	1.4	.9	2.0	1.3	–.1	–.1	6.0	3.8	–.1	–.1
Apr	1.1	.9	.3	.5	1.3	.9	1.9	1.2	.0	.1	5.4	3.3	.0	.1
May	1.0	.7	.0	–.6	1.3	1.1	1.8	1.5	.0	.1	4.2	3.5	.2	.2
June	–.2	.1	–.3	–.4	–.2	.1	–.2	.1	–.1	–.1	–.6	–.2	.0	.3
July	.8	.7	.1	.1	1.0	.9	1.4	1.1	.1	.3	3.4	2.5	.1	.3
Aug	–1.4	–1.4	–.1	–.2	–1.8	–1.7	–2.4	–2.4	–.1	–.1	–6.5	–6.7	.1	.1
Sept [2]	.8	1.0	1.2	1.1	.7	1.0	.9	1.3	.0	.1	2.6	3.7	.0	.1
Oct [2]	.7	.1	.8	1.0	.7	–.2	.6	–.3	1.0	–.1	–.1	–.8	.9	.0
Nov [2]	1.6	3.2	–.1	.0	2.1	4.1	2.8	5.5	.2	.3	6.9	14.1	.3	.4
Dec [2]	–.4	–.1	1.5	1.3	–.9	–.5	–1.3	–.6	–.1	.1	–3.4	–1.9	.0	.2

[1] Changes from December to December are based on unadjusted indexes.
[2] Data have been revised through August 2007; data are subject to revision four months after date of original publication.

Source: Department of Labor (Bureau of Labor Statistics).

Money Stock, Credit, and Finance

Table B–69.—*Money stock and debt measures, 1965–2007*

[Averages of daily figures, except debt end-of-period basis; billions of dollars, seasonally adjusted]

Year and month	M1 — Sum of currency, demand deposits, travelers checks, and other checkable deposits (OCDs)	M2 — M1 plus retail MMMF balances, savings deposits (including MMDAs), and small time deposits [2]	Debt [1] — Debt of domestic nonfinancial sectors	Percent change — From year or 6 months earlier [3] — M1	M2	From previous period [4] — Debt
December:						
1965	167.8	459.2	1,008.0	....	4.6	....
1966	172.0	480.2	1,075.5	2.5	4.6	6.7
1967	183.3	524.8	1,151.5	6.6	9.3	7.1
1968	197.4	566.8	1,243.3	7.7	8.0	8.0
1969	203.9	587.9	1,330.4	3.3	3.7	7.1
1970	214.4	626.5	1,420.2	5.1	6.6	6.8
1971	228.3	710.3	1,555.2	6.5	13.4	9.5
1972	249.2	802.3	1,711.2	9.2	13.0	10.0
1973	262.9	855.5	1,895.5	5.5	6.6	10.7
1974	274.2	902.1	2,069.9	4.3	5.4	9.2
1975	287.1	1,016.2	2,261.8	4.7	12.6	9.3
1976	306.2	1,152.0	2,505.3	6.7	13.4	10.8
1977	330.9	1,270.3	2,826.6	8.1	10.3	12.8
1978	357.3	1,366.0	3,211.2	8.0	7.5	13.8
1979	381.8	1,473.7	3,603.0	6.9	7.9	12.2
1980	408.5	1,599.8	3,953.5	7.0	8.6	9.5
1981	436.7	1,755.5	4,361.7	6.9	9.7	10.4
1982	474.8	1,910.1	4,783.4	8.7	8.8	10.1
1983	521.4	2,126.4	5,359.2	9.8	11.3	12.0
1984	551.6	2,309.8	6,146.2	5.8	8.6	14.8
1985	619.8	2,495.5	7,121.9	12.4	8.0	15.6
1986	724.7	2,732.2	7,965.7	16.9	9.5	11.9
1987	750.2	2,831.3	8,669.4	3.5	3.6	9.0
1988	786.7	2,994.3	9,450.3	4.9	5.8	9.0
1989	792.9	3,158.3	10,151.5	.8	5.5	7.2
1990	824.7	3,277.7	10,834.7	4.0	3.8	6.5
1991	897.0	3,378.3	11,301.4	8.8	3.1	4.3
1992	1,024.9	3,431.8	11,817.0	14.3	1.6	4.5
1993	1,129.6	3,482.5	12,395.7	10.2	1.5	4.8
1994	1,150.7	3,498.5	12,970.5	1.9	.5	4.6
1995	1,127.4	3,641.7	13,651.4	−2.0	4.1	5.3
1996	1,081.3	3,820.5	14,365.2	−4.1	4.9	5.2
1997	1,072.5	4,035.0	15,126.5	−.8	5.6	5.3
1998	1,095.5	4,381.8	16,153.0	2.1	8.6	6.8
1999	1,122.5	4,639.2	17,219.9	2.5	5.9	6.4
2000	1,087.4	4,921.7	18,074.8	−3.1	6.1	4.9
2001	1,181.9	5,433.5	19,213.4	8.7	10.4	6.4
2002	1,219.7	5,779.2	20,615.8	3.2	6.4	7.3
2003	1,306.1	6,071.2	22,325.5	7.1	5.1	8.1
2004	1,376.3	6,421.6	24,317.4	5.4	5.8	8.9
2005	1,374.5	6,691.7	26,528.0	−.1	4.2	9.1
2006	1,367.1	7,035.5	28,854.7	−.5	5.1	8.8
2007	1,364.4	7,447.1	....	−.2	5.9	....
2006: Jan	1,379.5	6,734.6	....	1.8	5.7	....
Feb	1,380.9	6,761.0	....	.6	5.5	....
Mar	1,385.1	6,776.0	27,186.2	1.2	4.9	10.0
Apr	1,380.3	6,794.8	....	.9	4.6	....
May	1,384.2	6,805.2	....	1.1	4.2	....
June	1,375.5	6,834.2	27,751.7	.1	4.3	8.3
July	1,371.3	6,861.8	....	−1.2	3.8	....
Aug	1,370.5	6,882.3	....	−1.5	3.6	....
Sept	1,361.8	6,905.9	28,249.3	−3.4	3.8	7.2
Oct	1,368.8	6,958.1	....	−1.7	4.8	....
Nov	1,371.6	6,993.7	....	−1.8	5.5	....
Dec	1,367.1	7,035.5	28,854.7	−1.2	5.9	8.6
2007: Jan	1,372.8	7,085.5	....	.2	6.5	....
Feb	1,367.7	7,113.0	....	−.4	6.7	....
Mar	1,370.5	7,163.5	29,439.6	1.3	7.5	8.0
Apr	1,378.1	7,210.3	....	1.4	7.2	....
May	1,375.3	7,230.0	....	.5	6.8	....
June	1,366.3	7,247.1	29,973.2	−.1	6.0	7.2
July	1,368.7	7,271.2	....	−.6	5.2	....
Aug	1,367.9	7,320.7	....	.0	5.8	....
Sept	1,365.8	7,350.7	30,640.9	−.7	5.2	8.9
Oct	1,368.7	7,377.6	....	−1.4	4.6	....
Nov	1,364.5	7,410.5	....	−1.6	5.0	....
Dec	1,364.4	7,447.1	....	−.3	5.5	....

[1] Consists of outstanding credit market debt of the U.S. Government, State and local governments, and private nonfinancial sectors.
[2] Money market mutual fund (MMMF). Money market deposit account (MMDA).
[3] Annual changes are from December to December; monthly changes are from six months earlier at a simple annual rate.
[4] Annual changes are from fourth quarter to fourth quarter. Quarterly changes are from previous quarter at annual rate.

Note.—The Federal Reserve no longer publishes the M3 monetary aggregate and most of its components. Institutional money market mutual funds is published as a memorandum item in the H.6 release, and the component on large-denomination time deposits is published in other Federal Reserve Board releases. For details, see H.6 release of March 23, 2006.

Source: Board of Governors of the Federal Reserve System.

TABLE B–70.—*Components of money stock measures, 1965–2007*

[Averages of daily figures; billions of dollars, seasonally adjusted]

Year and month	Currency	Nonbank travelers checks	Demand deposits	Other checkable deposits (OCDs)		
				Total	At commercial banks	At thrift institutions
December:						
1965	36.0	0.5	131.3	0.1	0.0	0.1
1966	38.0	.6	133.4	.1	.0	.1
1967	40.0	.6	142.5	.1	.0	.1
1968	43.0	.7	153.6	.1	.0	.1
1969	45.7	.8	157.3	.2	.0	.1
1970	48.6	.9	164.7	.1	.0	.1
1971	52.0	1.0	175.1	.2	.0	.2
1972	56.2	1.2	191.6	.2	.0	.2
1973	60.8	1.4	200.3	.3	.0	.3
1974	67.0	1.7	205.1	.4	.2	.4
1975	72.8	2.1	211.3	.9	.4	.5
1976	79.5	2.6	221.5	2.7	1.3	1.4
1977	87.4	2.9	236.4	4.2	1.8	2.3
1978	96.0	3.3	249.5	8.5	5.3	3.1
1979	104.8	3.5	256.6	16.8	12.7	4.2
1980	115.3	3.9	261.2	28.1	20.8	7.3
1981	122.5	4.1	231.4	78.7	63.0	15.6
1982	132.5	4.1	234.1	104.1	80.5	23.6
1983	146.2	4.7	238.5	132.1	97.3	34.8
1984	156.1	5.0	243.4	147.1	104.7	42.4
1985	167.7	5.6	266.9	179.5	124.7	54.9
1986	180.4	6.1	302.9	235.2	161.0	74.2
1987	196.7	6.6	287.7	259.2	178.2	81.0
1988	212.0	7.0	287.1	280.6	192.5	88.1
1989	222.3	6.9	278.6	285.1	197.4	87.7
1990	246.5	7.7	276.8	293.7	208.7	85.0
1991	267.1	7.7	289.6	332.5	241.6	90.9
1992	292.2	8.2	340.0	384.6	280.8	103.8
1993	321.6	8.0	385.4	414.6	302.6	112.0
1994	354.5	8.6	383.6	404.0	297.4	106.6
1995	372.8	9.0	389.0	356.6	249.0	107.6
1996	394.7	8.8	402.1	275.7	172.1	103.7
1997	425.3	8.4	393.6	245.2	148.3	96.8
1998	460.5	8.5	376.6	249.9	143.9	106.0
1999	517.8	8.6	352.8	243.4	139.6	103.7
2000	531.2	8.3	309.6	238.4	133.1	105.2
2001	581.2	8.0	335.2	257.4	142.0	115.5
2002	626.3	7.8	306.2	279.4	154.3	125.1
2003	662.5	7.7	325.8	310.1	175.2	134.8
2004	697.6	7.5	343.2	328.0	186.8	141.2
2005	723.9	7.2	324.9	318.5	180.5	138.0
2006	748.9	6.7	306.4	305.0	176.8	128.2
2007	759.0	6.3	293.1	306.1	173.0	133.1
2006: Jan	729.2	7.2	324.8	318.3	179.9	138.4
Feb	733.6	7.1	323.1	317.1	179.0	138.1
Mar	736.3	6.9	325.6	316.4	179.1	137.3
Apr	738.4	6.9	319.5	315.5	177.5	138.0
May	741.3	7.0	323.0	313.0	177.6	135.4
June	740.9	7.0	316.5	311.1	179.3	131.8
July	740.7	6.8	313.4	310.4	178.3	132.1
Aug	741.7	6.8	313.8	308.2	177.0	131.2
Sept	741.6	6.8	306.4	307.0	177.1	129.9
Oct	742.7	6.7	312.6	306.7	178.7	128.1
Nov	745.6	6.7	312.9	306.3	179.0	127.3
Dec	748.9	6.7	306.4	305.0	176.8	128.2
2007: Jan	750.5	6.7	308.0	307.6	177.6	130.0
Feb	751.0	6.6	305.2	304.9	176.1	128.7
Mar	752.5	6.6	303.9	307.5	176.2	131.3
Apr	754.4	6.6	306.9	310.3	176.8	133.5
May	755.4	6.6	304.7	308.6	175.8	132.7
June	756.0	6.5	302.5	301.3	171.2	130.1
July	758.0	6.5	301.9	302.3	171.4	130.9
Aug	758.1	6.4	300.7	302.6	171.0	131.6
Sept	759.2	6.4	296.1	304.1	170.9	133.1
Oct	761.6	6.4	296.1	304.7	172.1	132.5
Nov	761.2	6.3	295.5	301.4	171.4	130.0
Dec	759.0	6.3	293.1	306.1	173.0	133.1

See next page for continuation of table.

[Averages of daily figures; billions of dollars, seasonally adjusted]

Year and month	Savings deposits [1]			Small-denomination time deposits [2]			Retail money funds	Institutional money funds [3]
	Total	At commercial banks	At thrift institutions	Total	At commercial banks	At thrift institutions		
December:								
1965	256.9	92.4	164.5	34.5	26.7	7.8	0.0	0.0
1966	253.1	89.9	163.3	55.0	38.7	16.3	.0	.0
1967	263.7	94.1	169.6	77.8	50.7	27.1	.0	.0
1968	268.9	96.1	172.8	100.5	63.5	37.1	.0	.0
1969	263.7	93.8	169.8	120.4	71.6	48.8	.0	.0
1970	261.0	98.6	162.3	151.2	79.3	71.9	.0	.0
1971	292.2	112.8	179.4	189.7	94.7	95.1	.0	.0
1972	321.4	124.8	196.6	231.6	108.2	123.5	.0	.0
1973	326.8	128.0	198.7	265.8	116.8	149.0	.1	.0
1974	338.6	136.8	201.8	287.9	123.1	164.8	1.4	.2
1975	388.9	161.2	227.6	337.9	142.3	195.5	2.4	.5
1976	453.2	201.8	251.4	390.7	155.5	235.2	1.8	.6
1977	492.2	218.8	273.4	445.5	167.5	278.0	1.8	1.0
1978	481.9	216.5	265.4	521.0	185.1	335.8	5.8	3.5
1979	423.8	195.0	228.8	634.3	235.5	398.7	33.9	10.4
1980	400.3	185.7	214.5	728.5	286.2	442.3	62.5	16.0
1981	343.9	159.0	184.9	823.1	347.7	475.4	151.7	38.2
1982	400.1	190.1	210.0	850.9	379.9	471.0	184.3	48.8
1983	684.9	363.2	321.7	784.1	350.9	433.1	136.0	40.9
1984	704.7	389.3	315.4	888.8	387.9	500.9	164.8	62.4
1985	815.3	456.6	358.6	885.7	386.4	499.3	174.7	65.5
1986	940.9	533.5	407.4	858.4	369.4	489.0	208.2	86.4
1987	937.4	534.8	402.6	921.0	391.7	529.3	222.6	93.9
1988	926.4	542.4	383.9	1,037.1	451.2	585.9	244.1	93.9
1989	893.7	541.1	352.6	1,151.3	533.8	617.6	320.4	112.2
1990	922.9	581.3	341.6	1,173.4	610.7	562.7	356.8	140.5
1991	1,044.5	664.8	379.6	1,065.6	602.2	463.3	371.3	189.6
1992	1,187.2	754.2	433.1	868.1	508.1	360.0	351.5	213.9
1993	1,219.3	785.3	434.0	782.0	467.9	314.1	351.6	218.2
1994	1,151.3	752.8	398.5	818.1	503.6	314.5	378.4	213.0
1995	1,135.9	774.8	361.0	933.1	575.8	357.3	445.3	267.0
1996	1,274.8	906.0	368.8	948.8	594.2	354.6	515.6	327.2
1997	1,401.8	1,022.9	378.8	968.6	625.5	343.2	592.1	400.9
1998	1,605.0	1,188.5	416.5	952.4	626.4	326.1	728.9	549.6
1999	1,740.3	1,289.0	451.2	956.8	636.9	319.9	819.7	654.1
2000	1,878.8	1,424.6	454.2	1,047.6	700.2	347.5	908.0	808.2
2001	2,312.8	1,739.5	573.4	976.5	635.4	341.1	962.3	1,214.3
2002	2,778.2	2,060.4	717.8	896.0	590.8	305.2	885.3	1,265.7
2003	3,169.1	2,337.7	831.4	818.7	541.3	277.4	777.4	1,132.2
2004	3,518.3	2,631.0	887.3	829.9	551.0	278.8	697.1	1,082.8
2005	3,621.4	2,771.5	849.9	995.8	644.6	351.3	699.9	1,147.5
2006	3,698.6	2,905.7	792.9	1,170.4	758.0	412.4	799.4	1,344.3
2007	3,889.8	3,034.8	855.0	1,216.8	815.0	401.7	976.1	1,860.9
2006: Jan	3,639.0	2,782.6	856.4	1,010.4	654.1	356.4	705.7	1,161.9
Feb	3,644.5	2,783.2	861.3	1,026.9	664.9	362.0	708.7	1,168.8
Mar	3,631.5	2,778.0	853.5	1,044.4	676.4	368.0	715.0	1,178.7
Apr	3,635.3	2,796.2	839.1	1,060.3	686.4	373.9	718.9	1,192.0
May	3,620.9	2,776.1	844.7	1,075.6	695.3	380.3	724.5	1,207.8
June	3,629.3	2,784.5	844.8	1,091.4	704.6	386.9	738.0	1,226.2
July	3,632.2	2,789.8	842.4	1,110.9	716.4	394.4	747.4	1,238.6
Aug	3,626.9	2,779.4	847.5	1,128.7	726.3	402.4	756.1	1,257.5
Sept	3,634.9	2,791.6	843.3	1,144.0	733.7	410.3	765.1	1,268.6
Oct	3,653.5	2,850.1	803.5	1,157.5	750.8	406.8	778.2	1,289.4
Nov	3,668.0	2,868.7	799.3	1,165.3	755.1	410.2	789.0	1,307.1
Dec	3,698.6	2,905.7	792.9	1,170.4	758.0	412.4	799.4	1,344.3
2007: Jan	3,725.1	2,921.6	803.5	1,175.5	760.6	414.8	812.2	1,345.5
Feb	3,744.8	2,932.0	812.8	1,180.1	765.2	414.9	820.4	1,364.7
Mar	3,772.8	2,925.4	847.5	1,183.4	755.2	428.3	836.8	1,393.6
Apr	3,802.9	2,936.8	866.1	1,187.4	756.7	430.6	841.9	1,426.7
May	3,818.5	2,940.4	878.1	1,188.7	757.3	431.3	847.6	1,466.0
June	3,831.5	2,949.3	882.2	1,188.8	758.4	430.4	860.4	1,495.7
July	3,838.3	2,966.7	871.5	1,189.8	763.6	426.2	874.4	1,526.3
Aug	3,864.0	2,995.6	868.4	1,191.9	765.4	426.4	897.0	1,600.3
Sept	3,867.7	3,010.5	857.2	1,201.4	772.4	429.0	915.8	1,680.2
Oct	3,871.8	3,012.6	859.2	1,208.3	799.0	409.3	928.7	1,763.4
Nov	3,885.1	3,027.4	857.7	1,213.1	814.5	398.7	947.7	1,824.7
Dec	3,889.8	3,034.8	855.0	1,216.8	815.0	401.7	976.1	1,860.9

[1] Savings deposits including money market deposits accounts (MMDAs); data prior to 1982 are savings deposits only.
[2] Small-denomination deposits are those issued in amounts of less than $100,000.
[3] Institutional money funds are not part of non-M1 M2.
Note.—See also Table B–69.
Source: Board of Governors of the Federal Reserve System.

[Averages of daily figures [1]; millions of dollars; seasonally adjusted, except as noted]

Year and month	Adjusted for changes in reserve requirements [2]					Term auction credit (NSA) [3]	Other borrowings of depository institutions from the Federal Reserve (NSA) [3]				
	Reserves of depository institutions				Monetary base		Total	Primary	Secondary	Seasonal	Adjustment
	Total	Non-borrowed	Required	Excess (NSA) [3]							
December:											
1965	12,316	11,872	11,892	423	49,620		444			0	444
1966	12,223	11,690	11,884	339	51,565		532			0	532
1967	13,180	12,952	12,805	375	54,579		228			0	228
1968	13,767	13,021	13,341	426	58,357		746			0	746
1969	14,168	13,049	13,882	286	61,569		1,119			0	1,119
1970	14,558	14,225	14,309	249	65,013		332			0	332
1971	15,230	15,104	15,049	182	69,108		126			0	126
1972	16,645	15,595	16,361	284	75,167		1,050			0	1,050
1973	17,021	15,723	16,717	304	81,073		1,298			41	1,257
1974	17,550	16,823	17,292	258	87,535		727			32	548
1975	17,822	17,692	17,556	266	93,887		130			14	104
1976	18,388	18,335	18,115	274	101,515		53			13	40
1977	18,990	18,420	18,800	190	110,324		569			55	514
1978	19,753	18,885	19,521	232	120,445		868			135	734
1979	20,720	19,248	20,279	442	131,143		1,473			82	1,390
1980	22,015	20,325	21,501	514	142,004		1,690			116	1,571
1981	22,443	21,807	22,124	319	149,021		636			54	433
1982	23,600	22,966	23,100	500	160,127		634			33	415
1983	25,367	24,593	24,806	561	175,467		774			96	676
1984	26,913	23,727	26,078	835	187,252		3,186			113	469
1985	31,569	30,250	30,505	1,063	203,555		1,318			56	763
1986	38,840	38,014	37,667	1,173	223,416		827			38	486
1987	38,913	38,135	37,893	1,019	239,829		777			93	201
1988	40,453	38,738	39,392	1,061	256,897		1,716			130	342
1989	40,486	40,221	39,545	941	267,754		265			84	162
1990	41,766	41,440	40,101	1,665	293,300		326			76	227
1991	45,516	45,324	44,526	990	317,544		192			38	153
1992	54,421	54,298	53,267	1,154	350,912		124			18	105
1993	60,566	60,484	59,497	1,069	386,586		82			31	51
1994	59,466	59,257	58,295	1,171	418,339		209			100	109
1995	56,483	56,226	55,193	1,290	434,580		257			40	217
1996	50,185	50,030	48,766	1,418	452,051		155			68	87
1997	46,875	46,551	45,189	1,687	479,931		324			79	245
1998	45,168	45,052	43,656	1,512	513,920		117			15	101
1999	42,115	41,795	40,821	1,294	593,826		[4] 320			67	179
2000	38,680	38,471	37,356	1,325	584,944		210			111	99
2001	41,420	41,354	39,777	1,643	635,610		67			33	34
2002	40,357	40,278	38,349	2,008	681,623		80			45	35
2003	42,672	42,626	41,625	1,047	720,362		46	17	0	29	
2004	46,600	46,538	44,692	1,909	759,258		63	11	0	52	
2005	45,144	44,976	43,244	1,900	787,313		169	97	0	72	
2006	43,315	43,124	41,507	1,808	811,822		191	111	0	80	
2007	42,584	27,154	40,836	1,748	823,448	11,613	3,818	3,787	1	30	
2006: Jan	44,493	44,383	42,917	1,576	791,767		110	78	0	32	
Feb	44,273	44,220	42,722	1,550	796,502		53	21	2	30	
Mar	44,067	43,898	42,560	1,507	798,972		169	119	0	50	
Apr	44,819	44,572	42,994	1,825	801,486		248	164	0	84	
May	44,717	44,542	42,918	1,799	805,086		175	24	0	151	
June	45,243	44,990	43,460	1,783	805,165		253	16	0	237	
July	44,195	43,844	42,656	1,539	804,245		350	39	0	312	
Aug	42,935	42,566	41,410	1,524	804,637		369	26	0	343	
Sept	43,155	42,751	41,422	1,733	804,838		403	66	0	338	
Oct	42,914	42,685	41,246	1,667	805,254		229	24	0	205	
Nov	43,179	43,020	41,485	1,694	808,348		160	48	0	112	
Dec	43,315	43,124	41,507	1,808	811,822		191	111	0	80	
2007: Jan	42,171	41,960	40,665	1,506	813,455		211	187	0	24	
Feb	42,454	42,424	40,956	1,498	813,448		30	8	0	22	
Mar	42,321	42,267	40,686	1,635	814,991		54	21	5	28	
Apr	42,715	42,635	41,189	1,525	817,205		79	32	0	48	
May	43,197	43,093	41,760	1,436	818,799		103	14	0	90	
June	43,606	43,419	41,904	1,702	820,085		187	43	0	145	
July	41,915	41,653	40,251	1,664	821,476		262	45	0	217	
Aug	44,922	43,948	40,100	4,822	824,512		975	701	19	255	
Sept	42,540	40,973	40,798	1,742	821,732		1,567	1,345	0	221	
Oct	42,507	42,252	41,056	1,450	824,713		254	126	13	115	
Nov	42,646	42,281	40,970	1,676	825,653		366	315	0	50	
Dec	42,584	27,154	40,836	1,748	823,448	11,613	3,818	3,787	1	30	

[1] Data are prorated averages of biweekly (maintenance period) averages of daily figures.
[2] Aggregate reserves incorporate adjustments for discontinuities associated with regulatory changes to reserve requirements. For details on aggregate reserves series see *Federal Reserve Bulletin*.
[3] Not seasonally adjusted (NSA).
[4] Total includes borrowing under the terms and conditions established for the Century Date Change Special Liquidity Facility in effect from October 1, 1999 through April 7, 2000.

Source: Board of Governors of the Federal Reserve System.

[Monthly average; billions of dollars, seasonally adjusted [1]]

Year and month	Total bank credit	Securities in bank credit			Loans and leases in bank credit							
		Total securities	U.S. Treasury and agency securities	Other securities	Total loans and leases [2]	Commercial and industrial	Real estate			Consumer	Security	Other
							Total	Revolving home equity	Other			
December:												
1965	297.1	96.1	64.3	31.9	201.0	69.5	48.9	....	....	45.0	8.0	29.7
1966	318.6	97.2	61.0	36.2	221.4	79.3	53.8	....	....	47.7	8.3	32.4
1967	350.5	111.4	70.7	40.6	239.2	86.5	58.2	....	....	51.2	9.6	33.8
1968	390.5	121.9	73.8	48.1	268.6	96.5	64.8	....	....	57.7	10.5	39.2
1969	401.6	112.4	64.2	48.2	289.2	106.9	69.9	....	....	62.6	10.0	39.8
1970	434.4	129.7	73.4	56.3	304.6	111.6	72.9	....	....	65.3	10.4	44.5
1971	485.2	147.5	79.8	67.7	337.6	118.0	81.7	....	....	73.3	10.9	53.9
1972	555.3	160.6	85.4	75.2	394.7	133.6	98.8	....	....	85.4	14.4	62.5
1973	638.6	168.4	89.7	78.7	470.1	162.8	119.4	....	119.4	98.3	11.2	78.4
1974	701.7	173.8	87.9	85.9	527.9	193.0	132.5	....	132.5	102.1	10.6	89.6
1975	732.9	206.7	117.9	88.9	526.2	184.3	137.2	....	137.2	104.6	12.7	87.5
1976	790.7	228.6	137.3	91.3	562.1	186.3	151.3	....	151.3	115.9	17.7	91.0
1977	876.0	236.3	137.4	98.9	639.7	205.8	178.0	....	178.0	138.1	20.7	97.2
1978	989.4	242.2	138.4	103.8	747.2	239.0	213.5	....	213.5	164.6	19.1	110.9
1979	1,111.4	260.7	147.2	113.4	850.7	282.2	245.0	....	245.0	184.5	17.4	121.6
1980	1,207.1	296.8	173.2	123.6	910.3	314.5	265.7	....	265.7	179.2	17.2	133.6
1981	1,302.7	311.1	181.8	129.3	991.6	353.3	287.5	....	287.5	182.7	20.2	148.0
1982	1,412.3	338.6	204.7	133.9	1,073.7	396.4	303.8	....	303.8	188.2	23.6	161.7
1983	1,566.7	403.8	263.4	140.4	1,163.0	419.1	334.8	....	334.8	213.2	26.5	169.4
1984	1,733.4	406.6	262.9	143.7	1,326.9	479.4	380.8	....	380.8	253.6	34.1	179.0
1985	1,922.2	455.9	273.8	182.2	1,466.3	506.5	431.0	....	431.0	294.5	42.9	191.4
1986	2,106.6	510.0	312.8	197.2	1,596.5	544.0	499.9	....	499.9	314.5	38.6	199.5
1987	2,255.3	535.0	338.9	196.1	1,720.2	575.0	595.7	32.2	563.5	327.7	34.8	187.0
1988	2,445.4	561.4	365.9	195.5	1,884.0	612.0	676.6	42.6	634.0	354.9	39.8	200.7
1989	2,611.8	585.5	401.0	184.6	2,026.3	642.4	769.4	53.5	715.9	375.3	40.6	198.5
1990	2,756.4	635.8	457.5	178.4	2,120.6	644.8	856.7	66.4	790.3	380.8	43.8	194.5
1991	2,871.7	746.2	566.5	179.7	2,125.5	622.2	882.9	74.3	808.6	363.9	52.5	204.0
1992	2,989.6	842.8	666.5	176.3	2,146.8	598.0	905.9	78.5	827.4	356.2	60.6	226.1
1993	3,143.8	916.9	732.7	184.2	2,227.0	588.7	946.8	78.1	868.7	387.4	81.8	222.3
1994	3,317.6	940.2	722.5	217.7	2,377.4	647.9	1,010.5	80.5	930.0	447.9	70.9	200.2
1995	3,599.1	984.6	702.2	282.5	2,614.5	718.6	1,091.0	84.5	1,006.4	491.1	79.5	234.3
1996	3,755.4	984.6	703.0	281.5	2,770.9	778.6	1,143.8	90.9	1,052.9	512.2	70.7	265.6
1997	4,099.1	1,099.0	755.6	343.4	3,000.1	848.0	1,246.2	105.0	1,141.2	502.5	88.2	315.2
1998	4,534.1	1,237.4	797.0	440.4	3,296.7	940.9	1,337.0	103.9	1,233.1	496.9	135.2	386.7
1999	4,762.7	1,280.8	812.6	468.2	3,481.9	992.3	1,475.4	101.5	1,373.9	490.8	139.9	383.5
2000	5,221.4	1,347.4	790.1	557.3	3,874.0	1,080.3	1,658.1	130.2	1,528.0	540.2	160.6	434.8
2001	5,423.3	1,487.2	848.3	638.9	3,936.1	1,019.6	1,785.7	155.8	1,629.9	557.4	134.0	439.3
2002	5,886.5	1,715.0	1,022.6	692.3	4,171.5	956.8	2,030.8	213.7	1,817.1	588.0	171.8	424.2
2003	6,259.2	1,849.1	1,104.8	744.3	4,410.0	897.7	2,225.9	281.0	1,944.9	645.1	195.4	445.9
2004	6,805.8	1,936.2	1,153.3	782.8	4,869.6	920.5	2,568.2	399.9	2,168.2	697.0	194.2	489.7
2005	7,514.0	2,050.4	1,141.4	909.0	5,463.6	1,039.1	2,928.9	446.7	2,482.2	708.0	241.8	545.8
2006	8,349.0	2,227.4	1,196.0	1,031.4	6,121.7	1,193.8	3,369.5	471.3	2,898.1	741.8	266.0	550.7
2007	9,224.4	2,440.9	1,110.9	1,330.0	6,783.5	1,437.1	3,583.6	486.6	3,097.1	804.0	288.5	670.3
2006: Jan	7,569.6	2,066.8	1,152.6	914.1	5,502.8	1,053.8	2,955.3	447.3	2,507.9	712.2	232.9	548.6
Feb	7,652.7	2,104.4	1,180.8	923.7	5,548.3	1,063.0	2,979.5	446.9	2,532.6	711.8	239.7	554.3
Mar	7,724.9	2,115.7	1,185.8	929.9	5,609.2	1,074.3	3,009.7	450.2	2,559.5	722.5	244.8	557.9
Apr	7,815.7	2,168.9	1,198.2	970.7	5,646.9	1,091.6	3,033.2	446.1	2,587.1	727.5	235.1	559.5
May	7,929.1	2,204.5	1,194.9	1,009.7	5,724.6	1,111.8	3,059.1	442.4	2,616.7	734.5	251.2	567.9
June	7,939.6	2,187.3	1,200.5	986.7	5,752.4	1,119.8	3,101.8	444.8	2,657.0	729.2	231.6	570.0
July	7,987.1	2,192.5	1,212.4	980.1	5,794.6	1,131.2	3,140.7	452.0	2,688.7	722.5	229.9	570.3
Aug	8,049.0	2,205.6	1,221.1	984.5	5,843.4	1,160.4	3,142.4	448.1	2,694.2	728.4	237.6	574.5
Sept	8,071.8	2,192.5	1,210.8	981.8	5,879.2	1,164.8	3,165.0	450.6	2,714.4	727.8	249.9	571.8
Oct	8,225.2	2,216.2	1,222.9	993.2	6,009.0	1,178.2	3,313.6	466.4	2,847.1	729.5	252.5	535.3
Nov	8,274.5	2,225.0	1,215.3	1,009.7	6,049.5	1,183.5	3,330.5	468.1	2,862.4	734.5	261.6	539.6
Dec	8,349.0	2,227.4	1,196.0	1,031.4	6,121.7	1,193.8	3,369.5	471.3	2,898.1	741.8	266.0	550.7
2007: Jan	8,407.5	2,233.4	1,198.5	1,034.9	6,174.0	1,201.4	3,400.4	473.3	2,927.1	749.8	267.8	554.6
Feb	8,479.7	2,248.2	1,202.9	1,045.3	6,231.5	1,211.5	3,430.9	471.0	2,959.9	749.8	278.6	560.8
Mar	8,458.7	2,272.4	1,210.5	1,061.9	6,186.3	1,219.9	3,373.4	462.6	2,910.8	747.2	284.7	561.1
Apr	8,521.3	2,284.0	1,186.3	1,097.7	6,237.3	1,226.8	3,396.4	458.1	2,938.2	753.2	282.0	578.9
May	8,578.6	2,289.5	1,173.9	1,115.6	6,289.2	1,243.8	3,414.0	458.3	2,955.7	756.7	295.5	579.2
June	8,628.8	2,308.9	1,177.8	1,131.1	6,319.9	1,261.8	3,441.6	459.6	2,982.0	767.0	269.2	580.3
July	8,694.4	2,318.3	1,180.6	1,137.7	6,376.1	1,281.0	3,458.6	462.4	2,996.2	774.7	270.6	591.2
Aug	8,821.3	2,342.6	1,186.1	1,156.5	6,478.7	1,313.4	3,471.2	465.9	3,005.3	777.2	285.7	631.3
Sept	8,947.4	2,371.8	1,171.0	1,200.7	6,575.7	1,361.3	3,496.0	470.1	3,025.9	784.4	280.7	653.2
Oct	9,063.8	2,403.1	1,135.4	1,267.7	6,660.7	1,396.4	3,549.6	476.3	3,073.3	781.8	264.4	668.4
Nov	9,181.7	2,466.5	1,118.5	1,348.0	6,715.2	1,411.9	3,569.4	481.3	3,088.1	792.3	278.4	663.3
Dec	9,224.4	2,440.9	1,110.9	1,330.0	6,783.5	1,437.1	3,583.6	486.6	3,097.1	804.0	288.5	670.3

[1] Data are prorated averages of Wednesday values for domestically chartered commercial banks, branches and agencies of foreign banks, New York State investment companies (through September 1996), and Edge Act and agreement corporations.
[2] Excludes Federal funds sold to, reverse repurchase agreements (RPs) with, and loans to commercial banks in the United States.

Source: Board of Governors of the Federal Reserve System.

TABLE B–73.—*Bond yields and interest rates, 1929–2007*

[Percent per annum]

Year and month	U.S. Treasury securities — Bills (new issues)[1] 3-month	6-month	Constant maturities[2] 3-year	10-year	30-year	Corporate bonds (Moody's) Aaa[3]	Baa	High-grade municipal bonds (Standard & Poor's)	New-home mortgage yields[4]	Prime rate charged by banks[5]	Discount window (Federal Reserve Bank of New York)[5,6] Primary credit	Adjustment credit	Federal funds rate[7]
1929						4.73	5.90	4.27		5.50–6.00		5.16	
1933	0.515					4.49	7.76	4.71		1.50–4.00		2.56	
1939	.023					3.01	4.96	2.76		1.50		1.00	
1940	.014					2.84	4.75	2.50		1.50		1.00	
1941	.103					2.77	4.33	2.10		1.50		1.00	
1942	.326					2.83	4.28	2.36		1.50		[8]1.00	
1943	.373					2.73	3.91	2.06		1.50		[8]1.00	
1944	.375					2.72	3.61	1.86		1.50		[8]1.00	
1945	.375					2.62	3.29	1.67		1.50		[8]1.00	
1946	.375					2.53	3.05	1.64		1.50		[8]1.00	
1947	.594					2.61	3.24	2.01		1.50–1.75		1.00	
1948	1.040					2.82	3.47	2.40		1.75–2.00		1.34	
1949	1.102					2.66	3.42	2.21		2.00		1.50	
1950	1.218					2.62	3.24	1.98		2.07		1.59	
1951	1.552					2.86	3.41	2.00		2.56		1.75	
1952	1.766					2.96	3.52	2.19		3.00		1.75	
1953	1.931		2.47	2.85		3.20	3.74	2.72		3.17		1.99	
1954	.953		1.63	2.40		2.90	3.51	2.37		3.05		1.60	
1955	1.753		2.47	2.82		3.06	3.53	2.53		3.16		1.89	1.78
1956	2.658		3.19	3.18		3.36	3.88	2.93		3.77		2.77	2.73
1957	3.267		3.98	3.65		3.89	4.71	3.60		4.20		3.12	3.11
1958	1.839		2.84	3.32		3.79	4.73	3.56		3.83		2.15	1.57
1959	3.405	3.832	4.46	4.33		4.38	5.05	3.95		4.48		3.36	3.30
1960	2.928	3.247	3.98	4.12		4.41	5.19	3.73		4.82		3.53	3.22
1961	2.378	2.605	3.54	3.88		4.35	5.08	3.46		4.50		3.00	1.96
1962	2.778	2.908	3.47	3.95		4.33	5.02	3.18		4.50		3.00	2.68
1963	3.157	3.253	3.67	4.00		4.26	4.86	3.23	5.89	4.50		3.23	3.18
1964	3.549	3.686	4.03	4.19		4.40	4.83	3.22	5.83	4.50		3.55	3.50
1965	3.954	4.055	4.22	4.28		4.49	4.87	3.27	5.81	4.54		4.04	4.07
1966	4.881	5.082	5.23	4.92		5.13	5.67	3.82	6.25	5.63		4.50	5.11
1967	4.321	4.630	5.03	5.07		5.51	6.23	3.98	6.46	5.61		4.19	4.22
1968	5.339	5.470	5.68	5.65		6.18	6.94	4.51	6.97	6.30		5.16	5.66
1969	6.677	6.853	7.02	6.67		7.03	7.81	5.81	7.81	7.96		5.87	8.20
1970	6.458	6.562	7.29	7.35		8.04	9.11	6.51	8.45	7.91		5.95	7.18
1971	4.348	4.511	5.65	6.16		7.39	8.56	5.70	7.74	5.72		4.88	4.66
1972	4.071	4.466	5.72	6.21		7.21	8.16	5.27	7.60	5.25		4.50	4.43
1973	7.041	7.178	6.95	6.84		7.44	8.24	5.18	7.96	8.03		6.44	8.73
1974	7.886	7.926	7.82	7.56		8.57	9.50	6.09	8.92	10.81		7.83	10.50
1975	5.838	6.122	7.49	7.99		8.83	10.61	6.89	9.00	7.86		6.25	5.82
1976	4.989	5.266	6.77	7.61		8.43	9.75	6.49	9.00	6.84		5.50	5.04
1977	5.265	5.510	6.69	7.42	7.75	8.02	8.97	5.56	9.02	6.83		5.46	5.54
1978	7.221	7.572	8.29	8.41	8.49	8.73	9.49	5.90	9.56	9.06		7.46	7.93
1979	10.041	10.017	9.71	9.44	9.28	9.63	10.69	6.39	10.78	12.67		10.28	11.19
1980	11.506	11.374	11.55	11.46	11.27	11.94	13.67	8.51	12.66	15.27		11.77	13.36
1981	14.029	13.776	14.44	13.91	13.45	14.17	16.04	11.23	14.70	18.87		13.42	16.38
1982	10.686	11.084	12.92	13.00	12.76	13.79	16.11	11.57	15.14	14.86		11.02	12.26
1983	8.63	8.75	10.45	11.10	11.18	12.04	13.55	9.47	12.57	10.79		8.50	9.09
1984	9.58	9.80	11.89	12.44	12.41	12.71	14.19	10.15	12.38	12.04		8.80	10.23
1985	7.48	7.66	9.64	10.62	10.79	11.37	12.72	9.18	11.55	9.93		7.69	8.10
1986	5.98	6.03	7.06	7.68	7.78	9.02	10.39	7.38	10.17	8.33		6.33	6.81
1987	5.82	6.05	7.68	8.39	8.59	9.38	10.58	7.73	9.31	8.21		5.66	6.66
1988	6.69	6.92	8.26	8.85	8.96	9.71	10.83	7.76	9.19	9.32		6.20	7.57
1989	8.12	8.04	8.55	8.49	8.45	9.26	10.18	7.24	10.13	10.87		6.93	9.21
1990	7.51	7.47	8.26	8.55	8.61	9.32	10.36	7.25	10.05	10.01		6.98	8.10
1991	5.42	5.49	6.82	7.86	8.14	8.77	9.80	6.89	9.32	8.46		5.45	5.69
1992	3.45	3.57	5.30	7.01	7.67	8.14	8.98	6.41	8.24	6.25		3.25	3.52
1993	3.02	3.14	4.44	5.87	6.59	7.22	7.93	5.63	7.20	6.00		3.00	3.02
1994	4.29	4.66	6.27	7.09	7.37	7.96	8.62	6.19	7.49	7.15		3.60	4.21
1995	5.51	5.59	6.25	6.57	6.88	7.59	8.20	5.95	7.87	8.83		5.21	5.83
1996	5.02	5.09	5.99	6.44	6.71	7.37	8.05	5.75	7.80	8.27		5.02	5.30
1997	5.07	5.18	6.10	6.35	6.61	7.26	7.86	5.55	7.71	8.44		5.00	5.46
1998	4.81	4.85	5.14	5.26	5.58	6.53	7.22	5.12	7.07	8.35		4.92	5.35
1999	4.66	4.76	5.49	5.65	5.87	7.04	7.87	5.43	7.04	8.00		4.62	4.97
2000	5.85	5.92	6.22	6.03	5.94	7.62	8.36	5.77	7.52	9.23		5.73	6.24
2001	3.45	3.39	4.09	5.02	5.49	7.08	7.95	5.19	7.00	6.91		3.40	3.88
2002	1.62	1.69	3.10	4.61		6.49	7.80	5.05	6.43	4.67		1.17	1.67
2003	1.02	1.06	2.10	4.01		5.67	6.77	4.73	5.80	4.12	2.12		1.13
2004	1.38	1.58	2.78	4.27		5.63	6.39	4.63	5.77	4.34	2.34		1.35
2005	3.16	3.40	3.93	4.29		5.24	6.06	4.29	5.94	6.19	4.19		3.22
2006	4.73	4.81	4.77	4.80	4.91	5.59	6.48	4.42	6.63	7.96	5.96		4.97
2007	4.41	4.48	4.35	4.63	4.84	5.56	6.48	4.42	6.41	8.05	5.86		5.02

[1] Rate on new issues within period; bank-discount basis.

[2] Yields on the more actively traded issues adjusted to constant maturities by the Department of the Treasury. The 30-year Treasury constant maturity series was discontinued on February 18, 2002, and reintroduced on February 9, 2006.

[3] Beginning with December 7, 2001, data for corporate Aaa series are industrial bonds only.

See next page for continuation of table.

TABLE B–73.—Bond yields and interest rates, 1929–2007—Continued

[Percent per annum]

Year and month	U.S. Treasury securities					Corporate bonds (Moody's)		High-grade municipal bonds (Standard & Poor's)	New-home mortgage yields [4]	Prime rate charged by banks [5]	Discount window (Federal Reserve Bank of New York) [5,6]		Federal funds rate [7]
	Bills (new issues) [1]		Constant maturities [2]								Primary credit	Adjustment credit	
	3-month	6-month	3-year	10-year	30-year	Aaa [3]	Baa						
										High-low	High-low	High-low	
2003: Jan	1.17	1.21	2.18	4.05		6.17	7.35	4.88	6.12	4.25–4.25	2.25–2.25	0.75–0.75	1.24
Feb	1.16	1.18	2.05	3.90		5.95	7.06	4.80	5.82	4.25–4.25	2.25–2.25		1.26
Mar	1.13	1.12	1.98	3.81		5.89	6.95	4.72	5.75	4.25–4.25	2.25–2.25		1.25
Apr	1.14	1.15	2.06	3.96		5.74	6.85	4.71	5.92	4.25–4.25	2.25–2.25		1.25
May	1.08	1.09	1.75	3.57		5.22	6.38	4.35	5.75	4.25–4.25	2.25–2.25		1.26
June	.95	.94	1.51	3.33		4.97	6.19	4.32	5.51	4.25–4.00	2.25–2.00		1.22
July	.90	.95	1.93	3.98		5.49	6.62	4.71	5.53	4.00–4.00	2.00–2.00		1.01
Aug	.96	1.04	2.44	4.45		5.88	7.01	5.08	5.77	4.00–4.00	2.00–2.00		1.03
Sept	.95	1.02	2.23	4.27		5.72	6.79	4.91	5.97	4.00–4.00	2.00–2.00		1.01
Oct	.93	1.01	2.26	4.29		5.70	6.73	4.84	5.92	4.00–4.00	2.00–2.00		1.01
Nov	.94	1.02	2.45	4.30		5.65	6.66	4.74	5.92	4.00–4.00	2.00–2.00		1.00
Dec	.90	1.00	2.44	4.27		5.62	6.60	4.65	5.59	4.00–4.00	2.00–2.00		.98
2004: Jan	.89	.98	2.27	4.15		5.54	6.44	4.53	5.48	4.00–4.00	2.00–2.00		1.00
Feb	.92	.99	2.25	4.08		5.50	6.27	4.48	5.72	4.00–4.00	2.00–2.00		1.01
Mar	.94	.99	2.00	3.83		5.33	6.11	4.39	5.42	4.00–4.00	2.00–2.00		1.00
Apr	.94	1.06	2.57	4.35		5.73	6.46	4.84	5.49	4.00–4.00	2.00–2.00		1.00
May	1.04	1.31	3.10	4.72		6.04	6.75	5.03	5.77	4.00–4.00	2.00–2.00		1.00
June	1.27	1.58	3.26	4.73		6.01	6.78	5.00	5.81	4.25–4.00	2.25–2.00		1.03
July	1.35	1.68	3.05	4.50		5.82	6.62	4.82	5.96	4.25–4.25	2.25–2.25		1.26
Aug	1.48	1.72	2.88	4.28		5.65	6.46	4.65	5.88	4.50–4.25	2.50–2.25		1.43
Sept	1.65	1.86	2.83	4.13		5.46	6.27	4.49	5.72	4.75–4.50	2.75–2.50		1.61
Oct	1.75	2.00	2.85	4.10		5.47	6.21	4.43	5.82	4.75–4.75	2.75–2.75		1.76
Nov	2.06	2.26	3.09	4.19		5.52	6.20	4.48	5.91	5.00–4.75	3.00–2.75		1.93
Dec	2.20	2.45	3.21	4.23		5.47	6.15	4.40	6.02	5.25–5.00	3.25–3.00		2.16
2005: Jan	2.32	2.60	3.39	4.22		5.36	6.02	4.28	6.01	5.25–5.25	3.25–3.25		2.28
Feb	2.53	2.76	3.54	4.17		5.20	5.82	4.14	5.75	5.50–5.25	3.50–3.25		2.50
Mar	2.75	3.00	3.91	4.50		5.40	6.06	4.42	5.82	5.75–5.50	3.75–3.50		2.63
Apr	2.79	3.06	3.79	4.34		5.33	6.05	4.31	5.84	5.75–5.75	3.75–3.75		2.79
May	2.86	3.10	3.72	4.14		5.15	6.01	4.16	5.82	6.00–5.75	4.00–3.75		3.00
June	2.99	3.13	3.69	4.00		4.96	5.86	4.08	5.76	6.25–6.00	4.25–4.00		3.04
July	3.22	3.41	3.91	4.18		5.06	5.95	4.15	5.76	6.25–6.25	4.25–4.25		3.26
Aug	3.45	3.67	4.08	4.26		5.09	5.96	4.21	5.83	6.50–6.25	4.50–4.25		3.50
Sept	3.47	3.68	3.96	4.20		5.13	6.03	4.28	5.99	6.75–6.50	4.75–4.50		3.62
Oct	3.70	3.98	4.29	4.46		5.35	6.30	4.49	6.03	6.75–6.75	4.75–4.75		3.78
Nov	3.90	4.16	4.43	4.54		5.42	6.39	4.53	6.20	7.00–7.00	5.00–5.00		4.00
Dec	3.89	4.19	4.39	4.47		5.37	6.32	4.43	6.39	7.25–7.00	5.25–5.00		4.16
2006: Jan	4.20	4.30	4.35	4.42		5.29	6.24	4.31	6.12	7.50–7.25	5.50–5.25		4.29
Feb	4.41	4.51	4.64	4.57	4.54	5.35	6.27	4.41	6.40	7.50–7.50	5.50–5.50		4.49
Mar	4.51	4.61	4.74	4.72	4.73	5.53	6.41	4.44	6.53	7.75–7.50	5.75–5.50		4.59
Apr	4.59	4.72	4.89	4.99	5.06	5.84	6.68	4.60	6.64	7.75–7.75	5.75–5.75		4.79
May	4.72	4.81	4.97	5.11	5.20	5.95	6.75	4.61	6.69	8.00–7.75	6.00–5.75		4.94
June	4.79	4.95	5.09	5.11	5.15	5.89	6.78	4.64	6.79	8.25–8.00	6.25–6.00		4.99
July	4.96	5.09	5.07	5.09	5.13	5.85	6.76	4.64	6.81	8.25–8.25	6.25–6.25		5.24
Aug	4.98	4.99	4.85	4.88	5.00	5.68	6.59	4.43	6.87	8.25–8.25	6.25–6.25		5.25
Sept	4.82	4.90	4.69	4.72	4.85	5.51	6.43	4.30	6.72	8.25–8.25	6.25–6.25		5.25
Oct	4.89	4.91	4.72	4.73	4.85	5.51	6.42	4.32	6.69	8.25–8.25	6.25–6.25		5.25
Nov	4.95	4.96	4.64	4.60	4.69	5.33	6.20	4.17	6.55	8.25–8.25	6.25–6.25		5.25
Dec	4.85	4.88	4.58	4.56	4.68	5.32	6.22	4.17	6.37	8.25–8.25	6.25–6.25		5.24
2007: Jan	4.96	4.94	4.79	4.76	4.85	5.40	6.34	4.29	6.35	8.25–8.25	6.25–6.25		5.25
Feb	5.02	4.97	4.75	4.72	4.82	5.39	6.28	4.21	6.31	8.25–8.25	6.25–6.25		5.26
Mar	4.97	4.90	4.51	4.56	4.72	5.30	6.27	4.18	6.22	8.25–8.25	6.25–6.25		5.26
Apr	4.88	4.87	4.60	4.69	4.87	5.47	6.39	4.32	6.21	8.25–8.25	6.25–6.25		5.25
May	4.77	4.80	4.69	4.75	4.90	5.47	6.39	4.37	6.22	8.25–8.25	6.25–6.25		5.25
June	4.63	4.77	5.00	5.10	5.20	5.79	6.70	4.64	6.54	8.25–8.25	6.25–6.25		5.25
July	4.84	4.86	4.82	5.00	5.11	5.73	6.65	4.64	6.70	8.25–8.25	6.25–6.25		5.26
Aug	4.34	4.56	4.34	4.67	4.93	5.79	6.65	4.73	6.73	8.25–8.25	6.25–5.75		5.02
Sept	4.01	4.13	4.06	4.52	4.79	5.74	6.59	4.57	6.58	8.25–7.75	5.75–5.25		4.94
Oct	3.97	4.08	4.01	4.53	4.77	5.66	6.48	4.41	6.55	7.75–7.50	5.25–5.00		4.76
Nov	3.49	3.63	3.35	4.15	4.52	5.44	6.40	4.45	6.42	7.50–7.50	5.00–5.00		4.49
Dec	3.08	3.29	3.13	4.10	4.53	5.49	6.65	4.22	6.21	7.50–7.25	5.00–4.75		4.24

[4] Effective rate (in the primary market) on conventional mortgages, reflecting fees and charges as well as contract rate and assuming, on the average, repayment at end of 10 years. Rates beginning with January 1973 not strictly comparable with prior rates.

[5] For monthly data, high and low for the period. Prime rate for 1929-33 and 1947-48 are ranges of the rate in effect during the period.

[6] Primary credit replaced adjustment credit as the Federal Reserve's principal discount window lending program effective January 9, 2003.

[7] Since July 19, 1975, the daily effective rate is an average of the rates on a given day weighted by the volume of transactions at these rates. Prior to that date, the daily effective rate was the rate considered most representative of the day's transactions, usually the one at which most transactions occurred.

[8] From October 30, 1942 to April 24, 1946, a preferential rate of 0.50 percent was in effect for advances secured by Government securities maturing in one year or less.

Sources: Department of the Treasury, Board of Governors of the Federal Reserve System, Federal Housing Finance Board, Moody's Investors Service, and Standard & Poor's.

Table B–74.—*Credit market borrowing, 1999–2007*

[Billions of dollars; quarterly data at seasonally adjusted annual rates]

Item	1999	2000	2001	2002	2003	2004	2005	2006
NONFINANCIAL SECTORS								
Domestic	1,028.8	843.9	1,155.6	1,402.4	1,677.3	1,977.1	2,210.6	2,329.9
By instrument	1,028.8	843.9	1,155.6	1,402.4	1,677.3	1,977.1	2,210.6	2,329.9
Commercial paper	37.4	48.1	–83.0	–57.9	–35.1	16.8	–7.9	23.4
Treasury securities	–71.0	–294.9	–5.1	257.1	398.4	362.5	307.3	183.7
Agency- and GSE-backed securities [1]	–0.2	–1.0	–.5	.5	–2.4	–.6	–.4	–.3
Municipal securities	54.4	23.6	122.8	159.4	137.6	130.5	194.9	177.3
Corporate bonds	221.7	162.6	347.7	132.3	158.3	77.7	59.9	218.6
Banks loans n.e.c.	77.3	95.1	–87.2	–106.6	–77.0	10.8	137.6	173.4
Other loans and advances	26.1	77.4	4.4	15.7	5.5	20.4	47.7	47.3
Mortgages	570.8	556.4	705.8	893.9	987.6	1,243.9	1,377.0	1,402.2
Home	427.6	427.0	551.5	759.4	798.3	1,041.6	1,060.7	1,076.6
Multifamily residential	39.1	26.9	40.3	37.1	71.2	49.5	74.3	58.8
Commercial	100.0	105.1	110.3	90.5	119.4	150.2	237.4	259.3
Farm	4.1	–2.5	3.8	6.9	–1.3	2.7	4.6	7.5
Consumer credit	112.4	176.5	150.7	107.9	104.4	115.0	94.5	104.4
By sector	1,028.8	843.9	1,155.6	1,402.4	1,677.3	1,977.1	2,210.6	2,329.9
Household sector	494.0	583.9	671.5	833.7	980.5	1,077.4	1,135.7	1,203.1
Nonfinancial business	567.5	540.4	384.0	167.2	180.6	422.5	596.5	792.2
Corporate	370.2	341.7	215.2	12.1	90.1	171.8	256.3	447.0
Nonfarm noncorporate	194.3	196.8	162.2	148.0	92.1	244.7	327.5	326.9
Farm	3.0	1.9	6.7	7.1	–1.6	6.1	12.7	18.4
State and local governments	38.5	15.5	105.7	143.9	120.3	115.3	171.6	151.1
Federal Government	–71.2	–295.9	–5.6	257.6	396.0	361.9	306.9	183.4
Foreign borrowing in the United States	19.0	63.0	–13.7	92.9	36.9	124.8	102.8	250.4
Commercial paper	16.3	31.7	15.8	58.3	12.9	62.8	38.5	93.1
Bonds	7.9	21.2	–18.5	31.6	28.7	61.8	54.5	150.9
Bank loans n.e.c.	0.5	11.4	–7.3	5.3	–2.5	3.8	14.5	13.8
Other loans and advances	–5.7	–1.3	–3.8	–2.3	–2.1	–3.6	–4.6	–7.4
Nonfinancial domestic and foreign borrowing	1,047.7	906.9	1,141.9	1,495.3	1,714.3	2,101.9	2,313.5	2,580.3
FINANCIAL SECTORS								
By instrument	1,024.2	786.9	871.1	869.3	1,068.2	989.8	1,069.9	1,301.7
Open market paper	176.2	131.7	–124.5	–99.5	–59.7	26.6	214.5	200.7
GSE issues [1]	318.8	235.2	304.1	219.8	250.9	75.0	–84.0	45.2
Agency- and GSE-backed mortgage pool securities [1]	274.6	199.7	338.5	326.8	330.6	62.7	174.2	295.2
Corporate bonds	148.6	166.1	306.6	383.3	485.7	667.3	690.1	796.4
Banks loans n.e.c.	–7.9	6.9	18.7	21.1	21.4	58.1	17.0	–64.1
Other loans and advances	107.1	42.5	25.5	6.8	31.2	74.1	44.4	21.2
Mortgages	6.9	4.9	2.2	11.0	8.2	25.9	13.9	7.0
By sector	1,024.2	786.9	871.1	869.3	1,068.2	989.8	1,069.9	1,301.7
Commercial banking	67.2	60.0	52.9	49.7	48.5	78.4	85.1	177.4
U.S.-chartered commercial banks	41.8	36.8	30.2	29.9	13.2	18.7	36.9	107.5
Foreign banking offices in U.S.	–0.4	.0	–.9	–.4	–.1	.1	.0	–.3
Bank holding companies	25.8	23.2	23.6	20.3	35.4	59.5	48.2	70.2
Savings institutions	48.0	27.3	–2.0	–23.4	34.5	89.0	23.8	–111.9
Credit unions	2.2	.0	1.5	2.0	2.2	2.3	3.3	4.2
Life insurance companies	0.7	–.7	.6	2.0	2.9	3.0	.4	2.7
Government-sponsored enterprises	318.8	235.2	304.1	219.8	250.9	75.0	–84.0	45.2
Agency- and GSE-backed mortgage pools [1]	274.6	199.7	338.5	326.8	330.6	62.7	174.2	295.2
Asset-backed securities issuers	150.5	162.6	255.9	212.5	242.1	425.3	667.3	771.0
Finance companies	75.5	86.3	10.9	66.2	111.1	134.3	33.5	34.8
REITs	12.3	2.6	3.2	27.3	31.5	98.3	59.8	41.1
Brokers and dealers	–17.2	15.6	1.4	–1.7	6.4	15.2	.1	6.4
Funding corporations	91.6	–1.6	–96.0	–11.9	7.6	6.1	106.5	35.4
ALL SECTORS, BY INSTRUMENT								
Total	2,072.0	1,693.8	2,013.0	2,364.6	2,782.5	3,091.7	3,383.4	3,881.9
Open market paper	229.9	211.6	–191.6	–99.1	–82.0	106.2	245.1	317.1
Treasury securities	–71.0	–294.9	–5.1	257.1	398.4	362.5	307.3	183.7
Agency- and GSE-backed securities [1]	593.1	433.9	642.1	547.2	579.1	137.1	89.7	340.0
Municipal securities	54.4	23.6	122.8	159.4	137.6	130.5	194.9	177.3
Corporate and foreign bonds	378.2	349.9	635.8	547.2	672.7	806.8	804.4	1,166.0
Bank loans n.e.c.	69.8	113.3	–75.8	–80.2	–58.1	72.7	169.1	123.1
Other loans and advances	127.5	118.6	26.1	20.2	34.6	90.9	87.4	61.1
Mortgages	577.7	561.3	708.0	904.8	995.8	1,269.8	1,390.9	1,409.2
Consumer credit	112.4	176.5	150.7	107.9	104.4	115.0	94.5	104.4

[1] Government-sponsored enterprises (GSE).

See next page for continuation of table.

[Billions of dollars; quarterly data at seasonally adjusted annual rates]

Item	2006				2007		
	I	II	III	IV	I	II	III
NONFINANCIAL SECTORS							
Domestic	2,645.8	2,262.2	1,990.3	2,421.5	2,313.9	2,134.4	2,670.8
By instrument	2,645.8	2,262.2	1,990.3	2,421.5	2,313.9	2,134.4	2,670.8
Commercial paper	18.8	16.8	−37.7	95.6	−1.6	31.3	−48.6
Treasury securities	377.0	49.7	172.4	135.8	327.5	−70.7	435.9
Agency- and GSE-backed securities [1]	−1.0	.2	−1.0	.5	−1.3	−.1	−.8
Municipal securities	114.6	172.6	169.2	252.8	248.5	246.9	205.0
Corporate bonds	211.0	204.1	138.6	320.9	284.8	388.0	212.0
Banks loans n.e.c.	208.2	99.0	163.1	223.2	115.7	99.0	430.6
Other loans and advances	65.1	93.9	−30.0	60.1	69.7	64.1	196.3
Mortgages	1,590.8	1,498.2	1,296.1	1,223.7	1,157.7	1,246.6	1,089.9
Home	1,281.9	1,200.4	964.9	859.0	815.1	830.1	732.4
Multifamily residential	65.6	49.6	44.0	76.0	61.5	95.1	100.6
Commercial	235.6	241.3	279.6	280.7	275.8	317.1	251.8
Farm	7.7	6.9	7.6	7.9	5.3	4.4	5.1
Consumer credit	61.3	127.8	119.7	108.9	113.0	129.2	150.5
By sector	2,645.8	2,262.2	1,990.3	2,421.5	2,313.9	2,134.4	2,670.8
Household sector	1,322.2	1,351.0	1,076.3	1,063.1	921.2	1,004.6	924.8
Nonfinancial business	844.9	724.8	595.4	1,003.8	842.7	987.6	1,132.9
Corporate	488.4	401.5	262.9	635.3	537.2	603.1	661.5
Nonfarm noncorporate	336.5	306.6	318.6	345.7	282.9	377.5	462.3
Farm	19.9	16.7	13.9	22.9	22.6	7.0	9.2
State and local governments	102.8	136.4	147.2	218.2	223.8	212.9	178.1
Federal Government	376.0	49.9	171.4	136.3	326.2	−70.8	435.0
Foreign borrowing in the United States	140.1	115.7	518.1	227.7	158.2	257.8	−3.5
Commercial paper	83.4	−51.7	357.8	−17.2	8.8	22.4	−199.4
Bonds	60.8	144.6	180.2	218.0	174.8	191.1	170.1
Bank loans n.e.c.	5.2	30.8	−12.2	31.6	−22.5	47.1	26.5
Other loans and advances	−9.3	−8.0	−7.7	−4.6	−3.0	−2.9	−.7
Nonfinancial domestic and foreign borrowing	2,785.8	2,377.8	2,508.3	2,649.2	2,472.1	2,392.2	2,667.4
FINANCIAL SECTORS							
By instrument	1,370.7	1,593.7	939.9	1,302.4	1,170.5	1,418.5	2,321.1
Open market paper	190.9	331.7	80.7	199.6	206.5	357.0	−681.7
GSE issues [1]	−0.5	204.7	−73.9	50.3	28.3	161.4	556.6
Agency- and GSE-backed mortgage pool securities [1]	318.2	299.6	284.2	278.7	463.2	535.0	622.6
Corporate bonds	803.4	728.2	654.0	1,000.2	467.2	306.9	965.2
Banks loans n.e.c.	18.9	−15.7	−42.8	−216.8	51.0	48.8	103.4
Other loans and advances	20.8	38.1	29.9	−3.9	−30.5	.4	746.2
Mortgages	19.0	7.1	7.8	−5.8	−15.2	9.0	8.7
By sector	1,370.7	1,593.7	939.9	1,302.4	1,170.5	1,418.5	2,321.1
Commercial banking	85.7	171.8	51.6	400.6	90.7	147.3	496.0
U.S.-chartered commercial banks	49.0	58.7	14.9	307.6	8.6	22.4	355.1
Foreign banking offices in U.S.	0.2	−.2	−.2	−.9	−.4	.2	−.7
Bank holding companies	36.6	113.4	36.9	94.0	82.4	124.7	141.5
Savings institutions	0.5	−1.8	17.1	−463.3	−20.5	−24.9	363.8
Credit unions	−0.2	6.8	2.0	8.4	−10.5	10.6	37.9
Life insurance companies	2.8	1.3	2.4	4.3	4.9	12.6	26.9
Government-sponsored enterprises	−0.5	204.7	−73.9	50.3	28.3	161.4	556.6
Agency- and GSE-backed mortgage pools [1]	318.2	299.6	284.2	278.7	463.2	535.0	622.6
Asset-backed securities issuers	805.8	671.9	700.1	906.2	435.1	485.3	49.3
Finance companies	17.7	89.1	−36.6	69.0	13.9	9.3	119.7
REITs	61.4	56.5	32.8	14.0	2.2	−9.9	4.7
Brokers and dealers	35.1	6.5	5.0	−20.9	59.5	39.9	−29.3
Funding corporations	44.1	87.2	−44.8	55.0	103.6	51.9	73.0
ALL SECTORS, BY INSTRUMENT							
Total	4,156.5	3,971.5	3,448.2	3,951.5	3,642.5	3,810.7	4,988.5
Open market paper	293.0	296.7	400.8	278.0	213.7	410.6	−929.7
Treasury securities	377.0	49.7	172.4	135.8	327.5	−70.7	435.9
Agency- and GSE-backed securities [1]	316.7	504.6	209.3	329.5	490.2	696.3	1,178.4
Municipal securities	114.6	172.6	169.2	252.8	248.5	246.9	205.0
Corporate and foreign bonds	1,075.2	1,076.9	972.7	1,539.1	926.8	886.1	1,347.3
Bank loans n.e.c.	232.3	114.2	108.1	38.0	144.2	195.0	560.5
Other loans and advances	76.5	123.9	−7.8	51.6	36.2	61.7	941.9
Mortgages	1,609.9	1,505.3	1,303.9	1,217.9	1,142.5	1,255.6	1,098.6
Consumer credit	61.3	127.8	119.7	108.9	113.0	129.2	150.5

Source: Board of Governors of the Federal Reserve System.

TABLE B–75.—*Mortgage debt outstanding by type of property and of financing, 1949–2007*

[Billions of dollars]

End of year or quarter	All properties	Farm properties	Nonfarm properties				Nonfarm properties by type of mortgage					
							Government underwritten				Conventional [2]	
			Total	1- to 4-family houses	Multi-family properties	Com-mercial properties	Total [1]	1- to 4-family houses			Total	1- to 4-family houses
								Total	FHA-insured	VA-guar-anteed		
1949	62.3	5.6	56.7	37.3	8.6	10.8	17.1	15.0	6.9	8.1	39.6	22.3
1950	72.7	6.0	66.6	45.1	10.1	11.5	22.1	18.8	8.5	10.3	44.6	26.2
1951	82.1	6.6	75.6	51.6	11.5	12.5	26.6	22.9	9.7	13.2	49.0	28.8
1952	91.3	7.2	84.1	58.4	12.3	13.4	29.3	25.4	10.8	14.6	54.8	33.1
1953	101.1	7.7	93.4	65.9	12.9	14.5	32.1	28.1	12.0	16.1	61.3	37.9
1954	113.6	8.1	105.4	75.7	13.5	16.3	36.2	32.1	12.8	19.3	69.3	43.6
1955	129.9	9.0	120.9	88.2	14.3	18.3	42.9	38.9	14.3	24.6	78.0	49.3
1956	144.5	9.8	134.6	99.0	14.9	20.7	47.8	43.9	15.5	28.4	86.8	55.1
1957	156.5	10.4	146.1	107.6	15.3	23.2	51.6	47.2	16.5	30.7	94.6	60.4
1958	171.8	11.1	160.7	117.7	16.8	26.1	55.2	50.1	19.7	30.4	105.5	67.6
1959	190.8	12.1	178.7	130.8	18.7	29.2	59.3	53.8	23.8	30.0	119.4	77.0
1960	207.4	12.8	194.6	141.8	20.3	32.4	62.3	56.4	26.7	29.7	132.2	85.4
1961	228.0	13.9	214.1	154.6	23.0	36.5	65.6	59.1	29.5	29.6	148.5	95.5
1962	251.4	15.2	236.2	169.3	25.8	41.1	69.4	62.2	32.3	29.9	166.9	107.1
1963	278.5	16.8	261.6	186.4	29.0	46.2	73.4	65.9	35.0	30.9	188.2	120.5
1964	305.9	18.9	287.0	203.4	33.6	50.0	77.2	69.2	38.3	30.9	209.8	134.1
1965	333.3	21.2	312.1	220.5	37.2	54.5	81.2	73.1	42.0	31.1	231.0	147.4
1966	356.5	23.1	333.4	232.9	40.3	60.1	84.1	76.1	44.8	31.3	249.3	156.9
1967	381.0	25.0	356.0	247.3	43.9	64.7	88.2	79.9	47.4	32.5	267.8	167.4
1968	410.8	27.3	383.5	264.8	47.3	71.4	93.4	84.4	50.6	33.8	290.1	180.4
1969	441.4	29.2	412.2	283.2	52.2	76.9	100.2	90.2	54.5	35.7	312.0	193.0
1970	473.7	30.5	443.2	297.2	60.1	85.8	109.2	97.3	59.9	37.3	333.9	200.0
1971	524.2	32.4	491.8	325.6	70.1	96.2	120.7	105.2	65.7	39.5	371.1	220.4
1972	597.2	35.4	561.9	366.0	82.8	113.1	131.1	113.0	68.2	44.7	430.7	253.1
1973	672.4	39.8	632.6	407.1	93.2	132.3	135.0	116.2	66.2	50.0	497.5	290.9
1974	732.5	44.9	687.5	440.0	100.0	147.5	140.2	121.3	65.1	56.2	547.3	318.7
1975	791.9	49.9	742.0	481.2	100.7	160.1	147.0	127.7	66.1	61.6	595.0	353.5
1976	878.6	55.4	823.2	543.9	105.9	173.4	154.0	133.5	66.5	67.0	669.1	410.4
1977	1,010.2	63.8	946.4	639.7	114.3	192.3	161.7	141.6	68.0	73.6	784.6	498.1
1978	1,163.0	72.8	1,090.2	751.2	125.2	213.9	176.4	153.4	71.4	82.0	913.9	597.8
1979	1,328.3	86.8	1,241.6	867.7	135.0	238.8	199.0	172.9	81.0	92.0	1,042.6	694.8
1980	1,463.0	97.5	1,365.5	965.1	141.1	259.3	225.1	195.2	93.6	101.6	1,140.4	769.9
1981	1,587.8	107.2	1,480.6	1,042.8	139.2	298.6	238.9	207.6	101.3	106.2	1,241.7	835.2
1982	1,673.4	111.3	1,562.1	1,088.5	141.1	332.6	248.9	217.9	108.0	109.9	1,313.2	870.6
1983	1,867.3	113.7	1,753.5	1,210.6	154.3	388.6	279.8	248.8	127.4	121.4	1,473.7	961.7
1984	2,113.1	112.4	2,000.7	1,351.4	177.4	471.9	294.8	265.9	136.7	129.1	1,705.8	1,085.5
1985	2,371.4	94.1	2,277.3	1,529.9	205.9	541.6	328.3	288.8	153.0	135.8	1,949.0	1,241.1
1986	2,658.5	84.0	2,574.4	1,732.6	239.3	602.5	370.5	328.6	185.5	143.1	2,203.9	1,404.0
1987	2,995.4	75.8	2,919.6	1,959.5	262.1	698.0	431.4	387.9	235.5	152.4	2,488.2	1,571.6
1988	3,314.1	70.8	3,243.3	2,194.7	279.0	769.6	459.7	414.2	258.8	155.4	2,783.6	1,780.6
1989	3,602.7	68.8	3,534.0	2,444.6	289.9	799.5	486.8	440.1	282.8	157.3	3,047.1	2,004.5
1990	3,805.1	67.6	3,737.4	2,628.5	288.3	820.7	517.9	470.9	310.9	160.0	3,219.5	2,157.6
1991	3,945.8	67.5	3,878.3	2,786.3	284.9	807.1	537.2	493.3	330.6	162.7	3,341.1	2,293.0
1992	4,057.9	67.9	3,990.1	2,954.7	272.0	763.4	533.3	489.8	326.0	163.8	3,456.8	2,464.9
1993	4,191.3	68.4	4,122.8	3,114.0	269.1	739.7	513.4	469.5	303.2	166.2	3,609.4	2,644.6
1994	4,358.5	69.9	4,288.6	3,291.8	269.6	727.2	559.3	514.2	336.8	177.3	3,729.3	2,777.6
1995	4,545.3	71.7	4,473.6	3,459.4	275.5	738.7	584.3	537.1	352.3	184.7	3,889.3	2,922.3
1996	4,814.9	74.4	4,740.5	3,683.0	287.8	769.7	620.3	571.2	379.2	192.0	4,120.1	3,111.8
1997	5,128.6	78.5	5,050.1	3,917.7	299.8	832.6	656.7	605.7	405.7	200.0	4,393.4	3,312.0
1998	5,615.1	83.1	5,532.0	4,274.3	333.9	923.8	674.1	623.8	417.9	205.9	4,858.0	3,650.5
1999	6,224.9	87.2	6,137.7	4,699.6	375.0	1,063.1	731.5	678.8	462.3	216.5	5,406.2	4,020.8
2000	6,786.4	84.7	6,701.7	5,126.5	404.6	1,170.6	773.1	719.9	499.9	220.1	5,928.6	4,406.6
2001	7,494.4	88.5	7,405.9	5,678.0	446.5	1,281.4	772.7	718.5	497.4	221.2	6,633.2	4,959.5
2002	8,399.3	95.4	8,303.9	6,437.4	485.2	1,381.3	759.3	704.0	486.2	217.7	7,544.6	5,733.4
2003	9,395.1	94.1	9,300.9	7,227.8	564.9	1,508.3	709.2	653.3	438.7	214.6	8,591.8	6,574.5
2004	10,679.7	96.9	10,582.8	8,284.2	619.1	1,679.6	661.5	605.4	398.1	207.3	9,921.3	7,678.8
2005	12,070.6	101.5	11,969.1	9,344.8	691.5	1,932.7	606.6	550.4	348.4	202.0	11,362.5	8,794.4
2006	13,481.8	111.1	13,370.8	10,421.4	751.1	2,198.3	600.2	543.5	336.9	206.6	12,770.6	9,877.9
2006: I	12,455.5	103.4	12,352.1	9,653.1	708.4	1,990.7	599.9	543.7	343.3	200.4	11,752.2	9,109.4
II	12,847.0	105.2	12,741.8	9,966.4	719.8	2,055.6	594.9	539.1	339.8	199.3	12,146.9	9,427.3
III	13,180.9	108.4	13,072.5	10,216.7	732.5	2,123.3	599.1	542.7	338.6	204.2	12,473.4	9,674.0
IV	13,481.8	111.1	13,370.8	10,421.4	751.1	2,198.3	600.2	543.5	336.9	206.6	12,770.6	9,877.9
2007: I	13,751.5	112.4	13,639.0	10,614.4	767.6	2,257.1	597.9	541.0	335.6	205.4	13,041.2	10,073.4
II	14,082.4	115.1	13,967.3	10,835.5	789.9	2,341.9	598.3	541.7	335.6	206.1	13,369.0	10,293.8
III *p*	14,363.8	116.4	14,247.4	11,027.9	813.4	2,406.1	610.6	551.0	342.6	208.4	13,636.8	10,476.9

[1] Includes FHA-insured multifamily properties, not shown separately.
[2] Derived figures. Total includes multifamily properties, not shown separately, and commercial properties not shown here but are the same as nonfarm properties—commercial properties.

Source: Board of Governors of the Federal Reserve System, based on data from various Government and private organizations.

[Billions of dollars]

End of year or quarter	Total	Major financial institutions				Other holders	
		Total	Savings institutions [1]	Commercial banks [2]	Life insurance companies	Federal and related agencies [3]	Individuals and others [4]
1949	62.3	42.9	18.3	11.6	12.9	2.0	17.5
1950	72.7	51.7	21.9	13.7	16.1	2.6	18.4
1951	82.1	59.5	25.5	14.7	19.3	3.3	19.3
1952	91.3	66.9	29.8	15.9	21.3	3.9	20.4
1953	101.1	75.0	34.8	16.9	23.3	4.4	21.7
1954	113.6	85.7	41.1	18.6	26.0	4.7	23.2
1955	129.9	99.3	48.9	21.0	29.4	5.3	25.3
1956	144.5	111.2	55.5	22.7	33.0	6.2	27.1
1957	156.5	119.7	61.2	23.3	35.2	7.7	29.1
1958	171.8	131.5	68.9	25.5	37.1	8.0	32.3
1959	190.8	145.5	78.1	28.1	39.2	10.2	35.1
1960	207.4	157.5	86.9	28.8	41.8	11.5	38.4
1961	228.0	172.6	98.0	30.4	44.2	12.2	43.1
1962	251.4	192.5	111.1	34.5	46.9	12.6	46.3
1963	278.5	217.1	127.2	39.4	50.5	11.8	49.5
1964	305.9	241.0	141.9	44.0	55.2	12.2	52.7
1965	333.3	264.6	154.9	49.7	60.0	13.5	55.2
1966	356.5	280.7	161.8	54.4	64.6	17.5	58.2
1967	381.0	298.6	172.3	58.9	67.4	20.9	61.4
1968	410.8	319.7	184.3	65.5	70.0	25.1	66.1
1969	441.4	338.9	196.4	70.5	72.0	31.1	71.4
1970	473.7	355.9	208.3	73.3	74.4	38.3	79.4
1971	524.2	394.2	236.2	82.5	75.5	46.3	83.6
1972	597.2	449.9	273.6	99.3	76.9	54.5	92.8
1973	672.4	505.3	305.0	119.1	81.3	64.7	102.4
1974	732.5	542.6	324.2	132.1	86.2	82.2	107.7
1975	791.9	581.2	355.8	136.2	89.2	101.1	109.6
1976	878.6	647.5	404.6	151.3	91.6	116.7	114.4
1977	1,010.2	745.2	469.4	179.0	96.8	140.5	124.5
1978	1,163.0	848.2	528.0	214.0	106.2	170.6	144.3
1979	1,328.3	938.2	574.6	245.2	118.4	216.0	174.2
1980	1,463.0	996.8	603.1	262.7	131.1	256.8	209.4
1981	1,587.8	1,040.5	618.5	284.2	137.7	289.4	257.9
1982	1,673.4	1,021.3	578.1	301.3	142.0	355.4	296.7
1983	1,867.3	1,108.1	626.6	330.5	151.0	433.3	325.8
1984	2,113.1	1,247.8	709.7	381.4	156.7	490.6	374.7
1985	2,371.4	1,363.5	760.5	431.2	171.8	580.9	427.0
1986	2,658.5	1,476.5	778.0	504.7	193.8	733.7	448.2
1987	2,995.4	1,667.6	860.5	594.8	212.4	857.9	469.9
1988	3,314.1	1,834.3	924.5	676.9	232.9	937.8	542.1
1989	3,602.7	1,935.2	910.3	770.7	254.2	1,067.3	600.2
1990	3,805.1	1,918.8	801.6	849.3	267.9	1,258.9	627.4
1991	3,945.8	1,846.2	705.4	881.3	259.5	1,422.5	677.2
1992	4,057.9	1,770.4	627.9	900.5	242.0	1,558.1	729.4
1993	4,191.3	1,770.1	598.4	947.8	223.9	1,682.8	738.3
1994	4,358.5	1,824.7	596.2	1,012.7	215.8	1,788.0	745.8
1995	4,545.3	1,900.1	596.8	1,090.2	213.1	1,878.7	766.5
1996	4,814.9	1,981.9	628.3	1,145.4	208.2	2,006.1	826.9
1997	5,128.6	2,084.0	631.8	1,245.3	206.8	2,111.4	933.2
1998	5,615.1	2,194.6	644.0	1,337.0	213.6	2,310.9	1,109.7
1999	6,224.9	2,394.3	668.1	1,495.4	230.8	2,613.3	1,217.3
2000	6,786.4	2,619.0	723.0	1,660.1	235.9	2,834.4	1,333.1
2001	7,494.4	2,790.9	758.0	1,789.8	243.0	3,205.0	1,498.5
2002	8,399.3	3,089.3	781.0	2,058.3	250.0	3,592.2	1,717.8
2003	9,395.1	3,387.3	870.6	2,255.8	260.9	4,022.1	1,985.7
2004	10,679.7	3,926.3	1,057.4	2,595.6	273.3	4,093.9	2,659.5
2005	12,070.6	4,396.2	1,152.7	2,958.0	285.5	4,230.3	3,444.1
2006	13,481.8	4,780.8	1,074.0	3,403.1	303.8	4,547.6	4,153.4
2006: I	12,455.5	4,514.2	1,192.4	3,033.2	288.5	4,312.9	3,628.5
II	12,847.0	4,657.1	1,221.0	3,140.4	295.7	4,381.3	3,808.6
III	13,180.9	4,730.7	1,249.0	3,181.3	300.4	4,467.1	3,983.1
IV	13,481.8	4,780.8	1,074.0	3,403.1	303.8	4,547.6	4,153.4
2007: I	13,751.5	4,801.8	1,117.3	3,378.2	306.3	4,666.3	4,283.4
II	14,082.4	4,887.6	1,112.8	3,462.9	311.9	4,794.8	4,400.0
III ᵖ	14,363.8	4,977.1	1,146.9	3,513.8	316.3	4,972.9	4,413.9

[1] Includes savings banks and savings and loan associations. Data reported by Federal Savings and Loan Insurance Corporation-insured institutions include loans in process for 1987 and exclude loans in process beginning with 1988.

[2] Includes loans held by nondeposit trust companies but not loans held by bank trust departments.

[3] Includes Government National Mortgage Association (GNMA or Ginnie Mae), Federal Housing Administration, Veterans Administration, Farmers Home Administration (FmHA), Federal Deposit Insurance Corporation, Resolution Trust Corporation (through 1995), and in earlier years Reconstruction Finance Corporation, Homeowners Loan Corporation, Federal Farm Mortgage Corporation, and Public Housing Administration. Also includes U.S.-sponsored agencies such as Federal National Mortgage Association (FNMA or Fannie Mae), Federal Land Banks, Federal Home Loan Mortgage Corporation (FHLMC or Freddie Mac), Federal Agricultural Mortgage Corporation (Farmer Mac, beginning 1994), Federal Home Loan Banks (beginning 1997), and mortgage pass-through securities issued or guaranteed by GNMA, FHLMC, FNMA, FmHA, or Farmer Mac. Other U.S. agencies (amounts small or current separate data not readily available) included with "individuals and others."

[4] Includes private mortgage pools.

Source: Board of Governors of the Federal Reserve System, based on data from various Government and private organizations.

[Amount outstanding (end of month); millions of dollars, seasonally adjusted]

Year and month	Total consumer credit [1]	Revolving	Nonrevolving [2]
December:			
1959	56,010.68		56,010.68
1960	60,025.31		60,025.31
1961	62,248.53		62,248.53
1962	68,126.72		68,126.72
1963	76,581.45		76,581.45
1964	85,959.57		85,959.57
1965	95,954.72		95,954.72
1966	101,788.22		101,788.22
1967	106,842.64		106,842.64
1968	117,399.09	2,041.54	115,357.55
1969	127,156.18	3,604.84	123,551.35
1970	131,551.55	4,961.46	126,590.09
1971	146,930.18	8,245.33	138,684.84
1972	166,189.10	9,379.24	156,809.86
1973	190,086.31	11,342.22	178,744.09
1974	198,917.84	13,241.26	185,676.58
1975	204,002.00	14,495.27	189,506.73
1976	225,721.59	16,489.05	209,232.54
1977	260,562.70	37,414.82	223,147.88
1978	306,100.39	45,690.95	260,409.43
1979	348,589.11	53,596.43	294,992.67
1980	351,920.05	54,970.05	296,950.00
1981	371,301.44	60,928.00	310,373.44
1982	389,848.74	66,348.30	323,500.44
1983	437,068.86	79,027.25	358,041.61
1984	517,278.98	100,385.63	416,893.35
1985	599,711.23	124,465.80	475,245.43
1986	654,750.24	141,068.15	513,682.08
1987	686,318.77	160,853.91	525,464.86
1988 [3]	731,917.76	184,593.12	547,324.64
1989	794,612.18	211,229.83	583,382.34
1990	808,230.57	238,642.62	569,587.95
1991	798,028.97	263,768.55	534,260.42
1992	806,118.69	278,449.67	527,669.02
1993	865,650.58	309,908.02	555,742.56
1994	997,301.74	365,569.56	631,732.19
1995	1,140,744.36	443,920.09	696,824.27
1996	1,253,437.09	507,516.57	745,920.52
1997	1,324,757.33	540,005.56	784,751.77
1998	1,420,454.41	581,101.72	839,352.69
1999	1,532,055.98	610,509.36	921,546.62
2000	1,717,483.23	683,652.74	1,033,830.48
2001	1,867,199.37	716,650.81	1,150,548.55
2002	1,974,092.97	748,854.82	1,225,238.16
2003	2,077,958.10	770,450.42	1,307,507.68
2004	2,191,323.04	800,016.91	1,391,306.13
2005	2,284,875.88	824,963.31	1,459,912.57
2006	2,387,469.85	875,406.12	1,512,063.73
2006: Jan	2,295,350.95	826,986.09	1,468,364.86
Feb	2,298,170.10	828,193.98	1,469,976.12
Mar	2,299,756.33	829,176.25	1,470,580.08
Apr	2,305,469.58	830,599.08	1,474,870.50
May	2,320,019.67	838,719.26	1,481,300.41
June	2,331,242.11	846,471.77	1,484,770.34
July	2,342,640.85	850,345.33	1,492,295.52
Aug	2,354,459.42	855,548.91	1,498,910.51
Sept	2,360,703.20	858,586.79	1,502,116.41
Oct	2,362,903.89	863,346.55	1,499,557.33
Nov	2,381,861.30	872,955.01	1,508,906.28
Dec	2,387,469.85	875,406.12	1,512,063.73
2007: Jan	2,395,242.61	876,887.83	1,518,354.78
Feb	2,401,411.86	879,869.62	1,521,542.23
Mar	2,415,711.78	887,188.18	1,528,523.60
Apr	2,418,967.51	887,612.43	1,531,355.08
May	2,437,898.23	897,091.03	1,540,807.20
June	2,448,008.42	902,188.83	1,545,819.59
July	2,461,753.55	909,487.56	1,552,265.98
Aug	2,482,580.62	917,556.63	1,565,023.99
Sept	2,487,886.54	922,142.31	1,565,744.23
Oct	2,489,908.97	928,710.59	1,561,198.38
Nov [p]	2,505,358.25	937,463.50	1,567,894.76

[1] Covers most short- and intermediate-term credit extended to individuals. Credit secured by real estate is excluded.
[2] Includes automobile loans and all other loans not included in revolving credit, such as loans for mobile homes, education, boats, trailers, or vacations. These loans may be secured or unsecured. Beginning with 1977, includes student loans extended by the Federal Government and by SLM Holding Corporation.
[3] Data newly available in January 1989 result in breaks in these series between December 1988 and subsequent months.

Source: Board of Governors of the Federal Reserve System.

TABLE B–78.—*Federal receipts, outlays, surplus or deficit, and debt, fiscal years, 1940–2009*

[Billions of dollars; fiscal years]

Fiscal year or period	Total			On-budget			Off-budget			Federal debt (end of period)		Addendum: Gross domestic product
	Receipts	Outlays	Surplus or deficit (−)	Receipts	Outlays	Surplus or deficit (−)	Receipts	Outlays	Surplus or deficit (−)	Gross Federal	Held by the public	
1940	6.5	9.5	−2.9	6.0	9.5	−3.5	0.6	−0.0	0.6	50.7	42.8	96.8
1941	8.7	13.7	−4.9	8.0	13.6	−5.6	.7	.0	.7	57.5	48.2	114.1
1942	14.6	35.1	−20.5	13.7	35.1	−21.3	.9	.1	.8	79.2	67.8	144.3
1943	24.0	78.6	−54.6	22.9	78.5	−55.6	1.1	.1	1.0	142.6	127.8	180.3
1944	43.7	91.3	−47.6	42.5	91.2	−48.7	1.3	.1	1.2	204.1	184.8	209.2
1945	45.2	92.7	−47.6	43.8	92.6	−48.7	1.3	.1	1.2	260.1	235.2	221.4
1946	39.3	55.2	−15.9	38.1	55.0	−17.0	1.2	.2	1.0	271.0	241.9	222.7
1947	38.5	34.5	4.0	37.1	34.2	2.9	1.5	.3	1.2	257.1	224.3	233.2
1948	41.6	29.8	11.8	39.9	29.4	10.5	1.6	.4	1.2	252.0	216.3	256.0
1949	39.4	38.8	.6	37.7	38.4	−.7	1.7	.4	1.3	252.6	214.3	271.1
1950	39.4	42.6	−3.1	37.3	42.0	−4.7	2.1	.5	1.6	256.9	219.0	273.0
1951	51.6	45.5	6.1	48.5	44.2	4.3	3.1	1.3	1.8	255.3	214.3	320.6
1952	66.2	67.7	−1.5	62.6	66.0	−3.4	3.6	1.7	1.9	259.1	214.8	348.6
1953	69.6	76.1	−6.5	65.5	73.8	−8.3	4.1	2.3	1.8	266.0	218.4	372.9
1954	69.7	70.9	−1.2	65.1	67.9	−2.8	4.6	2.9	1.7	270.8	224.5	377.3
1955	65.5	68.4	−3.0	60.4	64.5	−4.1	5.1	4.0	1.1	274.4	226.6	394.6
1956	74.6	70.6	3.9	68.2	65.7	2.5	6.4	5.0	1.5	272.7	222.2	427.2
1957	80.0	76.6	3.4	73.2	70.6	2.6	6.8	6.0	.8	272.3	219.3	450.3
1958	79.6	82.4	−2.8	71.6	74.9	−3.3	8.0	7.5	.5	279.7	226.3	460.5
1959	79.2	92.1	−12.8	71.0	83.1	−12.1	8.3	9.0	−.7	287.5	234.7	491.5
1960	92.5	92.2	.3	81.9	81.3	.5	10.6	10.9	−.2	290.5	236.8	517.9
1961	94.4	97.7	−3.3	82.3	86.0	−3.8	12.1	11.7	.4	292.6	238.4	530.8
1962	99.7	106.8	−7.1	87.4	93.3	−5.9	12.3	13.5	−1.3	302.9	248.0	567.6
1963	106.6	111.3	−4.8	92.4	96.4	−4.0	14.2	15.0	−.8	310.3	254.0	598.7
1964	112.6	118.5	−5.9	96.2	102.8	−6.5	16.4	15.7	.6	316.1	256.8	640.4
1965	116.8	118.2	−1.4	100.1	101.7	−1.6	16.7	16.5	.2	322.3	260.8	687.1
1966	130.8	134.5	−3.7	111.7	114.8	−3.1	19.1	19.7	−.6	328.5	263.7	752.9
1967	148.8	157.5	−8.6	124.4	137.0	−12.6	24.4	20.4	4.0	340.4	266.6	811.8
1968	153.0	178.1	−25.2	128.1	155.8	−27.7	24.9	22.3	2.6	368.7	289.5	866.6
1969	186.9	183.6	3.2	157.9	158.4	−.5	29.0	25.2	3.7	365.8	278.1	948.6
1970	192.8	195.6	−2.8	159.3	168.0	−8.7	33.5	27.6	5.9	380.9	283.2	1,012.2
1971	187.1	210.2	−23.0	151.3	177.3	−26.1	35.8	32.8	3.0	408.2	303.0	1,079.9
1972	207.3	230.7	−23.4	167.4	193.5	−26.1	39.9	37.2	2.7	435.9	322.4	1,178.3
1973	230.8	245.7	−14.9	184.7	200.0	−15.2	46.1	45.7	.3	466.3	340.9	1,307.6
1974	263.2	269.4	−6.1	209.3	216.5	−7.2	53.9	52.9	1.1	483.9	343.7	1,439.3
1975	279.1	332.3	−53.2	216.6	270.8	−54.1	62.5	61.6	.9	541.9	394.7	1,560.7
1976	298.1	371.8	−73.7	231.7	301.1	−69.4	66.4	70.7	−4.3	629.0	477.4	1,736.5
Transition quarter ..	81.2	96.0	−14.7	63.2	77.3	−14.1	18.0	18.7	−.7	643.6	495.5	456.7
1977	355.6	409.2	−53.7	278.7	328.7	−49.9	76.8	80.5	−3.7	706.4	549.1	1,974.3
1978	399.6	458.7	−59.2	314.2	369.6	−55.4	85.4	89.2	−3.8	776.6	607.1	2,217.0
1979	463.3	504.0	−40.7	365.3	404.9	−39.6	98.0	99.1	−1.1	829.5	640.3	2,500.7
1980	517.1	590.9	−73.8	403.9	477.0	−73.1	113.2	113.9	−.7	909.0	711.9	2,726.7
1981	599.3	678.2	−79.0	469.1	543.0	−73.9	130.2	135.3	−5.1	994.8	789.4	3,054.7
1982	617.8	745.7	−128.0	474.3	594.9	−120.6	143.5	150.9	−7.4	1,137.3	924.6	3,227.6
1983	600.6	808.4	−207.8	453.2	660.9	−207.7	147.3	147.4	−.1	1,371.7	1,137.3	3,440.7
1984	666.5	851.9	−185.4	500.4	685.7	−185.3	166.1	166.2	−.1	1,564.6	1,307.0	3,840.2
1985	734.1	946.4	−212.3	547.9	769.4	−221.5	186.2	176.9	9.2	1,817.4	1,507.3	4,141.5
1986	769.2	990.4	−221.2	569.0	806.9	−237.9	200.2	183.5	16.7	2,120.5	1,740.6	4,412.4
1987	854.4	1,004.1	−149.7	641.0	809.3	−168.4	213.4	194.8	18.6	2,346.0	1,889.8	4,647.1
1988	909.3	1,064.5	−155.2	667.8	860.1	−192.3	241.5	204.4	37.1	2,601.1	2,051.6	5,008.6
1989	991.2	1,143.8	−152.6	727.5	932.9	−205.4	263.7	210.9	52.8	2,867.8	2,190.7	5,400.5
1990	1,032.1	1,253.1	−221.0	750.4	1,028.1	−277.6	281.7	225.1	56.6	3,206.3	2,411.6	5,735.4
1991	1,055.1	1,324.3	−269.2	761.2	1,082.6	−321.4	293.9	241.7	52.2	3,598.2	2,689.0	5,935.1
1992	1,091.3	1,381.6	−290.3	788.9	1,129.3	−340.4	302.4	252.3	50.1	4,001.8	2,999.7	6,239.9
1993	1,154.5	1,409.5	−255.1	842.5	1,142.9	−300.4	311.9	266.6	45.3	4,351.0	3,248.4	6,575.5
1994	1,258.7	1,461.9	−203.2	923.7	1,182.5	−258.8	335.0	279.4	55.7	4,643.3	3,433.1	6,961.3
1995	1,351.9	1,515.9	−164.0	1,000.9	1,227.2	−226.4	351.1	288.7	62.4	4,920.6	3,604.4	7,325.8
1996	1,453.2	1,560.6	−107.4	1,085.7	1,259.7	−174.0	367.5	300.9	66.6	5,181.5	3,734.1	7,694.1
1997	1,579.4	1,601.3	−21.9	1,187.4	1,290.7	−103.2	392.0	310.6	81.4	5,369.2	3,772.3	8,182.4
1998	1,722.0	1,652.7	69.3	1,306.2	1,336.1	−29.9	415.8	316.6	99.2	5,478.2	3,721.1	8,627.9
1999	1,827.6	1,702.0	125.6	1,383.2	1,381.3	1.9	444.5	320.8	123.7	5,605.5	3,632.4	9,125.3
2000	2,025.5	1,789.2	236.2	1,544.9	1,458.5	86.4	480.6	330.8	149.8	5,628.7	3,409.8	9,709.8
2001	1,991.4	1,863.2	128.2	1,483.9	1,516.4	−32.4	507.5	346.8	160.7	5,769.9	3,319.6	10,057.9
2002	1,853.4	2,011.2	−157.8	1,338.1	1,655.5	−317.4	515.3	355.7	159.7	6,198.4	3,540.4	10,377.4
2003	1,782.5	2,160.1	−377.6	1,258.7	1,797.1	−538.4	523.8	363.0	160.8	6,760.0	3,913.4	10,808.6
2004	1,880.3	2,293.0	−412.7	1,345.5	1,913.5	−568.0	534.7	379.5	155.2	7,354.7	4,295.5	11,499.9
2005	2,153.9	2,472.2	−318.3	1,576.4	2,070.0	−493.6	577.5	402.2	175.3	7,905.3	4,592.2	12,237.9
2006	2,407.3	2,655.4	−248.2	1,798.9	2,233.4	−434.5	608.4	422.1	186.3	8,451.4	4,829.0	13,015.5
2007	2,568.2	2,730.2	−162.0	1,933.2	2,276.6	−343.5	635.1	453.6	181.5	8,950.7	5,035.1	13,667.5
2008 (estimates)	2,521.2	2,931.2	−410.0	1,859.0	2,461.2	−602.2	662.2	470.1	192.2	9,654.4	5,428.6	14,311.5
2009 (estimates)	2,699.9	3,107.4	−407.4	2,004.4	2,615.5	−611.1	695.6	491.9	203.7	10,413.4	5,856.2	15,027.0

Note.—Fiscal years through 1976 were on a July 1-June 30 basis; beginning with October 1976 (fiscal year 1977), the fiscal year is on an October 1-September 30 basis. The transition quarter is the 3-month period from July 1, 1976 through September 30, 1976.

See *Budget of the United States Government, Fiscal Year 2009*, for additional information.

Sources: Department of Commerce (Bureau of Economic Analysis), Department of the Treasury, and Office of Management and Budget.

TABLE B–79.—*Federal receipts, outlays, surplus or deficit, and debt, as percent of gross domestic product, fiscal years 1934–2009*

[Percent; fiscal years]

Fiscal year or period	Receipts	Outlays		Surplus or deficit (−)	Federal debt (end of period)	
		Total	National defense		Gross Federal	Held by public
1934	4.8	10.7		−5.9		
1935	5.2	9.2		−4.0		
1936	5.0	10.5		−5.5		
1937	6.1	8.6		−2.5		
1938	7.6	7.7		−.1		
1939	7.1	10.3		−3.2	54.2	46.6
1940	6.8	9.8	1.7	−3.0	52.4	44.2
1941	7.6	12.0	5.6	−4.3	50.4	42.3
1942	10.1	24.3	17.8	−14.2	54.9	47.0
1943	13.3	43.6	37.0	−30.3	79.1	70.9
1944	20.9	43.6	37.8	−22.7	97.6	88.3
1945	20.4	41.9	37.5	−21.5	117.5	106.2
1946	17.6	24.8	19.2	−7.2	121.7	108.6
1947	16.5	14.8	5.5	1.7	110.3	96.2
1948	16.2	11.6	3.6	4.6	98.4	84.5
1949	14.5	14.3	4.9	.2	93.2	79.1
1950	14.4	15.6	5.0	−1.1	94.1	80.2
1951	16.1	14.2	7.4	1.9	79.6	66.9
1952	19.0	19.4	13.2	−.4	74.3	61.6
1953	18.7	20.4	14.2	−1.7	71.3	58.6
1954	18.5	18.8	13.1	−.3	71.8	59.5
1955	16.6	17.3	10.8	−.8	69.5	57.4
1956	17.5	16.5	10.0	.9	63.8	52.0
1957	17.8	17.0	10.1	.8	60.5	48.7
1958	17.3	17.9	10.2	−.6	60.7	49.2
1959	16.1	18.7	10.0	−2.6	58.5	47.8
1960	17.9	17.8	9.3	.1	56.1	45.7
1961	17.8	18.4	9.3	−.6	55.1	44.9
1962	17.6	18.8	9.2	−1.3	53.4	43.7
1963	17.8	18.6	8.9	−.8	51.8	42.4
1964	17.6	18.5	8.6	−.9	49.4	40.1
1965	17.0	17.2	7.4	−.2	46.9	38.0
1966	17.4	17.9	7.7	−.5	43.6	35.0
1967	18.3	19.4	8.8	−1.1	41.9	32.8
1968	17.7	20.6	9.5	−2.9	42.5	33.4
1969	19.7	19.4	8.7	.3	38.6	29.3
1970	19.0	19.3	8.1	−.3	37.6	28.0
1971	17.3	19.5	7.3	−2.1	37.8	28.1
1972	17.6	19.6	6.7	−2.0	37.0	27.4
1973	17.7	18.8	5.9	−1.1	35.7	26.1
1974	18.3	18.7	5.5	−.4	33.6	23.9
1975	17.9	21.3	5.5	−3.4	34.7	25.3
1976	17.2	21.4	5.2	−4.2	36.2	27.5
Transition quarter	17.8	21.0	4.9	−3.2	35.2	27.1
1977	18.0	20.7	4.9	−2.7	35.8	27.8
1978	18.0	20.7	4.7	−2.7	35.0	27.4
1979	18.5	20.2	4.7	−1.6	33.2	25.6
1980	19.0	21.7	4.9	−2.7	33.3	26.1
1981	19.6	22.2	5.2	−2.6	32.6	25.8
1982	19.1	23.1	5.7	−4.0	35.2	28.6
1983	17.5	23.5	6.1	−6.0	39.9	33.1
1984	17.4	22.2	5.9	−4.8	40.7	34.0
1985	17.7	22.9	6.1	−5.1	43.9	36.4
1986	17.4	22.4	6.2	−5.0	48.1	39.4
1987	18.4	21.6	6.1	−3.2	50.5	40.7
1988	18.2	21.3	5.8	−3.1	51.9	41.0
1989	18.4	21.2	5.6	−2.8	53.1	40.6
1990	18.0	21.8	5.2	−3.9	55.9	42.0
1991	17.8	22.3	4.6	−4.5	60.6	45.3
1992	17.5	22.1	4.8	−4.7	64.1	48.1
1993	17.6	21.4	4.4	−3.9	66.2	49.4
1994	18.1	21.0	4.0	−2.9	66.7	49.3
1995	18.5	20.7	3.7	−2.2	67.2	49.2
1996	18.9	20.3	3.5	−1.4	67.3	48.5
1997	19.3	19.6	3.3	−.3	65.6	46.1
1998	20.0	19.2	3.1	.8	63.5	43.1
1999	20.0	18.7	3.0	1.4	61.4	39.8
2000	20.9	18.4	3.0	2.4	58.0	35.1
2001	19.8	18.5	3.0	1.3	57.4	33.0
2002	17.9	19.4	3.4	−1.5	59.7	34.1
2003	16.5	20.0	3.7	−3.5	62.5	36.2
2004	16.4	19.9	4.0	−3.6	64.0	37.4
2005	17.6	20.2	4.0	−2.6	64.6	37.5
2006	18.5	20.4	4.0	−1.9	64.9	37.1
2007	18.8	20.0	4.0	−1.2	65.5	36.8
2008 (estimates)	17.6	20.5	4.2	−2.9	67.5	37.9
2009 (estimates)	18.0	20.7	4.5	−2.7	69.3	39.0

Note.—See Note, Table B–78.

Sources: Department of the Treasury and Office of Management and Budget.

TABLE B–80.—*Federal receipts and outlays, by major category, and surplus or deficit, fiscal years 1940–2009*

[Billions of dollars; fiscal years]

Fiscal year or period	Receipts (on-budget and off-budget)					Outlays (on-budget and off-budget)										Surplus or deficit (−) (on-budget and off-budget)
	Total	Individual income taxes	Corporation income taxes	Social insurance and retirement receipts	Other	Total	National defense Total	National defense Department of Defense, military	International affairs	Health	Medicare	Income security	Social security	Net interest	Other	
1940	6.5	0.9	1.2	1.8	2.7	9.5	1.7		0.1	0.1		1.5	0.0	0.9	5.3	−2.9
1941	8.7	1.3	2.1	1.9	3.3	13.7	6.4		.1	.1		1.9	.1	.9	4.1	−4.9
1942	14.6	3.3	4.7	2.5	4.2	35.1	25.7		1.0	.1		1.8	.1	1.1	5.4	−20.5
1943	24.0	6.5	9.6	3.0	4.9	78.6	66.7		1.3	.1		1.7	.2	1.5	7.0	−54.6
1944	43.7	19.7	14.8	3.5	5.7	91.3	79.1		1.4	.2		1.5	.2	2.2	6.6	−47.6
1945	45.2	18.4	16.0	3.5	7.3	92.7	83.0		1.9	.2		1.1	.3	3.1	3.1	−47.6
1946	39.3	16.1	11.9	3.1	8.2	55.2	42.7		1.9	.2		2.4	.4	4.1	3.6	−15.9
1947	38.5	17.9	8.6	3.4	8.5	34.5	12.8		5.8	.2		2.8	.5	4.2	8.2	4.0
1948	41.6	19.3	9.7	3.8	8.8	29.8	9.1		4.6	.2		2.5	.6	4.3	8.5	11.8
1949	39.4	15.6	11.2	3.8	8.9	38.8	13.2		6.1	.2		3.2	.7	4.5	11.1	.6
1950	39.4	15.8	10.4	4.3	8.9	42.6	13.7		4.7	.3		4.1	.8	4.8	14.2	−3.1
1951	51.6	21.6	14.1	5.7	10.2	45.5	23.6		3.6	.3		3.4	1.6	4.7	8.4	6.1
1952	66.2	27.9	21.2	6.4	10.6	67.7	46.1		2.7	.3		3.7	2.1	4.7	8.1	−1.5
1953	69.6	29.8	21.2	6.8	11.7	76.1	52.8		2.1	.3		3.8	2.7	5.2	9.1	−6.5
1954	69.7	29.5	21.1	7.2	11.9	70.9	49.3		1.6	.3		4.4	3.4	4.8	7.1	−1.2
1955	65.5	28.7	17.9	7.9	11.0	68.4	42.7		2.2	.3		5.1	4.4	4.9	8.9	−3.0
1956	74.6	32.2	20.9	9.3	12.2	70.6	42.5		2.4	.4		4.7	5.5	5.1	10.1	3.9
1957	80.0	35.6	21.2	10.0	13.2	76.6	45.4		3.1	.5		5.4	6.7	5.4	10.1	3.4
1958	79.6	34.7	20.1	11.2	13.6	82.4	46.8		3.4	.5		7.5	8.2	5.6	10.3	−2.8
1959	79.2	36.7	17.3	11.7	13.5	92.1	49.0		3.1	.7		8.2	9.7	5.8	15.5	−12.8
1960	92.5	40.7	21.5	14.7	15.6	92.2	48.1		3.0	.8		7.4	11.6	6.9	14.4	.3
1961	94.4	41.3	21.0	16.4	15.7	97.7	49.6		3.2	.9		9.7	12.5	6.7	15.2	−3.3
1962	99.7	45.6	20.5	17.0	16.5	106.8	52.3	50.1	5.6	1.2		9.2	14.4	6.9	17.2	−7.1
1963	106.6	47.6	21.6	19.8	17.6	111.3	53.4	51.1	5.3	1.5		9.3	15.8	7.7	18.3	−4.8
1964	112.6	48.7	23.5	22.0	18.5	118.5	54.8	52.6	4.9	1.8		9.7	16.6	8.2	22.6	−5.9
1965	116.8	48.8	25.5	22.2	20.3	118.2	50.6	48.8	5.3	1.8		9.5	17.5	8.6	25.0	−1.4
1966	130.8	55.4	30.1	25.5	19.8	134.5	58.1	56.6	5.6	2.5	0.1	9.7	20.7	9.4	28.5	−3.7
1967	148.8	61.5	34.0	32.6	20.7	157.5	71.4	70.1	5.6	3.4	2.7	10.3	21.7	10.3	32.1	−8.6
1968	153.0	68.7	28.7	33.9	21.7	178.1	81.9	80.4	5.3	4.4	4.6	11.8	23.9	11.1	35.1	−25.2
1969	186.9	87.2	36.7	39.0	23.9	183.6	82.5	80.8	4.6	5.2	5.7	13.1	27.3	12.7	32.6	3.2
1970	192.8	90.4	32.8	44.4	25.2	195.6	81.7	80.1	4.3	5.9	6.2	15.7	30.3	14.4	37.2	−2.8
1971	187.1	86.2	26.8	47.3	26.8	210.2	78.9	77.5	4.2	6.8	6.6	22.9	35.9	14.8	40.0	−23.0
1972	207.3	94.7	32.2	52.6	27.8	230.7	79.2	77.6	4.8	8.7	7.5	27.7	40.2	15.5	47.3	−23.4
1973	230.8	103.2	36.2	63.1	28.3	245.7	76.7	75.0	4.1	9.4	8.1	28.3	49.1	17.3	52.8	−14.9
1974	263.2	119.0	38.6	75.1	30.6	269.4	79.3	77.9	5.7	10.7	9.6	33.7	55.9	21.4	52.9	−6.1
1975	279.1	122.4	40.6	84.5	31.5	332.3	86.5	84.9	7.1	12.9	12.9	50.2	64.7	23.2	74.8	−53.2
1976	298.1	131.6	41.4	90.8	34.3	371.8	89.6	87.9	6.4	15.7	15.8	60.8	73.9	26.7	82.7	−73.7
Transition quarter ..	81.2	38.8	8.5	25.2	8.8	96.0	22.3	21.8	2.5	3.9	4.3	15.0	19.8	6.9	21.4	−14.7
1977	355.6	157.6	54.9	106.5	36.6	409.2	97.2	95.1	6.4	17.3	19.3	61.1	85.1	29.9	93.0	−53.7
1978	399.6	181.0	60.0	121.0	37.7	458.7	104.5	102.3	7.5	18.5	22.8	61.5	93.9	35.5	114.7	−59.2
1979	463.3	217.8	65.7	138.9	40.8	504.0	116.3	113.6	7.5	20.5	26.5	66.4	104.1	42.6	120.2	−40.7
1980	517.1	244.1	64.6	157.8	50.6	590.9	134.0	130.9	12.7	23.2	32.1	86.6	118.5	52.5	131.3	−73.8
1981	599.3	285.9	61.1	182.7	69.5	678.2	157.5	153.9	13.1	26.9	39.1	100.3	139.6	68.8	133.0	−79.0
1982	617.8	297.7	49.2	201.5	69.3	745.7	185.3	180.7	12.3	27.4	46.6	108.2	156.0	85.0	125.0	−128.0
1983	600.6	288.9	37.0	209.0	65.6	808.4	209.9	204.4	11.8	28.6	52.6	123.0	170.7	89.8	121.8	−207.8
1984	666.5	298.4	56.9	239.4	71.8	851.9	227.4	220.9	15.9	30.4	57.5	113.4	178.2	111.1	117.9	−185.4
1985	734.1	334.5	61.3	265.2	73.1	946.4	252.7	245.1	16.2	33.5	65.8	129.0	188.6	129.5	131.0	−212.3
1986	769.2	349.0	63.1	283.9	73.2	990.4	273.4	265.4	14.2	35.9	70.2	120.6	198.8	136.0	141.4	−221.2
1987	854.4	392.6	83.9	303.3	74.6	1,004.1	282.0	273.9	11.6	40.0	75.1	124.1	207.4	138.6	125.3	−149.7
1988	909.3	401.2	94.5	334.3	79.3	1,064.5	290.4	281.9	10.5	44.5	78.9	130.4	219.3	151.8	138.8	−155.2
1989	991.2	445.7	103.3	359.4	82.8	1,143.8	303.6	294.8	9.6	48.4	85.0	137.4	232.5	169.0	158.4	−152.6
1990	1,032.1	466.9	93.5	380.0	91.7	1,253.1	299.3	289.7	13.8	57.7	98.1	148.7	248.6	184.3	202.6	−221.0
1991	1,055.1	467.8	98.1	396.0	93.2	1,324.3	273.3	262.3	15.9	71.2	104.5	172.5	269.0	194.4	223.6	−269.2
1992	1,091.3	476.0	100.3	413.7	101.4	1,381.6	298.4	286.8	16.1	89.5	119.0	199.6	287.6	199.3	172.2	−290.3
1993	1,154.5	509.7	117.5	428.3	99.0	1,409.5	291.1	278.5	17.2	99.4	130.6	210.0	304.6	198.7	158.0	−255.1
1994	1,258.7	543.1	140.4	461.5	113.8	1,461.9	281.6	268.6	17.1	107.1	144.7	217.2	319.6	202.9	171.7	−203.2
1995	1,351.9	590.2	157.0	484.5	120.2	1,515.9	272.1	259.4	16.4	115.4	159.9	223.8	335.8	232.1	160.3	−164.0
1996	1,453.2	656.4	171.8	509.4	115.5	1,560.6	265.8	253.1	13.5	119.4	174.2	229.7	349.7	241.1	167.3	−107.4
1997	1,579.4	737.5	182.3	539.4	120.3	1,601.3	270.5	258.3	15.2	123.8	190.0	235.0	365.3	244.0	157.4	−21.9
1998	1,722.0	828.6	188.7	571.8	132.9	1,652.7	268.2	255.8	13.1	131.4	192.8	237.8	379.2	241.1	189.0	69.3
1999	1,827.6	879.5	184.7	611.8	151.7	1,702.0	274.8	261.2	15.2	141.1	190.4	242.5	390.0	229.8	218.2	125.6
2000	2,025.5	1,004.5	207.3	652.9	160.9	1,789.2	294.4	281.1	17.2	154.5	197.1	253.7	409.4	222.9	239.9	236.2
2001	1,991.4	994.3	151.1	694.0	152.0	1,863.2	304.8	290.2	16.5	172.3	217.4	269.8	433.0	206.2	243.4	128.2
2002	1,853.4	858.3	148.0	700.8	146.2	2,011.2	348.5	331.9	22.4	196.5	230.9	312.7	456.0	170.9	273.3	−157.8
2003	1,782.5	793.7	131.8	713.0	144.1	2,160.1	404.8	387.2	21.2	219.6	249.4	334.6	474.7	153.1	302.7	−377.6
2004	1,880.3	809.0	189.4	733.4	148.5	2,293.0	455.8	436.5	26.9	240.1	269.4	333.1	495.5	160.2	311.9	−412.7
2005	2,153.9	927.2	278.3	794.1	154.2	2,472.2	495.3	474.1	34.6	250.6	298.6	345.8	523.3	184.0	339.9	−318.3
2006	2,407.3	1,043.9	353.9	837.8	171.6	2,655.4	521.8	499.3	29.5	252.8	329.9	352.5	548.5	226.6	393.8	−248.2
2007	2,568.2	1,163.5	370.2	869.6	164.9	2,730.2	552.6	529.8	28.5	266.4	375.4	366.0	586.2	237.1	318.1	−162.0
2008 (estimates)	2,521.2	1,219.7	345.3	910.1	46.1	2,931.2	607.3	583.1	34.8	284.5	396.3	388.4	615.3	243.9	360.7	−410.0
2009 (estimates)	2,699.9	1,259.0	339.2	949.4	152.3	3,107.4	675.1	651.2	38.0	299.4	413.3	401.7	649.3	260.2	370.3	−407.4

Note.—See Note, Table B–78.

Sources: Department of the Treasury and Office of Management and Budget.

TABLE B–81.—*Federal receipts, outlays, surplus or deficit, and debt, fiscal years 2004–2009*

[Millions of dollars; fiscal years]

Description	Actual				Estimates	
	2004	2005	2006	2007	2008	2009
RECEIPTS, OUTLAYS, AND SURPLUS OR DEFICIT						
Total:						
Receipts	1,880,279	2,153,859	2,407,254	2,568,239	2,521,175	2,699,947
Outlays	2,293,006	2,472,205	2,655,435	2,730,241	2,931,222	3,107,355
Surplus or deficit (−)	−412,727	−318,346	−248,181	−162,002	−410,047	−407,408
On-budget:						
Receipts	1,345,534	1,576,383	1,798,872	1,933,150	1,858,960	2,004,383
Outlays	1,913,495	2,069,994	2,233,366	2,276,604	2,461,157	2,615,476
Surplus or deficit (−)	−567,961	−493,611	−434,494	−343,454	−602,197	−611,093
Off-budget:						
Receipts	534,745	577,476	608,382	635,089	662,215	695,564
Outlays	379,511	402,211	422,069	453,637	470,065	491,879
Surplus or deficit (−)	155,234	175,265	186,313	181,452	192,150	203,685
OUTSTANDING DEBT, END OF PERIOD						
Gross Federal debt	7,354,657	7,905,300	8,451,350	8,950,744	9,654,436	10,413,414
Held by Federal Government accounts	3,059,113	3,313,088	3,622,378	3,915,615	4,225,818	4,557,261
Held by the public	4,295,544	4,592,212	4,828,972	5,035,129	5,428,619	5,856,153
Federal Reserve System	700,341	736,360	768,924	779,632	....	....
Other	3,595,203	3,855,852	4,060,048	4,255,497	....	....
RECEIPTS BY SOURCE						
Total: On-budget and off-budget	1,880,279	2,153,859	2,407,254	2,568,239	2,521,175	2,699,947
Individual income taxes	808,959	927,222	1,043,908	1,163,472	1,219,661	1,259,041
Corporation income taxes	189,371	278,282	353,915	370,243	345,336	339,224
Social insurance and retirement receipts	733,407	794,125	837,821	869,607	910,125	949,377
On-budget	198,662	216,649	229,439	234,518	247,910	253,813
Off-budget	534,745	577,476	608,382	635,089	662,215	695,564
Excise taxes	69,855	73,094	73,961	65,069	68,835	68,946
Estate and gift taxes	24,831	24,764	27,877	26,044	26,757	26,313
Customs duties and fees	21,083	23,379	24,810	26,010	29,208	29,122
Miscellaneous receipts [1]	32,773	32,993	44,962	47,794	−78,747	27,924
Deposits of earnings by Federal Reserve System	19,652	19,297	29,945	32,043	31,358	31,652
All other [1]	13,121	13,696	15,017	15,751	−110,105	−3,728
OUTLAYS BY FUNCTION						
Total: On-budget and off-budget	2,293,006	2,472,205	2,655,435	2,730,241	2,931,222	3,107,355
National defense	455,847	495,326	521,840	552,568	607,263	675,084
International affairs	26,891	34,595	29,549	28,510	34,826	38,027
General science, space and technology	23,053	23,628	23,616	25,566	27,631	29,170
Energy	−166	429	782	−860	3,005	3,104
Natural resources and environment	30,725	28,023	33,055	31,772	35,549	35,546
Agriculture	15,440	26,566	25,970	17,663	20,967	19,070
Commerce and housing credit	5,266	7,567	6,188	488	7,361	4,182
On-budget	9,396	9,358	7,263	−4,605	6,426	3,111
Off-budget	−4,130	−1,791	−1,075	5,093	935	1,071
Transportation	64,627	67,894	70,244	72,905	80,268	83,901
Community and regional development	15,822	26,264	54,531	29,567	27,601	23,345
Education, training, employment, and social services	87,990	97,567	118,560	91,676	93,389	88,313
Health	240,134	250,614	252,780	266,432	284,499	299,393
Medicare	269,360	298,638	329,868	375,407	396,333	413,324
Income security	333,059	345,847	352,477	365,975	388,440	401,711
Social security	495,548	523,305	548,549	586,153	615,256	649,332
On-budget	14,348	16,526	16,058	19,307	18,728	22,890
Off-budget	481,200	506,779	532,491	566,846	596,528	626,442
Veterans benefits and services	59,779	70,151	69,842	72,847	86,618	91,875
Administration of justice	45,576	40,019	41,016	41,244	46,202	51,143
General government	22,347	17,010	18,215	17,457	19,809	21,534
Net interest	160,245	183,986	226,603	237,109	243,947	260,231
On-budget	246,473	275,822	324,325	343,112	358,258	382,081
Off-budget	−86,228	−91,836	−97,722	−106,003	−114,311	−121,850
Allowances						−495
Undistributed offsetting receipts	−58,537	−65,224	−68,250	−82,238	−87,742	−80,435
On-budget	−47,206	−54,283	−56,625	−69,939	−74,655	−66,651
Off-budget	−11,331	−10,941	−11,625	−12,299	−13,087	−13,784

[1] Includes Economic Growth Package.

Note.—See Note, Table B–78.

Sources: Department of the Treasury and Office of Management and Budget.

TABLE B–82.—*Federal and State and local government current receipts and expenditures, national income and product accounts (NIPA), 1959–2007*

[Billions of dollars; quarterly data at seasonally adjusted annual rates]

Year or quarter	Total government — Current receipts	Total government — Current expenditures	Total government — Net government saving (NIPA)	Federal Government — Current receipts	Federal Government — Current expenditures	Federal Government — Net Federal Government saving (NIPA)	State and local government — Current receipts	State and local government — Current expenditures	State and local government — Net State and local government saving (NIPA)	Addendum: Grants-in-aid to State and local governments
1959	123.0	115.8	7.1	87.0	83.6	3.3	40.6	36.9	3.8	3.8
1960	134.4	122.9	11.5	93.9	86.7	7.2	44.5	40.2	4.3	4.0
1961	139.0	132.1	6.9	95.5	92.8	2.6	48.1	43.8	4.3	4.5
1962	150.6	142.8	7.8	103.6	101.1	2.5	52.0	46.8	5.2	5.0
1963	162.2	151.1	11.1	111.8	106.4	5.4	56.0	50.3	5.7	5.6
1964	166.6	159.2	7.4	111.8	110.8	1.0	61.3	54.9	6.4	6.5
1965	180.3	170.4	9.9	120.9	117.6	3.3	66.5	60.0	6.5	7.2
1966	202.8	192.8	10.0	137.9	135.7	2.3	74.9	67.2	7.8	10.1
1967	217.6	220.0	−2.4	146.9	156.2	−9.4	82.5	75.5	7.0	11.7
1968	252.0	246.8	5.2	171.2	173.5	−2.3	93.5	86.0	7.5	12.7
1969	283.4	266.7	16.7	192.5	183.8	8.7	105.5	97.5	8.0	14.6
1970	286.7	294.8	−8.1	186.0	201.1	−15.2	120.1	113.0	7.1	19.3
1971	303.4	325.3	−21.9	191.7	220.0	−28.4	134.9	128.5	6.5	23.2
1972	346.8	355.5	−8.8	220.1	244.4	−24.4	158.4	142.8	15.6	31.7
1973	390.0	385.6	4.4	250.4	261.7	−11.3	174.3	158.6	15.7	34.8
1974	431.3	435.8	−4.4	279.5	293.3	−13.8	188.1	178.7	9.3	36.3
1975	441.6	508.2	−66.6	277.2	346.2	−69.0	209.6	207.1	2.5	45.1
1976	505.5	549.9	−44.4	322.5	374.3	−51.7	233.7	226.3	7.4	50.7
1977	566.8	597.7	−31.0	363.4	407.5	−44.1	259.9	246.8	13.1	56.6
1978	645.6	653.4	−7.8	423.5	450.0	−26.5	287.6	268.9	18.7	65.5
1979	728.2	726.5	1.7	486.2	497.5	−11.3	308.4	295.4	13.0	66.3
1980	798.0	842.8	−44.8	532.1	585.7	−53.6	338.2	329.4	8.8	72.3
1981	917.2	962.9	−45.7	619.4	672.7	−53.3	370.2	362.7	7.6	72.5
1982	938.5	1,072.6	−134.1	616.6	748.5	−131.9	391.4	393.6	−2.2	69.5
1983	999.4	1,167.5	−168.1	642.3	815.4	−173.0	428.6	423.7	4.9	71.6
1984	1,112.5	1,256.6	−144.1	709.0	877.1	−168.1	480.2	456.2	23.9	76.7
1985	1,213.5	1,366.1	−152.6	773.3	948.2	−175.0	521.1	498.7	22.3	80.9
1986	1,289.3	1,459.1	−169.9	815.2	1,006.0	−190.8	561.6	540.7	21.0	87.6
1987	1,403.2	1,535.8	−132.6	896.6	1,041.6	−145.0	590.6	578.1	12.4	83.9
1988	1,502.2	1,618.7	−116.6	958.2	1,092.7	−134.5	635.5	617.6	17.9	91.6
1989	1,626.3	1,735.6	−109.3	1,037.4	1,167.5	−130.1	687.3	666.5	20.8	98.3
1990	1,707.8	1,872.6	−164.8	1,081.5	1,253.5	−172.0	737.8	730.5	7.2	111.4
1991	1,758.8	1,976.7	−217.9	1,101.3	1,315.0	−213.7	789.2	793.3	−4.2	131.6
1992	1,843.7	2,140.4	−296.7	1,147.2	1,444.6	−297.4	845.7	845.0	.7	149.1
1993	1,945.8	2,218.4	−272.6	1,222.5	1,496.0	−273.5	886.9	886.0	.9	163.7
1994	2,089.0	2,290.8	−201.9	1,320.8	1,533.1	−212.3	942.9	932.4	10.5	174.7
1995	2,212.6	2,397.6	−184.9	1,406.5	1,603.5	−197.0	990.2	978.2	12.0	184.1
1996	2,376.1	2,492.1	−116.0	1,524.0	1,665.8	−141.8	1,043.3	1,017.5	25.8	191.2
1997	2,551.9	2,568.6	−16.7	1,653.1	1,708.9	−55.8	1,097.4	1,058.3	39.1	198.6
1998	2,724.2	2,633.4	90.8	1,773.8	1,734.9	38.8	1,163.2	1,111.2	52.0	212.8
1999	2,895.0	2,741.0	154.0	1,891.2	1,787.6	103.6	1,236.7	1,186.3	50.4	232.9
2000	3,125.9	2,886.5	239.4	2,053.8	1,864.4	189.5	1,319.5	1,269.5	50.0	247.3
2001	3,113.1	3,061.6	51.5	2,016.2	1,969.5	46.7	1,373.0	1,368.2	4.8	276.1
2002	2,958.7	3,240.8	−282.1	1,853.2	2,101.1	−247.9	1,410.1	1,444.3	−34.2	304.6
2003	3,035.6	3,428.1	−392.5	1,879.9	2,252.1	−372.1	1,494.2	1,514.5	−20.4	338.5
2004	3,254.1	3,623.2	−369.1	2,008.9	2,379.5	−370.6	1,594.3	1,592.8	1.5	349.1
2005	3,589.1	3,892.2	−303.1	2,243.4	2,561.6	−318.3	1,706.9	1,691.7	15.2	361.2
2006	3,934.8	4,130.3	−195.4	2,495.8	2,715.8	−220.0	1,797.7	1,773.0	24.6	358.6
2004: I	3,153.4	3,572.4	−419.0	1,939.5	2,350.6	−411.1	1,555.2	1,563.1	−7.9	341.3
II	3,221.6	3,597.7	−376.1	1,989.7	2,363.8	−374.1	1,582.5	1,584.5	−1.9	350.6
III	3,263.7	3,637.9	−374.2	2,023.5	2,385.4	−361.9	1,584.8	1,597.0	−12.3	344.6
IV	3,377.8	3,684.9	−307.1	2,082.8	2,418.2	−335.4	1,654.8	1,626.5	28.3	359.8
2005: I	3,531.9	3,797.9	−266.0	2,209.2	2,507.2	−298.0	1,681.1	1,649.1	32.0	358.3
II	3,592.2	3,853.9	−261.6	2,247.5	2,535.0	−287.5	1,705.6	1,679.7	25.9	360.8
III	3,537.6	3,926.5	−388.9	2,188.5	2,582.9	−394.3	1,709.3	1,703.8	5.4	360.2
IV	3,694.7	3,990.4	−295.6	2,328.3	2,621.4	−293.2	1,731.8	1,734.3	−2.5	365.4
2006: I	3,849.7	4,033.7	−184.0	2,436.5	2,656.2	−219.6	1,767.8	1,732.1	35.6	354.6
II	3,916.9	4,113.9	−197.0	2,471.5	2,711.4	−239.9	1,803.7	1,760.9	42.8	358.4
III	3,955.6	4,182.5	−226.9	2,513.1	2,752.3	−239.2	1,806.7	1,794.4	12.3	364.2
IV	4,017.3	4,191.1	−173.9	2,561.9	2,743.4	−181.5	1,812.4	1,804.8	7.6	357.1
2007: I	4,102.3	4,326.6	−224.3	2,619.7	2,838.2	−218.5	1,856.6	1,862.4	−5.8	374.0
II	4,183.9	4,377.2	−193.4	2,670.1	2,876.9	−206.8	1,889.9	1,876.5	13.4	376.1
III	4,200.8	4,446.4	−245.6	2,687.0	2,919.7	−232.6	1,892.8	1,905.8	−13.0	379.1

Note.—Federal grants-in-aid to State and local governments are reflected in Federal current expenditures and State and local current receipts. Total government current receipts and expenditures have been adjusted to eliminate this duplication.

Source: Department of Commerce (Bureau of Economic Analysis).

TABLE B–83.—*Federal and State and local government current receipts and expenditures, national income and product accounts (NIPA), by major type, 1959–2007*

[Billions of dollars; quarterly data at seasonally adjusted annual rates]

Year or quarter	Current receipts									Current expenditures					Net government saving
	Total	Current tax receipts				Contributions for government social insurance	Income receipts on assets	Current transfer receipts	Current surplus of government enterprises	Total ²	Consumption expenditures	Current transfer payments	Interest payments	Subsidies	
		Total ¹	Personal current taxes	Taxes on production and imports	Taxes on corporate income										
1959	123.0	107.1	42.3	41.1	23.6	13.8	0.3	0.8	1.0	115.8	80.7	26.8	7.3	1.1	7.1
1960	134.4	113.4	46.1	44.6	22.7	16.4	2.7	.9	.9	122.9	83.3	28.0	10.4	1.1	11.5
1961	139.0	117.1	47.3	47.0	22.8	17.0	2.9	1.1	.8	132.1	88.2	31.8	10.2	2.0	6.9
1962	150.6	126.1	51.6	50.4	24.0	19.1	3.2	1.2	.9	142.8	96.8	32.6	11.1	2.3	7.8
1963	162.2	134.4	54.6	53.4	26.2	21.7	3.4	1.3	1.4	151.1	102.7	34.1	12.0	2.2	11.1
1964	166.6	137.6	52.1	57.3	28.0	22.4	3.7	1.6	1.3	159.2	108.6	34.9	12.9	2.7	7.4
1965	180.3	149.5	57.7	60.8	30.9	23.4	4.1	1.9	1.3	170.4	115.9	37.8	13.7	3.0	9.9
1966	202.8	163.5	66.4	63.3	33.7	31.3	4.7	2.2	1.0	192.8	132.0	41.8	15.1	3.9	10.0
1967	217.6	173.9	73.0	68.0	32.7	34.9	5.5	2.5	.9	220.0	149.7	50.1	16.4	3.8	–2.4
1968	252.0	203.2	87.0	76.5	39.4	38.7	6.4	2.6	1.2	246.8	165.8	58.1	18.8	4.2	5.2
1969	283.4	228.5	104.5	84.0	39.7	44.1	7.0	2.7	1.0	266.7	178.2	63.7	20.2	4.5	16.7
1970	286.7	229.3	103.1	91.5	34.4	46.4	8.2	2.9	.0	294.8	190.2	76.8	23.1	4.8	–8.1
1971	303.4	240.4	101.7	100.6	37.7	51.2	9.0	3.1	–.2	325.3	204.7	91.6	24.5	4.7	–21.9
1972	346.8	274.0	123.6	108.1	41.9	59.2	9.5	3.6	.5	355.5	220.8	102.2	26.3	6.6	–8.8
1973	390.0	299.4	132.4	117.3	49.3	75.5	11.6	3.9	–.4	385.6	234.8	114.2	31.3	5.2	4.4
1974	431.3	328.3	151.0	125.0	51.8	85.2	14.4	4.5	–.9	435.8	261.7	134.7	35.6	3.3	–4.4
1975	441.6	334.4	147.6	135.5	50.9	89.3	16.1	5.1	–3.2	508.2	294.6	169.2	40.0	4.5	–66.6
1976	505.5	383.8	172.3	146.6	64.2	101.3	16.3	5.8	–1.8	549.9	316.6	181.9	46.3	5.1	–44.4
1977	566.8	431.2	197.5	159.9	73.0	113.1	18.4	6.8	–2.6	597.7	346.6	193.3	50.8	7.1	–31.0
1978	645.6	485.0	229.4	171.2	83.5	131.3	23.2	8.0	–1.9	653.4	376.5	207.9	60.2	8.9	–7.8
1979	728.2	538.2	268.7	180.4	88.0	152.7	30.8	9.1	–2.6	726.5	412.3	232.6	72.9	8.5	1.7
1980	798.0	586.0	298.9	200.7	84.8	166.2	39.9	10.7	–4.8	842.8	465.9	278.0	89.1	9.8	–44.8
1981	917.2	663.9	345.2	236.0	81.1	195.7	50.2	12.3	–4.9	962.9	520.6	314.2	116.7	11.5	–45.7
1982	938.5	659.9	354.1	241.3	63.1	208.9	58.9	14.8	–4.0	1,072.6	568.2	350.5	138.9	15.0	–134.1
1983	999.4	694.5	352.3	263.7	77.2	226.0	65.3	16.8	–3.1	1,167.5	610.6	378.4	156.9	21.2	–168.1
1984	1,112.5	763.0	377.4	290.2	94.0	257.5	74.3	19.6	–1.9	1,256.6	657.6	390.9	187.3	21.0	–144.1
1985	1,213.5	824.3	417.4	308.5	96.5	281.4	84.0	23.0	.8	1,366.1	720.2	415.7	208.8	21.3	–152.6
1986	1,289.3	869.2	437.3	323.7	106.5	303.4	89.8	25.6	1.3	1,459.1	776.1	441.9	216.3	24.8	–169.9
1987	1,403.2	966.1	489.1	347.9	127.1	323.1	86.1	26.8	1.2	1,535.8	815.2	459.7	230.8	30.2	–132.6
1988	1,502.2	1,019.4	505.0	374.9	137.2	361.5	90.5	28.2	2.5	1,618.7	852.8	488.8	247.7	29.4	–116.6
1989	1,626.3	1,109.7	566.1	399.3	141.5	385.2	94.3	32.2	4.9	1,735.6	901.4	533.1	274.0	27.2	–109.3
1990	1,707.8	1,161.9	592.8	425.5	140.6	410.1	98.7	35.6	1.6	1,872.6	964.4	586.1	295.3	26.8	–164.8
1991	1,758.8	1,180.3	586.7	457.5	133.6	430.2	98.1	44.6	5.7	1,976.7	1,014.1	622.5	312.7	27.3	–217.9
1992	1,843.7	1,240.2	610.6	483.8	143.1	455.0	90.5	50.5	7.6	2,140.4	1,047.8	749.5	313.2	29.9	–296.7
1993	1,945.8	1,318.2	646.6	503.4	165.4	477.7	87.6	55.1	7.2	2,218.4	1,072.2	796.3	313.6	36.4	–272.6
1994	2,089.0	1,426.1	690.7	545.6	186.7	508.2	86.6	59.5	8.6	2,290.8	1,104.1	831.2	323.4	32.2	–201.9
1995	2,212.6	1,517.2	744.1	558.2	211.0	532.8	92.1	59.1	11.4	2,397.6	1,136.5	872.5	354.6	34.0	–184.9
1996	2,376.1	1,642.0	832.1	581.1	223.6	555.2	100.2	66.0	12.7	2,492.1	1,171.1	921.4	365.3	34.3	–116.0
1997	2,551.9	1,780.5	926.3	612.0	237.1	587.2	103.7	67.9	12.6	2,568.6	1,216.6	947.8	371.4	32.9	–16.7
1998	2,724.2	1,911.7	1,027.0	639.8	239.2	624.2	102.4	75.5	10.3	2,633.4	1,256.0	969.6	372.4	35.4	90.8
1999	2,895.0	2,036.2	1,107.5	674.0	248.8	661.4	106.8	80.6	10.1	2,741.0	1,334.0	1,005.5	357.3	44.2	154.0
2000	3,125.9	2,206.8	1,235.7	708.9	255.0	702.7	117.4	93.7	5.3	2,886.5	1,417.1	1,062.4	362.8	44.3	239.4
2001	3,113.1	2,168.0	1,237.3	728.6	194.9	731.1	113.7	101.8	–1.4	3,061.6	1,501.6	1,160.6	344.1	55.3	51.5
2002	2,958.7	2,004.5	1,051.8	762.8	182.6	750.0	98.4	104.9	.9	3,240.8	1,616.9	1,270.4	315.1	38.4	–282.1
2003	3,035.6	2,050.3	1,001.1	807.2	233.1	778.6	95.8	109.2	1.7	3,428.1	1,736.5	1,343.2	300.6	47.9	–392.5
2004	3,254.1	2,213.4	1,046.3	863.8	293.3	828.8	99.1	117.0	–4.2	3,623.2	1,844.0	1,425.3	309.3	44.6	–369.1
2005	3,589.1	2,518.7	1,209.1	921.6	376.5	874.8	105.6	105.2	–15.1	3,892.2	1,965.7	1,521.7	346.2	58.5	–303.1
2006	3,934.8	2,769.8	1,354.3	967.3	435.5	927.6	111.9	139.5	–13.9	4,130.3	2,089.3	1,618.3	372.9	49.7	–195.4
2004: I	3,153.4	2,131.7	1,008.1	844.8	269.1	810.8	96.6	116.9	–2.5	3,572.4	1,808.8	1,416.6	304.9	43.7	–419.0
II ..	3,221.6	2,183.5	1,024.5	857.1	292.9	822.9	98.0	120.4	–3.3	3,597.7	1,831.3	1,418.2	303.7	42.9	–376.1
III ..	3,263.7	2,227.0	1,062.1	867.8	288.6	836.1	99.8	105.5	–4.7	3,637.9	1,859.4	1,421.7	312.5	44.2	–374.2
IV ..	3,377.8	2,311.5	1,090.7	885.5	322.6	845.5	102.2	125.1	–6.5	3,684.9	1,876.5	1,444.6	316.2	47.6	–307.1
2005: I	3,531.9	2,450.4	1,166.4	899.5	373.1	861.0	103.2	125.9	–8.5	3,797.9	1,922.0	1,499.1	322.5	54.3	–266.0
II ..	3,592.2	2,500.8	1,195.5	917.7	377.9	867.9	105.6	128.3	–10.4	3,853.9	1,944.0	1,508.5	343.3	58.1	–261.6
III ..	3,537.6	2,523.5	1,223.5	930.0	357.0	881.7	106.1	54.0	–27.7	3,926.5	1,993.0	1,527.4	346.5	59.6	–388.9
IV ..	3,694.7	2,600.0	1,251.0	939.2	397.9	888.5	107.4	112.7	–13.9	3,990.4	2,003.7	1,551.9	372.6	62.2	–295.6
2006: I	3,849.7	2,697.9	1,318.6	953.3	415.9	918.8	109.7	134.9	–11.7	4,033.7	2,052.3	1,575.3	352.8	53.2	–184.0
II ..	3,916.9	2,760.8	1,342.6	965.9	441.8	920.1	111.5	137.9	–13.4	4,113.9	2,076.7	1,608.0	379.6	49.7	–197.0
III ..	3,955.6	2,789.7	1,355.2	971.2	451.9	926.8	112.6	140.9	–14.5	4,182.5	2,101.0	1,640.0	393.1	48.3	–226.9
IV ..	4,017.3	2,830.7	1,401.0	978.9	432.5	944.6	113.7	144.3	–16.0	4,191.1	2,127.2	1,650.0	366.2	47.8	–173.9
2007: I	4,102.3	2,889.7	1,454.7	990.8	432.1	969.8	112.9	147.6	–17.8	4,326.6	2,156.5	1,729.6	393.5	47.0	–224.3
II ..	4,183.9	2,962.3	1,477.6	1,004.1	468.6	972.2	114.0	150.3	–15.0	4,377.2	2,205.7	1,716.3	407.9	47.3	–193.4
III ..	4,200.8	2,962.7	1,489.2	1,014.4	446.6	981.5	115.3	153.5	–12.2	4,446.4	2,242.1	1,749.1	408.6	46.6	–245.6

¹ Includes taxes from the rest of the world, not shown separately.
² Includes an item for the difference between wage accruals and disbursements, not shown separately.

Source: Department of Commerce (Bureau of Economic Analysis).

TABLE B–84.—*Federal Government current receipts and expenditures, national income and product accounts (NIPA), 1959–2007*

[Billions of dollars; quarterly data at seasonally adjusted annual rates]

Year or quarter	Current receipts									Current expenditures					Net Federal Govern- ment saving
	Total	Current tax receipts				Contri- butions for govern- ment social insur- ance	Income re- ceipts on assets	Current trans- fer re- ceipts	Current surplus of govern- ment enter- prises	Total 2	Con- sump- tion expen- ditures	Current trans- fer pay- ments 3	Interest pay- ments	Sub- si- dies	
		Total 1	Per- sonal current taxes	Taxes on produc- tion and imports	Taxes on corpo- rate income										
1959	87.0	73.3	38.5	12.2	22.5	13.4	0.0	0.4	−0.1	83.6	50.0	26.2	6.3	1.1	3.3
1960	93.9	76.5	41.8	13.1	21.4	16.0	1.4	.4	−.3	86.7	49.8	27.5	8.4	1.1	7.2
1961	95.5	77.5	42.7	13.2	21.5	16.5	1.5	.5	−.5	92.8	51.6	31.3	7.9	2.0	2.6
1962	103.6	83.3	46.5	14.2	22.5	18.6	1.7	.5	−.5	101.1	57.8	32.3	8.6	2.3	2.5
1963	111.8	88.6	49.1	14.7	24.6	21.0	1.8	.6	−.3	106.4	60.8	34.1	9.3	2.2	5.4
1964	111.8	87.8	46.0	15.5	26.1	21.7	1.8	.7	−.3	110.8	62.8	35.2	10.0	2.7	1.0
1965	120.9	95.7	51.1	15.5	28.9	22.7	1.9	1.1	−.3	117.6	65.7	38.3	10.6	3.0	3.3
1966	137.9	104.8	58.6	14.5	31.4	30.5	2.1	1.2	−.6	135.7	75.9	44.2	11.6	3.9	2.3
1967	146.9	109.9	64.4	15.2	30.0	34.0	2.5	1.1	−.6	156.2	87.1	52.6	12.7	3.8	−9.4
1968	171.2	129.8	76.4	17.0	36.1	37.8	2.9	1.1	−.3	173.5	95.4	59.3	14.6	4.1	−2.3
1969	192.5	146.1	91.7	17.9	36.1	43.1	2.7	1.1	−.5	183.8	98.4	65.1	15.8	4.5	8.7
1970	186.0	138.0	88.9	18.2	30.6	45.3	3.1	1.1	−1.5	201.1	98.6	80.0	17.7	4.8	−15.2
1971	191.7	138.7	85.8	19.1	33.5	50.0	3.5	1.1	−1.6	220.0	102.0	95.5	17.9	4.6	−28.4
1972	220.1	158.4	102.8	18.6	36.6	57.9	3.6	1.3	−1.1	244.4	107.7	111.9	18.8	6.6	−24.4
1973	250.4	173.1	109.6	19.9	43.3	74.0	3.8	1.3	−1.8	261.7	108.9	124.9	22.8	5.1	−11.3
1974	279.5	192.2	126.5	20.2	45.1	83.5	4.2	1.4	−1.8	293.3	118.0	145.7	26.0	3.2	−13.8
1975	277.2	187.0	120.7	22.2	43.6	87.5	4.9	1.5	−3.6	346.2	129.6	183.5	28.9	4.3	−69.0
1976	322.5	218.1	141.2	21.6	54.6	99.1	5.9	1.6	−2.2	374.3	137.2	198.5	33.8	4.9	−51.7
1977	363.4	247.4	162.2	22.9	61.6	110.3	6.7	1.9	−2.9	407.5	150.7	212.9	37.1	6.9	−44.1
1978	423.5	286.9	188.9	25.6	71.4	127.9	8.5	2.4	−2.1	450.0	163.3	232.7	45.3	8.7	−26.5
1979	486.2	326.2	224.6	26.0	74.4	148.9	10.7	2.8	−2.3	497.5	179.0	254.6	55.7	8.2	−11.3
1980	532.1	355.9	250.0	34.0	70.3	162.6	13.7	3.5	−3.6	585.7	207.5	299.1	69.7	9.4	−53.6
1981	619.4	408.1	290.6	50.3	65.7	191.8	18.3	3.8	−2.5	672.7	238.3	329.5	93.9	11.1	−53.3
1982	616.6	386.8	295.0	41.4	49.0	204.9	22.2	5.2	−2.4	748.5	263.3	358.8	111.8	14.5	−131.9
1983	642.3	393.6	286.2	44.8	61.3	221.8	23.8	6.0	−2.9	815.4	286.5	383.0	124.6	20.8	−173.0
1984	709.0	425.7	301.4	47.8	75.2	252.8	26.6	7.3	−3.4	877.1	310.0	396.5	150.3	20.6	−168.1
1985	773.3	460.6	336.0	46.4	76.3	276.5	29.1	9.4	−2.4	948.2	338.4	419.3	169.4	20.9	−175.0
1986	815.2	479.6	350.1	44.0	83.8	297.5	31.4	8.2	−1.5	1,006.0	358.2	445.1	178.2	24.5	−190.8
1987	896.6	544.0	392.5	46.3	103.2	315.9	27.9	10.7	−2.0	1,041.6	374.3	452.9	184.6	29.9	−145.0
1988	958.2	566.7	402.9	50.3	111.1	353.1	30.0	10.8	−2.3	1,092.7	382.5	481.9	199.3	29.0	−134.5
1989	1,037.4	621.7	451.5	50.2	117.2	376.3	28.6	12.4	−1.6	1,167.5	399.2	522.0	219.3	26.8	−130.1
1990	1,081.5	642.8	470.2	54.1	118.1	400.1	30.2	13.5	−5.1	1,253.5	419.8	569.9	237.5	26.4	−172.0
1991	1,101.3	636.1	461.3	62.2	109.9	418.6	30.1	17.9	−1.4	1,315.0	439.5	597.6	250.9	26.9	−213.7
1992	1,147.2	660.4	475.3	63.7	118.8	441.8	25.7	19.4	−.1	1,444.6	445.2	718.7	251.3	29.5	−297.4
1993	1,222.5	713.4	505.5	66.7	138.5	463.6	26.2	21.1	−1.8	1,496.0	441.9	764.7	253.4	36.0	−273.5
1994	1,320.8	781.9	542.7	79.4	156.7	493.7	23.4	22.3	−.4	1,533.1	440.8	799.2	261.3	31.8	−212.3
1995	1,406.5	845.1	586.0	75.9	179.3	519.2	23.7	19.1	−.6	1,603.5	440.5	839.0	290.4	33.7	−197.0
1996	1,524.0	932.4	663.4	73.2	190.6	542.8	26.9	23.1	−1.2	1,665.8	446.3	888.3	297.3	34.0	−141.8
1997	1,653.1	1,030.6	744.3	78.2	203.0	576.4	25.9	19.9	.3	1,708.9	457.7	918.8	300.0	32.4	−55.8
1998	1,773.8	1,116.8	825.8	81.1	204.2	613.8	21.5	21.5	−.1	1,734.9	454.6	946.5	298.8	35.0	38.8
1999	1,891.2	1,195.7	893.0	83.9	213.0	651.6	21.5	22.7	−.3	1,787.6	475.1	986.1	282.7	43.8	103.6
2000	2,053.8	1,313.6	999.1	87.8	219.4	691.7	25.2	25.7	−2.3	1,864.4	499.3	1,038.1	283.3	43.8	189.5
2001	2,016.2	1,252.2	994.5	85.8	164.7	717.5	24.9	27.1	−5.5	1,969.5	531.9	1,131.4	258.6	47.6	46.7
2002	1,853.2	1,075.5	830.5	87.3	150.5	734.3	20.2	24.8	−1.6	2,101.1	591.5	1,243.0	229.1	37.5	−247.9
2003	1,879.9	1,070.8	774.5	89.7	197.8	758.9	22.9	25.0	−2.3	2,252.1	662.7	1,328.7	212.9	47.8	−372.1
2004	2,008.9	1,152.3	797.4	94.6	250.3	805.2	23.8	28.8	−1.2	2,379.5	723.7	1,390.6	221.0	44.2	−370.6
2005	2,243.4	1,362.7	932.4	99.0	319.8	849.3	24.5	11.6	−4.8	2,561.6	768.5	1,479.1	255.9	58.2	−318.3
2006	2,495.8	1,537.5	1,053.2	98.6	373.1	901.6	24.7	35.2	−3.2	2,715.8	812.8	1,576.1	277.5	49.4	−220.0
2004: I	1,939.5	1,100.7	767.5	93.8	229.7	788.3	23.6	27.6	−.6	2,350.6	709.6	1,382.9	216.3	43.3	−411.1
II	1,989.7	1,139.0	785.8	94.3	249.8	799.6	23.4	28.5	−.8	2,363.8	721.2	1,383.2	215.3	42.6	−374.1
III	2,023.5	1,159.4	809.6	95.1	246.4	812.1	23.9	29.4	−1.4	2,385.4	734.6	1,382.5	224.4	43.9	−361.9
IV	2,082.8	1,209.9	826.6	95.3	275.3	820.9	24.2	29.9	−2.1	2,418.2	729.6	1,413.7	227.8	47.2	−335.4
2005: I	2,209.2	1,321.4	897.1	96.5	316.4	836.0	24.6	30.5	−3.3	2,507.2	759.1	1,460.6	233.5	54.0	−298.0
II	2,247.5	1,351.7	920.4	100.7	320.9	842.6	25.5	32.0	−4.2	2,535.0	761.7	1,462.0	253.6	57.7	−287.5
III	2,188.5	1,362.3	946.1	99.8	303.5	856.1	24.3	−48.2	−6.0	2,582.9	784.1	1,483.7	255.8	59.2	−394.3
IV	2,328.3	1,415.2	966.1	98.8	338.3	862.6	23.8	32.2	−5.6	2,621.4	769.0	1,510.1	280.5	61.8	−293.2
2006: I	2,436.5	1,488.0	1,022.7	98.7	356.4	892.8	24.2	33.8	−2.3	2,656.2	804.8	1,539.5	259.0	52.8	−219.6
II	2,471.5	1,521.1	1,032.9	99.0	378.6	894.1	24.6	34.6	−2.9	2,711.4	806.6	1,571.1	284.4	49.3	−239.9
III	2,513.1	1,555.3	1,057.4	99.3	387.1	900.9	24.8	35.5	−3.3	2,752.3	813.3	1,594.3	296.7	47.9	−239.2
IV	2,561.9	1,585.4	1,099.8	97.2	370.1	918.8	25.4	36.7	−4.3	2,743.4	826.4	1,599.6	270.0	47.4	−181.5
2007: I	2,619.7	1,619.0	1,138.8	97.9	370.3	944.0	24.6	38.1	−6.1	2,838.2	829.8	1,665.6	296.3	46.6	−218.5
II	2,670.1	1,663.2	1,151.7	98.3	401.3	946.3	25.1	38.5	−3.0	2,876.9	848.8	1,670.9	309.4	46.9	−206.8
III	2,687.0	1,666.6	1,170.1	101.4	382.5	955.6	25.3	39.4	.2	2,919.7	867.7	1,696.4	309.3	46.2	−232.6

[1] Includes taxes from the rest of the world, not shown separately.
[2] Includes an item for the difference between wage accruals and disbursements, not shown separately.
[3] Includes Federal grants-in-aid to State and local governments. See Table B–82 for data on Federal grants-in-aid.

Source: Department of Commerce (Bureau of Economic Analysis).

TABLE B–85.—*State and local government current receipts and expenditures, national income and product accounts (NIPA), 1959–2007*

[Billions of dollars; quarterly data at seasonally adjusted annual rates]

Year or quarter	Current receipts									Current expenditures						Net State and local government saving
	Total	Current tax receipts				Contributions for government social insurance	Income receipts on assets	Current transfer receipts [1]	Current surplus of government enterprises	Total [2]	Consumption expenditures	Government social benefit payments to persons	Interest payments	Subsidies	
		Total	Personal current taxes	Taxes on production and imports	Taxes on corporate income										
1959	40.6	33.8	3.8	28.8	1.2	0.4	1.1	4.2	1.1	36.9	30.7	4.3	1.8	0.0	3.8
1960	44.5	37.0	4.2	31.5	1.2	.5	1.3	4.5	1.2	40.2	33.5	4.6	2.1	.0	4.3
1961	48.1	39.7	4.6	33.8	1.3	.5	1.4	5.2	1.3	43.8	36.6	5.0	2.2	.0	4.3
1962	52.0	42.8	5.0	36.3	1.5	.5	1.5	5.8	1.4	46.8	39.0	5.3	2.4	.0	5.2
1963	56.0	45.8	5.4	38.7	1.7	.6	1.6	6.4	1.6	50.3	41.9	5.7	2.7	.0	5.7
1964	61.3	49.8	6.1	41.8	1.8	.7	1.9	7.3	1.6	54.9	45.8	6.2	2.9	.0	6.4
1965	66.5	53.9	6.6	45.3	2.0	.8	2.2	8.0	1.7	60.0	50.2	6.7	3.1	.0	6.5
1966	74.9	58.8	7.8	48.8	2.2	.8	2.6	11.1	1.6	67.2	56.1	7.6	3.4	.0	7.8
1967	82.5	64.0	8.6	52.8	2.6	.9	3.0	13.1	1.5	75.5	62.6	9.2	3.7	.0	7.0
1968	93.5	73.4	10.6	59.5	3.3	.9	3.5	14.2	1.5	86.0	70.4	11.4	4.2	.0	7.5
1969	105.5	82.5	12.8	66.0	3.6	1.0	4.3	16.2	1.5	97.5	79.9	13.2	4.4	.0	8.0
1970	120.1	91.3	14.2	73.3	3.7	1.1	5.2	21.1	1.5	113.0	91.5	16.1	5.3	.0	7.1
1971	134.9	101.7	15.9	81.5	4.3	1.2	5.5	25.2	1.4	128.5	102.7	19.3	6.5	.0	6.5
1972	158.4	115.6	20.9	89.4	5.3	1.3	5.9	34.0	1.6	142.8	113.2	22.0	7.5	.1	15.6
1973	174.3	126.3	22.8	97.4	6.0	1.5	7.8	37.3	1.5	158.6	126.0	24.1	8.5	.1	15.7
1974	188.1	136.0	24.5	104.8	6.7	1.7	10.2	39.3	.9	178.7	143.7	25.3	9.6	.1	9.3
1975	209.6	147.4	26.9	113.2	7.3	1.8	11.2	48.7	.4	207.1	165.1	30.8	11.1	.2	2.5
1976	233.7	165.7	31.1	125.0	9.6	2.2	10.4	55.0	.4	226.3	179.5	34.1	12.5	.2	7.4
1977	259.9	183.7	35.4	136.9	11.4	2.8	11.7	61.4	.3	246.8	195.9	37.0	13.7	.2	13.1
1978	287.6	198.2	40.5	145.6	12.1	3.4	14.7	71.1	.3	268.9	213.2	40.8	14.9	.2	18.7
1979	308.4	212.0	44.0	154.4	13.6	3.9	20.1	72.7	–.3	295.4	233.3	44.3	17.2	.3	13.0
1980	338.2	230.0	48.9	166.7	14.5	3.6	26.3	79.5	–1.2	329.4	258.4	51.2	19.4	.4	8.8
1981	370.2	255.8	54.6	185.7	15.4	3.9	32.0	81.0	–2.4	362.7	282.3	57.1	22.8	.4	7.6
1982	391.4	273.2	59.1	200.0	14.0	4.0	36.7	79.1	–1.6	393.6	304.9	61.2	27.1	.5	–2.2
1983	428.6	300.9	66.1	218.9	15.9	4.1	41.4	82.4	–.2	423.7	324.1	66.9	32.3	.4	4.9
1984	480.2	337.3	76.0	242.5	18.8	4.7	47.7	89.0	1.5	456.2	347.7	71.2	37.0	.4	23.9
1985	521.1	363.7	81.4	262.1	20.2	4.9	54.9	94.5	3.2	498.7	381.8	77.3	39.4	.3	22.3
1986	561.6	389.5	87.2	279.7	22.7	6.0	58.4	105.0	2.8	540.7	417.9	84.3	38.2	.3	21.0
1987	590.6	422.1	96.6	301.6	23.9	7.2	58.1	100.0	3.1	578.1	440.9	90.7	46.2	.3	12.4
1988	635.5	452.8	102.1	324.6	26.0	8.4	60.5	109.0	4.8	617.6	470.4	98.5	48.4	.4	17.9
1989	687.3	488.0	114.6	349.1	24.2	9.0	65.7	118.1	6.5	666.5	502.1	109.3	54.6	.4	20.8
1990	737.8	519.1	122.6	374.1	22.5	10.0	68.4	133.5	6.7	730.5	544.6	127.7	57.9	.4	7.2
1991	789.2	544.3	125.3	395.3	23.6	11.6	68.0	158.2	7.1	793.3	574.6	156.5	61.7	.4	–4.2
1992	845.7	579.8	135.3	420.1	24.4	13.1	64.8	180.3	7.7	845.0	602.7	180.0	61.9	.4	.7
1993	886.9	604.7	141.1	436.8	26.9	14.1	61.4	197.7	9.0	886.0	630.3	195.2	60.2	.4	.9
1994	942.9	644.2	148.0	466.3	30.0	14.5	63.2	211.9	9.0	932.4	663.3	206.7	62.0	.3	10.5
1995	990.2	672.1	158.1	482.4	31.7	13.6	68.4	224.1	12.0	978.2	696.1	217.6	64.2	.3	12.0
1996	1,043.3	709.6	168.7	507.9	33.0	12.5	73.3	234.1	13.9	1,017.5	724.8	224.3	68.1	.3	25.8
1997	1,097.4	749.9	182.0	533.8	34.1	10.8	77.8	246.6	12.3	1,058.3	758.9	227.6	71.4	.4	39.1
1998	1,163.2	794.9	201.2	558.8	34.9	10.4	80.9	266.8	10.2	1,111.2	801.4	235.8	73.6	.4	52.0
1999	1,236.7	840.4	214.5	590.2	35.8	9.8	85.3	290.8	10.4	1,186.3	858.9	252.4	74.6	.4	50.4
2000	1,319.5	893.2	236.6	621.1	35.5	11.0	92.2	315.4	7.7	1,269.5	917.8	271.7	79.5	.5	50.0
2001	1,373.0	915.8	242.7	642.8	30.2	13.6	88.8	350.8	4.0	1,368.2	969.8	305.2	85.5	7.7	4.8
2002	1,410.1	929.0	221.3	675.5	32.2	15.8	78.2	384.7	2.5	1,444.3	1,025.3	332.0	86.0	.9	–34.2
2003	1,494.2	979.4	226.6	717.5	35.3	19.8	72.9	422.7	–.6	1,514.5	1,073.8	353.0	87.7	.1	–20.4
2004	1,594.3	1,061.2	249.0	769.2	43.0	23.6	75.4	437.2	–3.0	1,592.8	1,120.3	383.8	88.4	.4	1.5
2005	1,706.9	1,156.0	276.7	822.6	56.7	25.5	81.0	454.8	–10.3	1,691.7	1,197.2	403.8	90.4	.4	15.2
2006	1,797.7	1,232.3	301.2	868.8	62.4	26.0	87.1	462.9	–10.7	1,773.0	1,276.5	400.8	95.4	.4	24.6
2004: I	1,555.2	1,031.0	240.6	751.0	39.4	22.5	73.0	430.5	–1.9	1,563.1	1,099.2	375.0	88.6	.4	–7.9
II	1,582.5	1,044.6	238.6	762.9	43.1	23.3	74.6	442.5	–2.5	1,584.5	1,110.2	385.6	88.3	.4	–1.9
III	1,584.8	1,067.5	252.5	772.7	42.3	24.0	75.9	420.6	–3.3	1,597.0	1,124.8	383.7	88.1	.4	–12.3
IV	1,654.8	1,101.6	264.1	790.1	47.3	24.6	78.0	455.1	–4.4	1,626.5	1,147.0	390.8	88.4	.4	28.3
2005: I	1,681.1	1,128.9	269.3	803.0	56.7	25.0	78.6	453.7	–5.1	1,649.1	1,162.9	396.8	89.0	.4	32.0
II	1,705.6	1,149.1	275.1	817.0	57.0	25.4	80.1	457.2	–6.2	1,679.7	1,182.3	407.4	89.7	.4	25.9
III	1,709.3	1,161.1	277.4	830.2	53.5	25.6	81.8	462.4	–21.7	1,703.8	1,208.9	403.8	90.7	.4	5.4
IV	1,731.8	1,184.8	284.9	840.3	59.6	25.8	83.6	445.9	–8.3	1,734.3	1,234.7	407.1	92.1	.4	–2.5
2006: I	1,767.8	1,209.9	295.9	854.6	59.4	26.0	85.5	455.7	–9.4	1,732.1	1,247.4	390.4	93.9	.4	35.6
II	1,803.7	1,239.7	309.7	866.9	63.2	26.0	86.9	461.6	–10.5	1,760.9	1,270.0	395.3	95.2	.4	42.8
III	1,806.7	1,234.4	297.7	872.0	64.8	26.0	87.8	469.6	–11.1	1,794.4	1,287.7	409.9	96.4	.4	12.3
IV	1,812.4	1,245.3	301.3	881.6	62.4	25.9	88.3	464.7	–11.7	1,804.8	1,300.8	407.5	96.1	.4	7.6
2007: I	1,856.6	1,270.6	315.9	893.0	61.8	25.8	88.3	483.6	–11.8	1,862.4	1,326.7	438.1	97.3	.4	–5.8
II	1,889.9	1,299.1	325.9	905.8	67.4	25.9	88.9	487.9	–12.0	1,876.5	1,355.9	421.5	98.6	.4	13.4
III	1,892.8	1,296.1	319.1	913.0	64.1	25.9	90.0	493.1	–12.4	1,905.8	1,374.3	431.7	99.3	.4	–13.0

[1] Includes Federal grants-in-aid. See Table B–82 for data on Federal grants-in-aid.
[2] Includes an item for the difference between wage accruals and disbursements, not shown separately.

Source: Department of Commerce (Bureau of Economic Analysis).

TABLE B–86.—*State and local government revenues and expenditures, selected fiscal years, 1938–2005*

[Millions of dollars]

Fiscal year [1]	General revenues by source [2]							General expenditures by function [2]				
	Total	Property taxes	Sales and gross receipts taxes	Individual income taxes	Corporation net income taxes	Revenue from Federal Government	All other [3]	Total [4]	Education	Highways	Public welfare [4]	All other [4, 5]
1938	9,228	4,440	1,794	218	165	800	1,811	8,757	2,491	1,650	1,069	3,547
1940	9,609	4,430	1,982	224	156	945	1,872	9,229	2,638	1,573	1,156	3,862
1942	10,418	4,537	2,351	276	272	858	2,123	9,190	2,586	1,490	1,225	3,889
1944	10,908	4,604	2,289	342	451	954	2,269	8,863	2,793	1,200	1,133	3,737
1946	12,356	4,986	2,986	422	447	855	2,661	11,028	3,356	1,672	1,409	4,591
1948	17,250	6,126	4,442	543	592	1,861	3,685	17,684	5,379	3,036	2,099	7,170
1950	20,911	7,349	5,154	788	593	2,486	4,541	22,787	7,177	3,803	2,940	8,867
1952	25,181	8,652	6,357	998	846	2,566	5,763	26,098	8,318	4,650	2,788	10,342
1953	27,307	9,375	6,927	1,065	817	2,870	6,252	27,910	9,390	4,987	2,914	10,619
1954	29,012	9,967	7,276	1,127	778	2,966	6,897	30,701	10,557	5,527	3,060	11,557
1955	31,073	10,735	7,643	1,237	744	3,131	7,584	33,724	11,907	6,452	3,168	12,197
1956	34,667	11,749	8,691	1,538	890	3,335	8,465	36,711	13,220	6,953	3,139	13,399
1957	38,164	12,864	9,467	1,754	984	3,843	9,252	40,375	14,134	7,816	3,485	14,940
1958	41,219	14,047	9,829	1,759	1,018	4,865	9,699	44,851	15,919	8,567	3,818	16,547
1959	45,306	14,983	10,437	1,994	1,001	6,377	10,516	48,887	17,283	9,592	4,136	17,876
1960	50,505	16,405	11,849	2,463	1,180	6,974	11,634	51,876	18,719	9,428	4,404	19,325
1961	54,037	18,002	12,463	2,613	1,266	7,131	12,563	56,201	20,574	9,844	4,720	21,063
1962	58,252	19,054	13,494	3,037	1,308	7,871	13,489	60,206	22,216	10,357	5,084	22,549
1963	62,890	20,089	14,456	3,269	1,505	8,722	14,850	64,816	23,776	11,136	5,481	24,423
1962-63	62,269	19,833	14,446	3,267	1,505	8,663	14,556	63,977	23,729	11,150	5,420	23,678
1963-64	68,443	21,241	15,762	3,791	1,695	10,002	15,951	69,302	26,286	11,664	5,766	25,586
1964-65	74,000	22,583	17,118	4,090	1,929	11,029	17,250	74,678	28,563	12,221	6,315	27,579
1965-66	83,036	24,670	19,085	4,760	2,038	13,214	19,269	82,843	33,287	12,770	6,757	30,029
1966-67	91,197	26,047	20,530	5,825	2,227	15,370	21,198	93,350	37,919	13,932	8,218	33,281
1967-68	101,264	27,747	22,911	7,308	2,518	17,181	23,599	102,411	41,158	14,481	9,857	36,915
1968-69	114,550	30,673	26,519	8,908	3,180	19,153	26,117	116,728	47,238	15,417	12,110	41,963
1969-70	130,756	34,054	30,322	10,812	3,738	21,857	29,973	131,332	52,718	16,427	14,679	47,508
1970-71	144,927	37,852	33,233	11,900	3,424	26,146	32,372	150,674	59,413	18,095	18,226	54,940
1971-72	167,535	42,877	37,518	15,227	4,416	31,342	36,156	168,549	65,813	19,021	21,117	62,598
1972-73	190,222	45,283	42,047	17,994	5,425	39,264	40,210	181,357	69,713	18,615	23,582	69,447
1973-74	207,670	47,705	46,098	19,491	6,015	41,820	46,542	198,959	75,833	19,946	25,085	78,095
1974-75	228,171	51,491	49,815	21,454	6,642	47,034	51,735	230,722	87,858	22,528	28,156	92,180
1975-76	256,176	57,001	54,547	24,575	7,273	55,589	57,191	256,731	97,216	23,907	32,604	103,004
1976-77	285,157	62,527	60,641	29,246	9,174	62,444	61,125	274,215	102,780	23,058	35,906	112,472
1977-78	315,960	66,422	67,596	33,176	10,738	69,592	68,435	296,984	110,758	24,609	39,140	122,478
1978-79	343,236	64,944	74,247	36,932	12,128	75,164	79,822	327,517	119,448	28,440	41,898	137,731
1979-80	382,322	68,499	79,927	42,080	13,321	83,029	95,467	369,086	133,211	33,311	47,288	155,276
1980-81	423,404	74,969	85,971	46,426	14,143	90,294	111,599	407,449	145,784	34,603	54,105	172,957
1981-82	457,654	82,067	93,613	50,738	15,028	87,282	128,925	436,733	154,282	34,520	57,996	189,935
1982-83	486,753	89,105	100,247	55,129	14,258	90,007	138,008	466,516	163,876	36,655	60,906	205,080
1983-84	542,730	96,457	114,097	64,529	17,141	96,935	153,571	505,008	176,108	39,419	66,414	223,068
1984-85	598,121	103,757	126,376	70,361	19,152	106,158	172,317	553,899	192,686	44,989	71,479	244,745
1985-86	641,486	111,709	135,005	74,365	19,994	113,099	187,314	605,623	210,819	49,368	75,868	269,568
1986-87	686,860	121,203	144,091	83,935	22,425	114,857	200,350	657,134	226,619	52,355	82,650	295,510
1987-88	726,762	132,212	156,452	88,350	23,663	117,602	208,482	704,921	242,683	55,621	89,090	317,527
1988-89	786,129	142,400	166,336	97,806	25,926	125,824	227,838	762,360	263,898	58,105	97,879	342,479
1989-90	849,502	155,613	177,885	105,640	23,566	136,802	249,996	834,818	288,148	61,057	110,518	375,094
1990-91	902,207	167,999	185,570	109,341	22,242	154,099	262,955	908,108	309,302	64,937	130,402	403,467
1991-92	979,137	180,337	197,731	115,638	23,880	179,174	282,376	981,253	324,652	67,351	158,723	430,526
1992-93	1,041,643	189,744	209,649	123,235	26,417	198,663	293,935	1,033,434	342,287	68,370	170,705	449,072
1993-94	1,100,490	197,141	223,628	128,810	28,320	215,492	307,099	1,077,665	353,287	72,067	183,394	468,916
1994-95	1,169,505	203,451	237,268	137,931	31,406	228,771	330,677	1,149,863	378,273	77,109	196,703	497,779
1995-96	1,222,821	209,440	248,993	146,844	32,009	234,891	350,645	1,193,276	398,859	79,092	197,354	517,971
1996-97	1,289,237	218,877	261,418	159,042	33,820	244,847	371,233	1,249,984	418,416	82,062	203,779	545,727
1997-98	1,365,762	230,150	274,883	175,630	34,412	255,048	395,639	1,318,042	450,365	87,214	208,120	572,343
1998-99	1,434,029	239,672	290,993	189,309	33,922	270,628	409,505	1,402,369	483,259	93,018	218,957	607,134
1999-2000	1,541,322	249,178	309,290	211,661	36,059	291,950	443,186	1,506,797	521,612	101,336	237,336	646,512
2000-01	1,647,161	263,689	320,217	226,334	35,296	324,033	477,592	1,626,066	563,575	107,235	261,622	693,634
2001-02	1,684,879	279,191	324,123	202,832	28,152	360,546	490,035	1,736,866	594,694	115,295	285,464	741,413
2002-03	1,763,212	296,683	337,787	199,407	31,369	389,264	508,702	1,821,917	621,335	117,696	310,783	772,102
2003-04	1,889,741	318,242	360,629	215,215	33,716	425,683	536,256	1,907,915	655,361	118,179	339,895	794,481
2004-05	2,020,926	335,678	383,264	240,930	43,138	438,156	579,760	2,014,357	689,376	123,900	366,661	834,421

[1] Fiscal years not the same for all governments. See Note.
[2] Excludes revenues or expenditures of publicly owned utilities and liquor stores and of insurance-trust activities. Intergovernmental receipts and payments between State and local governments are also excluded.
[3] Includes motor vehicle license taxes, other taxes, and charges and miscellaneous revenues.
[4] Includes intergovernmental payments to the Federal Government.
[5] Includes expenditures for libraries, hospitals, health, employment security administration, veterans' services, air transportation, water transport and terminals, parking facilities, transit subsidies, police protection, fire protection, correction, protective inspection and regulation, sewerage, natural resources, parks and recreation, housing and community development, solid waste management, financial administration, judicial and legal, general public buildings, other government administration, interest on general debt, and other general expenditures, not elsewhere classified.

Note.—Except for States listed, data for fiscal years listed from 1962-63 to 2004-05 are the aggregation of data for government fiscal years that ended in the 12-month period from July 1 to June 30 of those years; Texas used August and Alabama and Michigan used September as end dates. Data for 1963 and earlier years include data for governments fiscal years ending during that particular calendar year.

Data prior to 1952 are not available for intervening years.

Source: Department of Commerce (Bureau of the Census).

[Billions of dollars]

End of year or month	Total Treasury securities outstanding [1]	Marketable							Nonmarketable				
		Total [2]	Treasury bills	Treasury notes	Treasury bonds	Treasury inflation-protected securities			Total	U.S. savings securities [3]	Foreign series [4]	Government account series	Other [5]
						Total	Notes	Bonds					
Fiscal year:													
1969	351.7	226.1	68.4	78.9	78.8				125.6	51.7	4.1	66.8	3.1
1970	369.0	232.6	76.2	93.5	63.0				136.4	51.3	4.8	76.3	4.1
1971	396.3	245.5	86.7	104.8	54.0				150.8	53.0	9.3	82.8	5.8
1972	425.4	257.2	94.6	113.4	49.1				168.2	55.9	19.0	89.6	3.7
1973	456.4	263.0	100.1	117.8	45.1				193.4	59.4	28.5	101.7	3.7
1974	473.2	266.6	105.0	128.4	33.1				206.7	61.9	25.0	115.4	4.3
1975	532.1	315.6	128.6	150.3	36.8				216.5	65.5	23.2	124.2	3.6
1976	619.3	392.6	161.2	191.8	39.6				226.7	69.7	21.5	130.6	4.9
1977	697.6	443.5	156.1	241.7	45.7				254.1	75.4	21.8	140.1	16.8
1978	767.0	485.2	160.9	267.9	56.4				281.8	79.8	21.7	153.3	27.1
1979	819.0	506.7	161.4	274.2	71.1				312.3	80.4	28.1	176.4	27.4
1980	906.4	594.5	199.8	310.9	83.8				311.9	72.7	25.2	189.8	24.2
1981	996.5	683.2	223.4	363.6	96.2				313.3	68.0	20.5	201.1	23.7
1982	1,140.9	824.4	277.9	442.9	103.6				316.5	67.3	14.6	210.5	24.1
1983	1,375.8	1,024.0	340.7	557.5	125.7				351.8	70.0	11.5	234.7	35.6
1984	1,559.6	1,176.6	356.8	661.7	158.1				383.0	72.8	8.8	259.5	41.8
1985	1,821.0	1,360.2	384.2	776.4	199.5				460.8	77.0	6.6	313.9	63.3
1986	2,122.7	1,564.3	410.7	896.9	241.7				558.4	85.6	4.1	365.9	102.8
1987	2,347.8	1,676.0	378.3	1,005.1	277.6				671.8	97.0	4.4	440.7	129.8
1988	2,599.9	1,802.9	398.5	1,089.6	299.9				797.0	106.2	6.3	536.5	148.0
1989	2,836.3	1,892.8	406.6	1,133.2	338.0				943.5	114.0	6.8	663.7	159.0
1990	3,210.9	2,092.8	482.5	1,218.1	377.2				1,118.2	122.2	36.0	779.4	180.6
1991	3,662.8	2,390.7	564.6	1,387.7	423.4				1,272.1	133.5	41.6	908.4	188.5
1992	4,061.8	2,677.5	634.3	1,566.3	461.8				1,384.3	148.3	37.0	1,011.0	188.0
1993	4,408.6	2,904.9	658.4	1,734.2	497.4				1,503.7	167.0	42.5	1,114.3	179.9
1994	4,689.5	3,091.6	697.3	1,867.5	511.8				1,597.9	176.4	42.0	1,211.7	167.8
1995	4,950.6	3,260.4	742.5	1,980.3	522.6				1,690.2	181.2	41.0	1,324.3	143.8
1996	5,220.8	3,418.4	761.2	2,098.7	543.5				1,802.4	184.1	37.5	1,454.7	126.1
1997	5,407.5	3,439.6	701.9	2,122.2	576.2	24.4	24.4		1,967.9	182.7	34.9	1,608.5	141.9
1998	5,518.7	3,331.0	637.6	2,009.1	610.4	58.8	41.9	17.0	2,187.7	180.8	35.1	1,777.3	194.4
1999	5,647.2	3,233.0	653.2	1,828.8	643.7	92.4	67.6	24.8	2,414.2	180.0	31.0	2,005.2	198.1
2000	5,622.1	2,992.8	616.2	1,611.3	635.3	115.0	81.6	33.4	2,629.3	177.7	25.4	2,242.9	183.3
2001 [1]	5,807.5	2,930.7	734.9	1,433.0	613.0	134.9	95.1	39.7	2,876.7	186.5	18.3	2,492.1	179.9
2002	6,228.2	3,136.7	868.3	1,521.6	593.0	138.9	93.7	45.1	3,091.5	193.3	12.5	2,707.3	178.4
2003	6,783.2	3,460.7	918.2	1,799.5	576.9	166.1	120.0	46.1	3,322.5	201.6	11.0	2,912.2	197.7
2004	7,379.1	3,846.1	961.5	2,109.6	552.0	223.0			3,533.0	204.2	5.9	3,130.0	192.9
2005	7,932.7	4,084.9	914.3	2,328.8	520.7	307.1			3,847.8	203.6	3.1	3,380.6	260.5
2006	8,507.0	4,303.0	911.5	2,447.2	534.7	395.6			4,203.9	203.7	3.0	3,722.7	274.5
2007	9,007.7	4,448.1	958.1	2,458.0	561.1	456.9			4,559.5	197.1	3.0	4,026.8	332.6
2006: Jan	8,196.1	4,194.8	963.2	2,361.1	516.6	346.9			4,001.2	205.6	3.8	3,523.2	268.6
Feb	8,269.9	4,277.6	999.6	2,391.7	526.7	345.6			3,992.3	205.9	3.6	3,513.1	269.7
Mar	8,371.2	4,340.4	1,042.1	2,409.7	526.7	347.9			4,030.8	206.0	3.4	3,551.2	270.2
Apr	8,355.7	4,283.2	965.1	2,409.7	526.7	367.7			4,072.5	206.1	3.2	3,589.1	274.2
May	8,356.8	4,269.2	954.4	2,408.0	523.2	369.7			4,087.5	205.7	3.0	3,604.2	274.6
June	8,420.0	4,254.0	916.7	2,427.4	523.2	372.8			4,166.0	205.2	3.0	3,680.2	277.6
July	8,444.3	4,280.4	932.7	2,416.9	523.2	393.7			4,163.9	204.8	3.0	3,683.2	273.0
Aug	8,515.0	4,344.7	962.3	2,439.2	534.7	394.5			4,170.4	204.0	3.0	3,689.2	274.1
Sept	8,507.0	4,303.0	911.5	2,447.2	534.7	395.6			4,203.9	203.7	3.0	3,722.7	274.5
Oct	8,584.3	4,338.0	929.5	2,444.4	534.7	415.4			4,246.4	203.2	3.0	3,762.7	277.4
Nov	8,633.2	4,381.0	989.0	2,433.9	530.7	413.4			4,252.2	202.8	3.0	3,763.0	283.5
Dec	8,680.2	4,342.0	944.2	2,441.9	530.7	411.2			4,338.3	202.4	3.0	3,839.3	293.5
2007: Jan	8,707.6	4,347.4	932.1	2,459.7	530.7	411.0			4,360.1	201.4	3.0	3,853.8	302.0
Feb	8,778.1	4,408.6	982.1	2,460.5	540.5	411.5			4,369.6	200.9	3.0	3,859.4	306.3
Mar	8,849.7	4,468.8	1,033.1	2,468.5	540.5	412.7			4,380.9	200.3	3.5	3,859.2	317.8
Apr	8,840.2	4,412.4	944.1	2,482.7	540.5	431.1			4,427.8	199.8	3.5	3,897.3	327.2
May	8,829.0	4,378.3	919.1	2,463.0	547.3	435.0			4,450.7	199.2	3.0	3,912.3	336.3
June	8,867.7	4,339.1	869.1	2,471.0	547.3	437.8			4,528.6	198.6	3.0	3,989.3	337.7
July	8,932.4	4,403.4	892.1	2,494.1	547.3	456.0			4,529.0	198.1	3.0	3,994.2	333.7
Aug	9,005.6	4,496.2	1,014.1	2,450.0	561.1	457.0			4,509.4	197.4	3.0	3,976.4	332.6
Sept	9,007.7	4,448.1	958.1	2,458.0	561.1	456.9			4,559.5	197.1	3.0	4,026.8	332.6
Oct	9,079.1	4,464.7	938.1	2,482.1	561.1	469.4			4,614.4	196.9	3.0	4,081.4	333.1
Nov	9,149.3	4,543.3	1,035.0	2,465.0	558.5	470.7			4,606.1	196.6	3.0	4,073.7	332.8
Dec	9,229.2	4,536.6	1,003.9	2,488.5	558.5	471.7			4,692.6	196.5	3.0	4,164.3	328.9

[1] Data beginning with January 2001 are interest-bearing and non-interest-bearing securities; prior data are interest-bearing securities only.
[2] Data from 1986 to 2002 and 2005 to 2007 includes Federal Financing Bank securities, not shown separately.
[3] Through 1996, series is U.S. savings bonds. Beginning 1997, includes U.S. retirement plan bonds, U.S. individual retirement bonds, and U.S. savings notes previously included in "other" nonmarketable securities.
[4] Nonmarketable certificates of indebtedness, notes, bonds, and bills in the Treasury foreign series of dollar-denominated and foreign-currency-denominated issues.
[5] Includes depository bonds, retirement plan bonds, Rural Electrification Administration bonds, State and local bonds, special issues held only by U.S. Government agencies and trust funds and the Federal home loan banks, and, for the period July 2003 through February 2004, depositary compensation securities.

Note.—Through fiscal year 1976, the fiscal year was on a July 1–June 30 basis; beginning with October 1976 (fiscal year 1977), the fiscal year is on an October 1–September 30 basis.

Source: Department of the Treasury.

TABLE B–88.—*Maturity distribution and average length of marketable interest-bearing public debt securities held by private investors, 1969–2007*

End of year or month	Amount outstanding, privately held	Maturity class					Average length [1]	
		Within 1 year	1 to 5 years	5 to 10 years	10 to 20 years	20 years and over		
		Millions of dollars					Years	Months
Fiscal year:								
1969	156,008	69,311	50,182	18,078	6,097	12,337	4	2
1970	157,910	76,443	57,035	8,286	7,876	8,272	3	8
1971	161,863	74,803	58,557	14,503	6,357	7,645	3	6
1972	165,978	79,509	57,157	16,033	6,358	6,922	3	3
1973	167,869	84,041	54,139	16,385	8,741	4,564	3	1
1974	164,862	87,150	50,103	14,197	9,930	3,481	2	11
1975	210,382	115,677	65,852	15,385	8,857	4,611	2	8
1976	279,782	150,296	90,578	24,169	8,087	6,652	2	7
1977	326,674	161,329	113,319	33,067	8,428	10,531	2	11
1978	356,501	163,819	132,993	33,500	11,383	14,805	3	3
1979	380,530	181,883	127,574	32,279	18,489	20,304	3	7
1980	463,717	220,084	156,244	38,809	25,901	22,679	3	9
1981	549,863	256,187	182,237	48,743	32,569	30,127	4	0
1982	682,043	314,436	221,783	75,749	33,017	37,058	3	11
1983	862,631	379,579	294,955	99,174	40,826	48,097	4	1
1984	1,017,488	437,941	332,808	130,417	49,664	66,658	4	6
1985	1,185,675	472,661	402,766	159,383	62,853	88,012	4	11
1986	1,354,275	506,903	467,348	189,995	70,664	119,365	5	3
1987	1,445,366	483,582	526,746	209,160	72,862	153,016	5	9
1988	1,555,208	524,201	552,993	232,453	74,186	171,375	5	9
1989	1,654,660	546,751	578,333	247,428	80,616	201,532	6	0
1990	1,841,903	626,297	630,144	267,573	82,713	235,176	6	1
1991	2,113,799	713,778	761,243	280,574	84,900	273,304	6	0
1992	2,363,802	808,705	866,329	295,921	84,706	308,141	5	11
1993	2,562,336	858,135	978,714	306,663	94,345	324,479	5	10
1994	2,719,861	877,932	1,128,322	289,998	88,208	335,401	5	8
1995	2,870,781	1,002,875	1,157,492	290,111	87,297	333,006	5	4
1996	3,011,185	1,058,558	1,212,258	306,643	111,360	322,366	5	3
1997	2,998,846	1,017,913	1,206,993	321,622	154,205	298,113	5	5
1998	2,856,637	940,572	1,105,175	319,331	157,347	334,212	5	10
1999	2,728,011	915,145	962,644	378,163	149,703	322,356	6	0
2000	2,469,152	858,903	791,540	355,382	167,082	296,246	6	2
2001	2,328,302	900,178	650,522	329,247	174,653	273,702	6	1
2002	2,492,821	939,986	802,032	311,176	203,816	235,811	5	6
2003	2,804,092	1,057,049	955,239	351,552	243,755	196,497	5	1
2004	3,145,244	1,127,850	1,150,979	414,728	243,036	208,652	4	11
2005	3,334,411	1,100,783	1,279,646	499,386	281,229	173,367	4	10
2006	3,496,359	1,140,553	1,295,589	589,748	290,733	179,736	4	11
2007	3,634,666	1,176,510	1,309,871	677,905	291,963	178,417	4	10
2006: Jan	3,431,952	1,182,593	1,260,294	529,361	286,315	173,388	4	9
Feb	3,508,777	1,238,763	1,275,570	526,340	292,517	175,586	4	9
Mar	3,567,753	1,278,145	1,286,260	534,872	292,674	175,802	4	8
Apr	3,483,412	1,198,187	1,273,413	543,174	292,741	175,897	4	9
May	3,492,721	1,178,383	1,288,303	573,995	275,911	176,129	4	10
June	3,473,551	1,136,203	1,302,488	582,153	276,216	176,491	4	10
July	3,501,559	1,130,146	1,319,182	591,937	283,575	176,719	4	10
Aug	3,563,832	1,195,210	1,316,350	581,832	290,832	179,608	4	10
Sept	3,496,359	1,140,553	1,295,589	589,748	290,733	179,736	4	11
Oct	3,555,382	1,136,163	1,350,430	598,143	290,822	179,824	4	10
Nov	3,594,275	1,186,116	1,328,664	626,014	283,386	170,096	4	9
Dec	3,524,921	1,136,717	1,303,590	632,680	282,368	169,566	4	10
2007: Jan	3,554,471	1,124,464	1,335,480	634,734	290,298	169,494	4	10
Feb	3,613,660	1,171,311	1,332,822	640,611	298,399	170,517	4	10
Mar	3,649,732	1,220,193	1,324,286	636,049	298,554	170,648	4	9
Apr	3,611,093	1,128,525	1,357,728	655,774	298,188	170,878	4	10
May	3,573,898	1,123,310	1,305,310	682,977	286,028	176,272	4	11
June	3,514,691	1,075,672	1,296,936	679,143	286,376	176,564	4	11
July	3,598,529	1,102,053	1,349,349	677,402	292,887	176,838	4	11
Aug	3,702,458	1,215,692	1,333,432	682,935	291,975	178,425	4	10
Sept	3,634,666	1,176,510	1,309,871	677,905	291,963	178,417	4	10
Oct	3,671,046	1,171,587	1,332,632	696,633	291,857	178,337	4	10
Nov	3,749,458	1,272,770	1,309,028	692,196	310,684	164,780	4	9
Dec	3,781,877	1,295,981	1,309,642	700,562	310,814 ·	164,878	4	9

[1] Treasury inflation-protected securities—notes, first offered in 1997, and bonds, first offered in 1998—are included in the average length calculation from 1997 forward.

Note.—Through fiscal year 1976, the fiscal year was on a July 1–June 30 basis; beginning with October 1976 (fiscal year 1977), the fiscal year is on an October 1–September 30 basis.

Data shown in this table are as of January 16, 2008.

Source: Department of the Treasury.

[Billions of dollars]

End of month	Total public debt [1]	Federal Reserve and Government accounts [2]	Total privately held	De-pository institutions [3]	U.S. savings bonds [4]	Private [5]	State and local governments	Insurance companies	Mutual funds [6]	State and local governments	Foreign and international [7]	Other investors [8]
						Pension funds						
						Held by private investors						
1993: Mar	4,230.6	1,328.6	2,902.0	362.6	163.6	112.4	205.0	208.0	201.9	434.0	585.9	628.7
June	4,352.0	1,400.6	2,951.4	361.0	166.5	111.9	211.4	217.8	207.4	441.2	596.8	637.4
Sept	4,411.5	1,422.2	2,989.3	366.1	169.1	125.5	221.8	229.4	217.6	434.0	619.1	606.6
Dec	4,535.7	1,476.1	3,059.6	373.0	171.9	119.7	217.5	234.5	227.2	447.8	650.3	617.8
1994: Mar	4,575.9	1,476.0	3,099.9	397.4	175.0	120.1	224.3	233.4	212.8	443.4	661.1	632.3
June	4,645.8	1,547.5	3,098.3	383.9	177.1	129.4	220.6	238.1	204.6	425.2	659.9	659.5
Sept	4,692.8	1,562.8	3,130.0	364.0	178.6	136.4	217.4	243.7	201.5	398.2	682.0	708.1
Dec	4,800.2	1,622.6	3,177.6	339.6	179.9	140.1	215.6	240.0	209.4	370.0	667.3	815.7
1995: Mar	4,864.1	1,619.3	3,244.8	352.9	181.4	142.1	225.0	244.2	210.5	350.5	707.0	831.4
June	4,951.4	1,690.1	3,261.3	339.9	182.6	142.9	217.2	245.0	202.4	313.7	762.5	855.1
Sept	4,974.0	1,688.0	3,286.0	330.8	183.5	142.3	211.3	245.2	211.5	304.3	820.4	836.8
Dec	4,988.7	1,681.0	3,307.7	315.4	185.0	143.0	208.2	241.5	224.9	289.8	835.2	864.8
1996: Mar	5,117.8	1,731.1	3,386.7	322.1	185.8	144.7	213.5	239.4	240.8	283.6	908.1	848.8
June	5,161.1	1,806.7	3,354.4	318.7	186.5	144.9	221.1	229.5	230.4	283.3	929.7	810.3
Sept	5,224.8	1,831.6	3,393.2	310.9	186.8	141.6	213.4	226.8	226.4	263.7	993.4	830.1
Dec	5,323.2	1,892.0	3,431.2	296.6	187.0	140.4	212.8	214.1	227.2	257.0	1,102.1	794.0
1997: Mar	5,380.9	1,928.7	3,452.2	317.3	186.5	141.7	211.1	181.8	221.6	248.1	1,157.6	786.5
June	5,376.2	1,998.9	3,377.3	300.2	186.3	142.1	214.9	183.1	216.4	243.3	1,182.7	708.2
Sept	5,413.1	2,011.5	3,401.6	292.8	186.2	143.0	223.5	186.8	221.3	235.2	1,230.5	682.3
Dec	5,502.4	2,087.8	3,414.6	300.3	186.5	144.1	219.0	176.6	232.3	239.3	1,241.6	674.9
1998: Mar	5,542.4	2,104.9	3,437.5	308.3	186.2	141.3	212.1	169.5	234.6	238.1	1,250.5	696.9
June	5,547.9	2,198.6	3,349.3	290.9	186.0	139.0	213.2	160.6	230.8	258.5	1,256.0	614.4
Sept	5,526.2	2,213.0	3,313.2	244.5	185.9	135.5	207.8	151.4	231.7	271.8	1,224.2	660.3
Dec	5,614.2	2,280.2	3,334.0	237.4	186.6	133.2	212.6	141.7	257.6	280.8	1,278.7	605.4
1999: Mar	5,651.6	2,324.1	3,327.5	247.4	186.5	135.5	211.5	137.5	245.0	288.4	1,272.3	603.4
June	5,638.8	2,439.6	3,199.2	240.6	186.5	142.9	213.8	133.6	228.1	298.6	1,258.8	496.3
Sept	5,656.3	2,480.9	3,175.4	241.2	186.2	150.9	204.8	128.0	222.5	299.2	1,281.4	461.1
Dec	5,776.1	2,542.2	3,233.9	248.7	186.4	153.0	198.8	123.4	228.7	304.5	1,268.7	521.7
2000: Mar	5,773.4	2,590.6	3,182.8	237.7	185.3	150.2	196.9	120.0	222.3	306.3	1,106.9	657.2
June	5,685.9	2,698.6	2,987.3	222.2	184.6	149.0	194.9	116.5	205.4	309.3	1,082.0	523.5
Sept	5,674.2	2,737.9	2,936.3	220.5	184.3	147.9	185.5	113.7	207.8	307.9	1,057.9	510.8
Dec	5,662.2	2,781.8	2,880.4	201.5	184.8	145.0	179.1	110.2	225.7	310.0	1,034.2	490.0
2001: Mar	5,773.7	2,880.9	2,892.8	188.0	184.8	153.4	177.3	109.1	225.3	316.9	1,029.9	508.1
June	5,726.8	3,004.2	2,722.6	188.1	185.5	148.5	183.1	108.1	221.0	324.8	1,000.5	363.1
Sept	5,807.5	3,027.8	2,779.7	189.1	186.4	149.9	166.8	106.8	234.1	321.2	1,005.5	419.8
Dec	5,943.4	3,123.9	2,819.5	181.5	190.3	144.6	155.1	105.7	261.9	328.4	1,051.2	400.8
2002: Mar	6,006.0	3,156.8	2,849.2	187.6	191.9	150.6	163.3	114.0	266.1	327.6	1,067.1	381.0
June	6,126.5	3,276.7	2,849.8	204.7	192.7	149.0	153.9	122.0	253.8	333.6	1,135.4	304.6
Sept	6,228.2	3,303.5	2,924.8	209.3	193.3	151.4	156.3	130.4	256.8	338.6	1,200.8	287.9
Dec	6,405.7	3,387.2	3,018.5	222.9	194.9	150.8	158.9	139.7	281.0	354.7	1,246.8	268.9
2003: Mar	6,460.8	3,390.8	3,069.9	153.9	196.9	162.9	162.1	139.5	296.6	350.0	1,286.3	321.7
June	6,670.1	3,505.4	3,164.7	145.9	199.1	167.3	161.3	138.7	302.3	347.9	1,382.8	319.5
Sept	6,783.2	3,515.3	3,268.0	147.4	201.5	164.6	155.5	137.4	287.1	357.7	1,454.2	362.7
Dec	6,998.0	3,620.1	3,377.9	153.6	203.8	169.2	148.6	136.5	280.8	364.2	1,533.0	388.1
2004: Mar	7,131.1	3,628.3	3,502.8	163.2	204.4	167.0	143.6	141.0	280.8	374.1	1,677.1	351.5
June	7,274.3	3,742.8	3,531.5	159.6	204.6	170.2	134.9	144.1	258.7	381.2	1,739.6	338.6
Sept	7,379.1	3,772.0	3,607.0	139.6	204.1	170.6	140.8	147.4	255.0	381.7	1,798.7	369.1
Dec	7,596.1	3,905.6	3,690.6	125.2	204.4	170.5	151.0	149.7	254.1	389.1	1,853.4	393.2
2005: Mar	7,776.9	3,921.6	3,855.4	141.9	204.2	174.3	158.0	152.4	261.1	412.0	1,956.3	395.2
June	7,836.5	4,033.5	3,803.0	127.0	204.2	167.5	171.3	155.0	248.7	437.3	1,879.6	402.5
Sept	7,932.7	4,067.8	3,864.9	125.4	203.6	180.9	164.8	159.0	244.7	455.2	1,930.6	400.6
Dec	8,170.4	4,199.8	3,970.6	117.2	205.1	181.2	153.8	160.4	251.3	463.2	2,036.0	402.3
2006: Mar	8,371.2	4,257.2	4,114.0	115.4	206.0	183.0	153.0	161.3	248.7	465.7	2,084.5	496.3
June	8,420.0	4,389.2	4,030.8	117.4	205.2	188.4	150.9	161.2	244.2	476.7	1,979.8	506.9
Sept	8,507.0	4,432.8	4,074.2	113.9	203.7	191.2	151.6	160.6	235.7	478.2	2,027.3	512.0
Dec	8,680.2	4,558.1	4,122.1	115.1	202.4	193.2	153.0	159.0	250.7	497.7	2,105.0	445.9
2007: Mar	8,849.7	4,576.6	4,273.1	120.2	200.3	198.5	155.1	160.7	264.2	524.6	2,196.7	452.6
June	8,867.7	4,715.1	4,152.6	110.6	198.6	202.2	156.1	162.2	267.2	549.2	2,193.4	312.9
Sept	9,007.7	4,738.0	4,269.7	118.4	197.1	205.9	157.5	163.0	306.8	545.8	2,240.3	334.9
Dec	9,229.2	4,833.5	4,395.7	....	196.5							

[1] Face value.
[2] Federal Reserve holdings exclude Treasury securities held under repurchase agreements.
[3] Includes commercial banks, savings institutions, and credit unions.
[4] Current accrual value.
[5] Includes Treasury securities held by the Federal Employees Retirement System Thrift Savings Plan "G Fund."
[6] Includes money market mutual funds, mutual funds, and closed-end investment companies.
[7] Includes nonmarketable foreign series, Treasury securities, and Treasury deposit funds. Excludes Treasury securities held under repurchase agreements in custody accounts at the Federal Reserve Bank of New York. Estimates reflect benchmarks to this series at differing intervals; for further detail, see *Treasury Bulletin*.
[8] Includes individuals, Government-sponsored enterprises, brokers and dealers, bank personal trusts and estates, corporate and noncorporate businesses, and other investors.

Note.—Data shown in this table are as of January 16, 2008.

Source: Department of the Treasury.

TABLE B–90.—*Corporate profits with inventory valuation and capital consumption adjustments, 1959–2007*

[Billions of dollars; quarterly data at seasonally adjusted annual rates]

Year or quarter	Corporate profits with inventory valuation and capital consumption adjustments	Taxes on corporate income	Corporate profits after tax with inventory valuation and capital consumption adjustments		
			Total	Net dividends	Undistributed profits with inventory valuation and capital consumption adjustments
1959	55.7	23.7	32.0	12.6	19.4
1960	53.8	22.8	31.0	13.4	17.6
1961	54.9	22.9	32.0	13.9	18.1
1962	63.3	24.1	39.2	15.0	24.1
1963	69.0	26.4	42.6	16.2	26.4
1964	76.5	28.2	48.3	18.2	30.1
1965	87.5	31.1	56.4	20.2	36.2
1966	93.2	33.9	59.3	20.7	38.7
1967	91.3	32.9	58.4	21.5	36.9
1968	98.8	39.6	59.2	23.5	35.6
1969	95.4	40.0	55.4	24.2	31.2
1970	83.6	34.8	48.9	24.3	24.6
1971	98.0	38.2	59.9	25.0	34.8
1972	112.1	42.3	69.7	26.8	42.9
1973	125.5	50.0	75.5	29.9	45.6
1974	115.8	52.8	63.0	33.2	29.8
1975	134.8	51.6	83.2	33.0	50.2
1976	163.3	65.3	98.1	39.0	59.0
1977	192.4	74.4	118.0	44.8	73.2
1978	216.6	84.9	131.8	50.8	81.0
1979	223.2	90.0	133.2	57.5	75.7
1980	201.1	87.2	113.9	64.1	49.9
1981	226.1	84.3	141.8	73.8	68.0
1982	209.7	66.5	143.2	77.7	65.4
1983	264.2	80.6	183.6	83.5	100.1
1984	318.6	97.5	221.1	90.8	130.3
1985	330.3	99.4	230.9	97.6	133.4
1986	319.5	109.7	209.8	106.2	103.7
1987	368.8	130.4	238.4	112.3	126.1
1988	432.6	141.6	291.0	129.9	161.1
1989	426.6	146.1	280.5	158.0	122.6
1990	437.8	145.4	292.4	169.1	123.3
1991	451.2	138.6	312.6	180.7	131.9
1992	479.3	148.7	330.6	187.9	142.7
1993	541.9	171.0	370.9	202.8	168.1
1994	600.3	193.7	406.5	234.7	171.8
1995	696.7	218.7	478.0	254.2	223.8
1996	786.2	231.7	554.5	297.6	256.9
1997	868.5	246.1	622.4	334.5	287.9
1998	801.6	248.3	553.3	351.6	201.7
1999	851.3	258.6	592.6	337.4	255.3
2000	817.9	265.2	552.7	377.9	174.8
2001	767.3	204.1	563.2	370.9	192.3
2002	886.3	192.6	693.7	399.2	294.5
2003	993.1	243.3	749.9	424.7	325.1
2004	1,231.2	307.4	923.9	539.5	384.4
2005	1,372.8	392.9	979.9	601.4	378.6
2006	1,553.7	453.9	1,099.8	698.9	400.9
2004: I	1,184.0	282.5	901.5	473.9	427.7
II	1,227.4	307.1	920.3	500.7	419.6
III	1,218.7	302.5	916.2	528.5	387.7
IV	1,294.8	337.3	957.4	654.8	302.6
2005: I	1,376.7	389.0	987.7	566.0	421.7
II	1,404.0	393.8	1,010.3	588.1	422.2
III	1,297.9	373.1	924.8	612.6	312.2
IV	1,412.5	415.6	996.8	638.7	358.1
2006: I	1,515.5	432.8	1,082.6	662.5	420.2
II	1,575.5	460.0	1,115.6	685.6	430.0
III	1,592.5	470.4	1,122.1	711.1	411.1
IV	1,531.2	452.4	1,078.8	736.4	342.4
2007: I	1,547.7	452.5	1,095.2	759.4	335.8
II	1,642.4	490.1	1,152.2	784.2	368.0
III	1,621.9	469.4	1,152.5	807.7	344.7

Source: Department of Commerce (Bureau of Economic Analysis).

TABLE B–91.—*Corporate profits by industry, 1959–2007*

[Billions of dollars; quarterly data at seasonally adjusted annual rates]

Year or quarter	Total	Corporate profits with inventory valuation adjustment and without capital consumption adjustment												Rest of the world
		Domestic industries												
		Total	Financial			Nonfinancial								
			Total	Federal Reserve banks	Other	Total	Manufacturing[1]	Transportation[2]	Utilities	Wholesale trade	Retail trade	Information	Other	
SIC:[3]														
1959	53.5	50.8	7.6	0.7	6.9	43.2	26.5	7.1	....	2.9	3.3	....	3.4	2.7
1960	51.5	48.3	8.4	.9	7.5	39.9	23.8	7.5	....	2.5	2.8	....	3.3	3.1
1961	51.8	48.5	8.3	.8	7.6	40.2	23.4	7.9	....	2.5	3.0	....	3.4	3.3
1962	57.0	53.3	8.6	.9	7.7	44.7	26.3	8.5	....	2.8	3.4	....	3.6	3.8
1963	62.1	58.1	8.3	1.0	7.3	49.8	29.7	9.5	....	2.8	3.6	....	4.1	4.1
1964	68.6	64.1	8.8	1.1	7.6	55.4	32.6	10.2	....	3.4	4.5	....	4.7	4.5
1965	78.9	74.2	9.3	1.3	8.0	64.9	39.8	11.0	....	3.8	4.9	....	5.4	4.7
1966	84.6	80.1	10.7	1.7	9.1	69.3	42.6	12.0	....	4.0	4.9	....	5.9	4.5
1967	82.0	77.2	11.2	2.0	9.2	66.0	39.2	10.9	....	4.1	5.7	....	6.1	4.8
1968	88.8	83.2	12.8	2.5	10.3	70.4	41.9	11.0	....	4.6	6.4	....	6.6	5.6
1969	85.5	78.9	13.6	3.1	10.5	65.3	37.3	10.7	....	4.9	6.4	....	6.1	6.6
1970	74.4	67.3	15.4	3.5	11.9	52.0	27.5	8.3	....	4.4	6.0	....	5.8	7.1
1971	88.3	80.4	17.6	3.3	14.3	62.8	35.1	8.9	....	5.2	7.2	....	6.4	7.9
1972	101.2	91.7	19.1	3.3	15.8	72.6	41.9	9.5	....	6.9	7.4	....	7.0	9.5
1973	115.3	100.4	20.5	4.5	16.0	79.9	47.2	9.1	....	8.2	6.6	....	8.7	14.9
1974	109.5	92.1	20.2	5.7	14.5	71.9	41.4	7.6	....	11.5	2.3	....	9.1	17.5
1975	135.0	120.4	20.2	5.6	14.6	100.2	55.2	11.0	....	13.8	8.2	....	12.0	14.6
1976	165.6	149.0	25.0	5.9	19.1	124.1	71.3	15.3	....	12.9	10.5	....	14.0	16.5
1977	194.7	175.6	31.9	6.1	25.8	143.7	79.3	18.6	....	15.6	12.4	....	17.8	19.1
1978	222.4	199.6	39.5	7.6	31.9	160.0	90.5	21.8	....	15.6	12.3	....	19.8	22.9
1979	231.8	197.2	40.3	9.4	30.9	156.8	89.6	17.0	....	18.8	9.8	....	21.6	34.6
1980	211.4	175.9	34.0	11.8	22.2	141.9	78.3	18.4	....	17.2	6.2	....	21.8	35.5
1981	219.1	189.4	29.1	14.4	14.7	160.3	91.1	20.3	....	22.4	9.9	....	16.7	29.7
1982	191.0	158.5	26.0	15.2	10.8	132.4	67.1	23.1	....	19.6	13.4	....	9.2	32.6
1983	226.5	191.4	35.5	14.6	20.9	155.9	76.2	29.5	....	21.0	18.7	....	10.4	35.1
1984	264.6	228.1	34.4	16.4	18.0	193.7	91.8	40.1	....	29.5	21.1	....	11.1	36.6
1985	257.5	219.4	45.9	16.3	29.5	173.5	84.3	33.8	....	23.9	22.2	....	9.2	38.1
1986	253.0	213.5	56.8	15.5	41.2	156.8	57.9	35.8	....	24.1	23.5	....	15.5	39.5
1987	301.4	253.4	59.8	15.7	44.1	193.5	86.3	41.9	....	18.6	23.4	....	23.4	48.0
1988	363.9	306.9	68.7	17.6	51.1	238.2	121.2	48.4	....	20.1	20.3	....	28.3	57.0
1989	367.4	300.3	77.9	20.2	57.8	222.3	110.9	43.3	....	21.8	20.8	....	25.5	67.1
1990	396.6	320.5	94.4	21.4	73.0	226.1	113.1	44.2	....	19.2	20.7	....	29.0	76.1
1991	427.9	351.4	124.2	20.3	103.9	227.3	98.0	53.3	....	21.7	26.7	....	27.5	76.5
1992	458.3	385.2	129.8	17.8	111.9	255.4	99.5	58.4	....	25.1	32.6	....	39.7	73.1
1993	513.1	436.1	136.8	16.2	120.6	299.3	115.6	69.5	....	26.3	39.1	....	48.9	76.9
1994	564.6	487.6	119.9	18.1	101.8	367.7	147.0	83.2	....	30.9	46.2	....	60.4	77.1
1995	656.0	563.2	162.2	22.5	139.7	401.0	173.7	85.8	....	27.3	43.1	....	71.2	92.8
1996	736.1	634.2	172.6	22.1	150.5	461.6	188.8	91.3	....	39.8	51.9	....	89.7	101.9
1997	812.3	701.4	193.0	23.8	169.2	508.4	209.0	84.2	....	47.6	64.2	....	103.4	110.9
1998	738.5	635.5	165.9	25.2	140.7	469.6	173.5	78.9	....	52.3	73.4	....	91.5	103.0
1999	776.8	655.3	196.4	26.3	170.1	458.9	175.2	56.8	....	52.6	74.6	....	99.7	121.5
2000	759.3	613.6	203.8	30.8	173.0	409.8	166.3	43.8	....	56.9	70.1	....	72.8	145.7
NAICS:[3]														
1998	738.5	635.5	165.4	25.2	140.2	470.1	157.0	21.0	32.7	53.2	66.4	20.1	119.8	103.0
1999	776.8	655.3	194.3	26.3	168.0	461.0	150.6	16.1	33.1	55.5	65.2	10.5	130.1	121.5
2000	759.3	613.6	200.2	30.8	169.4	413.4	144.3	14.9	24.4	59.7	59.6	-17.6	128.2	145.7
2001	719.2	549.5	227.6	28.3	199.3	322.0	52.6	1.3	24.7	52.1	71.0	-25.6	145.9	169.7
2002	766.2	610.4	276.4	23.7	252.7	334.0	48.2	-9	10.6	49.3	79.4	-8.5	155.8	155.8
2003	894.5	729.0	317.3	20.1	297.2	411.8	76.0	7.3	11.6	55.2	86.8	3.2	171.7	165.5
2004	1,161.6	968.2	348.9	20.0	328.9	619.3	152.7	14.1	18.6	79.2	91.1	43.9	219.7	193.4
2005	1,543.4	1,325.2	423.6	26.6	397.1	901.6	251.2	28.2	28.4	95.2	114.4	74.8	309.5	218.2
2006	1,769.5	1,512.2	505.3	33.8	471.4	1,006.9	293.4	41.9	35.7	97.0	124.5	85.4	329.0	257.3
2005: I	1,513.0	1,309.0	464.8	23.1	441.8	844.2	244.2	25.0	30.2	89.0	99.6	62.2	293.8	204.0
II	1,559.3	1,347.6	429.3	25.9	403.3	918.4	244.9	29.8	30.4	107.4	122.6	74.1	309.4	211.6
III	1,495.4	1,255.0	364.8	26.9	338.0	890.2	252.5	31.1	19.9	87.2	108.5	79.7	311.3	240.4
IV	1,605.9	1,389.3	435.6	30.4	405.1	953.8	263.1	26.7	32.9	97.4	126.9	83.2	323.6	216.6
2006: I	1,708.8	1,466.7	478.7	30.9	447.8	987.9	276.1	34.0	31.7	93.3	119.4	85.3	348.1	242.1
II	1,784.6	1,525.2	521.0	33.8	487.3	1,004.2	298.0	45.9	35.3	85.4	119.6	83.2	336.7	259.4
III	1,816.2	1,566.4	500.3	35.9	464.4	1,066.1	319.5	47.7	37.8	118.1	126.9	81.5	334.5	249.8
IV	1,768.2	1,490.4	521.0	34.8	486.2	969.5	280.2	40.0	37.8	91.1	132.1	91.5	296.7	277.8
2007: I	1,775.6	1,477.7	493.0	38.5	454.5	984.7	298.9	39.1	36.4	97.8	134.3	109.5	268.7	297.9
II	1,876.8	1,562.1	546.4	39.2	507.2	1,015.7	347.0	45.8	41.2	104.9	134.4	92.9	249.5	314.6
III	1,859.4	1,518.3	514.2	38.4	475.8	1,004.1	296.8	55.4	46.4	109.8	140.2	100.8	254.7	341.0

[1] See Table B–92 for industry detail.
[2] Data on Standard Industrial Classification (SIC) basis include transportation and public utilities. Those on North American Industry Classification System (NAICS) basis include transporation and warehousing. Utilities classified separately in NAICS (as shown beginning 1998).
[3] SIC-based industry data use the 1987 SIC for data beginning in 1987 and the 1972 SIC for prior data. NAICS-based data use 1997 NAICS.

Note.—Industry data on SIC basis and NAICS basis are not necessarily the same and are not strictly comparable.

Source: Department of Commerce (Bureau of Economic Analysis).

TABLE B–92.—*Corporate profits of manufacturing industries, 1959–2007*

[Billions of dollars; quarterly data at seasonally adjusted annual rates]

Year or quarter	Total manufacturing	Corporate profits with inventory valuation adjustment and without capital consumption adjustment											
		Durable goods [2]							Nondurable goods [2]				
		Total [1]	Fabricated metal products	Machinery	Computer and electronic products	Electrical equipment, appliances, and components	Motor vehicles, bodies and trailers, and parts	Other	Total	Food and beverage and tobacco products	Chemical products	Petroleum and coal products	Other
SIC: [3]													
1959	26.5	13.7	1.1	2.2	....	1.7	3.0	3.5	12.9	2.5	3.5	2.6	4.3
1960	23.8	11.6	.8	1.8		1.3	3.0	2.7	12.2	2.2	3.1	2.6	4.2
1961	23.4	11.3	1.0	1.9		1.3	2.5	2.9	12.1	2.4	3.3	2.3	4.2
1962	26.3	14.1	1.2	2.4		1.5	4.0	3.4	12.3	2.4	3.2	2.2	4.4
1963	29.7	16.4	1.3	2.6		1.6	4.9	4.0	13.3	2.7	3.7	2.2	4.7
1964	32.6	18.1	1.5	3.3		1.7	4.6	4.4	14.5	2.7	4.1	2.4	5.3
1965	39.8	23.3	2.1	4.0		2.7	6.2	5.2	16.5	2.9	4.6	2.9	6.1
1966	42.6	24.1	2.4	4.6		3.0	5.2	5.2	18.6	3.3	4.9	3.4	6.9
1967	39.2	21.3	2.5	4.2		3.0	4.0	4.9	18.0	3.3	4.3	4.0	6.4
1968	41.9	22.5	2.3	4.2		2.9	5.5	5.6	19.4	3.2	5.3	3.8	7.1
1969	37.3	19.2	2.0	3.8		2.3	4.8	4.9	18.1	3.1	4.6	3.4	7.0
1970	27.5	10.5	1.1	3.1		1.3	1.3	2.9	17.0	3.2	3.9	3.7	6.1
1971	35.1	16.6	1.5	3.1		2.0	5.2	4.1	18.5	3.6	4.5	3.8	6.6
1972	41.9	22.7	2.2	4.5		2.9	6.0	5.6	19.2	3.0	5.3	3.3	7.6
1973	47.2	25.1	2.7	4.9		3.2	5.9	6.2	22.0	2.5	6.2	5.4	7.9
1974	41.4	15.3	1.8	3.3		.6	.7	4.0	26.1	2.6	5.3	10.9	7.3
1975	55.2	20.6	3.3	5.1		2.6	2.3	4.7	34.5	8.6	6.4	10.1	9.5
1976	71.3	31.4	3.9	6.9		3.8	7.4	7.3	39.9	7.1	8.2	13.5	11.1
1977	79.3	37.9	4.5	8.6		5.9	9.4	8.5	41.4	6.9	7.8	13.1	13.6
1978	90.5	45.4	5.0	10.7		6.7	9.0	10.5	45.1	6.2	8.3	15.8	14.8
1979	89.6	37.1	5.3	9.5		5.6	4.7	8.5	52.5	5.8	7.2	24.8	14.7
1980	78.3	18.9	4.4	8.0		5.2	-4.3	2.7	59.5	6.1	5.7	34.7	13.1
1981	91.1	19.5	4.5	9.0		5.2	.3	-2.6	71.6	9.2	8.0	40.0	14.5
1982	67.1	5.0	2.7	3.1		1.7	.0	2.1	62.1	7.3	5.1	34.7	15.0
1983	76.2	19.5	3.1	4.0		3.5	5.3	8.4	56.7	6.3	7.4	23.9	19.1
1984	91.8	39.3	4.7	6.0		5.1	9.2	14.6	52.6	6.8	8.2	17.6	20.1
1985	84.3	29.7	4.9	5.7		2.6	7.4	10.1	54.6	8.8	6.6	18.7	20.5
1986	57.9	26.3	5.2	.8		2.7	4.6	12.1	31.7	7.5	7.5	-4.7	21.3
1987	86.3	40.7	5.5	5.4		5.9	3.7	17.6	45.6	11.4	14.4	-1.5	21.3
1988	121.2	54.1	6.5	11.1		7.7	6.2	16.5	67.1	12.0	18.6	12.7	23.7
1989	110.9	51.2	6.4	12.2		9.3	2.7	14.2	59.7	11.1	18.2	6.5	23.9
1990	113.1	43.8	6.0	11.8		8.5	-1.9	15.9	69.2	14.3	16.8	16.4	21.7
1991	98.0	34.4	5.3	5.7		10.0	-5.4	17.3	63.6	18.1	16.2	7.3	22.0
1992	99.5	40.6	6.2	7.5		10.4	-1.0	17.4	59.0	18.2	16.0	-.9	25.6
1993	115.6	55.8	7.4	7.5		15.2	6.0	19.4	59.7	16.4	15.9	2.7	24.7
1994	147.0	74.4	11.1	9.1		22.8	7.8	21.3	72.6	19.9	23.2	1.2	28.3
1995	173.7	80.9	11.8	14.8		21.5	.0	25.8	92.8	27.1	27.9	7.1	30.6
1996	188.8	90.6	14.5	16.9		20.1	4.2	29.2	98.2	22.1	26.4	15.0	34.7
1997	209.0	103.1	17.0	16.7		25.3	4.8	33.0	105.9	24.6	32.3	17.3	31.7
1998	173.5	87.3	16.4	19.5		8.9	5.9	30.1	86.2	21.9	26.5	6.7	31.1
1999	175.2	78.8	16.2	12.4		5.3	7.3	35.3	96.4	28.1	25.2	4.3	38.9
2000	166.3	64.8	15.4	16.3		4.7	-1.5	28.8	101.5	25.7	16.0	29.1	30.7
NAICS: [3]													
1998	157.0	83.4	16.7	15.6	3.9	6.1	6.4	34.6	73.6	21.8	25.1	4.9	21.8
1999	150.6	72.3	16.5	12.4	-6.5	6.3	7.3	36.4	78.3	30.7	23.0	1.8	22.7
2000	144.3	60.0	15.5	8.2	4.0	5.6	-1.0	27.7	84.3	25.4	14.2	26.9	17.8
2001	52.6	-25.4	9.9	2.7	-48.5	1.9	-9.2	17.8	78.0	28.0	12.6	29.6	7.8
2002	48.2	-9.9	8.9	1.7	-35.3	-.1	-5.0	20.0	58.1	24.9	18.4	1.6	13.2
2003	76.0	-5.9	7.9	1.5	-15.6	2.1	-12.3	10.5	81.9	23.6	19.5	23.3	15.5
2004	152.7	38.3	11.9	7.2	-4.9	.3	-7.6	31.3	114.5	24.2	25.4	48.9	16.0
2005	251.2	85.1	17.3	16.0	10.1	-3.7	.1	45.3	166.0	27.8	29.7	89.8	18.7
2006	293.4	95.9	20.3	19.3	7.7	-1.9	-1.1	51.7	197.5	29.2	37.6	110.4	20.3
2005: I	244.2	80.2	16.3	12.1	5.5	-3.7	2.7	47.3	164.0	28.9	42.2	74.9	18.0
II	244.9	89.8	17.6	15.2	10.4	-4.3	2.9	47.9	155.1	26.7	26.2	81.5	20.7
III	252.5	87.0	19.1	17.0	11.7	-3.1	-.9	43.1	165.5	28.0	24.2	94.5	18.8
IV	263.1	83.7	16.2	19.9	12.8	-3.9	-4.3	42.9	179.4	27.7	26.1	108.4	17.2
2006: I	276.1	93.0	20.4	20.7	9.8	-3.4	-1.4	47.0	183.1	26.7	36.5	102.2	17.6
II	298.0	81.8	18.9	19.5	7.8	-2.9	-2.8	41.4	216.1	27.9	41.5	125.6	21.2
III	319.5	101.8	19.3	18.3	7.1	-1.6	-1.4	60.1	217.6	30.4	40.6	128.7	17.9
IV	280.2	107.2	22.5	18.7	6.2	.2	1.3	58.3	173.0	31.8	31.7	85.2	24.3
2007: I	298.9	113.0	23.3	21.8	9.0	1.3	4.6	52.9	185.9	30.1	41.0	94.9	20.0
II	347.0	117.2	22.2	22.5	7.7	.7	12.3	51.8	229.8	35.4	41.8	136.5	16.1
III	296.8	128.5	26.5	22.3	8.5	2.4	12.1	56.7	168.3	34.3	43.4	70.6	20.0

[1] For Standard Industrial Classification (SIC) data, includes primary metal industries, not shown separately.
[2] Industry groups shown in column headings reflect North American Industry Classification System (NAICS) classification for data beginning 1998. For data on SIC basis, the industry groups would be industrial machinery and equipment (now machinery), electronic and other electric equipment (now electrical equipment, appliances, and components), motor vehicles and equipment (now motor vehicles, bodies and trailers, and parts), food and kindred products (now food and beverage and tobacco products), and chemicals and allied products (now chemical products).
[3] See footnote 3 and Note, Table B–91.

Source: Department of Commerce (Bureau of Economic Analysis).

[Billions of dollars]

Year or quarter	All manufacturing corporations				Durable goods industries				Nondurable goods industries			
	Sales (net)	Profits Before income taxes [1]	Profits After income taxes	Stock-holders' equity [2]	Sales (net)	Profits Before income taxes [1]	Profits After income taxes	Stock-holders' equity [2]	Sales (net)	Profits Before income taxes [1]	Profits After income taxes	Stock-holders' equity [2]
1965	492.2	46.5	27.5	211.7	257.0	26.2	14.5	105.4	235.2	20.3	13.0	106.3
1966	554.2	51.8	30.9	230.3	291.7	29.2	16.4	115.2	262.4	22.6	14.6	115.1
1967	575.4	47.8	29.0	247.6	300.6	25.7	14.6	125.0	274.8	22.0	14.4	122.6
1968	631.9	55.4	32.1	265.9	335.5	30.6	16.5	135.6	296.4	24.8	15.5	130.3
1969	694.6	58.1	33.2	289.9	366.5	31.5	16.9	147.6	328.1	26.6	16.4	142.3
1970	708.8	48.1	28.6	306.8	363.1	23.0	12.9	155.1	345.7	25.2	15.7	151.7
1971	751.1	52.9	31.0	320.8	381.8	26.5	14.5	160.4	369.3	26.5	16.5	160.5
1972	849.5	63.2	36.5	343.4	435.8	33.6	18.4	171.4	413.7	29.6	18.0	172.0
1973	1,017.2	81.4	48.1	374.1	527.3	43.6	24.8	188.7	489.9	37.8	23.3	185.4
1973: IV	275.1	21.4	13.0	386.4	140.1	10.8	6.3	194.7	135.0	10.6	6.7	191.7
New series:												
1973: IV	236.6	20.6	13.2	368.0	122.7	10.1	6.2	185.8	113.9	10.5	7.0	182.1
1974	1,060.6	92.1	58.7	395.0	529.0	41.1	24.7	196.0	531.6	51.0	34.1	199.0
1975	1,065.2	79.9	49.1	423.4	521.1	35.3	21.4	208.1	544.1	44.6	27.7	215.3
1976	1,203.2	104.9	64.5	462.7	589.6	50.7	30.8	224.3	613.7	54.3	33.7	238.4
1977	1,328.1	115.1	70.4	496.7	657.3	57.9	34.8	239.9	670.8	57.2	35.5	256.8
1978	1,496.4	132.5	81.1	540.5	760.7	69.6	41.8	262.6	735.7	62.9	39.3	277.9
1979	1,741.8	154.2	98.7	600.5	865.7	72.4	45.2	292.5	876.1	81.8	53.5	308.0
1980	1,912.8	145.8	92.6	668.1	889.1	57.4	35.6	317.7	1,023.7	88.4	56.9	350.4
1981	2,144.7	158.6	101.3	743.4	979.5	67.2	41.6	350.4	1,165.2	91.3	59.6	393.0
1982	2,039.4	108.2	70.9	770.2	913.1	34.7	21.7	355.5	1,126.4	73.6	49.3	414.7
1983	2,114.3	133.1	85.8	812.8	973.5	48.7	30.0	372.4	1,140.8	84.4	55.8	440.4
1984	2,335.0	165.6	107.6	864.2	1,107.6	75.5	48.9	395.6	1,227.5	90.0	58.8	468.5
1985	2,331.4	137.0	87.6	866.2	1,142.6	61.5	38.6	420.9	1,188.8	75.6	49.1	445.3
1986	2,220.9	129.3	83.1	874.7	1,125.5	52.1	32.6	436.3	1,095.4	77.2	50.5	438.4
1987	2,378.2	173.0	115.6	900.9	1,178.0	78.0	53.0	444.3	1,200.3	95.1	62.6	456.6
1988 [3]	2,596.2	215.3	153.8	957.6	1,284.7	91.6	66.9	468.7	1,311.5	123.7	86.8	488.9
1989	2,745.1	187.6	135.1	999.0	1,356.6	75.1	55.5	501.3	1,388.5	112.6	79.6	497.7
1990	2,810.7	158.1	110.1	1,043.8	1,357.2	57.3	40.7	515.0	1,453.5	100.8	69.4	528.9
1991	2,761.1	98.7	66.4	1,064.1	1,304.0	13.9	7.2	506.8	1,457.1	84.8	59.3	557.4
1992 [4]	2,890.2	31.4	22.1	1,034.7	1,389.8	−33.7	−24.0	473.9	1,500.4	65.1	46.0	560.8
1993	3,015.1	117.9	83.2	1,039.7	1,490.2	38.9	27.4	482.7	1,524.9	79.0	55.7	557.1
1994	3,255.8	243.5	174.9	1,110.1	1,657.6	121.0	87.1	533.3	1,598.2	122.5	87.8	576.8
1995	3,528.3	274.5	198.2	1,240.6	1,807.7	130.6	94.3	613.7	1,720.6	143.9	103.9	627.0
1996	3,757.6	306.6	224.9	1,348.0	1,941.6	146.6	106.1	673.9	1,816.0	160.0	118.8	674.2
1997	3,920.0	331.4	244.5	1,462.7	2,075.8	167.0	121.4	743.4	1,844.2	164.4	123.1	719.3
1998	3,949.4	314.7	234.4	1,482.9	2,168.8	175.1	127.8	779.9	1,780.7	139.6	106.5	703.0
1999	4,148.9	355.3	257.8	1,569.3	2,314.2	198.8	140.3	869.6	1,834.6	156.5	117.5	699.7
2000	4,548.2	381.1	275.3	1,823.1	2,457.4	190.7	131.8	1,054.3	2,090.8	190.5	143.5	768.7
2000: IV	1,163.6	69.2	46.8	1,892.4	620.4	31.2	19.3	1,101.5	543.2	38.0	27.4	790.9
NAICS: [5]												
2000: IV	1,128.8	62.1	41.7	1,833.8	623.0	26.9	15.4	1,100.0	505.8	35.2	26.3	733.8
2001	4,295.0	83.2	36.2	1,843.0	2,321.2	−69.0	−76.1	1,080.5	1,973.8	152.2	112.3	762.5
2002	4,216.4	195.5	134.7	1,804.0	2,260.6	45.9	21.6	1,024.8	1,955.8	149.6	113.1	779.2
2003	4,397.2	305.7	237.0	1,952.2	2,282.7	117.6	88.2	1,040.8	2,114.5	188.1	148.9	911.5
2004	4,934.1	447.5	348.2	2,206.3	2,537.3	200.0	156.5	1,212.9	2,396.7	247.5	191.6	993.5
2005	5,411.5	524.2	401.3	2,410.4	2,730.5	211.3	161.2	1,304.0	2,681.0	312.9	240.2	1,106.5
2006	5,788.7	608.9	474.0	2,687.1	2,920.3	253.2	196.3	1,390.1	2,868.4	355.7	277.7	1,297.0
2005: I	1,258.4	117.6	89.8	2,351.3	642.5	45.3	34.4	1,279.1	616.0	72.3	55.5	1,072.2
II	1,352.2	137.8	106.7	2,389.1	692.1	62.2	47.6	1,294.3	660.0	75.6	59.1	1,094.8
III	1,384.2	142.1	108.5	2,437.8	684.2	56.4	43.8	1,319.7	700.1	85.7	64.7	1,118.0
IV	1,416.6	126.7	96.4	2,463.6	711.8	47.4	35.4	1,322.7	704.8	79.4	61.0	1,140.9
2006: I	1,397.4	149.1	119.8	2,606.1	702.1	63.9	51.7	1,351.7	695.3	85.2	68.1	1,254.4
II	1,485.6	159.8	122.4	2,674.4	748.0	64.5	49.5	1,389.7	737.6	95.3	72.9	1,284.6
III	1,467.1	164.4	126.3	2,738.8	729.4	66.6	50.8	1,409.5	737.8	97.8	75.5	1,329.3
IV	1,438.5	135.7	105.5	2,729.1	740.8	58.3	44.3	1,409.5	697.7	77.5	61.2	1,319.5
2007: I	1,418.0	149.6	117.6	2,801.9	724.5	63.0	48.9	1,457.8	693.5	86.6	68.7	1,344.0
II	1,541.2	172.9	135.6	2,889.4	771.3	77.3	61.9	1,484.1	769.9	95.6	73.7	1,405.4
III	1,554.7	159.1	90.2	2,937.8	774.4	71.5	20.9	1,496.3	780.3	87.7	69.3	1,441.5

[1] In the old series, "income taxes" refers to Federal income taxes only, as State and local income taxes had already been deducted. In the new series, no income taxes have been deducted.

[2] Annual data are average equity for the year (using four end-of-quarter figures).

[3] Beginning with 1988, profits before and after income taxes reflect inclusion of minority stockholders' interest in net income before and after income taxes.

[4] Data for 1992 (most significantly 1992:I) reflect the early adoption of Financial Accounting Standards Board Statement 106 (Employer's Accounting for Post-Retirement Benefits Other Than Pensions) by a large number of companies during the fourth quarter of 1992. Data for 1993 (1993:I) also reflect adoption of Statement 106. Corporations must show the cumulative effect of a change in accounting principle in the first quarter of the year in which the change is adopted.

[5] Data based on the North American Industry Classification System (NAICS). Other data shown are based on the Standard Industrial Classification (SIC).

Note.—Data are not necessarily comparable from one period to another due to changes in accounting principles, industry classifications, sampling procedures, etc. For explanatory notes concerning compilation of the series, see *Quarterly Financial Report for Manufacturing, Mining, and Trade Corporations,* Department of Commerce, Bureau of the Census.

Source: Department of Commerce (Bureau of the Census).

TABLE B–94.—*Relation of profits after taxes to stockholders' equity and to sales, all manufacturing corporations, 1959–2007*

Year or quarter	Ratio of profits after income taxes (annual rate) to stockholders' equity—percent [1]			Profits after income taxes per dollar of sales—cents		
	All manufacturing corporations	Durable goods industries	Nondurable goods industries	All manufacturing corporations	Durable goods industries	Nondurable goods industries
1959	10.4	10.4	10.4	4.8	4.8	4.9
1960	9.2	8.5	9.8	4.4	4.0	4.8
1961	8.9	8.1	9.6	4.3	3.9	4.7
1962	9.8	9.6	9.9	4.5	4.4	4.7
1963	10.3	10.1	10.4	4.7	4.5	4.9
1964	11.6	11.7	11.5	5.2	5.1	5.4
1965	13.0	13.8	12.2	5.6	5.7	5.5
1966	13.4	14.2	12.7	5.6	5.6	5.6
1967	11.7	11.7	11.8	5.0	4.8	5.3
1968	12.1	12.2	11.9	5.1	4.9	5.2
1969	11.5	11.4	11.5	4.8	4.6	5.0
1970	9.3	8.3	10.3	4.0	3.5	4.5
1971	9.7	9.0	10.3	4.1	3.8	4.5
1972	10.6	10.8	10.5	4.3	4.2	4.4
1973	12.8	13.1	12.6	4.7	4.7	4.8
1973: IV	13.4	12.9	14.0	4.7	4.5	5.0
New series:						
1973: IV	14.3	13.3	15.3	5.6	5.0	6.1
1974	14.9	12.6	17.1	5.5	4.7	6.4
1975	11.6	10.3	12.9	4.6	4.1	5.1
1976	13.9	13.7	14.2	5.4	5.2	5.5
1977	14.2	14.5	13.8	5.3	5.3	5.3
1978	15.0	16.0	14.2	5.4	5.5	5.3
1979	16.4	15.4	17.4	5.7	5.2	6.1
1980	13.9	11.2	16.3	4.8	4.0	5.6
1981	13.6	11.9	15.2	4.7	4.2	5.1
1982	9.2	6.1	11.9	3.5	2.4	4.4
1983	10.6	8.1	12.7	4.1	3.1	4.9
1984	12.5	12.4	12.5	4.6	4.4	4.8
1985	10.1	9.2	11.0	3.8	3.4	4.1
1986	9.5	7.5	11.5	3.7	2.9	4.6
1987	12.8	11.9	13.7	4.9	4.5	5.2
1988 [2]	16.1	14.3	17.8	5.9	5.2	6.6
1989	13.5	11.1	16.0	4.9	4.1	5.7
1990	10.6	7.9	13.1	3.9	3.0	4.8
1991	6.2	1.4	10.6	2.4	.5	4.1
1992 [3]	2.1	-5.1	8.2	.8	-1.7	3.1
1993	8.0	5.7	10.0	2.8	1.8	3.7
1994	15.8	16.3	15.2	5.4	5.3	5.5
1995	16.0	15.4	16.6	5.6	5.2	6.0
1996	16.7	15.7	17.6	6.0	5.5	6.5
1997	16.7	16.3	17.1	6.2	5.8	6.7
1998	15.8	16.4	15.2	5.9	5.9	6.0
1999	16.4	16.1	16.8	6.2	6.1	6.4
2000	15.1	12.5	18.7	6.1	5.4	6.9
2000: IV	9.9	7.0	13.9	4.0	3.1	5.1
NAICS: [4]						
2000: IV	9.1	5.6	14.3	3.7	2.5	5.2
2001	2.0	-7.0	14.7	.8	-3.3	5.7
2002	7.5	2.1	14.5	3.2	1.0	5.8
2003	12.1	8.5	16.3	5.4	3.9	7.0
2004	15.8	12.9	19.3	7.1	6.2	8.0
2005	16.7	12.4	21.7	7.4	5.9	9.0
2006	17.6	14.1	21.4	8.2	6.7	9.7
2005: I	15.3	10.8	20.7	7.1	5.4	9.0
II	17.9	14.7	21.6	7.9	6.9	9.0
III	17.8	13.3	23.1	7.8	6.4	9.2
IV	15.6	10.7	21.4	6.8	5.0	8.7
2006: I	18.4	15.3	21.7	8.6	7.4	9.8
II	18.3	14.2	22.7	8.2	6.6	9.9
III	18.4	14.4	22.7	8.6	7.0	10.2
IV	15.5	12.6	18.5	7.3	6.0	8.8
2007: I	16.8	13.4	20.5	8.3	6.8	9.9
II	18.8	16.7	21.0	8.8	8.0	9.6
III	12.3	5.6	19.2	5.8	2.7	8.9

[1] Annual ratios based on average equity for the year (using four end-of-quarter figures). Quarterly ratios based on equity at end of quarter.
[2] See footnote 3, Table B–93.
[3] See footnote 4, Table B–93.
[4] See footnote 5, Table B–93.

Note.—Based on data in millions of dollars.
See Note, Table B–93.

Source: Department of Commerce (Bureau of the Census).

TABLE B-95.—*Historical stock prices and yields, 1949-2003*

Year	Common stock prices [1]										Common stock yields (Standard & Poor's) (percent) [5]	
	NYSE indexes [2]						Dow Jones industrial average [2]	Standard & Poor's composite index (1941-43=10) [2]	Nasdaq composite index (Feb. 5, 1971=100) [2]	Dividend-price ratio [6]	Earnings-price ratio [7]
	Composite (Dec. 31, 2002= 5,000) [3]	December 31, 1965=50									
		Composite	Industrial	Transportation	Utility [4]	Finance					
1949		9.02					179.48	15.23		6.59	15.48
1950		10.87					216.31	18.40		6.57	13.99
1951		13.08					257.64	22.34		6.13	11.82
1952		13.81					270.76	24.50		5.80	9.47
1953		13.67					275.97	24.73		5.80	10.26
1954		16.19					333.94	29.69		4.95	8.57
1955		21.54					442.72	40.49		4.08	7.95
1956		24.40					493.01	46.62		4.09	7.55
1957		23.67					475.71	44.38		4.35	7.89
1958		24.56					491.66	46.24		3.97	6.23
1959		30.73					632.12	57.38		3.23	5.78
1960		30.01					618.04	55.85		3.47	5.90
1961		35.37					691.55	66.27		2.98	4.62
1962		33.49					639.76	62.38		3.37	5.82
1963		37.51					714.81	69.87		3.17	5.50
1964		43.76					834.05	81.37		3.01	5.32
1965		47.39					910.88	88.17		3.00	5.59
1966	487.92	46.15	46.18	50.26	90.81	44.45	873.60	85.26		3.40	6.63
1967	536.84	50.77	51.97	53.51	90.86	49.82	879.12	91.93		3.20	5.73
1968	585.47	55.37	58.00	50.58	88.38	65.85	906.00	98.70		3.07	5.67
1969	578.01	54.67	57.44	46.96	85.60	70.49	876.72	97.84		3.24	6.08
1970	483.39	45.72	48.03	32.14	74.47	60.00	753.19	83.22		3.83	6.45
1971	573.33	54.22	57.92	44.35	79.05	70.38	884.76	98.29	107.44	3.14	5.41
1972	637.52	60.29	65.73	50.17	76.95	78.35	950.71	109.20	128.52	2.84	5.50
1973	607.11	57.42	63.08	37.74	75.38	70.12	923.88	107.43	109.90	3.06	7.12
1974	463.54	43.84	48.08	31.89	59.58	49.67	759.37	82.85	76.29	4.47	11.59
1975	483.55	45.73	50.52	31.10	63.00	47.14	802.49	86.16	77.20	4.31	9.15
1976	575.85	54.46	60.44	39.57	73.94	52.94	974.92	102.01	89.90	3.77	8.90
1977	567.66	53.69	57.86	41.09	81.84	55.25	894.63	98.20	98.71	4.62	10.79
1978	567.81	53.70	58.23	43.50	78.44	56.65	820.23	96.02	117.53	5.28	12.03
1979	616.68	58.32	64.76	47.34	76.41	61.42	844.40	103.01	136.57	5.47	13.46
1980	720.15	68.10	78.70	60.61	74.69	64.25	891.41	118.78	168.61	5.26	12.66
1981	782.62	74.02	85.44	72.61	77.81	73.52	932.92	128.05	203.18	5.20	11.96
1982	728.84	68.93	78.18	60.41	79.49	71.99	884.36	119.71	188.97	5.81	11.60
1983	979.52	92.63	107.45	89.36	93.99	95.34	1,190.34	160.41	285.43	4.40	8.03
1984	977.33	92.46	108.01	85.63	92.89	89.28	1,178.48	160.46	248.88	4.64	10.02
1985	1,142.97	108.09	123.79	104.11	113.49	114.21	1,328.23	186.84	290.19	4.25	8.12
1986	1,438.02	136.00	155.85	119.87	142.72	147.20	1,792.76	236.34	366.96	3.49	6.09
1987	1,709.79	161.70	195.31	140.39	148.59	146.48	2,275.99	286.83	402.57	3.08	5.48
1988	1,585.14	149.91	180.95	134.12	143.53	127.26	2,060.82	265.79	374.43	3.64	8.01
1989	1,903.36	180.02	216.23	175.28	174.87	151.88	2,508.91	322.84	437.81	3.45	7.42
1990	1,939.47	183.46	225.78	158.62	181.20	133.26	2,678.94	334.59	409.17	3.61	6.47
1991	2,181.72	206.33	258.14	173.99	185.32	150.82	2,929.33	376.18	491.69	3.24	4.79
1992	2,421.51	229.01	284.62	201.09	198.91	179.26	3,284.29	415.74	599.26	2.99	4.22
1993	2,638.96	249.58	299.99	242.49	228.90	216.42	3,522.06	451.41	715.16	2.78	4.46
1994	2,687.02	254.12	315.25	247.29	209.06	209.73	3,793.77	460.42	751.65	2.82	5.83
1995	3,078.56	291.15	367.34	269.41	220.30	238.45	4,493.76	541.72	925.19	2.56	6.09
1996	3,787.20	358.17	453.98	327.33	249.77	303.89	5,742.89	670.50	1,164.96	2.19	5.24
1997	4,827.35	456.54	574.52	414.60	283.82	424.48	7,441.15	873.43	1,469.49	1.77	4.57
1998	5,818.26	550.26	681.57	468.69	378.12	516.35	8,625.52	1,085.50	1,794.91	1.49	3.46
1999	6,546.81	619.16	774.78	491.60	473.73	530.86	10,464.88	1,327.33	2,728.15	1.25	3.17
2000	6,805.89	643.66	810.63	413.60	477.65	553.13	10,734.90	1,427.22	3,783.67	1.15	3.63
2001	6,397.85	605.07	748.26	443.59	377.30	595.61	10,189.13	1,194.18	2,035.00	1.32	2.95
2002	5,578.89	527.62	657.37	431.10	260.85	555.27	9,226.43	993.94	1,539.73	1.61	2.92
2003 [3]	5,447.46		633.18	436.51	237.77	565.75	8,993.59	965.23	1,647.17	1.77	3.84

[1] Averages of daily closing prices.
[2] Includes stocks as follows: for NYSE, all stocks listed; for Dow Jones industrial average, 30 stocks; for Standard & Poor's (S&P) composite index, 500 stocks; and for Nasdaq composite index, over 5,000.
[3] The NYSE relaunched the composite index on January 9, 2003, incorporating new definitions, methodology, and base value. (The composite index based on December 31, 1965=50 was discontinued.) Subset indexes on financial, energy, and health care were released by the NYSE on January 8, 2004 (see Table B-96). NYSE indexes shown in this table for industrials, utilities, transportation, and finance were discontinued.
[4] Effective April 1993, the NYSE doubled the value of the utility index to facilitate trading of options and futures on the index. Annual indexes prior to 1993 reflect the doubling.
[5] Based on 500 stocks in the S&P composite index.
[6] Aggregate cash dividends (based on latest known annual rate) divided by aggregate market value based on Wednesday closing prices. Monthly data are averages of weekly figures; annual data are averages of monthly figures.
[7] Quarterly data are ratio of earnings (after taxes) for four quarters ending with particular quarter-to-price index for last day of that quarter. Annual data are averages of quarterly ratios.

Sources: New York Stock Exchange, Dow Jones & Co., Inc., Standard & Poor's, and Nasdaq Stock Market.

| Year or month | Common stock prices [1] | | | | | | | Common stock yields (Standard & Poor's) (percent) [4] | |
| | New York Stock Exchange (NYSE) indexes [2,3] (December 31, 2002=5,000) | | | | Dow Jones industrial average [2] | Standard & Poor's composite index (1941-43=10) [2] | Nasdaq composite index (Feb. 5, 1971=100) [2] | Dividend-price ratio [5] | Earnings-price ratio [6] |
	Composite	Financial	Energy	Health Care					
2000	6,805.89				10,734.90	1,427.22	3,783.67	1.15	3.63
2001	6,397.85				10,189.13	1,194.18	2,035.00	1.32	2.95
2002	5,578.89				9,226.43	993.94	1,539.73	1.61	2.92
2003	5,447.46	5,583.00	5,273.90	5,288.67	8,993.59	965.23	1,647.17	1.77	3.84
2004	6,612.62	6,822.18	6,952.36	5,924.80	10,317.39	1,130.65	1,986.53	1.72	4.89
2005	7,349.00	7,383.70	9,377.84	6,283.96	10,547.67	1,207.23	2,099.32	1.83	5.36
2006	8,357.99	8,654.40	11,206.94	6,685.06	11,408.67	1,310.46	2,263.41	1.87	5.78
2007	9,648.82	9,321.39	13,339.99	7,191.79	13,169.98	1,477.19	2,578.47	1.86	
2003: Jan	5,055.78	5,092.08	4,900.65	5,043.19	8,474.59	895.84	1,389.56	1.80	
Feb	4,738.56	4,723.86	4,802.42	4,788.19	7,916.18	837.62	1,313.26	1.95	
Mar	4,724.19	4,685.40	4,855.44	4,854.73	7,977.73	846.62	1,348.50	1.93	3.57
Apr	4,977.45	5,036.82	4,916.44	5,078.71	8,332.09	890.03	1,409.83	1.83	
May	5,269.96	5,357.20	5,190.65	5,316.27	8,623.41	935.96	1,524.18	1.75	
June	5,583.42	5,690.39	5,522.45	5,557.87	9,098.07	988.00	1,631.75	1.66	3.55
July	5,567.94	5,790.61	5,276.08	5,457.98	9,154.39	992.54	1,716.85	1.71	
Aug	5,580.87	5,776.36	5,368.25	5,263.19	9,284.78	989.53	1,724.82	1.78	
Sept	5,748.42	5,897.76	5,453.23	5,402.56	9,492.54	1,019.44	1,856.22	1.73	3.87
Oct	5,894.39	6,187.33	5,552.99	5,428.31	9,682.46	1,038.73	1,907.89	1.71	
Nov	5,989.42	6,282.53	5,474.84	5,521.85	9,762.20	1,049.90	1,939.25	1.69	
Dec	6,239.14	6,475.68	5,973.31	5,751.14	10,124.66	1,080.64	1,956.98	1.67	4.38
2004: Jan	6,569.76	6,827.35	6,323.29	6,000.57	10,540.05	1,132.52	2,098.00	1.62	
Feb	6,661.38	6,978.62	6,337.87	6,134.16	10,601.50	1,143.36	2,048.36	1.63	
Mar	6,574.75	6,914.60	6,455.53	5,908.76	10,323.73	1,123.98	1,979.48	1.68	4.62
Apr	6,600.77	6,792.05	6,638.65	6,028.53	10,418.40	1,133.08	2,021.32	1.68	
May	6,371.44	6,495.19	6,572.79	6,022.12	10,083.81	1,102.78	1,930.09	1.74	
June	6,548.06	6,683.10	6,780.86	6,063.65	10,364.90	1,132.76	2,000.98	1.70	4.92
July	6,443.45	6,569.52	6,971.57	5,823.34	10,152.09	1,105.85	1,912.42	1.77	
Aug	6,352.83	6,566.19	6,866.75	5,733.68	10,032.80	1,088.94	1,821.54	1.81	
Sept	6,551.90	6,773.95	7,270.08	5,890.05	10,204.67	1,117.66	1,884.73	1.78	5.18
Oct	6,608.98	6,792.44	7,593.71	5,668.02	10,001.60	1,118.07	1,938.25	1.79	
Nov	6,933.75	7,118.40	7,773.26	5,818.20	10,411.76	1,168.94	2,062.87	1.74	
Dec	7,134.42	7,354.73	7,843.99	6,006.46	10,673.38	1,199.21	2,149.53	1.72	4.83
2005: Jan	7,056.85	7,282.65	7,841.24	5,970.34	10,539.51	1,181.41	2,071.87	1.77	
Feb	7,241.89	7,377.10	8,646.71	6,052.78	10,723.82	1,199.63	2,065.74	1.76	
Mar	7,275.51	7,274.12	9,077.38	6,148.03	10,682.09	1,194.90	2,030.43	1.79	5.11
Apr	7,077.97	7,014.98	8,793.74	6,253.05	10,283.19	1,164.42	1,957.49	1.86	
May	7,094.02	7,092.20	8,513.39	6,432.30	10,377.18	1,178.28	2,005.22	1.86	
June	7,238.96	7,199.86	9,122.87	6,408.88	10,486.68	1,202.26	2,074.02	1.83	5.32
July	7,389.23	7,373.25	9,607.53	6,342.76	10,545.38	1,222.24	2,145.14	1.82	
Aug	7,482.93	7,374.01	10,034.26	6,383.81	10,554.27	1,224.27	2,157.85	1.82	
Sept	7,584.49	7,435.85	10,672.51	6,412.24	10,532.54	1,225.91	2,144.61	1.84	5.42
Oct	7,373.23	7,368.60	9,915.63	6,270.83	10,324.31	1,191.96	2,087.09	1.90	
Nov	7,585.75	7,800.01	9,998.62	6,297.57	10,695.25	1,237.37	2,202.84	1.85	
Dec	7,787.22	8,011.76	10,310.18	6,434.97	10,827.79	1,262.07	2,246.09	1.84	5.60
2006: Jan	8,007.35	8,187.86	10,965.30	6,604.09	10,872.48	1,278.72	2,289.99	1.83	
Feb	8,044.86	8,280.82	10,741.43	6,566.87	10,971.19	1,276.65	2,273.67	1.86	
Mar	8,174.34	8,459.04	10,702.23	6,653.63	11,144.45	1,293.74	2,300.26	1.85	5.61
Apr	8,351.28	8,572.54	11,467.85	6,519.78	11,234.68	1,302.18	2,338.68	1.85	
May	8,353.45	8,608.10	11,380.52	6,488.14	11,333.88	1,290.00	2,245.28	1.90	
June	7,985.59	8,225.13	10,690.86	6,395.87	10,997.97	1,253.12	2,137.41	1.96	5.86
July	8,103.97	8,340.25	11,360.86	6,566.19	11,032.53	1,260.24	2,086.21	1.94	
Aug	8,294.89	8,574.68	11,610.65	6,763.81	11,257.35	1,287.15	2,117.77	1.92	
Sept	8,383.29	8,789.30	10,807.75	6,910.95	11,533.60	1,317.81	2,221.94	1.87	5.88
Oct	8,651.02	9,101.77	11,020.11	6,975.17	11,963.12	1,363.38	2,330.17	1.83	
Nov	8,856.30	9,251.53	11,657.36	6,845.16	12,185.15	1,388.63	2,408.70	1.80	
Dec	9,089.55	9,461.77	12,078.39	6,931.01	12,377.62	1,416.42	2,431.91	1.79	5.75
2007: Jan	9,132.04	9,575.21	11,381.56	7,083.45	12,512.89	1,424.16	2,453.19	1.81	
Feb	9,345.98	9,732.63	11,658.11	7,174.03	12,631.48	1,444.79	2,479.86	1.82	
Mar	9,120.57	9,342.66	11,503.16	6,997.30	12,268.53	1,406.95	2,401.49	1.89	5.85
Apr	9,555.98	9,658.88	12,441.16	7,332.01	12,754.80	1,463.65	2,499.57	1.84	
May	9,822.99	9,864.01	13,031.00	7,474.48	13,407.76	1,511.14	2,562.14	1.81	
June	9,896.98	9,754.29	13,639.81	7,268.42	13,480.21	1,514.49	2,595.40	1.81	5.65
July	9,985.42	9,543.66	14,318.49	7,210.07	13,677.89	1,520.70	2,655.08	1.80	
Aug	9,440.44	8,963.67	13,250.28	6,957.87	13,239.71	1,454.62	2,539.50	1.92	
Sept	9,777.59	9,060.63	14,300.99	7,138.20	13,557.69	1,497.12	2,634.47	1.88	5.15
Oct	10,159.33	9,390.30	14,976.30	7,231.60	13,901.28	1,539.66	2,780.42	1.84	
Nov	9,741.15	8,522.71	14,622.23	7,127.40	13,200.58	1,463.39	2,662.80	1.95	
Dec	9,807.36	8,447.99	14,956.77	7,306.60	13,406.99	1,479.23	2,661.55	1.93	

[1] Averages of daily closing prices.

[2] Includes stocks as follows: for NYSE, all stocks listed (in 2007, over 2,750); for Dow Jones industrial average, 30 stocks; for Standard & Poor's (S&P) composite index, 500 stocks; and for Nasdaq composite index, in 2007, about 3,100.

[3] The NYSE relaunched the composite index on January 9, 2003, incorporating new definitions, methodology, and base value. Subset indexes on financial, energy, and health care were released by the NYSE on January 8, 2004.

[4] Based on 500 stocks in the S&P composite index.

[5] Aggregate cash dividends (based on latest known annual rate) divided by aggregate market value based on Wednesday closing prices. Monthly data are averages of weekly figures, annual data are averages of monthly figures.

[6] Quarterly data are ratio of earnings (after taxes) for four quarters ending with particular quarter-to-price index for last day of that quarter. Annual data are averages of quarterly ratios.

Sources: New York Stock Exchange, Dow Jones & Co., Inc., Standard & Poor's, and Nasdaq Stock Market.

TABLE B–97.—*Farm income, 1945–2007*

[Billions of dollars]

Year	Income of farm operators from farming						Production expenses	Net farm income
	Gross farm income							
	Total [1]	Cash marketing receipts			Value of inventory changes [3]	Direct Government payments [4]		
		Total	Livestock and products	Crops [2]				
1945	25.4	21.7	12.0	9.7	−0.4	0.7	13.1	12.3
1946	29.6	24.8	13.8	11.0	.0	.8	14.5	15.1
1947	32.4	29.6	16.5	13.1	−1.8	.3	17.0	15.4
1948	36.5	30.2	17.1	13.1	1.7	.3	18.8	17.7
1949	30.8	27.8	15.4	12.4	−.9	.2	18.0	12.8
1950	33.1	28.4	16.1	12.4	.8	.3	19.5	13.6
1951	38.3	32.8	19.6	13.2	1.2	.3	22.3	15.9
1952	37.7	32.5	18.2	14.3	.9	.3	22.8	14.9
1953	34.4	31.0	16.9	14.1	−.6	.2	21.5	13.0
1954	34.2	29.8	16.3	13.6	.5	.3	21.8	12.4
1955	33.4	29.5	16.0	13.5	.2	.2	22.2	11.3
1956	33.9	30.4	16.4	14.0	−.5	.6	22.7	11.2
1957	34.8	29.7	17.4	12.3	.6	1.0	23.7	11.1
1958	39.0	33.5	19.2	14.2	.8	1.1	25.8	13.2
1959	37.9	33.6	18.9	14.7	.0	.7	27.2	10.7
1960	38.6	34.0	19.0	15.0	.4	.7	27.4	11.2
1961	40.5	35.2	19.5	15.7	.3	1.5	28.6	12.0
1962	42.3	36.5	20.2	16.3	.6	1.7	30.3	12.1
1963	43.4	37.5	20.0	17.4	.6	1.7	31.6	11.8
1964	42.3	37.3	19.9	17.4	−.8	2.2	31.8	10.5
1965	46.5	39.4	21.9	17.5	1.0	2.5	33.6	12.9
1966	50.5	43.4	25.0	18.4	−.1	3.3	36.5	14.0
1967	50.5	42.8	24.4	18.4	.7	3.1	38.2	12.3
1968	51.8	44.2	25.5	18.7	.1	3.5	39.5	12.3
1969	56.4	48.2	28.6	19.6	.1	3.8	42.1	14.3
1970	58.8	50.5	29.5	21.0	.0	3.7	44.5	14.4
1971	62.1	52.7	30.5	22.3	1.4	3.1	47.1	15.0
1972	71.1	61.1	35.6	25.5	.9	4.0	51.7	19.5
1973	98.9	86.9	45.8	41.1	3.4	2.6	64.6	34.4
1974	98.2	92.4	41.3	51.1	−1.6	.5	71.0	27.3
1975	100.6	88.9	43.1	45.8	3.4	.8	75.0	25.5
1976	102.9	95.4	46.3	49.0	−1.5	.7	82.7	20.2
1977	108.8	96.2	47.6	48.6	1.1	1.8	88.9	19.9
1978	128.4	112.4	59.2	53.2	1.9	3.0	103.2	25.2
1979	150.7	131.5	69.2	62.3	5.0	1.4	123.3	27.4
1980	149.3	139.7	68.0	71.7	−6.3	1.3	133.1	16.1
1981	166.3	141.6	69.2	72.5	6.5	1.9	139.4	26.9
1982	164.1	142.6	70.3	72.3	−1.4	3.5	140.3	23.8
1983	153.9	136.8	69.6	67.2	−10.9	9.3	139.6	14.3
1984	168.0	142.8	72.9	69.9	6.0	8.4	142.0	26.0
1985	161.1	144.0	70.1	73.9	−2.3	7.7	132.6	28.5
1986	156.1	135.4	71.6	63.8	−2.2	11.8	125.0	31.1
1987	168.4	141.8	76.0	65.8	−2.3	16.7	130.4	38.0
1988	177.9	151.3	79.6	71.6	−4.1	14.5	138.3	39.6
1989	191.6	160.5	83.6	76.9	3.8	10.9	145.1	46.5
1990	197.8	169.3	89.1	80.2	3.3	9.3	151.5	46.3
1991	192.0	168.0	85.8	82.2	−.2	8.2	151.8	40.2
1992	200.6	171.5	85.8	85.7	4.2	9.2	150.4	50.2
1993	205.0	178.3	90.5	87.8	−4.2	13.4	158.3	46.7
1994	216.1	181.4	88.3	93.1	8.3	7.9	163.5	52.6
1995	210.8	188.2	87.2	101.0	−5.0	7.3	171.1	39.8
1996	235.8	199.4	92.9	106.5	7.9	7.3	176.9	58.9
1997	238.0	207.8	96.5	111.3	.6	7.5	186.7	51.3
1998	232.6	196.5	94.2	102.2	−.6	12.4	185.5	47.1
1999	234.9	187.8	95.7	92.1	−.2	21.5	187.2	47.7
2000	243.7	192.1	99.6	92.4	1.6	23.2	193.0	50.7
2001	251.9	200.1	106.7	93.4	1.1	22.4	196.8	55.0
2002	232.8	195.0	94.0	101.1	−3.4	12.4	192.7	40.1
2003	260.0	215.6	105.6	109.9	−2.4	16.5	200.3	59.7
2004	296.0	237.3	123.6	113.7	11.2	13.0	210.0	85.9
2005	299.6	240.7	124.9	115.9	−1.1	24.4	222.5	77.1
2006	291.5	239.3	119.3	120.0	−1.6	15.8	232.5	59.0
2007 *p*	341.7	282.2	139.6	142.6	5.8	12.1	254.2	87.5

[1] Cash marketing receipts, Government payments, value of changes in inventories, other farm-related cash income, and nonmoney income produced by farms including imputed rent of operator residences.

[2] Crop receipts include proceeds received from commodities placed under Commodity Credit Corporation loans.

[3] Physical changes in beginning and ending year inventories of crop and livestock commodities valued at weighted average market prices during the year.

[4] Includes only Government payments made directly to farmers.

Note.—Data for 2007 are forecasts.

Source: Department of Agriculture (Economic Research Service).

[Billions of dollars]

End of year	Total assets	Physical assets					Financial assets			Claims			
		Real estate	Live-stock and poultry[1]	Ma-chinery and motor vehicles	Crops[2]	Pur-chased inputs[3]	Total[4]	Invest-ments in coopera-tives	Other[4]	Total claims	Real estate debt[5]	Non-real estate debt[6]	Propri-etors' equity
1950	121.6	75.4	17.1	12.3	7.1		9.7	2.7	7.0	121.6	5.2	5.7	110.7
1951	136.0	83.8	19.5	14.3	8.2		10.2	2.9	7.3	136.0	5.7	6.9	123.4
1952	133.1	85.1	14.8	15.0	7.9		10.3	3.2	7.1	133.1	6.2	7.1	119.8
1953	128.7	84.3	11.7	15.6	6.8		10.3	3.3	7.0	128.7	6.6	6.3	115.8
1954	132.6	87.8	11.2	15.7	7.5		10.4	3.5	6.9	132.6	7.1	6.7	118.8
1955	137.0	93.0	10.6	16.3	6.5		10.6	3.7	6.9	137.0	7.8	7.3	121.9
1956	145.7	100.3	11.0	16.9	6.8		10.7	4.0	6.7	145.7	8.5	7.4	129.8
1957	154.5	106.4	13.9	17.0	6.4		10.8	4.2	6.6	154.5	9.0	8.2	137.3
1958	168.7	114.6	17.7	18.1	6.9		11.4	4.5	6.9	168.7	9.7	9.4	149.6
1959	172.9	121.2	15.2	19.3	6.2		11.0	4.8	6.2	172.9	10.6	10.7	151.6
1960	174.4	123.3	15.6	19.1	6.4		10.0	4.2	5.8	174.4	11.3	11.1	151.9
1961	181.6	129.1	16.4	19.3	6.5		10.4	4.5	5.9	181.6	12.3	11.8	157.5
1962	188.9	134.6	17.3	19.9	6.5		10.5	4.6	5.9	188.9	13.5	13.2	162.2
1963	196.7	142.4	15.9	20.4	7.4		10.7	5.0	5.7	196.7	15.0	14.6	167.1
1964	204.2	150.5	14.5	21.2	7.0		11.0	5.2	5.8	204.2	16.9	15.3	172.1
1965	220.8	161.5	17.6	22.4	7.9		11.4	5.4	6.0	220.8	18.9	16.9	185.0
1966	234.0	171.2	19.0	24.1	8.1		11.6	5.7	6.0	234.0	20.7	18.5	194.8
1967	246.1	180.9	18.8	26.3	8.0		12.0	5.8	6.1	246.1	22.6	19.6	203.9
1968	257.2	189.4	20.2	27.7	7.4		12.4	6.1	6.3	257.2	24.7	19.2	213.2
1969	267.8	195.3	22.8	28.6	8.3		12.8	6.4	6.4	267.8	26.4	20.0	221.4
1970	278.8	202.4	23.7	30.4	8.7		13.7	7.2	6.5	278.8	27.2	21.3	230.3
1971	301.8	217.6	27.3	32.4	10.0		14.5	7.9	6.7	301.8	28.8	24.0	248.9
1972	339.9	243.0	33.7	34.6	12.9		15.7	8.7	6.9	339.9	31.4	26.7	281.8
1973	418.5	298.3	42.4	39.7	21.4		16.8	9.7	7.1	418.5	35.2	31.6	351.7
1974[7]	449.2	335.6	24.6	48.5	22.5		18.1	11.2	6.9	449.2	39.6	35.1	374.5
1975	510.8	383.6	29.4	57.4	20.5		19.9	13.0	6.9	510.8	43.8	39.8	427.3
1976	590.7	456.5	29.0	63.3	20.6		21.3	14.3	6.9	590.7	48.5	45.7	496.5
1977	651.5	509.3	31.9	69.3	20.4		20.5	13.5	7.0	651.5	55.8	52.6	543.1
1978	777.7	601.8	50.1	78.8	23.8		23.2	16.1	7.1	777.7	63.4	60.4	653.9
1979	914.7	706.1	61.4	91.9	29.9		25.4	18.1	7.3	914.7	75.8	71.7	767.2
1980	1,000.4	782.8	60.6	97.5	32.8		26.7	19.3	7.4	1,000.4	85.3	77.2	838.0
1981	997.9	785.6	53.5	101.1	29.5		28.2	20.6	7.6	997.9	93.9	83.8	820.2
1982	962.5	750.0	53.0	103.9	25.9		29.7	21.9	7.8	962.5	96.8	87.2	778.5
1983	959.3	753.4	49.5	101.7	23.7		30.9	22.8	8.1	959.3	98.1	88.1	773.1
1984	897.8	661.8	49.5	125.8	26.1	2.0	32.6	24.3	8.3	897.8	101.4	87.4	709.0
1985	775.9	586.2	46.3	86.1	22.9	1.2	33.3	24.3	9.0	775.9	94.1	78.1	603.8
1986	722.0	542.4	47.8	79.0	16.3	2.1	34.4	24.4	10.0	722.0	84.1	67.2	570.7
1987	756.5	563.7	58.0	78.7	17.8	3.2	35.2	25.3	9.9	756.5	75.8	62.7	618.0
1988	788.5	582.3	62.2	81.0	23.7	3.5	35.9	25.6	10.4	788.5	70.8	62.3	655.4
1989	813.7	600.1	66.2	84.1	23.9	2.6	36.7	26.3	10.4	813.7	68.8	62.3	682.7
1990	840.6	619.1	70.9	86.3	23.2	2.8	38.3	27.5	10.9	840.6	67.6	63.5	709.5
1991	844.2	624.8	68.1	85.9	22.2	2.6	40.5	28.7	11.8	844.2	67.4	64.4	712.3
1992	867.8	640.8	71.0	84.8	24.2	3.9	43.0	29.4	13.6	867.8	67.9	63.7	736.2
1993	909.2	677.6	72.8	85.4	23.3	3.8	46.3	31.0	15.3	909.2	68.4	65.9	774.9
1994	934.7	704.1	67.9	86.8	23.3	5.0	47.6	32.1	15.5	934.7	69.9	69.0	795.8
1995	965.7	740.5	57.8	87.6	27.4	3.4	49.1	34.1	15.0	965.7	71.7	71.3	822.8
1996	1,002.9	769.5	60.3	88.0	31.7	4.4	49.0	34.9	14.1	1,002.9	74.4	74.2	854.3
1997	1,051.3	808.2	67.1	88.7	32.7	4.9	49.6	35.7	13.9	1,051.3	78.5	78.4	894.4
1998	1,083.4	840.4	63.4	89.8	29.9	5.0	54.7	40.5	14.2	1,083.4	83.1	81.5	918.7
1999	1,138.8	887.0	73.2	89.8	28.3	4.0	56.5	41.9	14.6	1,138.8	87.2	80.5	971.1
2000	1,203.2	946.4	76.8	90.1	27.9	4.9	57.1	43.0	14.1	1,203.2	84.7	79.2	1,039.3
2001	1,255.9	996.2	78.5	92.8	25.2	4.2	58.9	43.6	15.3	1,255.9	88.5	82.1	1,085.3
2002	1,304.0	1,045.7	75.6	93.6	23.1	5.6	60.4	44.7	15.8	1,304.0	95.4	81.8	1,126.8
2003	1,378.8	1,111.8	78.5	95.9	24.4	5.6	62.4	45.6	16.9	1,378.8	94.1	81.0	1,203.6
2004	1,584.8	1,307.6	79.4	102.2	24.4	5.7	65.5			1,584.8	96.9	86.1	1,401.9
2005	1,769.3	1,485.0	81.1	105.0	24.3	6.5	67.5			1,769.3	101.5	91.7	1,576.1
2006	1,979.1	1,682.4	80.7	113.1	22.7	6.5	73.7			1,979.1	109.0	98.3	1,771.8

[1] Excludes commercial broilers; excludes horses and mules beginning with 1959 data; excludes turkeys beginning with 1986 data.
[2] Non-Commodity Credit Corporation (CCC) crops held on farms plus value above loan rate for crops held under CCC.
[3] Includes fertilizer, chemicals, fuels, parts, feed, seed, and other supplies.
[4] Beginning in 2004, data available only for total financial assets. Data through 2003 for other financial assets are currency and demand deposits.
[5] Includes CCC storage and drying facilities loans.
[6] Does not include CCC crop loans.
[7] Beginning with 1974 data, farms are defined as places with sales of $1,000 or more annually.

Note.—Data exclude operator households. Beginning in 1959, data include Alaska and Hawaii.

Source: Department of Agriculture (Economic Research Service).

TABLE B–99.—*Farm output and productivity indexes, 1948–2004*

[1996=100]

Year	Farm output				Productivity indicators	
	Total	Primary output		Secondary output	Farm output per unit of total factor input	Farm output per unit of labor input
		Livestock and products	Crops			
1948	41	44	42	20	42	13
1949	41	47	40	18	40	13
1950	41	49	38	17	40	13
1951	43	52	40	18	41	15
1952	44	53	41	20	42	15
1953	45	54	42	21	43	16
1954	45	56	41	21	44	17
1955	46	58	42	23	44	18
1956	47	59	42	25	45	19
1957	46	58	41	29	45	20
1958	49	59	46	35	47	22
1959	51	62	46	53	48	24
1960	53	62	49	57	50	26
1961	53	65	48	56	51	27
1962	54	65	49	55	51	27
1963	56	67	51	56	52	29
1964	55	69	49	51	53	31
1965	57	67	52	51	54	32
1966	56	68	51	50	53	34
1967	58	70	53	52	56	38
1968	59	70	55	48	56	39
1969	60	70	57	46	56	40
1970	60	73	54	40	56	41
1971	64	74	61	40	60	45
1972	64	75	61	39	60	45
1973	67	76	65	42	62	48
1974	63	75	59	40	58	45
1975	66	70	67	41	64	48
1976	67	74	67	41	63	50
1977	71	75	72	40	67	54
1978	73	75	75	45	65	56
1979	78	77	82	44	67	59
1980	75	80	75	39	64	58
1981	81	82	86	32	72	63
1982	82	81	87	51	74	69
1983	71	83	67	53	65	61
1984	81	82	85	51	77	72
1985	85	84	89	60	82	82
1986	82	84	83	58	80	78
1987	84	86	84	68	83	78
1988	80	88	74	84	80	73
1989	86	88	84	91	87	82
1990	90	89	90	92	91	91
1991	90	92	89	97	90	91
1992	96	94	97	95	98	99
1993	91	95	88	100	92	99
1994	101	99	104	98	98	94
1995	96	101	92	108	92	89
1996	100	100	100	100	100	100
1997	104	101	105	111	101	105
1998	105	104	104	126	101	112
1999	108	107	105	133	102	115
2000	108	108	107	120	107	122
2001	108	107	106	126	107	124
2002	107	110	102	126	107	122
2003	108	110	105	122	111	131
2004	112	110	114	116	117	144

Note.—Farm output includes primary agricultural activities and certain secondary activities that are closely linked to agricultural production for which information on production and input use cannot be separately observed.

See Table B–100 for farm inputs.

Source: Department of Agriculture (Economic Research Service).

Year	Farm employment (thousands)[1]			Crops harvested (millions of acres)[3]	Selected indexes of input use (1996=100)										
	Total	Self-employed and unpaid family workers[2]	Hired workers		Total farm input	Capital input		Labor input			Materials input				
						Total	Durable equipment	Total	Hired labor	Self-employed	Total	Feed and seed	Energy	Agricultural chemicals	Purchased services
1948	9,759	7,433	2,326	356	97	108	66	326	279	349	48	60	77	20	43
1949	9,633	7,392	2,241	360	101	109	78	318	259	347	54	62	86	21	41
1950	9,283	6,965	2,318	345	102	112	90	306	270	324	55	62	88	25	43
1951	8,653	6,464	2,189	344	103	115	100	294	261	311	57	65	88	25	47
1952	8,441	6,301	2,140	349	104	117	109	287	255	304	58	64	93	26	51
1953	7,904	5,817	2,087	348	104	119	114	275	248	289	58	66	94	26	48
1954	7,893	5,782	2,111	346	102	120	120	270	234	288	56	61	97	27	47
1955	7,719	5,675	2,044	340	105	120	122	264	230	281	60	69	101	28	49
1956	7,367	5,451	1,916	324	105	120	124	247	210	267	63	71	101	30	51
1957	6,966	5,046	1,920	324	104	119	122	229	201	244	64	75	99	29	52
1958	6,667	4,705	1,962	324	105	118	121	219	203	227	68	79	105	30	54
1959	6,565	4,621	1,944	324	107	118	121	217	198	227	71	80	106	34	74
1960	6,155	4,260	1,895	324	106	118	123	205	198	208	71	80	109	34	72
1961	5,994	4,135	1,859	302	104	118	121	200	197	201	70	77	112	37	70
1962	5,841	3,997	1,844	295	106	118	119	201	197	202	72	80	113	41	71
1963	5,500	3,700	1,800	298	106	118	119	192	196	190	74	83	116	45	70
1964	5,206	3,585	1,621	298	105	119	121	181	177	182	74	81	123	49	68
1965	4,964	3,465	1,499	298	104	119	123	176	167	181	74	80	121	50	69
1966	4,574	3,224	1,350	294	105	119	126	164	150	170	78	86	120	55	69
1967	4,303	3,036	1,267	306	105	120	131	154	139	161	80	87	119	62	72
1968	4,207	2,974	1,233	300	106	121	137	153	135	162	81	88	123	66	71
1969	4,050	2,843	1,207	290	107	121	139	151	136	158	85	92	126	74	68
1970	3,951	2,727	1,224	293	107	120	140	144	137	147	86	95	126	79	65
1971	3,868	2,665	1,203	305	106	120	142	142	136	145	86	92	122	86	65
1972	3,870	2,664	1,206	294	107	119	142	141	135	144	88	95	118	94	64
1973	3,947	2,702	1,245	321	108	119	145	140	137	141	91	96	111	110	69
1974	3,919	2,588	1,331	328	108	120	153	140	146	136	90	96	97	115	69
1975	3,818	2,481	1,337	336	104	121	159	137	148	131	83	91	102	79	70
1976	3,741	2,369	1,372	337	107	123	164	135	150	128	88	95	111	89	74
1977	3,660	2,347	1,313	345	106	124	170	131	146	124	86	91	112	88	75
1978	3,682	2,410	1,272	338	113	126	175	129	137	125	97	104	119	92	88
1979	3,549	2,320	1,229	348	116	127	182	131	143	126	102	110	107	100	93
1980	3,512	2,302	1,210	352	116	130	189	128	141	121	102	116	98	100	83
1981	3,325	2,238	1,087	366	112	128	190	128	141	121	96	101	91	94	79
1982	3,260	2,135	1,125	362	111	127	187	119	126	114	96	113	88	83	88
1983	3,073	1,982	1,091	306	110	125	178	117	139	106	97	114	88	77	86
1984	2,932	1,919	1,013	348	106	120	170	114	130	105	93	103	92	90	83
1985	2,712	1,742	970	342	103	119	161	103	113	98	92	104	85	83	85
1986	2,678	1,732	946	325	102	115	150	105	109	103	91	104	101	81	78
1987	2,674	1,710	964	302	100	111	139	107	112	105	90	101	96	78	81
1988	2,679	1,719	960	297	100	109	131	109	117	105	91	99	102	78	81
1989	2,623	1,705	918	318	98	107	125	105	108	103	90	95	95	84	87
1990	2,538	1,646	892	322	99	105	121	99	109	93	94	102	92	88	84
1991	2,547	1,681	866	318	100	105	118	100	110	94	96	103	95	93	88
1992	2,510	1,644	866	319	98	103	114	97	103	94	95	102	94	93	85
1993	2,375	1,518	857	308	99	103	110	92	101	88	100	105	97	95	96
1994	2,623	1,783	840	321	103	101	106	107	101	111	102	106	100	94	100
1995	2,609	1,741	868	314	105	101	103	107	103	110	106	111	104	94	104
1996	2,447	1,615	832	326	100	100	100	100	100	100	100	100	100	100	100
1997	2,446	1,569	877	333	103	100	99	98	99	96	106	107	104	103	106
1998	2,299	1,419	880	326	104	99	98	94	106	87	113	116	115	105	112
1999	2,270	1,341	929	327	105	99	98	93	112	84	115	122	104	104	115
2000	2,150	1,260	890	325	102	98	98	89	106	79	110	120	94	103	108
2001	2,100	1,227	873	321	101	98	98	87	104	78	110	116	99	100	111
2002	2,148	1,262	886	316	100	98	99	88	105	79	108	114	106	99	104
2003	2,017	1,181	836	324	97	97	100	83	96	76	105	116	85	93	100
2004	2,012	1,187	825	321	96	97	102	78	85	75	104	117	82	94	101
2005	1,988	1,208	780	321	....	....	....	....	....	....	....	....	....	....	....
2006	1,900	1,148	752	312	....	....	....	....	....	....	....	....	....	....	....
2007 p	....	....	740	321	....	....	....	....	....	....	....	....	....	....	....

[1] Persons involved in farmwork. Total farm employment is the sum of self-employed and unpaid family workers and hired workers shown here.
[2] Data from Current Population Survey (CPS) conducted by the Department of Commerce, Census Bureau, for the Department of Labor, Bureau of Labor Statistics.
[3] Acreage harvested plus acreages in fruits, tree nuts, and vegetables and minor crops. Includes double-cropping.

Source: Department of Agriculture (Economic Research Service).

TABLE B–101.—*Agricultural price indexes and farm real estate value, 1975–2007*

[1990-92=100, except as noted]

Year or month	Prices received by farmers: All farm products	Crops	Livestock and products	Prices paid by farmers: All commodities, services, interest, taxes, and wage rates [1]	Production items: Total [2]	Feed	Livestock and poultry	Fertilizer	Agricultural chemicals	Fuels	Farm machinery	Farm services	Rent	Wage rates	Addendum: Average farm real estate value per acre (dollars) [3]
1975	73	88	62	47	55	83	39	87	72	40	38	48		44	340
1976	75	87	64	50	59	83	47	74	78	43	43	52		48	397
1977	73	83	64	53	61	82	48	72	71	46	47	57		51	474
1978	83	89	78	58	67	80	65	72	66	48	51	60		55	531
1979	94	98	90	66	76	89	88	77	67	61	56	66		60	628
1980	98	107	89	75	85	98	85	96	71	86	63	81		65	737
1981	100	111	89	82	92	110	80	104	77	98	70	89		70	819
1982	94	98	90	86	94	99	78	105	83	97	76	96		74	823
1983	98	108	88	86	92	107	76	100	87	94	81	82		76	788
1984	101	111	91	89	94	112	73	103	90	93	85	86		77	801
1985	91	98	86	86	91	95	74	98	90	93	85	85		78	713
1986	87	87	88	85	86	88	73	90	89	76	83	83		81	640
1987	89	86	91	87	87	83	85	86	87	76	85	84		85	599
1988	99	104	93	91	90	104	91	94	89	77	89	85		87	632
1989	104	109	100	96	95	110	93	99	93	83	94	91		95	668
1990	104	103	105	99	99	103	102	97	95	100	96	96	96	96	683
1991	100	101	99	100	100	98	102	103	101	104	100	98	100	100	703
1992	98	101	97	101	101	99	96	100	103	96	104	103	104	105	713
1993	101	102	100	104	104	102	94	96	109	93	107	110	100	108	736
1994	100	105	95	106	106	106	94	105	112	89	113	110	108	111	798
1995	102	112	92	109	108	103	82	121	116	89	120	115	117	114	844
1996	112	127	99	115	115	129	75	125	119	102	125	116	128	117	887
1997	107	115	98	118	119	125	94	121	121	106	128	116	136	123	926
1998	102	107	97	115	113	111	88	112	122	84	132	115	120	129	974
1999	96	97	95	115	111	100	95	105	121	94	135	114	113	135	1,030
2000	96	96	97	119	115	102	110	110	120	129	139	118	110	140	1,090
2001	102	99	106	123	120	109	111	123	121	121	144	120	117	146	1,150
2002	98	105	90	124	119	112	102	108	119	115	148	120	120	153	1,210
2003	107	111	103	128	124	114	109	124	121	140	151	125	123	157	1,270
2004	119	115	122	133	131	121	128	140	121	165	162	128	115	160	1,360
2005	115	111	120	142	139	117	138	164	123	216	173	132	123	165	1,650
2006	115	119	112	148	146	124	134	176	128	239	182	138	121	171	1,900
2007	138	143	132	158	156	151	130	209	130	263	189	143	119	177	2,160
2006: Jan	112	107	117	148	145	122	143	189	127	221	178	136	121	174	1,900
Feb	112	111	113	147	144	121	139	183	127	218	178	137	121	174	....
Mar	112	114	110	147	144	123	134	181	126	226	179	137	121	174	....
Apr	111	119	105	148	145	123	131	180	126	244	180	137	121	169	....
May	114	125	104	149	146	123	130	177	129	258	181	138	121	169	....
June	117	126	110	149	147	122	135	174	128	259	181	140	121	169	....
July	117	123	111	149	147	123	134	171	129	265	182	140	121	168	....
Aug	119	124	114	149	147	120	136	170	129	270	182	140	121	168	....
Sept	119	121	116	149	146	120	139	169	129	243	183	140	121	168	....
Oct	115	114	116	148	145	125	133	170	129	219	183	138	121	172	....
Nov	119	122	116	148	146	133	124	170	131	221	186	138	121	172	....
Dec	120	126	113	149	147	138	124	174	129	227	186	138	121	172	....
2007: Jan	123	130	116	152	148	140	122	182	129	219	186	142	119	179	2,160
Feb	127	137	120	153	150	148	124	186	129	222	187	142	119	179	....
Mar	133	141	126	155	153	150	130	202	130	240	189	142	119	179	....
Apr	134	140	129	157	156	148	133	209	130	258	189	142	119	176	....
May	137	141	134	157	156	147	131	210	130	263	189	142	119	176	....
June	138	140	137	158	156	149	128	211	130	262	189	144	119	176	....
July	140	141	140	158	157	149	133	212	130	265	189	144	119	173	....
Aug	140	141	139	158	158	149	135	216	131	262	189	144	119	173	....
Sept	141	142	139	159	158	151	135	214	130	270	189	144	119	173	....
Oct	141	148	132	160	159	155	132	213	133	281	190	143	119	178	....
Nov	146	155	136	161	161	161	129	220	132	309	191	143	119	178	....
Dec	151	165	136	162	163	169	127	227	131	304	192	143	119	178	....

[1] Includes items used for family living, not shown separately.
[2] Includes other production items not shown separately.
[3] Average for 48 States. Annual data are: March 1 for 1975, February 1 for 1976-81, April 1 for 1982-85, February 1 for 1986-89, and January 1 for 1990-2007.

Note.—Data on a 1990-92 base prior to 1975 have not been calculated by Department of Agriculture.

Source: Department of Agriculture (National Agricultural Statistics Service).

[Billions of dollars]

Year	Exports							Imports					Agricultural trade balance
	Total [1]	Feed grains	Food grains [2]	Oil-seeds and products	Cotton	Tobacco	Animals and products	Total [1]	Fruits, nuts, and vegetables [3]	Animals and products	Coffee	Cocoa beans and products	
1950	2.9	0.2	0.6	0.2	1.0	0.3	0.3	4.0	0.2	0.7	1.1	0.2	−1.1
1951	4.0	.3	1.1	.3	1.1	.3	.5	5.2	.2	1.1	1.4	.2	−1.1
1952	3.4	.3	1.1	.2	.9	.2	.3	4.5	.2	.7	1.4	.2	−1.1
1953	2.8	.3	.7	.2	.5	.3	.4	4.2	.2	.6	1.5	.2	−1.3
1954	3.1	.2	.5	.3	.8	.3	.5	4.0	.2	.5	1.5	.3	−.9
1955	3.2	.3	.6	.4	.5	.4	.6	4.0	.2	.5	1.4	.2	−.8
1956	4.2	.4	1.0	.5	.7	.3	.7	4.0	.2	.4	1.4	.2	.2
1957	4.5	.3	1.0	.5	1.0	.4	.7	4.0	.2	.5	1.4	.2	.6
1958	3.9	.5	.8	.4	.7	.4	.5	3.9	.2	.7	1.2	.2	(4)
1959	4.0	.6	.9	.6	.4	.3	.6	4.1	.2	.8	1.1	.2	−.1
1960	4.8	.5	1.2	.6	1.0	.4	.6	3.8	.2	.6	1.0	.2	1.0
1961	5.0	.5	1.4	.6	.9	.4	.6	3.7	.2	.7	1.0	.2	1.3
1962	5.0	.8	1.3	.7	.5	.4	.6	3.9	.2	.9	1.0	.2	1.2
1963	5.6	.8	1.5	.8	.6	.4	.7	4.0	.3	.9	1.0	.2	1.6
1964	6.3	.9	1.7	1.0	.7	.4	.8	4.1	.3	.8	1.2	.2	2.3
1965	6.2	1.1	1.4	1.2	.5	.4	.8	4.1	.3	.9	1.1	.1	2.1
1966	6.9	1.3	1.8	1.2	.4	.5	.7	4.5	.4	1.2	1.1	.1	2.4
1967	6.4	1.1	1.5	1.3	.5	.5	.7	4.5	.4	1.1	1.0	.2	1.9
1968	6.3	.9	1.4	1.3	.5	.5	.7	5.0	.5	1.3	1.2	.2	1.3
1969	6.0	.9	1.2	1.3	.3	.6	.8	5.0	.5	1.4	.9	.2	1.1
1970	7.3	1.1	1.4	1.9	.4	.5	.9	5.8	.5	1.6	1.2	.3	1.5
1971	7.7	1.0	1.3	2.2	.6	.5	1.0	5.8	.6	1.5	1.2	.2	1.9
1972	9.4	1.5	1.8	2.4	.5	.7	1.1	6.5	.7	1.8	1.3	.2	2.9
1973	17.7	3.5	4.7	4.3	.9	.7	1.6	8.4	.8	2.6	1.7	.3	9.3
1974	21.9	4.6	5.4	5.7	1.3	.8	1.8	10.2	.8	2.2	1.6	.5	11.7
1975	21.9	5.2	6.2	4.5	1.0	.9	1.7	9.3	.8	1.8	1.7	.5	12.6
1976	23.0	6.0	4.7	5.1	1.0	.9	2.4	11.0	.9	2.3	2.9	.6	12.0
1977	23.6	4.9	3.6	6.6	1.5	1.1	2.7	13.4	1.2	2.3	4.2	1.0	10.2
1978	29.4	5.9	5.5	8.2	1.7	1.4	3.0	14.8	1.5	3.1	4.0	1.4	14.6
1979	34.7	7.7	6.3	8.9	2.2	1.2	3.8	16.7	1.7	3.9	4.2	1.2	18.0
1980	41.2	9.8	7.9	9.4	2.9	1.3	3.8	17.4	1.7	3.8	4.2	.9	23.8
1981	43.3	9.4	9.6	9.6	2.3	1.5	4.2	16.9	2.0	3.5	2.9	.9	26.4
1982	36.6	6.4	7.9	9.1	2.0	1.5	3.9	15.3	2.3	3.7	2.9	.7	21.3
1983	36.1	7.3	7.4	8.7	1.8	1.5	3.8	16.5	2.3	3.8	2.8	.8	19.6
1984	37.8	8.1	7.5	8.4	2.4	1.5	4.2	19.3	3.1	4.1	3.3	1.1	18.5
1985	29.0	6.0	4.5	5.8	1.6	1.5	4.1	20.0	3.5	4.2	3.3	1.4	9.1
1986	26.2	3.1	3.8	6.5	.8	1.2	4.5	21.5	3.6	4.5	4.6	1.1	4.7
1987	28.7	3.8	3.8	6.4	1.6	1.1	5.2	20.4	3.6	4.9	2.9	1.2	8.3
1988	37.1	5.9	5.9	7.7	2.0	1.3	6.4	21.0	3.8	5.2	2.5	1.0	16.1
1989	40.1	7.7	7.1	6.4	2.2	1.3	6.4	21.9	4.4	5.0	2.4	1.0	18.2
1990	39.5	7.0	4.8	5.7	2.8	1.4	6.6	22.9	4.6	5.6	1.9	1.1	16.6
1991	39.3	5.7	4.2	6.4	2.5	1.4	7.1	22.9	4.6	5.5	1.9	1.1	16.5
1992	43.1	5.7	5.4	7.2	2.0	1.7	8.0	24.8	4.7	5.7	1.7	1.1	18.3
1993	42.9	5.0	5.6	7.3	1.5	1.3	8.0	25.1	5.0	5.9	1.5	1.0	17.7
1994	46.2	4.7	5.3	7.2	2.7	1.3	9.2	27.0	5.3	5.7	2.5	1.0	19.2
1995	56.3	8.2	6.7	9.0	3.7	1.4	10.9	30.3	5.9	6.0	3.3	1.1	26.0
1996	60.3	9.4	7.4	10.8	2.7	1.4	11.1	33.5	6.6	6.1	2.8	1.4	26.8
1997	57.2	6.0	5.2	12.1	2.7	1.6	11.3	36.1	6.9	6.5	3.9	1.5	21.0
1998	51.8	5.0	5.0	9.5	2.5	1.5	10.6	36.9	7.7	6.9	3.4	1.7	14.9
1999	48.4	5.5	4.7	8.1	1.0	1.3	10.4	37.7	8.5	7.3	2.9	1.5	10.7
2000	51.3	5.2	4.3	8.6	1.9	1.2	11.6	39.0	8.6	8.4	2.7	1.4	12.3
2001	53.7	5.2	4.2	9.2	2.2	1.3	12.4	39.4	9.0	9.2	1.7	1.5	14.3
2002	53.1	5.5	4.5	9.6	2.0	1.0	11.1	41.9	9.7	9.0	1.7	1.8	11.2
2003	59.4	5.4	5.0	11.7	3.4	1.0	12.2	47.4	10.8	8.9	2.0	2.4	12.0
2004	61.4	6.4	6.3	10.4	4.3	1.0	10.4	54.0	12.2	10.6	2.3	2.5	7.4
2005	63.2	5.4	5.7	10.2	3.9	1.0	12.2	59.3	13.4	11.5	3.0	2.8	7.4
2006	70.9	7.7	5.5	11.3	4.5	1.1	13.5	65.3	14.6	11.5	3.3	2.7	5.6
Jan–Nov:													
2006	64.3	6.8	5.0	10.0	4.3	1.0	12.3	59.7	13.3	10.5	3.0	2.4	4.5
2007	80.8	9.9	8.9	13.2	4.3	1.0	15.6	65.8	14.9	11.3	3.5	2.4	15.0

[1] Total includes items not shown separately.
[2] Rice, wheat, and wheat flour.
[3] Includes fruit, nut, and vegetable preparations. Beginning in 1989, includes bananas, but excludes yeasts, starches, and other minor horticultural products.
[4] Less than $50 million.

Note.—Data derived from official estimates released by the Bureau of the Census, Department of Commerce. Agricultural commodities are defined as (1) nonmarine food products and (2) other products of agriculture which have not passed through complex processes of manufacture. Export value, at U.S. port of exportation, is based on the selling price and includes inland freight, insurance, and other charges to the port. Import value, defined generally as the market value in the foreign country, excludes import duties, ocean freight, and marine insurance.

Source: Department of Agriculture (Economic Research Service).

Table B–103.—U.S. international transactions, 1946–2007

[Millions of dollars; quarterly data seasonally adjusted. Credits (+), debits (−)]

Year or quarter	Goods[1]			Services				Income receipts and payments			Unilateral current transfers net[2]	Balance on current account
	Exports	Imports	Balance on goods	Net military transactions[2]	Net travel and transportation	Other services, net	Balance on goods and services	Receipts	Payments	Balance on income		
1946	11,764	−5,067	6,697	−424	733	310	7,316	772	−212	560	−2,991	4,885
1947	16,097	−5,973	10,124	−358	946	145	10,857	1,102	−245	857	−2,722	8,992
1948	13,265	−7,557	5,708	−351	374	175	5,906	1,921	−437	1,484	−4,973	2,417
1949	12,213	−6,874	5,339	−410	230	208	5,367	1,831	−476	1,355	−5,849	873
1950	10,203	−9,081	1,122	−56	−120	242	1,188	2,068	−559	1,509	−4,537	−1,840
1951	14,243	−11,176	3,067	169	298	254	3,788	2,633	−583	2,050	−4,954	884
1952	13,449	−10,838	2,611	528	83	309	3,531	2,751	−555	2,196	−5,113	614
1953	12,412	−10,975	1,437	1,753	−238	307	3,259	2,736	−624	2,112	−6,657	−1,286
1954	12,929	−10,353	2,576	902	−269	305	3,514	2,929	−582	2,347	−5,642	219
1955	14,424	−11,527	2,897	−113	−297	299	2,786	3,406	−676	2,730	−5,086	430
1956	17,556	−12,803	4,753	−221	−361	447	4,618	3,837	−735	3,102	−4,990	2,730
1957	19,562	−13,291	6,271	−423	−189	482	6,141	4,180	−796	3,384	−4,763	4,762
1958	16,414	−12,952	3,462	−849	−633	486	2,466	3,790	−825	2,965	−4,647	784
1959	16,458	−15,310	1,148	−831	−821	573	69	4,132	−1,061	3,071	−4,422	−1,282
1960	19,650	−14,758	4,892	−1,057	−964	639	3,508	4,616	−1,238	3,379	−4,062	2,824
1961	20,108	−14,537	5,571	−1,131	−978	732	4,195	4,999	−1,245	3,755	−4,127	3,822
1962	20,781	−16,260	4,521	−912	−1,152	912	3,370	5,618	−1,324	4,294	−4,277	3,387
1963	22,272	−17,048	5,224	−742	−1,309	1,036	4,210	6,157	−1,560	4,596	−4,392	4,414
1964	25,501	−18,700	6,801	−794	−1,146	1,161	6,022	6,824	−1,783	5,041	−4,240	6,823
1965	26,461	−21,510	4,951	−487	−1,280	1,480	4,664	7,437	−2,088	5,350	−4,583	5,431
1966	29,310	−25,493	3,817	−1,043	−1,331	1,497	2,940	7,528	−2,481	5,047	−4,955	3,031
1967	30,666	−26,866	3,800	−1,187	−1,750	1,742	2,604	8,021	−2,747	5,274	−5,294	2,583
1968	33,626	−32,991	635	−596	−1,548	1,759	250	9,367	−3,378	5,990	−5,629	611
1969	36,414	−35,807	607	−718	−1,763	1,964	91	10,913	−4,869	6,044	−5,735	399
1970	42,469	−39,866	2,603	−641	−2,038	2,330	2,254	11,748	−5,515	6,233	−6,156	2,331
1971	43,319	−45,579	−2,260	653	−2,345	2,649	−1,303	12,707	−5,435	7,272	−7,402	−1,433
1972	49,381	−55,797	−6,416	1,072	−3,063	2,965	−5,443	14,765	−6,572	8,192	−8,544	−5,795
1973	71,410	−70,499	911	740	−3,158	3,406	1,900	21,808	−9,655	12,153	−6,913	7,140
1974	98,306	−103,811	−5,505	165	−3,184	4,231	−4,292	27,587	−12,084	15,503	−9,249	1,962
1975	107,088	−98,185	8,903	1,461	−2,812	4,854	12,404	25,351	−12,564	12,787	−7,075	18,116
1976	114,745	−124,228	−9,483	931	−2,558	5,027	−6,082	29,375	−13,311	16,063	−5,686	4,295
1977	120,816	−151,907	−31,091	1,731	−3,565	5,680	−27,246	32,354	−14,217	18,137	−5,226	−14,335
1978	142,075	−176,002	−33,927	857	−3,573	6,879	−29,763	42,088	−21,680	20,408	−5,788	−15,143
1979	184,439	−212,007	−27,568	−1,313	−2,935	7,251	−24,565	63,834	−32,961	30,873	−6,593	−285
1980	224,250	−249,750	−25,500	−1,822	−997	8,912	−19,407	72,606	−42,532	30,073	−8,349	2,317
1981	237,044	−265,067	−28,023	−844	144	12,552	−16,172	86,529	−53,626	32,903	−11,702	5,030
1982	211,157	−247,642	−36,485	112	−992	13,209	−24,156	91,747	−56,583	35,164	−16,544	−5,536
1983	201,799	−268,901	−67,102	−563	−4,227	14,124	−57,767	90,000	−53,614	36,386	−17,310	−38,691
1984	219,926	−332,418	−112,492	−2,547	−8,438	14,404	−109,073	108,819	−73,756	35,063	−20,335	−94,344
1985	215,915	−338,088	−122,173	−4,390	−9,798	14,483	−121,880	98,542	−72,819	25,723	−21,998	−118,155
1986	223,344	−368,425	−145,081	−5,181	−8,779	20,502	−138,538	97,064	−81,571	15,494	−24,132	−147,177
1987	250,208	−409,765	−159,557	−3,844	−8,010	19,728	−151,684	108,184	−93,891	14,293	−23,265	−160,655
1988	320,230	−447,189	−126,959	−6,320	−3,013	21,725	−114,566	136,713	−118,026	18,687	−25,274	−121,153
1989	359,916	−477,665	−117,749	−6,749	3,551	27,805	−93,142	161,287	−141,463	19,824	−26,169	−99,486
1990	387,401	−498,438	−111,037	−7,599	7,501	30,270	−80,864	171,742	−143,192	28,550	−26,654	−78,968
1991	414,083	−491,020	−76,937	−5,275	16,560	34,516	−31,136	149,214	−125,085	24,131	9,904	2,897
1992	439,631	−536,528	−96,897	−1,448	19,969	39,163	−39,212	133,767	−109,532	24,235	−35,100	−50,078
1993	456,943	−589,394	−132,451	1,383	19,714	41,040	−70,311	136,057	−110,741	25,316	−39,811	−84,805
1994	502,859	−668,690	−165,831	2,570	16,305	48,463	−98,493	166,521	−149,375	17,146	−40,265	−121,612
1995	575,204	−749,374	−174,170	4,600	21,772	51,414	−96,384	210,244	−189,353	20,891	−38,074	−113,567
1996	612,113	−803,113	−191,000	5,385	25,015	56,535	−104,065	226,129	−203,811	22,318	−43,017	−124,764
1997	678,366	−876,794	−198,428	4,968	22,152	63,035	−108,273	256,804	−244,195	12,609	−45,062	−140,726
1998	670,416	−918,637	−248,221	5,220	10,210	66,651	−166,140	261,819	−257,554	4,265	−53,187	−215,062
1999	683,965	−1,031,784	−347,819	2,593	7,085	73,051	−265,090	293,925	−280,037	13,888	−50,428	−301,630
2000	771,994	−1,226,684	−454,690	317	2,486	72,052	−379,835	350,918	−329,864	21,054	−58,645	−417,426
2001	718,712	−1,148,231	−429,519	−2,296	−3,254	69,943	−365,126	290,797	−259,075	31,722	−51,295	−384,699
2002	682,422	−1,167,377	−484,955	−7,158	−4,245	72,633	−423,725	281,215	−253,544	27,671	−63,587	−459,641
2003	713,415	−1,264,307	−550,892	−11,981	−11,475	77,433	−496,915	320,568	−275,147	45,421	−70,607	−522,101
2004	807,516	−1,477,094	−669,578	−13,518	−14,275	85,279	−612,092	401,942	−345,585	56,357	−84,414	−640,148
2005	894,631	−1,681,780	−787,149	−10,536	−12,945	96,259	−714,371	505,488	−457,430	48,058	−88,535	−754,848
2006	1,023,109	−1,861,380	−838,271	−13,942	−10,636	104,327	−758,522	650,462	−613,823	36,640	−89,595	−811,477
2006: I	243,880	−451,637	−207,757	−3,195	−3,075	24,315	−189,712	148,391	−137,929	10,462	−21,360	−200,611
II	252,458	−463,734	−211,276	−3,549	−3,111	25,359	−192,577	162,020	−151,352	10,668	−23,686	−205,595
III	260,285	−479,184	−218,899	−3,888	−2,456	25,936	−199,307	167,026	−161,177	5,850	−23,877	−217,334
IV	266,486	−466,825	−200,339	−3,310	−1,995	28,718	−176,926	173,025	−163,365	9,661	−20,673	−187,938
2007: I	270,116	−470,983	−200,867	−3,665	−1,711	28,662	−177,581	176,213	−168,735	7,478	−26,994	−197,097
II	279,339	−483,552	−204,213	−4,141	−59	29,983	−178,431	195,460	−182,791	12,669	−23,157	−188,919
III ᵖ	297,946	−497,646	−199,700	−4,278	1,042	29,783	−173,152	205,624	−185,168	20,456	−25,760	−178,456

[1] Adjusted from Census data for differences in valuation, coverage, and timing; excludes military.
[2] Includes transfers of goods and services under U.S. military grant programs.

See next page for continuation of table.

[Millions of dollars; quarterly data seasonally adjusted. Credits (+), debits (−)]

| Year or quarter | Capital account transactions, net | U.S.-owned assets abroad, excluding financial derivatives [increase/financial outflow (−)] | | | | Foreign-owned assets in the U.S., excluding financial derivatives [increase/financial inflow (+)] | | | Financial derivatives, net | Statistical discrepancy | |
		Total	U.S. official reserve assets [3]	Other U.S. Government assets	U.S. private assets	Total	Foreign official assets	Other foreign assets		Total (sum of the items with sign reversed)	Of which: Seasonal adjustment discrepancy
1946			−623									
1947			−3,315									
1948			−1,736									
1949			−266									
1950			1,758									
1951			−33									
1952			−415									
1953			1,256									
1954			480									
1955			182									
1956			−869									
1957			−1,165									
1958			2,292									
1959			1,035									
1960		−4,099	2,145	−1,100	−5,144	2,294	1,473	821		−1,019	
1961		−5,538	607	−910	−5,235	2,705	765	1,939		−989	
1962		−4,174	1,535	−1,085	−4,623	1,911	1,270	641		−1,124	
1963		−7,270	378	−1,662	−5,986	3,217	1,986	1,231		−360	
1964		−9,560	171	−1,680	−8,050	3,643	1,660	1,983		−907	
1965		−5,716	1,225	−1,605	−5,336	742	134	607		−457	
1966		−7,321	570	−1,543	−6,347	3,661	−672	4,333		629	
1967		−9,757	53	−2,423	−7,386	7,379	3,451	3,928		−205	
1968		−10,977	−870	−2,274	−7,833	9,928	−774	10,703		438	
1969		−11,585	−1,179	−2,200	−8,206	12,702	−1,301	14,002		−1,516	
1970		−8,470	3,348	−1,589	−10,229	6,359	6,908	−550		−219	
1971		−11,758	3,066	−1,884	−12,940	22,970	26,879	−3,909		−9,779	
1972		−13,787	706	−1,568	−12,925	21,461	10,475	10,986		−1,879	
1973		−22,874	158	−2,644	−20,388	18,388	6,026	12,362		−2,654	
1974		−34,745	−1,467	366	−33,643	35,341	10,546	24,796		−2,558	
1975		−39,703	−849	−3,474	−35,380	17,170	7,027	10,143		4,417	
1976		−51,269	−2,558	−4,214	−44,498	38,018	17,693	20,326		8,955	
1977		−34,785	−375	−3,693	−30,717	53,219	36,816	16,403		−4,099	
1978		−61,130	732	−4,660	−57,202	67,036	33,678	33,358		9,236	
1979		−64,915	6	−3,746	−61,176	40,852	−13,665	54,516		24,349	
1980		−85,815	−7,003	−5,162	−73,651	62,612	15,497	47,115		20,886	
1981		−113,054	−4,082	−5,097	−103,875	86,232	4,960	81,272		21,792	
1982	199	−127,882	−4,965	−6,131	−116,786	96,589	3,593	92,997		36,630	
1983	209	−66,373	−1,196	−5,006	−60,172	88,694	5,845	82,849		16,162	
1984	235	−40,376	−3,131	−5,489	−31,757	117,752	3,140	114,612		16,733	
1985	315	−44,752	−3,858	−2,821	−38,074	146,115	−1,119	147,233		16,478	
1986	301	−111,723	312	−2,022	−110,014	230,009	35,648	194,360		28,590	
1987	365	−79,296	9,149	1,006	−89,450	248,634	45,387	203,247		−9,048	
1988	493	−106,573	−3,912	2,967	−105,628	246,522	39,758	206,764		−19,289	
1989	336	−175,383	−25,293	1,233	−151,323	224,928	8,503	216,425		49,605	
1990	−6,579	−81,234	−2,158	2,317	−81,393	141,571	33,910	107,661		25,211	
1991	−4,479	−64,389	5,763	2,923	−73,075	110,809	17,388	93,421		−44,840	
1992	−557	−74,410	3,901	−1,667	−76,644	170,663	40,476	130,185		−45,617	
1993	−1,299	−200,551	−1,379	−351	−198,823	282,041	71,753	210,288		4,617	
1994	−1,723	−178,937	5,346	−390	−183,893	305,989	39,583	266,406		−3,717	
1995	−927	−352,264	−9,742	−984	−341,538	438,562	109,880	328,682		28,196	
1996	−735	−413,409	6,668	−989	−419,088	551,096	126,724	424,372		−12,188	
1997	−1,027	−485,475	−1,010	68	−484,533	706,809	19,036	687,773		−79,581	
1998	−766	−353,829	−6,783	−422	−346,624	423,569	−19,903	443,472		146,088	
1999	−4,939	−504,062	8,747	2,750	−515,559	740,210	43,543	696,667		70,421	
2000	−1,010	−560,523	−290	−941	−559,292	1,046,896	42,758	1,004,138		−67,937	
2001	−1,270	−382,616	−4,911	−486	−377,219	782,859	28,059	754,800		−14,274	
2002	−1,470	−294,646	−3,681	345	−291,310	797,813	115,945	681,868		−42,056	
2003	−3,480	−325,424	1,523	537	−327,484	864,352	278,069	586,283		−13,348	
2004	−2,369	−905,024	2,805	1,710	−909,539	1,461,766	397,755	1,064,011		85,775	
2005	−4,054	−426,875	14,096	5,539	−446,510	1,204,231	259,268	944,963		−18,454	
2006	−3,913	−1,055,176	2,374	5,346	−1,062,896	1,859,597	440,264	1,419,333	28,762	−17,794	
2006: I	−1,724	−344,032	513	1,049	−345,594	538,140	125,257	412,883	1,633	6,593	9,958
II	−1,008	−212,218	−560	1,765	−213,423	355,442	120,861	234,581	14,001	49,378	−252
III	−545	−209,898	1,006	1,570	−212,474	449,987	108,799	341,188	14,911	−37,121	−15,973
IV	−637	−289,028	1,415	962	−291,405	516,029	85,347	430,682	−1,783	−36,643	6,267
2007: I	−559	−449,454	−72	445	−449,827	616,602	152,193	464,409	14,800	15,708	11,335
II	−598	−465,466	26	−369	−465,123	619,272	70,464	548,808	−1,007	36,718	2,782
III *p*	−554	−155,739	−54	422	−156,107	249,126	39,016	210,110		85,622	−18,584

[3] Consists of gold, special drawing rights, foreign currencies, and the U.S. reserve position in the International Monetary Fund (IMF).

Source: Department of Commerce (Bureau of Economic Analysis).

TABLE B–104.—*U.S. international trade in goods by principal end-use category, 1965–2007*

[Billions of dollars; quarterly data seasonally adjusted]

Year or quarter	Exports							Imports						
			Nonagricultural products							Nonpetroleum products				
	Total	Agri-cultural prod-ucts	Total	Indus-trial sup-plies and materi-als	Capital goods except auto-motive	Auto-motive	Other	Total	Petro-leum and prod-ucts	Total	Indus-trial sup-plies and materi-als	Capital goods except auto-motive	Auto-motive	Other
1965	26.5	6.3	20.2	7.6	8.1	1.9	2.6	21.5	2.0	19.5	9.1	1.5	0.9	8.0
1966	29.3	6.9	22.4	8.2	8.9	2.4	2.9	25.5	2.1	23.4	10.2	2.2	1.8	9.2
1967	30.7	6.5	24.2	8.5	9.9	2.8	3.0	26.9	2.1	24.8	10.0	2.5	2.4	9.9
1968	33.6	6.3	27.3	9.6	11.1	3.5	3.2	33.0	2.4	30.6	12.0	2.8	4.0	11.8
1969	36.4	6.1	30.3	10.3	12.4	3.9	3.7	35.8	2.6	33.2	11.8	3.4	4.9	13.0
1970	42.5	7.4	35.1	12.3	14.7	3.9	4.3	39.9	2.9	36.9	12.4	4.0	5.5	15.0
1971	43.3	7.8	35.5	10.9	15.4	4.7	4.5	45.6	3.7	41.9	13.8	4.3	7.4	16.4
1972	49.4	9.5	39.9	11.9	16.9	5.5	5.6	55.8	4.7	51.1	16.3	5.9	8.7	20.2
1973	71.4	18.0	53.4	17.0	22.0	6.9	7.6	70.5	8.4	62.1	19.6	8.3	10.3	23.9
1974	98.3	22.4	75.9	26.3	30.9	8.6	10.0	103.8	26.6	77.2	27.8	9.8	12.0	27.5
1975	107.1	22.2	84.8	26.8	36.6	10.6	10.8	98.2	27.0	71.2	24.0	10.2	11.7	25.3
1976	114.7	23.4	91.4	28.4	39.1	12.1	11.7	124.2	34.6	89.7	29.8	12.3	16.2	31.4
1977	120.8	24.3	96.5	29.8	39.8	13.4	13.5	151.9	45.0	106.9	35.7	14.0	18.6	38.6
1978 [1]	142.1	29.9	112.2	34.2	47.5	15.2	15.3	176.0	42.6	133.4	40.7	19.3	25.0	48.4
1979	184.4	35.5	149.0	52.2	60.2	17.9	18.7	212.0	60.4	151.6	47.5	24.6	26.6	52.8
1980	224.3	42.0	182.2	65.1	76.3	17.4	23.4	249.8	79.5	170.2	53.0	31.6	28.3	57.4
1981	237.0	44.1	193.0	63.6	84.2	19.7	25.5	265.1	78.4	186.7	56.1	37.1	31.0	62.4
1982	211.2	37.3	173.9	57.7	76.5	17.2	22.4	247.6	62.0	185.7	48.6	38.4	34.3	64.3
1983	201.8	37.1	164.7	52.7	71.7	18.5	21.8	268.9	55.1	213.8	53.7	43.7	43.0	73.3
1984	219.9	38.4	181.5	56.8	77.0	22.4	25.3	332.4	58.1	274.4	66.1	60.4	56.5	91.4
1985	215.9	29.6	186.3	54.8	79.3	24.9	27.2	338.1	51.4	286.7	62.6	61.3	64.9	97.9
1986	223.3	27.2	196.2	59.4	82.8	25.1	28.9	368.4	34.3	334.1	69.9	72.0	78.1	114.2
1987	250.2	29.8	220.4	63.7	92.7	27.6	36.4	409.8	42.9	366.8	70.8	85.1	85.2	125.7
1988	320.2	38.8	281.4	82.6	119.1	33.4	46.3	447.2	39.6	407.6	83.1	102.2	87.9	134.4
1989 [1]	359.9	41.1	318.8	90.5	136.9	35.1	56.3	477.7	50.9	426.8	84.6	112.3	87.4	142.5
1990	387.4	40.2	347.2	97.0	153.0	36.2	61.0	498.4	62.3	436.1	83.0	116.4	88.2	148.5
1991	414.1	40.1	374.0	101.6	166.6	39.9	65.9	491.0	51.7	439.3	81.3	121.1	85.5	151.4
1992	439.6	44.1	395.6	101.7	176.4	46.9	70.6	536.5	51.6	484.9	89.1	134.8	91.5	169.6
1993	456.9	43.6	413.3	105.1	182.7	51.6	74.0	589.4	51.5	537.9	100.8	153.2	102.1	182.0
1994	502.9	47.1	455.8	112.7	205.7	57.5	79.9	668.7	51.3	617.4	113.6	185.0	118.1	200.6
1995	575.2	57.2	518.0	136.8	234.4	61.4	86.5	749.4	56.0	693.3	128.5	222.1	123.7	219.0
1996	612.1	61.5	550.6	138.7	254.0	64.4	93.6	803.1	72.7	730.4	136.1	228.4	128.7	237.1
1997	678.4	58.5	619.9	148.6	295.8	73.4	102.0	876.8	71.8	805.0	144.9	253.6	139.4	267.1
1998	670.4	53.2	617.3	139.4	299.8	72.5	105.5	918.6	50.9	867.7	151.6	269.8	148.6	297.7
1999	684.0	49.7	634.3	140.3	311.2	75.3	107.5	1,031.8	67.8	964.0	156.3	295.7	179.0	333.0
2000	772.0	52.8	719.2	163.9	357.0	80.4	117.9	1,226.7	120.3	1,106.4	181.9	347.0	195.9	381.6
2001	718.7	54.9	663.8	150.5	321.7	75.4	116.2	1,148.2	103.6	1,044.6	172.5	298.0	189.8	384.3
2002	682.4	54.5	627.9	147.6	290.4	78.9	110.9	1,167.4	103.5	1,063.9	164.6	283.3	203.7	412.2
2003	713.4	60.9	652.5	162.5	293.7	80.6	115.7	1,264.3	133.1	1,131.2	181.4	295.9	210.1	443.8
2004	807.5	62.9	744.6	192.2	331.4	89.2	131.7	1,477.1	180.5	1,296.6	232.5	343.6	228.2	492.4
2005	894.6	64.9	829.7	221.5	362.3	98.6	147.4	1,681.8	251.9	1,429.9	272.7	379.3	239.5	538.4
2006	1,023.1	72.9	950.2	263.2	413.9	107.2	166.0	1,861.4	302.4	1,559.0	300.1	418.3	256.7	583.9
2004: I	194.1	16.0	178.1	44.9	80.8	21.0	31.4	345.2	40.2	305.0	50.9	81.1	55.3	117.7
II	200.0	15.8	184.3	46.9	82.4	21.9	33.0	365.2	41.6	323.5	57.1	85.1	57.4	124.0
III	203.8	15.1	188.7	48.8	83.7	23.0	33.1	373.5	44.5	329.0	61.1	87.5	57.5	122.9
IV	209.5	16.0	193.5	51.6	84.6	23.3	34.1	393.3	54.1	339.1	63.4	89.9	57.9	127.9
2005: I	214.4	15.7	198.7	53.7	85.9	23.6	35.5	398.8	53.5	345.2	64.5	90.9	57.5	132.4
II	223.1	16.5	206.6	56.2	90.2	23.8	36.4	411.6	57.7	353.9	65.6	95.2	58.4	134.7
III	224.3	16.2	208.1	55.4	90.5	25.0	37.2	423.6	66.4	357.2	66.9	95.5	60.4	134.4
IV	232.9	16.6	216.3	56.2	95.7	26.2	38.2	447.8	74.2	373.6	75.6	97.8	63.2	136.9
2006: I	243.9	17.3	226.6	60.7	99.8	26.1	39.9	451.6	73.4	378.3	72.9	101.1	63.7	140.6
II	252.5	18.0	234.4	65.5	102.3	26.1	40.5	463.7	78.7	385.0	74.5	103.6	64.2	142.7
III	260.3	18.7	241.6	67.9	103.9	27.5	42.2	479.2	82.8	396.4	78.1	106.7	63.6	148.0
IV	266.5	18.8	247.6	69.0	107.9	27.4	43.3	466.8	67.6	399.2	74.5	106.9	65.2	152.6
2007: I	270.1	19.8	250.3	69.3	107.0	27.9	46.1	471.0	70.9	400.1	72.4	109.4	63.4	155.0
II	279.3	21.8	257.6	74.3	107.8	29.5	45.9	483.6	78.1	405.4	79.0	109.5	63.1	153.9
III [p]	297.9	25.8	272.2	77.1	114.7	32.2	48.2	497.6	81.9	415.8	79.1	112.8	67.1	156.8

[1] End-use commodity classifications beginning 1978 and 1989 are not strictly comparable with data for earlier periods. See *Survey of Current Business,* June 1988 and July 2001.

Note.—Data are on a balance of payments basis and exclude military. In June 1990, end-use categories for goods exports were redefined to include reexports (exports of foreign goods); beginning with data for 1978, reexports are assigned to detailed end-use categories in the same manner as exports of domestic goods.

Source: Department of Commerce (Bureau of Economic Analysis).

[Millions of dollars]

Item	1999	2000	2001	2002	2003	2004	2005	2006	2007 first 3 quarters at annual rate[1]
EXPORTS									
Total, all countries	683,965	771,994	718,712	682,422	713,415	807,516	894,631	1,023,109	1,129,868
Europe	168,298	184,657	178,229	160,045	168,314	189,416	207,895	241,274	280,128
Euro area[2]	104,631	114,930	111,026	103,837	109,898	124,762	135,686	153,696	177,047
France	18,498	20,161	19,693	18,871	16,849	21,083	22,228	23,990	27,179
Germany	26,359	28,921	29,363	26,027	28,290	30,842	33,584	40,743	48,552
Italy	9,878	10,951	9,715	9,810	10,286	10,420	11,245	12,272	13,549
United Kingdom	37,657	40,725	39,701	32,085	32,871	35,124	37,569	44,215	49,349
Canada	166,713	178,877	163,259	160,916	169,930	189,981	212,192	230,982	246,192
Latin America and Other Western Hemisphere	141,492	170,267	158,969	148,158	148,955	171,887	192,382	222,298	239,677
Brazil	13,116	15,257	15,790	12,267	11,125	13,727	15,173	19,088	23,488
Mexico	86,758	111,172	101,181	97,242	97,224	110,697	120,264	133,893	136,969
Venezuela	5,314	5,509	5,600	3,967	2,782	4,743	6,411	8,977	10,228
Asia and Pacific	179,847	211,043	188,731	185,665	198,047	221,860	237,511	274,532	302,387
China	13,047	16,141	19,108	22,040	28,287	34,638	41,799	55,038	62,705
India	3,682	3,668	3,754	4,097	4,977	6,091	7,973	9,990	16,236
Japan	56,073	63,473	55,879	49,670	50,252	52,288	53,265	57,593	61,143
Korea, Republic of	22,256	27,150	21,203	21,756	23,481	25,730	27,135	31,418	33,289
Singapore	16,009	17,620	17,337	15,977	16,147	19,252	20,259	24,255	25,603
Taiwan	17,430	23,832	17,394	17,886	16,987	21,296	21,453	22,645	25,620
Middle East	18,122	16,984	18,141	17,867	18,047	21,594	29,766	35,795	39,131
Africa	9,493	10,165	11,383	9,771	10,122	12,778	14,885	18,228	22,352
Memorandum: Members of OPEC[3]	18,315	17,625	19,503	17,808	16,554	21,579	31,304	39,108	44,069
IMPORTS									
Total, all countries	1,031,784	1,226,684	1,148,231	1,167,377	1,264,307	1,477,094	1,681,780	1,861,380	1,936,241
Europe	227,204	259,848	255,988	261,340	285,270	321,486	355,403	383,812	406,187
Euro area[2]	144,598	163,636	166,508	172,762	187,937	209,746	229,206	246,862	266,604
France	25,749	29,809	30,421	28,289	29,244	31,609	33,848	37,036	41,296
Germany	55,271	58,588	59,141	62,540	68,188	77,349	84,967	89,237	93,632
Italy	22,349	25,034	23,768	24,209	25,398	28,096	30,975	32,660	34,597
United Kingdom	38,975	43,379	41,185	40,597	42,610	46,087	50,800	53,187	55,431
Canada	201,752	234,084	219,243	212,225	224,955	259,871	290,384	306,067	315,908
Latin America and Other Western Hemisphere	169,043	210,186	199,660	205,193	218,526	256,746	295,915	334,877	340,799
Brazil	11,318	13,854	14,467	15,782	17,917	21,164	24,441	26,373	25,719
Mexico	110,574	136,829	132,279	135,701	139,695	158,096	173,034	201,196	210,305
Venezuela	11,335	18,623	15,251	15,093	17,136	24,921	33,978	37,134	35,885
Asia and Pacific	391,435	455,941	411,473	432,214	462,063	542,072	608,703	684,297	712,673
China	81,840	100,112	102,403	125,316	152,671	196,973	243,886	288,125	315,999
India	9,073	10,691	9,755	11,821	13,068	15,577	18,819	21,845	23,681
Japan	131,039	146,711	126,685	121,617	118,264	130,094	138,375	148,559	145,693
Korea, Republic of	31,160	40,309	35,207	35,606	37,238	46,177	43,791	45,811	48,225
Singapore	18,224	19,273	15,080	14,821	15,161	15,406	15,131	17,712	18,763
Taiwan	35,444	40,980	33,642	32,113	32,118	34,986	35,103	38,414	38,213
Middle East	25,365	38,977	36,424	34,304	41,469	51,283	62,468	71,907	72,517
Africa	16,985	27,648	25,443	22,101	32,024	45,636	65,210	80,420	88,153
Memorandum: Members of OPEC[3]	41,978	67,094	59,755	53,246	68,346	94,109	124,942	145,368	162,000
BALANCE (excess of exports +)									
Total, all countries	−347,819	−454,690	−429,519	−484,955	−550,892	−669,578	−787,149	−838,271	−806,373
Europe	−58,906	−75,191	−77,759	−101,295	−116,956	−132,070	−147,508	−142,538	−126,059
Euro area[2]	−39,967	−48,706	−55,482	−68,925	−78,039	−84,984	−93,520	−93,166	−89,557
France	−7,251	−9,648	−10,728	−9,418	−12,395	−10,526	−11,620	−13,046	−14,116
Germany	−28,912	−29,667	−29,778	−36,513	−39,898	−46,507	−51,383	−48,494	−45,077
Italy	−12,471	−14,083	−14,053	−14,399	−15,112	−17,676	−19,730	−20,388	−21,048
United Kingdom	−1,318	−2,654	−1,484	−8,512	−9,739	−10,963	−13,231	−8,972	−6,084
Canada	−35,039	−55,207	−55,984	−51,309	−55,025	−69,890	−81,889	−75,085	−69,716
Latin America and Other Western Hemisphere	−27,551	−39,919	−40,691	−57,035	−69,571	−84,859	−103,533	−112,579	−101,121
Brazil	1,798	1,403	1,323	−3,515	−6,792	−7,437	−9,268	−7,285	−2,232
Mexico	−23,816	−25,657	−31,098	−38,459	−42,471	−47,399	−52,770	−67,303	−73,335
Venezuela	−6,021	−13,114	−9,651	−11,126	−14,354	−20,178	−27,567	−28,157	−25,657
Asia and Pacific	−211,588	−244,898	−222,742	−246,549	−264,016	−320,212	−371,192	−409,765	−410,288
China	−68,793	−83,971	−83,295	−103,276	−124,384	−162,335	−202,087	−233,087	−253,293
India	−5,391	−7,023	−6,001	−7,724	−8,091	−9,486	−10,846	−11,855	−7,444
Japan	−74,966	−83,238	−70,806	−71,947	−68,012	−77,806	−85,110	−90,966	−84,549
Korea, Republic of	−8,904	−13,159	−14,004	−13,850	−13,757	−20,447	−16,656	−14,393	−14,937
Singapore	−2,215	−1,653	2,257	1,156	986	3,846	5,128	6,543	6,840
Taiwan	−18,014	−17,148	−16,248	−14,725	−15,131	−13,690	−13,650	−15,769	−12,595
Middle East	−7,243	−21,993	−18,283	−16,437	−23,422	−29,689	−32,702	−36,112	−33,388
Africa	−7,492	−17,483	−14,060	−12,330	−21,902	−32,858	−50,325	−62,192	−65,803
Memorandum: Members of OPEC[3]	−23,663	−49,469	−40,252	−35,438	−51,792	−72,530	−93,638	−106,260	−117,931

[1] Preliminary; seasonally adjusted.

[2] Euro area includes: Austria, Belgium, Finland, France, Germany, Greece (beginning in 2001), Ireland, Italy, Luxembourg, Netherlands, Portugal, Slovenia (beginning in 2007), and Spain.

[3] Organization of Petroleum Exporting Countries, consisting of Algeria, Angola (beginning in 2007), Indonesia, Iran, Iraq, Kuwait, Libya, Nigeria, Qatar, Saudi Arabia, United Arab Emirates, and Venezuela.

Note.—Data are on a balance of payments basis and exclude military. For further details, and additional data by country, see *Survey of Current Business,* January 2008.

Source: Department of Commerce (Bureau of Economic Analysis).

TABLE B–106.—*U.S. international trade in goods on balance of payments (BOP) and Census basis, and trade in services on BOP basis, 1981–2007*

[Billions of dollars; monthly data seasonally adjusted]

Year or month	Goods: Exports (f.a.s. value)[1,2]							Goods: Imports (customs value)[5]							Services (BOP basis)	
	Total, BOP basis[3]	Census basis (by end-use category)						Total, BOP basis	Census basis (by end-use category)						Exports	Imports
		Total, Census basis[3,4]	Foods, feeds, and beverages	Industrial supplies and materials	Capital goods except automotive	Automotive vehicles, parts, and engines	Consumer goods (nonfood) except automotive		Total, Census basis[4]	Foods, feeds, and beverages	Industrial supplies and materials	Capital goods except automotive	Automotive vehicles, parts, and engines	Consumer goods (nonfood) except automotive		
1981	237.0	238.7	....	....	....	....	....	265.1	261.0	....	....	....	....	....	57.4	45.5
1982	211.2	216.4	31.3	61.7	72.7	15.7	14.3	247.6	244.0	17.1	112.0	35.4	33.3	39.7	64.1	51.7
1983	201.8	205.6	30.9	56.7	67.2	16.8	13.4	268.9	258.0	18.2	107.0	40.9	40.8	44.9	64.3	55.0
1984	219.9	224.0	31.5	61.7	72.0	20.6	13.3	332.4	6330.7	21.0	123.7	59.8	53.5	60.0	71.2	67.7
1985	215.9	7218.8	24.0	58.5	73.9	22.9	12.6	338.1	6336.5	21.9	113.9	65.1	66.8	68.3	73.2	72.9
1986	223.3	7227.2	22.3	57.3	75.8	21.7	14.2	368.4	365.4	24.4	101.3	71.8	78.2	79.4	86.7	80.1
1987	250.2	254.1	24.3	66.7	86.2	24.6	17.7	409.8	406.2	24.8	111.0	84.5	85.2	88.7	98.7	90.8
1988	320.2	322.4	32.3	85.1	109.2	29.3	23.1	447.2	441.0	24.8	118.3	101.4	87.7	95.9	110.9	98.5
1989	359.9	363.8	37.2	99.3	138.8	34.8	36.4	477.7	473.2	25.1	132.3	113.3	86.1	102.9	127.1	102.5
1990	387.4	393.6	35.1	104.4	152.7	37.4	43.3	498.4	495.3	26.6	143.2	116.4	87.3	105.7	147.8	117.7
1991	414.1	421.7	35.7	109.7	166.7	40.0	45.9	491.0	488.5	26.5	131.6	120.7	85.7	108.0	164.3	118.5
1992	439.6	448.2	40.3	109.1	175.9	47.0	51.4	536.5	532.7	27.6	138.6	134.3	91.8	122.7	177.3	119.6
1993	456.9	465.1	40.6	111.8	181.7	52.4	54.7	589.4	580.7	27.9	145.6	152.4	102.4	134.0	185.9	123.8
1994	502.9	512.6	42.0	121.4	205.0	57.8	60.0	668.7	663.3	31.0	162.1	184.4	118.3	146.3	200.4	133.1
1995	575.2	584.7	50.5	146.2	233.0	61.8	64.4	749.4	743.5	33.2	181.8	221.4	123.8	159.9	219.2	141.4
1996	612.1	625.1	55.5	147.7	253.0	65.0	70.1	803.1	795.3	35.7	204.5	228.1	128.9	172.0	239.5	152.6
1997	678.4	689.2	51.5	158.2	294.5	74.0	77.4	876.8	869.7	39.7	213.8	253.3	139.8	193.8	256.1	165.9
1998	670.4	682.1	46.4	148.3	299.4	72.4	80.3	918.6	911.9	41.2	200.1	269.5	148.7	217.0	262.8	180.7
1999	684.0	695.8	46.0	147.5	310.8	75.3	80.9	1,031.8	1,024.6	43.6	221.4	295.7	179.0	241.9	281.9	199.2
2000	772.0	781.9	47.9	172.6	356.9	80.4	89.4	1,226.7	1,218.0	46.0	299.0	347.0	195.9	281.8	298.6	223.7
2001	718.7	729.1	49.4	160.1	321.7	75.4	88.3	1,148.2	1,141.0	46.6	273.9	298.0	189.8	284.3	286.2	221.8
2002	682.4	693.1	49.6	156.8	290.4	78.9	84.4	1,167.4	1,161.4	49.7	267.7	283.3	203.7	307.8	292.3	231.1
2003	713.4	724.8	55.0	173.0	293.7	80.6	89.9	1,264.3	1,257.1	55.8	313.8	295.9	210.1	333.9	304.3	250.4
2004	807.5	818.8	56.6	203.9	331.4	89.2	103.2	1,477.1	1,469.7	62.1	412.8	343.6	228.2	372.9	349.7	292.2
2005	894.6	906.0	59.0	233.0	362.3	98.6	116.1	1,681.8	1,673.5	68.1	523.8	379.3	239.5	407.2	388.4	315.7
2006	1,023.1	1,036.6	66.0	276.0	413.9	107.2	130.0	1,861.4	1,853.9	74.9	602.0	418.3	256.7	442.6	422.6	342.8
2006: Jan	80.6	81.4	5.2	20.9	33.0	8.8	10.3	152.2	151.5	6.2	50.2	33.9	21.5	34.9	34.0	27.6
Feb	80.9	81.8	5.1	20.9	33.3	8.8	10.3	148.8	148.2	6.0	49.0	32.8	21.2	34.5	33.6	28.1
Mar	82.4	83.3	5.2	22.2	33.5	8.6	10.5	150.7	150.0	6.3	47.0	34.4	21.0	36.4	34.1	28.0
Apr	82.3	83.2	5.2	22.3	33.6	8.6	10.3	150.9	150.4	6.1	48.5	34.2	21.3	35.4	34.4	28.2
May	83.9	84.9	5.4	23.1	33.9	8.5	10.7	155.9	155.3	6.1	52.7	34.6	21.0	36.1	34.1	28.6
June	86.3	87.2	5.5	23.6	34.8	9.0	10.9	156.9	156.3	6.1	51.9	34.7	21.9	36.8	34.8	28.7
July	85.1	86.2	5.6	22.9	33.9	9.4	10.9	158.8	158.2	6.2	53.9	35.2	21.1	36.9	34.8	28.7
Aug	87.4	88.6	5.8	23.5	34.9	9.3	11.2	161.6	160.9	6.4	55.0	35.8	21.3	37.4	35.2	28.6
Sept	87.8	89.1	5.7	24.5	35.2	8.8	10.9	158.7	158.1	6.4	51.9	35.8	21.2	37.9	35.5	28.8
Oct	88.2	89.5	5.7	24.3	35.5	8.8	11.2	153.7	153.0	6.4	46.8	35.5	21.1	38.1	36.4	29.1
Nov	88.8	90.4	5.6	24.0	36.1	9.1	11.3	155.0	154.4	6.4	46.9	35.7	21.4	38.8	37.1	29.3
Dec	89.5	91.0	5.9	23.8	36.4	9.5	11.4	158.1	157.5	6.5	48.3	35.7	22.6	39.3	37.6	29.3
2007: Jan	90.5	91.7	6.0	23.8	36.9	8.9	11.9	155.1	154.5	6.6	48.0	36.5	20.4	38.2	37.1	29.5
Feb	88.6	89.6	6.3	23.7	34.8	9.1	11.5	154.1	153.5	6.6	44.5	36.7	20.8	39.7	37.1	29.5
Mar	91.1	92.4	6.0	24.8	35.3	9.9	11.8	161.8	160.3	6.8	49.7	36.2	22.1	40.4	37.9	29.8
Apr	90.9	92.2	6.6	25.1	34.6	9.8	12.0	158.3	157.1	6.6	50.2	35.7	21.1	38.7	38.5	30.1
May	93.4	94.7	6.6	25.8	36.5	9.8	12.0	161.9	160.7	6.8	52.5	36.6	20.5	39.2	39.2	30.7
June	95.0	96.1	6.6	27.0	36.6	9.9	11.9	163.3	162.7	6.7	52.8	37.2	21.5	39.2	39.4	30.7
July	98.6	99.8	6.9	26.5	38.5	11.3	12.4	166.4	165.3	6.9	53.9	37.2	22.6	39.5	39.4	30.8
Aug	99.0	100.1	7.5	27.3	38.3	10.4	12.5	165.1	164.0	7.0	52.9	37.4	22.1	39.2	40.3	31.2
Sept	100.4	101.3	8.3	28.0	37.9	10.5	12.9	166.2	165.1	7.0	52.7	38.2	22.3	39.5	40.1	31.3
Oct	100.9	101.9	7.7	27.8	39.2	10.5	12.5	167.8	166.8	6.9	54.5	37.7	22.5	40.0	40.8	31.7
Nov p	101.0	102.4	8.1	28.0	38.3	10.9	12.3	173.7	173.0	7.0	59.2	37.8	22.6	40.8	41.4	31.8

[1] Department of Defense shipments of grant-aid military supplies and equipment under the Military Assistance Program are excluded from total exports through 1985 and included beginning 1986.

[2] F.a.s. (free alongside ship) value basis at U.S. port of exportation for exports.

[3] Beginning with 1989 data, exports have been adjusted for undocumented exports to Canada and are included in the appropriate end-use categories. For prior years, only total exports include this adjustment.

[4] Total includes "other" exports or imports, not shown separately.

[5] Total arrivals of imported goods other than in-transit shipments.

[6] Total includes revisions not reflected in detail.

[7] Total exports are on a revised statistical month basis; end-use categories are on a statistical month basis.

Note.—Goods on a Census basis are adjusted to a BOP basis by the Bureau of Economic Analysis, in line with concepts and definitions used to prepare international and national accounts. The adjustments are necessary to supplement coverage of Census data, to eliminate duplication of transactions recorded elsewhere in international accounts, and to value transactions according to a standard definition.

Data include international trade of the U.S. Virgin Islands, Puerto Rico, and U.S. Foreign Trade Zones.

Source: Department of Commerce (Bureau of the Census and Bureau of Economic Analysis).

[Millions of dollars]

Type of investment	1999	2000	2001	2002	2003	2004	2005	2006 P
NET INTERNATIONAL INVESTMENT POSITION OF THE UNITED STATES:	−766,237	−1,381,196	−1,919,430	−2,088,008	−2,140,361	−2,294,394	−2,238,359	−2,539,629
Financial derivatives, net [1]	....	....	....	....	....	....	57,915	58,935
Net international investment position, excluding financial derivatives	−766,237	−1,381,196	−1,919,430	−2,088,008	−2,140,361	−2,294,394	−2,296,274	−2,598,564
U.S.-OWNED ASSETS ABROAD	5,974,394	6,238,785	6,308,681	6,652,248	7,643,494	9,257,096	11,576,336	13,754,990
Financial derivatives, gross positive fair value [1]	....	....	....	....	....	....	1,190,029	1,237,564
U.S.-owned assets abroad, excluding financial derivatives	5,974,394	6,238,785	6,308,681	6,652,248	7,643,494	9,257,096	10,386,307	12,517,426
U.S. official reserve assets	136,418	128,400	129,961	158,602	183,577	189,591	188,043	219,853
Gold [2]	75,950	71,799	72,328	90,806	108,866	113,947	134,175	165,267
Special drawing rights	10,336	10,539	10,783	12,166	12,638	13,628	8,210	8,870
Reserve position in the International Monetary Fund	17,950	14,824	17,869	21,979	22,535	19,544	8,036	5,040
Foreign currencies	32,182	31,238	28,981	33,651	39,538	42,472	37,622	40,676
U.S. Government assets, other than official reserve assets	84,227	85,168	85,654	85,309	84,772	83,062	77,523	72,189
U.S. credits and other long-term assets [3]	81,657	82,574	83,132	82,682	81,980	80,308	76,960	71,635
Repayable in dollars	81,367	82,293	82,854	82,406	81,706	80,035	76,687	71,362
Other [4]	290	281	278	276	274	273	273	273
U.S. foreign currency holdings and U.S. short-term assets	2,570	2,594	2,522	2,627	2,792	2,754	563	554
U.S. private assets:	5,753,749	6,025,217	6,093,066	6,408,337	7,375,145	8,984,443	10,120,741	12,225,384
Direct investment at current cost	1,414,355	1,531,607	1,693,131	1,867,043	2,054,464	2,463,608	2,535,188	2,855,619
Foreign securities	2,551,949	2,425,534	2,169,735	2,079,891	2,953,778	3,553,387	5,432,264	5,432,264
Bonds	548,233	572,692	557,062	705,226	874,356	992,969	1,028,179	1,180,758
Corporate stocks	2,003,716	1,852,842	1,612,673	1,374,665	2,079,422	2,560,418	3,317,705	4,251,506
U.S. claims on unaffiliated foreigners reported by U.S. nonbanking concerns [5]	704,517	836,559	839,303	901,946	594,004	737,638	734,034	848,464
U.S. claims reported by U.S. banks, not included elsewhere [6]	1,082,928	1,231,517	1,390,897	1,559,457	1,772,899	2,229,810	2,505,635	3,089,037
FOREIGN-OWNED ASSETS IN THE UNITED STATES	6,740,631	7,619,981	8,228,111	8,740,256	9,783,855	11,551,490	13,814,695	16,294,619
Financial derivatives, gross negative fair value [1]	....	....	....	....	....	....	1,132,114	1,178,629
Foreign-owned assets in the United States, excluding financial derivatives	6,740,631	7,619,981	8,228,111	8,740,256	9,783,855	11,551,490	12,682,581	15,115,990
Foreign official assets in the United States	951,088	1,030,708	1,109,072	1,250,977	1,562,564	2,011,899	2,306,292	2,770,165
U.S. Government securities	693,781	756,155	847,005	970,359	1,186,500	1,509,986	1,725,193	2,104,696
U.S. Treasury securities	617,680	639,796	720,149	811,995	986,301	1,251,943	1,340,598	1,520,768
Other	76,101	116,359	126,856	158,364	200,199	258,043	384,595	583,928
Other U.S. Government liabilities [7]	21,141	19,316	17,007	17,144	16,421	16,287	15,866	18,999
U.S. liabilities reported by U.S. banks, not included elsewhere	138,847	153,403	134,655	155,876	201,054	270,387	296,647	296,687
Other foreign official assets	97,319	101,834	110,405	107,598	158,589	215,239	268,586	349,783
Other foreign assets	5,789,543	6,589,273	7,119,039	7,489,279	8,221,291	9,539,591	10,376,289	12,345,825
Direct investment at current cost	1,101,709	1,421,017	1,518,473	1,499,952	1,580,994	1,742,246	1,868,245	2,099,426
U.S. Treasury securities	440,685	381,630	375,059	473,503	527,223	561,610	643,793	594,243
U.S. securities other than U.S. Treasury securities	2,351,291	2,623,014	2,821,372	2,779,067	3,422,856	3,995,506	4,352,998	5,228,536
Corporate and other bonds	825,175	1,068,566	1,343,071	1,530,982	1,710,787	2,035,149	2,243,135	2,689,816
Corporate stocks	1,526,116	1,554,448	1,478,301	1,248,085	1,712,069	1,960,357	2,109,863	2,538,720
U.S. currency	250,657	255,972	279,755	301,268	317,908	332,737	351,706	364,277
U.S. liabilities to unaffiliated foreigners reported by U.S. nonbanking concerns [8]	578,046	738,904	798,314	897,335	450,884	508,296	557,840	740,365
U.S. liabilities reported by U.S. banks, not included elsewhere [9]	1,067,155	1,168,736	1,326,066	1,538,154	1,921,426	2,399,196	2,601,707	3,318,978
Memoranda:								
Direct investment abroad at market value	2,839,639	2,694,014	2,314,934	2,022,588	2,729,126	3,336,421	3,570,252	4,377,830
Direct investment in the United States at market value	2,798,193	2,783,235	2,560,294	2,021,817	2,454,877	2,717,383	2,806,029	3,222,479

[1] A break in series in 2005 reflects the introduction of U.S. Department of the Treasury data on financial derivatives.

[2] U.S. official gold stock is valued at market prices.

[3] Also includes paid-in capital subscriptions to international financial institutions and resources provided to foreigners under foreign assistance programs requiring repayment over several years. Excludes World War I debts that are not being serviced.

[4] Includes indebtedness that the borrower may contractually, or at its option, repay with its currency, with a third country's currency, or by delivery of materials or transfer of services.

[5] A break in series in 2003 reflects the reclassification of assets reported by U.S. securities brokers from non-bank-reported assets to bank-reported assets, and a reduction in counterparty balances to eliminate double counting.

[6] A break in series in 2003 reflects the reclassification of assets reported by U.S. securities brokers from non-bank-reported assets to bank-reported assets.

[7] Primarily U.S. Government liabilities associated with military sales contracts and other transactions arranged with or through foreign official agencies.

[8] A break in series in 2003 reflects the reclassification of liabilities reported by U.S. securities brokers from nonbank-reported liabilities to bank-reported liabilities, and a reduction in counterparty balances to eliminate double counting.

[9] A break in series in 2003 reflects the reclassification of liabilities reported by U.S. securities brokers from nonbank-reported liabilities to bank-reported liabilities.

Note.—For details regarding these data, see *Survey of Current Business,* July 2007.

Source: Department of Commerce (Bureau of Economic Analysis).

Year or quarter	United States [1]	Canada	Japan	France	Germany [2]	Italy	United Kingdom
Industrial production (Index, 2002=100) [3]							
1980	55.1	57.3	72.2	75.9	75.9	78.6	74.0
1981	55.9	57.6	72.9	75.1	74.5	76.8	71.7
1982	53.1	53.2	73.1	74.5	72.1	74.5	73.0
1983	54.5	56.1	75.5	74.5	72.5	72.7	75.7
1984	59.5	63.1	82.5	75.8	74.7	75.1	75.7
1985	60.3	66.3	85.5	76.3	78.3	75.2	79.9
1986	61.0	65.8	85.4	78.2	79.7	78.3	81.9
1987	64.1	68.5	88.3	79.6	80.1	80.3	85.1
1988	67.4	73.1	96.5	82.4	82.9	85.9	89.2
1989	68.1	72.9	102.1	85.3	87.0	89.2	91.1
1990	68.7	70.9	106.4	86.5	91.5	88.7	90.8
1991	67.7	68.3	108.4	86.3	94.1	87.8	87.7
1992	69.7	69.2	102.2	85.2	92.0	86.9	88.0
1993	72.0	72.5	98.6	81.9	85.0	84.9	90.0
1994	76.0	77.1	99.8	85.3	87.5	90.0	94.8
1995	79.8	80.6	103.1	87.0	88.1	95.4	96.5
1996	83.2	81.6	105.5	86.7	88.3	93.7	97.8
1997	89.2	86.2	109.3	90.4	91.0	97.4	99.2
1998	94.6	89.2	102.1	93.9	94.4	98.5	100.2
1999	99.1	94.4	102.4	96.1	95.5	98.4	101.6
2000	103.6	102.6	108.0	100.0	100.9	102.6	103.5
2001	100.0	98.4	101.2	101.3	101.1	101.4	102.0
2002	100.0	100.0	100.0	100.0	100.0	100.0	100.0
2003	101.1	100.1	103.0	99.6	100.4	99.4	99.7
2004	103.6	102.2	108.5	102.1	103.5	99.2	100.5
2005	106.9	103.9	109.8	102.3	106.9	98.4	98.5
2006	111.1	103.5	114.8	102.8	113.2	100.9	98.6
2007 ᵖ	113.4	....	117.8	....	....	....	....
2006: I	109.5	105.1	112.4	102.6	110.2	100.6	98.6
II	111.2	103.8	113.8	103.5	112.4	100.8	98.5
III	112.3	102.9	115.1	102.7	114.5	101.2	98.7
IV	111.9	102.0	117.7	102.6	115.8	102.8	98.5
2007: I	112.2	103.6	116.0	103.7	117.8	101.8	98.4
II	113.2	103.9	116.5	103.7	118.8	101.4	99.1
III	114.2	103.4	118.8	104.9	121.3	101.8	99.1
IV ᵖ	113.9	....	120.5	....	....	....	....
Consumer prices (Index, 1982-84=100)							
1980	82.4	76.1	91.0	72.2	86.7	63.9	78.5
1981	90.9	85.6	95.3	81.8	92.2	75.5	87.9
1982	96.5	94.9	98.1	91.7	97.0	87.8	95.4
1983	99.6	100.4	99.8	100.3	100.3	100.8	99.8
1984	103.9	104.7	102.1	108.0	102.7	111.4	104.8
1985	107.6	109.0	104.2	114.3	104.8	121.7	111.1
1986	109.6	113.5	104.9	117.2	104.6	128.9	114.9
1987	113.6	118.4	104.9	121.1	104.9	135.1	119.7
1988	118.3	123.2	105.6	124.3	106.3	141.9	125.6
1989	124.0	129.3	108.0	128.7	109.2	150.7	135.4
1990	130.7	135.5	111.4	132.9	112.2	160.4	148.2
1991	136.2	143.1	115.0	137.2	116.3	170.5	156.9
1992	140.3	145.3	117.0	140.4	122.2	179.5	162.7
1993	144.5	147.9	118.5	143.4	127.6	187.7	165.3
1994	148.2	148.2	119.3	145.8	131.1	195.3	169.3
1995	152.4	151.4	119.2	148.4	133.3	205.6	175.2
1996	156.9	153.8	119.3	151.4	135.3	213.8	179.4
1997	160.5	156.2	121.5	153.2	137.8	218.2	185.1
1998	163.0	157.8	122.2	154.2	139.1	222.5	191.4
1999	166.6	160.5	121.8	155.0	140.0	226.2	194.3
2000	172.2	164.9	121.0	157.6	142.0	231.9	200.1
2001	177.1	169.0	120.1	160.2	144.8	238.3	203.6
2002	179.9	172.8	119.0	163.3	146.7	244.3	207.0
2003	184.0	177.6	118.7	166.7	148.3	250.9	213.0
2004	188.9	180.9	118.7	170.3	150.8	256.4	219.4
2005	195.3	184.9	118.3	173.2	153.7	261.3	225.6
2006	201.6	188.5	118.7	176.2	156.3	266.9	232.8
2007 ᵖ	207.342	192.7	118.7	178.8	159.6	271.8	242.7
2006: I	198.9	187.1	118.1	174.8	155.3	264.6	228.2
II	202.3	189.2	118.7	176.5	156.3	266.7	232.2
III	203.4	189.3	119.0	176.8	156.9	268.1	234.2
IV	201.7	188.7	118.7	176.6	156.9	268.1	236.6
2007: I	203.756	190.5	118.0	176.8	157.9	269.2	238.5
II	207.662	193.3	118.6	178.6	159.2	271.0	242.4
III	208.235	193.3	118.8	179.0	160.1	272.4	243.3
IV ᵖ	209.716	193.3	119.3	180.7	161.3	274.5	246.5

[1] See Note, Table B–51 for information on U.S. industrial production series.
[2] Prior to 1991 data are for West Germany only.
[3] All data exclude construction. Quarterly data are seasonally adjusted.

Note.—National sources data have been rebased for industrial production and consumer prices.

Sources: National sources as reported by each country, Department of Labor (Bureau of Labor Statistics), and Board of Governors of the Federal Reserve System.

TABLE B–109.—Civilian unemployment rate, and hourly compensation, major industrial countries, 1980–2007

[Quarterly data seasonally adjusted]

Year or quarter	United States	Canada	Japan	France	Germany[1]	Italy	United Kingdom
	Civilian unemployment rate (Percent)[2]						
1980	7.1	7.3	2.0	6.5	2.8	4.4	6.9
1981	7.6	7.3	2.2	7.6	4.0	4.9	9.7
1982	9.7	10.7	2.4	[3]8.3	5.6	5.4	10.8
1983	9.6	11.6	2.7	8.6	[3]6.9	5.9	11.5
1984	7.5	10.9	2.8	10.0	7.1	5.9	11.8
1985	7.2	10.2	2.7	10.5	7.2	6.0	11.4
1986	7.0	9.3	2.8	10.6	6.6	[3]7.5	11.4
1987	6.2	8.4	2.9	10.8	6.3	7.9	10.5
1988	5.5	7.4	2.5	10.3	6.3	7.9	8.6
1989	5.3	7.1	2.3	9.6	5.7	7.8	7.3
1990	[3]5.6	7.7	2.1	[3]8.6	5.0	7.0	7.1
1991	6.8	9.8	2.1	9.1	[3]5.6	[3]6.9	8.9
1992	7.5	10.6	2.2	10.0	6.7	7.3	10.0
1993	6.9	10.8	2.5	11.3	8.0	[3]9.8	10.4
1994	[3]6.1	9.6	2.9	11.9	8.5	10.7	8.7
1995	5.6	8.6	3.2	11.3	8.2	11.3	8.7
1996	5.4	8.8	3.4	11.8	9.0	11.3	8.1
1997	4.9	8.4	3.4	11.7	9.9	11.4	7.0
1998	4.5	7.7	4.1	11.2	9.3	11.5	6.3
1999	4.2	7.0	4.7	10.5	[3]8.5	11.0	6.0
2000	4.0	6.1	4.8	9.1	7.8	10.2	5.5
2001	4.7	6.5	5.1	8.4	7.9	9.2	5.1
2002	5.8	7.0	5.4	8.8	8.6	8.7	5.2
2003	6.0	6.9	5.3	9.2	9.3	8.5	5.0
2004	5.5	6.4	4.8	9.5	10.3	8.1	4.8
2005	5.1	6.0	4.5	9.6	[3]11.2	7.8	4.8
2006	4.6	5.5	4.2	9.5	10.4	6.9	5.5
2007	4.6						
2006: I	4.7	5.7	4.3	9.8	11.0	7.3	5.3
II	4.7	5.4	4.2	9.7	10.6	6.9	5.5
III	4.7	5.6	4.2	9.4	10.1	6.7	5.6
IV	4.4	5.4	4.1	9.2	9.7	6.5	5.5
2007: I	4.5	5.4	4.0	9.0	9.2	6.3	5.5
II	4.5	5.2	3.8	8.8	8.9	6.1	5.4
III	4.7	5.2	3.8	8.6	8.6	6.0	5.4
IV	4.8						
	Manufacturing hourly compensation in U.S. dollars (Index, 1992=100)[4]						
1980	55.9	49.0	32.8	45.9	46.1	44.1	47.1
1981	61.6	53.8	36.0	41.7	39.3	39.4	47.5
1982	67.2	60.1	33.5	41.1	38.8	38.6	45.1
1983	69.3	64.3	36.1	39.7	38.6	39.6	41.9
1984	71.6	65.0	37.1	38.2	36.3	39.2	39.8
1985	75.3	65.0	38.5	40.1	37.2	40.9	42.3
1986	78.8	64.9	57.1	54.7	52.4	54.6	52.0
1987	81.3	69.6	68.2	66.7	66.0	66.1	64.5
1988	84.1	78.5	78.4	70.1	70.4	70.7	74.8
1989	86.6	85.5	77.4	69.3	69.1	72.8	73.5
1990	90.5	92.4	79.2	86.0	86.4	90.2	89.6
1991	95.6	100.7	90.9	88.0	86.0	93.6	99.9
1992	100.0	100.0	100.0	100.0	100.0	100.0	100.0
1993	102.0	94.8	117.2	97.5	100.3	82.8	88.8
1994	105.3	92.1	129.9	103.1	106.9	82.1	92.8
1995	107.3	93.9	146.1	117.5	127.6	84.7	97.3
1996	109.3	95.9	127.2	116.4	127.2	95.8	96.0
1997	112.2	96.7	118.1	105.4	112.5	89.8	104.1
1998	118.7	94.9	111.9	105.1	112.5	87.5	113.8
1999	123.4	96.8	128.8	104.0	110.3	85.1	117.5
2000	134.7	100.0	135.1	94.6	100.5	75.6	114.8
2001	137.8	98.9	121.4	94.3	100.5	76.3	114.7
2002	147.8	101.0	118.6	104.5	108.7	82.7	126.8
2003	158.2	116.7	125.3	128.8	133.1	102.0	145.2
2004	161.5	127.1	135.6	145.2	147.0	115.4	171.4
2005	168.3	141.8	134.7	144.4	148.8	119.0	177.4
2006	172.4	155.5	128.1	149.6	153.7	122.2	192.3

[1] Prior to 1991 data are for West Germany only.

[2] Civilian unemployment rates, approximating U.S. concepts. Quarterly data for France, Germany, and Italy should be viewed as less precise indicators of unemployment under U.S. concepts than the annual data.

[3] There are breaks in the series for France (1982 and 1990), Germany (1983, 1991, 1999, and 2005), Italy (1986, 1991, and 1993), and United States (1990 and 1994). For details on break in series in 1990 and 1994 for United States, see footnote 5, Table B–35. For details on break in series for other countries, see U.S. Department of Labor *Comparative Civilian Labor Force Statistics, Ten Countries: 1960–2006*, October 12, 2007.

[4] Hourly compensation in manufacturing, U.S. dollar basis; data relate to all employed persons (employees and self-employed workers). For details on manufacturing hourly compensation, see U.S. Department of Labor *International Comparisons of Manufacturing Productivity and Unit Labor Cost Trends, 2006*, September 27, 2007.

Source: Department of Labor (Bureau of Labor Statistics).

TABLE B–110.—Foreign exchange rates, 1985–2007

[Foreign currency units per U.S. dollar, except as noted; certified noon buying rates in New York]

Period	Australia (dollar)[1]	Canada (dollar)	China, P.R. (yuan)	EMU Members (euro)[1,2]	Germany (mark)[2]	Japan (yen)	Mexico (peso)	South Korea (won)	Sweden (krona)	Switzer-land (franc)	United Kingdom (pound)[1]
March 1973	1.2716	0.9967	2.2401		2.8132	261.90	0.013	398.85	4.4294	3.2171	2.4724
1985	0.7003	1.3659	2.9434		2.9420	238.47	0.257	872.45	8.6032	2.4552	1.2974
1986	.6709	1.3896	3.4616		2.1705	168.35	.612	884.60	7.1273	1.7979	1.4677
1987	.7014	1.3259	3.7314		1.7981	144.60	1.378	826.16	6.3469	1.4918	1.6398
1988	.7841	1.2306	3.7314		1.7570	128.17	2.273	734.52	6.1370	1.4643	1.7813
1989	.7919	1.1842	3.7673		1.8808	138.07	2.461	674.13	6.4559	1.6369	1.6382
1990	.7807	1.1668	4.7921		1.6166	145.00	2.813	710.64	5.9231	1.3901	1.7841
1991	.7787	1.1460	5.3337		1.6610	134.59	3.018	736.73	6.0521	1.4356	1.7674
1992	.7352	1.2085	5.5206		1.5618	126.78	3.095	784.66	5.8258	1.4064	1.7663
1993	.6799	1.2902	5.7795		1.6545	111.08	3.116	805.75	7.7956	1.4781	1.5016
1994	.7316	1.3664	8.6397		1.6216	102.18	3.385	806.93	7.7161	1.3667	1.5319
1995	.7407	1.3725	8.3700		1.4321	93.96	6.447	772.69	7.1406	1.1812	1.5785
1996	.7828	1.3638	8.3389		1.5049	108.78	7.600	805.00	6.7082	1.2361	1.5607
1997	.7437	1.3849	8.3193		1.7348	121.06	7.918	953.19	7.6446	1.4514	1.6376
1998	.6291	1.4836	8.3008		1.7597	130.99	9.152	1,400.40	7.9522	1.4506	1.6573
1999	.6454	1.4858	8.2783	1.0653		113.73	9.553	1,189.84	8.2740	1.5045	1.6172
2000	.5815	1.4855	8.2784	.9232		107.80	9.459	1,130.90	9.1735	1.6904	1.5156
2001	.5169	1.5487	8.2770	.8952		121.57	9.337	1,292.02	10.3425	1.6891	1.4396
2002	.5437	1.5704	8.2771	.9454		125.22	9.663	1,250.31	9.7233	1.5567	1.5025
2003	.6524	1.4008	8.2772	1.1321		115.94	10.793	1,192.08	8.0787	1.3450	1.6347
2004	.7365	1.3017	8.2768	1.2438		108.15	11.290	1,145.24	7.3480	1.2428	1.8330
2005	.7627	1.2115	8.1936	1.2449		110.11	10.894	1,023.75	7.4710	1.2459	1.8204
2006	.7535	1.1340	7.9723	1.2563		116.31	10.906	954.32	7.3718	1.2532	1.8434
2007	.8391	1.0734	7.6058	1.3711		117.76	10.928	928.97	6.7550	1.1999	2.0020
2006: I	.7389	1.1547	8.0498	1.2033		116.88	10.601	975.39	7.7689	1.2961	1.7532
II	.7472	1.1219	8.0104	1.2576		114.39	11.182	949.18	7.3938	1.2435	1.8286
III	.7572	1.1211	7.9654	1.2741		116.28	10.945	954.98	7.2435	1.2380	1.8751
IV	.7707	1.1390	7.8626	1.2898		117.76	10.885	937.88	7.0821	1.2356	1.9166
2007: I	.7865	1.1718	7.7582	1.3109		119.33	11.024	938.98	7.0089	1.2330	1.9548
II	.8316	1.0983	7.6784	1.3484		120.80	10.878	928.69	6.8641	1.2221	1.9862
III	.8471	1.0456	7.5578	1.3748		117.74	10.965	927.27	6.7402	1.1986	2.0213
IV	.8898	0.9811	7.4336	1.4482		113.23	10.849	921.26	6.4148	1.1468	2.0442

Trade-weighted value of the U.S. dollar

	Nominal				Real[7]		
	G-10 index (March 1973=100)[3]	Broad index (January 1997=100)[4]	Major currencies index (March 1973=100)[5]	OITP index (January 1997=100)[6]	Broad index (March 1973=100)[4]	Major currencies index (March 1973=100)[5]	OITP index (March 1973=100)[6]
1985	143.0	67.16	133.55	13.14	122.59	122.05	124.32
1986	112.2	62.35	109.77	16.49	107.22	99.71	128.81
1987	96.9	60.42	97.16	19.92	98.50	89.22	126.14
1988	92.7	60.92	90.43	24.07	91.96	84.18	115.25
1989	98.6	66.90	94.29	29.61	93.70	88.52	109.80
1990	89.1	71.41	89.91	40.10	91.17	85.15	109.45
1991	89.8	74.35	88.59	46.69	89.79	83.69	108.55
1992	86.6	76.91	87.00	53.13	87.90	82.55	104.95
1993	93.2	83.78	89.90	63.37	89.30	85.80	102.46
1994	91.3	90.87	88.43	80.54	89.14	85.45	102.54
1995	84.2	92.65	83.41	92.51	83.81	81.57	94.23
1996	87.3	97.46	87.25	98.24	85.75	86.49	91.46
1997	96.4	104.43	93.93	104.64	90.32	93.80	92.43
1998	98.8	115.89	98.45	125.89	98.05	98.88	104.55
1999		116.04	96.89	129.20	97.45	98.64	103.36
2000		119.45	101.58	129.84	101.19	105.30	103.52
2001		125.93	107.67	135.91	107.01	112.78	107.68
2002		126.67	105.99	140.36	107.15	111.15	109.94
2003		119.11	92.99	143.52	100.65	98.05	111.41
2004		113.63	85.37	143.38	96.19	91.04	110.17
2005		110.71	83.71	138.89	94.59	90.85	106.78
2006		108.52	82.46	135.38	93.48	90.78	104.26
2007		103.40	77.84	130.28	89.11	86.64	99.25
2006: I		110.24	84.79	135.78	94.31	92.68	103.85
II		108.50	81.95	136.26	94.08	90.61	105.86
III		107.96	81.55	135.55	93.76	90.35	105.44
IV		107.37	81.59	133.97	91.78	89.49	101.91
2007: I		107.16	81.87	132.92	91.74	90.25	100.90
II		104.60	79.33	130.78	90.86	88.56	100.93
III		102.71	77.01	130.00	88.71	85.95	99.16
IV		99.17	73.29	127.48	85.13	81.81	96.01

[1] U.S. dollars per foreign currency unit.
[2] European Economic and Monetary Union (EMU) members include Austria, Belgium, Finland, France, Germany, Greece (beginning in 2001), Ireland, Italy, Luxembourg, Netherlands, Portugal, Slovenia (beginning in 2007), and Spain.
[3] G-10 index discontinued after December 1998.
[4] Weighted average of the foreign exchange value of the dollar against the currencies of a broad group of U.S. trading partners.
[5] Subset of the broad index. Includes currencies of the Euro area, Australia, Canada, Japan, Sweden, Switzerland, and the United Kingdom.
[6] Subset of the broad index. Includes other important U.S. trading partners (OITP) whose currencies are not heavily traded outside their home markets.
[7] Adjusted for changes in consumer price indexes for the United States and other countries.

Source: Board of Governors of the Federal Reserve System.

TABLE B–111.—*International reserves, selected years, 1972–2007*

[Millions of special drawing rights (SDRs); end of period]

Area and country	1972	1982	1992	2002	2005	2006	2007 October	2007 November
All countries	146,658	361,166	753,827	1,890,007	3,000,359	3,414,461	3,974,378	4,022,678
Industrial countries [1]	113,362	214,025	424,749	762,781	965,053	978,157	990,002	990,765
United States	12,112	29,918	52,995	59,160	46,994	45,615	46,423	46,837
Canada	5,572	3,439	8,662	27,225	23,066	23,265	25,904	25,641
Euro area (incl. ECB) [1]				195,771	142,391	143,735	152,417	152,102
Austria	2,505	5,544	9,703	7,480	5,125	4,985	6,720	6,906
Belgium	3,564	4,757	10,914	9,010	6,022	6,095	6,598	6,644
Finland	664	1,420	3,862	6,885	7,416	4,372	4,474	4,415
France	9,224	17,850	22,522	24,268	22,597	31,412	35,913	34,752
Germany	21,908	43,909	69,489	41,516	35,440	31,561	31,987	31,764
Greece	950	916	3,606	6,083	476	502	544	555
Ireland	1,038	2,390	2,514	3,989	551	485	494	512
Italy	5,605	15,108	22,438	23,798	20,611	19,817	21,723	22,680
Luxembourg			66	114	171	148	138	137
Netherlands	4,407	10,723	17,492	7,993	7,069	7,902	7,110	6,730
Portugal	2,130	1,179	14,474	8,889	2,904	1,802	965	1,090
Slovenia			520	5,143	5,656	4,683	676	692
Spain	4,618	7,450	33,640	25,992	7,286	7,663	7,523	7,510
Australia	5,656	6,053	8,429	15,307	29,434	35,618	19,899	17,065
Japan	16,916	22,001	52,937	340,088	584,568	585,600	595,729	598,849
New Zealand	767	577	2,239	3,650	6,222	9,352	10,852	10,663
Denmark	787	2,111	8,090	19,924	23,115	19,833	22,108	22,116
Iceland	77	133	364	326	727	1,532	1,638	1,653
Norway	1,220	6,272	8,725	23,579	32,874	37,874	38,287	37,850
San Marino				135	248	318		
Sweden	1,453	3,397	16,667	12,807	15,645	16,649	17,802	17,923
Switzerland	6,961	16,930	27,100	31,693	26,847	26,773	28,243	28,123
United Kingdom	5,201	11,904	27,300	27,973	27,264	27,402	30,376	31,621
Developing countries: Total [2]	33,295	147,141	329,078	1,127,226	2,035,306	2,436,304	2,984,376	3,031,913
By area:								
Africa	3,962	7,737	13,049	54,011	113,205	147,969	174,779	175,972
Asia [2]	7,935	44,490	191,041	720,064	1,306,953	1,512,239	1,827,128	1,850,967
China, P.R. (Mainland)		10,733	15,441	214,815	575,454	710,920	927,541	943,299
India	1,087	4,213	4,584	50,174	92,704	113,895	163,827	167,153
Korea	485	2,556	12,463	89,272	147,166	158,804	165,464	164,685
Europe	2,680	5,359	15,488	135,806	296,579	403,906	518,479	532,506
Russia				32,840	123,499	196,921	277,872	284,848
Middle East	9,407	64,039	44,397	98,645	139,392	165,287	197,233	199,257
Western Hemisphere	9,089	25,563	65,102	118,700	179,177	206,902	266,757	273,211
Brazil	3,853	3,566	16,457	27,593	37,291	56,643	106,289	110,851
Mexico	1,072	828	13,800	37,223	51,816	50,702	53,215	53,740
Memorandum:								
Oil-exporting countries	9,927	67,108	46,392	110,079	187,027	236,971	284,453	288,823
Non-oil developing countries [2]	23,339	80,032	282,686	1,017,147	1,848,279	2,199,333	2,699,923	2,743,090

[1] Includes data for European Central Bank (ECB) beginning 1999. Detail does not add to totals shown.
[2] Includes data for Taiwan Province of China.

Note.—International reserves is comprised of monetary authorities' holdings of gold (at SDR 35 per ounce), SDRs, reserve positions in the International Monetary Fund, and foreign exchange.

U.S. dollars per SDR (end of period) are: 1.08570 in 1972; 1.10310 in 1982; 1.37500 in 1992; 1.35952 in 2002; 1.42927 in 2005; 1.50440 in 2006; 1.57190 in October 2007; and 1.59020 in November 2007.

Source: International Monetary Fund, *International Financial Statistics.*

TABLE B–112.—*Growth rates in real gross domestic product, 1989–2008*

[Percent change]

Area and country	1989–98 annual average	1999	2000	2001	2002	2003	2004	2005	2006	2007[1]	2008[1]
World	3.2	3.8	4.8	2.5	3.1	4.0	5.3	4.8	5.4	5.2	4.8
Advanced economies	2.7	3.5	4.0	1.2	1.6	1.9	3.2	2.5	2.9	2.5	2.2
Of which:											
United States	3.0	4.5	3.7	.8	1.6	2.5	3.6	3.1	2.9	1.9	1.9
Japan	2.0	−.1	2.9	.2	.3	1.4	2.7	1.9	2.2	2.0	1.7
United Kingdom	2.0	3.0	3.8	2.4	2.1	2.8	3.3	1.8	2.8	3.1	2.3
Canada	2.1	5.5	5.2	1.8	2.9	1.9	3.1	3.1	2.8	2.5	2.3
Euro area	....	3.0	3.8	1.9	.9	.8	2.0	1.5	2.8	2.5	2.1
Germany	2.5	1.9	3.1	1.2	*	−.3	1.1	.8	2.9	2.4	2.0
France	1.9	3.3	3.9	1.9	1.0	1.1	2.5	1.7	2.0	1.9	2.0
Italy	1.6	1.9	3.6	1.8	.3	*	1.2	.1	1.9	1.7	1.3
Spain	2.8	4.7	5.0	3.6	2.7	3.1	3.3	3.6	3.9	3.7	2.7
Netherlands	3.1	4.7	3.9	1.9	.1	.3	2.2	1.5	3.0	2.6	2.5
Belgium	2.3	3.3	3.9	.7	1.4	1.0	2.8	1.4	3.0	2.6	1.9
Austria	2.7	3.3	3.4	.8	.9	1.2	2.3	2.0	3.3	3.3	2.5
Finland	1.6	3.9	5.0	2.6	1.6	1.8	3.7	2.9	5.0	4.3	3.0
Greece	1.9	3.4	4.5	4.5	3.9	4.9	4.7	3.7	4.3	3.9	3.6
Portugal	3.6	3.9	3.9	2.0	.8	−.7	1.5	.5	1.3	1.8	1.8
Ireland	6.4	10.7	9.1	5.9	6.4	4.3	4.3	5.9	5.7	4.6	3.0
Luxembourg	4.9	8.4	8.4	2.5	3.8	1.3	3.6	4.0	6.2	5.4	4.2
Slovenia	....	5.4	4.1	3.1	3.7	2.8	4.4	4.1	5.7	5.4	3.8
Memorandum:											
Major advanced economies[2]	2.5	3.1	3.6	1.0	1.2	1.8	2.9	2.3	2.6	2.1	1.9
Newly industrialized Asian economies[3]	6.1	7.5	7.9	1.2	5.5	3.2	5.9	4.7	5.3	4.9	4.4
Other emerging market and developing countries	3.8	4.1	6.0	4.3	5.1	6.7	7.7	7.5	8.1	8.1	7.4
Regional groups:											
Africa	2.2	2.8	3.2	4.3	3.6	4.7	5.8	5.6	5.6	5.7	6.5
Central and eastern Europe	1.1	.5	4.9	.2	4.5	4.8	6.7	5.6	6.3	5.8	5.2
Commonwealth of Independent States[4]	....	5.2	9.0	6.3	5.3	7.9	8.4	6.6	7.7	7.8	7.0
Russia	....	6.4	10.0	5.1	4.7	7.3	7.2	6.4	6.7	7.0	6.5
Developing Asia	7.3	6.5	7.0	6.0	7.0	8.3	8.8	9.2	9.8	9.8	8.8
China	9.6	7.6	8.4	8.3	9.1	10.0	10.1	10.4	11.1	11.5	10.0
India	5.7	6.9	5.4	3.9	4.5	6.9	7.9	9.0	9.7	8.9	8.4
Middle East	4.5	1.9	5.4	3.0	4.0	6.6	5.6	5.4	5.6	5.9	5.9
Western Hemisphere	3.1	.3	3.9	.5	.3	2.4	6.0	4.6	5.5	5.0	4.3
Brazil	2.0	.3	4.3	1.3	2.7	1.1	5.7	2.9	3.7	4.4	4.0
Mexico	3.4	3.8	6.6	*	.8	1.4	4.2	2.8	4.8	2.9	3.0

[1] All figures are forecasts as published by the International Monetary Fund.

[2] Includes Canada, France, Germany, Italy, Japan, United Kingdom, and United States.

[3] Includes Hong Kong SAR (Special Administrative Region of China), Korea, Singapore, and Taiwan Province of China.

[4] Includes Mongolia, which is not a member of the Commonwealth of Independent States, but is included for reasons of geography and similarities in economic structure.

* Figure is zero or negligible.

Note.—For details on data shown in this table, see *World Economic Outlook* published by the International Monetary Fund.

Sources: Department of Commerce (Bureau of Economic Analysis) and International Monetary Fund.